Second Edition

The Handbook of
SOCIAL
POLICY

Second Edition

The Handbook of
SOCIAL
POLICY

James Midgley
University of California, Berkeley

Michelle Livermore
Louisiana State University

editors

SAGE

Los Angeles • London • New Delhi • Singapore

For information:

SAGE Publications, Inc.
2455 Teller Road
Thousand Oaks,
  California 91320
E-mail: order@sagepub.com

SAGE Publications India Pvt. Ltd.
B 1/I 1 Mohan Cooperative
  Industrial Area
Mathura Road, New Delhi 110 044
India

SAGE Publications Ltd.
1 Oliver's Yard
55 City Road
London EC1Y 1SP
United Kingdom

SAGE Publications
Asia-Pacific Pte. Ltd.
33 Pekin Street #02-01
Far East Square
Singapore 048763

Printed in the United States of America.

Library of Congress Cataloging-in-Publication Data

The handbook of social policy / edited by James Midgley,
Michelle Livermore. — 2nd ed.
    p. cm.
Includes bibliographical references and index.
ISBN 978-1-4129-5076-3 (cloth: alk paper)
ISBN 978-1-4129-5077-0 (pbk. : alk paper)
    1. United States—Social policy. 2. Social service—United States. 3. Public welfare—United States. I. Midgley, James. II. Livermore, Michelle.

HN65.H345 2009
361.6'10973—dc22   2008001219

This book is printed on acid-free paper.

08   09   10   11   12   10   9   8   7   6   5   4   3   2   1

Acquisitions Editor:	Kassie Graves
Editorial Assistant:	Veronica Novak
Production Editor:	Tracy Buyan
Copy Editor:	Karen E. Taylor
Typesetter:	C&M Digitals (P) Ltd.
Proofreader:	Wendy Jo Dymond
Indexer:	Joan Shapiro
Cover Designer:	Candice Harman
Marketing Manager:	Carmel Schrire

Contents

Preface

It was about 10 years ago that Jim Nageotte, who was then with Sage Publications, first proposed the idea of publishing a series of handbooks in the fields of social work and social policy. We were honored to respond to his invitation to produce *The Handbook of Social Policy*—the first in the new series. Following the handbook's publication in 2000, a number of additional handbooks dealing with different social work and welfare issues have appeared. We are now delighted to be working with Kassie Graves and her colleagues at Sage on the revised and updated edition of *The Handbook of Social Policy*. We were also pleased to learn from her that the first edition has been widely used not only as a reference source but also as an advanced, graduate-level text and that there is demand for a new edition.

We believe that the quality of the contributions, and the expertise of the authors who wrote for the first edition, was primarily responsible for the handbook's popularity. We are most fortunate that many of those who contributed to the first edition were willing to update their original chapters. They are acknowledged to be among the leading scholars working in the field of social policy today, and we are grateful for their participation. It has been a great pleasure to work with them and to coordinate their different contributions which, taken together, compose a "state of the art" overview of social policy in the United States today.

Many thanks to Kassie Graves for her confidence in this project and to her and Veronica Novak for their encouragement and support. Karen Taylor coped extremely well with a heavy demand to finish the copyediting. Many thanks also to Tracy Buyan, who saw the book through production. Thanks also to Carmel Schrire for her efforts to ensure that the book is properly marketed.

We are sorry that Martin Tracy decided not to participate in the production of the second edition. He was adamant that retirement meant retirement and that he intended to avoid the demands of editing a major work such as *The Handbook of Social Policy*. We respect his determination to pursue his well-earned retirement goals and wish him the very best. His informal advice and support are also greatly appreciated.

As with the first edition, we have enjoyed working on this project and have benefited from the extensive knowledge of the contributors. We hope that the book will be helpful to those who wish to have a broad overview of social policy and the many complex issues that affect the policy-making process, We also hope that it will stimulate further reflection and in-depth reading of the many interesting and important issues raised by the contributors. Social policy is a continuously evolving field requiring constant review, documentation, and analysis. We sincerely hope that *The Handbook of Social Policy* will prove to be a useful resource for students, administrators, social workers, and policy makers concerned with the well-being of all who live in the United States today.

James Midgley
Michelle Livermore

Introduction

Social Policy and Social Welfare

This book is about government social policies and the way they affect peoples' welfare. As will be shown in the next chapter, policies are courses of action adopted by formal organizations. They prescribe, govern, and routinize the activities of formal organizations. By prescribing courses of action, policies standardize decision making, enhance organizational efficiency, and help organizations achieve their goals.

Policies are used in all types of organizations including commercial and industrial firms, nonprofit agencies, religious organizations, universities, and multinational corporations. They are used to prescribe the ways governmental agencies function and seek to achieve their goals. In addition, the government formulates and implements policies that affect the lives of citizens and their many activities. Policies formulated and implemented by governments are known as public policies. They are used by governments to deal with major issues that affect a country's social, economic, environmental, and political affairs. Governments throughout the world use policies to discharge their obligations and to carry out their many complex functions. Policies designed to maintain law and order, ensure national defense, promote economic development, protect the environment, foster communications, and control urban growth are just some examples of the way governments prescribe courses of action, routinize their activities, and meet their goals. In addition, they have adopted policies designed to enhance the welfare of their citizens.

Policies designed to enhance peoples' welfare or well-being are known as social policies. These policies are concerned with many aspects of social welfare, including health, housing, education, income, and nutrition, to name but a few. Social policies have also been formulated to meet the needs of groups of people such as needy children, people with disabilities, low-income families, and elderly people. Some social policies govern particular social service programs while others operate in more complex ways through the tax system, directing resources toward particular groups of people.

Although government social policies make an important contribution to the well-being of the country's citizens, the welfare of the population is not only determined by government policies. Many other activities and circumstances also affect social well-being, including the income people derive from employment; their educational achievements; the support they receive from family members, friends, and neighbors; the services provided by nonprofit and religious organizations; local events in the communities in which people live; the state of the economy; and a host of other factors. However, government social policies are particularly important because they are intended to improve the well-being of people today and they mobilize sizable resources to achieve this goal.

This book is primarily concerned with social policy in the United States and with the complex system of services and programs provided by the federal, state, and county governments. Although social policies are developed and implemented at all levels of government, the role of the federal government is particularly important, and this book will pay special attention to its social policies, services, and programs. However, the role of the states and local governments will also be considered. Although the book deals with social policy in the United States, the editors and contributors are mindful of the fact that the government of the United States both influences social policies in other countries and is influenced by developments from abroad. In today's increasingly globalized world, the peoples of different nations are more closely linked together and are affected by international events.

The idea that governments should formulate social policies with the specific intention of improving the well-being of their citizens is a relatively recent one. For most of human history, governments were primarily concerned with maintaining law and order and with national defense. Earlier generations would have been surprised by the now widely accepted idea that the federal and state governments should be involved in social welfare. It is only since the 19th century that the power and resources of the government have been used to raise the educational levels of the population, provide housing, subsidize the incomes of people with low incomes, seek to improve health through public medical services, and in other ways improve peoples' well-being. In earlier times, families and local communities, as well as the church and voluntary agencies, were primarily responsible for welfare. During the 20th century, largely because of the efforts of social reformers, trade unionists, and progressive politicians, government involvement increased rapidly, and the social services have expanded to consume a growing proportion of national income.

Because the role of the government in social welfare is now so extensive, it is desirable that social policies should be subjected to academic scrutiny. Accordingly, the term *social policy* is used not only to refer to actual government social policies and programs but also to the academic study of these policies and programs. Social scientists have only been studying the social policies of government systematically for about 50 years but a good deal of information is now available about the way social policies are formulated and how these policies are implemented through the social services, legal regulations, the tax system, and the courts. They have also traced the history of social policy, studied the ideologies that influence social policy making, and assessed the impact of government welfare provision. The result is an evolving body of knowledge that has illuminated the many complex ways government policies affect the well-being of citizens.

The social services are specifically intended to improve social welfare, and not surprisingly, they have been a primary focus of social policy scholarship. A good deal of academic effort has been devoted to documenting the major social services, tracing their historical evolution, describing their legislative basis, and reporting on their cost and coverage. The goals of the different social services have also been studied, particularly with reference to outcomes. Part IV of this book contains accounts of the major social services and the way they address social needs and enhance people's well-being in the United States today.

Social policy scholarship has also been concerned with theoretical issues. Several typologies or models of different types of social welfare provision have been constructed. These models have also been used to classify the social welfare systems of different countries. In addition, social policy scholars have sought to explain reasons for the expansion of government social welfare provision in the 20th century, and a variety of interesting and plausible analyses have emerged. Explanatory accounts of the functions that social policies serve have also been offered. While some of these accounts contend that governments introduce social welfare programs to meet social needs and enhance well-being, others stress the political or economic functions of social policies. Part II of the book, which deals with the history of social policy in the United States, touches on many of these issues.

Social policy scholars have been particularly interested in the values and ideologies that shape social policies. This stimulating area of inquiry has shown that social policy making is not based entirely on rational, technocratic decision-making techniques but is significantly influenced by values and ideological beliefs. These beliefs give expression to the value preferences of politicians, different interest groups, academic writers, and members of the public and permeate the policy-making process. As is shown in Part III of this book, many academic social policy scholars are interested in the way values and ideologies influence social policy decisions. Of course, many social policy scholars also express their own normative preferences by advocating for the adoption of one or another approach or by criticizing policies with which they disagree. This tendency has led to vigorous debates within the field and arguments for and against particular policy proposals.

Normative social policy debates reveal that the field is a controversial one in which there are many disagreements about social policy issues. Indeed, the way social policy has been defined in this introduction to the handbook will not be universally accepted. Some social policy scholars will challenge the idea that governments introduce social policies to enhance the welfare of citizens believing instead that governments represent sectional interests and are not much concerned with the general well-being of the population. Others take issue with the idea that governments should be responsible for social welfare programs. Some believe that government welfare programs are bureaucratic, wasteful, and economically harmful. They seek to curtail government involvement and encourage individuals and their families to take responsibility for their own welfare. Others believe that nonprofit organizations, faith-based organizations, and local community groups should assume a greater responsibility for people's welfare.

Critics of conventional social policy interpretations make many valid points and temper the enthusiasm for government involvement that previously dominated social policy scholarship. These critics have raised awareness of the limitations of government and of the rather naive belief that the government is composed of caring politicians, competent civil servants, and dedicated planners who use their political authority and technical skills to formulate policies that invariably improve the well-being of the population. But, although it is true that governments have adopted policies that have a negative impact on people's welfare, it is simplistic to claim that governments never act in the best interests of their citizens. Many examples of well-designed and effective social policies can be given. Indeed, Part II of this book reveals that many social policies were introduced because of the campaigns of social reformers who sought to address social wrongs and promote positive social change through government intervention. Social policy scholarship is challenged to disentangle the many different ways social policies affect people's welfare and to assess the outcomes of social policies. As will be appreciated, this is a complex and demanding task, but it is an interesting and rewarding one. As scholars study the social policy-making process, analyze the ideological and political dimensions of social policy, and assess the outcomes of social policies, a good deal of useful information that can improve social policy and enhance peoples' future welfare is being collected.

The Scope of This Book

The Handbook of Social Policy is an attempt to document the now substantial body of knowledge about government social policies that has been accumulated since the study of social policy first emerged as an organized field of academic endeavor about 50 years ago. The handbook has been compiled specifically for readers in the United States, and it is, therefore, primarily concerned with the social policies of the country's federal and state governments. However, many of the authors make references to other countries, and in the final section, a chapter by two distinguished scholars, examines American social policy in the international context by linking social policy in the United States to developments in other nations.

The handbook hopes to provide a "state of the art" account of American social policy at the beginning of the 21st century. It is divided into five parts. Part I, which deals with the nature of social policy, seeks to define social policy and to examine the wider social, economic, political, and cultural context in which social policies are formulated. It is also concerned with two technical aspects of social policy, namely, policy analysis and policy practice. Attention is given to the impact of social policy and the different ways the effects of social policies and programs are assessed.

Part II examines the history of social policy in the United States from the colonial period up to the present. This part of the book covers more than three hundred years of social policy development and shows how changing social, political, and economic realities have contributed to a continuously evolving system of governmental social welfare that, at different times, has sought to expand the role of government in social welfare and, at other times, to retrench its role. The chapters in this part of the book seek to provide an historical overview that will acquaint readers with the most critical events in the history of American social policy and to show how its evolution has been affected by wider social, economic, political, and cultural forces as well as the efforts of campaigners to bring about progressive improvements in social conditions.

Part III of the book is concerned with the political economy of social policy. Although the process of social policy making involves technical activities in which research, needs assessments, policy analysis, and other factors play an important role, it is also influenced by ideological beliefs. Indeed, many social policy writers claim that ideologies play a critically important role in social policy. Because of their importance, various competing political economy or normative approaches, as they are also known, will be examined. These approaches reflect different ideological preferences. After describing the institutional approach, which has long dominated social policy thinking, attention is given to the conservative approach, critical social policy, welfare pluralism, feminist perspectives, multicultural approaches, the developmental perspective, and, finally, the ecological approach.

Part IV of the book covers the major social services. As was noted earlier, academic research into the social services is now well developed, and, today, many different aspects of social service provision in the United States have been documented and analyzed. Scholars have gathered a great deal of information about the legislative basis for social service provision, the administrative aspects of social service delivery, the costs of the social services, and their impact on different client groups and the population at large. The chapters in this part of the book seek to document these different aspects of social service provision and to highlight issues arising out of the study of various social services. The section covers the most familiar social services, such as child welfare, social security, and mental health, but it also includes chapters on urban development, education, and employment services, which are not always regarded as forming an integral part of social policy.

The concluding part of the book contains two chapters. As mentioned earlier, one of these examines American social policy in international context. The last chapter, which is written jointly by the editors, speculates on the future of social policy. Although it is extremely difficult to predict future trends in social policy, factors that will in all likelihood shape social policy in the years to come will be discussed and, it is hoped, will help readers to discern the way social policy will evolve.

Although the handbook seeks to provide an overview of the social policy field in the United States, given the complexity of the subject and the now substantial body of knowledge that has accumulated about the way government social policies affect peoples' well-being, this is a formidable task. The task is made more difficult by length constraints. The editors are only too aware that it has only been possible to provide an overview of very complex issues and that some topics may not have received the in-depth analysis they deserve. It is also the case that some issues, which are referred to in some of the chapters, would have benefited from separate, more detailed treatment. For example, the impact of the tax system on social welfare is mentioned in several chapters, but it could have been addressed in a chapter of its own. This is also true of the way social policy interacts with the nonprofit sector and the wider civil society. Despite these limitations, it is hoped that the book will meet the needs of readers who wish to familiarize themselves with the field of social policy in the United States today. It should also serve as a pointer for further reading. The authors have provided not only helpful summaries of their topics but also informative bibliographies that will facilitate the further, in-depth study of the field or of particular aspects of the field that may interest different readers. We hope that the handbook will satisfy the need for a comprehensive yet accessible introduction to a vast field of endeavor, one that has, over the years, made a significant difference to the lives and the well-being of the people of the United States.

PART I

The Nature of
Social Policy

Part I of the handbook provides a framework for the rest of the book. It deals broadly with issues of definition, the context of social policy, and matters of policy analysis, policy practice, and evaluation.

The first chapter shows that the term *social policy* is a complex one that has been defined differently by different scholars. It notes that the term is used to describe both the activities of government that affect peoples' well-being and the academic study of these activities. It offers a broad interpretation of the field that seeks to accommodate diverse perspectives and interpretations.

Chapter 2 offers an account of the way social policy is formulated and implemented in the United States. It pays particular attention to the role of the federal, state, and local governments in formulating and implementing social policies. It examines the way the legislative process, the actions of the executive branch, and the decisions of the courts shape social policy today.

The economic context in which social policy operates is examined in Chapter 3. The chapter shows that social policy is formulated and implemented not only within a fiscal framework but also within a wider economic environment in which growth, employment, productivity, and other economic factors are important determinants of social welfare.

The next two chapters are concerned with issues of policy analysis and policy practice. As will be seen, these fields are closely related. Chapter 4 is concerned with the steps that characterize the policy-making process and facilitate effective decision making. Chapter 5 deals with the implementation of social policy and with the role of professional policy practitioners in ensuring that policy decisions are efficiently translated into tangible programs that have a positive impact on peoples' well-being.

The last chapter in Part I discusses the impact of social policy. Although it is often assumed that social policies and programs are carefully evaluated to ensure that they meet their goals, this is not always the case. Emphasizing the need for rigorous evaluation, Chapter 6 shows how the impact of social policies can be assessed and how their wider effects can be measured.

1

The Definition of Social Policy

James Midgley

As was noted in the introduction to this book, policies are courses of action adopted by formal organizations. They prescribe, govern, and routinize the activities of these organizations. They govern their internal functioning, direct the activities of their members, and shape their relations with other organizations. They also specify how organizations should function in the wider social, economic, and political environment. They standardize decision making, enhance organizational efficiency, and facilitate goal attainment.

Policies are necessitated by the increasing complexity and pace of organizational life. They are critically important if organizations are to attain their goals. Without policies, managers and staff would spend a good deal of time trying to decide how to act in different situations, and there would also be considerable duplication, confusion, and wastage. Efficiency would also be impeded if different managers responded differently to the same problems and issues. By defining goals, prescribing courses of action, and routinizing decision making, policies enhance the effectiveness of formal organizations in an increasingly complex and changing world.

Usually, policies are written down in documentary form, and for this reason, they are actually prescriptive statements about goals, decision making, and organizational activities. Although many organizations codify their policies in manuals and other publications, most people working in organizations learn about policies through experience. Of course, many organizations offer training programs in which employees are informed about policies. Generally, all employees are required to be familiar with the organization's policies, but policies are of primary concern to administrators and managers who are also responsible for monitoring and reviewing policies. The terms *administration* and *management* are often used interchangeably, but the former term, administration, is sometimes used to refer to the implementation of policies while management refers to the direction or supervision of policy implementation. Managers are closely involved in the policy-making process, but usually, organizations have governing bodies or boards that have the ultimate control over which policies should be adopted.

Policies play a particularly important role in large, formal organizations such as corporations, universities, religious and nonprofit organizations, hospitals, and government agencies. Government agencies are particularly dependent on policies. They are complex organizations that make extensive use of policies to define goals and standardize decision making. Taken as a whole, the government, with its different departments and branches, is often the largest and most complex of a nation's organizations. In addition, governments formulate and implement policies that profoundly affect the lives and everyday activities of their citizens. Today, a country's economic, social, cultural, environmental, and political affairs are shaped to an extraordinary extent by government policies. As noted in the introduction to this book, governments around the world have adopted policies that, for example, promote economic development, maintain law and order, govern relationships with other countries, defend the nation against external threats, protect the environment, foster communications, and control urban growth. Policies formulated and implemented by governments are known as public policies. These policies are unique in that they are enshrined in enforceable laws and regulations. Unlike other organizations and bodies, governments can ensure that people comply with their policies by using their powers of coercion.

The term *the state* is often used by social scientists to refer to the government and its different braches. The state thus consists of the legislature, the executive branch, the judiciary, the military, and law enforcement agencies, as well as many specialized agencies and quasi-governmental bodies. Conventionally, the legislative branch of government is considered to be responsible for making policies while the executive branch implements policies. The task of the judicial branch is to interpret policies. However, the roles of the three branches of government overlap considerably, and all branches may be involved in the policy making, interpretation, and implementation process. Although some scholars use the term *government* to refer only to the administrative branch, others use the term to refer to all the branches of government. As was noted earlier, the term *the state* is usually preferred when all the braches of government are being discussed.

Governments have also adopted policies designed to enhance the welfare of their citizens. As noted in the introduction, these policies are known as social policies. They deal with many aspects of social welfare, including health, housing, education, and income, and they are also used to meet the needs of groups of people such as children, elderly people, single mothers, and people with disabilities. Social policies also govern the operations of social service agencies responsible for particular social services such as social security, school meals, probation, and foster care. Social policies also operate through the tax system to direct resources toward particular groups of people. The courts also play a very important role in social policy by making judicial decisions on many issues that affect people's lives. In addition, governments may promote social well-being through policies and programs that are not usually classed as social policies. For example, economic policy is regarded as separate from social policy, but by ensuring steady economic growth, creating jobs, managing inflationary tendencies, encouraging investments, and directing the economy in other ways, economic policy contributes to welfare goals.

The documentation, analysis, and interpretation of government policies are among the major preoccupations of legal scholars, organizational experts, and social scientists. They have acquired extensive knowledge about a wide range of public policies. The academic study of these policies is now well established at universities. Indeed, most universities today have academic departments or schools devoted to the study of public policies. In addition, public policies are also studied by specialized research institutes or "think tanks" and by government agencies concerned with policy analysis.

The social policies of governments are also being extensively documented, analyzed, debated, and evaluated by social scientists. Although social policies have been subjected to systematic academic inquiry only since the middle decades of the last century, a good deal of knowledge about these policies, their history, objectives, and effects has been acquired, and many important social policy issues are currently being analyzed. Social policy inquiry takes place within schools of public policy; inside academic departments of economics, political science, and sociology; and at schools of social work and social welfare. Although social policy is still a relatively new field of academic inquiry, it has grown rapidly in recent years.

The term *social policy* thus involves two aspects: first, it refers to the actual policies and programs of governments, policies that affect people's welfare and, second, it connotes an academic field of inquiry concerned with the description, explanation, and evaluation of these policies. In seeking to define social policy, this chapter deals with these two aspects separately. But first, it examines the concept of social welfare, which is the primary goal of government social policy.

Social Policy and Social Welfare

Scholars have shown that social policies have many different functions. Although these functions have been extensively discussed in the literature, the primary reason for introducing a social policy is to enhance conditions of social well-being in society. This can be done in many different ways. For example, governments can provide services to meet the needs of particularly vulnerable or disadvantaged groups such as foster children, low-income families living in inner-city areas, or people with mental illness. Social well-being can also be enhanced by directing resources to particular groups of people through income maintenance programs such as social security or otherwise through the tax system. Governments can also improve conditions of social well-being by controlling pollution or enhancing educational opportunities for children.

When social policies have a widespread, positive effect, social conditions in society as a whole improve, producing a condition of social welfare or social well-being. Because the notion of social welfare is a key element in social policy, its meaning must be defined at the outset. Accordingly, social welfare will be defined in this book as a condition or state of human well-being that exists when peoples' needs are met, problems are managed, and opportunities are maximized. The opposite of the condition of social welfare is social illfare. Social illfare exists when human needs are not met, when social problems are not effectively managed, and when there are very limited opportunities for improving life chances.

This definition transcends the conventional definition of social welfare as a range of services provided by charities and government social services agencies to poor, needy, and vulnerable people. This conventional meaning of the term implies that only some particularly unfortunate or needy people have welfare needs that should be addressed by charitable organizations and public welfare departments. This narrow meaning fails to capture the original significance of the term, which defines social welfare in a positive way, stressing the importance of well-being for all people and, indeed, for society as a whole. The broader definition of social welfare offered in this book reflects the term's original meaning, which is derived from the greeting *farewell*. This greeting connotes a sense of going and being well. It is a pity that the term has now been so narrowly defined and that it has even acquired a pejorative connotation. Hopefully, the broader, more positive meaning of the term will be revived, and its more encompassing connotation will, in future, be more widely accepted.

Over the years, social policy scholars have devoted a good deal of effort to defining the concept of social welfare. Initially, they stressed the importance of meeting social needs and suggested that a condition of social welfare exists when basic human needs for nutrition, health, shelter, security, and income have been met. Others emphasized the importance of managing problems, arguing that a condition of social well-being exists when social problems such as crime and delinquency, substance abuse, family violence, and child neglect are effectively controlled. Although the two elements of meeting needs and managing social problems have been widely employed in the social policy literature, the definition offered earlier extends on them by highlighting the role of opportunities in social welfare. Obviously, conditions of social welfare are more likely to exist in societies that create and sustain opportunities for people to maximize their life chances and accomplish their goals. The role of governments in providing educational and other opportunities for people to fulfill their life goals is a crucial one.

In addition, the wider sociopolitical and economic context is also important when discussing social welfare. Broader conditions, such as peace, democratic participation, and human rights, are obviously highly relevant when seeking to understand conditions of social well-being. People can best experience social well-being if they live in peaceful societies that respect human rights and encourage full participation in the political life of the community through democratic institutions. This is equally true when they live in societies that are experiencing economic development and have educational and employment opportunities that allow them to realize their potential. Although it is still possible for people to meet their needs and manage their problems in undemocratic and conflict-ridden societies, peace, human rights, and democratic political participation are vital for conditions of social welfare to be realized.

When social policy scholars discuss conditions of social welfare, they usually refer to society as a whole, but, obviously, a condition or state of social well-being can be associated with individuals, families, groups, organizations, neighborhoods, and communities as well. In addition, it can pertain to groups of countries in different regions of the world and even to the world as a whole. The ability to meet needs, manage problems, and achieve goals is as much a feature of the lives of individuals and families, organizations and communities as it is of societies. However, it is at the societal and community levels that contextual notions of peace, human rights, and democratic participation are most relevant. Subjective experiences of well-being, such as feelings of contentment, satisfaction, and happiness, are most relevant to individuals and families.

It is difficult to measure the extent to which people, families, organizations, communities, and societies have attained a condition of social well-being. Nevertheless, research in the field has become increasingly sophisticated, and social scientists now use a variety of statistical techniques to operationalize the concept. One technique is to use social surveys to ask people whether they feel that their needs are met and whether they are contented and satisfied with their lives (Layard, 2005). These "happiness" studies have become quite popular in recent years. Although surveys of individual happiness and satisfaction are aggregated to obtain insights into the degree of happiness in communities and societies as a whole, they are subjective and have obvious methodological limitations.

For this reason, social scientists seeking to measure social welfare have often made use of social indicators based on census results, population registration procedures, and routine statistics collected by government agencies. Using data collected through these sources, they are able to gain insights into conditions of social welfare in different communities by comparing life expectancy estimates, adult literacy rates, infant mortality rates, school attendance data, the incidence of crime, and many other indicators. These indicators show that some communities have far higher levels of welfare than others. While some have high incomes; good standards of health, education, and housing; and low rates of crime and other social problems, many others are characterized by poverty, low standards of living, and high rates of violence. These indicators have also been used to measure conditions of social welfare at the international level, and as is well known, there are very significant differences in social conditions in different parts of the world today. As this research reveals, the notion of social welfare is not some abstract or academic idea but a tangible feature of peoples' experience and of social life.

Different institutionalized practices or mechanisms have evolved in all societies to promote conditions of social welfare. Traditionally, individuals and their families have been the primary source of well-being, and the family has been the locus of efforts to meet needs, manage problems, and even to help their members maximize opportunities. Families have historically nurtured and protected their members (and especially their young) and have cared for them in times of illness or other adversities. Individual family members are expected to contribute to the well-being of others in the family and also to be self-reliant and responsible. In addition, the family's welfare efforts are usually supplemented by those of relatives, friends, neighbors, and the local community. These activities comprise what social policy scholars often call nonformal welfare institutions.

External agents such as churches, mosques, temples, and faith-based and secular philanthropic agencies also contribute to social welfare, particularly by supplementing the role of the family and by providing a residual "safety net" that comes into operation when individuals and their families are unable to cope with the challenges they face. Faith-based welfare organizations and nonprofit agencies comprise what social policy scholars call formal welfare institutions. The government's social welfare policies and programs are also considered to form a part of the formal welfare system.

Governments have historically played a minor role in social welfare, and it was only during the 20th century that the state's contribution to meeting peoples' needs, managing social problems, and maximizing citizens' opportunities expanded. As mentioned in the introduction, social reformers, trade unionists, and progressive political leaders played a critical role in the expansion of government involvement, but other factors, such as industrialization, urbanization, the decline in the extended family, and cultural changes, are also relevant.

In addition, many arguments in favor of a greater role for government have been formulated by the advocates of state welfare. One of these concerns the fact that social well-being is affected by many complex events that are beyond individual and family control. For example, economic growth, which depends largely on business enterprise and the incentives created by governments, has a direct bearing on employment opportunities and incomes and, thus, on the welfare of individuals and families. When the economy expands, employment opportunities increase with positive implications for incomes and the social well-being of individuals and families.

On the other hand, when the economy experiences a recession, employment opportunities decline with negative implications for employment and incomes. These developments have grave consequences for the well-being of individuals and families but also for communities and society as a whole.

Many social policy scholars believe that individuals and families cannot adequately meet their own needs when faced with economic adversities such as unemployment. They believe that government intervention is needed. They also believe that governments should intervene in the economy to promote economic growth and prevent unemployment. Some social policy writers disagree and want government involvement to be strictly limited to providing support for philanthropic and faith-based organizations, which, they contend, are more efficient than government in dealing with adverse social conditions.

The policy efforts of governments to improve conditions of social welfare and to address those forces that create conditions of illfare are now a feature of public life in all countries of the modern world. They transcend the traditional individual and family responsibility approach as well as the "safety-net" approach. They include a wide range of services, programs, legal regulations, tax incentives, and judicial decisions. All have a tangible impact on social welfare and deserve further scrutiny.

Social Policy as a Government Activity

Governments affect the welfare of people through social policies in many different ways. Although they formulate policies and enact laws that are specifically intended to enhance the well-being of citizens, it has been noted already that social welfare may be enhanced through other types of interventions, such as economic, transportation, environmental, and other policies. Although these policies may not be intended to have a direct impact on social welfare, they nevertheless affect social conditions. However, social policy scholars have focused primarily on social legislation that allocates resources for social welfare programs and creates and authorizes a variety of social service programs. The study of these social services was a major preoccupation of social policy scholarship over the years. More recently, attention has focused on the way the fiscal system and the judicial process also affect conditions of social welfare. For example, the federal government uses the tax system to subsidize the incomes of low-income workers through the Earned Income Tax Credit (or EITC) and to subsidize mortgages and thus promote home ownership. Similarly, the federal courts have shaped policies that address racial, gender, and other forms of discrimination. They have also ruled on educational matters, health, urban development, and many other social issues.

Government social policies are authorized, codified, and implemented through *legislation*. A wide variety of laws and regulations are used to promote social welfare. They are used primarily to enable government agencies to introduce particular services or to change existing services or to terminate services. The government's budget is also governed by statute and determines the way a government funds its own social programs or contracts with nonprofit and commercial agencies to provide social services. Similarly, the tax system and the way it is used by government to promote welfare are also governed by legislation.

Governments obviously use *budgetary allocations* to enhance conditions of social welfare. These allocations are used to fund a great variety of government programs but, of particular interest, is the way they are used to finance income maintenance and support programs and the specialized social services that address the needs of groups of people who have traditionally been the primary concern of the social welfare system. Because governments are able to mobilize significant resources through the tax system, budgetary allocations are a very important factor in social welfare, and, usually, the amounts of the funds allocated to different services and programs are hotly contested.

Social services are regarded by many social policy scholars as the primary means by which governments seek to enhance the well-being of their citizens. Throughout the world, governments have adopted policies and enacted statutes that govern the way these social services operate and meet their goals. Conventionally, the term *social services* has been used to connote government programs operating in the fields of health, education, housing, income security, and family welfare. The last two fields are often classified under the heading of "social welfare policy." Social workers have played a major role in implementing welfare policies and, particularly, in using family and community welfare policies to discharge their professional obligations.

In addition to using legislation to create social service programs and fund these programs, governments also enact laws that impose mandates designed to improve social welfare. This mechanism is known as *statutory regulation.* Legislation of this kind is regularly enacted to require employers, homeowners, educational institutions, commercial firms, hospitals, and many others to adopt measures that have a direct impact on social welfare. Many areas of welfare, including housing, health, incomes, employment, and education, are shaped by government regulation. The minimum wage, rent control, affirmative action, school attendance, adequate safety at work, and a host of other statutory prescriptions and proscriptions all affect peoples' welfare. Of course, administrative decisions and the use of executive orders by the executive branch of government may also function as a regulatory mechanism. However, it is expected that administrative decisions and executive orders will be compatible with the laws enacted by Congress and that they will generally support the intent of social welfare legislation.

A third way in which government influences social welfare is through the *tax system.* The use of the tax system for social purposes is known as fiscal welfare. As Christopher Howard (1997) has shown, governments use the tax code to create incentives or disincentives that have a direct impact on social welfare. For example, tax incentives to save for retirement, to create educational accounts for children, or to obtain a mortgage to finance the purchase of a home are widely utilized by ordinary citizens and clearly affect their welfare.

Of particular interest to social policy scholars is the way the government uses statutory regulation and the tax system to encourage business corporations to provide occupational benefits for their workers. The commercial tax code contains numerous incentives of this kind (Hacker, 2002; Morris, 2006). The provision of social benefits by commercial and industrial enterprises is known as *occupational welfare*. Together with fiscal welfare, occupational welfare provisions play a major role in improving the well-being of those in regular wage employment (Jacoby, 1997). However, because temporary workers and immigrants do not always participate fully in the tax system, they do not usually benefit from these provisions. Many social policy scholars believe that both fiscal and occupational welfare disproportionately benefit high-income families and the middle class.

In addition to the direct actions of the legislature and the executive branch of government, the courts make a major contribution to social welfare through the *judicial process*. The courts play a significant role in social policy in the United States; they not only interpret government legislation but also take constitutional issues into account when deciding cases that affect the welfare of individuals or groups of people. These decisions influence many aspects of social welfare, ranging from access to social services to wider social issues such as civil rights, immigration, affirmative action, gay rights, and abortion. In addition, the courts have also ruled on a number of issues that are directly related to the social welfare system, such as whether claimants have a constitutional right to be provided with income benefits and social services.

Interest Groups and the Functions of Social Policy

Although social policies are usually formulated by elected officials through the legislative process, the policy-making process is complicated because the courts, the executive branch, and others are also involved. In addition, the role of interest groups in lobbying for or against particular policies should be recognized. Interest groups play a very important role in social policy making and exert a great deal of pressure on politicians. These groups are very active in seeking to influence the policy-making process and include business lobbies, professional associations, trade unions, nonprofit groups, state and municipal governments, and local communities. They may be represented by professional lobbyists, but they may also use personal contacts, campaign funding support, and electoral pressures to achieve their goals. The media, as well, play an important role in influencing policy. The exposure of social problems or injustices may galvanize public support and facilitate legislative action. Editorial opinion may also exert considerable influence on the way government policies are formulated and implemented. In addition, academics and the research staff of foundations and think tanks contribute to social policy formulation. Civil servants and professional government staff, too, play a key role by sharing their experience and knowledge with politicians.

A good deal of public policy research into the role of these different interest groups has now been undertaken, and it shows that the conventional view of social policy making is rather simplistic. This view considers social policy making as a technical, rational activity designed to produce the best policy that maximizes efficiency in the attainment of policy goals. Social policy makers may indeed aspire to be rational and efficient, but they cannot ignore the influence of many interest groups and constituencies in the policy-making process. In addition, interest groups play a significant role in the *implementation* of policies. Professional associations, trade unions, and others may be actively involved in the implementation of policies, and they also provide social services of their own. They undoubtedly have an effect on the way policies are translated into practice. Obviously, civil servants, planners, and other government officials also affect the implementation of policies in profound ways. Faith-based organizations, nonprofit agencies, and commercial firms that contract with the government to provide services also affect the implementation of policy.

Although, at first, it may appear that social policies can be readily understood by reading the statutes or studying the way the different social services operate, clearly, both the formulation and implementation of policy are complicated. In addition, government policies may have very complex effects. Although the legislation that enshrines policies may have clearly stated goals, it may also have "hidden" or unstated goals. Social policies and programs as well may have unintended consequences, may fail to achieve their goals, and may even have contradictory goals and effects.

Unfortunately, social policies may be introduced with the deliberate intention of negatively affecting the well-being of some groups of people. An example is the adoption of racist or discriminatory policies. The exclusion of immigrants from receiving social welfare benefits is another example of the use of social policy to diminish the welfare of a particular group of people. While these policies are often said to serve the interests of society as a whole, they have a negative effect on the welfare of some groups of people and create more illfare than welfare among these groups.

Recent debates about welfare reform revealed the extent to which a social policy has stated as well as "hidden" goals. The Personal Responsibility and Work Opportunity Reconciliation Act of 1996 (which is often referred to as the welfare reform legislation) has the stated goal of ending welfare dependency by promoting work among those who receive benefits, thereby promoting self-sufficiency and lifting them out of poverty. But many scholars have shown that the policy has not really met this goal and that many "welfare leavers," as they are known, in fact work intermittently and earn low wages. They also claim that it has hidden goals as well as other effects that benefit different groups of people. One hidden goal is simply to reduce the number of people receiving benefits. There is little doubt that the policy has met this unstated objective. As is well known, the number of people receiving income benefits has declined by well over 60% since the mid-1990s. In addition, political leaders of both major parties claim that welfare reform has been a resounding success, and the media generally endorse this position with the result that the issue of welfare is no longer a major topic in national elections as was previously the case. Many experts believe that the Democratic Party has benefited from this policy because it is no longer accused in national elections of condoning welfare dependency and abuse. In examining the impact of social policy, scholars often seek to determine who gains and who loses from the policy.

Although social policies are ostensibly introduced to enhance people's well-being, the complex ways that social policies work, their stated and unstated goals, and their effectiveness, as well as their unintended consequences, have become key themes of social policy scholarship. Today, social policy scholars are very interested in the motives of social policy makers and the hidden reasons for adopting social policies. A good deal of social policy scholarship has examined the motives of social policy makers and the way governments use social policy to achieve a variety of objectives. Much normative theory in the social policy field has been concerned with this issue and has attributed the emergence of social policy to factors other than the promotion of social welfare. These factors include the interests of different economic, political, and cultural groups and the way governments exert social control of people and respond to sectional interests. Social policy scholars have recognized the role of ideological beliefs and values in social policy, and they now stress the ways ideologies and normative theories influence social policy formulation and implementation. However, much more needs to done to understand the nuances of social policy and the different and intricate ways policies affect peoples' well-being. As is shown in the next section, social policy is now well established as a specialized field of academic inquiry, and it continues to provide new information and insights into what is a large and complex subject.

Social Policy as an Academic Field

Although the study of social policy only emerged as a distinct field of academic inquiry about 50 years ago, social thinkers and commentators have written about the subject for many centuries and have produced numerous accounts of the causes of social problems and of the way human welfare can be enhanced. These commentaries have also speculated about the actions of the state and its effects on peoples' welfare. In addition, these commentaries have been prescriptive, making recommendations for improving social conditions, and, sometimes, these recommendations have been formulated as utopian blueprints setting out a vision for an ideal society. Although utopian writings are frequently dismissed, they inspired social reformers in the 19th century to campaign for progressive social change. They also influenced the expansion of government involvement in social welfare in the 20th century.

The evolution of social policy as an academic field of study was significantly influenced by the idea that scientific principles should be adopted to study social welfare issues. Early pioneers of the study of social policy, such as the 19th century French mathematician Auguste Comte, believed that scientific methods could be applied not only to explain natural phenomena but also to analyze and improve social conditions. Comte outlined the basis for a science of society that he called sociology. He argued that the science of sociology should explain not only how societies function but also how they can be improved. The belief that scientific methods should be used to study social phenomena is known as positivism. The idea that social science scholarship should seek to improve social conditions is known as the normative approach. Although positive and normative approaches are today often regarded as antithetical, Comte believed that they were compatible. Today, Comte is widely regarded as one of the founders of sociology. Because his ideas have direct relevance for the emergence of social policy, he is also regarded by some as a founder of the applied social science of social policy.

The use of scientific methods in social welfare was fostered by the widespread employment of the census in Europe in the 19th century. The census permitted the collection of a large amount of statistical data on social conditions, and it provided information on which proposals for social reform could be based. The availability of census data was complemented by the findings of early ethnographic studies of the living conditions of low-income workers and poor people. This research involved careful studies of poor communities and the lives of their members. Formative ethnographic studies also resulted in the emergence of the social survey at the end of the 19th century. The survey was a powerful tool that activists used to collect information about poverty, to draw attention to social injustice, and to campaign for social reform.

The surveys of poverty undertaken by Charles Booth and Seebohm Rowntree in England and by Paul Kellogg in the United States informed many middle-class citizens about the harsh conditions under which poor people lived, engendering a degree of sympathy for their plight. The findings of these surveys were also used by social reformers to pressure governments to take ameliorative action. Leading reformers, such as Beatrice and Sidney Webb in England and Jane Addams and her followers in the United States, made effective use of survey and census data to campaign for progressive social change.

By the 1930s, social science information was frequently being used in government social policy making. Statistical data about the extent of unemployment and poverty during the Great Depression played a significant role in the development of New Deal social policies. Also relevant were the results of carefully documented social policy innovations that had previously sought to address these problems. The enactment of the nation's first unemployment insurance statute in Wisconsin in 1932 was influenced by a group of economists at the University of Wisconsin who documented its effects. Their research helped persuade the Roosevelt administration that social security could significantly reduce the incidence of poverty among the unemployed, elderly, and other needy groups (Leuchtenburg, 1963; Skocpol & Ikenbery, 1995).

The rapid expansion of government social service programs, which followed the New Deal in the United States and the publication of the Beveridge Report in Britain, also played a major role in the creation of social policy as an academic subject. Although government social welfare policies had previously been studied at universities, often at schools of social work, the massive expansion of government social welfare intervention at the time facilitated a much more systematic examination of government social policies and their effects on people's well-being.

In 1950, the London School of Economics (LSE) in England appointed Richard Titmuss to the first professorial position in social policy. The school had been a pioneer of social work education having collaborated with the Charity Organisation Society to establish the first social work training program in Britain in the early years of the 20th century, and its program was well regarded. However, academic leaders at the LSE believed that more emphasis should be placed on scholarly research than on the professional training of social workers, and on the recommendation of T. H. Marshall, the head of LSE's sociology department, a search for a professor with expertise in social policy was launched. Although Titmuss was not a university graduate, he had written several books on social issues and was highly respected. He was appointed to the position.

Titmuss had a major influence on the subsequent development of social policy as an academic subject. His publications were widely read, and he initiated a research agenda that drew international attention. He also recruited new faculty whose academic work further enhanced the subject's reputation. Their publications were widely read in Britain and in other countries as well, and they also exerted considerable influence on politicians and government officials concerned with welfare issues. Their research was particularly important to the British Labour Party. When the party won the 1964 election, Titmuss and his colleagues played a major role in shaping the government's social policy agenda (Reisman, 1977). Titmuss's work was ideologically aligned with social democratic thinking, and he believed strongly that government should assume responsibility for social welfare. Governments, he argued, should formulate and implement social policies that address the problems of poverty, social deprivation, and inequality.

In the 1960s and 1970s, many other British universities also established interdisciplinary departments of social policy or social administration, as they are also known, and many of Titmuss's former students were recruited to staff these departments. Their approach to the study of social policy was largely based on the social democratic perspective that Titmuss and his colleagues had adopted at the London School of Economics, and generally, most British social policy scholars urged governments to play an active role in promoting the welfare of their citizens.

Titmuss's writings were also well received by academics in the United States and soon began to influence social policy making in America as well. However, academic departments of social policy similar to those in Britain have not emerged in the United States. Here, the study of social policy is pursued in other academic settings, for example, in schools of public policy and social work and within academic departments of sociology, political science, and economics. While social policy is not established as a distinctive academic field in the United States to the same extent as it is in Britain and other English-speaking nations, the different disciplinary perspectives from which social policy is studied in America have contributed significantly to the understanding of government social policies and their effects.

Although many social policy scholars believe that social policy investigation should be based on scientific research and be dispassionate, much social policy writing evokes values and beliefs about the desirability of different social policies, and often these beliefs shape the way social policy scholars approach the subject and evaluate the effects of social policies. Some social policy scholars are critical of this tendency, arguing that the study of social policy should avoid ideological issues and be based on objective, scientific methods of investigation. This view reflects the positivist approach, although, as was noted earlier, Comte did not see any contradiction between positivism and using social science knowledge for social welfare purposes. Despite disagreements on this issue, much social policy scholarship today is characterized by both positive and normative forms of inquiry.

Some social policy scholars believe that government social policies are intrinsically value laden and permeated with ideological beliefs. They reject the idea that the policy-making process can be impartial and based exclusively on rational and objective criteria. They argue that the values and beliefs of policy makers invariably affect the ways policies are formulated, and, for this reason, they contend that the academic study of social policy cannot and should not avoid normative issues. They argue that even detached writings, which purport to provide a factual account of government policies, usually reflect the normative preferences of their authors. Consequently, instead of seeking to be ideologically neutral, social policy scholars should, they contend, identify the values and beliefs inherent in social policies and explicate the normative position of those engaged in the social policy process.

Today, this view is more widely accepted, and a good deal of social policy writing is now explicitly normative. Since the 1970s, when British scholars such as Vic George and Paul Wilding (1976) first analyzed the role of ideology in social policy, the field has been characterized by vigorous normative debates. However, the social democratic influence on social policy has waned, and this approach has now been challenged by other normative approaches such as radical populism, Marxism, critical theory, feminism, multiculturalism, postmodernism, conservatism, and market liberalism (or neoliberalism, as it is more commonly known). This diversification has fostered a vibrant body of normative theory that stresses the political economy dimensions of social policy scholarship. Part III of this book discusses the major political economy perspectives in social policy thinking today and reveals that the normative approach to social policy has generated important debates about how social welfare can be enhanced.

Features of Social Policy Inquiry

Although social policy is still a relatively new academic subject, social policy scholars have now produced a substantial literature that has described, analyzed, and evaluated the social policies of governments in the United States and many other countries as well. Their research has also exerted considerable influence on the social policy-making process. This sizable and complex field of study is difficult to summarize, but describing its salient features in terms of the purposes of social policy inquiry may be helpful. Four primary purposes of social policy scholarship can be identified.

First, academic inquiry into social policy has been concerned with understanding the *policy-making process* and the way policies are implemented. This research draws extensively on organization and management theory as well as quantitative techniques, and a substantial literature on the subject has now been published. Studies of the policy-making process are particularly concerned with the way the process is influenced by rational and technical decisions. The field also considers the implementation of policy. Known as administration or, increasingly, as policy practice, these academic studies have clarified the steps, skills, and procedures involved in implementing social policies. They have also exposed the challenges facing managers seeking to direct the implementation of social policies.

Second, social policy inquiry has sought to describe and analyze the *social conditions* that social policies and programs are intended to change. This analysis was a major preoccupation of social policy scholarship in the 19th century when, as noted earlier, social scientists collected a great deal of information about the incidence of poverty and deprivation in European and North American cities. They were primarily motivated by the aim of using this information for social reform purposes. Since then, studies of the extent of social need, the causes of social problems, and the way people maximize opportunities and improve their life chances have become commonplace. In addition to social surveys, sophisticated analyses of administrative and census data have been used to study and describe social conditions. Documentary and ethnographic methods are also used for this purpose.

Third, as mentioned earlier, much social policy scholarship has been concerned with describing and documenting the *social services*. When social policy first emerged as a systematic field of academic inquiry in the 1950s, many scholars devoted a great deal of attention to tracing the historical evolution of the social services, documenting their legislative basis, analyzing social service budgetary allocations, studying their target client groups, and assessing their effectiveness. Although the *historical descriptive method*, as this approach is known, was pioneered in the Western world, other regions have adopted it, and many studies of the social services in other countries have now been published.

Descriptive studies have given rise to the construction of *conceptual representations* or *typologies* of social policies. Typologies of social policy that seek to classify particular social policy approaches, or even the features of the social policies of nation states as a whole, are now commonplace. One of the first of these was Harold Wilensky and Charles Lebeaux's (1965) residual-institutional typology, which is still used today. It has since been augmented by many other typologies, including those of Titmuss (1974), Mishra (1984), and Esping-Andersen (1990).

Third, social policy inquiry has sought to *explain* why and how social policies emerge to respond to social conditions. Although still relatively underdeveloped, social policy inquiry has made considerable progress in formulating theoretical explanations. Research in the field has been largely concerned with explaining reasons for the introduction of social service programs and the social functions they serve in society. Social policy scholars, particularly in Britain, have also sought to incorporate the insights of sociological and political science theories into these analyses.

Finally, social policy inquiry has sought to *evaluate* the effectiveness of social policy and to determine its outcomes. Given the subject's normative nature, evaluative research is central to the field. Much social policy research is concerned, either directly or indirectly, with assessing the effectiveness of government social policy interventions. Nevertheless, many social policy writers recognize that evaluative research, while technically sophisticated, is not always used in practice. While evaluation forms a central component of service delivery, social programs are regularly implemented without adequate thought being given to assessing their outcomes. This is not only the case with the social services but with far more complicated areas of social policy investigation such as the effects of fiscal and regulatory policies on social welfare. Despite its importance, evaluation remains a neglected topic in social policy.

_____ **The Future of Social Policy**

For much of the postwar period, social policy has been dominated by the assumption that peoples' welfare can best be enhanced through government intervention. However, since the 1980s, this assumption has been challenged by academic writers on the political right who believe that government involvement in social welfare is inefficient, unnecessary, and even harmful (Friedman, 1962; Gilder, 1981; Mead, 1986, 1992; Murray, 1984, 2006; Olasky, 1992, 1996). Their ideas have inspired conservative political leaders in the United States and other countries. With the electoral successes of conservative governments, social policies have changed significantly over the last two decades to incorporate greater privatization, decentralization, and the increased participation of nongovernmental and particularly faith-based agencies in service delivery. Budgetary allocations for the social services have also been reduced, and the seemingly inexorable expansion of state welfare since the Second World War has been halted. These developments have created a new social and political climate for social policy, posing new challenges for those working in the field. Some of these challenges are examined further in the final chapter of this book.

_____ **References**

Esping-Andersen, G. (1990). *Three worlds of welfare capitalism.* Cambridge, UK: Polity Press.

Friedman, M. (1962). *Capitalism and freedom.* Chicago: University of Chicago Press.

George, V., & Wilding, P. (1976). *Ideology and social welfare.* London: Routledge and Kegan Paul.

Gilder, G. (1981). *Wealth and poverty.* London: Buchan and Enright.

Hacker, J. S. (2002). *The divided welfare state.* New York: Cambridge University Press.

Howard, C. (1997). *The hidden welfare state: Tax expenditure and social policy in the United States.* Princeton, NJ: Princeton University Press.

Jacoby, S. M. (1997). *Modern manors: Welfare capitalism since the New Deal.* Princeton, NJ: Princeton University Press.

Layard, R. (2005). *Happiness: Lessons from a new science.* New York: Penguin.

Leuchtenburg, W. E. (1963). *Franklin Roosevelt and the New Deal.* New York: Harper.

Mead, L. M. (1986). *Beyond entitlement: The social obligations of citizenship.* New York: Free Press.

Mead, L. M. (1992). *The new politics of poverty: The nonworking poor in America.* New York: Basic Books.

Mishra, R. (1984). *The welfare state in crisis.* Brighton, UK: Wheatsheaf Press.

Morris, C. R. (2006). *Apart at the seams: The collapse of private pension and health care protections.* New York: Century Foundation Press.

Murray, C. (1984). *Losing ground: American social policy 1950–1980.* New York: Basic Books.

Murray, C. (2006). *In our hands: A plan to replace the welfare state.* Washington, DC: AEI Press.

Olasky, M. (1992). *The tragedy of American compassion.* Washington, DC: Regnery.

Olasky, M. (1996). *Renewing American compassion.* Washington, DC: Regnery.

Reisman, D. A. (1977). *Richard Titmuss: Welfare and society.* London: Heinemann Educational Books.

Skocpol, T., & Ikenbery, G. R. (1995). The road to social security. In T. Skocpol (Ed.), *Social policy in the United States* (pp. 136–166). Princeton, NJ: Princeton University Press.

Titmuss, R. M. (1974). *Social policy: An introduction.* London: Allen & Unwin.

Wilensky, H., & Lebeaux, C. (1965). *Industrial society and social welfare.* New York: Free Press.

2 An Overview of American Social Policy

Diana M. DiNitto

To use an inelegant phrase, social policy has effects from "womb to tomb." The wide-ranging effects of social policy necessitate an overview of this subject that is very board. Even narrowly defined, social policy functions consume most of the federal budget and a growing percentage of state and local budgetary allocations (U.S. Census Bureau, 2005; U.S. Congress, 2004). The stakes involved are not only monetary; they are also ideological because Americans have divergent views of social policy.

The Many Contexts of Social Policy

When we consider the contexts of social policy, no social unit is more important than the family. Families are expected to provide food, shelter, and other necessities for their members and to direct their young to conform to the norms and laws of society. Social policy helps families or surrogate families carry out these many social functions, for example, by providing a public school education and by establishing health care facilities. There is, however, no overarching social policy for families in the United States. Many other developed countries have family policies that are much broader than those in the United States, which has long operated under the premise that social policy should be used to intervene in family affairs only as a last resort. Libertarians support this laissez-faire or reactive posture. Others prefer more proactive policies, such as the public provision of health care, child care, and elder care.

Both the family and governments are intimately involved in social welfare functions, and often, there is considerable tension between these social institutions in carrying out socially prescribed mandates. For example, parents may disagree with a school district's decision as to whether or not to classify their child as needing services under the Individuals with Disabilities Education Act. Gaps in social policy can also interfere with the family's ability to carry out its functions. For example, families may be unable to obtain preventive or remedial health care for their members. Many other gaps between families' roles and the policies available to assist them also have to do with families' financial constraints, such as lack of affordable child care while parents work. Other tensions involve ideological differences. For instance, families might disagree with mandates about the limits of discipline as defined in their state's child abuse statutes, or parents may oppose state laws that allow minors to obtain an abortion without their consent.

Religion has long been a motivator for doing charitable works. Even with the vast expansion of government aid, churches continue to supplement public and private responses to those in need. Church-related organizations generally support social legislation such as public assistance and minimum wage laws. Most churches, however, demur from overt political activity, preferring to go about their work in other ways. A major exception is the fundamentalist religious right, which has attempted to influence social policy through direct political involvement, especially on the issue of abortion.

Some writers have gained notoriety for their position that social policy has spawned a series of misguided social programs (e.g., Olasky, 1992, 1996). They see public relief as an impersonal and ineffective system of entitlements that should be replaced by a more personal relationship with the givers, often established through religious organizations. Evangelicals embrace the position that they can provide the spiritual guidance as well as other services that may be necessary to help lift the downtrodden out of poverty or degradation. In 1996, Congress passed the Personal Responsibility and Work Opportunity Reconciliation Act (PRWORA), a major revision of the Aid to Families with Dependent Children (AFDC) program and other public assistance programs. The 1996 act allows monies to be channeled to religious groups for programs to aid public assistance recipients, providing greater opportunities for religious organizations' involvement in social welfare. President George W. Bush's establishment of the White House Office of Faith-Based and Community Initiatives was another step in the merger of religion and social policy functions.

The country's economic situation also plays a major role in social welfare programs. In their well-known book *Regulating the Poor*, Piven and Cloward (1971) took the position that "the key to understanding relief-giving is in the functions it serves for the larger economic and political order, for relief is a secondary and supportive institution" (p. xii). They saw a direct relationship between the number of people needed in the workforce and the expansion and contraction of social welfare programs to fit the situation. Corporate enterprises, from small businesses to multinational conglomerates, have a vested interest in legislation that affects workers (minimum wage legislation, health care legislation, and tax policy such as

Social Security taxes). The labor movement is equally concerned about these issues. Corporations pour vast sums of money into promoting legislation and supporting candidates that are "pro business." Labor unions and professional organizations do the same to protect their interests.

The country's economic (budgetary and monetary) policies also affect social welfare. There are different views about the economic policies that promote the well-being of the greatest number of people. A notable contrast involves the Reagan and Clinton administrations. According to Keynesian economics, when unemployment is high, prices are expected to drop to accommodate the reduction in workers' incomes, and when unemployment is low, prices are expected to rise as workers earn more and demand more goods and services. However, during the 1970s, both unemployment and inflation remained high, causing President Reagan to adopt a policy of "supply side" economics. It included both attempts to cut the rate of growth of government expenditures and tax cuts in the hope that people would save and invest more, thus boosting the economy. Benefits were supposed to accrue to everyone, even trickling down to those in the lower income brackets. But the greatest benefits seemed to go to the wealthy who gained substantially from the tax cuts. Poverty failed to abate, income inequality was exacerbated, and annual budget deficits and the accompanying national debt skyrocketed (see DiNitto, 2007).

The Clinton administration's policy, referred to as "enterprise economics" focused on government investment in human capital (education and training of workers), technology (communication systems), and infrastructure (transportation systems) that affect a broad spectrum of people (Dye, 1998). There were also tax increases during this period, including the addition of two higher personal income tax brackets. Although it is difficult to know the exact impact of these policies, during the late 1990s, the country's economic picture was much brighter—with employment high and inflation low. Federal budgeting involves considerable use of "smoke and mirrors," but deficits and the debt abated as Republicans and Democrats finally came to some agreement over balancing the budget. Even in good times, some Americans remain outside the economic mainstream. They have been referred to as the *underclass* (Wilson, 1987), those who remain the concern of the public sector and who rely especially on the social policies called public assistance or welfare.

There have long been ideological differences among Americans over the role of government in social welfare. For decades, those who wished to prevent government intervention in health care programs (the American Medical Association prominent among them) and other aspects of social welfare claimed that federally sponsored programs would propel the country toward socialism. But during the New Deal era of the 1930s, Republicans and Democrats banded together to ease the financial hardship faced by so many. During the Great Society era of the 1960s, Congress and the president again worked together to alleviate poverty for those who had not benefited from the affluence of the previous decade.

In the last few decades, rifts over social policy have become increasingly apparent. In 1994, Republicans offered a ten point "Contract with America" to represent their conservative budgetary and social agenda. Democratic President Bill Clinton vetoed two major welfare reform bills delivered by the Republican-controlled Congress because he thought they were too punitive. In 1996, he finally approved a major reform, but he was still unhappy with some provisions, such as denying most aid to immigrants residing legally in the country. On the other hand, he supported provisions limiting the time that families can receive Temporary Assistance for Needy Families (TANF), the program that replaced AFDC. Some of his closest social welfare advisors quit in protest over the new law.

Opinion polls also show that the American public holds different views about public assistance policy, but often, responses fluctuate based on what questions are asked. For example, Americans say they want to help those in need, even though many claim to disdain welfare programs (Weaver, Shapiro, & Jacobs, 1995). One might say that Republicans and conservatives favor limited social programs, and Democrats and liberals, greater intervention, while Libertarians believe in a hands-off approach. These are overly simplistic descriptions. A Republican may be conservative on spending issues but support abortion or gay rights, which are considered traditional liberal positions (DiNitto, 2007). A Catholic Democrat may want the Food Stamp Program expanded, tougher work requirements for TANF recipients, and the right to an abortion overturned. Within both major political parties there are conservatives, liberals, and moderates depending on the issue involved.

Politics in the United States can rightfully be called special interest politics. Individuals and groups often pool their resources by donating to political action committees (PACs) in order to support candidates who share their positions. To garner the money needed to run for political office, candidates become beholding to these special interest groups. Big money politics breeds corruption. Some candidate or organization is always being investigated for violating campaign contribution rules. Most Americans believe that cases like that of powerful lobbyist Jack Abramoff, who pleaded guilty in 2006 to felony charges of conspiracy, corruption, and tax evasion, are not isolated (Harris Poll, 2006). We might assume that elected officials would prefer not to be at the mercy of special interests. We can also assume that proposed ethics and campaign finance reform legislation frequently fails in Congress because few candidates believe they can win without special interest money.

Groups supportive of social welfare legislation may not have the biggest coffers, but they still form PACs. The National Association of Social Workers' PAC is called Political Action for Candidate Election (PACE). Social workers and other groups act as proxies for the poor, children, and other disenfranchised groups that cannot easily represent themselves in the political process (Keller, 1981). Nonetheless, they are sometimes accused of being more concerned about their own professional interests than those of their clients.

The media are said to have a liberal bias (Goldberg, 2002), but this point is debatable given that big business controls the major media (Fiorina &

Peterson, 2002) and conservative media personalities flood radio, television, newspapers, the Internet, and other media to challenge liberal views. There is widespread agreement that the media play a key role in social policy development. The media's ability to bring social problems and proposed solutions to the public's attention is widely recognized (Dye & Zeigler, 1991; Hewitt, 1996). Prior to mass means of communication, it was difficult to mobilize Americans behind issues. Today, Americans are bombarded with so much media coverage that they may also become desensitized to many social issues (DiNitto, 2007) unless the issue affects them directly or results in widespread devastation, as was the case following the terrorist attacks on the World Trade Center and the Pentagon on September 11, 2001, and after hurricanes Katrina and Rita hit the U.S. Gulf Coast in 2005.

Other influences shaping social policy are the relationships among the public, not-for-profit (voluntary), and private (proprietary) sectors. The once sharp distinctions among them have blurred. The inability of governments and voluntary organizations to solve social problems has led to privatization—allowing profit-making entities to provide services, such as residential programs for people with disabilities and even child protective services, once thought to be the clear purview of state and local governments (Kamerman & Kahn, 1989). Some people think that privatization results in governments abrogating their responsibilities along with providing fewer and poorer quality services (see, for example, Katz, 2001). Others believe that private entities can do the job at least as well and more efficiently. In a capitalist society, entrepreneurs are constantly seeking new ventures. The foray into social welfare, like other ventures, can be motivated by profit as well as the desire to do good.

Class distinctions may also influence social policy. To quote James Madison (1787/1911), "the most common and durable source of faction has been the various and unequal distribution of property. Those who hold and those who are without property have ever formed distinct interests in society." Many Americans want to have their cake and eat it too. For example, in 2007, most Republicans, Democrats, and Independents did not think it "necessary to increase taxes to reduce the budget deficit" (Harris Poll, 2007), but if programs had to be cut, substantially more favored cutting space programs than welfare or defense programs. Least popular was cutting social welfare programs that affect broad segments of the population (Medicare, Social Security, education, and Medicaid). However, Americans in upper income brackets tend to be the most liberal on many social welfare issues. For example, in a 1996 public opinion poll, those earning $75,000 or more were more likely than those who earned less to oppose cuts in social spending and restrictions on abortions, and they were most supportive of school busing (Saad, 1996).

Race has also had a profound effect on social policy. Slavery was abolished in 1865, but the "separate but equal" doctrine set forth in the 1896 U.S. Supreme Court decision in *Plessy v. Ferguson* supported racial segregation. This changed in 1954, when the high court decided in *Brown v. the Board of Education of Topeka, Kansas* that separate facilities were not equal facilities. The Civil Rights Act of 1964 was another milestone in securing opportunity regardless of an individual's race or national origin. Affirmative action programs in schools and in workplaces followed, but, in the 1990s, the call was for an end to race-based preferences. Black Americans, those of Hispanic origins, and other ethnic groups have made considerable social and economic progress, but on average, these groups still do not earn the same as whites, even with the same education (U.S. Census Bureau, 2006a). Social program spending cuts are often considered direct affronts to these groups because these programs help offset the economic effects of discrimination. Many people feel that preferential treatment may no longer be in order but that affirmative action is still needed to ensure that people of all ethnic and racial groups have a fair chance.

Gender must also be considered in social policy analysis. From the bedroom to the boardroom and from the state legislatures to the houses of Congress, gender politics is a sensitive issue. Women continue to earn less than men even when they have the same education or work at the same jobs (U.S. Census Bureau, 2006a). Since women's poverty rates are much higher than men's (U.S. Census Bureau, 2006b), women constitute most of the adults receiving public assistance. The more generous federal social insurance legislation of the 1930s was written with men as the primary breadwinners in mind (Gordon, 1990, 1994). At the same time, federal Aid to Families with Dependent Children legislation to help female-headed households was built on states' more penurious public assistance programs. Women also took the brunt of welfare reform as a backlash grew over the rising numbers of public assistance cases in which mothers were not married to (or cohabitating with) the child's father, the mother did not work, and the father did not pay child support.

The feminist political movement has resulted in some gains for women, such as the Equal Pay Act of 1963 and the 1972 Title IX education amendments to the 1964 Civil Rights Act. Child support enforcement legislation has also made it more difficult for fathers to shirk their financial responsibility to their children. For many women, the crowning social policy would be an amendment to the U.S. Constitution guaranteeing women equal rights.

Many more issues should be included in this overview of U.S. social welfare policy, including the aging of the population, the millions of U.S. citizens under age 65 without health insurance, immigration, the lack of affordable housing, domestic violence, and the right to life and the right to die. All these issues have a direct bearing on social welfare.

Social Policy Functions of Governments _____

The federal government, state and municipal governments, and entities such as school districts and hospital districts make social policy. Federalism is the constitutional division of powers among the federal and state governments. The Constitution grants the federal government 18 powers, including the power to tax and spend for the "general welfare" and the power granted by the "necessary and proper" clause, which allows the federal government to do many things it deems necessary (see, for example, Dye & Zeigler, 2006). The Constitution also reserves powers for the states (and the people). Social welfare functions are generally considered among the states' powers, though local governments initially took responsibility for those in need.

During the late 1800s and early 1900s, heavy industrialization, urbanization, immigration, and World War I brought rapidly changing conditions and many social problems (Dye, 1998). During the Progressive Era (1900 to 1919), the states' role in social welfare also grew rapidly as local governments needed assistance with these mounting concerns. States passed child labor laws; instituted mothers' aid for women whose husbands died, deserted, or became disabled; adopted workers' compensation laws; and provided aid to poor people who were elderly or blind (Axinn & Stern, 2005; Day, 2006).

Dual federalism, which emphasized separate federal and state government functions, became *cooperative federalism* as the federal government ventured into the social policy arena (Dye, 1998; Jost, 1996). The federal Children's Bureau was established in 1912 to address the problems of the country's youngest citizens. The Sheppard-Towner Act of 1921 allowed the bureau to establish maternal and child health clinics. This was a beginning, but the defining event that led the federal government to exercise the major role it does today in social policy was the Great Depression.

The stock market crash of 1929 and the Great Depression that followed caused widespread suffering. The federal government responded initially with temporary strategies—soup kitchens and public works (jobs) programs. The more permanent strategies came in President Roosevelt's New Deal, embodied in the Social Security Act of 1935. The act made the federal government a full partner with the states in alleviating poverty through public assistance programs. Using the model the states had adopted, the act established a program for poor families with children—Aid to Dependent Children (ADC)—and programs for people who were poor and aged or blind—Old Age Assistance (OAA) and Aid to the Blind (AB), respectively. More important, the federal government adopted a new strategy to prevent poverty through the national social insurance program called Old Age Insurance or, more commonly, Social Security. It also adopted an unemployment compensation program to be administered primarily by the states. The act contained additional provisions to assist the states in providing for maternal and child health and welfare. The Social Security Act cast the federal government's net quite wide in addressing social policy issues. None of this could have been accomplished without the introduction in 1913 of the federal income tax, which gave the federal government a large source of revenue that could be tapped to address these problems (see Dye, 1998).

Federal intervention increased in the 1950s. Many more workers were included under the Social Security retirement program. Social Security Disability Insurance was established for people who became disabled during their working years. The federal government also stepped in to help the states by adding a public assistance program called Aid to the Permanently and Totally Disabled (APTD).

The federal government increased its role in social policy again during the 1960s with its War on Poverty and the programs of the Great Society. These strategies began emerging during the Kennedy administration, but it was President Johnson whose rhetoric included the war analogy. Some of the experimental strategies of that war, which varied from community to community, did not survive. Others remain well known today, especially the Head Start preschool program. Great Society initiatives also included the Food Stamp Program to assist poor and low-income individuals and families obtain an adequate diet, the Medicaid program to help certain categories of poor people gain access to medical care (e.g., children receiving public assistance), and the Medicare program to provide health care access to virtually all the population aged 65 and older.

Except for some administrative costs paid by the states, the Food Stamp Program is funded by the federal government, which also sets eligibility rules. The program is available to more poor and low-income Americans than any other public assistance program. Medicaid, the most expensive of all the public assistance programs, is a joint federal-state program and relies on funding and rule making by both the federal and state governments. Medicare, a social insurance program, is the most highly centralized and entirely under federal purview.

Beginning in the 1950s, the federal government embraced another role by providing funding to the states for social services to families receiving public assistance (Kahn, 1979; Morris, 1979). This role expanded in the 1960s with the hope that social services could help parents address the personal problems that might be preventing them from leaving the welfare rolls. The federal government also stepped up its role in helping the states provide services for people with intellectual disabilities and mental illnesses through the Mental Retardation Facilities and Community Mental Health Centers Construction Act of 1963. It ventured further into social services for older people with the Older Americans Act in 1965.

In 1974, the joint federal and state programs of Old Age Assistance, Aid to the Blind, and Aid to the Permanently and Totally Disabled were transformed into the Supplemental Security Income (SSI) program. Under SSI, the federal government sets eligibility requirements, provides a basic payment to all recipients, and does most of the program administration. This "federalization" was intended to bring an end to the unequal treatment of poor people who were aged, blind, or otherwise disabled across the states. Most states supplement the federal minimum payment, but, once again, the federal role in public assistance had grown.

In 1965, national defense consumed 43% of the federal budget, and social welfare (social insurance, health, and public assistance), 24%. By 1975, defense was 26% and social welfare, 42%. Political scientist Aaron Wildavsky (1979) called it the "revolution no one noticed." Eventually, critics such as George Gilder (1981) and Charles Murray (1984) did take note, contending that many of the country's social welfare problems can be blamed on social policy itself. They believe that public assistance programs (primarily AFDC) emasculated men in their role of breadwinner, causing their self-esteem to plummet along with their worth to society. They blame these programs for family break up and entrapment in lives of degradation and despair.

Gilder's work caught the attention of President Reagan, who wanted to turn much of the role the federal government had assumed in social welfare back to the states, an approach known as the New Federalism or devolution. Reagan successfully combined many smaller categorical grant programs for specific functions into block grants for broader functions. These block grants allow the states more flexibility in determining how the money is spent. President Bush also encouraged devolution, looking to the states as laboratories to test new approaches in delivering the Aid to Families with Dependent Children (AFDC) program. President Clinton went even further, helping to make many of these experiments federal policy by signing the Personal Responsibility and Work Opportunity Reconciliation Act of 1996. The act changed AFDC, a categorical entitlement program, into the block grant called Temporary Assistance for Needy Families (TANF). Some other attempts to turn public assistance programs, such as the Food Stamp Program, into block grants have failed. There is no doubt, however, that the current era of public assistance is characterized by devolution.

The federal government continues to retain full responsibility for administering Social Security and Medicare, the country's major social insurance programs. There has been interest in privatizing Social Security. Even if employees were allowed to divert only a portion of their Social Security taxes into private investments, this would be a radical departure from the way Social Security has operated. The possibility is a whittling away of the government's role in social insurance. Given the risky nature of the stock market, such a move could place more people in need of public assistance during their retirement. Medicare is already privatized in that most participants obtain their health services from physicians and other medical providers in the private sector.

State Governments' Role

Prior to federal intervention, growing social problems caused states to aid local governments with a number of social welfare programs. Even with the Social Security Act, the states maintained key roles in financing public assistance and social service programs and determining eligibility requirements and the payments or services to be provided. In the ensuing years, the federal government took on more social welfare responsibilities. For several decades, federalization was the prevailing social policy philosophy. In fact, the original Aid to Dependent Children (ADC) program was intended to diminish in importance as Social Security grew to cover nearly all retired workers and their dependents, long-term disabled workers and their dependents, and survivors of deceased workers. The growth of programs such as Aid to Families with Dependent Children and an increase in the number of families that received benefits for long periods of time resulted in dissatisfaction with public assistance. There was a widespread feeling that more should be done to help families become self-sufficient.

Presidents Ronald Reagan and George H. W. Bush and many Congress members were convinced that less federal red tape would allow the states to improve delivery of public assistance and social service programs (mental health, substance abuse, and so forth). As states tried to cope with AFDC's perceived failure, they invented a wide variety of new approaches—capping payments to families that had more children while on AFDC, cutting benefits to families with children who missed too much school, allowing AFDC families to keep more job earnings while still receiving benefits, and allowing them to save money for education or to start a business. While Congress argued over President Clinton's proposed Health Security Act (which was soundly defeated) and Congress members offered their own health care proposals, the states were taking concrete steps to cover more individuals and families through managed health care arrangements and laws requiring employers to cover more employees. The states continue to assume a great deal of responsibility for services such as mental health, substance abuse, and vocational rehabilitation. Under the leadership of President George W. Bush, the country has remained in the era of "devolutionist federalism."

One program that some states and localities continue to operate without federal help is General Assistance (GA) or General Relief. Following the Social Security Act, GA expenditures dropped considerably as the federal government stepped in to help. GA programs vary widely from place to place, but they continue to have an important function by helping those ineligible for federal or federal-state social welfare programs. Traditionally, these were needy people who did not qualify for AFDC, Old Age Assistance, Aid to the Blind, or Aid to the Permanently and Totally Disabled; able-bodied adults who did not qualify for unemployment insurance and were unable to find work; and individuals who could not pay their medical bills (MacIntyre, 1964). A contemporary study of California's GA program describes many recipients as those with mental disabilities, immigrants, and individuals recently released from correctional facilities (Moon & Schneiderman, 1995). There is still a need to fill in the cracks of federal and federal-state social welfare programs, but many jurisdictions have cut back on General Assistance (Gallagher, 1999).

Local Governments' Role

Historically, relief in the United States consisted of communities compensating families that took in needy people. Communities also developed "outdoor relief," which was provided to people in their own homes, and "indoor relief," which was provided in institutions such as almshouses or workhouses. Once the key player in public assistance, local governments now have the smallest role. Today, local jurisdictions' primary tasks concern broad social functions, such as public safety (police and fire protection) and public school education. Local governments do provide support for social service programs, for example, community mental health centers, shelters for women victimized by spousal violence, and senior citizens centers. Many cities operate some type of social welfare or social service department, and some offer General Assistance even if their state does not have a required GA program.

Legislative, Executive, and Judicial Authority in Social Policy Making

Social policy is made by federal, state, and local legislative bodies; by the executive authority of elected officials (the president, governors, and other state and municipal officials) and appointed officials (agency heads); and by the judiciary (the Supreme Court and other federal, state, and municipal courts). This system of checks and balances may not make for a speedy policy process, but it does help to ensure that policy issues get thorough consideration in a pluralistic, democratic society.

Legislative Processes

Both branches of Congress have a number of committees and subcommittees that are responsible for social policy. Many of the largest social programs (Social Security, Medicare, Medicaid, TANF, SSI) come under the jurisdiction of the House Committee on Ways and Means. The House Committee on Agriculture with its Subcommittee on Department Operations, Oversight, Nutrition, and Forestry is responsible for the Food Stamp Program and most other nutrition programs. The Senate Committee on Finance oversees Social Security and many functions of the Department of Health and Human Services, such as child welfare and child support enforcement, Medicaid and Medicare, and social services. The Senate also has a Committee on Agriculture, Nutrition, and Forestry. Many other congressional committees are also responsible for parts and parcels of social policy.

A high degree of congressional involvement is warranted, but the complex legislative system can make for overlapping and even contradictory social policies. Some of these overlaps and contradictions result from the different ideologies of the major political parties. They also result from the many steps involved in seeing a bill become a law as well as the special interests and regional interests that want a say in legislation. For example, states with heavy agricultural interests are particularly concerned about the many programs of the U.S. Department of Agriculture. States with large immigrant populations want input into legislation affecting the U.S. Citizenship and Immigration Services, immigrants' entrance into the country, and the social welfare benefits immigrants can receive.

In addition to the policies that each state's legislative body generates, state legislatures must often respond to laws that Congress has passed and other federal mandates. For example, when Congress passed the Personal Responsibility and Work Opportunity Reconciliation Act of 1996, state legislatures had to transform their AFDC programs to make them conform to the new TANF program legislation or risk losing funding. Each time the federal government expands Medicaid eligibility to include more categories of people, the states have had to generate the match money to serve these individuals, even if some states would not have chosen to do so. A recent battle over unfunded mandates concerns Congress's No Child Left Behind Act, which requires states and school districts to see that students meet standards in reading and math, among other provisions.

The federal and state governments also have different social policy traditions. Congress has instituted automatic cost of living adjustments (COLAs) in the Social Security, SSI, and Food Stamp programs. States rarely choose to make automatic adjustments in public assistance programs. There are different social welfare traditions among the states as well. Some states, many of them in the Northeast, are known for more generous social welfare programs than are the poorer states of the South.

Municipal governments (city councils, county commissions) also deliberate about social programs. Although the financial stakes are smaller, citizen participation in local policy making is often the greatest because it is closest to home. Some cities run elaborate social welfare programs, as might be expected in a place like New York City where considerable resources are directed to public aid. Many municipalities are much smaller and have limited funds to distribute among many worthy causes. For local social service programs, even a few thousand dollars of operating funds can be critical. Local elected officials might want to support all these programs, but because they cannot really do enough for any of them, many appoint a group of citizens to study the requests and make funding recommendations. This might deflect some of the heat local officials experience when a group feels slighted by the council's or commission's budget decisions (DiNitto, 2007).

A government's budget is its most important policy document. This blueprint for spending expresses the government's values or priorities. Many individuals and groups try to influence the allocation of the scarce monetary resources available. Each year the Office of Management and Budget, part of the Executive Office of the President, works with the federal agencies to develop a budget for the following year. Based on this work, the president presents a budget for the operation of the entire federal government to Congress. Congress then does its work through House and Senate budget committees and a joint Congressional Budget Office as well as

House and Senate appropriations committees and subcommittees. Appropriations acts must be passed by both houses and signed by the president. Wildavsky (1988) calls this legislatively centered, decentralized, and fragmented process one that "distinguishes the American budgetary process from that of any other democratic nation" (p. viii).

Although the media reports the bitter battles that often ensue in passing a budget, much federal spending is considered uncontrollable because so many legislatively mandated programs are in place. Many of them are social welfare programs, primarily the large social insurance programs, which are hardly likely to be eliminated or even reduced by much. The president's proposed budget for fiscal year 2009 is $3.1 trillion, making the federal government very big business. Everyone seems to want a piece of the pie. State and local budgets are much smaller, but sometimes, the smaller the stakes, the more bitter the battles.

Actions of the Executive Branch

Elected government executives—the president, governors, and mayors— also make social policy decisions. The president and governors can veto legislation, though the respective legislative body may overturn these vetoes with sufficient votes. Elected government heads also make policy through executive decisions. Examples are President Harry S. Truman's decision to desegregate the military and President Clinton's order to establish a uniform policy of nondiscrimination against gay men and lesbians in federal government employment. Executive orders have also been used to deny federal contracts to employers who practice gender discrimination and for many other purposes.

The executive branch is composed of agencies responsible for administering government functions. At the federal level, the vast Department of Health and Human Services is but one of the agencies responsible for carrying out social policy. Departments such as Agriculture, Labor, and Justice; the independent Social Security Administration and the Legal Services Corporation; and many other entities also administer social policy. The states have their own bureaucratic agencies that administer social policy. Some have a large social welfare umbrella agency that encompasses many functions. Others use a more decentralized approach with several separate agencies to carry out health, public assistance, child and adult protective services, mental health, substance abuse, developmental disabilities, vocational rehabilitation, aging services, and other functions.

Elected government executives appoint commissions and agency heads to oversee the operation of these social welfare agencies. These appointed officials and agency employees (civil servants) make policy in the form of rules and regulations that must be developed when a piece of legislation lacks the specificity to be implemented. Many of these rules and regulations are published in the *Federal Register* or similar state publications or are otherwise made available for public review. Sometimes, it takes years before rules and regulations are issued, reviewed, contested, revised, and finally put into place. The Rehabilitation Act of 1973 was the first to provide certain protections for people with disabilities, but implementing regulations were not issued until 1977 (World Institute on Disability, 1992). Many other agency decisions are not subject to formal review, but they become standard operating procedures that can have a profound effect on social policy and on the people the agency is intended to serve.

Decisions of the Courts

When people are unhappy with a policy decision, they may appeal to the courts, and when they disagree with a lower court decision, they try to appeal to a higher court. The U.S. Supreme Court is often the ultimate authority. It plays a critical role in social policy. For example, in 1968, it ruled that "man-in-the-house rules" could not be used to "flatly deny" children Aid to Families with Dependent Children (AFDC), and in 1979, it ruled that it was unconstitutional to provide AFDC benefits to unemployed fathers but not to unemployed mothers. The U.S. Supreme Court has also played a major role in the quest to end racial discrimination, in the right to obtain an abortion, and in more recent decisions to restrict abortion rights. Without these decisions, the course of social policy might be quite different than it is today.

The role of judges is to interpret the laws and the constitutions of the federal and state governments, but there are conservative justices, liberal justices, and those whose decisions are not so predictable. Since many Supreme Court decisions are split, the high court offers majority and minority opinions with its rulings. The president makes nominations to the Supreme Court and to other federal courts, and the Senate decides whether or not to approve them. This is serious business because judges and Supreme Court justices are permitted to serve for life. The nine Supreme Court justices have been called the most elite of policy makers (Dye & Zeigler, 2006).

Pluralism and Incrementalism

With all the players and processes involved, it is no wonder that social policies are overlapping and conflicting. This mass of social policy may be difficult for the public to comprehend and for people in need to traverse, but many people get to see some of their desires enacted. This system may be preferable to highly centralized policy making that may leave some people out entirely. Such an approach may also prevent large social policy errors from occurring.

Another safeguard is that, at all levels, social policy making is largely incremental, and often with good reason (Lindblom, 1959). It is difficult for policy makers or others to accurately predict the short- or long-term impacts a major policy change will have. Governments are able to avoid the costly mistakes that might ensue from major shifts in policy paradigms by funding demonstration programs, allowing states to obtain waivers from federal requirements in order to try new approaches, and relying on private groups to execute their own initiatives. Many people have portrayed the change from AFDC to TANF as a radical departure from long-held social policy, yet many states had tried these approaches before Congress passed the Personal Responsibility and Work Opportunity Reconciliation Act.

Health care policy in the United States is one example of incrementalism. In 1993, President Clinton proposed a sweeping change of the nation's health care system. Other national health care proposals have been introduced to Congress, and all have failed. Instead, Congress and the states have made a succession of more modest changes—expanding Medicaid eligibility, offering tax incentives to employers who provide employee health care benefits, and adding the Children's Health Insurance Program in 1997 to cover more low-income children. Changes have also been made in the Social Security program. Changes in this largest of social welfare programs have generally been made incrementally after a great deal of consideration, and radical proposals for change, such as privatization, have been met with widespread skepticism. Policy making is not a single event. Policy is constructed and reconstructed time and time again, but the wheels of policy making tend to turn slowly.

In summary, political, economic, and social institutions affect social policy development, and social policy affects these institutions. Federal, state, and local governments share functions in making and carrying out social policy, but the balance of responsibilities among the three levels of government has shifted with the times. The legislative, executive, and judicial branches of government all play important roles in these processes. In a pluralistic and democratic society like the United States, policy making is decentralized and fragmented, resulting in overlapping and even conflicting policies. Policy making is also incremental. Whatever the virtues of incrementalism, social policy making almost always moves slowly.

References

Axinn, J., & Stern, M. (2005). *Social welfare: A history of the American response to need* (6th ed.). Needham Heights, MA: Allyn & Bacon.

Day, P. J. (2006). *A new history of social welfare* (5th ed.). Boston: Allyn & Bacon.

DiNitto, D. M. (2007). *Social welfare: Politics and public policy* (6th ed.). Boston: Allyn & Bacon.

Dye, T. R. (1998). *Understanding public policy* (9th ed.). Upper Saddle River, NJ: Prentice Hall.

Dye, T. R., & Zeigler, H. (1991). *American politics in the media age* (4th ed.). Pacific Grove, CA: Harbrace.

Dye, T. R., & Zeigler, H. (2006). *The irony of democracy: An uncommon introduction to American politics* (13th ed.) Belmont, CA: Thomson Wadsworth.

Fiorina, M. P., & Peterson, P. E. (2002). *The new American democracy* (Alternate 2nd ed.). New York: Longman.

Gallagher, L. J. (1999, September 1). *A shrinking portion of the safety net: General Assistance from 1989–1998.* Washington, DC: Urban Institute. Retrieved April 22, 2007, from http://www.urban.org/publications/309197.html

Gilder, G. (1981). *Wealth and poverty.* New York: Bantam.

Goldberg, B. (2002). *Bias: A CBS insider exposes how the media distort the news.* Washington, DC: Regnery.

Gordon, L. (1990). *Women, the state, and welfare.* Madison: University of Wisconsin Press.

Gordon, L. (1994). *Pitied but not forgotten: Single mothers and the history of welfare.* New York: Free Press.

Harris Poll. (2006, January 24). *Very few U.S. adults believe the Jack Abramoff case is an isolated incident* (Harris Poll® #9). Retrieved April 21, 2007, from http://www.harrisinteractive.com/harris_poll/index.asp?PID=633

Harris Poll. (2007, April 10). *Closing the budget deficit: U.S. adults strongly resist raising any taxes except "sin taxes" or cutting major programs* (Harris Poll®#30). Retrieved April 21, 2007, from http://www.harrisinteractive.com/harris_poll/index.asp?PID=746

Hewitt, C. (1996). Estimating the number of homeless: Media misrepresentation of an urban problem. *Journal of Urban Affairs, 18*(3), 431–447.

Jost, K. (1996, September 13). The states and federalism. *Congressional Quarterly Researcher, 6*(34), 795–815.

Kahn, A. (1979). *Social policy and social services.* New York: Random House.

Kamerman, S., & Kahn, A. J. (1989). *Privatization and the welfare state.* Princeton, NJ: Princeton University Press.

Katz, M. B. (2001). *The price of citizenship: Redefining the American welfare state.* New York: Metropolitan Books.

Keller, B. (1981, April 16). Special treatment no longer given advocates for the poor. *Congressional Quarterly Weekly, 39*(16), 659–664.

Lindblom, C. (1959). The science of "muddling through." *Public Administration Review, 19,* 79–88.

MacIntyre, D. M. (1964). *Public assistance: Too much or too little.* Ithaca: New York State School of Industrial and Labor Relations, Cornell University.

Madison, J. (1911). *The Federalist, No. X.* In A. Hamilton, J. Madison, & J. Jay, *The Federalist, or, the new constitution* (pp. 41–48). London: Dent. (Original work published 1787, November 23)

Moon, A., & Schneiderman, L. (1995). *Assessing the growth of California's General Assistance program.* Berkeley, CA: California Policy Seminar. Retrieved January 13, 2008, from http://www.sen.ca.gov/ftp/SEN/COMMITTEE/STANDING/HEALTH/_home/WELFARE/resear02.htm

Morris, R. (1979). *Social policy of the American welfare state: An introduction to policy analysis.* New York: Harper & Row.

Murray, C. (1984). *Losing ground: American social policy, 1950–1980.* New York: Basic Books.

Olasky, M. (1992). *The tragedy of American compassion.* Washington, DC: Regnery Gateway.

Olasky, M. (1996). *Renewing American compassion.* New York: Free Press.

Piven, F. F., & Cloward, R. (1971). *Regulating the poor: The functions of public welfare.* New York: Random House.

Saad, L. (1996, May). Issues referendum reveals populist leanings. *The Gallup Poll Monthly, 368,* 2–6.

U.S. Census Bureau. (2005). [Table 424 & Table 440]. *Statistical abstract of the United States: 2007* (126th ed.). Washington, DC: Author. Retrieved April 20, 2007, from http://www.census.gov/compendia/statab

U.S. Census Bureau. (2006a, August 29). [Table PINC-04 & Table PINC-06]. *Current population survey 2006: Annual demographic survey, March supplement.* Retrieved April 22, 2007, from http://pubdb3.census.gov/macro/032006/perinc/toc.htm

U.S. Census Bureau. (2006b, August 29). [Table POV01]. *Current population survey 2006: Annual demographic survey, March supplement.* Retrieved April 22, 2007, from http://pubdb3.census.gov/macro/032006/pov/new01_000.htm

U.S. Congress, House Committee on Ways and Means. (2004). *2004 green book: Background material and data on programs within the jurisdiction of the Committee on Ways and Means* (Appendix I). Washington, DC: Government Printing Office. Retrieved April 20, 2007, from http://waysandmeans.house.gov/Documents.asp?section=813

Weaver, R. K., Shapiro, R. Y., & Jacobs, L. R. (1995). Trends: Welfare. *Public Opinion Quarterly, 59*(4), 606–627.

Wildavsky, A. (1979). *Speaking truth to power: The art and craft of policy analysis.* Boston: Little, Brown.

Wildavsky, A. (1988). *The new politics of the budgetary process.* Glenview, IL: Scott, Foresman and Co.

Wilson, W. J. (1987). *The truly disadvantaged: The inner city, the underclass, and public policy.* Chicago: University of Chicago Press.

World Institute on Disability. (1992). *Just like everyone else.* Oakland, CA: Author.

3 Economic Dimensions of Social Policy

Jane Waldfogel

This chapter examines the economic context in which social policy in the United States is formulated and implemented. It traces the historical growth of expenditures on social programs and describes current social welfare spending with reference to the major program areas to which resources are allocated. It compares social spending in the United States with that in other countries and asks whether spending on social welfare is sufficient or inadequate. In discussing this issue, and in examining wider questions of social welfare allocation, the chapter refers to the principles that economists use to decide issues of social spending and, in particular, to principles related to efficiency, equity, and other social goals. As is shown, economists differ in the way they apply these principles to current economic conditions, social welfare programs, and social expenditure.

The Economic Context for Social Policy

Social welfare programs are designed to promote economic security by protecting individuals from risks that anyone could potentially face in a market society. These risks include the loss of income due to one's own unemployment, injury, disability, or retirement; the loss of income due to a family member's unemployment, injury, disability, retirement, or death, for individuals who are dependent children or spouses; inadequate income to afford an extraordinary and irregular purchase such as health care or education; and income poverty.

Programs to insure individuals against these types of risk are present in virtually all industrialized countries, although, of course, individual countries vary a great deal in the type of programs they provide and in the generosity of those programs. And many countries go beyond these narrow aims to promote other goals such as equality of opportunity or social inclusion.

What principles are used to decide when government intervention is justified and what types of programs are warranted? Governments do not intervene unless it is generally agreed that there is a problem. Economists refer to this as the need to identify a market failure, which basically means that "if it isn't broken, don't fix it." However, even when there is an agreed-upon problem, before government intervenes, it must also be agreed that government as opposed to private intervention is the best solution and that government intervention will not do more harm than good. Two basic principles play a key role in these decisions.

The first principle is economic efficiency, which has three different aspects. Macro-efficiency is concerned with the effect of the overall level of social welfare expenditures on the economy; micro-efficiency considers the relative merits of spending on one social program versus others; and incentives efficiency has to do with the potentially adverse effects of social welfare policy on individuals' behavior (Barr, 1998). In making decisions about social welfare policy, then, one would want to minimize, to the extent possible, the adverse effects of those decisions on the overall economy (macro-efficiency) and on individuals' decisions about employment, saving, and so on (incentive efficiency), and one would want to be sure to allocate expenditures where they could do the most good relative to other social welfare expenditures (micro-efficiency) as well as to other government expenditures (macro-efficiency).

The second principle underlying social welfare policy is equity. Economists typically differentiate two types of equity: vertical equity or redistribution, which is the principle that a social welfare system should redistribute income from those who have more to those who have less, and horizontal equity or fairness, which is the principle that similarly situated people should be treated equally (Barr, 1998). Thus, all else being equal, one would tend to prefer social welfare policies that help make the poor better off and that treat individuals fairly. One would also prefer programs that make their intended recipients better off; this form of equity gain is sometimes referred to as *target efficiency*.

What happens when these principles collide? Obviously, trade-offs must be made (Okun, 1975), but social theorists disagree on how to resolve this question. Liberal theorists such as John Rawls (1972) place equity and social justice first and would promote equity even at the price of some efficiency losses. Conservative theorists such as Milton Friedman (1962) see efficiency as primary and worry a great deal about adverse incentives and also about restrictions on personal freedom; they, therefore, tend to have a much more skeptical view of social welfare programs.

Other principles that are relevant to the design of social welfare programs tend to vary by country and over time. In the United States, one important goal of social welfare policy has been to promote equality of opportunity. In the 19th century, universal public schools were introduced as a way to help integrate immigrants into American society, and more recently, reducing racial inequality was a key goal of the 1960s' War on Poverty. As another example, in much of Europe currently, an important goal of social policy is to promote social solidarity and social inclusion. Thus, in many European countries, social policy aims to reduce income inequality and relative poverty as well as absolute poverty.

Generally speaking, the size, structure, and generosity of a country's social welfare system will reflect how these questions about efficiency and equity, and about other social goals, have been answered over time. A country's social welfare system will also reflect that society's assumptions and norms, for instance, about gender or family responsibility. A good example of how efficiency, equity, and other concerns interact to shape social welfare policy arises when we consider the decision of whether to provide services universally or to target them to low-income or other specific groups (Garfinkel, 1982; Titmuss, 1968). If the aim of a social welfare program is to reduce poverty, for instance, then it seems obvious that the best way to deliver the program would be to target it to those who are poor. This approach has the advantage of targeting the benefits to those who need them most, which would improve both efficiency and equity. However, income testing also imposes costs. Identifying poor people and ensuring that benefits are provided only to them creates administrative costs for the system and stigma for the recipients. Stigma is costly in that it may diminish recipients' well-being and may also deter some potential recipients from taking up the benefit. Income testing can also create adverse work incentives. Because, in order to maintain targeting, families that work and earn more must then have their benefits reduced, there is an incentive for families to keep their earnings low. In the extreme case, if benefits are reduced dollar for dollar as earnings rise, families have an incentive not to work at all (or to work "off-the-books"). This kind of "poverty trap" impedes the efficiency of the program and also lowers families' well-being relative to what it might be under a better-designed program.

Universal benefits, in contrast, impose much lower administrative costs, do not stigmatize their recipients, and do not have large adverse effects on work effort because they are provided to all residents regardless of income or other characteristics. They also have the advantage of promoting social solidarity and social inclusion. However, universal benefits are also likely to do a poorer job of redistributing income since they provide benefits to rich and poor alike. Of course, the extent to which they are redistributive will depend on the extent to which they are funded through progressive taxation.

Indicator targeting offers an attractive intermediate solution to the targeting versus universalism dilemma. If, for instance, families with children are at much higher risk of poverty than other families or households, then the presence of children could be used as an indicator, and benefits could be targeted accordingly. Compared to income targeting, this kind of targeting costs much less to administer, does not stigmatize recipients, and poses fewer problems in terms of adverse incentives (although one might worry about fertility effects). However, it may be less efficient in terms of reaching its intended targets. Thus, whether this kind of indicator targeting makes sense from a target efficiency and equity perspective will depend on what share of families with children are poor and on what share of poor people live in families with children. In the extreme case, if all families with children were poor and all poor people were found in families with children, targeting to families with children would be the most efficient way to redistribute resources to the poor. In the United States, about one-sixth of families with children are poor and about two-thirds of poor people are found in families with children (U.S. Census Bureau, 2006). Therefore, although entirely replacing income testing with indicator targeting would not be warranted, some additional targeting to families with children might be.

How Much Does the United States Spend on Social Programs?

In 2003, the United States spent over $2 trillion on social welfare programs. Even when one takes the overall size of the U.S. economy into account, this figure is a large amount, representing one-fifth of the country's gross domestic product or GDP. (The GDP represents the total amount of goods and services produced in a country each year.) It is important to note that the $2 trillion figure and the figures reported below capture only a portion of the American social welfare system. As is customary in analyses of social welfare expenditures, they do not include private social welfare expenditures (such as spending on health insurance by individuals and employers) nor do they include tax expenditures (such as the Earned Income Tax Credit, child care tax credits, and tax deductions for mortgage interest and property tax payments). If these expenditures were included, the American social welfare system would look even larger (see Garfinkel, Smeeding, & Rainwater, in press).

The historical data on total social welfare expenditures and on these expenditures as a share of GDP, shown in Table 3.1, allow us to place the current figures in historical perspective. Table 3.1 shows a dramatic increase in total social welfare expenditure levels over time; however, the total expenditure figures must be interpreted cautiously because they are not adjusted for inflation or for increases in the size of the population. Therefore, Table 3.1 also shows expenditures as a share of GDP. This percentage provides a better measure of how much government is spending on social welfare as a share of the total size of the economy.

In 1929, the earliest year shown for which comparable data are available, social welfare spending by government at all levels amounted to under 4% of GDP. By 1940, that share had more than doubled, reflecting the increase in spending at the federal level after the passage of the Social Security Act of 1935. Spending as a share of GDP did not rise again until the War on

Table 3.1   Social Welfare Expenditures in the United States, 1929–2003

	Total Federal, State, and Local Expenditures on Social Welfare (in Millions of Dollars)	Expenditures as a Percent of Gross Domestic Product (GDP)
1929	3921	3.9
1940	8795	9.2
1950	23508	8.8
1955	32844	8.5
1960	52293	10.0
1965	77175	11.0
1970	145856	14.2
1975	290080	18.2
1980	492213	18.1
1985	731874	17.8
1990	1048809	18.5
1995	1505000	20.3
2000	1933949	19.7
2003	2334480	21.3

SOURCES: U.S. Social Security Administration (1981, Table 1; 1990, Table 2; 1999) and Organisation for Economic Co-operation and Development (OECD, 2007).

NOTE: Expenditures are expressed as a share of gross national product (GNP), instead of GDP, for the years 1929 and 1940.

Poverty in the 1960s, which resulted in a jump in the share of GDP spent on social welfare from 11% in 1965 to over 14% in 1970 and over 18% in 1975. Spending on social welfare programs then held steady from the mid-1970s until the 1990s, when the share increased only slightly to 20% in 1995, similar to its level of 21% in 2003 (the latest year for which data are currently available). But, as we shall see below, the distribution of expenditures by type of program has changed a good deal over time.

Expenditures by Type of Program

Although the public often thinks of social welfare as public assistance or welfare, social welfare includes a much broader range of programs. One of these is social insurance, which covers the risks of unemployment, injury, disability, or death, and is provided on a universal basis to all individuals who have worked and paid into the social security system. In addition to what is termed *welfare*, various other means-tested programs are also included in the definition of social welfare. These programs are targeted to needy individuals and families and include educational assistance, housing, food stamps, and medical services.

Until fairly recently, education was the largest social welfare program as a share of GDP. As we can see in Table 3.2, it was not until 1960 that spending on social insurance exceeded spending on education for the first time, and it was not until 1980 that spending on social insurance began to take up twice as large a share of the GDP as education.

The increase in spending on social insurance has been driven by demographic, economic, and political factors: the increasing share of the population that is over retirement age; rapidly rising health care costs for retirees; and rising levels of retirement benefits, reflecting an increased willingness on the part of Congress to spend money on older Americans.

In contrast to social insurance, spending on public assistance or welfare has risen much more gradually, and in 1995 (the most recent year for which this kind of detailed breakdown is available), it constituted only about 3.4% of GDP, about a third of the share taken up by social insurance. Spending on public assistance, like spending on social insurance, is affected by demographic, economic, and political changes. The rising share of children living in female-headed families that are at greater risk of poverty due to the lack of a second earner, economic downturns such as the Great Depression in the 1930s, and political changes such as the welfare expansions of the 1970s or the welfare cutbacks of the 1980s have all had an effect on the share of GDP that is allocated to public assistance.

Table 3.2 Expenditure on Major Types of Social Welfare Programs in the United States as a Percent of Gross Domestic Product, 1929–1995

	Social Insurance	Public Aid	Health & Medical	Education	Veterans, Housing, & Other
1929	0.3	0.1	0.3	2.4	0.8
1940	1.3	3.8	0.6	2.7	0.8
1950	1.8	0.9	0.8	2.5	2.8
1955	2.4	0.8	0.8	2.8	1.7
1960	3.7	0.8	0.9	3.4	1.2
1965	4.0	0.9	0.9	4.0	1.2
1970	5.3	1.6	0.9	5.0	1.4
1975	7.7	2.6	1.0	5.1	1.8
1980	8.5	2.7	1.0	4.5	1.4
1985	9.0	2.4	0.9	4.2	1.3
1990	9.0	2.6	1.1	4.5	1.3
1995	9.5	3.4	1.2	5.0	1.3

SOURCES: U.S. Social Security Administration (1981, 1990, 1997, 1999).

NOTE: Expenditures are expressed as a share of gross national product (GNP), instead of GDP, for the years 1929 and 1940.

As noted earlier, education was the largest single component of the social welfare system until the 1960s, and at 5% of GDP, it continues to take up about a quarter of all social welfare spending. The remaining categories—health and medical, veterans, housing, and other—are less important, together making up only about 2.5% of GDP and only a little over one-tenth of overall social welfare spending.

Thus, only a small share of social welfare expenditures (about 16%) is spent on public assistance or welfare. The largest single item, and the one that is growing most rapidly, is social insurance, which, in the United States, is mainly composed of retirement and health care benefits for the elderly.

How Do U.S. Expenditures Compare to Those of Other Countries?

Another useful way to place United States social welfare expenditures in context is to compare them to social welfare expenditures by other Western industrialized countries. Table 3.3 shows social welfare expenditures as a share of GDP for 21 countries that are members of the Organisation for Economic Co-operation and Development (OECD) at four points in time: 1960, 1975, 1990, and 2003. Table 3.3 ranks countries by the share of their GDP that they dedicate to social welfare spending in 2003 (the most recent year for which comparable data are available). As in the earlier tables, the figures in this table refer only to public spending and do not include tax expenditures (see discussion in Adema & Ladaique, 2005; Garfinkel et al., in press).

Table 3.3 shows that the U.S. share of GDP devoted to social welfare—21.3 percent—is below the OECD average of 25.4 percent; indeed, the United States ranks 19th out of the 21 countries on this measure, with only two countries—Japan and Ireland—spending less as a share of their economies. Moreover, the United States ranking has been pretty consistent over time (in 1960 and 1990, only four countries spent a lower share of GDP on social welfare than the United States; in 1975, only three countries did). If private spending and tax expenditures were included in this table, the United States would rank higher, but it would still be outspent by many other countries.

Judging the Economic Impact of Social Welfare Expenditures

With spending on social welfare at an all-time high in the United States and yet low by international standards, how are we to judge whether we are now spending too much or too little on social welfare? This section examines three possible tests that can be used to decide this issue. The first test concerns macro-efficiency, that is, whether social welfare spending has negative effects on the economy as a whole. The second concerns possible adverse incentives

Table 3.3 Government Social Welfare Expenditure as a Percentage of Gross Domestic Product in OECD Countries, 1960, 1975, 1990, 2003

Country	1960	1975	1990	2003
1. Sweden	15.6	27.4	39.6	37.4
2. France	14.4	26.3	31.9	33.8
3. Denmark	9.0	27.1	33.9	33.4
4. Belgium	na	28.7	30.6	31.7
5. Germany	17.1	27.8	27.5	31.5
6. Norway	11.0	23.2	35.5	31.2
7. Austria	17.4	26.0	29.9	30.9
8. Portugal	na	na	20.8	28.7
9. Italy	13.7	20.6	26.7	28.4
10. Finland	14.9	21.9	33.8	28.1
11. Switzerland	8.2	19.0	20.5	26.1
(12) OECD average	12.3	21.9	27.9	25.4
12. Greece	na	10.0	19.5	25.1
13. Netherlands	12.8	29.3	34.4	25.0
14. United Kingdom	12.4	19.6	27.6	24.9
15. Spain	na	na	23.8	24.0
16. New Zealand	12.7	19.0	19.8	23.4
17. Australia	9.5	17.3	17.7	22.1
18. Canada	11.2	20.1	25.5	21.8
19. United States	9.9	18.7	20.1	21.3
20. Japan	7.6	13.7	15.3	20.9
21. Ireland	11.3	22.0	25.2	20.1

SOURCES: Data for 1960, 1975, and 1990 are from Table 4.1 (p. 94) in Kamerman and Kahn (1997b). Data for 2003 are from OECD (2006, 2007).

NOTE: Countries ranked by percentage in 2003. The 1990 figures for Greece, Italy, and New Zealand are from 1985; 1990 figure for Switzerland is from 1984.

associated with social welfare spending. The third test takes into account the well-being of the intended targets of the social welfare expenditures, that is, those who are the recipients of social welfare benefits and participants in the programs. Returning to the framework outlined at the start of the chapter, one can think of the first two tests as reflecting concerns about efficiency and the third as reflecting concerns about equity (as well as target efficiency), keeping in mind that trade-offs between the two are unavoidable.

Measuring the impact of the welfare state on economic efficiency is no easy task. Many analysts take it as given that strong economic performance in the United States is due at least in part to the fact that its welfare state is smaller and its labor market less tightly regulated than those of other Western industrialized nations, but the comparative evidence on such effects is not very strong (Blank, 1994; Burtless, 1994).

Looking within the United States, there is not much evidence of large adverse effects of social welfare expenditures on our economy over time. Most analysts would agree with Lampman (1985) that, if there is a point at which welfare state spending would interfere with the smooth functioning of the economy, we have not reached it in the United States. This is not to say that such a point could not be reached (see, e.g., Freeman, Topel, & Swedenborg's 1997 work on Sweden) but rather that we have not come close to it.

There has been a great deal of work, and controversy, in recent years on the potentially adverse effects of welfare on family formation. Charles Murray (1984) and other conservatives argued forcefully that the American social welfare system creates perverse incentives that encourage out-of-wedlock childbearing and divorce and thus leads to the formation and maintenance of female-headed families. But evidence of such effects is lacking (see Moffitt, 1998 for a comprehensive review; see also earlier discussions in Ellwood, 1988; Garfinkel & McLanahan, 1986).

There has also been a great deal of research on the effects of welfare on work incentives, and here the evidence of adverse effects is stronger (Blank, 1997). The issue, however, is not so much whether too much or too little is being spent on welfare as it is how that spending is allocated. As a result, the welfare system has undergone a series of reforms to improve work incentives, including the passage of the Personal Responsibility and Work Opportunity Reconciliation Act in 1996, with most states now using both positive and negative incentives ("carrots and sticks") to encourage work effort.

We also have some evidence with regard to equity, and here we can more clearly address the question of whether we are now spending too little or too much on social welfare. If we can agree that a desired outcome of social insurance spending is to reduce economic insecurity and poverty among older Americans, then the increased spending on social insurance seems to be money well spent, since it reduced the poverty rate among those over 65 from nearly 30% in 1966 to just 10% today (U.S. Census Bureau, 2006). The poverty statistics for older Americans also suggest that, although spending for social insurance is now at record-high levels, we may not be spending enough or we may be spending inefficiently. Even after receiving social insurance, about 25% of the elderly poor (constituting about 10% of all elderly) are still poor (Danziger & Weinberg, 1994). If we want to eliminate poverty among older Americans, we will have to either spend more or shift some spending from the nonpoor elderly to the poor elderly. However, this latter option would run the risk of undermining Social Security's universal appeal.

What, though, are we to make of the spending on public assistance? We spend more on means-tested public assistance, as a share of our economy, than at any point since the Great Depression, and yet, poverty rates among families with children remain stubbornly high. One in six children in the United States is poor, and for children under the age of 6, the rate is one in five (U.S. Census Bureau, 2006). And public assistance has not made much of a dent in the problem. Even before the welfare reforms of the 1990s, only about 6% of poor female-headed families were moved out of poverty by public assistance (Danziger & Weinberg, 1994).

Not everyone agrees that these high child poverty rates mean that we are spending too little on public assistance. Some would argue that aid itself may increase poverty in the long run by, for example, inducing young women to have children out of wedlock. However, it is clear in an accounting sense that, if we spent more on public assistance and raised benefit levels for poor families, then, at least in the short run, the incomes of poor families would be higher. This is not to say that public assistance is the only, or even the best, strategy to raise the incomes of poor families; as we shall see below, many countries use universal benefits to fight child poverty.

Here, although cross-national comparisons can be perilous, the comparative data are certainly suggestive. Deborah Mitchell (1991) used data held by the Luxembourg Income Study to compare the social welfare systems of 10 industrialized countries across an array of measures and found that the United States ranked last in its effectiveness in reducing the poverty rate (the share of the population in poverty) and the poverty gap (the amount that would be needed to raise poor families' incomes up to the poverty line), and next to last in reducing income inequality (as measured by the Gini coefficient). In a study focused on families with children, Lee Rainwater and Tim Smeeding (1996) studied 18 industrialized countries participating in the Luxembourg Income Study and found that the United States social welfare system did the poorest job of bringing families with children out of poverty. Rainwater and Smeeding found that the high level of child poverty in the United States, compared to levels in other countries, reflects not just the fact that many children live in single-parent families or families with low earnings but also the fact that the U.S. social welfare system does a poorer job of alleviating child poverty among these families. These results make sense given the relatively low amount spent on social welfare in the United States as compared to expenditures in other countries, as shown in Table 3.3. In social welfare, as in other domains, the old adage holds: you get what you pay for.

In thinking about the adequacy of spending on social welfare, it is important not to forget the smaller components of the system. For instance, health and medical expenditures make up only a relatively small share of the social welfare system, reflecting the fact that the United States, unlike most other industrialized nations, has no system of universal health insurance. Although many Americans receive coverage privately, through their employers or through policies they purchase on their own, at any given point in time, about 16% of Americans have no health insurance, and an even higher percentage lack health insurance at some point during the year (U.S. Census Bureau, 2006). Whether it would be better, in terms of both efficiency and equity, to move toward a universal system of health insurance in the United States continues to be actively debated.

The United States also lags behind other countries in the provision of universal benefits for families with young children. Most other industrialized countries have some form of universal child allowance or child benefit. This allowance is typically provided to families with children of all ages, but it plays a particularly important role for families with preschoolers, as these families can use the allowance to offset the costs of a parent staying at home or the cost of child care. In addition, most other countries provide other universal supports to families with young children, including paid maternity leave and publicly provided or subsidized child care for preschool-aged children (Kamerman & Kahn, 1997a). In the United States, in contrast, virtually all benefits for young children are targeted, although not necessarily to the lowest income families. Cash welfare benefits and a broad range of in-kind benefits (including day care programs such as Head Start and nutritional programs such as the Women, Infants, and Children program and Food Stamps) are targeted to poor families, as is the Earned Income Tax Credit for those with earnings. However, there are also an array of nonrefundable tax credits and tax deductions that mainly benefit nonpoor families since they can be claimed only by families that pay income taxes and, in the case of mortgage interest and property tax deductions, only by families owning property.

Would it be advantageous for the United States to move toward a universal early childhood allowance or some other type of universal early childhood program? Advocates of early childhood intervention point to the potential benefits in terms of child health and development, particularly in light of what we now know about the importance of children's experiences in the preschool years. Moreover, to the extent that young children are at a disproportionately high risk of poverty, establishing a benefit for them could be an effective form of indicator targeting, with potentially much lower administrative and stigma costs than targeting on the basis of low income. However, there would also be costs entailed in moving toward more universal benefits for young children, and thus the merits of such a move depend on both efficiency and equity concerns. If the money for a universal early childhood allowance came from other programs where the spending was less effective, then it would be an improvement in terms of efficiency. Whether incentives would be improved is a more complicated question, since a universal program could avoid some of the adverse incentives of targeted welfare programs but might introduce others (for instance, fertility incentives) that might or might be not be seen as positive. Whether equity would be improved is a complicated question as well. If the new program was less redistributive than the ones it replaced, then equity would be adversely affected. However, if the program was at least as redistributive, then equity would be improved since social solidarity and social inclusion would be enhanced with all families receiving the same universal benefit.

Social Spending: Too Much or Too Little? _____

Although social welfare spending has increased dramatically in the United States since 1929, the share of our economy that is devoted to social welfare continues to be low by international standards. Although we now spend a fifth of every dollar in our economy on the "welfare state," most modern industrialized nations spend more.

It has also been shown that, contrary to popular perceptions, most social welfare spending in the United States does not go to welfare. Cash and other forms of assistance to the poor make up only a small share (16%) of the social welfare expenditures and a tiny share (3.4%) of the total economy. The largest component of the welfare state, and the one that is growing most rapidly, is social insurance, which benefits the retired and the disabled and which now makes up about half of social welfare expenditures. Indeed, social insurance alone now takes up nearly 10% of GDP, as much as the entire welfare state took up in 1960.

It is also clear from this review that there are no easy answers as to whether the right amount is being spent on the social welfare system. The answer depends on which programs and which populations are being considered. Spending on social insurance for the elderly, for example, has been high enough to substantially reduce poverty among its target population, whereas spending on public assistance and other programs for children has not.

Whether more or less should be spent on social welfare also depends on how much weight one places on efficiency versus equity concerns. Nevertheless, it is fair to conclude that there is little evidence from studies of efficiency that too much is being spent on the social welfare system, and some evidence that, in terms of enhancing equity, too little is being spent. Particularly concerning in this regard are the programs such as public aid that seem to be inadequately funded as well as the programs such as universal health insurance and universal child allowances that do not exist at all.

Ultimately, an assessment of the social welfare system will also be affected by what we see as the aims of social welfare policy. In the United States, we tend to think of those aims fairly narrowly, as we saw above, whereas many European countries are now moving to a broader conception that includes notions of reducing social exclusion and inequality. If, in the future, we decided as a nation that we wished to achieve those aims, and to assess the adequacy of our system in those terms, we would probably find that our current spending levels and patterns are even more inadequate than they appear today.

References

Adema, W., & Ladaique, M. (2005). *Net social expenditures, 2005 edition: More comprehensive measures of social support* (OECD Social Employment and Migration Working Paper No. 29). Paris: OECD Directorate for Employment, Labour, and Social Affairs.

Barr, N. (1998). *The economics of the welfare state* (3rd ed.). Oxford, UK: Oxford University Press.

Blank, R. (Ed.). (1994). *Social protection versus economic flexibility: Is there a trade-off?* Chicago: University of Chicago Press.

Blank, R. (1997). *It takes a nation: A new agenda for fighting poverty.* Princeton, NJ: Princeton University Press.

Burtless, G. (1994). Public spending on the poor: Historical trends and economic limits. In S. Danziger, G. Sandefur, & D. Weinberg (Eds.), *Confronting poverty: Prescriptions for change* (pp. 51–84). Cambridge, MA: Harvard University Press.

Danziger, S., & Weinberg, D. (1994). The historical record: Trends in family income, inequality, and poverty. In S. Danziger, G. Sandefur, & D. Weinberg (Eds.), *Confronting poverty: Prescriptions for change* (pp. 18–50). Cambridge, MA: Harvard University Press.

Ellwood, D. (1988). *Poor support.* New York: Basic Books.

Freeman, R., Topel, R., & Swedenborg, B. (1997). *The welfare state in transition: Rethinking the Swedish model.* Chicago: University of Chicago Press.

Friedman, M. (1962). *Capitalism and freedom.* Chicago: University of Chicago Press.

Garfinkel, I. (1982). *Income-tested transfers: The case for and against.* New York: Academic Press.

Garfinkel, I., & McLanahan, S. (1986). *Single mothers and their children: A new American dilemma.* Washington, DC: Urban Institute.

Garfinkel, I., Smeeding, T., & Rainwater, L. (in press). *The American welfare state: Laggard or leader?* New York: Russell Sage Foundation.

Kamerman, S. B., & Kahn, A. J. (1997a). *Starting right: How America neglects its youngest children and what we can do about it.* New York: Oxford University Press.

Kamerman, S. B., & Kahn, A. J. (1997b). Investing in children: Government expenditures for children and their families in western industrialized countries. In G. A. Cornia & S. Danziger (Eds.), *Child poverty and deprivation in the industrialized countries, 1945–1995* (pp. 91–121). Oxford, UK: Oxford University Press.

Lampman, R. (1985). *Balancing the books.* Washington, DC: National Conference on Social Welfare.

Mitchell, D. (1991). *Income transfers in ten welfare states.* Aldershot, UK: Avebury.

Moffitt, R. (1998). The effect of welfare on marriage and fertility: What do we know and what do we need to know?" In R. Moffitt (Ed.), *The effect of welfare on family and reproductive behavior* (pp. 50–97). Washington, DC: National Research Council.

Murray, C. (1984). *Losing ground: American social policy 1950–1980.* New York: Basic Books.

Okun, A. (1975). *Equality and efficiency: The big trade-off.* Washington, DC: Brookings Institution Press.

Organisation for Economic Co-operation and Development (OECD). (2006). *Education at a glance.* Paris: Author.

Organisation for Economic Co-operation and Development (OECD). (2007). *Society at a glance.* Paris: Author.

Rainwater, L., & Smeeding T. (1996). *Doing poorly: The real income of American children in comparative perspective* (Working Paper No. 127). Walferdange, Luxembourg: Luxembourg Income Study.

Rawls, J. (1972). *A theory of justice.* Oxford, UK: Oxford University Press.

Titmuss, R. (1968). Universal and selective social services. In *Commitment to welfare* (pp. 113–123). London: Allen & Unwin.

U.S. Census Bureau. (2006). Income, poverty, and health insurance coverage in the United States: 2005. In *Current population reports* (pp. 60–231). Washington, DC: Government Printing Office.

U.S. Social Security Administration. (1981). *Social Security Bulletin* (Annual Statistical Supplement). Washington, DC: Government Printing Office.

U.S. Social Security Administration. (1990, February). *Social Security Bulletin, 53*(2).

U.S. Social Security Administration. (1997, Fall). *Social Security Bulletin, 60*(3).

U.S. Social Security Administration. (1999, Fall). *Social Security Bulletin, 62*(3).

4

Policy Analysis

Bruce Jansson

Policy selection lies at the heart of the policy-making process. Confronting policy issues or problems, policy practitioners and advocates must develop policy alternatives to address them and select a preferred alternative in the course of policy deliberations. This process is commonly called *policy analysis* (Patton & Sawicki, 1993; Weimer & Vining, 1992).

After discussing the rational approach to policy analysis and the criticisms made of this approach, the chapter concludes that "pure" approaches or models seldom exist. Rather, values, data collection, and political considerations usually influence policy analysis, even if the relative emphasis on them differs between situations and among policy analysts.

The Rational Approach

The rational approach to policy analysis came of age in the 1960s as economists and systems analysts assumed major roles in policy selection (Heineman, Bluhm, Peterson, & Kearny, 1997). Rationalists were perturbed by the lack of rigor in the selection of policies in governmental and corporate settings, believing that empirical data were rarely used to compare and contrast policy alternatives or to evaluate existing policies (Meltsner, 1976). With the support of such government officials as Robert McNamara and Lyndon Johnson, ambitious projects were undertaken known as Planning, Programming, and Budgeting Systems (PPBS), zero-based budgeting, and management by objectives (MBO). PPBS identified major objectives of government programs, requiring that alternative methods of achieving them be subjected to rigorous empirical analysis before making policy choices. Zero-based budgeting proposed periodically erasing existing policies and programs so that an array of policies could be compared to ascertain which of them would best achieve specific policy goals. Spurred by these early efforts, the rational approach to policy selection has dominated the policy field in subsequent decades in academic settings and in some governmental arenas. Indeed, about thirty journals currently focus on policy analysis from a rational perspective (Einbinder, 1996).

The basic logic of the rational approach is described by a decision-making matrix that can be used in organizational, corporate, or governmental settings (Jansson, 2008; Patton & Sawiki, 1993). After studying a problem or issue, analysts identify objectives they wish to achieve and then operationalize them into one or more criterion. They identify policy alternatives and select the one that best meets the criteria. Assume, for example, that staff in a hospital want to increase responsiveness of services to Hispanic patients when few Hispanic medical staff or translators exist. They identify four alternative policy options: a cultural course for medical staff, a computerized list of Spanish-speaking employees (who can be mobilized to assist in specific cases), hiring interpreters, and recruiting 40 bilingual undergraduate volunteers from local colleges. They select four criteria: cost, effectiveness in helping patients with translations, political feasibility, and ease of implementation. Because they have identified multiple criteria, they must weight them, ranking them with numbers that cumulatively total 1.0 to establish the relative importance of each of them. (They rank cost as .3, effectiveness in helping patients with translations as .3, political feasibility as .2, and ease of implementation as .2.) Drawing on the informed estimates of organizational consultants and existing research, they rank the four policy options from 1 (worst) to 10 (best) with respect to each of the criteria, ranking hiring more interpreters as worst (1) while giving the best score to the computerized list of Spanish-speaking employees (8). They derive a score for each policy option with respect to each criterion by multiplying the rankings of the four options on each of the criteria by the weight of the criteria. After totaling the scores of each option, they select the option of recruiting 40 bilingual undergraduate volunteers because its total score (7.8) exceeds that of the other policy alternatives.

In governmental contexts, a rational approach to social policies often involves using a single criterion, such as efficiency, effectiveness, cost-effectiveness, or cost-benefit measurements. When using *efficiency* as a criterion, policy makers select the alternative that is least expensive; when using *effectiveness*, they select the alternative that brings the best outcomes. They might compare two job-training strategies for welfare recipients, for example, choosing the one that most effectively removes recipients from the rolls. Or they might identify several outcomes, such as the extent to which recipients leave the rolls and the level of earnings of graduates 6 months later, selecting job training as the option that yields the best aggregate benefits.

Rationalists sometimes couple several criteria into a single measure. In the case of *cost-effectiveness* criteria, for example, they examine both the cost and the effectiveness of policy alternatives, selecting the policy option that is both efficient and effective (Chambers, Wedel, & Rodwell, 1992). Under this approach, a job-training strategy for welfare recipients that placed many of them in jobs at a relatively low cost per placement would receive a high score as compared with a strategy that was equally effective but more costly. *Cost-benefit* analyses aim to measure the net benefits to society when the costs to society are compared with the benefits to society (Weimer & Vining, 1992). Analysts estimate the costs of a policy alternative by gauging how much it costs to implement it and combining these costs with its estimated *opportunity costs*. (The opportunity cost is the interest that could have been earned on the funds had they not been expended.) They then estimate the value of the benefits rendered to society by the policy alternative, such as (in the case of a job-training strategy for recipients) increases in tax revenues from enhanced job earnings and averted welfare payments for recipients who leave the rolls. Analysts then compare the ratio of costs to benefits: a policy alternative with a 1:1 ratio, where costs equal benefits, would be regarded as inferior to a policy alternative with a 1:5 ratio, where society receives benefits far exceeding the cost of a policy option.

Criteria that rely on quantitative data are often supplemented by ones that require qualitative information, such as the political or implementation feasibility of options. Moreover, value-based criteria can be included, such as social justice, confidentiality, and self-determination (Jansson, 2008).

While comparisons of policy alternatives in the context of one or more criterion often yield important findings, policy analysts provide a relatively static analysis of dynamic phenomena. Many analysts use a systems framework to study complex phenomenon and to gauge the likely effects of specific policies. Take the case of the welfare dependency of single heads of households, for example, as portrayed in Figure 4.1, which identifies an array of factors that, singly and in tandem, influence the likely outcomes of the Personal Responsibility and Work Opportunities Act of 1996 (Jansson, 2008). Susceptible populations (on the left of Figure 4.1) are persons not currently on the rolls, but at risk (in varying degrees) of becoming recipients. Neither susceptible or current recipients are homogenous populations; as the typology in Figure 4.1 suggests, they include recipients with different skill levels, job experience, levels of disability, motivation to leave the rolls, and longevity on the rolls. These various factors describe, singly and in tandem, the likelihood that specific persons will obtain and keep jobs. Nor is postwelfare experience understandable in simple terms, since it involves work activity for varying lengths of time, at different levels of remuneration, and with varying levels of state subsidies for short or extended periods. The welfare issue is associated, moreover, with various indirect effects; as rolls diminish, for example, local costs associated with foster care, homelessness, and general relief may increase if large numbers of former recipients find jobs that pay them only at or near the minimum wage.

A dynamic view of such problems as welfare, moreover, requires that contextual factors be included, such as familial, community, and economic ones (see Figure 4.1). Recipients live in families and communities whose cultures, patterns of interaction, and characteristics may profoundly influence the outcomes of welfare policies. The ability of recipients to obtain assistance from

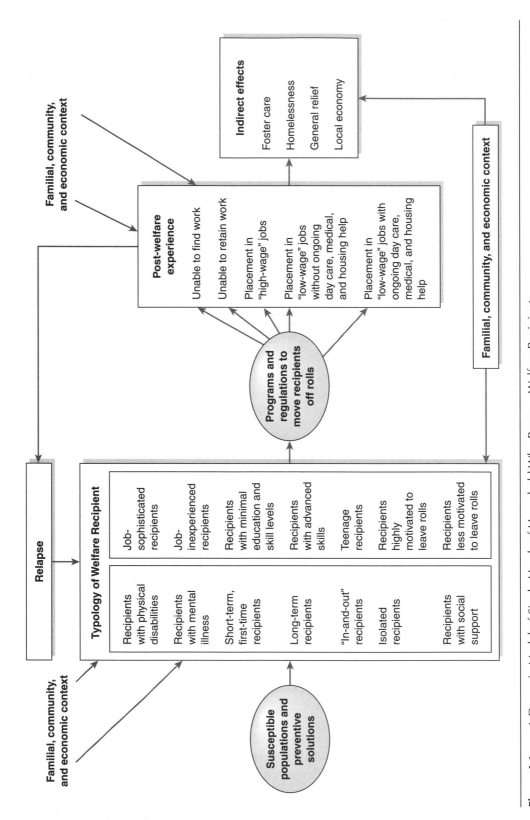

Figure 4.1 A Dynamic Model of Single Heads of Household Who Become Welfare Recipients

SOURCE: Jansson (1999).

relatives, such as help with child care or financial assistance, may influence the ability of recipients to survive on low wages. Economic realities, such as up- or downturns in a local economy, can facilitate or frustrate efforts to diminish the size of rolls. The decisions of thousands of employers to hire— or not to hire—welfare recipients powerfully influence the ability of government to reduce the rolls. Indeed, many employers may not hire recipients unless given substantial and ongoing subsidies.

Were policy analysts desirous of analyzing the likely effects of the Personal Responsibility and Work Opportunity Reconciliation Act, they would have to examine complex interactions between the various elements outlined in Figure 4.1 (Wolch & Sommer, 1997). Moreover, they would need to identify possible contingencies, such as the effects of an economic upturn, on the one hand, and of an economic downturn, on the other hand. The power to predict likely outcomes of this legislation becomes weaker as the complexity of interactions *and* the range of possible future events increases. Yet, modeling and simulations of likely policy outcomes in the context of a systems framework is often preferable to statical analyses that only examine the interactions of several factors.

The Role of Research

The rubric of policy analysis includes research into the causes of specific social problems, since analysts' perceptions of these causes powerfully shape the kinds of policy options they will consider. Reanalyzing data reported by Herrnstein and Murray in *The Bell Curve* (1994), sociologists at the University of California at Berkeley contended, for example, that welfare dependence stems from a system of inequality that places certain persons at particular risk of welfare dependence (Fischer et al., 1996). These sociologists disputed Herrnstein and Murray's contention that welfare dependence was primarily caused by intelligence, arguing that *cognitive skills*—a term they preferred to "intelligence"—are themselves caused by such environmental factors as the parental home and the adolescent community. Women who enter adolescence with multiple and interacting deficits in their environments, such as coming from low-income families, being tracked into noncollege classes in school, and living in communities with primarily low-paying service jobs, are more likely than others to become welfare recipients, regardless of their innate abilities. The Berkeley sociologists' analysis led them to support an array of interventions in communities and schools, as well as job-training and educational programs for recipients themselves.

If correlational data provide important insights into the causes of social problems, other strategies are used by policy analysts, as well. They compare persons with and without a social problem, in order to infer from their differences why certain persons develop this problem. They follow people through time to discover when they develop a problem, such as following teen women over time to discern why some of them become pregnant and join welfare rolls. They evaluate existing programs to find clues to the causes of a problem. If an evaluation of job-training programs discovers, for example, that a program that offers expansive child care benefits yields better outcomes than other programs, a policy analyst might deduce that inadequate child care is a cause of welfare dependency. Analysts also get information directly from persons who are experiencing a specific problem, by observing them (as in anthropological studies) or by interviewing them (Jansson, 2008).

Epidemiological research in public health also provides useful insights to policy analysts who seek measures to prevent social problems (Bloom, 1981). It identifies negative factors that place persons at varying degrees of risk of developing a problem as well as strengths or environmental supports that immunize some persons from developing specific problems. These findings, in turn, are linked to research on interventions, whether to diminish or reduce at-risk factors or to bolster strengths or environmental supports. Policy analysts seek preventive strategies that focus resources on true positives (persons who will develop a problem) rather than false positives (people with at-risk signs who do not develop a problem) or false negatives (persons lacking at-risk signs who develop a problem).

Marketing research is also used by policy analysts. As Aaron, Mann, and Taylor (1994) note, values profoundly shape the actions and choices of the people that policies aim to help, influence, or regulate, even if academics and policy analysts often "take values, habits, and social norms as given [and] beyond analysis and the reach of public policy" (p. 1). Influenced by economists to emphasize incentives, analysts often assume that mere provision of services or resources will suffice, not sufficiently considering how consumers' values and norms profoundly shape how they respond to specific services, resources, or opportunities. Analysts use survey research, focus groups, and client satisfaction studies to obtain data about the perceptions, values, and desires of potential or actual users of social programs (Kotler, 1989).

Other empirical techniques are available to policy analysts. They can use multiple regression techniques to predict future trends, for example, using historical data to predict future rates of crimes (Gupta, 1994). They can use decision trees to illuminate the relative merits of alternative choices (Behn & Vaupel, 1982). They can use geographical analysis to locate specific problems and to analyze their causes (Maguire, 1991; Queralt & Witte, 1998). They can use the Delphi technique to elicit policy alternatives, criteria, and rankings from informed experts (Gupta, 1994). They can use needs assessment techniques to gauge the incidence, prevalence, and location of specific social problems (Mayer, 1985).

Policy analysis that is grounded in the use of empirical data has many advantages. By basing policy selection on data, policy analysts can avoid selection that is based upon best guesses, tradition, professional wisdom, or political considerations. An empirical approach forces policy analysts to structure their inquiry systematically. It fosters critical discussion of options, criteria, rankings of options, and choices by publicly disclosing assumptions and data. It can be used in agency as well as governmental settings (Kettner, Moroney, & Martin, 1990).

Criticisms of the Rational Model

Despite its currency in academic, think-tank, and government settings, critics cite political, value-based, and methodological problems with the rational model of policy analysis. Rationalists usually assume that decision makers will use their analytic findings to make policy choices, whether in organizational or legislative settings, but this assumption is often incorrect (Heineman et al., 1997). Mann and Ornstein (1995) contend, for example, that Congress does not usually make important health policy decisions in a rational way, responding instead to political pressures from interest groups, partisan competition, or ideology. A dramatic example of indifference to empirical data was demonstrated when President Bill Clinton decided in 1998 not to allow Secretary of Health and Human Services Donna Shalala to announce public funding of sterilized needles to drug addicts, even though scientific evidence demonstrated that this policy would markedly reduce transmission of HIV without stimulating additional use of drugs, as was alleged by many conservatives. Often ignored when they conflict with ideological preferences or strongly held beliefs, rationalists' arguments are frequently overridden, as well, when legislators and political leaders believe that empirical findings conflict with their political interests. Indeed, such leaders as Lyndon Johnson *began* his "analysis" with political questions, not even considering policy initiatives until he was convinced that he could build sufficient support for them. Most legislators and political leaders have scant knowledge of research, economics, or statistics, making them unlikely to read technical analyses. Some conservatives are relatively hostile to the use of science in policy making, as illustrated by their opposition to initiatives to reduce global warming during the administration of George W. Bush, even when most scientists believed definitive data documented its growth.

Indeed, many political scientists contend that an "iron triangle" of interest groups, bureaucrats, and legislators often shapes policy on the basis of interests and tradition (Smith, 1988). When rationalists seek elimination of a specific program on the grounds that it is ineffective, for example, they are often opposed by its defenders, whose resources and power would decline if it were eliminated.

Public opinion can also promote opposition to rationalists' arguments, as illustrated by widespread indifference to technical arguments opposing the death penalty and gun control in specific jurisdictions, not to mention the investment of resources in job training and child care to help welfare recipients leave the rolls.

Politics shapes policy analysis in other ways as well. Desirous of enacting policies that bring political benefits—and wanting to enact policies when windows of opportunity exist—public officials seldom wait for extended technical analyses of alternative policies. Indeed, Smith (1988) likens policy innovation to surfing as politicians try to ride waves of media coverage and public opinion that support specific innovations, afraid that the waves will dissipate if they fail to move rapidly. Public officials often develop policies in uncharted areas before extensive evaluative or social science data exists, forcing policy analysts to choose between policy options while considering scant information. Few people could accurately predict in 1996, for example, the likely effects of the Personal Responsibility and Work Opportunity Reconciliation Act because only the scattered precedents of waiver programs in various states preceded its enactment.

As the previously described study by Herrnstein and Murray (1994) suggests, participants in policy debates often opportunistically use data to support positions that they held *before* they commenced their policy analysis. Already believing that welfare recipients were parasites and should be dealt with in a punitive fashion, Herrnstein and Murray (1994) marshaled empirical data to support this position, even though many social scientists subsequently criticized their research methodology.

Other critics question whether rationalists overstate the scientific nature of their work, since values intrude at many points (Hawkesworth, 1988; Jansson, 1990). Analysts use conceptual lenses to order reality, such as ecological, medical, deviance, or other perspectives (Rubington & Weinberg, 1989). These lenses powerfully influence their perceptions of problems, the kinds of variables they include in their research, and their interpretation of data. As some advocates of rational approaches concede, the selection and weighting of criteria are primarily determined by values, ideology, or political considerations. Different analysts use different—and conflicting—criteria that reflect their value premises when they examine welfare policy, for example. Whereas some conservative analysts may tend to prioritize rapid reduction of welfare rolls, relatively liberal analysts are more likely to favor improving the economic condition of recipients over an extended period. Liberal analysts are less likely to want reduction in rolls at the price of erosion of the economic condition of recipients, framing welfare reform as an antipoverty initiative rather than as a cost-saving device. While some welfare analysts use a short time frame to compare alternatives, selecting alternatives that demonstrate success in a year or less, other analysts advocate longer time frames.

Interpretations of data are also shaped by values. When faced with ambiguous data, analysts must decide whether "the glass is half full or half empty." In the case of evaluations of programs, for example, data rarely suggest overwhelming success, even when statistically significant differences exist between control and experimental groups. Deciding where to establish the minimum thresholds of success required to declare a policy to be meritorious is a value-laden enterprise. Nor is it easy to decide whether adverse side effects of a policy possess sufficient magnitude to rescind it. In the case of evaluations of a guaranteed income, for example, analysts differed regarding whether the heightened divorce rates that accompanied a guaranteed income constituted sufficient grounds for rejecting the policy itself.

The values of analysts also shape how they define specific social problems. If some analysts define poverty in absolute terms, perhaps subscribing to the market-basket approach of the federal government, others define it in relative terms by focusing on the extent of economic disparities between different social classes. In each case, the analysts must decide what thresholds must be exceeded to bring someone into poverty—also a value-laden choice. As Rein (1983) notes, "the facts we attend to depend upon the construction we impose on reality" (p. 86). Indeed, the decision that a condition in the external world is or is not a "problem" is highly shaped by cultural and value considerations, as history and comparative studies amply reveal. If reading and learning disorders were not commonly viewed as problems in the 1960s, for example, they were widely seen a major problems three decades later.

When viewing the same data, moreover, analysts may interpret their findings in strikingly different fashion. Take the example of the failure of most job-training programs to markedly improve the earnings of former welfare recipients over an extended period when these earnings are compared with those of welfare recipients not receiving any job training (Grubb, 1996). Most short-term earnings improvements erode with time, meaning that, in the long term, trainees tend to have incomes roughly commensurate with persons who were not trained. This adverse finding prompts some people to abandon training altogether or to rely on job placement and referral programs. Others conclude that these negative findings should lead to *increased* public funding of job training and remedial education, contending that the ineffectiveness of past programs stems from their short-term and fragmented nature. Grubb (1996) advocates that many low-income persons receive an extended sequence of training and education, often spread over many years, that yields credentials that have been demonstrated to catapult persons into jobs that pay relatively high wages.

Ethical objections have been raised against some technical approaches. Cost-benefit studies can yield findings, for example, that discriminate against certain kinds of populations. When applied to programs to assist populations that cannot work, such as terminally ill persons, cost-to-benefit ratios are likely to be relatively high because these people cannot produce monetary benefits to society by working (Heineman et al., 1997).

The work of policy analysts is also influenced by political realities. When identifying policy options, for example, analysts frequently do not consider options that lack political feasibility, such as drastic shifts from the status quo. When they work in legislative or bureaucratic settings—or conduct analysis under contract in academic settings—the views of their sponsors often influence their work, such as by focusing them toward certain policy options that sponsors favor.

A Six-Step Policy Analysis Framework

Policy analysis is a dynamic form of practice that includes conceptual work, linkages with other persons and groups, and presentations. Somewhat abbreviating Bardach's eight-step model (2005), I propose a six-step model in Figure 4.2 (Jansson, 2008).

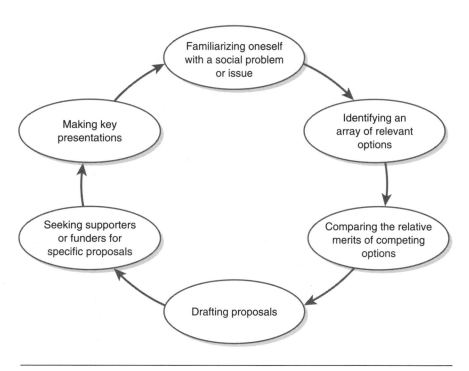

Figure 4.2   A Six-Step Model of Policy Analysis

1. *Policy analysts familiarize themselves with a specific social problem or issue—or interrelated problems or issues.* Policy analysis begins with the selection of a specific social problem or issue. Or the problem or issue can involve defects in the implementation of specific programs or regulations.
   Policy advocates need to ask

- What political, fiscal, cultural, or other factors led to a specific festering problem or issue? This question can often be stated by using words like "too many people possess XYZ condition or problem," such as homelessness, poverty, or lack of access to specific services, or "too few persons with depression receive optimal services for their condition." Alternatively, they can use a value-based perspective to state a specific problem, such as by contending that too many low-income persons lack adequate housing when compared with the broader population.

- What remedies or solutions (if any) currently exist for the social problem or issue, and why are they insufficient either in strategy, relative size, or implementation? Can they be reformed or changed—and, if so, how—or are new remedies or solutions needed?
- What is the magnitude of current expenditures on the program or issue? From what sources do these funds come? Are they sufficient or insufficient?
- Does the current problem or issue pose adverse consequences for specific persons, communities, and society? What are they, and what is the level or amount of these consequences? Do the adverse consequences suggest that the problem requires urgent action? (If policy advocates cannot make a strong case that the problem or issue is significant, they will find it difficult to generate support for solutions from decision makers.)

Policy advocates sometimes develop strategies for preventing specific problems. They need to examine relevant literature from various disciplines, such as social science and public health, and other research, including Internet sites, all of which discuss prevention strategies for specific social problems.

They also need to ask questions concerning who will address the social problem or issue that they are analyzing—and to whom their policy analysis will be directed:

- In what specific policy arenas can remedies for this social problem or issue be developed and enacted, including local, state, or federal legislatures; specific local, state, or federal bureaucracies; the courts; the private sector; specific social agencies, whether public ones or nongovernmental organizations (NGOs); and nonpublic entities such as faith-based or for-profit organizations?
- Or should the issue or problem be addressed by a combination of these organizations, such as by a strategy that links public and nonpublic agencies?

Even at the outset, policy analysts often involve other persons in their work. Policy advocacy usually involves collaborative work by task forces, teams, coalitions, or advocacy groups that seek solutions to specific social problems or issues.

2. *Policy analysts brainstorm an array of relevant policy, programmatic, and resource options that, singly and together, might define a strategy for addressing the social problem or issue.* These can consider several or many options, depending on the complexity of the proposal that is ultimately developed during the analytic process.

3. Policy analysts analyze the relative merits of competing options so that, on balance, they can select a specific one from two or more options. To make these comparisons of options, they must first identify specific criteria that they will use to contrast the options and to decide, on balance, which of them is meritorious.

The term *trade-offs* is used to describe how policy analysts deal with the fact that specific policy options often rank high on one or more criteria but lower on others. Faced with this situation, policy analysts might conclude that, *on balance,* they prefer a specific policy option even though it does not rank high on all criteria.

4. Policy analysts draft a specific policy proposal that flows from their brainstorming and conceptual work during the preceding three stages of policy analysis. The proposals can be relatively simple or complex, relatively modest or ambitious, or relatively inexpensive or costly. They can propose new policies or modifications of existing ones. They can propose new programs or improvements in existing ones. They often include proposed budgets.

Policy advocates often get feedback during the drafting process from other policy advocates and from decision makers, and they may modify their proposals as needed. They might decide, for example, to downsize or to expand proposals. They could decide to delete certain contentious provisions or to add some that they think might have sufficient political support.

5. Policy analysts seek supporters for their proposals—although, they will have involved other persons in their work from the outset.

6. Policy analysts make key presentations to public officials or decision makers to persuade them that a policy proposal is meritorious.

Different Models—Or Variations on a Theme?

A strong case can be made, then, that policy analysis remains an art rather than a science (Bardach, 2005; Heineman et al., 1997; Majone, 1989). It often contains rational elements, such as sophisticated use of data to illuminate social issues and to select policy options. Indeed, with the explosion of social science, economic, and medical research, most policy analysts *have* to use some data to buttress their case if their arguments are to merit consideration by decision makers.

But the *relative* emphasis given to rational, value, and political factors varies between analysts and specific analytic projects. Value-based analysts are likely to identify value-focused criteria and policy options that conform to their personal beliefs (Gil, 1981; Moroney, 1985). Whereas analysts in conservative think tanks often select policies that advance devolution, rights, and choice, analysts in liberal think tanks are more likely to favor policy options that promote equality, social justice, and fairness. To the extent that analysts use legal arguments to support or oppose specific policy options, they use normative criteria drawn from legal precedents or the Constitution, such as opposing (or supporting) on constitutional grounds a policy that legalizes euthanasia (Turnbull, 1981).

Legislative aides and some civil servants are likely to emphasize political criteria. When circumstances favor it, such as when tidal shifts in public opinion occur or when the balance of power changes markedly in a legislative setting, they may support policy options that propose sweeping changes from the status quo (Brown, 1990; Kingdon, 1997). More typically, they favor incremental shifts because these are less likely to attract opposition from persons and groups who support existing policies (Lindblom, 1959).

University-based and some think-tank analysts are more likely to emphasize rational analysis. Emancipated from the political process, possessing resources and time to complete sophisticated studies, and working in a setting that accords quantitative work considerable prestige, they frequently develop extended research projects.

Yet, few of these analysts can escape values or political realities—and most of them have to use data at some point. Rather than using distinct models of policy analysis, then, perhaps different analysts place differing emphasis on rational, political, and value-focused criteria. Different emphases can be used sequentially and iteratively. Perhaps policy analysts begin with a rational model that locates specific options and produces data to determine their relative merit. Then, perhaps, the analysts decide to factor political realities into their analysis as they realize that their preferred (rational) option has virtually no chance of selection. Then, they might decide to include value-based criteria, shifting their choice yet again. Or perhaps the inclusion of political and value-based criteria leads them to add new options to their analysis, thus enriching their deliberations.

Different emphases may exist within a specific analytic project when complex proposals are developed in legislative settings. Take the development of a federal shelter program as discussed by Jansson (2008). In this situation, a policy practitioner develops a multifaceted piece of legislation that includes incorporating a mission for the program, locating the program in the federal bureaucracy, determining its auspices, and determining myriad other policies. With respect to some of these policy choices, political considerations will likely prevail, such as whether a powerful faction will oppose the legislation, no matter its overall merit, if a certain policy is chosen. With respect to other issues, legislators may be willing to be governed by rational considerations. With respect to yet other issues, values may predominate. So policy analysts need to be agile, emphasizing different kinds of criteria as they engage in different projects. If they want decision makers to use their products, moreover, they need to place their work in a broader political and cultural context. Policy analysis is embedded in a larger policy-making process that includes agenda building, policy analysis, policy enactment, policy implementation, and policy assessment (Jansson, 2008). If policy analysts want their work to influence decisions within this broader context, they need to include important stakeholders in their projects from the outset and at multiple points during the analytical process, both to gain insights and to increase the chances that their work will influence decisions. They need to disseminate their results to advocacy groups and decision makers in a manner that makes a convincing case (Bardach, 2005). In short, excessively narrow definitions of policy analysis that emphasize only technical skills place analysts in a restrictive niche. To avoid relegating their work to the sidelines of the policy-making process, policy analysts need to couple their technical skills with political, interactional, and value-clarifying ones.

References

Aaron, H., Mann, T., & Taylor, T. (Eds.). (1994). *Values and public policy.* Washington, DC: Brookings Institution Press.

Bardach, E. (2005). *A practical guide for policy analysis: The eightfold path to a more effective problem solving* (2nd ed.). Washington, DC: CQ Press.

Behn, D., & Vaupel, J. (1982). *Quick analysis for busy decision makers.* New York: Basic Books.

Bloom, M. (1981). *Primary prevention: The possible science.* Englewood Cliffs, NJ: Prentice Hall.

Brown, R. (1990). *The logic of congressional action.* New Haven, CT: Yale University Press.

Chambers, D., Wedel, K., & Rodwell, M. (1992). *Evaluating social programs.* Boston: Allyn & Bacon.

Einbinder, S. (1996). Policy analysis. In R. L. Edwards & J. G. Hopps (Eds.), *Encyclopedia of social work* (19th ed., Vol. 3, pp. 1849–1855). Silver Spring, MD: NASW Press.

Fischer, C., Hout, M., Jankowski, M., Lucas, S., Swidler, A., & Voss, K. (1996). *Inequality by design.* Princeton, NJ: Princeton University Press.

Gil, D. (1981). *Unraveling of social policy* (3rd ed.). Cambridge, MA: Schenkman.

Grubb, W. (1996). *Learning to work.* New York: Russell Sage Foundation.

Gupta, D. (1994). *Decisions by the numbers.* Englewood Cliffs, NJ: Prentice Hall.

Hawkesworth, M. (1988). *Theoretical issues in policy analysis.* Albany: State University of New York Press.

Heineman, R., Bluhm, W., Peterson, S., & Kearny, E. (1997). *The world of the policy analyst.* Chatham, NJ: Chatham House.

Herrnstein, R. J., & Murray, C. (1994). *The bell curve: Intelligence and class structure in American life.* New York: Free Press.

Jansson, B. (1990). Blending social change and technology in macro-practice: Developing structural dialogue in technical deliberations. *Administration in Social Work, 14,* 13–28.

Jansson, B. (2008). *Becoming an effective policy advocate: From policy practice to social justice.* Pacific Grove, CA: Brooks/Cole.

Kettner, P., Moroney, R., & Martin, L. (1990). *Designing and managing programs.* Newbury Park, CA: Sage.

Kingdon, J. (1997). *Agendas, alternatives, and public choices.* Boston: Little, Brown.

Kotler, P. (1989). *Principles of marketing* (4th ed.). Englewood Cliffs, NJ: Prentice Hall.

Lindblom, C. (1959). The science of muddling through. *Public Administration Review, 19*(2), 79–81.

Maguire, D. (1991). An overview and definition of GIS. In D. Maguire, M. Goochild, & D. Rhind (Eds.), *Geographical information systems: Principles and applications* (Vol. 1, pp. 9–20). New York: John Wiley & Sons.

Majone, G. (1989). *Evidence, argument, and persuasion in the policy process.* New Haven, CT: Yale University Press.

Mann, T., & Ornstein, N. (1995). *How congress shapes health policy.* Washington, DC: Brookings Institution Press.

Mayer, R. (1985). *Policy and program planning.* Englewood Cliffs, NJ: Prentice Hall.

Meltsner, A. (1976). *Policy analysts in the bureaucracy.* Berkeley: University of California Press.

Moroney, R. (1985). Policy analysis within a value theoretical framework. In R. Haskins & J. Gallagher (Eds.), *Models for analysis of social policy* (pp. 78–101). Norwood, NJ: Ablex.

Patton, C., & Sawicki, D. (1993). *Basic methods of policy analysis and planning.* Englewood Cliffs, NJ: Prentice Hall.

Queralt, M., & Witte, A. (1998). A map for you? Geographic information systems in the social services. *Social Work, 43,* 455–469.

Rein, M. (1983). Value-critical policy analysis. In D. Callhan & B. Jennings (Eds.), *Ethics, the social sciences, and policy analysis* (pp. 83–111). New York: Plenum.

Rubington, E., & Weinberg, M. (1989). *The study of social problems* (4th ed.). New York: Oxford University Press.

Smith, H. (1988). *The power game: How Washington works.* New York: Ballantine Books.

Turnbull, H. (1981). Two legal analysis techniques and public policy analysis. In R. Haskins & J. Gallagher (Eds.), *Models for analysis of social policy* (pp. 153–173). Norwood, NJ: Ablex.

Weimer, D., & Vining, A. (1992). *Policy analysis: Concepts and practice.* Englewood Cliffs, NJ: Prentice Hall.

Wolch, J. & Sommers, H. (1997). *Era of welfare reform.* Los Angeles: Southern California Inter-University Consortium on Homelessness and Poverty.

5

Policy Practice and Advocacy

Richard Hoefer

Social workers were policy practitioners long before the term was coined. Jane Addams, for example, not only founded Hull House, a settlement house in Chicago, but also was a leader in the Progressive Party and influenced the national political scene (Day, 2006). Grace Abbott worked at Hull House and, with her sister Edith, taught at one of the first schools of social work, the Chicago School of Civics and Philanthropy, before being appointed to the staff of the federal Children's Bureau. In that position, she was able to prohibit child labor in companies holding federal government contracts during World War I. Later, she headed the Children's Bureau (Day, 2006). Harry Hopkins assisted Franklin D. Roosevelt (governor of New York state and later U.S. president) in designing and implementing social programs to help unemployed workers during the Great Depression (Day, 2006).

More recent examples abound as well, with social workers active in the electoral realm at all levels. Elected officials include, at the national level, United States Senators Barbara Mikulski (D-MD) and Debbie Stabenow (D-MI) and Representatives Susan Davis (CA), Barbara Lee (CA), Ed Towns (NY), and Ciro Rodriguez (TX). The National Association of Social Workers (NASW) further counted 69 social workers elected at the state level, 30 at the county or borough level, 44 at the city level, and 28 serving on school boards (NASW, 2007). Innumerable other social workers are active in additional ways, affecting social policy by being active in coalitions, interest groups, and agencies and by acting independently to challenge injustice and to work for social justice.

This chapter explores the meanings of policy practice and advocacy, explains the ethical imperative for policy practice and advocacy, and discusses a model of advocacy practice to affect social policy that fits within the generalist model of social work practice.

_____ What Are Policy Practice and Advocacy?

Jansson (2003) defines _policy practice_ as "efforts to change policies in leg-islative, agency and, community settings, whether by establishing new policies, improving existing ones, or defeating the policy initiatives of other people" (p. 13). Policy practice is thus not limited to social workers, as anyone, whether liberal, conservative, radical, or reactionary, can try to change policy. Jansson also defines the term _policy advocacy_ as "policy practice that aims to help relatively powerless groups, such as women, children, poor people, African Americans, Asian Americans, gay men and lesbians, and people with disabilities, improve their resources and oppor-tunities" (p. 13).

Adopting a perspective similar to Jansson's concept of advocacy practice, but working in an Israeli context, Gal and Weiss (2000) state, "Policy-practice is a form of social work intervention that is intended to influence social policy. It is linked to an understanding of the role of social workers which places the struggle for social justice at the forefront of social work activity" (p. 487).

Wyers (1991) discusses five different though overlapping perspectives regarding policy practice. His emphasis is on what the individual social worker does rather than on the process and goal of the social worker's acts.

> In this article, policy-practice is defined as a direct social work practice mode with the potential to strengthen the social work profession's abil-ities to meet its century-long commitments of providing policy-informed services to those in need of them. (p. 241)

Wyers (1991) sees social workers who are policy practitioners as pol-icy experts, change agents in external and internal work environments, policy conduits, and, sometimes, as policy itself. This emphasis on the role of the social worker in policy practice is different than other authors' perspectives.

Similar to the term _policy practice_, the word _advocacy_ has an unclear and diffuse set of definitions. Schneider and Lester (2001) synthesize over 90 different definitions to define social work advocacy as "the exclusive and mutual representation of a client(s) or a cause in a forum, attempting to systematically influence decision making an in an unjust or unresponsive system(s)" (p. 65). Barker (1995), in the _Social Work Dictionary,_ defines advocacy as "the act of directly representing or defending others" (p. 11). Mickelson (1995), in an entry in the _Encyclopedia of Social Work_, defines advocacy as "the act of directly representing, defending, intervening, sup-porting or recommending a course of action on behalf of one or more indi-viduals, groups, or communities, with the goal of securing or retain social justice" (p. 95).

Hoefer (2006) discusses what he terms *advocacy practice*, which is defined as

> that part of social work practice where the social worker takes action in a systematic and purposeful way to defend, represent or otherwise advance the cause of one or more clients at the individual, group, organizational, or community level in order to promote social justice. (p. 8)

The context for Hoefer is that advocacy practice fits into social work's general problem-solving approach, which is often termed *generalist social work* (see, for an example of a generalist social work text, Kirst-Ashmon & Hull, 2006). This approach directly contradicts Schneider and Lester (2001), who state, "Advocacy is not a form of problem solving" (p. 71). Hoefer (2006) argues, however, that, because advocacy has the goal of achieving greater social justice, it is a tool to fix the problems of oppression and injustice, and "all social workers should understand the principles and processes of advocacy" (p. 2).

Adopting a vision of advocacy or policy practice as a problem-solving approach to promote social justice helps to promote its adoption by social workers of all types, and at micro, mezzo, and macro levels of practice. Drawing upon the National Association of Social Workers' *Code of Ethics*, the next section explains the ethical imperative for policy practice and the connections between the code's call for advocacy and the realization of social justice.

The Ethical Imperative for Policy Practice and Advocacy

Social workers are called to conduct advocacy by the National Association of Social Workers' *Code of Ethics* (1999). While the need for social action is mentioned in several sections of the code ("Preamble," "Ethical Principles," and sections 3.07, 6.01, 6.02, and 6.04), one clear call to become an advocate is in the preamble: "Social workers promote social justice and social change with and on behalf of clients" (NASW, 1999). Social action can take place in many ways, including advocacy. Later, in section 6.01, the idea is amplified:

> Social workers should promote the general welfare of society, from local to global levels, and the development of people, their communities, and their environment. Social workers should advocate for living conditions conducive to the fulfillment of basic human needs and should promote social, economic, political, and cultural values and institutions that are compatible with the realization of social justice. (NASW, 1999)

Note that action is never taken just to be taking action—in fact, particular goals for action are proclaimed, chief among them being the realization of social justice. Advocacy is thus intended to bring about social policies that have specific goals, such as making sure that all humans have "equal access to the resources, employment, services, and opportunities they require to meet their basic human needs and to develop fully" (NASW, 1999, section 6.04a). In addition, "Social workers should act to expand choice and opportunity for all persons, with special regard for vulnerable, disadvantaged, oppressed, and exploited people and groups" (NASW, 1999, section 6.04b).

It is one thing to know that one must, in theory, support social justice through advocacy in order to be an ethical social worker. It is another thing, however, to know what this means in practice. Knowing that one is obligated as a social worker to engage in social policy practice and advocacy is not the same thing as knowing what to do as an advocate or when to do it. This is particularly true if policy practice or advocacy is seen as something different than or outside of a social worker's normal actions. The next section discusses how advocacy can be seen as a special case of the generalist model of social work and the advantages of so viewing it.

The Generalist Model of Social Work and Advocacy

One advantage of placing policy or advocacy practice in a problem-solving or generalist framework is that it brings together all types of social workers by using a common language. Social work students receive training in the problem-solving method from the start of their education. Placing advocacy within this previously encountered framework assists in lowering anxiety on the part of potential advocates and allows social workers a flatter learning curve.

With minor variations, many authors propose a similar problem-solving process for social workers (see Table 5.1). Sheafor and Horejsi (2006) write on social work practice, Kirst-Ashmon and Hull (2006) discuss generalist practice in a macro context, and Boyle, Hull, Mather, Smith, and Farley (2006) describe direct social work practice. Hoefer (2006) focuses on advocacy practice. Still, the practice process is described very similarly across texts and foci. No matter what they call themselves, direct practitioners, macro practitioners, clinicians, community organizers, or group workers, all social workers can relate to advocacy practice described in terms that they are familiar with and that make sense to them.

Another advantage of locating advocacy within a generalist practice model is that it brings together under one umbrella all different types of advocacy. No longer is legal advocacy so different from legislative, agency, or community advocacy (Ezell, 2001). It is also easier to see commonalities between client or case advocacy and cause advocacy (Schneider & Lester, 2001). The remainder of this chapter will expand on the conceptualization of advocacy practice for social justice as shown in Table 5.1.

Table 5.1   Stages of Social Work Practice Across Types of Practice

Social Work Practice	Generalist Macro Practice	Direct Practice	Advocacy Practice
Sheafor and Horejsi (2006)	Kirst-Ashmon and Hull (2006)	Boyle, Hull, Mather, Smith, and Farley (2006)	Hoefer (2006)
Intake and Engagement	Engagement	Engagement	Getting Involved
Data Collection and Assessment	Assessment	Assessment	Understanding the Issue
Planning and Contracting	Planning	Planning	Planning
Intervention and Monitoring	Implementation	Intervention	Advocating
Final Evaluation	Evaluation	Evaluation	Evaluating
Termination	Termination	Termination	
	Follow-Up		Ongoing Monitoring

Advocacy Practice for Social Justice _____

As is shown in Table 5.1, Hoefer (2006) lists six phases of advocacy practice: (1) getting involved, (2) understanding the issue, (3) planning, (4) advocating, (5) evaluating, and (6) ongoing monitoring. This section describes each phase and provides examples.

Phase 1: Getting Involved

Social workers have been shown to be more politically active than the general public and about as active as other groups of professionals (Ezell, 1993; Pawlak & Flynn, 1990; Wolk, 1981). Yet, activists constantly exhort social workers to do more, including joining action alert e-mail lists, contacting legislators, testifying before commissions, voting, or running for office, among other activities. The question rightly arises as to why social workers become active in advocacy.

Putting work by political scientists Verba, Schlozman, and Brady (1995) together with research on social workers' involvement in advocacy, Hoefer (2006) describes seven variables that affect levels of social worker activism.

These variables are

- educational level, which, for social workers, tends to be higher than the national average. Social work education describes the need for activism to promote social justice, and it includes knowledge of political structures and organizational processes;
- values, which emphasize promoting the needs and rights of vulnerable populations;
- sense of professional responsibility, which is molded by education and personal values toward the belief that social workers "should" be actively advocating for social justice;
- interest in advocacy, which varies from one social worker to the next and from one period of life to another;
- participation in other organizations, which provides a deeper understanding of how "the world" works and how individuals and organizations operate to achieve their goals;
- skills, which includes abilities in areas such as research, public speaking, negotiation, and persuasion; and
- time, a limiting factor for all organizations and advocates, as there are only so many hours in a day.

Each of these variables can be affected to increase or decrease the likelihood of advocacy being conducted by social workers. Organizations wishing to promote advocacy among volunteers or employees can provide additional education and skills training, emphasize social work values and professional responsibilities for conducting advocacy, promote engagement in other organizations, and structure time on the job for advocacy to occur.

Phase 2: Understanding the Issue

Once the decision to become active has been made, a natural tendency to jump into advocacy surfaces. This reaction must be resisted, however, because it is unlikely that effective advocacy can take place without an individual fully understanding an issue and then planning an effective strategy to make a change.

Hoefer (2006) suggests a five-step process to take to understand an issue. These steps are to (1) define the issue, (2) decide who is affected and how they are affected by the issue, (3) decide what the main causes of the issue are, (4) generate possible solutions to the issue, and (5) review proposed solutions to determine their impact on social justice (p. 53).

Defining the issue is necessary so that advocates can focus on what they are trying to change. A good definition helps us to concentrate our efforts and not drift to related concerns. Examples of good issue definitions are, for example, "Families are running out of nutritious food before the end of the month" and "Child protective services workers have caseloads that are twice the recommended levels."

It is important to define the issue in a way that does not suggest just one possible solution. The examples just provided could be addressed in more than one way. Running out of food before the end of the month may be due to inadequate incomes, not enough food available from food banks, wasteful spending or lack of food preparation skills, or having only high-cost stores accessible to clients, among other reasons. High caseloads could be caused by too few workers, too many children being abused, a lack of alternatives for permanent placement of children, and so on. An example of a problematic definition of an issue is "Child protective workers are not paid enough." The solution to this issue is embedded in its definition in a way that is not true of the earlier examples.

Deciding who is affected and how is important so that we understand the scope of the issue. We must also remember that, in most cases, while we see the negative side of the current situation and wish to change it, it is likely that at least someone is benefiting from the situation just the way it is. This "silver lining" must be understood and reckoned with, as those benefiting from the status quo can be expected to resist change.

Deciding on the main causes of the issue is important but can be frustrating. Individuals and organizations will usually not admit that they are at fault for causing damage to others and will seek to deflect attention from their actions. Usually, the most we can do is to focus on how we have defined the issue of concern and then look for proximate causes of that issue.

Generating possible solutions to the issue is one of the most creative steps of the advocacy process. Techniques such as brainstorming, thinking win-win, considering a new approach that restructures the situation (Nagel, 2002), trying the opposite of what is usually done, or focusing on "what can be done" (loosely based on May [1981]) can be used to create fresh insights and to develop new alternatives to old policies or procedures.

The final step in understanding the issue is to evaluate the different possible solutions according to how well they promote social justice. While advocates must always weigh the practicality of their proposals and the chances of getting them adopted, they should also strive for possible solutions that most fully promote social justice. One possible approach to evaluating proposals is De Bono's "six hats" method, where participants "put on" different "thinking hats" to examine the idea from different perspectives (De Bono, 1999). Another method is to use a scorecard (Patton & Sawicki, 1993), where each possible solution is rated on criteria related to social justice, such as respect for basic human rights, promotion of social responsibility, commitment to individual freedom, and support for self-determination (criteria listed here are suggested in the work of Abbott, 1988). One preferred solution may emerge from this analysis of all options. The lesser-preferred solutions should still be kept in mind, however, if the most desirable answer is not achievable.

With the desire to be involved and a deep understanding of the issue, complete with a preferred solution in hand, the social worker is only now ready to plan the advocacy effort.

Phase 3: Planning

The planning process can be seen as developing a road map for getting from "here" to "there." "Here" is the current situation, and "there" is the solution developed in the previous phase. By the end of the planning process, advocates should be able to answer four questions:

1. What do you want?

2. Who can get you what you want?

3. When can or should you act?

4. How can you act to get what you want?

Hoefer (2006) suggests a tool dubbed an *advocacy map* as an aid to the planning process. Based on logic modeling used in program planning and evaluation (W. K. Kellogg Foundation, 2004), an advocacy map clearly shows the connections between an advocacy effort's resources, actions, and desired outcomes, in the short, medium, and long term. It also relates all of these to an ultimate social justice outcome, thus keeping a focus on why the advocacy is being done. In the example outlined in Figure 5.1, the advocate has chosen a case that is seen as possibly needing a micro-level intervention as well as macro-level interventions. This case shows the multidimensional nature of many problems that advocates face, with partial solutions potentially coming at different levels of intervention.

The advocacy map in Figure 5.1 has several elements. First, it is dated because the plan can (and probably will) change as different ideas are tried and possible roadblocks are encountered. Knowing when a plan was developed enables advocates to work with the latest version at all times.

Second, the definition of the problem or issue is listed so that it remains in mind. Third, the map outlines resources, actions, and outcomes. Column 1 shows the resources that are available to use. These resources will always include the client (at whatever level of intervention) and the social worker or advocate. Other resources may be available too. Column 2 indicates what actions should be taken by each resource. These actions should then lead to accomplishing short-term outcomes (Column 3), which then lead to medium-term outcomes (Column 4), which, in turn, will lead to the long-term outcome or outcomes (Column 5). At the end of the process, at least some progress will have been made toward improving social justice for members of society (Column 6). A completed advocacy map, then, makes clear who is supposed to do what, for what purpose, and how social justice will be enhanced if all goes according to plan.

The next question to answer is, who can get you what you want? In many cases, the answer will become obvious during the advocacy mapping process. At other times, however, advocates may not yet be clear which specific individual should be contacted to create changes. In Figure 5.1, for

Date: September 29, 2008

Definition of problem/issue being addressed: Families face food insecurity, that is, they are running out of nutritious food before the end of the month

Resources (Col. 1)	Tasks (Col. 2)	Short-Term Outcomes (Col. 3)	Medium-Term Outcomes (Col. 4)	Long-Term Outcomes (Col. 5)	Social Justice Outcomes for Society (Col. 6)
Adults in families	Examine shopping patterns to ensure food dollars are being used wisely Plan meals so that leftover food can be used effectively Apply for food assistance programs (governmental and nonprofit)	Food money is used only for nutritious meals Little or no food spoils or is wasted A larger food budget or additional nutritious food in the home	Food budget lasts longer	Problems caused by poor nutrition are avoided	Healthy citizens with no nutrition-related ailments
Social Worker/ Advocate	Assist adults in families to receive training in food budgeting, shopping, and preparation Research policies of governmental and nonprofit food assistance programs As needed, advocate for individual clients to receive program benefits	Client gains additional knowledge regarding preparing a food budget, shopping for and preparing food Understand client eligibility for programs Enhance ability of clients to receive food assistance	Client food budget lasts longer and meals are more nutritious Have clients receive maximum benefits allowed Increased amounts of food for families at risk of hunger Altered policies or more resources allocated to eliminate food insecurity	Problems caused by poor nutrition are avoided	Healthy citizens with no nutrition-related ailments

Resources (Col. 1)	Tasks (Col. 2)	Short-Term Outcomes (Col. 3)	Medium-Term Outcomes (Col. 4)	Long-Term Outcomes (Col. 5)	Social Justice Outcomes for Society (Col. 6)
	Create a coalition of advocates to work for different eligibility criteria, increased benefit levels, and so on	Educate community and decision makers about problems of food insecurity	Higher quality or more food eaten by clients at risk of food insecurity		
	Promote major grocery store coming into low-income areas	More choice for clients on where to shop for food (perhaps with better quality food or lower costs)			
Community-based food programs	Provide training in food shopping and meal preparation	Clients facing food insecurity have additional knowledge in these areas	Clients are able to consume adequate amounts of nutritious food every day	Problems caused by poor nutrition are avoided	Healthy citizens with no nutrition-related ailments
	Find more sources of nutritious food for clients	Clients facing food insecurity have more food and more food choices than before			
Major chain grocery stores	Locate in low-income areas	Store provides nutritious food at costs that allow a profit to be made	Profit is made while offering low-income persons access to higher quality and lower cost food than before	Problems caused by poor nutrition are avoided	Healthy citizens with no nutrition-related ailments

Figure 5.1   Sample Advocacy Map

75

example, the advocacy map indicates that training should be provided to improve knowledge about shopping and meal preparation. The social worker may not know who can provide this service. The advocate also is supposed to work with a major grocery store chain to bring in a new shopping alternative. Just which chain or who in the corporate office to contact is not yet known. Thus, the target of advocacy action (which can be a group, such as a city council or legislative committee) may need to be determined after the map is created.

The third question—when should you act?—can be answered—when you are prepared. Once the plan is in place and a target has been identified, little reason exists to wait. There is never a "perfect time" when the stars are all aligned and success is assured. Finally, the fourth question—how can you act to get what you want?—leads us into a discussion of educating, negotiating, and persuading.

Educating

Most politicians (and their aides) cover a geographic district that encompasses many constituents, who experience a wide variety of issues. Other decision makers, whether in a private nonprofit or other organization, are also similarly spread thin, having numerous and diverse duties. By necessity, such politicians and officials know a little about many issues but tend not to know that much about any particular issue. Further, they may not have had any exposure to many topics. Thus, much of an advocate's job turns out to be educating such generalists in the issue that is of concern to the advocate. In some cases, particularly within a bureaucracy (at whatever level), however, the targets of advocacy are well-respected experts in their field. In these cases, the advocate needs to be very knowledgeable in order to be credible. It is useful to think about the type of person your target is— a generalist or a specialist—when planning your advocacy.

If the advocate is in an educating position, then the discussion may feel rather one-sided, with the advocate doing most of the talking. If the advocate is able to bring new information to the table and provide rationales for the positions being espoused, progress may be quick. Very often, however, the target will not commit to any action until additional information is collected.

Negotiating

Negotiating is a process of coming to an agreed upon decision. Negotiation theory suggests that preparation for the advocate is essential. Before starting any negotiation, an advocate should develop an initial position, fallback positions, and a limit. The initial position is probably more than the advocate expects to receive, but not outrageously more. Fallback positions contain some concessions compared to the initial position, but are outcomes that the advocate can live with. A limit is the worst acceptable position for the advocate. Anything less than the limit as an outcome is simply unacceptable, with no agreement being preferable. If one plans to negotiate, it is imperative to develop these positions.

With these positions laid out in advance of a negotiation session, the advocate has an easier time knowing how to react to the counteroffers being made during negotiations. A clear prioritizing of desired outcomes is also beneficial. Thus, while it is true that almost no one gets all that is hoped for, skilled negotiators can often find common ground so that the negotiation process concludes with an agreement that all sides can live with.

Persuading

Negotiation, by its nature, tends to lead to compromises in which the parties do not achieve all of their desired outcomes. With persuasion, however, it is possible to have one party adopt the other party's position entirely, so both see the outcome as positive. Hoefer (2006) adopts a communication perspective for his treatment of persuasion techniques. He argues that advocacy can be thought of as a specialized case of persuasion. Every time persuasion is attempted, four variables are important: the context, the message, the sender, and the receiver. Some behaviors improve the odds of persuasion happening, whereas others decrease this likelihood. Planning for persuasion must focus on how to improve the advocate's chances of achieving agreement with the target.

People's reactions to various proposals will be colored by the context or frame they use to understand the situation. If the social worker advocates can have their framework for discussion adopted by the target, persuasion is easier. For example, an advocacy effort might want to address a problem by arguing that the current situation is unfair to children who need services. Or advocates may decide to oppose another group's proposals by arguing that, while the goal is laudable, it can be accomplished in other ways. Other typical advocacy frames are discussed by Hoefer (2006, pp. 98–102).

Messages are also critically important. Booth-Butterfield (1996) lists six general principles of persuasive messages: intent, organization, sidedness, repetition and redundancy, rhetorical questions, and fear appeals. He advises that it is usually not a good idea to announce to the target your intent to persuade him or her. This is because targets begin to justify their behavior more strongly once it is clear that the advocate wishes to change it. Two situations run counter to this general rule, however. First, if the situation is clearly one of advocacy, it is best to be honest about it. Second, if your target agrees with most of what you want, and you want to make only small changes, you gain points by saying up front what you are after.

Well-organized messages are more persuasive than poorly organized presentations. This should be kept in mind, as advocates frequently want to "shoot from the hip" in a rush to begin. Instead, it is more powerful to take the time to organize the message logically and coherently, paying attention to other elements of what makes for a persuasive message.

Sometimes, advocates wonder if they should present only their side of a controversial position or if they should present the "other side" as well. Cialdini (2000) argues that talking about opposing viewpoints is often a good strategy, but only if those views are also attacked. Otherwise, stick with a one-sided presentation of ideas.

Repetition, repeating one's message in the same way, and redundancy, presenting the same theme repeatedly but in a different way, help a persuasive message sink in, as most targets are not paying careful attention. Both are powerful elements of persuasive messages. Rhetorical questions are useful in persuasion efforts because they are disguised statements. Targets hear them as questions yet accept them as facts, which can then be taken for granted in later conversation (Cialdini, 2000). This is especially true if the target is not paying complete attention to the advocate.

Appealing to your target's fears is another way to be persuasive. A fear appeal is a type of message that focuses on the negative things that will occur if the target takes some action or fails to take some action. To be effective, however, the advocate must not stop at scaring the target but must provide a plan to reassure the target that his or her fears can be assuaged. That plan is, of course, what the advocate is pushing for.

One of the most important elements of persuasion is the sender. Targets react not just to the context and the message but also to the advocate. The sender must, first and foremost, be credible. Credibility is composed of three factors: expertise, trustworthiness, and likeability. Advocates have some control over the target's perception of them regarding these factors, and, if needed, can work to improve in these three areas.

The last element of persuasion relates to the receiver or target of the message. Advocates must understand their targets well enough to know how to convince them to convince themselves and adopt the advocate's views as their own. In this way, the target is the best (and only true) persuader. The advocate should focus on what needs of the target will be at play and should show the target how the advocate's plan achieves something of importance to the target (Bedell, 2000). Bedell suggests that three personal needs are usually the most prominent in the minds of targets: the need to win, the need for security, and the need for acceptance. Thus, advocates should strive to meet these (usually unexpressed) needs in order to help targets convince themselves that it is preferable to adopt the advocate's suggested course of action.

Digesting all this information on planning an advocacy effort can seem daunting. Yet, it is vital to take each part in turn and plan carefully before beginning advocacy. Even if done informally, each step adds an important element and increases the power of the advocacy effort.

Phase 4: Advocating

At this stage, the advocate actually contacts the target and puts the plans into motion. Over preparation is better than under preparation when you are sitting across the table from the one person who can provide you with the outcome you desire. Advocates still have decisions to make at this point in regard to the manner and format of their presentation.

Research indicates some things to keep in mind when one is considering the manner of making the pitch. A general template for the advocate is to describe the problem and then provide the solution. Accuracy and clarity are vital. Timing (at least, keeping things brief) means a lot. Advocates should be able to tailor their message to the amount of time available, whether this is a 15-minute appointment or the few seconds of an elevator ride. The advocate should also decide whether the effort will be a one-shot try or part of a longer-term plan.

The format of the message may be oral or written. Oral advocacy includes both individual or small group face-to-face interaction and telephone contacts, with the former considered more effective when it is possible. Testimony before an official body is also oral advocacy. Written communication has an important place in advocacy practice as well. It can include letters, faxes, e-mail messages, letters to the editor, editorials, reports, briefs, and petitions. Increasingly, Web sites act as open libraries of persuasive information. The printed word often carries weight simply because it is connected with a physical object. This means it continues to exist and can be an effective advocacy tool long after it has been delivered.

Communication with the target is the part of advocacy that is the most exciting and usually the only part that one sees in the movies or on television shows. But it is really only the tip of the iceberg; preparation is the larger portion. When it is over, one hopes that results can be seen quickly, but one of the rules for advocates is to be patient (Richan, 1996) for it may take a great deal of time to see the fruits of one's labors.

Phase 5: Evaluating

Of all the phases of advocacy, probably the least well developed is the step of evaluating it, despite the acknowledgement of its importance (Clark, 2001; Hoefer, 2006; Weiss, 2007). Hoefer (2006) suggests that advocates can use their advocacy maps to determine the extent of task completion and outcome attainment. Doing this provides a more formal and quantitative approach to advocacy evaluation, especially when compared with informal discussions over a cold drink, which is sometimes considered state of the art. Laney, Scobie, and Fraser (2005) discuss the importance of evaluating the context of advocacy, monitoring several stakeholders for signs of change, and looking for alterations within one's own organization; these changes involve the organization's reputation, the target's positions, and the relationships amongst the organization, the target, and external sources, as well as altered perspectives expressed by the media and the public.

New resources for evaluating advocacy are emerging, as discussed in a recent issue of *The Evaluation Exchange*, published by the Harvard Family Research Project within the Harvard Graduate School of Education. Several points were made summarizing the issue, including these:

- Advocacy evaluation is particularly challenging when approached with a traditional program evaluation mindset.
- Advocates must often become their own evaluators.
- Evaluation creativity is important. (Harvard Family Research Project, 2007)

Phase 6: Ongoing Monitoring

The final phase of advocacy in the generalist social work approach is to monitor the situation that was the impetus for the process's start. Frequently, this job is ignored, as a new case or cause captures our attention. But the hard-won gains of advocacy can be lost if attention is completely diverted from the seemingly won battle. Hoefer (2006) discusses three areas where ongoing monitoring is most important: "influencing the way the program rules are written, advocating in the budgetary process, and monitoring program evaluation" (p. 161).

Influencing the executive side of government or of an organization is different from lobbying the legislative or policy-setting side of these same bodies. One main difference is that legislative policy makers expect to be the objects of advocacy, whereas those responsible for implementation feel less accountable to outsiders. This leads to a second important difference: it can be quite difficult to find out who the correct target for advocacy should be, as those implementing policies frequently do not consider themselves public figures. This situation is as true for private organizations, such as nonprofits or businesses, as it is for government agencies. It may take persistence and many efforts to locate and develop a relationship with people in such positions. Still, such efforts are worthwhile and can mean the difference between achieving one's goals or not.

Conclusion _____

Social policy and advocacy are inextricably intertwined in the field of social work. A long history exists within the profession of working to create change for social justice. Using the process described here, an extension of the generalist model of social work, students and practitioners can take their place in the struggles for social justice still occurring. While cynics doubt that the system is capable of improvement and decry as corrupt working within the system, most social workers are willing to take their code of ethics seriously by advocating the elimination of clear disparities in society and working for the achievement of social justice. Using the methods discussed here can lead to better outcomes for our most vulnerable populations. It is both our duty and our privilege to conduct advocacy for social justice.

References

Abbott, A. (1988). *Professional choices: Values at work*. Silver Spring, MD: NASW Press.

Barker, R. (1995). Advocacy. *The social work dictionary* (3rd ed.). Washington, DC: NASW Press.

Bedell, G. (2000). *Three steps to yes: The gentle art of getting your way*. New York: Crown Business.

Booth-Butterfield, S. (1996). *Dual process persuasion*. Retrieved June 28, 2004, from http://www.as.wvu.edu/~sbb/com221/chapters/dual.htm

Boyle, S., Hull, G., Mather, J., Smith, L., & Farley, O. W. (2006). *Direct practice in social work*. Boston: Allyn & Bacon.

Cialdini, R. (2000). *Influence: Science and practice* (4th ed.). Boston: Pearson, Allyn & Bacon.

Clark, C. (2001). *Making change happen: Advocacy and citizen participation*. Washington, DC: Just Associates.

Day, P. (2006). *A new history of social welfare* (5th ed.). Boston: Allyn & Bacon.

De Bono, E. (1999). *Six thinking hats*. Boston: Little, Brown.

Ezell, M. (1993). The political activities of social workers: A post-Reagan update. *Journal of Sociology and Social Welfare, 20*(4), 81–97.

Ezell, M. (2001). *Advocacy in the human services*. Belmont, CA: Wadsworth.

Gal, J., & Weiss, I. (2000). Policy-practice in social work and social work education in Israel. *Social Work Education, 19*(5), 485–499.

Harvard Family Research Project. (2007, Spring). Advocacy and policy change [Issue title]. *The Evaluation Exchange: A Periodical on Emerging Strategies in Evaluation, 13*(1).

Hoefer, R. (2006). *Advocacy practice for social justice*. Chicago: Lyceum.

Jansson, B. (2003). *Becoming an effective policy advocate* (4th ed.). Pacific Grove, CA: Brooks/Cole.

Kirst-Ashmon, K., & Hull, G. (2006). *Generalist practice with organizations and communities* (3rd ed.). Pacific Grove, CA: Brooks/Cole.

Laney, M., Scobie, J., & Fraser, A. (2005). *The how and why of advocacy: Guidance notes 2.1*. London: British Overseas NGOs for Development. Retrieved May 22, 2005, from http://www.bond.org.uk/publs/guidance/2.1howwhyadvocacy.pdf

May, P. (1981). Hints for crafting alternative policies. *Policy Analysis, 7*(2), 227–244.

Mickelson, J. (1995). Advocacy. In R. L. Edwards & J. G. Hopps (Eds.), *Encyclopedia of social work* (19th ed., Vol. 1, pp. 95–100). Washington, DC: NASW Press.

Nagel, S. (2002). *Handbook of public policy evaluation.* Thousand Oaks, CA: Sage.

National Association of Social Workers (NASW). (1999). *Code of ethics.* Retrieved May 9, 2007, from http://www.socialworkers.org/pubs/code/code.asp

National Association of Social Workers (NASW). (2007). *Demographics of social workers in elected offices, 2005.* Retrieved May 9, 2007, from http://www.social workers.org/pace/characteristics.asp

Patton, C., & Sawicki, D. (1993). *Basic methods of policy analysis and planning* (2nd ed.). Englewood Cliffs, NJ: Prentice Hall.

Pawlak, E., & Flynn, J. (1990). Executive directors' political activities. *Social Work, 35*(4), 307–312.

Richan, W. (1996). *Lobbying for social change.* New York: Haworth.

Schneider, R. L., & Lester, L. (2001). *Social work advocacy: A new framework for action.* Belmont, CA: Brooks/Cole.

Sheafor, B., & Horejsi, C. (2006). *Techniques and guidelines for social work practice* (7th ed.). Boston: Allyn & Bacon.

Verba, S., Schlozman, K., & Brady, H. (1995). *Voice and equality: Civic voluntarism in American politics.* Cambridge, MA: Harvard University Press.

W. K. Kellogg Foundation. (2004). *Logic model development guide.* Battle Creek, MI: W. K. Kellogg Foundation.

Weiss, H. (2007). From the director's desk. *The Evaluation Exchange: A Periodical on Emerging Strategies in Evaluation, 13*(1), 1–32.

Wolk, J. (1981). Are social workers politically active? *Social Work, 26*(4), 283–288.

Wyers, N. (1991). Policy practice in social work: Models and issues. *Journal of Social Work Education, 27*(3), 241–250.

6

The Impact of Social Policy

Pranab Chatterjee and Diwakar Vadapalli

There is increasing recognition today that social policies and programs should be carefully evaluated to determine whether they do, in fact, meet their stated objectives. Although it has often been assumed that social policies have a positive impact, this assumption has been called into question by many critics of government social programs. This chapter discusses the ways in which the impact of social policies can be assessed. It describes the principles and techniques used in different types of evaluation. Although evaluation research has become increasingly sophisticated, values and ideologies continue to play an important role in deciding which policy approaches work best.

The Logic of Impact Analysis

Rossi and Freeman (1985, 1993) and Rossi, Lipsey, and Freeman (2004) observe that there are four phases of social policy evaluation. These are needs assessment, selection of a program to respond to needs, impact evaluation, and cost-benefit analysis. Upon outlining the four phases of evaluation, they discuss many experimental, quasi-experimental, and time-series designs that can be used for program evaluation. Mohr (1995) singled out the idea of impact evaluation and called it an attempt to isolate the direct effects of a policy (or, more precisely, a program derived from a policy) apart from any confounding environmental effects. Earlier, Suchman (1967) suggested that a program is a form of social experiment, and any evaluation of it leads to the conclusion that the program does or does not produce given social ends. Following Suchman's ideas, Riecken and Boruch (1974) listed ways of evaluating the impact of social experiments, many of which can be construed as preludes to new forms of social policy. Schalock (2001), using these contributions, defined outcome-based evaluation as evaluation that uses valued and objective person- and organization-referenced outcomes to analyze a program's effectiveness, impact, or efficiency. Suchman (1967), in his earlier work, had stated that, if any one program does not produce given social ends, one should conclude that it is a case of *program* failure.

However, if it seems that a substantial number of programs, all similar in nature, do not produce given ends, then it indicates a case of *theory* failure. In other words, the theory that generated the programs (as interventions to bring about a change) has been developed on faulty premises.

The groundwork of Rossi and Suchman on impact analysis (both of social programs and of the parent policies or theories on which they rest) is based on the assumption that quantitative analysis and multivariate design will produce knowledge about the impact of social policies and programs. Ask a typical policy analyst, academic, or program administrator about the impact of social policy and one will be provided with a sheaf of statistics supporting one perspective or another. This has come to be regarded as not just natural but the most appropriate response. On the matter of overemphasis on numbers, Zerbe (1998) has observed, "Hard numbers drive out soft" (p. 429).

Designing Impact Analysis: Some Issues

For example, an intervention designed to improve economic conditions in an urban neighborhood might well appear to be very successful, until one becomes aware that a regional upturn in the economy has occurred throughout the evaluation period and, although the neighborhood economy is much improved, it has, in fact, lagged far behind the rapid growth evident across the rest of the region. To reliably sort out program effects from environmental and other confounding influences is a daunting task. The significant achievements of impact analysis have been to spark an awareness of the need for such an analysis if program effectiveness is ever to be convincingly established and to offer a cookbook of strategies for attempting to achieve valid statistical evaluations.

Perhaps the best case for the use of quasi–experimental designs in impact analysis was made by Campbell (1969), when he proposed that the evaluation of a policy in one state, province, or country is possible by comparing the posttests in two nearly identical states, provinces, or countries, where one has experienced a policy and the other has not. However, this form of impact analysis often results in doing two case studies, which defeats the entire purpose of quasi-experimentation with valid samples and controls.

Impact analysis typically suggests a spectrum of research approaches from experimental to quasi-experimental and strongly recommends that the evaluator stick as closely to the classic controlled experiment and statistical analysis strategies as possible. Of course, it is rarely possible to approach these conditions in social experimentation and evaluation, so the main thrust of an impact analysis is on quasi-experimental strategies and somewhat less powerful statistical analyses. The notion of qualitative strategies is usually dismissed as neither rigorous nor practical enough to warrant consideration.

The product resulting from an impact analysis is a methodologically and statistically sophisticated document detailing relationships and relative levels of importance among a number of variables. In keeping with the values of science in the modern age, it is widely accepted that rigorous attention to methodological and statistical norms will produce an objective analysis of the program under study, so the resulting information may safely be used to determine the fate of a particular policy and the fates of all those stakeholders upon which it has an impact.

Information of this statistical kind has become the lingua franca of decision makers for many easily appreciated reasons. It is a manageable way to consider very large numbers, whether dollars or populations. It appears to offer a nearly irrefutable assessment, apparently devoid of bias or ideology. It is not presented as personal or emotional and is perceived as dispassionate and objective. It does indeed provide one of the most useful approximations available of valid grounds for a judgment as to the effect of a particular policy or program. And it allows for the easy flow of information from one venue to another, for example, from the budget office to the program designers to states, counties, and beyond.

The methodological and statistical achievements of impact analysis have, however, contributed to certain strategies for the evaluation of policy (Rossi & Freeman, 1985). Crane (1982) suggested that a useful impact analysis clearly depends on the formulation of evaluative hypotheses, which may take the following form:

Null hypothesis: The true effect is zero.

Alternative hypothesis: The true effect is at least equal to the threshold effect. (pp. 86–88)

Mohr (1995), using Deniston's ideas (1972a, 1972b), listed further elements of impact evaluation, when he defined "a problem relative to a given [policy or] program as *some predicted condition that will be unsatisfactory without the intervention of the program and satisfactory, or at least more acceptable, given the program's intervention*" (p. 14). Yet, troubling questions persist. In order to be statistically malleable, complex phenomena must be reduced to measurable form. If this is not possible (as it frequently is not) *indicators* must be developed. That is, one kind of information must be made to substitute for another. So, for example, educational level or occupational title is often used as a proxy for income or socioeconomic status because respondents to surveys are loath to reveal their actual earnings. One potential difficulty arises when indicators are used not as indicators but as actual measures. The potential for misunderstanding inherent in the process is important enough that it has led to the establishment of nationwide panels charged with the production of increasingly more reliable indicators.

For example, there are no existing measures that are called "measures of the impact of social policy." However, the Human Development Index (HDI), developed by the United Nations, can be used as a somewhat direct measure of conditions in a society, and it can be then speculated whether one or another of these conditions is the outcome of a certain kind of social policy. The HDI represents three equally weighted indicators of the quality of human life: longevity, as shown by life expectancy at birth; knowledge, as shown by adult literacy and mean years of schooling; and income, as purchasing power parity dollars per capita (United Nations Development Programme, 1994, pp. 108, 220). Using 0.875 as a boundary, 35 states from Canada through Portugal could be said to rate high as welfare societies in 1993. In contrast, 10 countries from the former planned economies of Eastern Europe can be seen to rate below the 0.875 threshold. The data are presented in Table 6.1.

The data from Table 6.1 can now be placed in the design parameters shown in Table 6.2. In this posttest only design, the impact of economic and social policies show that market-oriented policies produce higher HDI levels than planning-oriented policies.

The data presented in Table 6.1 are standardized data and can be placed in most any design parameters. Statistical impact analysis works well with such data.

Perhaps a "better" form of impact analysis would emerge if the Human Development Index measures were available for two different times (e.g., Time 1 and Time 2), and then one could see where planned and market economies were in Time 1 and whether, at Time 2, the gain or loss of planned economies is greater or less than those of market economy societies. This better design would be called a pretest-posttest design (Campbell & Stanley, 1963; Cook & Campbell, 1979; Mohr, 1995).

A yet better design for impact analysis would emerge if prestest-postest measures were available for societies that were comparable to the societies described in Table 6.1 in Time 1 but that did not experience industrial development to the same extent as the market economy societies and planned economy societies did. Actually, this effort can be simulated by going back to the posttest design (as shown in Table 6.2). Take, for example, the case of Afghanistan, which has not experienced any form of industrialization or social policy, and note its HDI level in 1993 (which is 0.229). Then, consider the ethnically similar neighboring societies of Uzbekistan or Turkmenistan or Tajikistan and look at their HDI levels in 1993, which are 0.679, 0.695, and 0.616, respectively, as reported by United Nations Development Programme (1996). Such data can be grouped together for a posttest design (as shown in Table 6.3) to see the impact of economic and social policies driven by forced industrialization and planned economy.

Table 6.1   Market Versus Planned Economy Societies and Their Human Development Index (HDI) Measures, 1993

State	HDI	State	HDI
Market economy societies			
Canada	0.951	Denmark	0.924
Switzerland	0.926	Belgium	0.929
Japan	0.938	Iceland	0.919
Austria	0.928	Finland	0.935
Sweden	0.933	Luxembourg	0.895
Norway	0.937	New Zealand	0.927
France	0.935	Israel	0.908
Australia	0.929	Barbados	0.908
United States	0.940	Ireland	0.919
Netherlands	0.938	Italy	0.914
United Kingdom	0.924	Spain	0.933
Germany	0.920	Hong Kong	0.909
Greece	0.909	Argentina	0.885
Cyprus	0.909	Costa Rica	0.884
Bahamas	0.895	Uruguay	0.883
South Korea	0.886	Chile	0.882
Malta	0.886	Singapore	0.881
Portugal	0.878		
Former planned economy societies			
Czech Republic	0.872	Russia	0.804
Slovakia	0.864	Bulgaria	0.773
Hungary	0.855	Belarus	0.787
Latvia	0.820	Ukraine	0.719
Poland	0.819	Lithuania	0.719

SOURCE: United Nations Development Programme (1996).

Table 6.2   Impact of Economic and Social Policies in Market Versus Planned Societies, With Posttest Measures

Market economy societies $(N_1=35)$	Time 1 (Undetermined)	Time 2 (1993) (Higher in Human Development Index)
Planned economy societies $(N_2=10)$	Time 1 (Undetermined)	Time 2 (1993) (Lower in Human Development Index)

Table 6.3   Four Societies, Where Three Have Had Economic and Social Policies, With Posttest
Measures

Three societies with industrialization and economic and social policies (N_1=3)

Time 1	Time 2 (1993)	
(Undetermined)	(Higher in Human Development Index)	
	Uzbekistan	0.679
	Turkmenistan	0.695
	Tajikistan	0.616

One society without significant industrialization and without economic or social policies (N_2=1)

Time 1	Time 2 (1993)	
(Undetermined)	(Lower in Human Development Index)	
	Afghanistan	0.229

The existence of standardized data on nations, as shown above, makes it possible to do several types of statistical analysis: time series observation, posttest only observation, and several types of quasi-experimental observation.

The *National Human Development Report* produced by the Planning Commission of the Government of India (2002) contains HDI data for states and union territories. The availability of such data at a within-nation level allowed for comparisons between different states and regions and also between urban and rural populations. This report also presents data that was computed for the same states in 1981 and 1991, which allowed for comparison in time, as suggested earlier. In the absence of such data, as is the case for some countries and many within-nation regions, when one is interested in seeing whether policies targeted to only a region within a nation have had any impact, one has to resort to other indicators that are often not comparable to the HDI levels.

Lack of acceptable and standardized outcome measures is one principal problem in impact analysis. However, there are other issues as well. Coleman (1975) listed some considerations in the following terms.

For policy research,

(1) partial information available at the time an action must be taken is better than complete information after that time;

(2) the ultimate product is not a "contribution to existing knowledge" in the literature, but a social policy modified by the research results;

(3) results that are, with high certainty, approximately correct are more valuable than results which are more elegantly derived but possibly grossly incorrect;

(4) it is necessary to differently treat policy variables which are subject to policy manipulation, and situational variables which are not;

(5) the research problem enters from outside any academic discipline and must be carefully translated from the real world of policy or the conceptual world of a client without loss of meaning; and

(6) the existence of competing or conflicting interests should be reflected in the commissioning of more than one research group, under the auspices of different interested parties where possible. Even in the absence of explicitly conflicting interests, two or more research projects should be commissioned to study a given policy problem. (pp. 22–34)

Ideological Biases in Impact Analysis

But beyond methodological considerations lie questions of another order. There is, for example, a growing literature regarding the value-laden nature of the ostensibly objective evaluation process. Every aspect of evaluation reflects a decision made, often, according to a particular perspective or value system. When one measures poverty, for example, what is it that is being measured? Income, perhaps. But income relative to what?

Economist Mollie Orshansky developed the federal poverty thresholds in 1964 for the Social Security Administration (Fisher, 1997). They are based upon what has been termed the *economy budget*, that is, the amount a careful homemaker would spend on food for a family of a particular size for "temporary or emergency use when funds are low." This decision was to locate the American standard of poverty below the level of "minimum comfort" and even below the level of "minimum adequacy" at the level of "minimum subsistence." The problem is, this measure presumes the family in question has access to a working stove connected to utilities, owns a substantial collection of cookware, and has a working refrigerator, not to mention having had the opportunity to learn nutritious cooking techniques and basic budgeting and shopping strategies. It seems that, at the levels of poverty often addressed in evaluation reports, few of these assumptions are valid, yet they remain the de facto standard of American poverty.

Serious attempts at redefining poverty, either according to different levels of income or from different perspectives (for example, poverty defined as the inability to afford *satisfactory* housing as opposed to simply affording shelter of any kind or, most notably, the ability to financially support a socially rewarding lifestyle as opposed to affording simple existence) have been the subject of intense debate since the turn of the century. The United States alone, for example, has produced 60 different "poverty levels" between the 1900s and the 1990s (Fisher, 1996).

Effectiveness Analysis

One simple question can be derived from the above discussions. It can be stated in the following form: Is a given policy, including any programs generated from that policy, effective? Obviously, such a question about effectiveness requires clarity of goals (or ends to be achieved) of social policy.

The idea of effectiveness analysis is borrowed from the field of organizational studies and, more specifically, from the concept of organizational effectiveness (Cameron & Whetten, 1983; Price, 1968, 1972; Mintzberg, 1993). In effectiveness analysis, one sees organizational behavior as rational, goal-directed behavior and begins the analysis of effectiveness by assessing how much of the goal has been or is being reached by the organization. This model originates in the classic works of Max Weber (1925/1947) and is called the rational model of organizational studies (Haas & Drabek, 1973). Building on this model, Price (1972) proposed that organizations with single goals are likely to be more effective than organizations with multiple goals. Similarly, he suggests that organizations with high degrees of goal specificity are more likely to be effective than organizations that have diffuse goals, and so on. Also building on this model, Etzioni (1964) proposed that effectiveness can be studied from two perspectives: a goal perspective and a system perspective. The goal perspective tries to decipher the organizational goals and then attempts to assess whether or how much of the goals have been reached. In this context, it often becomes important to differentiate between *stated goals* and *pursued goals*. That is, the organization may claim that it is in business to pursue Goal X, but, in reality, it is pursuing Goal Y. The second perspective proposed by Etzioni, the systems perspective, calls for a comparative approach to effectiveness evaluation. Here, one assesses the impact of two or more similar organizations in the pursuit of similar ends and attempts to come to some conclusions about which one is more effective in this pursuit and why.

Most of the reasoning behind the studies of rational bureaucracies and their effectiveness can be transferred to the study of the impact analysis of social policy. One just needs to substitute *social policy* for *organization*. After all, the implementation of social policy often requires a rational bureaucracy, where the policy sets the goal and the organization responsible for program execution attempts to attain that goal.

The lessons learned from the studies of organizational effectiveness can be used in the studies of policy effectiveness (assuming that the concept of effectiveness is similar to that of impact). These lessons are that policy goals are often not clearly stated; that there may be multiple and conflicting goals set by a social policy; and that, within two or more cultural contexts, the same form of policy execution may produce different outcomes due to the cultural context in which policies are executed (Boje, Gephart, & Thatchenkery, 1996; Haas & Drabek, 1973; Newstrom & Davis, 1993).

Taking these issues into account, Hudson (1997) has commented that "there can be no effectiveness unless there is change, [and] a measure of effectiveness is a measure of change" (pp. 70–71). He has also offered a set of equations that formally assess change with a probabilistic model.

The term *goal analysis* was popularized by Mager (1972). In this small but comprehensive work, he outlines how to decipher the attainable goals, ensure these are the goals being pursued, and do impact analysis of a program or of a policy behind that program.

Efficiency Analysis

In organizational behavior, the concept of efficiency analysis has long been popular. It was formally introduced by Taylor (1916/1987) and can be referred to as an early form of cost-benefit analysis. Taylor showed that an organization can be effective but not necessarily efficient, especially if the unit cost of production is too high or if the goals of production cannot be met within a specified time period.

The lessons learned from efficiency analysis (Haas & Drasbek, 1973; Newstrom & Davis, 1993) are already used by Rossi & Freeman (1985) as they offered designs for cost-benefit evaluation. They can be translated to policy analysis by asking, first, whether the policy under question is effective but not necessarily efficient and, second, whether the policy under question is effective but not useful under the time constraints.

Manifest and Latent Beneficiaries of Social Policy

Clearly, defining poverty and assessing its effects are complex and troublesome issues for researchers of all kinds, and particularly for policy makers. There are issues on at least two additional levels that are more troubling still. Since the early 1970s, social scientists have begun examining the policy process in a reflexive manner that has generated several important new insights.

Among these important insights is the notion, now supported through research, that policies may state program goals or identify target populations that are not the actual focus of the policy. That is, social policy is directed at both *manifest beneficiaries*—for example, the poor or minorities—and at what may be termed *latent beneficiaries*—for example, providers of services or the policy makers themselves (Chatterjee, 1999). This process is common enough in a variety of contexts. In fact, the entire edifice of gentlemanly compromise, which has produced such an impressive history of social development in America, is grounded in the shared willingness of elected representatives to allow such fictions to pass, as often as not, without question.

The question of who benefits by given social policies has been dealt with from several perspectives in recent times. Bartik (1991) has used it in relation to policies intended to promote regional and local economic development. Clotfeller (1991, 1992) has asked this very question in great detail about policies that create and support the nonprofit sector in market economies.

An examination of recent American social welfare policy may help make clear some of the more important issues. For example, in an environment that is perceived by many as increasingly blaming of the beneficiaries of welfare, it has also been increasingly fashionable to discuss the wealth of opportunity that only awaits ambition and personal commitment to hard work. A policy outgrowth of these two streams of thought has been the recent drive for welfare reform under it many names, such as welfare-to-work, workfare, and so on.

The idea publicly put forth is that the beneficiaries of the programs will be the presently poor who prepare diligently for new careers and pull themselves up with a helping hand from the government. By limiting the amount and the duration of benefits available, legislatures expect to eliminate or curtail the culture of poverty, welfare dependency, work aversion or avoidance, and the other problems of recent welfare strategies. This public message has been well received and oft repeated. However, it fails to tell the whole story.

For example, who are the beneficiaries of this program? The manifest beneficiaries, of course, are the poor who will finally be given just what they need, no less and no more, to succeed in America. But what of the latent beneficiaries, those who stand to benefit from the program, but not as publicly? Earlier welfare strategies created an entire industry of service providers and program administrators (as well as the hundreds of college and professional programs to train them and the thousands of professors to staff those programs and institutions and to evaluate them). The present approach will benefit the career training industry and whatever bureaucratic mechanism becomes necessary to monitor the quality of the work of its graduates.

Private industry is likely to benefit from the sudden influx of recently trained, poorly experienced, low-cost workers created by the welfare reform effort. Those who currently provide services to low-paid workers without government benefits, such as child care, insurance, and medical care, will see their market expanding.

A further step away from the manifest beneficiaries are the institutions and individuals who theorize, consult, and write about social problems, as well as those who conduct research. With so many new and untried interventions in the field, it will be a time of extraordinary opportunity for those who can produce the kinds of research and theoretical products deemed most useful to policy makers and others with a stake in welfare change.

Finally, the legislators themselves stand to benefit. By appealing to the taxpayer's natural instinct to save money by reducing government, they have frequently been able to solidify their political positions. By reducing benefits to the poorest, least politically powerful groups, they have been able to do so with little risk.

The same process of identifying latent beneficiaries may be applied to any social welfare legislation, whether it originates from the left or right, from conservative or liberal. It is important to do so in order to understand fully why social welfare policy takes the form it does, who supports its passage and implementation, and what the real stakes are in an evaluation process. It may make little difference to policy makers if a program is perceived to fail its manifest beneficiaries, so long as latent beneficiaries are pleased with the results.

Of late, a number of social theorists have written in essential agreement with Charles Lemert's (1997) assessment of the social policy process: "The more sensible post-modernists, being generally respectful of much in modernity, are rigorously skeptical of the prospects that modernity's grand ideals ever will, or ever were truly meant to, become the true *manifest* structure of world things." That is, there is a widening realization that policy is not infrequently created for reasons other than those offered publicly by policy makers themselves.

Stakeholder-Based Analysis

Stakeholder-based analysis, like effectiveness and efficiency analysis, has also been popular in studies of organizational behavior (Cooperrider & Dutton, 1998; Harrison & Shirom, 1998). Here, the critical question is, who wants know about the impact of a given policy? It is entirely possible that groups such as policy makers, politicians, and disinterested social scientists, using their various tool bags, conclude that a given policy is poorly effective. On the other hand, those involved as the policy's target population or those who benefit from the programs generated by a given policy may hold a very different position than the groups mentioned above. Nowakowski (1987), shifting the "who wants to know" question, offered plans to do research from the client's perspective. In the discipline called organizational development, which is usually located in business schools and where training is offered to individuals who would serve as consultants to various organizations, a similar approach is called *appreciative inquiry* (Cooperrider, 1986; Srivastava & Cooperrider, 1990). An important point in appreciative inquiry is to study a client's organization in such a way that the client benefits from the organization development consultant's knowledge but does not get alienated if the consultant makes some constructive criticisms.

Translated to the realm of the impact analysis of social policy, appreciative inquiry would mean a study of social policy that is sensitive to the needs of the clients who commissioned the study, who may be stakeholders in the programs derived from that policy, and who may be beneficiaries of some or all parts of that policy's execution.

Impact Analysis or Satisfaction Analysis?

We could proceed to contrast these strategies across the entire evaluation process. However, it is important to note that the whole concept of impact analysis as analysis by impartial third-party scientists to see whether a given policy X produces outcome Y should be differentiated from the question whether given policy X produces satisfaction in given group G and whether given group G wants the programs derived from that social policy continued. What we have here will suffice to make the real point, which is that several of the attempts to define a new evaluation process really amount to attempts to shift the ability to define concepts and standards from policy makers to those who must live with policy consequences. This work is more than simply political in nature (although, clearly, it could reduce or bolster the influence of groups espousing any number of ideological or political views). Rather, it represents a serious-minded attempt to get inside the black box at the heart of so many important social policy questions. That is, the developing strategies attempt to discover not only what policies work but also why they work and in what contexts, what their meaning is to each class of stakeholder, and what approaches may best be applied in which particular contexts.

Use of Focus Groups

The concept of the *focus group* originated in the 1930s (Rice, 1931), and it was developed to gather specific types of information from key informants in a group setting. Typically, a focus group is somewhere between seven and ten in size and is selected by the researcher (Krueger, 1988). In this group, the researcher creates a relaxed atmosphere to elicit information about certain subjects. The discussions carried on in this group become an important source of data for the researcher. Roethlisberger and Dickson (1939) used a version of it during their famous studies of employee participation and productivity. Merton, Fiske, and Kendall (1956) produced the first book on the subject, and they outlined how it is an important tool for policy research. Krueger (1988) has outlined how focus groups can be used *before a program begins*, corresponding with the idea of needs assessment in the sequence described by Rossi and Freeman (1985, 1993). Focus groups can also be used *during a program* or *after a program*, strategies that Rossi and Freeman call program monitoring and impact evaluation, respectively. However, it is entirely possible that focus groups may yield information that is different from formal, multivariate, instrument-generated information captured through a postest or a pretest-posttest design.

The use of focus groups is comparable with what is called the *Delphi method*, in which selected purposive groups are used for community-level agenda building (Linstone & Turoff, 1975).

The Interpretive Model in Policy Research _____

It has become increasingly common for conscientious theorists to recommend that researchers employ a variety of approaches in conducting policy evaluations (Porter, 1995). A particularly eloquent statement of the case from a more general perspective than simply policy studies has been made by Robert Alford

(1998). He suggests that there are three paradigms of inquiry: multivariate, interpretive, and historical. At the macro level, the multivariate model studies *structure,* the interpretive method studies *culture,* and the historical method studies *context.* Knowledge is obtained, in the multivariate model, through *data;* in the interpretive model, through *observation;* and, in the historical model, through *evidence.* The following case example illustrates how impact evaluation from a different paradigm may lead to different forms of outcome.

An Example From Delinquency Research

A metropolitan city in the United States gets a large grant to set up a delinquency prevention program, and the program is to be administered through its park district. The theory behind the program is the opportunity theory of Cloward and Ohlin (1964), which suggests that the reason for delinquent behavior by working- and lower-class youth is their lack of opportunity. Given proper opportunity, the theory further suggests, delinquent behavior in these youth is likely to be reduced. Arnold (1964) pronounced that this was a failed idea, and Lewis (1966) claimed that working-class and lower-class youth are products of a culture of poverty.

Nevertheless, influenced by opportunity theory, a city sets up a program of delinquency prevention, and approximately 150 teenagers are recruited into it. The program consists of counseling by young adult counselors two to three times a week, participation in recreational group work throughout the week, and a stipend of a few hundred dollars a month. A multivariate program evaluation of this looks as shown in Table 6.4.

In this multivariate (the research included other variables besides x) pretest-posttest model, x represented the rate of being apprehended by juvenile authorities. At Time 1, it was found that

$$x_1 = x_3$$

(that is, apprehension rates in the program group and the comparison group are approximately equal). However, at Time 2, it was found that

$$x_2 > x_1; \; x_2 > x_3; \; x_2 > x_4; \; \text{and} \; x_1 = x_2 = x_4 \text{ (approximately)}.$$

This multivariate model of policy and program analysis leads to the conclusion that the program is not effective. In fact, it seems to increase delinquency and certainly does not lead to delinquency reduction.

Table 6.4   Pretest-Posttest Comparison in Delinquency Prevention: An Example

	Time 1	*Time 2 (about a year later)*
Program group	x_1	x_2
A comparable group	x_3	x_4

However, an interpretive study, which collected information through a series of open-ended interviews with program staff and through some observations of interactions between the program staff and the counselors in the program, revealed the following scenario: The counselors are not professionally trained helping persons. They are young adult members from the same community in their early twenties, some of whom are graduates of a nearby community college. The counselors have developed a work group themselves, and a work group culture has formed. Within that work group culture, the counselors often brag about their advisees and take pride in the fact that their advisees are indeed very tough, perhaps even tougher than the advisees of their peer counselors. One of the secretaries said the following about these counselors: "Boy, they treat those kids [teenagers in the program group who are targets of intervention] like some rich people treat their Doberman pinschers!"

The secretary's observation is indeed a very important symbolic statement: the work group culture of the counselors, themselves only a few years older than the teenagers in the program, has created a status system. Within that status system, a program teenager confers status on his or her counselor by being "bad," "tough," and more unruly than others. The teenagers are rewarded by their counselors for being deviant. Whatever the counselors do toward delinquency reduction during their formal interactions with these teenagers, the culture of the work group and the status system within that work group give an important message to the inner city youth, and that message is that they are to be rewarded for their "toughness."

The case makes clear, we think, the usefulness of an interpretive model in program and policy evaluation. Alford (1998), writing from a more general perspective than that of policy studies, supports our view, and he makes some particularly eloquent statements about the importance of using various approaches in the analytical work of the social scientist:

the emphasis on the multivariate [quantitative] paradigm as the only "real" social science is impoverishing, a mark of the insecurity of the discipline, not a sign of its scientific maturity. . . . (p. 4)

Developing coherent arguments that recognize historical processes, symbolic meanings, and multivariate relations is the best way to construct an adequate explanation of a complex social phenomenon. (p. 19)

Conclusion

These considerations may encourage reflection upon what the most significant impact of recent social welfare policy in America might be. That is, it has become increasingly evident to observers from many political points of view that the policy creation and evaluation processes are not objective in the sense science is usually taken to be; that statistics, alone, may mask more than they reveal; and that any meaningful evaluation of the impact of social welfare policy must, as a matter of course, incorporate sophisticated statistical analysis, provide historical perspective on the problem being addressed and on previous attempts at solutions, and provide rigorously collected and analyzed qualitative data from the perspective of every stakeholder (that is, beneficiary) group involved. Further, an effective evaluation of policy impact must first seek to unearth and clearly state the goals of the policy under consideration from the points of view of all those who supported it and worked for its passage and implementation.

References

Alford, R. A. (1998). *The craft of inquiry.* New York: Oxford University Press.

Arnold, R. (1964). Mobilization for youth: Patchwork or solution? *Dissent, 11,* 347–354.

Bartik, T. J. (1991). *Who benefits?* Kalamazoo, MI: W.E. Upjohn Institute.

Boje, D. M., Gephart, R. P., Jr., & Thatchenkery, T. J. (Eds.). (1996). *Postmodern management and organization theory.* Thousand Oaks, CA: Sage.

Cameron, K., & Whetten, D. A. (1983). *Organizational effectiveness: A comparison of multiple models.* New York: Academic Press.

Campbell, D. T. (1969). Reforms as experiments. *American Psychologist, 24,* 409–429.

Campbell, D. T., & Stanley, J. C. (1963). *Experimental and quasi–experimental designs in research.* Chicago: Rand McNally.

Chatterjee, P. (1999). *Repackaging the welfare state.* Washington, DC: NASW Press.

Chatterjee, P., Olsen, L., & Holland, T. P. (1976). Evaluation research: Some possible contexts of theory failure. *Journal of Sociology and Social Welfare, 3*(4), 384–408.

Clotfeller, C. T. (1991). *Economic challenges in higher education.* Chicago: University of Chicago Press.

Clotfeller, C. T. (Ed.). (1992). *Who benefits from the nonprofit sector?* Chicago: University of Chicago Press.

Cloward, R., & Ohlin, L. E. (1964). *Delinquency and opportunity.* New York: Free Press.

Coleman, J. S. (1975). Problems of conceptualization and measurement in studying policy impacts. In K. M. Dolbeare (Ed.), *Public policy evaluation* (pp. 19–40). Beverly Hills, CA: Sage.

Cook, T. D., & Campbell, D. T. (1979). *Quasi–experimentation: Design and analysis issues for field studies.* Chicago: Rand McNally.

Cooperrider, D. L. (1986). *Appreciative inquiry: Toward a methodology for understanding and enhancing organizational innovation.* Unpublished doctoral dissertation, Case Western Reserve University, Cleveland, OH.

Cooperrider, D. L., & Dutton, J. E. (1998). *Organizational dimensions of global change.* Thousand, Oaks, CA: Sage.

Crane, J. A. (1982). *The evaluation of social policies.* The Hague, Netherlands: Kluwer-Nijhoff.

Deniston, O. L. (1972a). *Evaluation of disease control programs.* Washington, DC: U.S. Department of Health, Education, and Welfare, Public Health Service,

Health Services and Mental Health Administration, Communicable Disease Center.

Deniston, O. L. (1972b). *Program planning for disease control programs.* Washington, DC: U.S. Department of Health, Education, and Welfare, Public Health Service, Health Services and Mental Health Administration, Communicable Disease Center.

Etzioni, A. (1964). *Modern organizations.* Englewood Cliffs, NJ: Prentice Hall.

Fisher, G. M. (1996, Summer). Relative or absolute: New light on the behavior of poverty lines over time. *GSS/SSS Newsletter,* pp. 10–12.

Fisher, G. M. (1997, Winter). The development and history of the behavior of poverty lines over time. *GSS/SSS Newsletter,* pp. 6–7.

Haas, J. E., & Drabek, T. E. (1973). *Complex organizations: A sociological reader.* New York: Macmillan.

Harrison, M., & Shirom, A. (1998). *Organizational diagnosis and assessment.* Thousand Oaks, CA: Sage.

Hudson, W. (1997). Assessment tools as outcome measures in social work. In E. J. Mullen & J. L. Magnabosco (Eds.), *Outcomes measurement in the human services* (pp. 68–80). Washington, DC: NASW Press.

Krueger, R. A. (1988). *Focus groups: A practical guide for applied research.* Newbury Park, CA: Sage.

Lemert, C. (1997). *Postmodernism is not what you think.* Malden, MA: Blackwell.

Lewis, O. (1966). *La vida: A Puerto Rican family in the culture of poverty—San Juan and New York.* New York: Vintage.

Linstone, H. A., & Turoff, M. (1975). *The Delphi method: Techniques and applications.* Reading, MA: Addison-Wesley.

Mager, R. F. (1972). *Goal analysis.* Belmont, CA: Lear Siegler/Fearon.

Merton, R. K., Fiske, M., & Kendall, P. L. (1956). *The focused interview.* Glencoe, IL: Free Press.

Mintzberg, H. (1993). *Structure in fives: Designing effective organizations.* Englewood-Cliffs, NJ: Prentice Hall.

Mohr, L. B. (1995). *Impact analysis for program evaluation.* Thousand Oaks, CA: Sage.

Newstrom, J. W., & Davis, K. (1993). *Organizational behavior: Human behavior at work.* New York: McGraw-Hill.

Nowakowski, J. (1987). *The client perspective on evaluation.* San Francisco: Jossey-Bass.

Planning Commission, Government of India. (2002, March). *National Human Development Report 2001.* New Delhi: Oxford University Press.

Porter, T. M. (1995). *Trust in numbers: The pursuit of objectivity in science and public life.* Princeton, NJ: Princeton University Press.

Price, J. (1968). *Organizational effectiveness: An inventory of propositions.* Homewood, IL: Richard Irwin.

Price, J. (1972, Winter). The study of organizational effectiveness. *The Sociological Quarterly, 13,* 3–15.

Rice, S. (1931). *Methods in social science.* Chicago: University of Chicago Press.

Riecken, H. W., & Boruch, R. F. (Eds.). (1974). *Social experimentation: A method for planning and evaluating social intervention.* New York: Academic Press.

Roesthlisberger, F. J., & Dickson, W. J. (1939). *Management and the worker.* Cambridge, MA: Harvard University Press.

Rossi, P. H., & Freeman, H. E. (1985). *Evaluation: A systematic approach* (3rd ed.). Beverly Hills, CA: Sage.

Rossi, P. H., & Freeman, H. E. (1993). *Evaluation: A systematic approach* (6th ed.). Newbury Park, CA: Sage.

Rossi, P. H., Lipsey, M. W., & Freeman, H. E. (2004). *Evaluation: A systematic approach* (7th ed.). Thousand Oaks, CA: Sage.

Schalock, R. L. (2001). *Outcome-based evaluation.* New York: Plenum Press.

Srivastava, S., & Cooperrider, D. (1990). *Appreciative management and leadership.* San Francisco: Jossey-Bass.

Suchman, E. A. (1967). *Evaluative research: Principles and practice in public service and social action programs.* New York: Russell Sage Foundation.

Taylor, F. (1987). The principles of scientific management. In J. M. Shafritz & J. S. Ott (Eds.), *Classics of organization theory* (pp. 66–81). Chicago: Dorsey. (Original work published 1916)

United Nations Development Programme. (1994). *Human development report 1994.* New York: Oxford University Press.

United Nations Development Programme. (1996). *Human development report 1996.* New York: Oxford University Press.

Weber, M. (1947). *The theory of social and economic organization* (A. M. Henderson & T. Parsons, Trans.). New York: Free Press. (Original work published as part of *Wirtschaft und Gesellschaft* in 1925)

Zerbe, R. O. (1998). Is cost-benefit analysis legal? Three rules. *Journal of Policy Analysis and Management, 17*(3), 419–456.

PART II

The History
of Social Policy

Part II of the handbook summarizes more than 300 years of social welfare history, focusing on the way government has formulated policies that affect the well-being of America's diverse peoples.

Chapter 7 provides an account of social policy during the colonial era and the early years of the Republic, showing how the poor laws dominated government action in the field. It also describes the way slavery and policies toward Native Americans have caused great harm and suffering. It dramatically illustrates the point that social policies are not always benevolent.

Chapter 8 highlights a period at the end of the 19th century during which efforts were made to enhance the well-being of the nation's citizens through activist government intervention. Known as the Progressive Era, this period witnessed considerable expansion of government regulation that brought about improved working conditions for poor people, particularly in industrial occupations. It was also characterized by the expansion of the social services and the enactment of legislation that afforded a greater measure of protection to children and other vulnerable groups.

The next chapter shows how the involvement of government in social welfare increased dramatically in the 1930s. Faced with the problems of mass unemployment and poverty resulting from the Great Depression, the Roosevelt administration introduced various measures intended to revive the economy, create jobs, and meet the needs of the unemployed and poor. These and similar programs adopted at the time are loosely referred to as the New Deal. Although the public works, relief, and job training programs that were central to the New Deal were eventually disbanded, the Social Security Act of 1935 continues to function today, providing social protection to millions of Americans.

As shown in Chapter 10, The Johnson administration's Great Society programs perpetuated the trend toward the expansion of government involvement in social welfare. These programs strengthened the existing social services and introduced new programs such as Medicare and Medicaid. They also encouraged local participation in poverty alleviation and translated into law the civil rights movement's struggle against racism and oppression. These developments fostered the integration of millions of African Americans into the nation's political life.

The final chapter in Part II traces the efforts of the Reagan administration to halt the apparently inexorable trend toward increasing government involvement in social welfare. It shows how budgetary retrenchments, privatization, contracting of services, and other policy innovations reshaped social policy in America. The chapter also discusses the policies of the Clinton administration, which sought to implement a "new Democrat" agenda but is largely remembered for terminating the Aid to Families with Dependent Children (AFDC) program in 1996. It concludes by examining the policy innovations of the Bush administration, which focused unsuccessfully on Social Security privatization but was more successful in promoting a faith-based approach to social welfare.

7

Social Policy From Colonial Times to the Civil War

Phyllis J. Day

Throughout history, social policy's evolution has been a repetition of past ideologies rather than of forward movement. As our nation developed, based on European policies toward "outsiders" and the disadvantaged, two patterns emerged. The first was colonialism along North America's eastern coast, beginning with the Dutch East India Company and English merchants and settlers. The second, often ignored, was Spanish invasions in areas touched by the Gulf Stream in the South and up from Central America in the Southwest.

The latter brought *conquistadores* and Catholic priests, the first seeking gold, the second souls. Established self-supporting Native American communities were wiped out, their people starved and decimated by the enormous tributes demanded by the conquerors. Priests tended the welfare of this newly poor population in missions based on Catholic social policy: hospices for the needy, alms for the poor, hospitals for the sick, and shelter for the aged, homeless, or dependent. By the 1600s, there were 3,000 Catholic missionaries in the Southwest, their missions the major social welfare system (Day, 1997).

Social Policy Under Colonial Rule

In Florida and the Caribbean, as early as 1502, Spanish-appointed governors set up forced labor systems that promised wages, "protection," and Christian instruction for Native American laborers. In reality, this meant starvation and work slavery often resulting in death. Runaways were killed, others committed suicide, and multitudes died from overwork and disease (Morgan, 1993). By the end of the 1600s, most native populations in the area were extinct (Morgan, 1993). As in the Southwest, in this region social welfare depended on Catholic missions.

Meanwhile, northern colonists entered into a vast experiment: the Protestant work ethic reinforced by Puritan morality. The Dutch East India Company, needing satisfied workers, required each settlement to provide preachers, schoolmasters, and "comforters" of the sick, unhappy, ill, and disabled. The church collected donations and fines for alms while church and Company encouraged neighbors to set up mutual aid societies and help one another. Courts, Company, and church established and controlled schools. The able-bodied poor—vagabonds and idlers—were "bonded" to *patroons,* often for life, in return for their keep.

After ousting Dutch rule, colonists brought Elizabethan Poor Laws to America, laws expressly intended to control the laboring poor and established a system of poor relief to maintain an available low-wage workforce. Religion and governance were inseparable; their major social and economic theme was wealth as morality and poverty as immorality. Even the "worthy poor"—aged, disabled, children—required they work to their full capacities.

Slavery and Indenture

Social policies legitimated both harsh colonial poor laws and the institutions of slavery and indenture, which provided two of the country's most important labor groups. Enforced work "taught" morality to slaves and indentured servants while adding to their masters' wealth, and masters supported their workers. Other poor people depended on colonial poor relief systems. In the agricultural South, slaves were property by law, as any animal was property. Providing for them, then, was not social policy but animal husbandry that kept them able to work, produce, and reproduce. Not all slave owners agreed, but slave holding itself gave the institution legal, moral, and social legitimation.

About half of all white immigrants in the colonial era—a quarter million people, half of them women—came to America as indentured servants (Hymowitz & Weissman, 1980). Some came willingly, selling their indentures, or legal work bonds, to ship captains in return for passage to America. Colonists bought the bonds, often of families, although captains could and did separate husbands from wives and children from their parents. Children could not be sold, but they could be "given" to colonists to work for their keep, boys usually until age 18 and girls to age 21.

However, forced indenture was common: America became a dumping ground for England's unwanted—paupers, beggars, criminals (many charged with small offenses and given the choice of death or deportation), political dissidents (such as the Irish), and dependent or unwanted children. England deported 300 to 400 children ages 10 to 15 as indentured servants (Compton, 1980). "Newlanders" or "man-stealers" provided more, kidnapping people to sell off to America. Indenture was usually from five to seven years, although the time was doubled for political dissenters.

Colonial Poor Relief

In the colonies, churches, private philanthropy, and local governments merged to help the worthy poor, reform the nonworking poor, and control the workforce. Work became a social, civic, and religious obligation, and those who failed in it—nonworking able-bodied persons, vagabonds, rogues, criminals, unwed pregnant women, and poor women with children—were considered dangerous to community safety and morality. Like criminals, they were branded, flogged, put in stocks and pillories, auctioned off to the highest bidder or "sold" to the lowest, banished or "warned out," or even hanged.

Colonies depended on private citizens and associations to take care of special groups such as the insane, blind, deaf, and retarded. In addition, religions, craft societies, and ethnic groups developed mutual aid systems and even almshouses for their own needy people. For example, Quakers gave alms, sent Friendly Visitors to the sick and old, and established the Friends Almshouse in 1713. Service to the country elicited new social policies: veterans' pensions were established shortly after the Revolution and the Marine Hospital Service was begun in 1789.

American Poor Laws had three major tenets: local responsibility, family responsibility, and categorization of the poor.

Local responsibility. By 1636, Plymouth and Massachusetts were "placing" the poor to work, and by 1642, all towns had to supply their basic necessities (Day, 1997). Town supervisors investigated the poor to determine their worthiness, and they dispensed poor relief from monies collected from poor taxes, church and private donations, and fines for such errors as refusing to work at harvest time, selling at short weight, not attending church, or bringing a pauper into town. Poor relief eligibility depended on owning property or having lived in the town a set number of years. Newcomers were ineligible for poor relief. If they wanted to settle, they had to prove they would not become town dependents. By 1725, strangers had to register with town councils within 20 days or leave, and by 1767, many town councils forbade immigration without permission. Massachusetts, in 1793, required people to stay five years without being warned out before they were granted residency status (Grob, 1976).

Family responsibility. By 1675, laws required families to enforce community social, moral, and economic customs. They had to "take in" and support poor or ill relatives and to provide bond for immigrating relatives in case they became poor. All children under age 21 had to live with families to insure their moral upbringing, and those without families were placed to work for their keep or, if from the upper classes, indentured to learn a trade.

Categorization of poor. Following the English model, colonial towns categorized their poor and dependent into three categories: worthy poor, unworthy poor, and dependent children.

Worthy poor were widows, the incapacitated or ill, and the aged: poor through no fault of their own. "Outdoor relief" so that they could remain in their homes was an option, but placement with relatives was preferred. If neither was possible, they were sold to the lowest bidders—those who would charge the town the least for their care. Often, awarding these payments for care became a business, with profits gleaned from cutting back food, clothing, shelter, and medical care. Mortality among the poor was so high that, at least in larger towns, almshouses were built to offer alternative care. However, these too were run as businesses, with results similar to those found in private care homes.

The unworthy poor were able-bodied, nonemployed men and women, including widows; vagrants, idlers, and strangers; and the mentally impaired. Reasons for their poverty were irrelevant, but the cause was usually considered to be personal defect or often crime. Male paupers could be put to work on town projects until these were completed; then, they would be "auctioned off," often for life, with proceeds going to the town. Women, along with their children, were "farmed out" to local homes, or, if they could not be placed, "warned out" to other towns or into the forests, where many simply disappeared. As early as 1639, eight years after Boston was settled, courts could return the poor to their former towns or deport them from the country. Workhouses and houses of correction proliferated during the 1700s, becoming increasingly popular for placement because they could force inmates to work to help earn the costs of their care.

Dependent children included orphans, children born out of wedlock, unwanted children, and children of the poor, all of whom communities "owned." An overriding concern was that children not follow their parents into poverty. By 1641, courts could bond them out: in Virginia, for example, two children from every poor family could be indentured to flax-houses for piecework, their wages paid to the town (Day, 1997). Courts sold most poor children to families to work for board and room, with the expectation that they receive a Christian education and that boys learn to read and girls learn housekeeping. Often, these children were considered cheap labor, ill-used or worked to death by their "hosts." Runaways, incorrigibles, and "criminal children" went to workhouses or jails (later reform schools). Childhood was an unknown concept, and children were punished as adults, up to and including hanging.

The Institution as Social Policy

From colonial days, towns preferred to place their poor or deviant people in institutions, which enforced work and morality, rather than provide outdoor relief, which was admittedly more humane. Despite proof otherwise, institutions were thought cheaper: their "pay-by-the-head" schemes were considered easier to budget, and inmates' work, whether inside or contracted out, was thought more likely to reduce town costs. However, as supervisors profited on costs by reducing inmates' food, heat, clothing, and medical care, mortality rates skyrocketed. Investigations found these institutions inhumane, places of "filth and misery, and the most degrading, unrelieved suffering" (Grob, 1976, p. 16).

In the 1700s, first almshouses and then workhouses, houses of correction, and penal institutions spread across the country, warehouses for society's unwanted people. Unsegregated by sex, age, physical condition, or reason for incarceration, the worthy poor (aged, ill, physically disabled) were housed with vagabonds, rogues, and idlers; criminals; able-bodied women; dependent children from ages one month to 14 years, often placed with their mothers; and the "insane" (Day, 1997). Obstreperous or violent inmates were whipped, chained, or shackled and often left to die in their own excrement. Many of the aged or ill died quickly, and only 3% of children under age one survived (Grob, 1976).

After the Revolution, though outdoor relief remained common and acceptable in the South, northern almshouses and workhouses increased and diversified, becoming forerunners of hospitals, mental hospitals, orphanages, reform schools, and penitentiaries. Sections set aside for the ill and insane became the first public hospitals. Later, with the medical profession's growth, they became teaching hospitals for new treatments. Medical customs and faith, rather than science, dictated treatment, the most common of which included bleeding, violent purges, heavy doses of mercury-based drugs, and the use of opium. People who went to public hospitals had about a 50/50 chance of dying. Experimental treatments on them, if successful, could be transferred to paying patients. Women (and women slaves in the South) were particularly vulnerable after the ovum was discovered in 1824. Although female slaves were rarely afflicted with the "women's problems" of the upper class, exploration of their organs offered new explanations for those ills.

The first law for the so-called insane (dated 1676) was intended to protect towns from their bizarre behavior, often thought to be demonic possession. Although families were responsible for members with mental illness at first, they often whipped and beat them to get rid of "devils"; shackled them in outside pens, basements, or attics without heat despite the cold northern winters; and neglected their most basic care. Whether to better their conditions or get rid of them, persons with mental illness were institutionalized. Almshouses became the answer, though treatment was horrific. Almshouses began to segregate persons with mental illness from other inmates and so became the first so-called insane asylums. They attracted researchers, among them Benjamin Rush, who later instituted private asylums where "moral treatment" was available to paying patients. Although inhumane by today's standards, these asylums were still better than almshouse care.

Almshouses and workhouses also set institutional patterns for both juvenile and adult offenders. The industrial reformatory movement began with the New York House of Refuge for boys in 1825. Intended to reform inmates through moral training, religion, and labor, it used indeterminate sentencing at the discretion of a judge or reformatory administrator, along with "organized persuasion" rather than coercive restraint. In like manner, penitentiaries, first established by Quakers in 1823, took the able-bodied poor from almshouses, workhouses, and jails and tried to rehabilitate them through silence, isolation, and meditation. Along with later penology and prison models, they became standards for prisons and corrections. Another principle was developed at this time: philanthropists Isaac Hopper and John Augustus developed the concept of probation. Hopper began helping discharged prisoners find work, and Augustus supervised offenders charged with minor offenses to keep them from imprisonment.

From the Revolution to the Civil War

The Enlightenment, which helped create the intellectual framework of the Revolution, had little effect on social policies for the poor or unwanted. After the Revolution, abetted by the new Constitution, the nation continued to violate treaties with Native Americans and other non-Caucasians; to enslave Africans and their descendants (redefined as two-thirds of a person); and to deny equal rights to women and to unpropertied workers. In northern factories, laborers worked when owners dictated, depending on charities or starving when factories closed. For all intents and purposes, throughout a massive change in government, social policies still focused on work morality for the poor and excluded the "different" from civil and citizen rights.

The context changed, of course, through expansion to the West, burgeoning immigration, and leadership in international trade. A cycle of wars and depressions followed the Revolution, the worst from 1815 through 1819, reaching a peak in 1819 where, with 500,000 workers unemployed, whole families starved or froze to death in the northern winter (Mencher, 1967). At times, a third of the labor force was unemployed and wages fell 30% to 50% (Compton, 1980). Yet, despite unemployment and minuscule wages, the monied elite still issued reports blaming the poor for "idleness, ignorance, spend-thriftiness, hasty marriages, use of pawnbrokers, lottery, houses of prostitution and gambling"(Mencher, 1967, pp. 527–528).

New York Secretary of State J. V. N. Yates believed intemperance to be the major cause of poverty, estimating in 1824 that it affected two-thirds of the poor. Yet, after blaming the poor and calling for better ways to control them, he reported that only 27% of those he studied could actually work—the others were old, ill, disabled, or children (Yates, 1824/1900). Social policy in the 1800s was a split reality: one part pondered the causes and cures of poverty, another *experienced* poverty, illness, the drudgery and dangers of work, and brutal punishments for the "idle" or "different." Two trends in social policy strengthened: a trend toward state rather than local authority, first seen when states required counties to build poorhouses and to use state standards, and a trend toward institutionalization as the answer to every social problem.

The number of immigrants, mostly from the impoverished classes of Europe, rose steadily, from 129,000 in the 1820s to 540,000 by the end of the 1830s, peaking at more than 1.75 million in the 1850s. Six million people came to America between 1820 and 1860 (Coll, 1972). Moreover, in the United States, migration from farms to cities increased with the new technologies of the Industrial Revolution. Urban population grew at a rate of 40% to 50% per decade. In New York alone, the urban population grew from 5.5% in 1796 to 27.4% in 1855 (Seller, 1984). As the proportion of wage laborers increased, employers could lower wages more drastically.

Almshouses in immigration ports, supported (unwillingly) by local towns, were the first stops for poverty-stricken or ill immigrants. Not until 1847 did the Board of Immigration collect taxes and impose fines on immigrants, crews, and ships to support almshouses or reimburse local communities for outdoor relief, medical help, education, transportation, and job placement (Compton, 1980). Cities became human warrens of crowding, disease, plagues, crime, and unemployment, with little if any minimum sanitation or safety standards. By 1859, 1 out of every 20 urban residents lived in cellars, averaging 6 to 20 per room, with an estimated 10,000 abandoned, orphaned, or runaway children living in the streets (Hymowitz & Weissman, 1980).

The depression of 1837–1838 broke the back of private charity and gave impetus to new social reform, not only for poverty-related problems but on such issues as the morality of slavery, women's suffrage, and temperance. A women's movement arose, enabled in part by the decline of the extended family and the expectation that single women would care for children. Among its leaders were the Grimké sisters of Georgia, Elizabeth Cady Stanton, Susan B. Anthony, and Sojourner Truth, who began to speak out publicly for women's rights and the emancipation of slaves. Frederick Douglass, freed slave and orator, joined them at Seneca Falls, the first women's conference, held in 1848.

While men studied and supported poverty reform movements, women became active in them as "friendly visitors." In New York, Robert Hartley established the Association for Improving the Condition of the Poor (AICP), which divided the city into wards where friendly visitors investigated needs and distributed relief and friendly advice. The association led the way to planned giving, cooperation among agencies, and accurate record keeping, and it became the model for later charity organization societies. At first opposed to almsgiving, the AICP adopted it as a major purpose when data collected by friendly visitors proved poverty lay in society's institutions. The AICP became the poor's advocate, opening health dispensaries, crippled children's hospitals, public bathhouses, and asylums for the care and instruction of children (Mencher, 1967).

In 1840, Dorothea Dix began to investigate the conditions of the mentally ill in Massachusetts asylums, and pleading that the state had moral and legal obligations to these people, she gained state care for them. She pursued her cause in other states, which refused responsibility. However, her proposal to the United States Congress to use proceeds of set-aside public lands to care for the indigent mentally ill passed as the Ten Million Acre Bill of 1848, with an additional 2.5 million acres to support the indigent deaf. President Franklin Pierce vetoed the legislation in 1851, saying that the federal government could not impinge on states' rights and that the bill would open the door for all indigents seeking federal aid.

By 1830, there were more than a hundred private charities, among them organizations for freedmen, Chinese immigrants, and Finnish and Polish women; the American Female Guardian Society; Homes for the Friendless; the Mission to Children of the Disabled; and the American Temperance Society. Religious groups played their part: Protestants advocated better housing, sanitation, and moral improvement; gave religious tracts along with food and clothing; and established in Boston both the first American Young Men's Christian Association for rural boys in the cities, which was founded in 1851, and the first American group to call itself the Young Women's Christian Association, which was founded in 1866. Irish and Italian Catholics began highly successful outdoor relief programs for immigrants and built orphanages, schools, and hospitals. For their newcomers, Jews set up mutual aid societies, especially for education and work.

Reformers demanded special schools for the blind, deaf, and retarded and campaigned for better treatment of criminals, delinquents, and the mentally ill. Public schools, always a goal in the colonies, became firmly established by the middle 1800s. Their purpose, in addition to education, was to provide supervision for children and take them out of the men's job market. Reform schools based on new penology principles trained the incorrigible to conform to society and work rules, readying them for labor in the Industrial Revolution.

Three social movements set the stage for the social work profession today—the Charity Organization Society (COS) movement, the child-saving movement, and the settlement house movement. The first two reached fruition in the middle 1800s, the latter at the turn of the century. Charity organization societies developed in all the larger cities, with structures and processes modeled on the Association for Improving the Condition of the Poor. Originally aimed at cooperation and referral among city agencies, and designed, in part, to prevent "double-dipping" by the needy, the COS developed procedures for charity distribution, registered a city's poor, worked with police to clean up city crime and delinquency, and collected and collated accurate data, leading to more reform. Programs for training social workers began under COS auspices because these societies were the major professional associations of the time.

The thousands of children roaming city streets led Charles Loring Brace in 1853 to establish the child-saving movement. He believed that no help should be given that kept pauper families together, and he determined to relocate poor children, placing them with families in the West so that they could learn the benefits of hard work in a new environment. Over the next 20 years, haphazardly and without follow-up, his agents took (often kidnapped) over 50,000 children, loaded them into freight trains, and shipped them west, where they were picked over and chosen stop after stop. Unfortunately, many were taken for cheap labor, mistreated, and overworked. Many ran away, got lost, died, or simply disappeared.

Saving children became a hallmark of the times, spreading through public and private charities. It led to provision of nurseries and day care for poor children, new health care, and food distribution. An orphanage movement began, taking children from almshouses. Work morality was still the major emphasis, however, so orphans experienced rigid discipline, work schedules, and harsh punishments. Also, the orphanages continued to be run on the almshouse profit-making model, with mortality rates of about 20% (Compton, 1980).

Women and Non-White Populations

Social policies continued to oppress women and people of color throughout this era. Some white women won victories in education and the professions, and because of their scarcity, women migrating to the West had citizen rights. However, most women remained subservient to male rule. Poor women were considered almost as prostitutes, selling their labor and being used sexually by men of the upper class. Women of color underwent inhumane treatment: hard work, being bred for children sold away as slaves, rape, mutilation, and of course death, since owners could inflict any punishment on their property.

Cotton production's importance continued slave imports until 1859, as did breeding programs to produce prime workers. Prices of "good slaves" rose from $300 in 1820 to over $1000 in 1859, and the slave population grew from 1.5 million to almost 4 million (Bennett, 1966). Rebellions begun by folk leaders such as Gabriel Prosser, Denmark Vesey, and Nat Turner in the early 1800s were brutally put down, and state slave codes dictated proper behavior and forbade assembly and education. The Missouri Compromise of 1829 ensured the continuance of slavery in the South, ordering that any new free state be matched by the creation of a new slave state. Updated in 1850, it mandated a new and harsher Fugitive Slave Act. In 1857, the Dred Scott decision reaffirmed slaves as property, and though escaped slaves flocked to join the Union army, Lincoln ordered them returned to their owners. Although free people of African descent were living in the United States from 1826, even in the North they had no citizen rights.

For Native Americans, every treaty was broken as they were systematically robbed of their lands. Andrew Jackson, perhaps the most anti–Native American president, signed the Indian Removal Act of 1830, which led to the infamous Trail of Tears, a journey during which thousands of the more than 70,000 Native Americans sent beyond the Allegheny River died. The westward movement brought an estimated 250,000 white settlers between 1840 and 1860, encouraged by legislation such as the Kansas-Nebraska Act of 1854 and the Homestead Act in 1863, and the bison-based economy of the Plains societies was destroyed by hunters riding the Transcontinental Railroad, which was completed in 1869.

Southwest and Mexican Hispanics were also in the path of white settlers, whose encroachment included the annexation of Texas in 1845. This precipitated the Mexican War of 1845, ending with the Treaty of Guadalupe Hidalgo in 1848, in which the United States demanded Texas, New Mexico, and the California Coast. Border clashes continued, led by Mexican hero Juan Cortina against local militia and the Texas Rangers, but white squatters continued their assault on Mexican territory, and the white migration wave soon reduced the Southwest Spanish culture to peonage.

Although a smaller group, Chinese people also bore the brunt of race hatred in America. Men shanghaied from China after the devastation of the Opium Wars in the mid-19th century became American debt slaves, though nominally free, put to work in gold mines and on the railroad until its completion. The Chinese Exclusion Act of 1882 effectively ended any rights they had in the United States until after World War II.

Conclusion _____

In the Civil War, the real issue was the states' rights to profit in international trade: unrestricted shipping of cotton based on slave labor for the South or using the South's cotton for manufacturing in the North by the laboring poor. This battle for profit, overlaid on the yeasty mix of civil, moral, and religious reform of the 1800s, exploded into war with ourselves. Yet, basically, it was a logical outcome—a result of the 400-year-old experiment in work ethic morality that wed wealth to the use of others as cogs in the profit-making machine. Social policies throughout that time rose and fell according to what was required for profit. Perhaps this experiment and its success were necessary to build our nation. How would we know?

References _____

Bennett, L. J. (1966). *Before the Mayflower: A history of the Negro in America.* Chicago: Johnson.

Coll, B. (1972). Public assistance in the United States: Colonial to 1860. In E. W. Martin (Ed.), *Comparative development in social welfare* (pp. 128–158). London: Allen & Unwin.

Compton, B. (1980). *Introduction to social welfare and social work: Structure, function, and process.* Homewood, IL: Dorsey.

Day, P. J. (1997). *A new history of social welfare* (2nd ed.). Needham Heights, MA: Allyn & Bacon.

Grob, G. N. (Ed.). (1976). Maryland report on almshouses. In *State and public welfare in nineteenth century America*. New York: Arno.

Hymowitz, C., & Weissman, M. (1980). *A history of women in America*. New York: Bantam.

Mencher, S. (1967). *From poor house to poverty programs*. Pittsburgh, PA: University of Pittsburgh Press.

Morgan, T. (1993). *Wilderness at dawn: The settling of the North American continent*. New York: Simon & Schuster.

Seller, M. (1984). *Immigrant women*. Philadelphia: Temple University Press.

Yates, J. V. N. (1900). Report of the Secretary of State in 1824 on the relief and settlement of the poor. In *34th Annual Report of the State Board of Charities of the State of New York* (Vol. 1, pp. 939–963). (Reprinted from the original 1824 report)

8

Social Policy and the Progressive Era

John M. Herrick

From the 1890s to the 1920s, the United States experienced rapid growth as large industrial cities became magnets for immigration and centers of economic power. By 1916, at least half the country's population of 100 million lived in urban settings of at least 8,000 people (Coll, 1970). Large corporations grew powerful and demanded workers to labor in oftentimes dangerous conditions such as steelmaking and meatpacking. Facilitated by new modes of transportation, including electric streetcars and automobiles, urban residents separated themselves by social class, income, race, and ethnicity, producing a new geography of social problems. Middle-class suburbs distanced residents from inner cities with high rates of crime, disease, and poverty, largely populated by working-class immigrants, many from central Europe, and African Americans, who left the South for better lives. While economic growth brought prosperity, periodic "panics" such as the depression of 1893–1894 and the panic of 1907, resulted in unemployment and hardship for many workers and families whose well-being depended on wages. Without unemployment insurance or other protections, unemployed or injured workers had little choice except to seek whatever relief or assistance was available or find employment elsewhere. Some cities offered temporary outdoor relief, financial assistance, or temporary work, but those who could not obtain jobs soon joined the needy aged, the poor, and the infirm, and widows and children were forced to turn to whatever public or private relief was available.

Many towns, cities, and counties maintained poorhouses or poor farms, almshouses, and workhouses, where indoor relief was given to residents who had no other means of support. Many of these institutions became the city or county homes of the late 19th century, but they continued to serve as visible reminders of what might happen to those who could not support themselves. Outdoor relief was given by local government authorities inconsistently, resulting in hardship to destitute persons. Relief was administered by different local officials, some elected, others appointed, who most often had little training for their tasks, wanted to conserve relief funds, and distrusted the motives of relief applicants. The poor law tradition of settlement, which required residency for a specific time in the locality where a poor person sought relief, created hardship and uncertainty for those who moved regularly to seek employment. Eligibility criteria for assistance varied widely across political jurisdictions in the states (Wagner, 2005). As late as 1931, New Hampshire had 700 local officials overseeing relief in 245 different towns, cities, and counties (Brown, 1940). Any consideration of social policy in the Progressive Era must acknowledge how little uniform social policy aimed at supporting persons in need existed at the turn of the 20th century. Poor law relief would be criticized at the end of the 19th century by social welfare reformers who were part of a broad-based effort to address social problems. Muckrakers, both journalists and novelists, exposed in popular newspapers and books the dangers to workers in meatpacking and other hazardous industries, encouraging reformers to work for workplace protections. They often sensationalized the political corruption that they exposed in big city governments and alerted the public that reforms were needed. Labor unrest and strikes raised concern about social stability and signaled conflict between workers and industrialists. The Spanish-American War, begun in 1898, created an American empire stretching from Cuba to the Philippines in hopes of securing markets that would shore up the domestic economy, but it also raised questions about the direction of American society and its ability to provide opportunities for its citizenry (Schoonover, 2003). At the turn of the 20th century, the American social fabric faced unprecedented changes that challenged the status quo.

The Reform Impulse

In the decades after the Civil War, both farmers and urban workers agitated for government protection from businesses, which dominated economic markets and threatened their well-being. Agrarian populists and socialists both gained adherents who demanded government action to protect their interests. Unable to influence national political parties or create successful third party alternatives, farmers and labor focused on state-level policy reform, demonstrating how federalism functioned to weaken and fragment policy reform and strengthen the status quo. Fearing both working-class radicals and exploitive industrialists, an emerging middle class, often supported by business interests, attempted to rationalize the rapidly changing society by advocating social and political reforms to protect their vision of a progressive America. Progressives' influence was possible because of expanding personal and social opportunities for educated women and men. By 1910, 40% of college students were women with new career opportunities in such fields as law, medicine, and social work. Urban reformers included Protestants imbued with a call for social action and reform based on the Social Gospel that called Christians to address social problems. Both women and men, blacks and whites, practiced the Social Gospel across the country. Recent scholarship has noted that progressive civic professionalism, which combined a sense of civic responsibility, humanistic values, and a sense of calling, characterized the work of leading Progressive Era reformers such as Jane Addams and Mary Richmond, both seen as founders of professional social work (Edwards & Gifford, 2003). Religious social reformers were challenged by conservative fundamentalists in all major denominations, who believed reform must be personal rather than social (Mencher, 1967). Progressives saw a collective need for reform while clinging to the cherished belief that individual hard work would lead to success if opportunities were freely available.

It should be noted that the realities of race, class, and gender often circumscribed opportunity in the Progressive Era. The limits imposed by race were especially evident in popular culture. One of the first popular motion pictures, D. W. Griffith's *The Birth of a Nation*, portrayed the Ku Klux Klan in the South as chivalrous protectors of Southern white women from predatory blacks during Reconstruction after the Civil War. Many Progressive Era reformers shared widely held racial stereotypes and discriminated against persons of color, leading to separation between white and black reformers. Black reformers established separate, parallel social agencies and services, such as settlement houses, because they were so often excluded from participation in mainstream social services. Progressive causes were often moralistic, frequently echoing social class biases, as demands were made for government action to stop alcohol and drug abuse, to protect young women from the evils of prostitution, and for the regulation of dance halls and places where vice was thought to be commercialized. Some settlement house workers favored prohibition of liquor, even though many immigrant residents of settlement neighborhoods drank wine and liquor as part of their cultures. Much reform, echoing earlier charity, focused on the plight of the poor. Public assistance for the poor in public institutions such as poorhouses was still available for the destitute elderly and for those with disabilities, but it had been curtailed in many areas. In 1923, 2,046 almshouses had custody of 85,899 "inmates," as they were labeled, across the country (Patterson, 2000, p. 29). The most extensive national social policy after the Civil War was the establishment of pensions for Union Civil War veterans (Skocpol, 1992). By 1906, 90% of living Union soldiers were receiving pensions, which, in effect, functioned as old age or disability pensions. Race mattered: black veterans were excluded. Civil War pensions were criticized by reformers who lamented the corruption associated with their administration (Amenta, 1998; Orloff, 1988).

In the absence of national policies aimed at assisting the poor, voluntary and private welfare developed alongside public poor assistance. Charity organization societies, begun in the 19th century by reformers who felt outdoor relief, money, or in-kind charitable support for the poor often did little good since it seemed to encourage dependency and discourage self-sufficiency among recipients, attempted to apply sound business principles in collecting and distributing charity. Like Progressive reformers bent on eliminating the graft and corruption associated with patronage awards by political machines, the Charity Organization Society (COS) movement wanted to keep politics out of public relief. Mary Richmond, a longtime COS worker, exemplified civic professionalism. She wrote influential training guides for COS caseworkers that detailed innovative methods for helping clients or "cases." Although she held fast to traditional maternalist notions of women and work, maintaining that women should be dependent wives and mothers, Richmond opened career opportunities for women in the fledgling profession of social work. In her pathbreaking training manual *Social Diagnosis*, published in 1917, Richmond described social casework as a method that examined the role of environment as well as personal characteristics as contributors to well-being (Ehrenreich, 1985). Like other COS leaders, Richmond opposed public relief, arguing that it could corrupt recipients. She clashed with Jane Addams and other women reformers who argued for public support for those in need. Social reform, Richmond eventually argued, including legislative action, was a necessary complement of social casework, a stance that demonstrated her vision of social work as a field with enormous civic responsibility (Agnew, 2003). By 1915, COS offices were located in 327 cities (Pimpare, 2004, p. 53), where the new "scientific" methods of charity work challenged the tradition of poor law relief in almshouses and poor houses, by offering relief to those "cases" ascertained as most amenable to casework assistance. Other Progressive reformers in the social settlement movement, led by an impressive group of women including Jane Addams, Florence Kelley, and Edith Abbott, studied the problems of workers in settlement neighborhoods and began to study environmental and structural contributors to individual problems, eventually calling for government reforms to protect workers against exploitation. Realizing that individual social problems demanded more than COS-style personal moral rehabilitation through casework, they aimed to close the gap between the classes through social and political action. Other Progressives in universities looked to innovative social policies in Europe and integrated them into their prescriptions for social reform (Rodgers, 2003).

Political Reform

Progressive political reform was complex. The Democratic, Republican, Progressive, and Socialist parties offered voters competing visions for coping with new realities. Legislative innovation, much of it the legacy of earlier populist concerns, aimed at making government more responsive to "the people." The direct election of senators, a federal income tax, the initiative and referendum, women's suffrage, and administrative reforms were all part of Progressive Era state building. At the turn of the century, state and federal bureaucracies, necessary institutions for administering social policy, were still developing, which may partially explain why the United States seemed to lag behind European nations such as Germany in the development of social insurance. It is also noteworthy that, when the government attempted to regulate business, as happened with railroads, powerful railroad lobbyists were often able to influence regulatory policy to protect their interests. Political and social reforms promoting popular access to government to counter the influence of powerful interests, perhaps paradoxically, allowed expansion of racial segregation in the South through popular Jim Crow laws, which solidified white subjugation of African Americans (McGerr, 2003).

Interpreting the Progressive Era

Progressive responses to a changing society were complex, and their purposes and functions are debated by scholars. Most often, the Progressive Era is seen as a period when reforms attempted to grapple with social change by seeking social policy responses that would promote market stability by providing measures of protection and security for those seen as vulnerable to the vicissitudes of social change: workers, women, families, and children (Davis, 1967).

Early scholars saw the Progressive Era as a time when liberal reformers battled against conservative corporate elites to gain protections and opportunities for common people. Vernon Louis Parrington's (1927) *Main Currents in American Thought* and Charles and Mary Beard's (1916/1927) *The Rise of American Civilization*, written from a liberal-progressive perspective, saw the Progressive Era as a time when democratic interests attempted to wrest power from monopolistic, corporate, conservative elites. Popular sentiment, fueled by the sensationalistic, muckraking journalism exemplified by Upton Sinclair's (1906) *The Jungle* and Frank Norris's (1901/1967) *The Octopus,* portrayed gigantic, inhumane meat processors and greedy railroads as exploiters of labor and dangers to public health and helped create popular demand for reform.

Writing after World War II, a group of influential historians reassessed the Progressive Era and found the motives of Progressives to be somewhat suspect. Richard Hofstadter, a prominent historian, was awarded a Pulitzer Prize for the *Age of Reform: From Bryan to F.D.R.,* written in 1955, in which he concluded that profound status anxiety among Progressives was the reason for their altruistic reforms. Hofstadter's neoconservative analysis found that Progressive reformers, threatened by social change and challenged by calls for improvements by labor and a growing cadre of reformers, were struggling to achieve respectability and status in a dynamic, changing society where white elites controlled major institutions.

Still other historians, influenced by the behavioral sciences, examined the rise of complex organizations and bureaucracies in the Progressive Era and noted increasing professionalization in many fields, including social work, and growing bureaucratization, developments that downplayed individualistic values and stressed the importance of rational planning and the use of scientific methods to promote efficiency. Proponents of what Samuel P. Hays (1959) called the "Gospel of Efficiency," these reformers wanted a planned, efficient society, amenable to the findings and recommendations of expert social scientists whose studies could lead the way to a progressive future (O'Connor, 2001).

Historians writing in the 1960s found that Progressive Era reforms aimed at curtailing the power of large corporations did not create opportunities for small business but stifled competition, promoted market stability, and curtailed labor unrest (Wiebe, 1962). In *The Search for Order, 1877–1920*, Robert Wiebe (1967) explored how middle-class professionals promoted social stability by creating bureaucracies to carry out the complex business of the regulation and rationalization of dynamic society while creating new opportunities for middle-class experts such as themselves.

Other historians, influenced by critiques of American culture and society in the 1960s, saw Progressive reform as fundamentally conservative. Gabriel Kolko (1963), an influential New Left historian, felt Progressive economic reform was directly influenced by powerful business elites who shared assumptions with political reformers about what was needed to protect property relationships and social order in the face of challenges from labor and others demanding change (Grob & Billias, 1972; Weinstein, 1968).

There is less disagreement about the strategies used by Progressive reformers to achieve goals of conflict mediation and social progress. Since much social policy reform was initiated and driven by women who focused on the needs of women and children, scholars have labeled their work as maternalistic reform, which often collided with paternalistic traditions and power structures (Skocpol, 1996). Gwendolyn Mink (1995) has questioned the motives of COS proponents of scientific social casework who felt they could transform intended beneficiaries into semblances of the middle-class reformers themselves, creating inevitable class, gender, cultural, and racial tensions. Other scholars found that the reforms implemented by states and municipalities were often influenced by the biases and prejudices of local administrators, resulting in conservative, antiprogressive outcomes (Ladd-Taylor, 1994; Lasch-Quinn, 1997; Mink, 1995; Muncy, 1991). Examination of municipal reform shows how uniquely it conformed to local needs and expectations—from the work of Chicago's able women reformers to create a better city (Flanagan, 2002) to Linda Gordon's (1999) study of the dynamics of racism in child welfare reform in Arizona. Shelton Stromquist's (2006) recent study of the Progressive Era is reminiscent of those of earlier historians, who saw the resolution of social conflict as central to reformist motivation. His reformers wanted to promote order and harmony among all social classes. Knight's (2005) biography of Jane Addams is supportive of this argument, emphasizing Addams's belief that settlement reformers at Hull House, nearly all women, aimed to close the gap between the classes—inspired by a vision of America in which difference could be reconciled for the greater good. During the Pullman strike of 1896, Addams worked tirelessly for mediation of the dispute, encouraging the railway union and its leader, Eugene V. Debs, to bargain with the arrogant George Pullman. Eventually, the union agreed, but Pullman would not bargain. President Cleveland sent in federal troops and an injunction was served on the union, creating tensions that finally erupted into violence. The union was broken, and Addams and her colleagues were criticized by labor for not being more supportive and by business for their support of union troublemakers and radicals. Hull House lost contributors, but Addams continued to believe that social problems could be settled by people of good will who opted for conciliation and avoidance of conflict.

These conflicting interpretations of the Progressive Era reflect ongoing scholarly debate about the meaning and function of reform in American history. They demonstrate the complexity and futility of attempting to explain Progressive Era reforms simplistically.

Studies for Reform

Careful definition and articulation of social problems by trained professionals who provide scientific analyses and recommendations that offer realistic solutions have become the hallmark of modern social scientific approaches to social intervention. During the Progressive Era, reformers undertook pioneering studies of social conditions that argued for social policies to assist the disadvantaged and poor (Lasch-Quinn, 1997). Borrowing techniques from earlier social studies, such as Charles Booth's (1902) multivolume *Life and Labour of the People of London*, which brought the existence of considerable poverty to the attention of British policy makers, reformers used new social science methods to describe social problems, especially quantitative analyses. *Poverty*, written in 1904 by Robert Hunter, a socialist who had lived at Jane Addams's Hull House, is a pioneering attempt to discover and describe American poverty. Hunter estimated that 10 million Americans out of a total population of 82 million were poor according to a normative income standard he developed (Leiby, 1978). He acknowledged that many people were poor because of economic conditions that were beyond their control, so they deserved assistance. His thinking is redolent of old poor law distinctions between the worthy and unworthy poor. He admitted that others were more or less permanently poor because of laziness or sloth, character traits that should disqualify them from aid; these themes resonate to this day in discussions of antipoverty policy.

Perhaps the most important Progressive Era analysis of American social conditions, the *Pittsburgh Survey* (1909–1914), was completed from 1907 to 1914 under the direction of Paul U. Kellogg, a journalist, social reformer, and ally of Progressive social settlement leaders. Supported by the Russell Sage Foundation, which financed much social research, Kellogg found that workers in Pittsburgh's industries needed workplace protections and support when injured. His findings were often cited in state efforts to develop workmen's compensation programs as well as in industrial safety campaigns. Kellogg went on to serve as founder and editor of *The Survey*, an important magazine devoted to social welfare issues and an advocate for social policy reforms from 1909 until 1952. Kellogg was active in the National Conference of Charities and Corrections (NCCC), founded in the late 19th century, a forum for reformers representing a diverse array of settings from corrections to the COS. The NCCC Committee on Occupational Standards examined working conditions and made policy recommendations for workers' compensation, industrial health, limits on hours of labor, the prohibition of child labor, and minimum wages for female workers. These recommendations were incorporated into the platform of the Progressive Party in 1912.

The American Association for Labor Legislation, an important source of social policy advocacy, reported on its activities in *The Survey*, and Kellogg printed articles on discrimination against immigrants and "Negroes," women's suffrage, tenement safety concerns, the need for more parks and playgrounds and better hospitals, the problems of juveniles and the need for juvenile courts, and how social insurance could protect workers from sickness and accidents and provide for their needs in old age (Chambers, 1971; Coll, 1970; O'Connor, 2001; Woodroofe, 1971).

Major Reforms of the Progressive Era

Progressive reforms were difficult to achieve since prevailing theories of government held that the federal government generally did not possess the constitutional authority to enact social policy reforms. Consequently, the states were the main arenas for contests to enact social policy reform (Amenta, 1998, p. 62; Coll, 1970). National women's organizations, including the Women's Trade Union League and the General Federation of Women's Clubs, promoted social policies that would support women. The American Association for Labor Legislation advocated for old age insurance and social insurance, and the Fraternal Order of the Eagles, which had members across the country, supported old age pensions.

Reforms were not easily won. In 1905, the U.S. Supreme Court held in *Lochner v. New York* that a New York state law limiting the working hours of bakers to 10 hours a day and 60 hours per week to protect them from inherently dangerous and unhealthy work was unconstitutional since it interfered with employees' and employers' "liberty of contract." Some state courts did, however, uphold state laws establishing maximum 12-hour workdays for women (Moss, 1996).

Charles Noble (1997) argues that whenever reforms threatened relationships between labor and capital or supported labor unions, they usually failed. Reformers learned that success was possible by using maternalist approaches that linked reform to women's accepted domestic roles. In 1908, the U.S. Supreme Court reversed the Lochner decision, upholding Oregon's 10-hour workday for women in *Mueller v. Oregon*, relying on a brief submitted by Louis D. Brandeis, a social reformer and later a justice of the U.S. Supreme Court, that included sociological findings about the ill effects of harsh working conditions and lengthy workdays on women workers. By distributing Brandeis's brief to supporters of protective legislation for women workers, other organizations promoted this change. Proponents included the Russell Sage Foundation; the National Consumers' League led by Florence Kelley, an ally of Jane Addams; and the American Association for Labor Legislation, founded in 1906 to research labor conditions and promote policies supporting workers. The Muller decision was precedent for other judicial rulings protecting women in the workplace. By 1917, 41 states had enacted protective laws for women workers, setting the hours and conditions of work. Although seen by Progressives as victories, these laws can be viewed as supportive of women's traditional maternalist roles since they kept women from competing with men for similar and often well-paying jobs and encouraged them to stay in the home, thereby supporting a "family ethic" that relegated women to traditional familial roles (Abramovitz, 1996).

Other maternalist social policy initiatives had mixed results. In Massachusetts, a commission investigated working conditions in specific industries and recommended minimum wage scales for women. In 1910, the Russell Sage Foundation created a Committee on Women's Work spearheaded by Mary Van Kleeck, a skilled social researcher. The committee's publications linked low wages to women's poverty (Bremner, 1956). The United States Bureau of Labor's influential *Report on Conditions of Women and Child Wage Earners in the United States,* published from 1910 to 1913, found there were no agreed upon standards governing women's wages, which Mary van Kleeck and other reformers argued led to exploitation of women workers. She observed, "It is the worker nearest starvation who is most likely to accept starvation wages" (Bremner, 1956, p. 238).

By 1917, the momentum for minimum wage legislation had stalled. Little headway was made at the state level, and opposition by business contributed to lack of action. After World War I, opposition to minimum wage legislation continued. In 1923, the U.S. Supreme Court in *Adkins v. Children's Hospital* held a District of Columbia minimum wage law to be unconstitutional because it interfered with the right of contract. Mimi Abramovitz (1996) argued that, in general, maternalist protective legislation limited women's opportunities by confining their labor to specific occupations, which often paid low wages, and maintaining a "sex segregated labor market" that "channeled women back into the home" (p. 188). The lack of success in creating solid standards regulating wages reflects the differential success of Progressive social policy efforts owing to the strength of opposition to those reforms viewed as harmful to business interests and the inability of Progressives to create effective political coalitions that might achieve lasting social welfare policy reform with broad social impact.

Housing

Investigation of social conditions in urban areas led to policy responses aimed at providing measures to improve housing. New York, Chicago, and Boston saw many successful efforts to reform the living conditions of the poor, most notably in efforts to demolish unsafe tenements and to strengthen housing codes aimed at safety. New York City's Tenement House Law of 1901 and Chicago's ordinance of 1902, which was largely the result of Jane Addams and her Hull House colleagues' skillful advocacy, are examples of successful Progressive Era housing reforms. By 1917, 40 cities and 11 states had new tenement house codes and regulations that attempted to improve sanitary conditions (Bremner, 1956).

The idea of public housing, which was attacked vehemently by those who felt provision of housing was not a government responsibility, was proposed by the American Federation of Labor (AFL) at its national convention in 1914, when it asked that the federal government provide loans to cities to finance the construction of municipal housing. In 1915, Massachusetts adopted a constitutional amendment that allowed the state to construct low cost housing (Bremner, 1956). Although the number of public housing efforts begun in the Progressive Era was modest, they became precedents for government subsidization of housing during the 1930s in response to the Great Depression (Lubove, 1963).

Child Welfare and Mothers' Pensions

Campaigns to "save" children have long been part of reform efforts in the United States. Progressive Era reformers continued these efforts, and, between 1900 and 1917, there were numerous enactments by municipalities and states that created juvenile courts, improved recreational opportunities and parks and playgrounds, extended periods of compulsory school attendance, and established standards to protect children's health. The crusade against child labor, as Bremner (1956) noted, was one of the areas where Progressive reformers achieved considerable success. John Spargo's (1906) *The Bitter Cry of the Children* alerted sympathetic readers that there were over 2 million child laborers in the United States. Jane Addams told the National Conference of Charities and Corrections in 1903 that working boys and girls would grow up without schooling or skills they could use in the market place, leading to unproductive, wasted lives (Bremner, 1956).

Child welfare reformers were acutely aware of arguments supporting child labor, most notably that children's wages were necessary for support of families, particularly for families led by single mothers. Progressives parried with demands for living wages for family breadwinners that would obviate the need for children's income.

By 1900, 28 states had adopted laws regulating child labor, and more followed during the Progressive Era. In 1904, a National Child Labor Committee was founded by Felix Adler, long active in New York campaigns to improve tenements; he was helped in this by Jane Addams and Lillian Wald from New York City's Henry Street settlement. The National Child Labor Committee studied children's well-being, lobbied for child welfare, and recommended standards governing child labor, including the prohibition of child laborers below the age of 14 in manufacturing (Bremner, 1956).

In 1909, after persistent lobbying by the National Child Labor Committee, a White House Conference on the Care of Dependent Children was held. It urged creation of a federal children's bureau, which would investigate children's welfare throughout the nation. The plan was supported by President Theodore Roosevelt, and the Children's Bureau in the Department of Labor and Commerce was created in 1912, but its mandate was limited to research and investigation without any regulatory power (Skocpol, 1992).

In 1916, child labor reformers succeeded in passing federal legislation mandating prohibition from interstate commerce of items produced by child labor. Success was brief, however, when the courts held the federal law to be unconstitutional, demonstrating the strength of the longstanding belief that the marketplace should not be regulated and business should be able to operate as freely as possible in order to promote the common good.

In the 1920s, child labor reformers lobbied unsuccessfully for a constitutional amendment prohibiting child labor. A loose coalition of antireform groups, reflecting the conservatism of the 1920s, succeeded in preventing state ratification of the amendment. This proved to be a bitter defeat for reformers and symbolized the reactionary conditions of the 1920s as the nation reassessed its priorities after World War I. It is noteworthy, however, that, by 1930, all states had created some form of child protection laws (Day, 1997).

The White House Conference of 1909 also recommended that, whenever possible, children should not be removed from their homes despite the presence of poverty. This was a reversal of practices long in effect that forced impoverished female-headed families apart by placing their children in orphanages or other institutions. Although the 1909 Conference did not support public relief for families, in 1911, Illinois became the first state to provide this support, a mothers' or widows' pension for needy single mothers, recognizing that mothers were needed at home to care for their children. Widows, not single mothers, were the preferred beneficiaries, and they had to either give up their full-time jobs or take part-time jobs, often for low pay, to obtain what were frequently meager pensions.

The experience in Illinois was scrutinized by reformers, including those in the COS who had long opposed outdoor relief, fearing that public pensions would be open to administrative fraud and corruption and encourage dependency and pauperism among recipients (Leiby, 1978; Pumphrey & Pumphrey, 1983). Edward T. Devine, former secretary of the New York Charity Organization Society and director of the New York School of Social Work, equated mothers' pensions with public relief that would subsidize immorality and be injurious to the character of parents (Mencher, 1967, p. 305). Eventually, some COS leaders concluded that public relief—mothers' pensions—augmented by professional social casework could prevent family breakup. Despite reservations, 20 states adopted mothers' pension laws by 1913, and, by 1926, all but 8 states had enacted them (Patterson, 2000).

Southern states with the greatest number of African American residents were the last states to adopt mothers' pension laws (Abramovitz, 1996). Although mothers' pensions were eventually seen as acceptable forms of outdoor relief, means tests were used to limit assistance to physically, mentally, and morally "fit" women, presaging welfare restrictions placed on women in New Deal welfare reforms.

Having an illegitimate child could prevent a mother from receiving aid. Widows with young children were the preferred recipients. Levels of mothers' pension support varied across states, and it is questionable whether assistance was adequate for achieving even a modest standard of living (Lubove, 1986; Moss, 1996; Patterson, 2000; Skocpol, 1992). The 1919 White House Conference on Children reported that assistance to women was inadequate for raising children in many states, resulting in the need for outside employment (Abramovitz, 1996).

Despite their shortcomings, mothers' pensions were precedent setting. Government agreed to support women and their children, clear recognition that family life was superior to institutional residency for needy children. Caseworkers, often COS personnel, supervised mothers and children receiving assistance, assuring that middle-class, maternalist norms of female behavior would be enforced by careful scrutiny of pension recipients, a practice that has characterized much discretionary social policy in the United States (Coll, 1970; Gordon, 1994; Mink, 1995; Skocpol, 1996).

Linda Gordon (1994) found that single or divorced women were seen as unworthy of assistance in most states, evidence of the strength of social norms supporting traditional views of the family. She argued that workers' compensation, whose beneficiaries were primarily men, eventually became seen as an entitlement program, less open to discretionary determination of eligibility than mothers' pensions primarily because of gender bias in social policy. Nevertheless, by 1926, only five states continued to give assistance only to widows, and some jurisdictions gave support to divorced mothers or to women whose husbands were incapacitated or imprisoned (Day, 1997). Clearly, mothers' pensions were only palliative. They did little to address fundamental causes of social inequality and poverty, but they did demonstrate widespread public awareness and support for needy mothers and children. However inadequate mothers' pensions were, however few mothers of color were assisted, however these pensions reflected maternalist bias, they did support family life and often removed women from the labor market, at least temporarily. When mothers had to work outside the home to supplement public assistance, they were forced to join the ranks of temporary, low-paid female workers, thereby supplying labor demand and enforcing social norms regulating women's work. In the 1930s, mothers' pensions became important precedents for federal efforts to support women and children during the Great Depression.

Workers' Compensation

During the Progressive Era, reformers saw workers' insurance as a rational response to the growing recognition of the dangers of the workplace. Industrial accidents claimed lives and created loss of wages because of injury. The United States Bureau of Labor and the Russell Sage Foundation conducted comparative studies of foreign social insurance systems, providing data for use by reformers seeking protection for workers. Isaac M. Rubinow's (1913) *Social Insurance* also informed reformers. The Progressive Party's "Social and Industrial Justice" recommendations in its 1912 platform called for old age and unemployment insurance.

Before workers' compensation, assistance for job-related injuries was uncertain (Bremner, 1956). Workers might be covered under employer or private insurance, or they could attempt to use common law remedies by suing employers for negligence, an expensive and uncertain process. Statistics on the number of industrial accidents in 1913 revealed at least 25,000 fatalities and injuries. Between 1909 and 1913, 30 state commissions studied workers' accidents and recommended systems of workers' compensation. The first effective state legislation was enacted in 1911, and by 1921, 42 of 48 states had workers' compensation laws requiring businesses to insure workers against industrial accidents (Amenta, 1998, p. 64). Supported by reform-minded organizations like the American Association for Labor Legislation and, at times, by conservative groups such as the National Association of Manufacturers and the National Civic Federation, workers' compensation legislation showed widespread acceptance of social policy that would support injured workers and their families.

Why were workers' compensation laws so widely adopted? One explanation is that workers' compensation laws were seen by business as more acceptable than the unpredictable consequences of negligence lawsuits brought by workers (Moss, 1996). Within the emerging culture of corporate capitalism, workers' compensation statutes came to be accepted by business as appropriate rationalizations of marketplace uncertainly. The new laws also usually excluded agricultural and domestic laborers, many of whom were women and African Americans (Alston & Fearie, 1985; Moss, 1996). They often did not provide compensation for occupational diseases, nor did they provide benefits sufficient to secure an adequate standard of living. Furthermore, most state laws were voluntary so that employers could elect not to provide compensation insurance for their workers. Approximately 30% of workers in states with compensation laws in 1920 were not covered (Bremner, 1956). Despite these limitations, workers' compensation laws signify a shift from "rugged individualism" to acceptance of state intervention to protect individuals from occupational accidents (Orloff, 1988).

Health Insurance and Unemployment Insurance

Progressive reformers, feeling some justifiable success with the enactment of workers' compensation statutes, turned to health insurance as a solution to the many problems created by illness. Prominent reformers such as Jane Addams and Paul Kellogg saw health insurance as a logical goal that complemented other reforms, but they did not anticipate the strength of opposition to the notion. Insurance companies; labor, medical, and dental associations; drug producers; and other powerful interests opposed public health insurance, sometimes arguing that it was un-American, an especially potent argument after World War I (Chambers, 1967; Day, 1997).

In retrospect, it seems curious that so many Americans have objected to the idea of public health insurance even though they generally agreed that workers' compensation is acceptable. Unemployment insurance was also controversial. By 1930, not a single state had enacted unemployment insurance (Patterson, 2000). Not until 1932, during the hard times of the Great Depression, did Wisconsin became the first state to pass unemployment insurance legislation (Skocpol & Ikenbery, 1995). The failure of Progressive Era efforts to enact unemployment insurance reflects widespread belief that it might encourage carelessness or idleness among workers, echoing old fears that relief would corrupt its beneficiaries.

The Elderly and Categorical Assistance

The 1912, the Progressive Party platform recommended the establishment of social insurance that would cover the elderly. By 1914, only Arizona had a modest form of old age pension, which was very circumscribed in its delineation of eligibility. In 1915, it was declared unconstitutional. Very few workers in private employment had any form of old age protection, indicating the strongly held belief that it was the responsibility of individuals to save for their old age. Railroad workers were the exception. By 1908, 72 railroads, employing a million workers, had established old age pensions (Mencher, 1967, p. 306). In the 1920s, other businesses practiced corporate welfare by establishing workers' pensions that varied in the amount of benefits awarded to loyal workers. Middle-class reformers did not generally advocate old age pensions after the recession of 1913–1915. The American Association for Labor Legislation also did not support old age pensions, opting instead for unemployment insurance, workers' compensation, and safety laws in hazardous industries. In 1923, Montana and Nevada became the first states to enact old age assistance, setting precedents for federal old age insurance during the New Deal of the 1930s as the nation responded to the Depression. In 1907, Wisconsin became the first state to provide assistance to the blind (Brown, 1940, p. 26). These reforms signaled willingness by some states to provide relief to needy recipients in their homes, outside of institutions.

The Legacy of the Progressive Era

Social policy reflects the possible, and the parameters of the possible are most often decided by elites whose beliefs determine allocation of resources to those who are economically and socially vulnerable. Progressive Era reformers seldom proffered structural solutions to the social problems they studied. Most often, they offered remedies that would support those with temporary needs, such as widows and injured workers (Patterson, 2000).

There were, of course, Progressive Era policy initiatives that had a widespread effect on the political system. The long struggle for women's suffrage could claim victory in 1919, the same year the Volsted Act became federal law and brought prohibition of the manufacture and sale of alcoholic beverages. Prohibition was supported by some social reformers and derided by others. Its impact was felt by New York City settlement workers whose neighborhoods, often teeming with immigrants, did not understand the rationale for prohibition and often ignored it (Herrick, 1970).

Progressive reform was mainly an urban phenomenon. Social policy reformers were urban focused and reflected the views of their times. Child labor and its elimination, a central concern of pre–World War I reform, targeted children working in industry, not the 60% of child laborers working in rural agricultural labor. Protecting women workers from unsafe and exploitive working conditions also focused on industrial workers, not on women working in rural areas. Debates about the legacy of Progressive reforms, particularly its meaning for women, enrich our understanding of the era.

Progressive reformers generally shared a "new" view of poverty, which broke from older beliefs that saw poverty as the result of individual character flaws. Rather than emphasizing personal rehabilitation as the main solution to poverty, they felt reform of the social conditions linked to poverty could prevent it. Consequently, they focused their energies on housing reform, eliminating dangers to workers, regulating working conditions, eliminating child labor, and lobbying for workers' compensation, aid to widows with children, and old age pension laws. In order to create a more just and humane society and to preserve social order, Progressive reformers, many of whom were women, believed that reducing dependency and strengthening families necessitated policy changes aimed at ameliorating conditions that, if left unattended, would lead to social instability. While the Progressives never did achieve comprehensive social insurance, their accomplishments foreshadowed the social policy enactments of the 1930s. Even modest old age assistance and mothers' pensions were precedents for social insurance initiatives in the 1930s. It should also be noted that traditions of federalism militated against federal involvement in social policy development. A well-developed federal bureaucracy to administer social policy initiatives did not develop until the 1930s. Consequently, most Progressive Era social policy reform occurred in the states (Skocpol, 1992).

According to prominent historian Arthur Schlesinger, Jr. (1957), World War I brought the generation of Progressive reformers to maturity. Much of their domestic program had been enacted as legislation and regulations. Reformers associated with the Progressive Party had, by 1916, become disillusioned with President Wilson's stance on domestic reform and absorbed with international issues as the nation moved toward war. Most opposed Wilson, and the decline of the Progressive Party is seen by many historians as symbolic of the waning of liberal reform and the end of the Progressive Era (Margulies, 1969). Jane Addams and other prominent women reformers became active in the peace movement during World War I, arguing that war was inimical to all they cherished. Henry F. May (1959), analyzing intellectual history from 1912 to 1917, characterized the end of the Progressive Era as "The End of American Innocence," a diminishing of the American "belief in Progress," which had been implicitly assumed by Progressive social reformers. Clearly, although some Progressive social policies had been enacted, the 1920s witnessed a general retreat from social policy development, which would not resurface until the era of the Great Depression. Some reformers continued to express hope that the unfinished business of the Progressive Era, such as the wholesale prohibition of child labor and the provision of social insurance, would someday be addressed. However, it took massive economic breakdown before the nation created a new reform agenda in the 1930s (Chambers, 1967).

References

Abramovitz, M. (1996). *Regulating the lives of women: Social welfare policy from colonial times to the present* (Rev. ed.). Boston: South End Press.

Agnew, E. (2003). Shaping a civic profession: Mary Richmond, the Social Gospel, and social work. In W. J. Deichmann Edwards & C. De Swarte Gifford (Eds.), *Gender and the social gospel* (pp. 116–135). Urbana: University of Illinois Press.

Alston, L. J., & Fearie, J. P. (1985). Labor costs, paternalism, and loyalty in southern agriculture: A constraint on the growth of the welfare state. *Journal of Economic History, 45,* 95–117.

Amenta, E. (1998). *Bold relief: Institutional politics and the origins of modern American social policy.* Princeton, NJ: Princeton University Press.

Beard, C., & Beard, M. E. (1927). *The rise of American civilization.* New York: Macmillan. (Original work published 1916)

Booth, C. (1902). *Life and labour of the people in London.* New York: Macmillan.

Bremner, R. H. (1956). *From the depths: The discovery of poverty in the United States.* New York: New York University Press.

Brown, J. (1940). *Public relief, 1929–1939.* New York: Henry Holt.

Chambers, C. A. (1967). *Seedtime of reform: American social service and social action.* Ann Arbor: University of Michigan Press.

Chambers, C. A. (1971). *Paul U. Kellogg and* The Survey. Minneapolis: University of Minnesota Press.

Coll, B. (1970). *Perspectives in public welfare: A history.* Washington, DC: Government Printing Office.

Davis, A. (1967). *Spearheads for reform: The social settlements in the Progressive Era, 1890–1914.* New York: Oxford University Press.

Day, P. (1997). *A new history of social welfare* (2nd ed.). Boston: Allyn & Bacon.

Edwards, W. J. D., & Gifford, C. D. S. (Eds.). (2003). *Gender and the social gospel.* Urbana: University of Illinois.

Ehrenreich, J. (1985). *The altruistic imagination: A history of social work and social policy in the United States.* Ithaca, NY: Cornell University Press.

Flanagan, M. (2002). *Seeing with their hearts: Chicago women and the vision of the good city.* Princeton, NJ: Princeton University Press.

Gordon, L. (1994). *Pitied but not entitled: Single mothers and the history of welfare, 1890–1935.* New York: Free Press.

Gordon, L. (1999). *The great Arizona orphan abduction.* Cambridge, MA: Harvard University Press.

Grob, G. N., & Billias, G. A. (1972). The progressive movement: Liberal or conservative? In G. N. Grob & G. A. Billias (Eds.), *Interpretations of American history* (Vol. 2, pp. 159–176). New York: Free Press.

Hays, S. P. (1959). *Conservation and the gospel of efficiency: The progressive conservation movement, 1890–1920.* Cambridge, MA: Harvard University Press.

Herrick, J. M. (1970). *A holy discontent: The history of the New York City social settlements in the interwar era, 1919–1941.* Unpublished doctoral dissertation, University of Minnesota.

Hofstader, R. (1955). *The age of reform: From Bryan to F.D.R.* New York: Vintage.

Hunter, R. (1904). *Poverty.* New York: Macmillan.

Kellogg, P. U. (1909–1914). *The Pittsburgh Survey* (Vols. 1–6). New York: Charities Publication Committee.

Knight, L. (2005). *Citizen: Jane Addams and the struggle for democracy.* Chicago: University of Chicago Press.

Kolko, G. (1963). *The triumph of conservation: A reinterpretation of American history, 1900–1916.* Chicago: Quadrangle Books.

Ladd-Taylor, M. (1994). *Mother-work: Women, child welfare, and the states, 1890–1930.* Urbana: University of Illinois Press.

Lasch-Quinn, E. (1997). Progressives and the pursuit of agency. *Reviews in American History, 25,* 253–257.

Leiby, J. (1978). *A history of social welfare and social work in the United States.* New York: Columbia University Press.

Lubove, R. (1963). *The progressives and the slums: Tenement house reform in New York City, 1890–1917.* Pittsburgh, PA: University of Pittsburgh Press.

Lubove, R. (1986). *The struggle for social security, 1900–1935.* Pittsburgh, PA: University of Pittsburgh Press.

Margulies, H. (1969). Recent opinion on the decline of the progressive era. In M. Plesur (Ed.), *The 1920s: Problems and paradoxes* (pp. 39–58). Boston: Allyn & Bacon.

May, H. (1959). *The end of American innocence: A study of the first years of our own time, 1912–1917.* Chicago: Quadrangle Books.

McGerr, M. (2003). *A fierce discontent: The rise and fall of the Progressive movement in America, 1870–1920.* New York: Free Press.

Mencher, S. (1967). *Poor law to poverty program: Economic security in England and the United States.* Pittsburgh, PA: University of Pittsburgh Press.

Mink, G. (1995). *The wages of motherhood: Inequity in the welfare state, 1917–1942.* Ithaca, NY: Cornell University Press.

Moss, D. A. (1996). *Socializing security: Progressive Era economists and the origins of American social policy.* Cambridge, MA: Harvard University Press.

Muncy, R. (1991). *Creating a female dominion in American reforms, 1890–1935.* New York: Oxford University Press.

Noble, C. (1997). *Welfare as we knew it: A political history of the American welfare state.* New York: Oxford University Press.

Norris, F. (1967). *The octopus: A story of California.* Port Washington, NY: Kennikat Press. (Original work published 1901)

O'Connor, A. (2001). *Poverty knowledge: Social science, social policy, and the poor in twentieth-century U.S. history.* Princeton, NJ: Princeton University Press.

Orloff, A. (1988). The political origins of America's belated welfare state. In M. Weir, A. Orloff, & T. Skocpol (Eds.), *The Politics of social policy in the United States* (pp. 37–80). Princeton, NJ: Princeton University Press.

Parrington, V. (1927). *Main currents in American thought* (Vols. 1–3). New York: Harcourt, Brace & World.

Patterson, J. (2000). *America's struggle against poverty in the twentieth century.* Cambridge, MA: Harvard University Press.

Pimpare, S. (2004). *The new Victorians.* New York: New Press.

Pumphrey, M., & Pumphrey, R. (1983). The widows' pension movement, 1900–1930: Preventive child-saving or social control? In W. Trattner (Ed.), *Social welfare or social control? Some historical reflections of regulating the poor* (pp. 51–66). Knoxville: University of Tennessee Press.

Richmond, M. (1917). *Social diagnosis.* New York: Russell Sage.

Rodgers, D. (2003). *Atlantic crossings: Social politics in a progressive age.* Cambridge, MA: Belknap Press of Harvard University.

Rubinow, I. M. (1913). *Social insurance, with special reference to American conditions.* New York: Henry Holt.

Schlesinger, A. M., Jr. (1957). *The crisis of the old order, 1919–1933.* Boston: Houghton Mifflin.

Schoonover, T. (2003). *Uncle Sam's war of 1898 and the origins of globalization.* Lexington: University of Kentucky Press.

Sinclair, U. (1906). *The jungle.* New York: The Jungle Publishing.

Skocpol, T. (1992). *Protecting soldiers and mothers: The political origins of social policy in the United States.* Cambridge, MA: Harvard University Press.

Skocpol, T. (1996). The trouble with welfare. *Reviews in American History, 24,* 641–646.

Skocpol, T., & Ikenbery, G. R. (1995). The road to social security. In T. Skocpol (Ed.), *Social policy in the United States* (pp. 136–166). Princeton, NJ: Princeton University Press.

Spargo, J. (1906). *The bitter cry of the children.* New York: Macmillan.

Stromquist, S. (2006). *Reinventing "The People": The progressive movement, the class problem, and the origins of modern liberalism.* Urbana: University of Illinois Press.

Wagner, D. (2005). *The poorhouse, America's forgotten institution.* Lanham, MD: Rowman & Littlefield.

Weinstein, J. (1968). *The corporate ideal in the liberal state, 1900–1918.* Boston: Beacon Press.

Wiebe, R. H. (1962). *Businessmen and reform: A study of the progressive movement.* Cambridge, MA: Harvard University Press.

Wiebe, R. H. (1967). *The search for order, 1877–1920.* New York: Hill and Wang.

Woodroofe, K. (1971). *From charity to social work in England and the United States.* Toronto: University of Toronto Press.

9

Social Policy of the New Deal

Robert Leighninger and Leslie Leighninger

S cholars consider the New Deal a defining moment in American public life (Bordo, Goldin, & White, 1998). A major change in American attitudes toward government and the economy took place, and social policies were formulated that were to define public life for the rest of the century. Other scholars, although not denying the changes, point out the continuities underlying them (Dubofsky, 1979/1992). It seems fair to conclude, however, that the efforts of Franklin Roosevelt's government to pull the country out of a catastrophic depression produced a degree of creative experimentation in social policy that has never been equaled in U.S. history.

Interpretations of the social and political meaning of the New Deal are numerous and varied. The standard liberal view of an overthrow of conservative business domination and the inauguration of a new era of rights for common working people prevailed into the 1960s (Schlesinger, 1957). But by the end of the decade, revisionist historians had begun painting a very different picture of the triumph of capitalism and the maintenance of the status quo despite apparent upheaval (Bernstein, 1968/1992).

Since then, more complicated analyses have been made of the many political and economic forces contending during the period. Some see the emergence of a "broker state" within which a variety of interests compete (Lowi, 1969). A related perspective, sometimes called *corporatism*, sees advances in the security and welfare of common people being achieved because it was in the economic interests of the holders of wealth and power (Ferguson, 1989).

One particularly interesting account focuses on *state capacity* and party alignment in the formation and implementation of New Deal policy. In this view, the government can have some autonomy in what does and does not become policy. The state is not simply responding to popular forces or powerful interest groups (Finegold & Skocpol, 1995).

Still other analysts have focused on the ways in which New Deal policies were shaped by assumptions about gender, race, and class. These historians picture a national agenda that, in many ways, ignored the needs of women (especially single mothers), African Americans and other minorities, and chronically low-paid workers (Gordon, 1994; Jones, 1985; Patterson, 1994; Sitkoff, 1984; Smith, 1995).

In documenting specific New Deal policy initiatives, this chapter tries to see how these interpretations might improve understanding of policy formation and successful implementation. It looks particularly at the relationships of federal, state, and local government, public and private interest, and centralized and decentralized administration. It will also look at the roles of minorities and women as they participated in and were affected by New Deal policy making.

Economic Reforms

Initial blame for the depression fell on bankers and financiers, so the first reform efforts included the Securities Act of 1933, the Securities Exchange Act of 1934, and the Banking Acts of 1933, 1934, and 1935. They all aimed at curbing reckless speculation. But it was clear that agriculture and industry would need major support. The Agricultural Adjustment Act and the National Industrial Recovery Act were both enacted in Roosevelt's first "hundred days."

The central strategy of the Agricultural Adjustment Act was to bring farm prices up by reducing production. This, in turn, would boost farmers' incomes so that they might buy more farm machinery, thus helping the industrial sector recover. Farmers were paid subsidies for not producing. Soil conservation was another hoped-for result.

Farmers themselves had lobbied for programs that maintained high levels of production and dumped the result overseas. Cutbacks were against all their instincts. But the program was made law and found wide support. It remains the basis for modern farm policy. The reason for this success despite strong skepticism from a powerful interest group, say Finegold and Skocpol (1995), was that the Department of Agriculture (DOA) had strong institutions and relationships that could both create a successful policy and implement it effectively. Its Bureau of Agricultural Economics and its partners in the land grant colleges across the South and the West were accustomed to thinking holistically about American agriculture and its role in the world market. They could take a larger view. They also had working relationships with farmers through the Agricultural Extension Service and Experiment Stations. Thus, the DOA could ground its theories in practical experience. The southern congressmen who controlled key committees could see the benefits for their constituents, so the passage of the act was speedy.

Sharecroppers and tenant farmers were important casualties of the Agricultural Adjustment Act. The price supports paid to landowners under the act were rarely shared with their farm workers. The result was a massive uprooting of poor farmers and a boost to large landowners. When government lawyers tried to protect sharecroppers, they were fired (Biles, 1994). The Resettlement Administration and Farm Security Administration tried to compensate for this forced migration by creating new farming communities (Baldwin, 1968; Conkin, 1959).

There was no similar state capacity in the business sector. Efforts to mobilize the economy during World War I had been ad hoc and managed by corporate executives who returned to private life after the war, leaving nothing behind. The National Industrial Recovery Act created the National Recovery Administration (NRA), which brought such executives back together and, with labor leaders, encouraged them to develop agreements in each industry on which production levels, prices, and wages would return the economy to health. The NRA's symbol was the blue eagle with the motto: "We do our part."

There were, however, no established relationships or organizations for implementing the National Recovery Act. Noncompliance was widespread, and the policy was a total failure. Some say it may even have delayed recovery (Finegold & Skocpol, 1995). Both statutes were declared unconstitutional by the conservative Supreme Court. The basic policy of the Agricultural Adjustment Act was quickly revised to avoid further challenges. The National Recovery Act was abandoned.

One part of the National Industrial Recovery Act had a rebirth, however. Its section 7a was the first federal guarantee of collective bargaining, and the act also regulated minimum wages and maximum hours. Subsequent legislation resurrected and strengthened these provisions. The Wagner National Labor Relations Act of 1935 was, in part, a response to the loss of section 7a. Crucial to the act's development was the emergence of a new industrial unionism, soon to be embodied in the Congress of Industrial Organizations (CIO), and the mobilization of the Keynesian left wing of the New Deal following the Supreme Court's rulings. These two groups coalesced around beliefs in a planned economy, the redistribution of income, and the necessity of expanding mass consumption (Fraser, 1989). Growing business opposition to Roosevelt following the breakup of the National Recovery Administration pulled him closer to labor. Also, the increased number of liberal urban Democrats in Congress after the 1934 elections established a more favorable climate for progressive labor legislation (Finegold & Skocpol, 1995).

The Wagner Act strengthened labor's right to organize and engage in collective bargaining. Policy makers believed that this spur to unionization would lead to wage increases and thus to increased consumption. Union membership did grow. Yet, because of opposition to the act by southern farm interests, tenant farmers (both black and white) were excluded from its provisions.

The Fair Labor Standards Act proved more difficult to pass. This legislation represented the chance to reinstall the wage and hours protections and a child labor prohibition included in the National Industrial Recovery Act. In fact, Secretary of Labor Frances Perkins had kept a version of the standards bill in her desk drawer as a hedge against the demise of the National Recovery Administration. When the bill was introduced in 1938, it encountered heavy resistance from business and farm interests. The women's reform network of the New Deal had been active in the act's development, especially the child labor ban, and along with labor interests carried out a strong lobbying effort (Ware, 1981). The legislation passed, but in a weakened form. Again, agricultural along with other workers were excluded from certain provisions in the act. The last major legislation of a waning New Deal, the Fair Labor Standards Act, along with the Wagner Act, managed nonetheless to give some support to the emergence of the modern labor movement in the 1930s.

The New Deal also carried out an important experiment in federally backed regional planning, through a program initiated by the Tennessee Valley Authority Act of 1933. The Authority focused on the Tennessee River valley area, an economically underdeveloped part of the South involving seven states, which faced continued problems of flooding and soil erosion. The program set up an independent corporation to construct dams, carry out flood control, build power plants, and produce and sell electrical power. It also sought to improve the welfare of the people of the region and to do this through a process emphasizing decentralized decision making and grassroots democracy (Hargrove & Conkin, 1983).

Like many New Deal reforms, the Tennessee Valley Authority (TVA) produced a mixed record. As implemented, the stress on grassroots democracy led to local control by southern whites bent on excluding African Americans from most benefits. Blacks received the least skilled and lowest paid construction jobs and were denied admission to its training programs (Sitkoff, 1984). Members of the TVA's board debated the appropriate balance between government and business in regional planning, and, although its public power system prevailed over the private utility companies, it favored the interests of large commercial farmers over those of tenants and sharecroppers (Bernstein, 1968/1992; Olson, 1985). Yet, the program made major contributions to the region, including construction of sixteen huge dams; the electrification of the entire Tennessee Valley; and, by altering water levels, the elimination of malaria as a serious health problem (Biles, 1984; Kyle, 1958).

Relief

One of the most pressing challenges of the New Deal was to do something for the phenomenal number—25% of the U.S. population in 1933—left unemployed by the Depression. This was "a disaster without equal in the twentieth century" (Bordo et al., 1998, p. 7). Over a million people wandered the country seeking work. Many cities and states, particularly in the South, provided little or no aid to their out-of-work citizens. Shelby County, Tennessee spent more on golf course maintenance than relief (Biles, 1994). Private social agencies and those cities that attempted to provide aid found their resources woefully inadequate. Early calls by social workers and others for federally financed relief had been rebuffed by President Hoover. Roosevelt, who as governor of New York had established a statewide relief system, was far more receptive.

In early 1933, Congress appropriated an initial $500 million for a federal relief effort. Roosevelt established the Federal Emergency Relief Administration (FERA) and put social worker Harry Hopkins, former head of the New York State program, in charge. Shrewd, hard-driving, and with genuine humanitarian impulses, Hopkins quickly built a massive federal/state program to get relief out as fast as possible. While the FERA put greatest emphasis on emergency work relief programs, a good amount of money was expended on cash relief to the needy, including single mothers (Gordon, 1994; Trattner, 1999).

Hopkins tried to steer a path that avoided the potential of corruption in state administration of relief as well as the intensive casework screening approach of private social agencies. To increase federal control, he bypassed existing state welfare departments and set up separate state relief organizations. He also ruled that federal relief was to be administered solely by public agencies; although, in an attempt to enhance the professionalism of welfare services, he approved regulations calling for supervision of relief workers by trained social workers (Jansson, 2001). Despite all this, the FERA was in some ways a traditional relief program; for example, recipients of both work and cash relief had to undergo a means test. Yet, overall, the FERA spent about $4 billion and affected some 20 million people (Trattner, 1999). Its public work programs were its greatest and most tangible contribution (Olson, 1985).

Work relief was championed by many, even though it might be more expensive, because it would allow workers to retain their skills and their self-respect. In the process, they might perform needed services and construct useful public facilities. Economic advisors, particularly Alvin Hansen, supported public works programs because they believed that public investment would stimulate consumer spending and encourage greater private investment (Brinkley, 1996; Rosenof, 1997).

The first such program, and one of the most popular of the New Deal, was aimed at youth. The Civilian Conservation Corps (CCC) recruited young men ages 17 to 24 to stop soil erosion, plant trees, fight forest fires, create parks, build or repair roads and bridges, and do other work in rural and suburban areas. Next, the Public Works Administration (PWA) was given the task of constructing traditional, heavy-duty public works projects: dams, tunnels, airports, and larger public buildings. Secretary of the Interior Harold Ickes was chosen to direct the program. It became clear almost immediately, however, that the agency was not going to have enough of an impact on unemployment soon enough to relieve the misery of the Depression because large projects required careful planning and relied on skilled workers and heavy machinery. As the winter of 1933 approached, the Civil Works Administration (CWA) was created to employ more unskilled laborers in labor-intensive projects such as road building. The CWA lasted only until March of 1934, but it provided useful experience for the creation of the Works Progress Administration (WPA) the following spring (Schwartz, 1984).

The Works Progress Administration engaged in construction of public facilities but provided other services as well. It staffed clinics, supervised playgrounds, preserved historic records and buildings, revived traditional crafts, excavated archeological sites, painted pictures, produced plays and concerts, and recycled clothing and toys. Under the WPA, the National Youth Administration (NYA) helped students stay in school by providing part-time jobs, offered vocational training to out-of-school youth, and over-saw construction projects like those of the other agencies (Amenta, 1998; MacMahon, Millet, & Ogden, 1941).

The Depression, the ecological disaster in the Dust Bowl, and the New Deal's own agricultural policies displaced many farm families. The Department of Agriculture began a variety of programs to aid destitute farmers, later con-solidated in the Resettlement Administration (RA) and still later run by the Farm Security Administration. These included loans to small farmers; orga-nization of farm cooperatives, camps for migrant workers, and planned suburban "greenbelt" towns; and efforts to move urban families back to the land and to relocate farmers from marginal and depleted land to commu-nities where they might farm successfully. The Farm Security Administration did much to explain the reality of rural poverty to the rest of the nation through a photography program that employed the talents of Walker Evans, Dorothea Lange, and Gordon Parks.

The organization and administration of federal relief programs varied widely. Federal Emergency Relief Administration monies were allocated to state and local governments, half as matching grants and half at Hopkins's discretion. Hopkins used the discretionary funds to maximize state dona-tions, rewarding states for spending more of their own money on relief (Wallis & Oates, 1998). The Civil Works Administration was centrally organized; workers were recruited and paid directly from Washington. The Works Progress Administration was run through state and city offices with strong central leadership. Local sponsorship of projects was required and local financial participation was encouraged but negotiable. In contrast, Public Works Administration projects were locally initiated and designed. They were financed by a combination of federal grants and local money. Part or all of the local portion could be loaned by the PWA. The projects were reviewed by the PWA for financial and structural soundness, but Washington made no attempt to dictate what projects communities should want nor how they should look (Williams, 1939/1968).

The Civilian Conservation Corps was a very unusual collaboration of government branches. The Department of Labor recruited participants; the Department of Agriculture and the Department of the Interior chose the projects for them to work on, some of which involved the Forest Service or the National Park Service; and the training, billeting, and supervision of the boys was done by the U.S. Army (Salmond, 1967).

The programs for farmers were all fairly centralized. Rexford Tugwell, head of the Resettlement Administration, was the major New Deal voice for national planning. Participants were screened by social workers and their conduct monitored (Alanen & Elden, 1987). One observer found considerable parallels between the ideology and administration of New Deal resettlement efforts and those of Mussolini (Ghirardo, 1989).

Most of the relief programs maintained policies of nondiscrimination, but enforcement was another matter. African Americans often had difficulty qualifying for aid under the Federal Emergency Relief Administration and, once qualified, received less money than whites (Jones, 1985). Jobs in the Works Progress Administration were supposed to be awarded without discrimination, but state and local managers were usually allowed to do as they pleased (Wye, 1992). Aubrey Williams, head of the National Youth Administration, was more aggressive in enforcing nondiscrimination and in targeting black colleges and vocational training programs for support. He employed the noted African American educator Mary McLeod Bethune to direct a Division of Negro Affairs.

Particularly strong on civil rights was Public Works Administration's Ickes. He desegregated the public areas of the Department of the Interior and hired black professional and clerical staff. He allocated half of PWA's housing projects to blacks, though he did not try to desegregate them in the South. Since PWA projects were locally initiated, the agency had no control over what was proposed, but an estimated $40 million worth of schools, hospitals, and libraries for African Americans in the South was approved (Sitkoff, 1984).

Although Civilian Conservation Corps Director Robert Fechner was a segregationist and tried to inhibit recruitment of African Americans, the organization was 11% black by 1938. Over 40,000 black enrollees learned to read in the CCC. Eighty thousand Native Americans also participated (Biles, 1994; Leake & Carter, 1988).

The National Youth Administration did not make enrollment of women a priority, but it did not discourage them. By 1941, its ranks were half female. Women played little role in the Public Works Administration since it concentrated on heavy construction. But the Federal Emergency Relief Administration had a Women's Division, the Civil Works Administration had women's projects, and the Works Progress Administration had a Division of Women's and Professional Projects, all directed by Ellen Woodward (Swain, 1994). These projects tended to support traditional women's roles: sewing, child care, nursing, clerical work. But the New Deal gave more prominence to women in leadership positions—including the first woman cabinet officer, Secretary of Labor Frances Perkins—than any earlier administration.

The impact of work relief on the reduction of unemployment and the stimulation of the economy were slow but substantial. Millions of people had been kept working and their families kept fed. The Civilian Conservation Corps saved millions of acres of land from erosion and trees from forest fires, and planted 3 billion new trees. It refurbished and extended national parks and added over 800 state parks for our enjoyment. Although the record of rural resettlement was modest, it rescued many farm families and migrant workers from disaster and included the propagation of soil conservation and scientific farming methods (Biles, 1994; Cannon, 1996). The greenbelt communities remain as models of safe, healthy, comfortable places that nurture family growth and community life (Hughes, 2007).

The Federal Emergency Relief Administration (FERA) ended in 1935. When full employment returned at the end of the decade, sped by preparations for World War II, the rest of these programs were closed. But their effects survive 60 years later. The FERA set important precedents for the public assistance titles of the Social Security Act. The combined building legacy of the various agencies of the New Deal is the least noticed but perhaps most important accomplishment of its relief approach. Today, there is scarcely a community that was of even modest size in the 1930s that does not contain a school, civic building, park, waterworks, or other public structure contributed by one of these agencies, most still in use (Federal Works Administration, 1946; Leake & Carter, 1988; R. Leighninger, 2007; Public Works Administration, 1939).

Social Security and Institutionalized Public Welfare

Early in 1935, in what would become a frequently quoted statement, President Roosevelt declared that "the Federal Government must and shall quit this business of relief." Roosevelt and Hopkins had never intended public cash relief to be an ongoing federal responsibility. Although they saw the continuation of federal work relief as an important tool in combating unemployment, even this could be terminated once employment levels had sufficiently recovered. At the same time, Roosevelt and his advisors realized the necessity of establishing permanent programs to deal with shortcomings in the American economic system. These ideas led to three interrelated policy developments in 1935: the closing down of the Federal Emergency Relief Administration, the formation of the Works Progress Administration, and the creation of what is arguably the most long-lasting contribution of the

New Deal—the social insurance and public assistance programs of the Social Security Act.

In order to end federal involvement in relief, or "the dole," responsibility for general cash relief was transferred from the Federal Emergency Relief Administration to the states. Although it was clear that states had fewer resources for this job, the Works Progress Administration was expected to take up the slack through its expanded jobs program. Social workers and their organizations vociferously opposed these policy decisions, arguing that neither the WPA nor states and localities could handle all those in need. They saw federal funding of general relief as the necessary cornerstone of a permanent federal welfare program, but this proposal was rejected by the Roosevelt administration (Coll, 1995; L. Leighninger, 1987).

In order to structure a program to protect people, particularly workers and the elderly, "against the hazards and vicissitudes of life," Roosevelt had established a Committee on Economic Security (CES) in 1934. Frances Perkins chaired the committee; Hopkins was one of its members. A large advisory group included employers, labor leaders, social workers, and representatives of civic groups. The CES was further supported by a technical board headed by Arthur Altmeyer, an economist from Wisconsin. Control of the process rested largely in the hands of Perkins and Edwin Witte, another Wisconsin economist, who held the powerful job of the committee's executive director. Thus, many groups had input, although some more than others, into the creation of the Social Security Act (Coll, 1995). Together, they attempted to develop a politically, economically, and administratively feasible national economic security program.

When Roosevelt spoke of protecting workers and the elderly, he had in mind a social insurance program along the lines of those created earlier in Europe and promoted by an American social insurance movement since the early 1900s. Two versions of unemployment insurance were debated, one a state system developed in Wisconsin, with employer funds providing the resources, and the other a federal program financed by general revenues. Witte, an author of the Wisconsin legislation, was influential in getting this program, which was paid partially out of workers' paychecks and partially by employer contributions, adopted by the Committee on Economic Security. The federal incentive for the states' adoption of the program was a new 5% payroll tax on employers. If a state enacted employer-based insurance, the federal government would forgive the tax (Berkowitz, 1991).

Providing for the security of the elderly was a more politically charged issue. By the mid-1930s, the Townsend Plan had achieved wide acceptance. Devised by a California physician, the plan proposed payment of a flat grant of $200 a month to everyone over 60. Financed by federal taxation, the measure would bolster the economy by requiring recipients to spend the entire amount within 30 days. This and other solutions to the problems of the elderly, such as Louisiana Senator Huey Long's Share Our Wealth program, captured public interest far more than a social insurance program. Public attention helped lead to the creation of two mechanisms for supporting the elderly: social insurance and a federal-state old age public assistance measure. The latter received far more acceptance than the former during passage and implementation of the Social Security Act (Leiby, 1978).

To assure passage of a permanent program of social insurance for the elderly, Roosevelt strongly influenced the Committee on Economic Security to recommend a plan financed by taxes on employers and employees. This peculiarly American approach contrasted with the European system of support through general revenues but resonated with American values of hard work and self-help. By tying old age insurance to a contributory system and designating that taxes would be kept in a separate trust fund, Roosevelt felt he had insulated the program from future attempts by Congress to change appropriation levels (Achenbaum, 1987; Berkowitz, 1991). Thus, the opportunity to use general taxes to create real income redistribution and a higher level of aid for the elderly was lost. Also, due in part to pressure from southern congressmen, the act omitted coverage for agricultural and domestic workers (a large proportion of the African American workforce).

In addition to old age assistance, public assistance programs were created for two other categories: children in families with one caretaker and people who were blind. All three programs were joint endeavors, with states receiving matching funds from the federal government. It was up to the states to apply for participation. Acceptance was predicated on the existence of a specific state agency to implement the program applying uniform policies and procedures throughout the state (an attempt to avoid local control over public relief). As shaped by congressional debate, dominated by southern Democrats, certain aspects of the proposed public assistance titles were toned down. Within certain general restrictions, states would be in charge of eligibility standards, could impose such requirements as good moral character, and were free to set minimum levels of payment (Coll, 1995).

The final shape of the Social Security Act thus established a two-tier system for dealing with poverty and dependence. The insurance titles of the legislation were universal entitlements covering workers or former workers; the public assistance titles were means-tested programs with residency requirements, designed primarily for people considered unemployable. To use Berkowitz's terms, the lower tier was predicated on a poor law notion of assistance based on location, the higher on assistance based on occupation (Berkowitz, 1991).

The nature of the public assistance titles reflected the thinking of prominent social workers in and out of government. This was particularly true of the development of Aid to Dependent Children (ADC), in which Katharine Lenroot, chief of the U.S. Children's Bureau, was very influential. The Committee on Economic Security asked the Children's Bureau to present a proposal for aiding dependent children. Assisted by former bureau head Grace Abbott, Lenroot set up a program similar to existing state mothers' pensions. ADC, like those pensions, assumed that widowed, deserted, and other single women caring for children should be given a stipend to enable them to stay at home rather than work. In what some historians have labeled a *maternalistic* approach by white women of privilege, Lenroot suggested that ADC should require careful investigations of applications for relief and that the program should be staffed by skilled caseworkers (Gordon, 1994; Mink, 1995).

Although the Children's Bureau developed ADC, it was not successful in its bid to gain administrative responsibility for the program. However, it did receive control over a system of public child welfare services. Instead, ADC, along with Old Age Assistance and Assistance to the Blind, was assigned to the new Social Security Board, under a Bureau of Public Assistance (BPA). BPA's director was Jane Hoey, a trained social worker who had worked with Hopkins in New York. One of Hoey's major concerns was developing a professionalized public social service, using professional social workers wherever possible. Her goal was not so much the provision of in-depth casework services as the development of a fair and adequate system of assistance. Hoey battled with state officials over issues of patronage in hiring public assistance staff, discrimination against African American and Hispanic applicants, and inadequate grant levels. Since much of the control over ADC was lodged in the states, Hoey had to rely mostly on persuasion in these endeavors (L. Leighninger, 1987). The Social Security Amendments of 1939 improved things by mandating merit systems for state public assistance personnel and increasing the federal match for ADC payments.

The story of the development and implementation of ADC underscores the fact that women played important roles in New Deal policy making, particularly regarding labor standards and public welfare. Frances Perkins's position as secretary of labor gave her influence over a broad spectrum of policies. She, like many women activists, received invaluable support from Eleanor Roosevelt. Yet, New Deal programs for women generally provided less security and lower coverage than they did for men. The gendered nature of New Deal social policies has come under increasing scrutiny (Mettler, 1998). Perspectives on the influence of gender in policy development range from the fairly single-faceted gender lens of Linda Gordon to the more comprehensive approach of analysts like Suzanne Mettler (1998), who sees gender specific policies as emerging out of a complex interplay of "institutional factors, political imperatives, and unintended consequences of policy design" (p. xii).

Impact of New Deal Policies

The New Deal had a major impact, not only in dealing with the immediate challenge of the Great Depression but in more far-reaching areas of life as well. Its impact can be felt in the development of the nation's infrastructure, in its social welfare policies, in housing, and in civil rights.

Infrastructure

A vast amount of physical and cultural infrastructure was built in the nine years that the Public Works Administration and other agencies were in operation. We are still using most of it over 70 years later. Ronald Reagan Washington National Airport, Hoover Dam, the Triborough Bridge, Skyline Drive, the Key West Overseas Highway, the San Antonio River Walk, Denver's Red Rocks Amphitheatre, Mount Hood's Timberline Lodge, Mount Mansfield's ski trails, and universities across the country are just a few examples. The impact on our education, health, commerce, and recreation was immense (R. Leighninger, 2007; Short & Stanley-Brown, 1939). Ironically, even New Dealers came to question the cost-effectiveness of work relief (Patterson, 1994) without ever factoring into this calculation the long-term value of what was built.

Social Insurance, Health, and Welfare Policies

The Social Security Act created two long-lasting responses to economic insecurity: institutionalized entitlements to old age and unemployment insurance and more traditional public assistance measures. The first favored male workers and former workers and was legitimized by stressing recipient contributions to the system. The second concentrated on women and children and was sanctioned by the more tenuous criterion of need. Widows and survivors were soon added to Social Security, and a large proportion of women now benefit from the program. Yet, public welfare, with its smaller, less stable, and more stigmatized provision of aid, has remained the dominant program for poor women and minorities. A system of national health care benefits would have mitigated the situation, but such a system was politically unachievable during the New Deal era, and was proven equally elusive in future decades.

Current debates about Social Security, health care, and public welfare reflect some of the same questions and issues that the United States grappled with during the New Deal. In his State of the Union address in 2005, President George W. Bush warned that the country's largest and costliest social program was headed for bankruptcy unless major changes were made. The president's proposal of "strengthening and saving the program" through adding individual private investment accounts to the traditional system brought forth a heated discussion among politicians and the public (Popple & Leighninger, 2008, pp. 210–214).

Health care affordability and accessibility continue to be major concerns for many Americans. What is the appropriate balance between private and public health care delivery systems? Is managed care, particularly as delivered by for-profit companies, the best structure for delivering health services? Should states, counties, and cities continue to be the main providers of publicly financed health care, which is often limited to certain population groups, such as children and those receiving public welfare? Or can the country develop a national health care system such as those in England, Holland, and Sweden?

And finally, public welfare, or Temporary Assistance to Needy Families, continues to be a controversial program. States vary in their rules for eligibility, the amount of money they provide to families, and their requirements for work activities. While the national program limits the time that families may receive federal assistance to five years, some states impose shorter limits. As researchers for the Urban Institute note, "Understanding not just the broad outline of the program but some of the nuances of how individual states have implemented their policies is important for both policy-makers and low-income families" (Rowe & Giannarelli, 2006, p. 7).

Housing

A two-tiered housing policy emerged from the New Deal, one part hugely successful, the other a dismal failure. For the middle-class home buyer, low-interest mortgages from the Federal Housing Administration, a Public Works Administration offshoot, made the American dream of a single-family home a reality. For the working poor, PWA offered the first public housing in America: well planned, well built, and well appointed. Its first occupants were the envy of even middle-class apartment dwellers (Straus & Wegg, 1938). But the attempt to continue this standard of building failed. The Wagner-Steagall Housing Act of 1937 was passed only after being gutted by southern senators. The result was that the agency it created, the United States Housing Authority, was severely limited in what it could construct. Its projects were more regimented, more easily worn down, and more vulnerable to the stigma of "poor-people's housing." Nonetheless, they were sorely needed, and most are still used (R. Leighninger, 2007; Radford, 1996).

Civil Rights

African Americans, particularly southern sharecroppers, were hit harder than most citizens by the depression, and they received far less help from the New Deal than they needed. But they did receive help. Jobs through New Deal agencies such as the Public Works Administration were a key to the survival of many black families. Federal employment of African Americans tripled in the 1930s, including employment in the professional ranks of lawyers, engineers, economists, and scientists

(Biles, 1994). It was also important that federal programs established policies of apportioning jobs to African Americans in proportion to their presence in the population—and made some attempt to enforce these policies. All of these measures raised African American expectations for future progress.

Ickes and Williams and their African American appointees Robert Weaver and Mary McLeod Bethune, along with Will Alexander of the Farm Security Administration, First Lady Eleanor Roosevelt, and others, were visible to the nation in support of civil rights. A political basis for later challenges to segregation was under construction. And it is not unimportant to that challenge that seven of eight Roosevelt appointees to the Supreme Court would support it (Biles, 1994; Sitkoff, 1984).

The New Deal and Society

Abe Fortas, who held various positions in the federal government during and after the 1930s, describes the New Deal not as a radical change but as "a successful effort to salvage the existing way of life, using objectives, procedures, and methods that were in existence" (Louchheim, 1983, p. 225). It is true that many elements of the New Deal program drew on prior policies, and Roosevelt worked within the context of a capitalist system; a federal form of government; and American values of hard work, self-help, and limited government interference. Yet, all these factors were stirred around and some transformed by the onset of the Depression and by subsequent attempts to deal with it. An air of excitement hung in the nation's capital during the New Deal years; great numbers of talented young people were drawn to Washington to improvise and innovate (Louchheim, 1983). These innovations often drew on existing political and economic arrangements, yet, in the process, these arrangements were modified and recast.

The relationship between federal, state, and local governments shifted in interesting ways. Contrary to the current criticisms of "big government," although the federal government grew and took on more responsibilities in the 1930s, this did not diminish state or local powers. Federal programs encouraged state and local participation, creating stronger governments at all levels (Wallis & Oates, 1998). Localities were enabled to do things they wanted to do but could not without national support. But, rather than turning all control over to localities, the federal government retained some direction and oversight. The importance of this can be seen in efforts, not always successful, to prevent local discrimination and graft.

The United States retained its capitalist system, yet that system now had to accommodate a more powerful labor movement. New rules regulated the labor-capital relationship. Social Security provided protections beyond the capacity (or willingness) of the private sector. Comprehensive economic planning measures achieved some success and would be revived during World War II.

On the other hand, as Patterson (1994) has noted, the New Deal did relatively little to change long-term structural causes of poverty: low-paid and irregular employment, discrimination against minorities, and women's inequality in the work place. It abandoned tenant farmers in the interest of promoting agribusiness. It produced two-tiered programs, such as those in welfare and housing, that greatly benefited the middle class while stigmatizing the poor.

During the New Deal, there was a national change in attitudes about the relationship of government to the economy. The Great Depression, and the country's slowness to recover from it, convinced people that a balanced budget and an unobstructed market were inadequate and even inappropriate responses to their problems. Forceful government intervention was needed. The many successes of that intervention produced a new confidence in government efficacy that lasted another four decades. And this tended to obscure, for a while, the failures and inadequacies of New Deal programs. But the confidence gradually eroded and came to be replaced by an equally lopsided belief—that governments, particularly big ones, can do nothing right. A closer look at the myths and the realities of New Deal programs could give us the confidence and wisdom to construct more effective policies in the future.

References

Achenbaum, W.A. (1987). *Social security: Visions and revisions.* New York: Cambridge University Press.

Alanen, A. R., & Elden, J. Y. (1987). *Main street ready-made: The New Deal community of Greendale, Wisconsin.* Madison: State Historical Society of Wisconsin.

Amenta, E. (1998). *Bold relief: Institutional politics and the origins of modern American social policy.* Princeton, NJ: Princeton University Press.

Baldwin, S. (1968). *Power and poverty: The rise and decline of the Farm Security Administration.* Chapel Hill: University of North Carolina Press.

Berkowitz, E. D. (1991). *American's welfare state: From Roosevelt to Reagan.* Baltimore: Johns Hopkins University Press.

Bernstein, B.J. (1992). The New Deal: The conservative achievements of liberal reform. In M. Dubofsky (Ed.), *The New Deal: Conflicting interpretations and shifting perspectives* (pp. 1–24). New York: Garland. (Reprinted from *Towards a new past: Dissenting essays in American history*, pp. 263–288, by B. J. Bernstein, Ed., 1968, New York: Pantheon Books)

Biles, R. (1994). *The New Deal and the south.* Lexington: University of Kentucky Press.

Bordo, M. D., Goldin, C., & White, E. N. (Eds.). (1998). *The Defining Moment: The Great Depression and the American economy in the twentieth century.* Chicago: University of Chicago Press.

Brinkley, A. (1996). *The end of reform: New Deal liberalism in recession and war.* New York: Vintage.

Cannon, B. Q. (1996). *Remaking the agrarian dream: New Deal rural resettlement in the mountain west.* Albuquerque: University of New Mexico Press.

Coll, B. D. (1995). *Safety net: Welfare and Social Security, 1929–1979.* New Brunswick, NJ: Rutgers University Press.

Conkin, P. (1959). *Tomorrow a better world: The New Deal community program.* Ithaca, NY: Cornell University Press.

Dubofsky, M. (1992). Not so "turbulent years": Another look at the American 1930's. In M. Dubofsky (Ed.), *The New Deal: Conflicting interpretations and shifting perspectives* (pp. 123–146). New York: Garland. (Originally published 1979 in *Amerikastudien, 24,* 5–20)

Federal Works Administration. (1946). *Final Report on the WPA program, 1935–1943.* Washington, DC: Government Printing Office.

Ferguson, T. (1989). Industrial conflict and the coming of the New Deal: The triumph of multinational liberalism. In S. Fraser & G. Gerstle (Eds.), *The rise and fall of the New Deal order, 1930–1980* (pp. 3–31). Princeton, NJ: Princeton University Press.

Finegold, K., & Skocpol, T. (1995). *State and party in America's New Deal.* Madison: University of Wisconsin Press.

Fraser, S. (1989). The "labor question." In S. Fraser & G. Gerstle (Eds.), *The rise and fall of the New Deal order, 1930–1980* (pp. 55–84). Princeton, NJ: Princeton University Press.

Ghirardo, D. Y. (1989). *Building new communities: New Deal America and fascist Italy.* Princeton, NJ: Princeton University Press.

Gordon, L. (1994). *Pitied but not entitled: Single mothers and the history of welfare, 1890–1994.* New York: Free Press.

Hargrove, E., & Conkin, P. (Eds.). (1983). *TVA: Fifty years of grass-roots bureaucracy.* Urbana: University of Illinois Press.

Hughes, C. (2007, January 28). Merging the old with the new in suburban Washington. *New York Times,* p. BU21.

Jansson, B. S. (2001). *The reluctant welfare state: American social welfare policies—Past, present, and future* (4th ed.). Pacific Grove, CA: Brooks/Cole.

Jones, J. (1985). *Labor of love, labor of sorrow: Black women, work, and the family from slavery to the present.* New York: Vintage.

Kyle, J. (1958). *The building of TVA: An illustrated history.* Baton Rouge: Louisiana State University Press.

Leake, F. E., & Carter, R. S. (1988). *Roosevelt's tree army: A brief history of the civilian conservation corps.* St. Louis, MO: National Association of Civilian Conservation Corps Alumni.

Leiby, J. (1978). *A history of social welfare and social work in the United States.* New York: Columbia University Press.

Leighninger, L. (1987). *Social work: Search for identity.* Westport, CT: Greenwood.

Leighninger, R. (2007). *Long range public investment: The forgotten legacy of the New Deal.* Columbia: University of South Carolina Press.

Louchheim, K. (Ed.). (1983). *The making of the New Deal: The insiders speak.* Cambridge, MA: Harvard University Press.

Lowi, T. J. (1969). *The end of liberalism: Ideology, policy, and the crisis of public authority.* New York: Norton.

MacMahon, A., Millett, J., & Ogden, G. (1941). *The administration of federal work relief.* Chicago: Public Administration Service.

Mettler, S. (1998). *Dividing Citizens: Gender and federalism in new deal public policy.* Ithaca, NY: Cornell University Press.

Mink, G. (1995). *The wages of motherhood: Inequality in the welfare state.* Ithaca, NY: Cornell University Press.

Olson, J. S. (1985). *Historical dictionary of the New Deal.* Westport, CT: Greenwood.

Patterson, J. T. (1994). *America's struggle against poverty, 1900–1994.* Cambridge, MA: Harvard University Press.

Popple, P., & Leighninger, L. (2008). *The policy-based profession: An introduction to social welfare policy analysis for social workers* (4th ed.). Boston: Allyn & Bacon.

Public Works Administration. (1939). *America builds: The record of PWA.* Washington, DC: Government Printing Office.

Radford, G. (1996). *Modern housing for America: Policy struggles in the New Deal era.* Chicago: University of Chicago Press.

Rosenof, T. (1997). *Economics in the long run: New Deal theorists and their legacies, 1933–1993.* Chapel Hill: University of North Carolina Press.

Rowe, G., & Giannarelli, L. (2006, July). Getting on, staying on, and getting off welfare: The complexity of state-by-state policy choices. *New Federalism: Issues and Options for States* (Series A, No. A-70). Washington, DC: Urban Institute.

Salmond, J. (1967). *The Civilian Conservation Corps, 1933–1942.* Durham, NC: Duke University Press.

Schlesinger, A. M. (1957). *The age of Roosevelt.* New York: Houghton-Mifflin.

Schwartz, B. (1984). *The Civil Works Administration, 1933–1934: The business of emergency employment in the New Deal.* Princeton, NJ: Princeton University Press.

Short, C. W., & Stanley-Brown, R. (1939). *Public buildings: A survey of architecture of projects constructed by federal and other governmental bodies between the years 1933 and 1939 with the assistance of the Public Works Administration.* Washington, DC: Government Printing Office. (The first half of this volume was reprinted by DeCapo Press, New York, 1986)

Sitkoff, H. (1984). The impact of the New Deal on black southerners. In J. C. Cobb & M. V. Namorato (Eds.), *The New Deal and the south* (pp. 117–134). Jackson: University of Mississippi Press.

Smith, S. L. (1995). *Sick and tired of being sick and tired: Black women's health activism in America, 1890–1950.* Philadelphia: University of Pennsylvania Press.

Straus, M. W., & Wegg, T. (1938). *Housing comes of age.* New York: Oxford University Press.

Swain, M. H. (1994). *Ellen S. Woodward: New Deal advocate for women.* Jackson: University of Mississippi Press.

Trattner, W. I. (1999). *From poor law to welfare state: A history of social welfare in America* (5th ed.). New York: Free Press.

Wallis, J. J., & Oates, W. E. (1998). The impact of the New Deal on American federalism. In M. D. Bordo, C. Goldin, & E. N. White (Eds.), *The defining moment: The Great Depression and the American economy in the twentieth century* (pp. 155–180). Chicago: University of Chicago Press.

Ware, S. (1981). *Beyond suffrage: Women in the New Deal.* Cambridge, MA: Harvard University Press.

Williams, J. K. (1968). *Grants-in-aid under the Public Works Administration.* New York: AMS Press. (Originally published 1939)

Wye, C. G. (1992). The New Deal and the Negro community: Toward a broader conceptualization. In M. Dubofsky (Ed.), *The New Deal: Conflicting interpretations and shifting perspectives* (pp. 247–269). New York: Garland.

10 Social Policy and the Great Society

Michael Reisch

From 1940 to 1960, economic growth, a progressive income tax, and modestly redistributive policies provided many Americans with a better life and hope for a brighter future. Spurred by the favorable postwar economic climate and increased military spending due to the cold war, the gross national product of the United States increased over 150% and unemployment ranged between 3% and 5%. Dramatic demographic shifts, especially the northern migration of over 4 million African Americans, accompanied this rapid economic expansion.

During these decades, the social policies established by the New Deal, particularly the 1935 Social Security Act, helped maintain a floor on workers' spending power. They also contributed substantially to the physical transformation of cities and laid the foundation for the postwar growth of suburbs (Patterson, 2001). Other policies, however, in such areas as housing, employment, and education, sustained and exacerbated long-standing discrimination against racial minorities and contributed to the creation of urban ghettos (Massey & Denton, 1993; Sugrue, 1996). Yet, the long-term implications of these demographic and social trends were little understood by policy makers at the time (Lemann, 1991).

By the end of the Eisenhower years, the boom that fueled the postwar recovery had begun to slow down. Facing increased competition from European countries (whose recovery had been assisted by the American Marshall Plan), the economies of Northern and Midwestern states began to decline, and industrial unemployment among unskilled and semiskilled blue-collar workers increased. While over two-thirds of Americans still lived in cities affected by this decline, the growth of suburbs and the appearance of universal material well-being fostered by the media, particularly television, contributed to the increasing "invisibility of the poor" (Harrington, 1962/1981). A quarter century after the passage of the Social

Security Act, severe and chronic poverty lurked below the surface of the nation's well-being, particularly in urban ghettos and isolated rural areas. The recognition that the New Deal had not solved the problem of poverty was a major factor in the emergence of the War on Poverty and Great Society programs described in this chapter.

Background to the War on Poverty

During the 1940s and 1950s, the repressive political climate of the cold war and McCarthyism abetted conservatives' efforts to roll back the New Deal. Social activism declined, particularly in social work, and openly antiwelfare political attitudes reemerged (Jones, 1992; Reisch & Andrews, 2001; Schrecker, 1998). Social policy advances of the postwar period, such as the expansion of Social Security and the growth of private family service and mental health agencies, largely aided middle-income persons. The perception grew, however, that the preponderance of tax dollars were being spent on increasing numbers of "undeserving" urban welfare recipients, many of whom were African American or Latino. This resentment of the urban poor, which later undermined federal antipoverty efforts in the 1960s, resulted partly from a shift in the demographic makeup of urban areas and the racial composition of the welfare rolls (Brown, 1999; Danziger & Weinberg, 1994; Edsall, 1991; Katz, 2001; Piven & Cloward, 1995; Quadagno, 1994). At the time, the linkages between interracial tensions, the emerging civil rights movement, and the needs of welfare recipients were unclear to all but a few analysts (Hamilton & Hamilton, 1997).

During these years policy makers also paid little attention to the status of women, who were encouraged to give up their wartime employment and return to the domestic sphere (Stoltzfus, 2003). Abortion was illegal, as was contraception in many states, and proponents of feminist-oriented policies, including child care, received scant support among politicians or in the media (Abramovitz, 1999).

Although the seeds of the modern gay rights movement had been planted in coastal cities during the war, gays and lesbians continued to be highly stigmatized. Many remained closeted, and virtually no attention was paid to issues that affected this population. In fact, the suggestion of homosexuality was often used by investigators to cast suspicion on the loyalty of defendants and witnesses in the anticommunist hearings of the era (Schrecker, 1998).

Just as the 1954 *Brown* decision and the 1957 Montgomery bus boycott awakened white Americans to the realities of segregation, Michael Harrington's (1962/1981) classic exposé, *The Other America*, and other, lesser known works, such as Caudill's (1963) *Night Comes to the Cumberlands*, forced Americans to rediscover those segments of the population bypassed by postwar economic and social progress. In Harrington's "Other America," over 40 million people lived in poverty, approximately one-third of them children. Poverty moved to the front page for the first time since the Great Depression (Axinn & Stern, 2008; Patterson, 2001).

Images of Poverty

Prior to the New Deal, the nation's conception of poverty was closely linked to individually focused, often moral explanations. Several factors shaped this view of poverty: the expectation of chronic material scarcity, the physical proximity of social classes in urban environments, and the extent of social interaction between the poor and nonpoor components of the population (Reisch, 1996). Although the Depression changed many attitudes about poverty and unemployment, it did not eliminate societal prejudices toward the poor, particularly prejudices against those from racial or ethnic minority groups. In fact, many New Deal programs discriminated against African Americans and women, and the centerpiece of the New Deal, the Social Security Act, incorporated both racial and gender biases in its basic structure (Brown, 1999; N. Rose, 1995). As a consequence, social welfare programs continued to reflect pre–New Deal myths about the poor and to stigmatize those who received public assistance (Axinn & Stern, 1988). Highly publicized antiwelfare campaigns during the 1950s, such as the one in Newburgh, New York, focused increased attention on these issues.

It is also important to note that New Deal policies had not eliminated poverty or unemployment, which remained as high as 17% in 1939. Instead, four factors contributed to the decline in poverty in the postwar era: wage increases that resulted from greater labor-management cooperation, spurred in part by the cold war; the growth of two-earner households (which would soon produce serious social consequences); the increase in family income from private pensions and investments; and the impact of government transfers such as social insurance and public assistance programs. The primary beneficiaries of these advances were the elderly and white workers, who began to leave urban areas in the postwar decades. Poverty seemed to disappear because aggregate economic growth, the structure of suburbs, and the images of American society conveyed by popular culture masked its persistence (Axinn & Stern, 1988; Danziger & Weinberg, 1994). The "rediscovery of poverty" that inspired the policy reforms of the 1960s must be understood in this context.

The War on Poverty and the Great Society thus rested on misconceptions about the extent of poverty and misinterpretations of contemporary analyses of poverty and the poor (Harrington, 1962/1981; Lewis, 1966/1996). The popular "culture of poverty" thesis assumed that the poor were different from the nonpoor and, by implication, somehow inferior in terms of values and behaviors. These differences, it was argued, were transmitted from generation to generation. By defining the needs of low-income persons as the product of individual or cultural deficiency, rather than institutional or resource deficiency, analysts, policy makers, and most of the general public came to view poverty as a normal state for large segments of the urban population (Ryan, 1971). This definition justified existing patterns of inequitable resource distribution.

In the late 1950s, however, new perspectives on social problems emerged within American universities, views that eventually shaped structurally oriented social policy responses to poverty in the 1960s. In such areas as juvenile delinquency and urban poverty, scholars began to focus on issues of opportunity rather than pathology. This view initially caused a schism between its proponents (largely sociologists) and mainstream social workers, who tended to regard family dysfunction as the source of deviant behavior. Despite these differences, the work of Richard Cloward and Lloyd Ohlin (1960) inspired the development of a new kind of social service organization in cities such as Chicago and New York (Helfgot, 1981; Lemann, 1988, 1989). Initiatives implemented by the Kennedy and Johnson administrations emulated this model and reinvigorated the community organization component within the social work profession (Reisch & Wenocur, 1986).

Initiatives by the Kennedy Administration

Beginning with the West Virginia primary, the 1960 presidential campaign brought issues of poverty to the attention of the American people, primarily through the speeches of Senator John F. Kennedy. Consciously evoking Franklin D. Roosevelt, Kennedy repeatedly referred to the hunger and deprivation he had seen (Matusow, 1984). Ironically, powerful media images of rural deprivation in places like Appalachia and the Mississippi Delta distorted efforts to deal with problems that had structural and not personal causes, much as they had in the 1930s.

A major influence on the Kennedy administration was the Ford Foundation's "grey areas" project, which funded community action agencies' initiatives to address the physical and social needs of low-income urban residents. Another influence was Mobilization for Youth, a New York City project originally designed and implemented in the late 1950s by the Henry Street Settlement. By 1960, Mobilization for Youth had become an independent agency and, in 1962, the Kennedy administration provided it with $12.6 million in funding (Gillette, 1996).

Economists like John Kenneth Galbraith and Walter Heller, whose ideas emphasized the expansion of economic opportunity rather than income support, also influenced Kennedy's antipoverty efforts. The creation of the Area Redevelopment Agency in 1961 brought increased federal attention and funding to economically depressed regions such as rust belt cities and the Mississippi Delta. The Manpower Development and Training Act of 1962 continued the American trend of stressing employment over public assistance, a trend that led to a series of welfare "reforms" over the next three and a half decades.

Continuing the pattern of social policies established during the New Deal, President Kennedy also proposed legislation designed to maintain consumption levels of low-income families, both the working poor and the welfare poor. These included the extension of Aid to Families with Dependent Children (AFDC) benefits to the children of unemployed workers (a program given the acronym AFDC-UP), an increase in the minimum wage, and the expansion of public housing projects. A complementary approach appeared in the 1962 Public Welfare Amendments, which increased federal support for the public social services (Jones, 1992; Katz, 2001; Patterson, 2001).

With the exception of child welfare services, social services had been omitted from the original Social Security Act. In 1956, however, the federal government began to reimburse states for one half of the social services that they provided welfare recipients. These matching funds provided inadequate incentives for many states, and few chose to take advantage of the government's offer. The 1962 amendments attempted to address this problem by providing a higher federal matching rate (75%) and incorporating a comprehensive social services strategy into broader federal efforts to combat poverty.

The 1962 amendments also emphasized preventive and rehabilitative services. They expanded eligibility for services to former and potential welfare recipients with a particular emphasis on family preservation. Initially, this prevention-oriented strategy appeared to offer a greater chance for reducing poverty, particularly in the African American community. Subsequently, under less sympathetic administrations, it led to punitive policies that mandated work in order to receive benefits (Goldberg & Collins, 2001; Katz, 1989; Katz, 2001).

Other key components of these reforms were the development of services to the elderly, particularly the elderly poor; limitations on social workers' caseloads; support for individual counseling and information and referral services; and the introduction of case management via individualized service plans. Financial incentives included authorization for state governments to contract for services (which spurred the growth of nonprofit agencies), the absence of a ceiling on federal expenditures for social services, and permission for states to conduct home visits to determine clients' eligibility (Gillette, 1996). By providing the emerging welfare rights movement with a powerful symbolic issue, this latter development led to unexpected and eventually explosive consequences. In addition, these reforms failed to address the specific needs of women as workers, beneficiaries, or mothers, particularly the issue of child care (Abramovitz, 1999).

Separating Services From Income Support

Despite its preventive focus, this service strategy did not stem the growth of welfare caseloads and, between 1962 and 1967, welfare rolls increased by nearly 50%. Neither the growing activism of welfare rights organizations nor the relaxation of eligibility requirements completely explains this increase. Basic flaws in the service strategy itself undermined its intentions. As later studies revealed, the low level of public assistance provided insufficient support for clients to take advantage of the services provided (Bell, 1983; Goldberg & Collins, 2001; Katz, 1989; Patterson, 2001).

The 1967 amendments to the Social Security Act attempted to correct this problem by further strengthening the social service provisions within public welfare, with a new focus on a work-based alternative to welfare. They placed greater emphasis on moving clients from welfare to work through job training and child care in addition to counseling. Yet, the new Work Incentive Program (WIN) ultimately made public assistance more restrictive through the initiation of so-called "workfare" requirements. It also had little impact on labor force participation among AFDC recipients (Goldberg & Collins, 2001).

Changes in the structure of social services abetted this new policy focus. Perhaps the most important organizational shift was the formal separation of the administration of federally funded social services from the administration of cash assistance. This division occurred as a result of the Department of Health, Education, and Welfare's reorganization, which created the Social and Rehabilitation Service. Regulations mandating this separation first appeared in 1972, although local governments had begun to split their administration as early as 1969 (Patterson, 2001).

Proponents of separation, including welfare rights and feminist organizations, asserted that it would promote better relationships between social service workers and AFDC recipients because workers would no longer have the ability to deny cash benefits to clients. They also argued that many of the problems of welfare recipients were merely the result of poverty, not pathology. Requiring all beneficiaries to receive social services, they argued, perpetuated the view of clients as humans in need of fixing rather than as people who merely need financial assistance (Gillette, 1996; Ginzberg & Solow, 1974; Nadasen, 2005).

From the federal government's perspective, separation also had desirable fiscal consequences. Since 1962, the costs of public social services had increased dramatically, largely because states had transferred their service expenditures to the public sector to take advantage of the 75% match. Separation prevented states from claiming this rate for the administrative costs of cash assistance programs, which had a lower matching rate of 50%.

Despite these efforts to curtail spending, AFDC rolls more than doubled from the late 1960s to the early 1970s, while federal spending for social services increased by over 500%. A combination of factors produced this dramatic surge in expenditures. These included vague legislative definitions of a social service, liberal eligibility requirements, and sophisticated applications of the law's purchase of service authority by the states (Derthick, 1975).

A similar pattern emerged in the area of mental health policy. The Community Mental Health Centers Act of 1963 emphasized prevention over treatment and a community rather than an institutionally based approach to mental health services. Yet, in some ways, the movement for deinstitutionalization spawned by this legislation inadvertently worsened the plight of the chronically mentally ill and contributed to the growing problem of homelessness in the 1980s and 1990s (Blau, 1992). This occurred because lawmakers designing community-based rehabilitation programs focused more on the fiscal savings provided by deinstitutionalization than on the needs of the mentally ill (S. M. Rose & Black, 1985).

The War on Poverty and the Great Society

In January 1964, two months after the assassination of President Kennedy, President Lyndon Johnson proclaimed an "unconditional" War on Poverty in his first State of the Union address. Soon, the *Economic Report of the President* proposed a broad range of economic and social policies designed to achieve this lofty objective. Acknowledging the complexity of a problem like poverty, the Johnson administration's legislative package included economic stimuli, full employment programs, urban and rural rehabilitation, expanded educational and labor opportunities for youth and adults, new health care initiatives, and increased assistance for the elderly and the disabled (Danziger, 1991; Gillette, 1996).

The primary instrument of the War on Poverty was the Economic Opportunity Act. This legislation created such programs as the Job Corps, VISTA (Volunteers in Service to America, a domestic version of the Peace Corps), Upward Bound, the Neighborhood Youth Corps, Community Action, Head Start, Legal Services, Foster Grandparents, and the Office of Economic Opportunity (OEO). Later that year, the landmark Civil Rights Act further promoted an equal opportunity agenda through the prohibition of racial, ethnic, or gender discrimination in employment and the establishment of the Equal Employment Opportunity Commission (EEOC). In three whirlwind years, the Johnson administration augmented these efforts by expanding existing entitlement programs.

In 1965, through the enactment of Medicare and Medicaid, Congress created a mandatory program of hospital insurance, an optional program of physician care for the elderly and the disabled, and a joint federal-state health insurance program for low-income persons. In the same year, Congress established the Department of Housing and Urban Development (HUD), funded an array of services for the aged through the Older Americans Act, and created the Food Stamp Program under the auspices of the Department of Agriculture. In addition, the Elementary and Secondary School Education Act overturned long-standing precedents and directed federal aid to local schools in order to equalize educational opportunities for children. Expanding on the Civil Rights Act, the Voting Rights Act gave these reforms a political dimension by prohibiting the denial of the right to vote (Matusow, 1984).

In 1966, the Model Cities Act targeted certain urban areas with comprehensive services. Emphasizing the concept of community control, funds for the Model Cities Program would pass through municipal governments yet be controlled by boards comprised equally of elected officials, low-income people, and representatives of community organizations. Shortly, this proved to be an explosive formula, and tensions between largely white politicians and African American and Latino activists escalated. This conflict weakened support for the administration's policy agenda, which collapsed in two years under the pressures of foreign war and inflation (Lemann, 1988, 1989). Despite these emerging tensions, the Housing and Urban Redevelopment Act of 1968 expanded federal funding for low-income housing and, through the creation of Section 8 housing, enabled poor tenants to rent apartments outside of stigmatized and increasingly ghettoized projects. Additional growth in this area occurred in 1974 through the Housing and Community Development Act.

The Idea of the Great Society

After Johnson's landslide victory over Barry Goldwater in the November 1964 presidential election, he unveiled the concept of the Great Society in his 1965 State of the Union address. Drawing upon a deep reservoir of public support, his own well-honed legislative skills, and the support of large Democratic majorities in Congress, Johnson soon pushed through a social policy agenda second only to Roosevelt's (Ginzberg & Solow, 1974).

From the outset, the concept of the Great Society was closely linked with a civil rights agenda, the movement toward community control, and efforts to ameliorate the plight of poor children. Its centerpiece was the creation of semiautonomous community action programs in virtually every city in the United States. Together with VISTA and the local legal assistance services established under the Equal Opportunity Act, the community action programs increased the role of neighborhood residents in shaping the policies and programs that affected their lives. Under the leadership of local activists, these initiatives led to the development of alternative centers of political power in low-income urban neighborhoods.

Opposition to such programs soon emerged among some big city mayors, who regarded the community action programs and efforts to empower low-income community residents as potential threats to their political dominance (Katz, 1989; Matusow, 1984). The racially egalitarian implications of the Great Society initiatives also led to attacks on antipoverty programs, even popular and successful ones like Head Start, particularly in Southern states such as Mississippi. Echoing sentiments previously expressed during the McCarthy period, both rural and urban conservative critics of the Office of Economic Opportunity and the Great Society alleged that these programs promoted a socialist agenda and that their proponents were communists. Consequently, as early as 1966, conservative Democrats joined Republicans in calling for major reductions in federal spending for such purposes (Quadagno, 1994).

Yet, despite the charges of opponents, the policies of the Johnson administration did not constitute a fundamental shift from traditional approaches to the problem of poverty. Changes in public assistance policies and the development of programs within the Office of Economic Opportunity (OEO), such as the Job Corps, emphasized employment incentives and training over income maintenance. This approach was consistent with the longstanding American preference for employment over welfare. In addition, the federal government provided states with financial incentives to develop social services leading to self-care and self-support, which reinforced American values such as political decentralization, individualism, and self-reliance. Finally, the shift in focus from subsistence to prevention (even if only in theory) occurred primarily for reasons of cost efficiency and out of reluctance to expand public assistance benefits. The planning and community development components of the OEO spurred nearly as much opposition as its expectation of "maximum feasible participation" by community residents. In fact, the underlying assumption of all such policies was that economic growth, rather than resource redistribution, was the key to solving urban problems (Gillette, 1996).

In the late 1960s, however, several developments underscored the insufficiency of this strategy. Cities like Detroit and Newark erupted in a series of increasingly violent disturbances. Welfare rolls grew rapidly in the midst of prosperity. Organized welfare recipients and urban residents took seriously the government's promise of "maximum feasible participation" by the community in the design and implementation of so-called community action programs (Moynihan, 1969). Fearing a challenge to their political power from alarmed middle-income residents and newly organized low-income groups, urban politicians persuaded the federal government to dismantle or cut many antipoverty initiatives, particularly community action programs (Lemann, 1988, 1989; S. M. Rose, 1972). In an increasingly conservative political climate, the policy emphasis shifted from inducements to receive services to coercive pressures to seek employment (Edsall, 1991; Katz, 1989, 2001; Patterson, 2001).

At the same time, by the mid-1960s, the nature of the country's economic growth itself intensified the poverty and isolation of low-income urban and rural communities. Even at the height of the War on Poverty, a late-1966 study revealed that a majority of Americans earned less than was needed to live a "decent life." This created the appearance that the problems of poverty were beyond solution—the consequence of a growing "underclass"—and justified the retreat of social policy from addressing the needs of disadvantaged communities (Katz, 1989).

The attack on the urban poor, in particular, during the late 1960s coincided with a major shift in the locus of American economic and political power—a shift that initially went unnoticed. Large corporations began to move the base of their manufacturing operations away from the traditional industrial centers of the Northeast and Midwest (the so-called Rust Belt) to the newer cities of the Sun Belt, to the suburban areas that soon ringed older cities, and to factories abroad.

Beginning with the 1968 election, these economic shifts were accompanied by political changes of considerable magnitude. The power of states in which the old New Deal coalition (which consisted of organized labor, white ethnics, African Americans, and intellectuals) did not exist increased as their populations and economic bases expanded (Matusow, 1984). Such states, in which unions were weak and racial minorities scarce, supported increasingly antiurban, antiwelfare policies at the local and national levels (Edsall, 1991). Since state governments had considerable discretion in establishing eligibility criteria and benefit levels, this "power shift" exacerbated existing disparities in income among and within regions (Sale, 1976). As multinational corporations and their political allies grew stronger, the influence of unions and the social movements of the 1960s declined. This removed an effective counterweight and a force for progressive social policy development from the nation's political equation. Simultaneously, ongoing "white flight" from urban centers weakened the tax base of cities and created what O'Connor (1973) termed the "fiscal crisis of the state," symbolized by the budget problems encountered by New York and Cleveland in the mid-1970s.

The foreign policy of the Johnson administration exacerbated these developments. By refusing to choose between the "guns" of the Vietnam War and the "butter" of the Great Society, Johnson brought about an increase in inflation. This slowed economic growth, diminished support for increasingly expensive antipoverty programs, and fostered renewed receptivity to arguments that explained poverty in personal rather than structural terms (Ginzberg & Solow, 1974; Katz, 1989; Lemann, 1988, 1989). The continuing militancy of welfare recipients and community action leaders, the spread of civil unrest in urban ghettos, and the growing cost of public assistance further contributed to this political shift. In the 1968 election, Richard Nixon eked out a narrow victory by effectively exploiting these fears and social tensions and appealing to racial and class resentments in carefully coded language (Matusow, 1984).

Welfare Rights and the War on Poverty

Between 1966 and 1973, as the civil rights movement shifted its focus to Northern cities, a social movement of welfare recipients, the National Welfare Rights Organization (NWRO), transformed the political debate over welfare and economic justice. Led by Dr. George Wiley, a chemist and former organizer with the Congress of Racial Equality (CORE), and inspired by the antipoverty strategy developed by Richard Cloward and Francis Fox Piven at Mobilization for Youth, the NWRO sought to organize female welfare recipients to fight on their own behalf (Kotz & Kotz, 1977; Nadasen, 2005; Piven & Cloward, 1977; West, 1981).

In a few years, the NWRO grew from a patchwork of local grassroots groups to a social movement and, in the process, reframed the national debate over poverty. Unlike the liberal creators of the Great Society programs whose benign paternalism they frequently criticized, NWRO activists argued that poor people were entitled to public aid as a matter of legal and human rights. Their philosophy and tactics "pushed the postwar welfare state to new limits [and] articulated a historically remarkable theory of citizenship . . . [which] reconfigured familiar Anglo-American ideas about rights and obligations" (Kornbluh, 1997, p. 103).

A short-lived alliance between the National Welfare Rights Organization and the Office of Economic Opportunity–sponsored Community Legal Services produced a legal strategy to create a constitutional right to subsistence that complemented the former's confrontational political tactics. Spearheaded by the Center for Social Welfare Policy and Law, this approach initially met with considerable success. In 1966, 10 years after the Warren Supreme Court had hinted its receptivity to arguments recognizing the unconstitutionality of wealth-based discrimination, the Court established the principle that such discrimination was equivalent to "invidious" racial discrimination. This principle expanded the concept of fundamental rights to include those rights not explicitly listed in the Constitution. Inspired by these decisions, welfare rights advocates tried to convince the Court to find a "right to live" within the Equal Protection Clause of the 14th Amendment. Relying on natural law tradition and universalist arguments, they sought to eradicate the distinction between positive and negative rights. By 1968, prospects looked hopeful that this bold strategy would prevail (Bussiere, 1997).

Yet, the strategy ultimately failed for three reasons. First, the initial success of advocates, which relied on a selective, maternalist ideology with roots in the Progressive Era and on a judicially oriented approach, contained the seeds of this failure because it inadvertently undermined the foundation of their legal arguments. Second, at the organizational level, the strategy failed because grassroots National Welfare Rights Organization leaders increasingly resisted the use of a maternalist argument in support of welfare rights. This resistance reflected internal conflicts within the organization between male founders such as Wiley and female community-based leaders such as Johnnie Tillmon (Nadasen, 2005; West, 1981).

The principle explanation for the NWRO's failure, however, lies in the advocates' legal strategy, not in the contradictions of their ideology or in their intraorganizational conflicts. Early judicial victories led to natural rights being defined as mere statutory entitlements rather than as constitutional guarantees. Thus, in the late 1960s, just as antipoverty programs were beginning to lose their broad base of public support in the aftermath of civil disturbances, judicial decisions neutralized the universal appeal of advocates' arguments and limited the redistributive potential of the policy changes they proposed (Bussiere, 1997; Nadasen, 2005; West, 1981).

The Court's focus on procedural rather than substantive rights and its definition of welfare as a statutory rather than a constitutional entitlement also made welfare recipients dependent on the political whims of elected officials. By the early 1970s, this approach had succeeded in getting 6 million more people on public assistance and significantly increasing both total welfare spending and average benefit levels. Yet, in the long run, it inadvertently "tended to set different groups of poor people against each other in the pluralist political arena . . . in a fierce competition for diminishing public resources" (Bussiere, 1997, p. 119). It fostered a climate in which advocates for disadvantaged groups were ill prepared, a decade later, to defend against the antiwelfare policies of the Reagan-Bush era. The failure of the "right to welfare" campaign thus resulted from the same philosophical limitations that plagued the Great Society programs. These included an emphasis on procedural rights (opportunity) instead of group outcomes, a negative conception of liberty, and hostility to the role of local communities.

Social Policies Under Nixon, Ford, and Carter

Although he initially maintained many of the social policies of the Johnson administration, President Nixon sought to continue the war in Southeast Asia and simultaneously control the inflation it had produced by reducing the domestic side of the federal budget. A major component of his strategy was a shift in the administration of antipoverty programs to states and localities. From 1968 to 1972, grants to states for services increased by over one-third to $500 million. These funds were controlled largely by elected officials rather than community action programs or neighborhood residents.

Nixon also tried to replace Aid to Families with Dependent Children (AFDC) with a Family Assistance Program (FAP) that would provide a guaranteed annual income, but, in 1970, a unique congressional coalition of liberals and conservatives rejected the proposal (Moynihan, 1973). In 1972 and 1973, however, Congress passed the State and Local Fiscal Assistance Act and the .Comprehensive Employment and Training Act (CETA). This legislation established the concept of revenue sharing and led ultimately to the dismantling of the Office of Economic Opportunity, effectively ending the Great Society concept (Ginzberg & Solow, 1974; Katz, 2001; Matusow, 1984; Patterson, 2001).

The most significant social policy accomplishments of the Nixon administration, however, were the Social Security Amendments of 1972, which centralized and standardized aid to the disabled and low-income elderly and indexed Social Security benefits to inflation. Other programs, such as food stamps, child nutrition, and railroad retirement were also linked to cost-of-living adjustments (or COLAs). These reforms prompted predictions that official poverty in the United States might be eliminated by 1980.

In 1971 and 1972, in another attempt to curtail the growth of federal social services expenditures, the Nixon administration proposed a controversial ceiling of $2.5 billion, effective in 1973. Only 10% of these funds, to be distributed to the states on the basis of their population, could be used for services to former or potential welfare recipients (Bixby, 1990; Derthick,

1975). The controversy that this proposal generated ultimately led to the passage of Title XX of the Social Security Act in January 1975. This legislation reinforced the popular concept of federal *revenue sharing*, which provided states with maximum flexibility in planning social services while promoting fiscal accountability.

Guided by four basic principles, Title XX shaped the direction of both public and nonprofit social services during the Ford and Carter administrations and sought to alter the provision of social services to low-income persons without creating any new programs. The two most important principles were the prevention, reduction, or elimination of welfare dependency and the prevention or remediation of abuse, neglect, or exploitation of children and vulnerable adults (through an emphasis on family preservation, rehabilitation, and reunification). Two other principles were the prevention or reduction of inappropriate institutional care through the provision of alternative forms of assistance and targeting at least 50% of state funds to low-income persons.

In the late 1970s, the implementation of Title XX led to a rapid increase in federal social service expenditures at a time when economic stagnation undermined government's ability to sustain these costs. The combination of a legislatively imposed spending ceiling and the increased rate of inflation, however, effectively froze state Title XX budgets and undermined local efforts to develop innovative and comprehensive forms of services. In addition, fiscal inefficiency, program redundancy, uneven regulations and standards, and lack of integration often plagued state programs developed under Title XX (Gilbert, 1977). The growing power of suburban legislators led to a disproportionate distribution of benefits to middle-income families, further undermining the legislation's original intent to target programs for the inner-city poor. As a result, the final battle of the War on Poverty, the last echo of the Great Society concept—an attempt to develop a national social services strategy—was lost largely due to insufficient resources and a lack of political commitment (Edsall, 1991; Katz, 1989).

In sum, there was a general failure during the Nixon, Ford, and Carter administrations to assist the growing proportion of low-income and working-class families that were left behind in rapidly declining older cities. At the same time as the problems of these cities and their residents were becoming increasingly severe and resistant to solution, the country's fiscal policies at all levels had become more regressive. Reflecting an antipoor, antiurban bias, states and local governments froze social welfare expenditures and, succumbing to the growing pressure of antitax crusades, created formidable barriers to revenue enhancement, such as Proposition 13 in California. Additionally, during the 1970s, state governments failed to adjust the size of public assistance payments to keep pace with high rates of inflation. Consequently, even prior to the antiwelfare policies of presidents Reagan and Bush, the plight of low-income populations in the United States had become increasingly grave (Edsall, 1991; Jones, 1992; Katz, 1989; Patterson, 2001; Quadagno, 1994).

The Impact of the Great Society on Social Policy

In conjunction with sustained economic growth, the antipoverty policies of the Great Society produced a decline in the official poverty rate from 19% in 1964 to 11.1% in 1973. The poverty rate was now nearly one half what it was at the end of the Eisenhower era. Between 1959 and 1969, the per capita incomes of the bottom 20% of households increased faster than those of any other groups while real median family income grew by 40% (Danziger & Weinberg, 1994).

Yet, the decline in poverty varied significantly among demographic groups. Throughout the 1970s, poverty rates continued to decrease among the elderly, largely as a consequence of benefit indexing and Medicare. A virtual freeze on AFDC benefits after 1973, however, and a decline in the purchasing power of wages due to inflation produced a steady increase in poverty among women and children, particularly children of color. Thus, despite continuing growth in social spending in the 1970s, economic stagflation and unevenly distributed social policies prevented further reductions in poverty. By 1980, the poverty rate had risen to 13% (Patterson, 2001).

There are several ways of interpreting these developments. Conservative critics of government social spending, such as Charles Murray (1984) and Lawrence Mead (1986), argued that government policies from 1950 to 1980 produced negligible social benefits and, in fact, harmed those they sought to assist. These critics asserted that economic growth and not government intervention produced any reduction in poverty that occurred during this period. This view became popular during the Reagan administration, rationalizing deep cuts in antipoverty programs (Katz, 1989).

A liberal perspective on the War on Poverty and the Great Society (Danziger, 1991; Lemann, 1988, 1989) asserted that a combination of antipoverty and growth-promoting economic policies achieved some success in reducing poverty, established a stronger safety net, and cushioned the poor, to some extent, from the economic shocks of the 1970s. Social spending increases particularly benefited the elderly, whose poverty rate plummeted between 1960 and 1980 as a result of the passage of Medicare and Medicaid, the expansion of Social Security benefits, and the creation of a broad network of social services for the aging. "Poverty rose during the 1970s primarily among those groups for whom spending did not accelerate," such as children and single adults (Danziger, 1991, p. 53). Neoliberals agreed with conservatives that Great Society initiatives, such as the Model Cities Program, were wasteful or counterproductive, but they supported the liberal view that their underlying goals were worthwhile (Keisling, 1984).

Radical perspectives on this period (Abramovitz, 1992; Piven & Cloward, 1995; Quadagno, 1994) maintained that the rise and fall of social spending in the 1960s and 1970s occurred for several reasons. One was the desire of the government to dampen growing social unrest by controlling access to the labor market and its benefits (Piven & Cloward, 1995). Another was the use of social spending to reinforce prevailing gender roles regarding work and the family (Abramovitz, 1999). A third influence was persistent institutional racism, a perspective shared by some liberal analysts as well (Edsall, 1991). These analyses argued that social action, not government benevolence, produced the modest reforms of the 1960s and that, ultimately, egalitarian goals ran counter to what O'Connor (1973) termed the *accumulation function* of capitalist political economies.

The Great Society's Influence on Social Service Delivery

Analysts across the ideological spectrum generally agreed that the new social policy directions inspired by the Great Society had several significant implications for the design and implementation of social services. In the late 1960s and early 1970s, many nonprofit agencies became the beneficiaries of government efforts to contract out mandated, publicly funded services under various rubrics, including community participation and control, decentralization, the New Federalism, or revenue sharing. In fact, the primary motives were cost efficiency and political expediency.

Initially, this policy shift increased the accessibility of services to those most in need and began to reverse the trend among nonprofits since the late 1930s toward serving primarily a white, middle-income clientele. Rapidly, these agencies came to depend largely on government revenues to maintain fiscal solvency. Beginning in the mid-1970s, however, this reliance on public funds began to backfire, a trend that continues today (Gilbert, 1977; Salamon, 1993).

As economic growth stalled, social service providers encountered growing numbers of clients with increasingly complex and chronic problems. At the same time, economic stagnation and declining political support for social spending led to a withdrawal of government funding for programs directed at the effects of poverty. Increasing racial and class stratification exacerbated these trends in the 1980s (Katz, 1989; Massey & Denton, 1993; Wilson, 1996).

As urban areas became more dramatically divided along income and racial lines, nonprofit community-based organizations that served low-income areas had fewer sources of potential income. Consequently, when policy makers promoted the concepts of privatization and agency self-sufficiency beginning in the late 1970s, many nonprofit organizations lacked the resources to respond effectively to the burgeoning social costs being thrust upon them. This hampered their ability to respond to dramatic increases in homelessness and drug abuse and the emergence of the HIV/AIDS epidemic in the 1980s (Blau, 1992; Willinger & Rice, 2003).

In sum, policy changes in the 1970s altered the government's role in social service delivery and further compounded the effects of the formal separation of income maintenance and services. These effects included an increase in the public use of the private sector through contracting and greater decentralization of policy planning, which produced more variations in the scope, coverage, and quality of services. Another development was more universal coverage in child care and family planning programs. Finally, policy changes in the 1970s resulted in the creation of block grants by the Carter administration, which combined formerly categorical programs into broad programmatic areas. In return for acquiring greater control of spending patterns, states accepted a federally imposed ceiling on total social welfare expenditures. This last development became particularly significant in the 1980s and 1990s when political leaders tried to dismantle the remnants of the Great Society.

References

Abramovitz, M. (1992). The Reagan legacy: Undoing race, class, and gender accords. In J. Midgley (Ed.), The Reagan legacy and the American welfare state [Special issue]. *Journal of Sociology and Social Welfare, 22*(4), 91–110.

Abramovitz, M. (1999). *Regulating the lives of women: American social policy from colonial times to the present* (2nd ed.). Boston: South End Press.

Axinn, J., & Stern, M. (1988). *Dependency and poverty: Old problems in a new world.* Lexington, MA: Lexington Books.

Axinn, J., & Stern, M. (2008). *Social welfare: A history of the American response to need* (7th ed.). Boston: Allyn & Bacon.

Bell, W. (1983). *Contemporary social welfare.* New York: Macmillan.

Bixby, A. K. (1990). Public social welfare expenditures, fiscal years 1965–1987. *Social Security Bulletin, 53*(2), 10–26.

Blau, J. (1992). *The visible poor: Homelessness in the United States.* New York: Oxford University Press.

Brown, M. (1999). *Race, money, and the American welfare state.* Ithaca, NY: Cornell University Press.

Bussiere, E. (1997). *(Dis)entitling the poor: The Warren Court, welfare rights, and the American political tradition.* University Park: Pennsylvania State University Press.

Caudill, H. (1963). *Night comes to the Cumberlands: A biography of a depressed area.* Boston: Little, Brown.

Cloward, R., & Ohlin, L. (1960). *Delinquency and opportunity: A theory of delinquent gangs.* London: Routledge and Kegan Paul.

Danziger, S. (1991, September–October). Relearning lessons of the war on poverty. *Challenge,* pp. 53–54.

Danziger, S., & Weinberg, D. (1994). The historical record: Trends in family income, inequality, and poverty. In S. Danziger, G. D. Sandefur, & D. H. Weinberg (Eds.), *Confronting poverty: Prescriptions for change,* (pp. 18–50). Cambridge, MA: Harvard University Press.

Derthick, M. (1975). *Uncontrollable spending for social services grants.* Washington, DC: Brookings Institution Press.

Edsall, T. (1991). *Chain reaction: The impact of race, rights, and taxes on American politics.* New York: Norton.

Gilbert, N. (1977). The transformation of social services. *Social Service Review,* *53*(3), 75–91.

Gillette, M. (1996). *Launching the war on poverty: An oral history,* New York: Twayne Publishers.

Ginzberg, E., & Solow, R. M. (Eds.). (1974). *The Great Society: Lessons for the future.* New York: Basic Books.

Goldberg, G. S., & Collins, S. D. (2001). *Washington's new poor law: Welfare "reform" and the roads not taken, 1935 to the present.* New York: Apex Press.

Hamilton, D. C., & Hamilton, C. V. (1997). *The dual agenda: Race and social welfare policies of civil rights organizations.* New York: Columbia University Press.

Harrington, M. (1981), *The other America: Poverty in the United States* (Rev. ed.). New York: Macmillan. (Original work published 1962)

Helfgot, J. (1981). *Professional reforming: Mobilization for Youth and the failure of social science.* Lexington, MA: Lexington Books.

Jones, J. (1992). *The dispossessed: America's underclasses from the civil war to the present.* New York: Basic Books.

Katz, M. (1989). *The undeserving poor: From the war on poverty to the war on welfare.* New York: Pantheon Books.

Katz, M. (2001). *The price of citizenship: Redefining the American welfare state.* New York: Henry Holt.

Keisling, P. (1984, December). Lessons of the great society. *The Washington Monthly,* pp. 50–53.

Kornbluh, F. (1997). To fulfill their "rightly needs": Consumerism and the national welfare rights movement. *Radical History Review, 69,* 76–113.

Kotz, N., & Kotz, M. (1977). *A passion for equality: George Wiley and the movement.* New York: Norton.

Lemann. N. (1988, December). The unfinished war: Part I. *Atlantic Monthly,* pp. 37–56.

Lemann. N. (1989, January). The unfinished war: Part II. *Atlantic Monthly,* pp. 53–68.

Lemann, N. (1991). *The promised land: The great black migration and how it changed America.* New York: Alfred Knopf.

Lewis, O. (1996). *La Vida: A Puerto Rican family in the culture of poverty—San Juan and New York.* New York: Random House. (Original work published 1966)

Massey, D. S., & Denton, N.A. (1993). *American apartheid: Segregation and the making of the underclass.* Cambridge, MA: Harvard University Press.

Matusow, A. J. (1984). *The unraveling of America: A history of liberalism in the 1960s.* New York: Harper & Row.

Mead, L. (1986). *Beyond entitlement: The social obligations of citizenship.* New York: Free Press.

Moynihan, D. P. (1969). *Maximum feasible misunderstanding.* New York: Free Press.

Moynihan, D. P. (1973). *The politics of a guaranteed income: The Nixon administration and the family assistance plan.* New York: Random House.

Murray, C. (1984). *Losing ground: American social policy, 1950–1980.* New York: Basic Books.

Nadasen, P. (2005). *Welfare warriors: The welfare rights movement in the United States.* New York: Routledge.

O'Connor, J. (1973). *The fiscal crisis of the state.* New York: St. Martin's Press.

Patterson, J. (2001). *America's struggle against poverty in the twentieth century.* Cambridge, MA: Harvard University Press.

Piven, F. F., & Cloward, R. (1977). *Poor people's movements: How they succeed, why they fail*. New York: Vintage Books.

Piven, F. F., & Cloward, R. (1995). *Regulating the poor: The functions of public welfare* (Rev. ed.). New York: Vintage Books.

Quadagno, J. (1994*)*. *The color of welfare: How racism undermined the war on poverty*. New York: Oxford University Press.

Reisch, M. (1996). Urbanisation et politique sociale aux États-Unis [Urbanization and social politics of the United States]. *Revue M, 85–86,* 9–14.

Reisch, M., & Andrews, J. L. (2001). *The road not taken: A history of radical social work in the United States*. Philadelphia: Brunner Routledge.

Reisch, M., & Wenocur, S. (1986). The future of community organization in social work: Social activism and the politics of profession-building. *Social Service Review, 60*(1), 70–91.

Rose, N. (1995). *Workfare or fair work: Women, welfare and government programs*. New Brunswick, NJ: Rutgers University Press.

Rose, S. M. (1972). *The betrayal of the poor: The transformation of community action*. Cambridge, MA: Schenkman.

Rose, S. M., & Black, B. L. (1985). *Advocacy and empowerment: Mental health care in the community*. Boston: Routledge and Kegan Paul.

Ryan, W. (1971). *Blaming the victim*. New York: Vintage.

Sale, K. (1976). *Power shift: The rise of the Southern rim and the challenge to the Eastern establishment*. New York: Random House.

Salamon, L. M. (1993). The marketization of welfare: Changing nonprofit and for-profit roles in the American welfare state. *Social Service Review, 67*(1), 17–39.

Schrecker, E. (1998). *Many are the crimes: McCarthyism in America*. Boston: Little, Brown.

Stoltzfus, E. (2003). *Citizen, mother, worker: Debating public responsibility for child care after the Second World War*. Chapel Hill: University of North Carolina Press.

Sugrue, T. (1996). *The origins of the urban crisis: Race and inequality in postwar Detroit*. Princeton, NJ: Princeton University Press.

West, G. (1981). *The national welfare rights movement: The social protest of poor women*. New York: Praeger.

Willinger, B. I., & Rice, A. (Eds.). (2003). *A history of AIDS social work in hospitals: A daring response to an epidemic*. Binghamton, NY: Haworth Press.

Wilson, W. J. (1996). *When work disappears: The world of the new urban poor*. New York: Alfred Knopf.

11

Social Policy

Reagan and Beyond

David Stoesz

Following a half-century of liberal hegemony in social policy, a series of Republican presidents consolidated conservatism as the dominant ideology in America. Beginning with the Social Security Act of 1935, liberals had crafted a public philosophy that had eclipsed conservatism up to that time, at least with respect to domestic policy. Further elaborated during the Great Society of the mid-1960s, liberalism was so ascendant that few would have prophesied its demise. Even Republican presidents, such as Nixon, affirmed the American welfare state and further expanded its provisions. Yet, the liberal plan to replicate the northern European welfare state in the United States faltered. The Reagan presidency pushed social policy to the Right, away from unconditional federal entitlements and toward temporary state-managed, work-oriented benefits—in the words of one commentator, "the work-ethic state" (Kaus, 1992). Conservative momentum not only contributed to a right-wing welfare reform agenda signed by a Democratic president, but Republicans also introduced their own domestic policy initiatives, reforming education through the No Child Left Behind Act, even adding a new entitlement, the prescription drug benefit through Part D of Medicare. In this fundamental shift, the United States paralleled Great Britain, leading the way to a new formulation of social policy among the industrialized nations (Yergin & Stanislaw, 1998).

Antecedents to Conservatism

The conservative assault on the liberal welfare state was waged on both philosophical and programmatic fronts. In the most sweeping of philosophical treatments, Milton and Rose Friedman (1988) posited three epochs in the "tides of man": the rise of laissez-faire during the 19th century (the Adam

Smith tide), the rise of the welfare state during the 20th century (the Fabian [Marxist] tide), and the resurgence of free markets during the coming century (the Hayek tide). In naming the latter after Frederich von Hayek, the Friedmans honored a philosopher, little known to liberals, who not only foretold the demise of communism, but also predicted the globalization of capitalism. Hayek would become a cornerstone of the intellectual foundations of the most influential institutions promoting conservatism in America: the economics department of the University of Chicago and the Heritage Foundation in Washington, D.C.

Conservative strategy was abetted by academics who had reservations about liberal social policy in general, and welfare policy in particular. George Gilder (1981) suggested that liberal social programs induced dependency on the part of the poor; what the poor needed most was not more government programs, but "the spur of their own poverty" (p. 118). Charles Murray (1984) proposed even more draconian measures: "scrapping the entire federal welfare and income support structure for working-aged persons, including Aid to Families with Dependent Children, Medicaid, Food Stamps, Unemployment Insurance, Workers Compensation, subsidized housing, disability and the rest" (pp. 227–228). More moderately, Lawrence Mead (1986) proposed making receipt of welfare conditional on specific behavioral standards. While the research and conclusions of Gilder, Murray, and Mead were hotly disputed by liberal scholars, conservatives were securing the endorsements of neoconservatives, former liberals, such as Daniel Patrick Moynihan, who had become disillusioned with the liberal direction of social policy (Moynihan, 1988).

The conservative case against the welfare state would have consisted of little more than ideological sniping had not wealthy individuals and corporations funded the establishment of a network of policy institutes to promote the conservative agenda. During the 1980s, policy institutes, or "think tanks," that subscribed to conservative philosophy blossomed around the nation. The American Enterprise Institute, the Heritage Foundation, the Cato Institute, and the Hudson Institute of Washington, D.C., were complemented by the Manhattan Institute of New York City and the Hoover Institution of Stanford (Smith, 1991). Assuming an aggressive stance compared to the more staid liberal institutes, such as the Brookings Institution, the conservative think tanks viewed their mission as if it were a crusade. Writing shortly after the Reagan presidential election victory, a Heritage Foundation vice president observed that conservative think tanks could "deploy formidable armies on the battlefield of ideas—forces which [conservative] traditionalist movements previously lacked" (Pines, 1982, p. 254).

The Reagan Presidency

The conservative strategy against the welfare states was threefold: (1) end liberal dominance of social policy, (2) whenever possible reroute public policy through the states or the private sector, and (3) preclude the prospect of a resurgence in social entitlements (Blumenthal & Edsall, 1988). The end of the millennium would demonstrate how enormously successful conservatives had become in redefining public philosophy, though few would have credited a compliant Democratic Party with this transformation. An example of Democratic sclerosis can be found in testimony preceding the first Reagan legislation targeting liberal social programs, the 1981 Omnibus Budget and Reconciliation Act (OBRA). Democrats were so bewildered by the conservative legislative assault that, when the administration's new director of the Office of Management and the Budget, David Stockman, "cooked" the budget numbers affirming the soundness of the Reagan proposal, the House Democratic leadership was completely hoodwinked.

By 1983, the consequences of the 1981 OBRA were clear. Some 408,000 families had been terminated from welfare; another 299,000 had their benefits reduced. Among the casualties were the working poor. Thirty-five percent of adults who persisted in working while on public assistance were removed from the program. In addition to cuts in cash welfare, OBRA consolidated many categorical programs into block grants, in the process cutting appropriations. Accompanying the construction of the Social Services Block Grant, for example, was a 25% reduction in funding (Stoesz, 1996).

The most profound impacts of the Reagan presidency on social policy were the 1983 amendments to the Social Security Act. To block a rapidly hemorrhaging trust fund, Reagan established a bipartisan commission under the direction of Alan Greenspan to restore the program's health. The suggestions of the Greenspan Commission, later adopted by Congress, promised to keep Social Security solvent well into the 21st century. The 1983 amendments to Social Security were incremental adjustments, but the consequences of these changes had radical implications. Modest changes included advancing the age of eligibility for benefits, increasing the federal withholding tax, including federal and nonprofit employees in the program, a six-month delay in benefit increases, and modifying the indexing formula. Altogether, the Greenspan Commission assured that Social Security would generate unprecedented surpluses in anticipation of the retirement of baby boomers. Conveniently, the surplus generated by the 1983 Social Security amendments cushioned the massive federal budget deficits that grew during subsequent decades.

The Family Support Act (FSA) of 1988 anticipated the most incisive strike against the welfare state, the 1996 welfare reform legislation known as the Personal Responsibility and Work Opportunity Reconciliation Act. Foremost, FSA mandated that mothers on public assistance who did not have exempting conditions would be required to participate in education, training activities, or find work in exchange for benefits. The FSA incorporated incentives as well as penalties: the carrot consisted on the Job Opportunities and Basic Skills (JOBS) program that included "transitional benefits" (the continuation of child care, Medicaid, and transportation for one year after securing a job); the stick was the termination of benefits for recipients who refused to participate in "welfare-to-work." FSA was budgeted at only $3.34 billion over five years. Significantly, during this period, states were encouraged to obtain federal waivers for innovative demonstrations designed to wean poor mothers from public assistance and assist them in becoming economically self-sufficient (Stoesz & Karger, 1989).

The Reagan legacy extended far beyond these legislative triumphs, however. His vice president assumed the White House, and, although the first Bush presidency was limited to one term, it witnessed an underappreciated addition to social policy: the Americans with Disabilities Act (ADA). Liberals praised the implementation of ADA since it extended civil rights to the disabled; conservatives lauded ADA for a different reason. Contrary to traditional disability programs, such as Supplemental Security Income, which assumed that the disabled would need assistance because they could not participate in activities such as work, the ADA evolved from a different orientation: the disabled were entitled to—indeed, would insist on—being involved in the mainstream. Rather than being unable to work, the disabled, according to the ADA, were capable employees if only barriers to the labor market were removed.

Another legacy of the Reagan presidency was its influence on the Democratic Party. Reflecting on the failed presidential candidacies of Jimmy Carter in 1980, Walter Mondale in 1984, and Michael Dukakis in 1988, Charles Peters, editor of the *Washington Monthly* coined the term *neoliberalism* in proposing an alternative to the welfare liberalism that had guided the Democratic Party. "We still believe in liberty and justice and a fair chance for all, in mercy for the afflicted, and help for the down and out," wrote Peters, attempting to pull Democrats to the Right, "but we no longer automatically favor unions and big government or oppose the military and big business" (Peters, 1983, p. 12). Peters was not alone among progressively oriented Democrats who perceived the party as having moved too far to the Left.

The Clinton Presidency

Success of the conservative ideological juggernaut led Democratic leaders to reassess the party's adherence to welfare liberalism. During the late-1980s, several prominent Democrats—Paul Tsongas, Richard Gebhardt, Sam Nunn, and Bill Bradley—founded the Democratic Leadership Council (DLC) to pull the party toward the center. The DLC hired Al From as its political director and soon established a think tank, the Progressive Policy Institute (PPI), under the direction of Will Marshall. The DLC and PPI scored a major victory when the Democratic presidential ticket featured two additional founders: Bill Clinton and Al Gore. After a decade of frustration, Democrats had found the key to the White House. Success, however, entailed one significant concession: abandoning welfare liberalism.

Much of Clinton's presidential victory was attributed to his claim to be a "new Democrat," one who eschewed sentimental liberalism as much as retrograde conservatism. As a Democratic nominee, Clinton had identified himself as pursuing a "new covenant" that would reflect a "third way" in American politics. As president, however, Clinton proved less capable of moving beyond his ubiquitous references to "change" and toward the institutionalization of a post-liberal and post-conservative orientation to social policy. Indeed, the tentativeness of Clinton's control of the executive branch was conspicuous during the ill-fated initiatives of 1993.

Confronted, on entering the White House, by the massive deficits generated by the Reagan-Bush era, Clinton found little fiscal room for his investment strategy to rebuild the nation's physical and social infrastructure. Clinton resolved the dilemma by siding with Federal Reserve Chairman Alan Greenspan, who advised against massive tax increases that would be necessitated by major new federal initiatives. Accordingly, Clinton's 1993 budget consisted of much line-item reshuffling with only token allocations for those projects that had identified candidate Clinton as a "new" Democrat. The primary exception was a major expansion of the Earned Income Tax Credit for low-wage workers, an income subsidy program long favored by conservatives as an alternative to welfare. Clinton's 1993 budget squeaked through a Democratic Congress by single votes in both chambers, the slimmest margin in the history of the Republic.

A minimalist budget notwithstanding, 1993 would become most associated with failed health care reform. The Clinton Health Security Act (HSA) was the product of a protracted and elaborate planning process managed by White House adviser and corporate savant Ira Magaziner and overseen by First Lady Hillary Rodham Clinton. HSA was designed as a national health insurance program that would be administered by health alliances, which would subscribe large numbers of members over entire regions. By extending a health maintenance organization approach to health care to the entire population, HSA was an industry-friendly proposal. The requirement that employers would have to finance much of the initiative and the elimination of small health insurers spelled the demise of the HSA, however. In the face of the increasingly bitter opposition by the business community, Clinton admitted defeat of the HSA. Years later, planners of the HSA would be fined by the courts for having plotted the scheme in violation of federal requirements that such planning be open to the public.

The 1993 budget and health reform initiatives were soon overshadowed by the 1994 mid-term congressional election. White House ineptitude and Democratic intransigence in Congress bred contempt among voters, who took revenge at the polls, electing the first Republican-controlled Congress in 40 years. A shocked Clinton took stock of his political fortunes and quickly veered Right. After the disastrous 1994 congressional election, Clinton showed his conservative colors by announcing in his 1996 State of the Union address that "the era of big government is over." Democrat survivors in Congress were heartened by Clinton's embrace of an increase in the minimum wage, elevating it in two stages to $5.15 per hour; yet, any suspicion of the president's inherent liberal tendencies were soon dashed. After vetoing two welfare reform proposals forwarded by a conservative

Congress, Clinton signed the third. Thus, on the eve of his 1996 reelection campaign, Clinton appeared to sacrifice the well-being of America's poor children on the altar of his reelection.

In signing the 1996 Personal Responsibility and Work Opportunity Reconciliation Act (PRWORA), Clinton cashiered the 60-year-old entitlement for poor families. Aid to Families with Dependent Children was replaced with Temporary Assistance for Needy Families (TANF), a block grant that was devolved to the states. In place of the open-ended entitlement, states would receive finite funding, the amount predicated on caseload levels of the early 1990s. Beyond a few requirements—states must have 75% of one adult from two-parent households in the labor market by 1997, 25% of single heads of households in the labor market by 1997, and 50% of single heads of households working by 2002—states were free to exercise latitude in managing their block grants. PRWORA established a 5-year lifetime limit on receipt of welfare and allowed the states to establish shorter time limits. The only funding restriction was that 80% of the block grant had to be committed to "maintenance of effort," in other words, to welfare recipients (Karger & Stoesz, 1997).

Response to PRWORA was immediate and volatile. The conservative reaction to federal welfare reform was euphoric. Since passage of Family Support Act in 1988, some 40 states had received federal waivers to experiment with welfare reform, most of which focused on pushing mothers on public assistance into the labor market. Conservatives touted state and local welfare reforms that reduced caseloads sharply, increasing earnings of welfare recipients and leaving localities and states with substantial savings. Contrary to liberal fears that welfare reform would provoke a "race to the bottom" in which states would compete in lowering benefits to make welfare less and less desirable, states tended to retain benefits levels; some, such as Wisconsin, actually increased programs to help welfare recipients find and keep jobs (Vobejda, 1998). In the absence of evidence indicating otherwise, conservatives were free to pronounce welfare reform a uniform success both in terms of the increasing work experience of welfare beneficiaries as well as the absence of the disastrous consequences voiced by liberal critics.

Liberals, on the other hand, were horrified. Speaking for many, Peter Edelman (1997), an advocate for the poor as well as the husband of Children's Defense Fund executive Marian Wright Edelman, condemned PRWORA as "the worst thing that Bill Clinton has done." Citing evidence of tentative attachment to the labor market, liberal policy analysts contended that the benefits of welfare-to-work programs were temporary and that long-term consequences were cause for much less optimism, particularly once time limits were considered (Stoesz, 1996). If, as conservatives claimed, the benefits were universal, liberals contended that was largely because states had tracked neither those families that had left public assistance voluntarily nor those who had been terminated involuntarily from aid. Although state welfare demonstrations did yield positive outcomes, liberals pointed out that these were quite modest over the long run and vaulted relatively few families out of poverty (Friedlander & Burtless, 1995; Gueron & Pauly, 1991).

In fairness, the Clinton presidency featured a number of progressive policies. Immediately upon entering office, the president reversed several abortion-restrictive executive orders. Clinton's adherence to affirmative action was unshakable, even when states and localities reversed their commitment to equality by race and gender. The Clinton presidency oversaw the establishment of "empowerment zones" in order to reverse the deterioration of urban and rural regions, a long-overdue increase in the minimum wage, and the extension of health care to the nation's poor children. And the Clinton AmeriCorps initiative reacquainted tens of thousands of Americans with the virtue of volunteerism while providing essential services to disadvantaged communities. Compared to earlier initiatives, such as Johnson's War on Poverty, however, Clinton's initiatives appeared modest if not puny.

As president, Clinton behaved less like a liberal Democrat and more like a moderate Republican: his social policy reinforced the work ethic, while diminishing welfare entitlements; tax policy afforded modest wage subsidies to the working poor; the administration's social policy innovations were small scale and overshadowed by reversals (the demise of health care reform) or inaction (the failure to reform social insurance, particularly Medicare and Social Security). Just at the point when Clinton seemed poised to use an anticipated budget surplus for program innovation, his presidency was rocked by a sex scandal. Despite Clinton's two-term presidency—the first since Franklin Delano Roosevelt—the Democratic Party seemed unable to attract promising pols. Except for the vice president and first lady, Clinton's following of "new" young Democrats appeared to be few in number. After signing the 1996 welfare reform legislation on the eve of his presidential campaign, the primary question regarding a Clinton reelection was whether it represented not a second term of the Clinton presidency but rather the fifth term of Ronald Reagan's.

The millennium found American social policy in a period of transformation. Since the 1980s, the policy template of welfare liberalism—federally assured benefits available unconditionally as an open-ended entitlement—seemed an artifact of the New Deal and the War on Poverty. In order to reform the welfare state, the Reagan and Bush administrations introduced a conservative direction in social policy, one that clearly resonated with American voters. Rather than revive liberalism, Clinton actually furthered the conservative momentum in public policy. Liberal human service professionals, for their part, reacted defensively to conservatism in Congress and the White House. Social policy advocates defended the American welfare state, whenever possible protecting the more vulnerable public assistance program while keeping a wary eye on the social insurances. Despite the opportunities to redefine social policy so that it would be more consonant with a service- and information-oriented postindustrial environment, the liberal reflex was to defend the industrial era welfare state (Gans, 1995).

The Presidency of George W. Bush

The presidency of George W. Bush further propelled public policy to the Right. Invoking "compassionate conservatism," Bush advocated a series of initiatives that challenged policy areas traditionally held by liberal Democrats. Although Congress failed to pass the Bush "faith-based services" agenda, the White House used an executive order to divert $2 billion to religiously inspired service providers. Bush recruited congressional Democrats to pass the No Child Left Behind Act, an educational reform requiring that states demonstrate the proficiency of local schools vis-à-vis a rigorous testing agenda. Subsequently, Bush squeezed through Congress a prescription drug benefit, adding Part D to Medicare. At the same time, the White House was successful in executing a series of tax cuts, transforming the budget surplus inherited from the Clinton presidency into looming deficits. The tax cuts had been a staple of conservative activist Grover Norquist, director of Americans for Tax Reform, who advocated a "starve the beast" strategy of entitlement reform. Conceding that social programs were well defended politically, Norquist contended that social spending could be contained and new entitlements precluded by deep reductions in federal revenues, hence a series of tax cuts. Norquist quipped that the objective was to reduce government "down to the size where we can drown it in the bathtub" (Gourevitch, 2004, p. 37).

The conservative juggernaut ran aground during the second term of George W. Bush's presidency. Capitalizing on public sympathy after the terrorist attack of September 11, 2001, the Bush White House oversaw a rapid mobilization of the military and the creation of the Department of Homeland Security in order to prosecute a "war on terrorism." Through misuse of intelligence, Bush convinced Congress to authorize an invasion of Iraq. Public support of the commander in chief contributed to Bush's reelection. After a successful military invasion, however, the project faltered due to poor advance planning and inept nation building (Chandrasekaran, 2006). Compounding problems related to the nation's military adventure in Iraq, the worst natural disaster in the nation's history struck. Hurricane Katrina wiped out dozens of communities along the Gulf Coast and inundated large parts of New Orleans. After applauding relief efforts, President Bush was forced to admit bungling by the Federal Emergency Management Agency and to remove its director. By the 2006 midterm elections, the ineptitude of the Bush White House was causing congressional Republicans to distance themselves from the president.

The Future of Social Policy

As the minority party, Democrats stubbornly held to traditional positions. In one of their few victories during the second Bush presidency, liberals effectively nixed Republican attempts to privatize Social Security. Democrats complained bitterly that the Bush tax cuts were exacerbating economic inequality in America—to the point that the chasm between rich and poor rivaled the period of the robber barons prior to the Progressive Era. Yet, Democratic liberals were unable to craft a convincing vision for future social policy. "The Democrats have generally spent their energy defending past accomplishments, from Social Security to Medicare, rather than seeking to refocus that basic commitment to the middle class and the poor into ideas that reflect how the nation has changed since those laws were passed," noted a journalist (Clymer, 2003, p. 1). "American liberalism, as both a body of ideas and a political coalition, is a shadow of its former self," echoed two British observers. "It is remarkable how far the best liberal thinkers have been reduced to reacting to conservative arguments" (Micklethwait & Wooldridge, 2004, p. 383). In a reversal of Harry Hopkins's strategy of taxing the rich to fund benefits for the poor and working classes, in return for which they would vote Democratic, conservatives used tax cuts to allow people to keep their income, enabling them to use it as they wished and, in the process, bypassing the social welfare bureaucracy—a strategy that encouraged people to vote Republican.

The 2006 midterm election was a referendum on Bush's leadership and, therein, on the future of conservatism. Democrats regained both chambers of Congress, a victory that surprised the president who quickly made conciliatory overtures to Democrats. Chastened conservatives took stock. Conservative philosopher William Buckley, founder of the *National Review* magazine, opined that "The conservative movement is in a sense inanimate, compared to 20 or 30 years ago" (Kirkpatrick & DeParle, 2006, p. WK-4). Similarly, right-wing pundit David Brooks (2006) wrote that the election was a watershed in the nation's ideological history: "Say goodbye to the era of conservative dominance that began in 1980" (p. A31). The Democratic takeover of Congress notwithstanding, conservative apologists cited two reasons that their movement was far from finished: First, many of the Democrats who had defeated Republicans were ideologically center-right, favoring gun rights, opposing abortion, and advocating the containment of federal spending. Second, Democrats had yet to craft an alternative platform for governing that would reassert liberalism as the nation's public philosophy. In this respect, the 2006 midterm election may have been a midcourse correction in conservative governance.

The impending 2008 presidential election may well find the nation beset by ideological gridlock due to an intransigent conservative president and a fractious Congress. The result may lead to a rethinking of ideological conventions. Compassionate conservatism rang hollow with respect to the pressing problems with which many Americans struggled: faulty schools, lack of health insurance, stagnant incomes, and escalating college tuition. Yet, liberals were reluctant to restructure Social Security and Medicare despite the enormous costs expected with the retirement of 70 million baby boomers. In response to this political stalemate, radical pragmatism has been proposed, a strategy that was post-conservative as well as post-liberal. Radical pragmatism consisted of three themes: accelerate upward mobility by wage supplements and asset building, empower citizens by expanding choice with respect to the services and benefits they receive, and restructure government through reassigning public responsibilities to local entities, thus downsizing the welfare bureaucracy (Stoesz, 2005). Just as today's dominant ideologies, liberalism and conservatism, were manifestations of the industrial era, radical pragmatism is more congruent with the circumstances of the postindustrial era.

References

Blumenthal, S., & Edsall, T. (1988). *The Reagan legacy.* New York: Pantheon.

Brooks, D. (2006, November 9). The middle muscles in. *New York Times,* pp. A31, A33.

Chandrasekaran, R. (2006). *Imperial life in the emerald city.* New York: Knopf.

Clymer, A. (2003, May 26). Democrats seek a stronger focus, and money. *New York Times.* Available at http://nytimes.com

Edelman, P. (1997, March). The worst thing Bill Clinton has done. *Atlantic Monthly, 279,* 43–58.

Friedlander, D., & Burtless, G. (1995). *Five years after.* New York: Russell Sage Foundation.

Friedman, M., & Friedman, R. (1988). The tide in the affairs of men. In A. Anderson & D. Bark (Eds.), *Thinking about America* (pp. 455–468). Stanford, CA: Hoover Institution.

Gans, H. (1995). *The war against the poor.* New York: Basic Books.

Gilder, G. (1981). *Wealth and poverty.* New York: Basic Books.

Gourevitch, P. (2004, April 12). Fight on the right. *The New Yorker, 8,* 34–39.

Gueron, J., & Pauly, E. (1991). *From welfare to work.* New York: Russell Sage Foundation.

Karger, H., & Stoesz, D. (1997). *American social welfare policy* (3rd ed.). New York: Longman.

Kaus, M. (1992). *The end of equality.* New York: Basic Books.

Kirkpatrick, D., & DeParle, J. (2006). For conservatives, it's back to basics. *New York Times,* Section 4, pp. 1, 4.

Mead, L. (1986). *Beyond entitlement.* New York: Free Press.

Micklethwait, J., & Wooldridge, A. (2004). *The right nation.* New York: Penguin.

Moynihan, D. (1988). *Came the revolution.* San Diego, CA: Harcourt Brace Jovanovich.

Murray, C. (1984). *Losing ground.* New York: Basic Books.

Peters, C. (1983). A new politics. *Public Welfare, 18,* 12–14.

Pines, B. (1982). *Back to basics.* New York: William Morrow.

Smith, J. (1991). *The idea brokers.* New York: Free Press.

Stoesz, D. (1996). *Small change: Domestic policy under the Clinton presidency.* New York: Longman.

Stoesz, D. (2005). *Quixote's ghost: The right, the liberati, and the future of social policy.* New York: Oxford University Press.

Stoesz, D., & Karger, H. (1989, March–April). When welfare reform fails. *Tikkun, 4,* 23–25, 118–122.

Vobejda, B. (1998). Fewer welfare recipients. *Washington Post Weekly,* February 16.

Yergin, D., & Stanislaw, J. (1998). *The commanding heights.* New York: Simon & Schuster.

PART III

The Political Economy of Social Policy

This part of the handbook provides an overview of the major theoretical and ideological orientations in social policy thinking today. These orientations provide very different insights into social policy and offer very different normative perspectives on how social policy affects social well-being. They reveal that social policy is not a technical or politically neutral activity but rather that it draws on wider ideological beliefs about how social life should be organized and how the ideals of the Good Society can be realized. These beliefs comprise a rich and complex political economy, which frames discussions about social policy today.

The first chapter in Part III discusses the institutional approach to social policy. Systematically formulated by scholars at the London School of Economics in England in the 1950s and 1960s, it advocates extensive government involvement in social welfare. The institutionalists dominated the social policy field for many years. Their ideas also had considerable appeal in the United States and provided a normative basis for social policy, which was widely accepted in social work and social policy circles.

The institutional approach was challenged by conservative thinkers whose ideas about social policy became ascendant in the 1980s. As shown in Chapter 13, the conservative approach has generally been critical of state intervention and has advocated a larger role for families, the nonprofit sector, and commercial providers in social welfare. It stresses the importance of personal responsibility and individual effort. However, the conservative approach gives expression to diverse normative themes. Indeed, not all conservatives are opposed to government intervention in social welfare. Some believe governments have an important role to play in promoting individual responsibility and traditional values.

Chapter 14 discusses the critical approach to social policy. Although this approach is rooted in Marxist thought, it has incorporated a variety of perspectives that transcend classical Marxist analysis. These include the perspectives of the Frankfurt school as well as the insights of critical post-modernists, feminists, and multiculturalists. Critical ideas also characterize radical populist movements that have challenged both conservative and institutional social policy approaches.

The pluralist approach, which is discussed in the next chapter, advocates a mix of government, nonprofit, and commercial interventions in social welfare. Pluralism opposes the emphasis on government exclusivity that characterizes institutionalist thought and rejects the institutionalists' claim that government is the best agent for promoting peoples' welfare. Although recognizing that government has a role to play, pluralists believe that social well-being can be promoted by a variety of agents.

Drawing on the insights of critical theory, Chapter 16 offers a feminist perspective on social policy. It shows that the gender dimension has, until fairly recently, been seriously neglected in social policy analysis. It demonstrates that gender issues are central to the field and that social policy scholarship must pay more attention to these issues.

Chapter 17 makes a similar point about issues of race and cultural diversity. Even though social policy invariably has implications for race and ethnicity, it is only recently that proper attention to these dimensions of social life has been paid. Historical accounts of the evolution of social policy have tended to downplay the importance of race and cultural diversity and, as the authors of Chapter 17 show, this has distorted historical realities. As they point out, a proper analysis of social policy in the United States must examine the ever-present reality of race and ensure that issues of ethnicity are properly recognized.

As discussed in Chapter 18, social development is a relatively new perspective in social policy even though it originated in the developing countries in the 1950s. It is based on the argument that people's welfare is inextricably linked to the economy and that social and economic policies need to be harmonized. Economic development policies that raise the standards of living of all should be actively fostered and should be linked to social welfare policies and programs that contribute positively to economic development.

The relationship between social policy and the environment is examined in Chapter 19. Although environmental issues have been neglected by social policy scholars, greater public concern about the future of the environment requires that social policy analysis take these issues into account. The authors argue for the adoption of ecologically sensitive social policies that not only enhance peoples' welfare but do so in conjunction with sustainable development policies that link issues of social welfare to wider environmental concerns.

12

The Institutional Approach to Social Policy

James Midgley

Like other normative approaches to social policy, the institutional approach reflects a number of values and beliefs about how peoples' welfare can best be enhanced. The most fundamental of these is that social well-being is best promoted through collective action and the pooling of resources. Institutionalists point out that, throughout history, people have not only relied on their own efforts and the support of their families but have formed local, community-based associations and organizations that augment individual and family resources to promote the well-being of the community as a whole. Cooperatives of many kinds have also emerged to pool resources and encourage collective action to attain economic, cultural, and social goals. During the period of rapid industrialization in the 19th century, workers formed trade unions and other associations to protect their interests and promote their well-being. In the 20th century, as working people and their representatives were able to exercise significant political influence, the agency of government was increasingly used to promote welfare goals. Progressive social legislation that regulated employment and working conditions and created new social service and income maintenance and support programs became the new collective means for achieving social well-being. As a result of these developments, supporters of the institutional approach believe that social welfare can best be enhanced through the agency of government. Inspired by progressive liberalism and social democratic ideology, they contend that social needs should be addressed through a range of statutory interventions, including fiscal measures, legal regulations, and the provision of a comprehensive system of social services. They claim that these interventions *institutionalize* social programs, embedding them in the very fabric of society.

Institutional ideas were widely applied in social policy making during the 20th century, and they legitimated and even shaped the expansion of government intervention in social welfare. Institutional social policies and programs are characterized by their statutory authority, public funding, bureaucratic direction, and universality of coverage. One of the most frequently cited examples of an institutional social program is the British national health service, which provides a range of tax-funded medical and health services to all citizens, irrespective of their ability to pay. Tax-funded child benefits and universal social insurance programs are also typical of institutional social welfare.

Although most Western nations have programs of this kind, those in Western Europe, and particularly in Scandinavia, are usually extolled for exemplifying institutional ideals. Because these countries introduced extensive social service programs that cater to the population as a whole, they are often described as *welfare states*. It is claimed that these welfare states successfully modified the economic market to combine the wealth-generating power of capitalism with social goals and that they found a viable middle way between unfettered capitalism and authoritarian communism.

This chapter describes the institutional approach. It traces it historical origins in the progressive reforms of social democratic and liberal governments that sought to expand statutory social welfare at the end of the 19th century and during the 20th century. The writings of academic thinkers who advocated institutional ideas are also discussed. After summarizing the salient features of the institutional approach, the chapter concludes with a brief appraisal of its contribution, as well as an assessment of its potential role in shaping social policy making in the future.

History of the Institutional Approach

The evolution of the institutional approach was propelled both by ideas and by developments in the world of politics and policy making. Academic scholars played a critical role in formulating institutional principles, drawing on religious teachings, progressive social thought, utopianism and socialism. Their writings melded with the activism of working people, the campaigns of social reformers, and the political programs of progressive governments committed to harnessing the resources and power of the state to promote social welfare goals.

As was noted earlier, the institutionalist agenda is motivated by the belief that peoples' welfare can best be enhanced through the agency of government. Historically, the governments of the Western countries played a very limited role in social welfare, and social well-being was regarded as the product of individual effort, supported by families and kin, and, in the case of those who could not meet their own needs, as the benevolent work of the church and the charities. It was during the reign of Elizabeth I that the state first began to assume a significant role in social welfare. The Elizabethan Poor Law of 1601 is regarded as a milestone in the evolution of public welfare, laying the foundation for the expansion of state involvement both in Britain and the United States.

The idea that governments should alleviate social distress and enhance the welfare of their citizens gained momentum during the late 19th century. Reform-minded politicians, intellectuals, trade union members, religious leaders, and middle-class activists believed that governments could ameliorate social wrongs and improve social conditions, and they urged political leaders to take action to address these ills. They drew extensively on the findings of social surveys and statistical studies to expose social injustice and social neglect, and they campaigned for the regulation of working conditions, the prohibition of child labor, the end of economic exploitation, and the introduction of social services. Because of these activities, the end of the 19th century is known as the Progressive Era. As was shown in Chapter 8, the efforts of progressive reformers resulted in the creation of new social programs such as mothers' pensions and workmen's compensation. However, efforts to introduce health or unemployment insurance and comprehensive contributory retirement pensions were not successful at the time.

Another important development was the introduction of social insurance. Social insurance originated in Germany in the 1880s and was soon adopted in other European countries. In the United States, the campaign to introduce social insurance resulted in the enactment of the Social Security Act in 1935. The Social Security Act is regarded by many social policy writers as the crowning achievement of the New Deal and the nation's single most important social welfare program. Social Security is also one of a few social programs in the United States to be based on institutional ideas.

Many scholars believe that the New Deal institutionalized the principle of government responsibility for social welfare (Dolgoff & Feldstein, 1980). However, others do not think that the American people have ever fully accepted the principle of government welfare responsibility, and they contend that the United States remains a "reluctant welfare state" (Jansson, 2005). Nevertheless, the New Deal did lay the foundations for the subsequent expansion of social policy during the 1960s when President Johnson's War on Poverty and Great Society programs were established. Together with the Progressive Era, periods of social policy expansion such as the New Deal and the War on Poverty were significant not only because government involvement in social welfare increased but also because they popularized the idea that social welfare is the legitimate responsibility of the state.

Theoretical Ideas

By the 1950s, academic writers began to formulate theories about the role of the state in social welfare. Scholars such as Harold Wilensky and Charles Lebeaux (1958) were among the first to provide an explanation of the growth of government involvement in social welfare in the 20th century.

They expounded the thesis that the expansion of government responsibility is an inevitable by-product of industrialization. Because industrialization undermined traditional welfare institutions (such as the extended family) and created new social problems that demanded concerted action, governments were compelled to intervene. Marxist writers (Ginsberg, 1979; Gough, 1979; Offe, 1984) rejected this interpretation, arguing instead that the state became involved in social welfare to prevent social unrest and preserve the interests of capitalism. Social democratic scholars (Korpi, 1983; Stephens, 1979) took a different position, claiming that the expansion of government involvement in social welfare was the result of the struggle of working-class movements and their allies to use the state for progressive social purposes. These theoretical explanations were augmented by normative accounts that were less concerned with the causes of the expansion of government involvement in social welfare than with its legitimation. Although Wilensky and Lebeaux sought to explain the expansion of government social programs, they formulated an important typology of two major social policy approaches that subsequently had a powerful influence on normative thinking about social welfare. They argued that social policies and programs could be classified as either residual or institutional. The residual approach, they suggested, advocated a very limited role for government while the institutional approach favored extensive government intervention and urged the provision of comprehensive social services and income maintenance and support programs. Their use of the term *institutional* social policy was soon adopted by other scholars who favored government social welfare provision.

T. H. Marshall and Richard Titmuss of the London School of Economics in England made a major contribution to the development of the institutional approach, and their writings were very influential not only in Britain but in other parts of the world as well. Their writings were well received in the United States, and both helped popularize the institutional approach in the country's social policy circles. Titmuss visited the United States on many occasions and became friendly with several academic leaders in the field of social policy as well as a number of key federal government policy makers.

Marshall (1950) argued that government social welfare provision is the culmination of the historical evolution of citizenship rights. Historically, the rights of citizenship were not accorded to all human beings. Slaves, peasant farmers, laborers, and workers were not regarded as citizens and were not permitted to share the rights enjoyed by the aristocracy. However, the ambit of citizenship was gradually extended as civil and then political rights were granted. Marshall contends that the development of citizenship also requires the extension of social rights. People who live in poverty, and who are badly housed and poorly educated, cannot be regarded as citizens in the proper sense of the term. For this reason, the state must ensure that they have rights to an adequate income, housing, and education. The government must establish these rights in law and guarantee that they will be fulfilled. Marshall's ideas provided an appealing normative basis for state intervention in social welfare. Social rights are as sacred as civil and political rights and should be guaranteed and fulfilled by the state.

Titmuss did not develop Marshall's thesis to any significant extent but, in various publications (1958, 1968, 1971, 1974), he offered a compatible set of ideas that provided additional normative justifications for government welfare. He injected a strong ethical element into the debate, arguing that social welfare should be the collective moral responsibility of citizens. Because the state represents its citizens, he believed that it is the proper agency through which they discharge their collective responsibility and give expression to their altruistic intentions. In modern industrial societies, government welfare provision is the most efficient way of expressing altruism. He claimed that the use of the market is not only inefficient but morally repugnant. Institutionalized altruism through the state increases reciprocity and promotes social solidarity. Also, because the social services redistribute resources, society becomes more equal and feelings of solidarity increase. Altruism, solidarity, and equality all promote the ideals of the Good Society.

Diverse influences permeate Titmuss's writings. He was an active member of the British Fabian society and committed to its brand of democratic socialism. He was also a great admirer of Richard Tawney, the British Christian socialist, and it is clear that Christian and utopian elements inform Titmuss's work. He was also influenced by earlier institutionalist writers such as the 19th century economist Thorstein Veblen, who railed against the excesses of affluence in American society. Veblen inspired Titmuss's own brand of social criticism, which was fiercely directed at the proponents of individualism and the free market.

Titmuss drew a sharp distinction between economic and social goods. The former, he believed, are appropriately bought and sold on the economic market. The latter should only be delivered through collective means of provision. He was particularly critical of commercial social services in the United States, which he believed undermined the altruistic and moral imperatives of social welfare. Nevertheless, as noted earlier, his ideas were well received in the United States and had a significant influence on the expansion of government social programs. Many social policy scholars in the United States accepted his view that social welfare is an expression of altruism. Many also agreed with Marshall that access to the social services and income maintenance is a social right.

As was reported in the first chapter of this book, Titmuss played in major role in promoting the academic study of social policy at the London School of Economics where he greatly enhanced the scholarly agenda of the Department of Social Science and Administration. The department had been founded in 1911 as a social work training program, but after his appointment as its first full professor in 1950, Titmuss expanded its scope and recruited an interdisciplinary faculty who soon increased its reputation and influence in government circles. Most British universities followed the example of the London School of Economics and established similar academic departments that promoted scholarly inquiry into social policy. These developments also helped strengthen social policy teaching and research at schools of social work and public policy in the United States.

The electoral successes of radical right-wing political groups in the 1980s posed a serious challenge to the proponents of the institutional approach. Budgetary retrenchment, privatization, contracting out, decentralization, and other innovations introduced by right-wing governments in different countries facilitated the emergence of a far more pluralistic social welfare system than institutionalists such as Titmuss would have approved, or even envisaged. Many commentators now believe that the institutional approach has run its course and that economic, demographic, electoral, and attitudinal changes will further undermine state involvement in social welfare. Apart from a small group of American writers who are known as neo-institutionalists (Evans, Rueschemeyer, & Skocpol, 1985), there appears to be limited support for the institutional approach in social policy circles today. This is not the case in most Western European nations, but, even here, government responsibility for social welfare has been heavily criticized (Alesina & Giavazzi, 2006; Sinn, 2007), and few now believe that the state's involvement in social welfare will expand further. On the other hand, a number of social policy scholars continue to promote institutionalist ideas. Gøsta Esping-Andersen's (1990) widely cited typology of different welfare regimes advocated *decommodification* in social welfare. Decommodification refers to the rights of citizens to receive social services and income maintenance benefits without having to meet employment and other requirements. Others have campaigned for the introduction of universal income support programs, such as a guaranteed or basic income, to be paid to all citizens irrespective of their income and needs (Fitzpatrick, 1999; Standing, 2002; Van Parijs, 1992). They draw on institutionalist ideas, but so far, their proposals have not been implemented on a significant scale.

Features of the Institutional Approach

As was noted earlier, the term *institutional* social welfare was coined by Wilensky and Lebeaux, who contrasted the narrow role government historically played in providing residual social services to the most conspicuously needy with the institutional approach that creates comprehensive social programs for all citizens. They claimed that a gradual historic shift from residual to institutional welfare was taking place and that this shift was resulting in the acceptance of social welfare as a normal, first-line function of society. Social welfare, they argued, was being institutionalized.

Wilensky and Lebeaux's account made a significant and durable contribution to the articulation of the institutional approach. However, their work did not fully encompass all of the dimensions of this approach. At the time their book was published, Titmuss had not articulated his own theory of collective altruism, which provided a moral legitimation for state social welfare. Nor did they discuss Marshall's ideas on social rights. Although drawn from their definition, it is extended in the following account by examining these and other contributions.

State Collectivism and Institutionalism

Collectivist ideology accords prime importance to collective forms of association in which people share resources and decision making. Cooperatives, trade unions, communes, and, ultimately, the state are examples of collectives. Collectivists believe that the state is jointly owned by its citizens and that shared decision making is a function of representative democracy. They also believe that the state is the most effective agent for meeting social needs.

Institutionalists are essentially collectivists even though they differ in the extent to which they advocate state responsibility for social welfare. Most believe that government should not merely augment but transcend the traditional role of the extended family, the community, and philanthropic endeavor and assume a fundamental responsibility for social welfare. Others advocate a less extensive role for the state. While many institutionalists support a pluralistic conception that includes public support for nonprofit agencies, most reject commercial services, accepting Titmuss's view that the market is an inappropriate mechanism for meeting social needs. Marxists are collectivists, but most contend that the provision of statutory social services by liberal and social democratic governments in capitalist society does little to promote social welfare. For this reason, institutional collectivism is usually associated with social democracy and progressive liberalism.

Although the Marxist critique of the institutional approach exerted some influence in academic circles in the 1970s, it was eclipsed by the Radical Right. As was noted earlier, right-wing movements and governments mounted an effective attack on institutional ideas and began to dominate social policy thinking in the 1980s. Critiques offered by Milton Friedman (1962), Martin Feldstein (1974), and other economists claimed that government social programs had weakened the economy and were responsible for the high unemployment and inflation that characterized the 1970s. Social policy writers such as George Gilder (1981) and Charles Murray (1984) argued that government social programs had failed miserably to eradicate poverty and instead had created an impoverished underclass of people who became dependent on government aid. Murray was applauded by many Republican politicians for his insistence that state welfare had done more harm than good. Lawrence Mead (1986, 1997) attacked Marshall's notion of social rights claiming that it had been abused. Rights, he contends, are not unconditional but involve reciprocal obligations. Many of those claiming social benefits do not discharge their obligations to society and should not be provided with services or financial aid.

The writings of these and other critics of government welfare contributed significantly to the retrenchment of public social programs and the declining influence of institutionalist thinking in social policy circles in the 1980s.

Universality and Selectivity

Institutionalists believe that government intervention should be comprehensive and universal in scope. Although governments have been involved in social welfare on an organized basis since Elizabethan times, their involvement has historically been targeted at the most needy through means-tested programs. The institutional approach requires that government social programs cater for all citizens, irrespective of income, and ensure that they are protected against the contingencies of modern life. Titmuss (1968) was a severe critic of selective, means-tested social services. These services were not only meager but also stigmatized recipients and were often punitive. Although he campaigned for their replacement with universal social services, means-tested approaches continued to dominate social provisions in most Western countries even during the most generous years of the welfare state. In the United States, means-tested programs such as Aid for Families with Dependent Children (AFDC), which has been replaced by the Temporary Assistance for Needy Families (TANF) program, have long been criticized for their stigmatizing and punitive effects.

It is for this reason that institutionalists favor the adoption of universal social services such as social security, health insurance, and child allowances. An added dimension to their universalism is the idea that government social services should be culturally accepted and embedded in society. Together with fiscal measures and statutory regulation, the social services should meet social needs, subsidize incomes, redistribute resources, and raise standards of living for all. This means that social welfare must transcend its traditional safety net function and become an integral component of modern social life.

Critics of universalism reject these arguments and claim that there is no point in spending public revenues on those who do not need assistance. By targeting the social services, the government is better able to focus scarce resources on the poor. Their ideas have recently been used to criticize Social Security, which is one of the few universal social programs in the United States. Critics contend that it would be more cost effective if Social Security were replaced with a means-tested program catering for the elderly poor and by commercially managed savings accounts that would accumulate the contributions of workers and provide an adequate income when they retire. Those who have accumulated sufficient savings and have private pensions would then be spared the expense of paying onerous Social Security taxes. Although President George W. Bush attempted to introduce private savings accounts, his proposals were rejected by the Congress, and Social Security remains intact. Nevertheless, it continues to be condemned by writers on the political right for being wasteful, harmful to economic growth, and unnecessary (Blahous, 2000; Feldstein, 1998; Tanner, 2004).

Institutionalism and Social Rights

Reference was made earlier to Marshall's (1950) theory of social rights, which provided an appealing normative rationale for the institutional perspective. Marshall argued that the ideal of citizenship requires that civil and political rights be accompanied by social rights. By ensuring social rights, governments foster social justice and meet the ideals of the welfare state. Although Marshall's ideas were widely adopted and formed the basis for the legal campaigns fought by welfare recipients in the 1960 and 1970s (Nadasen, 2005), they were attacked scholars such as Lawrence Mead (1986, 1997) who, as was shown earlier, argued that the payment of income benefits to people who refuse to work or meet their social obligations to society amounts to a travesty of the social rights idea. Although he agrees that citizens do have social rights, Mead argues that they are also obligated to do their best to meet their own social needs and contribute to the well-being of society as a whole through working and being responsible citizens. It is only when they are unable to work and contribute to society that they have a legitimate right to claim assistance.

Mead's writing inspired the Republican Party's approach to welfare reform, which resulted in the enactment of the Personal Responsibility and Work Opportunity Reconciliation Act in 1996. This legislation rejects the argument that income benefits should be paid to needy people on the basis that they have a right to an adequate income. Instead, workfare and many other requirements now accompany the payment of these benefits. These requirements are believed by the proponents of the legislation to have a desirable impact on the lifestyles of the poor. Others are less sanguine about the future well-being of those who have been adversely affected by this legislation. They point out that relatively few welfare leavers, as they are known, have found employment in regular, well-paid jobs that meet their social needs (Acs & Loprest, 2004; Besharov, 2003; Goldberg & Collins, 2001). Some even believe that this legislation was never intended to help needy people find employment and become self-sufficient but that it, in fact, functions to control the poor and particularly poor women of color with children, who have historically been the victims of negative stereotypes and discriminatory practices (Bell, 2006; Mink, 1998).

Institutionalism, Pragmatism, and the Middle Way

Although the institutional approach is inspired by progressive liberalism and social democratic ideas, it lacks the ideological fervor that has characterized much of the social policy literature of the Radical Right and Marxist

Left. It is not that institutionalists have no ideological commitment but rather that their ideological proclivities are tempered by a historical preference for empiricism and pragmatism.

The historical development of the institutional approach was significantly influenced by the use of empirical research for social reform purposes. Studies of poverty, child labor, and other social ills were effectively used by social reformers to expose social problems and promote social change. Institutionalism has also been influenced by the philosophical methodology of pragmatism. Pragmatism stresses the need to test the veracity of knowledge through experience. It rejects a priori theories, requiring that intellectual claims be verified before being accepted. Pragmatism contributed to a distrust in institutional circles of grand theories, such as Marxism, that offered appealing but abstract explanations and prescriptions.

This preference for pragmatic thinking has prompted the criticism that institutionalism is both atheoretical and ideologically limited. Robert Pinker (1971) lamented the lack of theoretical sophistication in institutionalist thinking, while Karl Popper (1961) characterized institutionalists as engaging in "piecemeal social engineering." However, as Ramesh Mishra (1977) observed, pragmatism is consistent with the institutionalists' reform agenda. Unlike Marxism and other grand theories that are committed to the radical transformation of society, the reformism espoused by institutionalists is much more likely to be concerned with practical matters and incremental social reform.

Although the reformism of the institutionalist approach has been ridiculed by radicals on both the political right and left, institutionalists claim that their middle-way position between unfettered capitalism and authoritarian communism has fostered significant social improvements and high standards of living in those nations that have implemented institutional ideas. The Western European welfare states have made significant social gains by combining social welfare with economic growth. The wealth-generating vigor of capitalism has been successfully harmonized with social welfare. In addition, this blending has been achieved without coercion or intrusive authoritarian statism. However, it is interesting that, with the collapse of Soviet communism in the 1990s, the middle way adopted by institutionalists should have been challenged by the claim that institutionalism is itself an extreme position and that a new "Third Way" between free-market capitalism and social democratic institutionalism needs to be found (Giddens, 1998, 2000).

In this regard, several scholars have speculated on whether the European welfare state is a manifestation of socialism or capitalism. Some writers believe that the welfare state gives expression to democratic socialist ideas, while others contend that it is essentially capitalist in nature (Ginsberg, 1979; Gough, 1979; Marshall, 1971; Offe, 1984). On the other hand, Pinker (1979) argued that the welfare state should not be regarded as a variant of either capitalism or socialism but as a new and distinctive social formation with its own unique features.

As was noted earlier, the institutionalists' claim that the welfare state represents the best form of social organization has been challenged by both the political left and right. Marxists argue that the welfare state legitimizes capitalism and fails to address fundamental social needs and injustices. Those on the political right argue that it has sapped the vitality of enterprise, impeded economic growth, created a dependent and unproductive underclass, and undermined cherished moral values. These latter ideas have gained significant electoral support and have seriously undermined the institutionalist position.

Altruism and the Moral Imperatives of Social Policy

Reference was previously made to the work of Richard Titmuss, who formulated a conception of social policy that emphasized the moral aspects of institutionalizing social welfare. His analysis went beyond an account of the advantages of engaging the state in social policy. It is not only that the state has the authority and resources to address social needs effectively but also that its involvement has the desirable moral consequence of facilitating the expression of altruism, enhancing solidarity, promoting social inclusion, and fostering compassion. If people recognize that they "own" the state, that it represents their collective interests, they will be willing to pay their taxes to fund social service programs not only to help the needy but also to enhance the welfare of all. In this way, social policy serves fundamental moral purposes.

The moral elements in Titmuss's writings are most systematically developed in his best-selling book *The Gift Relationship* (1971). Using blood procurement and distribution as a case study, he argued, on the basis of a wealth of empirical data, that voluntary donation is the most effective way of meeting the need for blood. He was appalled by the use of the commercial market to supply blood in the United States, contending that the use of the market for this purpose is both inefficient and morally reprehensible. He also insisted that social policy is not primarily about management and policy theories or technical issues but about values and ideals. A system of social welfare based on desirable social values is infinitely superior to one based on technical arguments about the advantages of collective versus market provision.

Although Titmuss claimed the high moral ground in his advocacy of state welfare, writers on the political right, such as Murray (1984), have responded with a value position of their own. As was noted earlier, Murray contends that government involvement in social welfare has had a negative moral impact, undermining marriage and the family, promoting profligacy, weakening the values of self-reliance, and creating widespread dependency. As Murray's contrasting position suggests, moral imperatives in social welfare are not absolutes but dependent on ideological persuasion. Mead's (1986) insistence that social rights must be accompanied by social responsibilities offers another moral challenge to Titmuss's theory of altruism and the morality of the institutionalist position.

The Future of Institutionalism

It was noted earlier that the institutional approach has been undermined by economic realities, ideological opposition, attitudinal changes, and other factors. The policy changes introduced by Radical Right governments during the 1980s have significantly weakened the institutionalist position. Although many institutionalists hoped that the election of President Clinton in 1992 would restore their influence, it was clear by the time of the 1996 election that the political right continued to take the initiative and frame debates on social policy. The election of President George W. Bush in 2000 and his reelection in 2004 gave little cause for optimism, and many institutionalists observed with despair the tax cuts introduced by his administrations, the further programmatic retrenchments in social programs, and the campaign to partially privatize Social Security. The invasion of Iraq and the huge military costs incurred by the federal government as a result of its neo-imperial adventurism were equally depressing in view of the fact that these resources could have been used to meet educational, health, and other vital social welfare needs.

While institutionalism continues to exert considerable influence in Europe, many believe that its impact on social policy thinking in the United States is now depleted. On the other hand, some writers believe that its basic premises remain valid and that a reformulation of some of its tenets could ensure its long term vitality. Some proponents of a rejuvenated institutionalism (Gilbert & Gilbert, 1989) recommend that institutionalists adopt a more pluralistic stance, recognizing the inadequacies of state-managed social services and the need for contracting these services out on a more substantial scale to other providers. Others (Etzioni, 1993) believe that institutional ideas should be united with communitarian beliefs and that the state should actively encourage community participation in social policy formulation and implementation. Still others (Midgley, 1995, 1999; Sherraden, 1991) suggest that institutional beliefs about state responsibility for social welfare should stress the role of the state in promoting social investments that enhance the capacity of people to participate in the productive economy. However, while these different proposals may offer new directions for the institutional approach, it remains to be seen whether they will reinvigorate a set of ideas that previously exerted such a profound influence on social policy.

References

Acs, G., & Loprest, P. (2004). *Leaving welfare.* Kalamazoo, MI: UpJohn Institute.

Alesina, A., & Giavazzi, F. (2006). *The future of Europe: Reform or decline.* Cambridge: MIT Press.

Bell, H. (2006). Putting mothers to work. In J. Henrici (Ed.), *Doing without: Women and work after welfare reform* (pp. 155–171). Tucson: University of Arizona Press.

Besharov, D. (Ed.). (2003). *Family and child well-being after welfare reform.* New Brunswick, NJ: Transaction.

Blahous, C. P. (2000). *Reforming social security for ourselves and our prosperity.* Westport, CT: Praeger.

Dolgoff, R., & Feldstein, D. (1980). *Understanding social welfare.* New York: Longman.

Esping-Andersen, G. (1990). *The three worlds of welfare capitalism.* Princeton, NJ: Princeton University Press.

Etzioni, A. (1993). *The spirit of community: Rights, responsibilities and the communitarian agenda.* New York: Crown.

Evans, P., Rueschemeyer, D., & Skocpol, T. (Eds.). (1985). *Bringing the state back in.* New York: Cambridge University Press.

Feldstein, M. (1974). Social security, induced retirement and aggregate capital accumulation. *Journal of Political Economy, 83*(4), 447–475.

Feldstein, M. (Ed.). (1998). *Privatizing social security.* Chicago: University of Chicago Press.

Fitzpatrick, T. (1999). *Freedom and security: An introduction to the basic income debate.* New York: Palgrave Macmillan.

Friedman, M. (1962) *Capitalism and freedom.* Chicago: University of Chicago Press.

Giddens, A. (1998). *The third way: The renewal of social democracy.* Cambridge, UK: Polity Press.

Giddens, A. (2000). *The third way and its critics.* Cambridge, UK: Polity Press.

Gilbert, N., & Gilbert, B. (1989). *The enabling state: Modern welfare capitalism in America.* New York: Oxford University Press.

Gilder, G. (1981). *Wealth and poverty.* London: Buchan and Enright.

Ginsberg, N. (1979). *Class, capital, and social policy.* London: Macmillan.

Goldberg, G. S., & Collins, S. D. (2001). *Washington's new poor law: Welfare reform and the roads not taken, 1936 to the present.* New York: Apex Press.

Gough, I. (1979). *The political economy of the welfare state.* London: Macmillan.

Jansson, B. (2005). *The reluctant welfare state: A history of American social welfare policies* (5th ed.). Pacific Grove, CA: Brooks/Cole.

Korpi, W. (1983). *The social democratic class struggle.* London: Routledge and Kegan Paul.

Marshall, T. H. (1950). *Citizenship and social class and other essays.* Cambridge, UK: Cambridge University Press.

Marshall, T. H. (1971). Value problems of welfare capitalism. *Journal of Social Policy, 1*(1), 15–32.

Mead, L. (1986). *Beyond entitlement: The social obligations of citizenship.* New York: Basic Books.

Mead, L. (Ed.). (1997). *The new paternalism: Supervisory approaches to poverty.* Washington, DC: Brookings Institution Press.

Midgley, J. (1995). *Social development: The developmental perspective in social welfare.* Thousand Oaks, CA: Sage.

Midgley, J. (1999). Growth, redistribution and welfare: Toward social investment. *Social Service Review, 77*(1), 3–21.

Mink, G. (1998). *Welfare's end.* Ithaca, NY: Cornell University Press.

Mishra, R. (1977). *Society and social policy: Theories and practice of welfare.* London: Macmillan.

Murray, C. (1984). *Losing ground: American social policy 1950–1980.* New York: Basic Books.

Nadasen, P. (2005). *Welfare warriors: The welfare rights movement in the United States.* New York: Routledge.

Offe, C. (1984). *Contradictions of the welfare state.* Cambridge, MA: MIT Press.

Pinker, R. (1971). *Social theory and social policy.* London: Heinemann.

Pinker, R. (1979). *The idea of welfare.* London: Heinemann.

Popper, K. (1961). *The poverty of historicism.* London: Routledge and Kegan Paul.

Sherraden, M. (1991). *Assets and the poor: A new American welfare policy.* Armonk, NY: M. E. Sharpe.

Sinn, H. W. (2007). *Can Germany be saved? The malaise of the world's first welfare state.* Cambridge: MIT Press.

Standing, G. (2002). *Beyond the new paternalism: Basic security as equality.* London: Verso.

Stephens, J. (1979). *The transition from capitalism to socialism.* London: Macmillan.

Tanner, M. D. (Ed.). (2004). *Social security and its discontents: Perspectives on choice.* Washington, DC: Cato Institute.

Titmuss, R. M. (1958). *Essays on the welfare state.* London: Allen & Unwin.

Titmuss, R. M. (1968). *Commitment to welfare.* London: Allen & Unwin.

Titmuss, R. M. (1971). *The gift relationship.* London: Allen & Unwin.

Titmuss, R. M. (1974). *Social policy: An introduction.* London: Allen & Unwin.

Van Parijs, P. (Ed.). (1992). *Arguing for basic income: Ethical foundations for a radical reform.* London: Verso.

Wilensky, H., & Lebeaux, C. (1958). *Industrial society and social welfare.* New York: Russell Sage Foundation.

13 Conservative Approaches to Social Policy

Leon Ginsberg

For some 30 years, conservative ideas about social welfare and government have dominated American politics. In the United States, the term conservative refers to the ideological belief that traditional American values should govern the society. These values include a strong belief in the free-market economic system, the family, and traditional religious and cultural beliefs. The 1980 election of Ronald Reagan (Ginsberg, 1987) and the election and reelection of Bill Clinton and George W. Bush as presidents were major influences in shaping the conservative direction of the nation. Clinton called for fundamental changes in American social welfare policy in 1992 and was one of the most conservative post–World War II Democratic presidential candidates. Since 1935, when the Social Security Act was passed, many political figures supported and often expanded social welfare programs, a trend that Reagan, Clinton, and the U.S. Congress of the 1990s and early 21st century modified. In current American political conservatism, the most central issues have included policies about national defense, social welfare policy, and taxation as well as other fiscal policy.

The election in 1994 of Republican majorities in both houses of Congress, majorities promising the conservative "Contract with America" (Gillespie & Schellhas, 1994), laid other bases for shifts in social welfare policy. The election of Newt Gingrich, who led the development of this "contract" (Gingrich, 1995), as Speaker of the U.S. House was another step toward major changes, which were popularly called welfare reform. Gingrich resigned from the House of Representatives in 1998 but remains well known for his work in changing American policy. His Web site, www.newt.org, says he was the "architect of the 'Contract with America'" that led the Republican Party to victory in 1994 by capturing the majority in the U.S. House for the first time in 40 years. Under his leadership, Congress passed welfare reform, passed the first balanced budget in a generation, and passed the first tax cuts in

16 years. In addition, the Congress restored funding to strengthen defense and intelligence capabilities, an action later lauded by the bipartisan 9/11 Commission." Gingrich's Web site also says that, under his leadership, "The 61-year-old entitlement for welfare was ended, restoring the work ethic and putting people to work across the country, fundamentally changing millions of lives" (Gingrich Communications, 2008). Gingrich is referring to the Work Opportunity and Personal Responsibility Act of 1996, which Congress passed and President Clinton signed. It is the most far-reaching conservative social policy legislation in modern U.S. history, and it is discussed later in this chapter. However, the trend toward conservative government social policies, which continued to dominate until 2006, was interrupted by the election of small Democratic Party majorities in the U.S. House of Representatives and the Senate.

The chapter begins by outlining the key features of the conservative tradition and then traces its historical evolution. Key features of current conservative political thought are also discussed. Attention is given to the role of conservative think tanks and the media in promoting the conservative agenda. The remainder of the chapter discusses conservative thought and social policy with reference to economics, religion, business interests, and current social welfare programs.

Basic Concepts of Conservatism

Conservatism, as it is understood and practiced in the United States, is a blend of a variety of economic, political, and philosophical concepts. Its origins were in the 18th century, primarily in England. It has had a variety of adherents and points of view, but many believe that conservatism began with early economic thinkers, especially Adam Smith (1789/1991). Smith propounded the notion of laissez-faire economics and was an early advocate of free enterprise. Essentially, *laissez-faire,* a French term, means that governments should leave the economy alone. Smith believed that an invisible hand governs financial interactions and that free economic pursuits build economies and create wealth. In fact, he called his major work *The Wealth of Nations* (1789/1991). Smith's ideas remain widely accepted and popular today. They are fundamental to American economic activity and law, which attempt to guarantee competition, the pursuit of free economic development, the avoidance of monopolies, and relatively little government interference. One author, Peter Watson (2005,) calls *The Wealth of Nations* one of the best scientific books of all time. According to Watson, Smith discovered that economics followed certain laws and order. Smith was not opposed to helping others and believed that, although people would always pursue their self-interest, they would also share sympathy with others.

One criticism of free-enterprise economics is that, after periods of growth and prosperity, such economies may collapse. Social welfare programs, their advocates believe, mitigate the fractured economies that cycle with economic growth. Otherwise, the human consequences of unbridled economic activity are severe, as they were during the Great Depression. However, many proponents of unfettered free enterprise believe that social welfare programs interfere with the natural order of economic activity (Friedman & Friedman, 1980).

Also basic to the development of conservative political ideas was England's Edmund Burke (1729–1797), a member of the House of Commons who was one of the earliest writers and thinkers on the subject (Rathbone & Stephenson, 1985; Stearns, 2001). He believed in the virtue of conserving tradition and in respect for government. Burke's writings reacted to the French Revolution, which he considered excessive. The assassinations of political leaders, the dramatic and violent break with earlier traditions, and the general chaos associated with the Revolution disturbed him. He developed, from his observations, the theory of conservatism (although he did not use the term, himself) and the need for conservative policies. Loyalty to the government and its authority, ties between government and the church, and limiting suffrage were part of his beliefs. He also reacted negatively to the social consequences of industrialization.

Parenthetically, conservatism and liberalism, which many view as opposites, are similar terms for some. In fact, when this writer discussed the worldwide movement toward less government involvement in social welfare and called it conservative, the president of the International Federation of Social Workers (Elis Envall, personal communication, May 22, 1998) said his organization launched a study group on neoliberalism to explore the same issues. The classic definitions of liberalism, then, are similar to the current American definitions of conservatism. In the U.S. context, those identified as liberals (or as *progressive*—a currently more popular designation whose advent parallels the denigration of the term liberal) are thought to usually support government involvement in human affairs such as social welfare. Although American conservatives consider themselves equally interested in human betterment, they believe that government intervention usually causes more harm than good.

In the United States, conservatism generally describes those who oppose any government involvement in human affairs. Conservative thinkers are often especially negative toward government social welfare programs, and especially those of the federal government. In recent times, conservatives and liberals have diverged over the propriety of the government's military actions in Iraq, with many conservatives largely supporting the policies, which were pro-military and supportive of involvement in Iraq, and liberals generally opposing such involvement.

American conservative ideas about human welfare have a number of basic elements. Conservatives believe that individuals are fundamentally, perhaps solely, responsible for themselves and their families. Each person must take care of himself or herself through employment or other sources of financial support and provide for his or her family, which today means a spouse and children. In earlier times, family responsibility laws often extended to siblings, parents, grandparents, and even nieces and nephews. Conservatives also value order and are disturbed by disorder.

Conservatives also believe in a limited role for government. Government should be involved, most say, in no more than maintaining international relations through diplomacy, operating a money system, and maintaining a defense force. Related to this, they believe that people do not legally owe responsibility to each other. One's only responsibility is to one's self. Therefore, concepts such as social welfare entitlements are an anathema to many conservative thinkers. However, that does not mean conservatives are unwilling to support humane assistance. But help for individuals ought to come from family and voluntary or religious charities, and not the government. If government programs are desired, they ought to be organized and provided at the lowest levels, such as the state, county, or city. Also, the worthy or truly needy poor are distinguished from the unworthy poor, a classic distinction in social welfare history. The worthy poor are children, older adults, and those with physical and some mental disabilities. The unworthy are the unemployed and those who are disabled by substance abuse. Thus, help should be means tested rather than universal. People who seek help should prove their need and account for other assets or earnings before being helped.

Conservatives also emphasize religion, law, and patriotic loyalty. Citizens should be raised and continuously encouraged to be supportive and loyal to their basic institutions such as the church and the government. Conservatives (and most other Americans, as well) have a strong belief in private property because this is seen as fundamental to a just society. Finally, conservatives are more skeptical than others about the perfectibility of human beings, especially through governmental efforts.

History of Modern American Conservative Thought

For much of American history, conservative political thought dominated national life and social policy as well. Ideas of human services and social responsibility, such as those that essentially became encoded in the Social Security Act of 1935, were practically unheard of in mainstream American government until the 20th century. The spacious agrarian America of the 18th and 19th centuries saw little room for grand schemes of social welfare. Families were supposed to take care of themselves; farm families could provide themselves with sufficient food and housing through subsistence economic activity. Of course, as Day (1997) suggests, social welfare institutions have a long history in the United States. Private and local government programs such as orphanages and charitable organizations similar to those operated in England were imported to the United States. And social reformers such as Jane Addams and her colleagues at Hull House in Chicago worked to change the environment for the urban poor (Davis & McCree, 1969). They pressed for social reforms and government involvement through many avenues, including the White House conferences on children, which began in 1909 (Coll, 1977). Institutions such as the Children's Bureau were established in the federal government, but these efforts were more advisory to state governments than administrators of federal social welfare programs. In addition, it was widely expected that the federal government should not be involved in social welfare. One example was President Franklin Pierce's veto of a bill to provide federal funds for the construction and operation of asylums. It had been promoted by Dorothea Dix and her supporters (Axinn & Levin, 1996). Generally, Congress stayed away from national social welfare programs, which were assumed to be the responsibilities of the states.

Therefore, many modern American conservative pronouncements date from the 1930s, when the Franklin Delano Roosevelt New Deal brought federal government social welfare programs to the United States for the first time. The Social Security Act of 1935, which is still the basic social welfare law of the United States, although it has been modified through amendments extensively and regularly, provided programs to overcome the poverty that arose from the Great Depression. Roosevelt's administration also tried food stamps as a means for providing surplus food to low-income people, a program that became national, after a gap of several years, during President Johnson's Great Society programs (Johnson, 1998).

Herbert Hoover, who served as president during the early years of the Depression and who was defeated by Roosevelt in 1932, partly because of the angry public response to the economic difficulties, wrote frequently about his opposition to the New Deal and its programs (Hoover, 1956). He was one of the earliest conservative critics of the New Deal, and many of his charges against government social welfare are echoed by contemporary as well as later conservative thinkers, writers, and politicians.

The major human services efforts of the New Deal, as they evolved, included paid work for unemployed people through programs such as the Works Progress Administration and the Civilian Conservation Corps; prevention of poverty for older adults, survivors, and people with disabilities through the Social Security program; and welfare help such as Supplemental Security Income and Aid to Families with Dependent Children. Subsequently, other presidents augmented these social welfare programs even though they were considered to be conservative. For example, President Richard M. Nixon proposed the most generous public assistance program in U.S. history, the Family Assistance Plan, which was not passed by Congress (Moynihan, 1969).

An important modern political influence on modern American conservative thinking was Barry Goldwater, who was the 1964 candidate for president on the Republican ticket. Goldwater was a long-term senator from

Arizona. Senator Goldwater took a strong conservative posture on social programs, including Social Security and public welfare (Goldwater, 1990). He opposed a variety of federal programs introduced by President Lyndon B. Johnson, such as the Economic Opportunity Act of 1965 and Head Start. Goldwater also opposed Johnson's civil and voting rights legislation. Although not racially prejudiced, he opposed these initiatives on the grounds that they were not federal government issues. He was an articulate opponent of almost all federal initiatives for solving human problems such as civil rights deprivations and poverty. He remained strongly opposed to any efforts to impose regulations and special help for disadvantaged groups by the federal government, strictly on the basis of his conservative ideology, which he explained in his *The Conscience of a Conservative* (Goldwater, 1990). In the 1964 presidential election, he was defeated handily by Johnson.

Among the most influential conservative social welfare policy makers was President Ronald Reagan, who served from 1981 to 1989. Reagan's position on government, which he developed as governor of California and brought to the United States federal government, was that government had no business engaging in other than the classic government functions of operating a money system, maintaining international relations, and providing a national defense. His presidential objectives included reducing the size of the federal government and removing the federal government, to whatever extent was possible, from the fields of human services and social welfare. He worked to achieve those goals by reducing large portions of the federal bureaucracy and giving the states block grants to operate formerly specifically defined federal programs. He also proposed, and Congress accepted, reductions on the amount of funding the federal government would provide to the states for social services. Increasingly, under the Reagan administration, the states became the operators of the social welfare programs with significantly reduced federal involvement and supervision. However, in his last year in office, Reagan signed into law the Family Support Act of 1988, which provided job training for welfare recipients. He also supported economic policies that had, before Roosevelt, been rejected by conservatives. Those policies included the theories of John Maynard Keynes, whose economic concepts informed Roosevelt's New Deal. Reagan, and later George W. Bush, appeared to believe in the basic Keynesian theory of the value to the economic system of deficit financing of government.

It is important to note that not only the conservative Republicans called for major changes in social welfare—so did President Bill Clinton. Clinton made political campaign promises in 1992 of ending the Aid to Families with Dependent Children, in other words, of reformulating a major welfare program. He spoke favorably about time limits on the receipt of public assistance, for example, which became part of the 1996 Personal Responsibility and Work Opportunity Reconciliation Act. When Congress passed the 1996 legislation, Clinton signed the bill. Although many of

President Clinton's supporters doubted that he wanted to reform welfare as radically as it was in 1996, he clearly had supported similar kinds of action in his own political campaigns. Some of his closest colleagues and supporters (Edelman, 1997) said President Clinton did not need to support such a bill in order to win reelection and that he could have achieved similar objectives while supporting and more fully implementing Reagan's Family Support Act of 1988, which was already the law. However, the changes contained in the new law were popular not only with conservative politicians but also with the larger public.

Current Conservative Political Thought

As mentioned above, social welfare changed dramatically under the leadership of the Republican Congress, which was elected in 1994. For the first time since the 1950s, both the Senate and the House of Representatives had majority Republican membership. Newt Gingrich, the Speaker of the House of Representatives, considers himself as the progenitor of the conservative resurgence. Both Gingrich and Congressman Dick Armey (1996), who became his second-in-command, wrote and spoke often about changing the federal approach to social welfare (Gillespie & Schellhas, 1994; Gingrich, 1995). Both were influential in formulating the Contract with America and both have now left Congress. Armey wrote about the elimination of income tax and replacing it with a "flat tax" (Armey, 1996). By 1996, with the passage of the 1996 welfare reform legislation, they had succeeded in implementing many of the reforms long sought by conservative social thinkers. These included placing time limits on the receipt of federally financed welfare assistance, requiring teenage mothers to live with their parents or other responsible adults in order to receive help, and insisting upon work as a condition for receiving aid.

Of course, many other political figures in both major political parties have supported conservative approaches to social welfare. Altogether, it appears they constituted a majority of policy makers in the late 20th century and early in the 21st—at least until the 2006 election. Southern members of the Senate and Congress from both parties tend toward conservative positions. So do many governors throughout the nation who have implemented welfare-tightening policies that go beyond the provisions of the federal requirements.

Among the best-known intellectual conservative thinkers in recent times have been Milton Friedman, Charles Murray, and Irving Kristol. They have been supported by a number of minority-group thinkers and writers who have questioned some of the premises of the modern social welfare programs of the United States. Milton Friedman, a Nobel prize–winning economist from the University of Chicago, made his reputation and contribution to economic thinking in the area of monetarism. However, his basic concepts about social welfare are grounded in his belief that the Social Security system and other social welfare programs are ill advised and inappropriate under American law and tradition (Friedman & Friedman, 1980).

Writing with his wife Rose in 1980, Friedman argued that the Social Security retirement program or Old Age, Survivors, and Disability Insurance ought to be eliminated. They say the trust fund approaches of Social Security are propagandistic, and the benefits are really paid out of current collections from younger workers to retirees. The Friedmans questioned whether Social Security is a reliable insurance program. Instead, he and his wife call it a tax combined with transfer payments. They also believed that the Social Security tax is regressive in that lower-income people pay a greater percentage of their earnings than do the wealthiest people. Ideally, they suggested, people would buy their own retirement and life insurance on the private market. The Friedmans generally believed that it is an improper and inefficient arrangement for government to engage in large-scale insurance schemes. They may be correct in believing that the burden of Social Security payments falls most heavily on the lowest-paid workers in terms of percentages of income paid. The rate is the same for all workers, but there is a ceiling on the amount on which the tax is paid. Workers who exceed that maximum therefore pay a lower rate. However, Social Security advocates view Social Security not as a tax-supported government program but as an insurance program in which premiums earn benefits. The higher the wages earned, the higher the premiums. And there is a maximum of benefits, just as there is a ceiling on the amount on which the premiums are paid. Some of these ideas are reflected in some current thinking about Social Security in which younger workers doubt that they will ever receive Social Security benefits. That belief has, at times, seemed to be widespread among younger workers even though the Social Security program is considered viable for the next few decades and could, with minor adjustments in the benefit ages and other elements, be made solvent for all of the foreseeable future. Threats to the continuation of Social Security as it exists are usually avoided by political figures, and Congress generally shuns proposals for its basic modification. In 2001, President George W. Bush proposed allowing workers to invest part of their Social Security taxes in individual savings accounts that could be invested in stocks and bonds and thereby grow more rapidly for the benefit of the worker (Social Security Administration, n.d.). The proposal was widely criticized and did not gain congressional approval.

The Friedmans were also noteworthy proponents of a negative income tax to replace existing programs of poverty assistance, such as the former program known as Aid to Families with Dependent Children (AFDC). They suggested that poverty could be overcome through the income tax system. Low wage earners with families would receive more than they paid in taxes in the form of refunds. In fact, the United States established such an arrangement many years ago and called it the Earned Income Tax Credit (EITC) by which low-income people receive a rebate on their income taxes, frequently more than they paid in taxes, if they are among the working poor and have families. The EITC and the negative income tax are similar in concept.

Much of Irving Kristol's early writing was liberal, but his current work is considered conservative or neoconservative. He supports the kinds of changes made in social welfare policy although he doubted such ideas would prevail (Kristol, 1996). His son, William Kristol, is a prominent current conservative spokesperson.

George Gilder is a major critic of elements of social welfare programs (Gilder, 1981, 1995). He questions the correctness of ideas such as entitlements and urges the elimination of federally supported welfare programs. He also thought that AFDC was incorrect in its permanence as a support for clients. He prefers shorter-term, crisis-based assistance and would probably be more supportive of the new program, discussed later, Temporary Assistance for Needy Families (TANF). Gilder suggests that the welfare assistance programs such as AFDC kept people poor because being poor was a condition for receiving help. In essence, people were paid to forego work. He especially thinks that the former program, prior to the 1996 reforms, made men irresponsible because it was usually women who were eligible for and who received aid. Married men work harder than bachelors, he notes, and, without AFDC, men would have to be the supporters of many women and children. The deterioration of American communities, Gilder suggests, is a result of welfare assistance, an idea he shares with Charles Murray.

Charles Murray's book *Losing Ground* (1984) made the compelling case that public assistance programs and social welfare services of all kinds cause the problems they are supposed to resolve. He thinks that assistance programs for low-income families give assistance to women with children and reduce the importance of men in low-income families, which, in turn, causes social problems and economic decline in low-income communities. Murray believes he is correct about not only public assistance and Social Security but also such programs as unemployment compensation and virtually anything else directly for the benefit of people. Murray describes himself as a libertarian with strong antigovernment program convictions. He proposes doing away with all government assistance programs. This proposal has recently been reinstated in his new book, *In Our Hands: A Plan to Replace the Welfare State* (2006).

Collaborating with the late R. J. Hernnstein, Murray has also attempted to demonstrate that significant differences in IQ reflect significant differences among groups of people (Hernnstein & Murray, 1994). The ideas outlined in the book *The Bell Curve* caused an uproar, partly because it made the case that there were group IQ differences that left some groups disadvantaged while others fared better. Minority groups, especially African Americans, as well as many statisticians and scientists believed their conclusions were in error. Missed in the book by many advocates of human services and equity for disadvantaged people is a lengthy discussion on the need to create a more humane society that would simplify work, participation in government, and other elements of everyday life. The authors believed that many of the problems of disadvantage resulted from a society that is too complicated as much as from more traditional economic difficulties. On the opposite side of the argument, Murray and Hernnstein suggest that the United States was becoming a "custodial state," caring for and supervising the lives of large numbers of citizens who are incapable of taking care of themselves. They argue that such a state of affairs will create even greater problems, including a growing underclass isolated in public housing, the resurgence of virulent racism, and the growth of social welfare programs resulting from government's ever more adamant insistence on changing the behavior of disadvantaged people.

David Frum (1996) is another prominent conservative writer. He suggests that current laws make it difficult for society to enforce morality. For example, landlords may find that antidiscrimination laws make it difficult to require their tenants to be married. Communities cannot discriminate against people born out of wedlock, which also does little to discourage non-married unions. Similarly, restaurants and other public facilities cannot reject customers whose appearance or behavior might be unacceptable to the proprietors. Therefore, social legislation may conflict with efforts to promote morality.

One of the principle concerns of many conservative thinkers is affirmative action, although few oppose equal opportunity for all people without regard to their ethnicity or gender. Their concern is that affirmative action is "reverse discrimination" or some kind of effort to give special preferences to selected groups. Although that is not the intention of affirmative action programs, the belief that it is has caused some states to reduce or eliminate affirmative action efforts. Although most organized minority groups, such as those involving African Americans, Hispanics, Asian Americans, Latinos, and Native Americans, support affirmative action efforts, there are some minority writers who represent a conservative point of view. One of the most prominent is Robert Woodson, director of the National Center for Neighborhood Enterprise and formerly an employee of the American Enterprise Institute and the Urban League. Woodson, who was educated as a professional social worker, doubts the virtues of affirmative action and even the motives and performance of some elected African American officials. He has expressed concern about some African American politicians, whom he believes have used their political successes and their positions to better their own conditions, without being equally concerned about the most disadvantaged among their own ethnic group. Woodson (1981) is a supporter of the mediating structures approach, which is discussed in more detail later, for, among other things, preventing youth crime. Essentially, that approach suggests that social problems be solved through structures that exist between individuals and government. The large bureaucracies that dispense assistance and services to disadvantaged people can often be more oppressive than supportive and may also create dependency rather than fostering independence, Woodson suggests.

Another minority writer questions much of what has occurred in some elements of the civil rights movement is Thomas Sowell (1983, 2005) of the Hoover Institution in California. Sowell has written often about the inadequacies of affirmative action and the necessity for equal treatment and self-help. In some ways, his writings, which appear in books, professional journals, and magazines, are similar to the writings of Murray and Gilder, although he differs with Murray about some of the conclusions in *The Bell Curve*. He favors self-help and believes that minority group members who are disadvantaged can, through their own efforts, resolve their social and economic problems as have other groups of Americans. Sowell also believes that affirmative action, which he equates with preference for selected groups, is a source of conflict in the United States as well as in other nations that make such efforts. Another conservative African American writer is Glenn Loury (1987), a noted social scientist who questions some of the policy activities designed to bring equality to minority group people. Dinesh D'Souza, who is also a fellow at the Hoover Institution, is another well-known minority conservative thinker who does not hesitate to attack liberals. He published a book in 2007 (*The Enemy at Home*) suggesting that the Left, which is often treated as synonymous with liberal, had a hand in causing the September 11, 2001, attacks on New York City.

Although most of the prominent writers on conservative social welfare issues are men, some women also advocate similar approaches. Phyllis Schlafly (1977) is one of the best known conservative writers. She presents her views in a newspaper column, in her books, and in lectures. She calls her organized efforts the Eagle Forum. Of course, the late Ayn Rand (1984, 1989), the author of several novels and other books on economic freedom, is a major figure in conservative writing and in conservative circles. Peg Luksik (1996) of Pennsylvania has headed an organization called the National Parents Commission, which takes conservative social policy positions. Ann Coulter has published several recent books decrying liberal influence in the United States. Her most recent is entitled *Godless: The Church of Liberalism* (2006). She is outspoken, and many regard her proclamations about her opponents as intemperate. Many of these ideas are to be found in an encyclopedia of American conservatism that was published in 2006 (Frohnen, Beer, & Nelson, 2006).

Conservative Think Tanks and the Media

In addition to these writers and academics, several organizations study conservative ideas and provide support for conservative thinkers and writers. The Heritage Foundation, which has its headquarters in Washington, D.C., is one of the primary sources of conservative literature and information.

The American Enterprise Institute also takes a generally conservative posture. It has been the organizational affiliation of Charles Murray and, for a time, Robert Woodson.

In January 2008, Douglas J. Besharov of the American Enterprise Institute published a statement on social welfare conservatism. His ideas are similar to those presented by other authors in this chapter, although no others are quite so specific. Besharov (2008) argued that six principles underlie a conservative approach to dealing with social problems:

1. "A preference for limited government." He suggests that conservatives are wary of any expansion of government and believe that any expansion can be a part of "an unchecked upward spiral."

2. "A desire to means-test or otherwise target government benefits." He believes that universal programs contribute to the expansion of government. He describes as crude the argument that only if the middle class is supportive of a program will it succeed politically. He says there is no good evidence to support such a theory. Targeted programs are less expensive than universal programs and contribute less to the expansion of government.

3. "A concern about the behavioral consequences of assistance."

4. "A deference to mediating institutions." These are generally nonprofit and often religious organizations. Letting them develop and manage programs as they choose and operating social welfare services through them, rather than making them extensions of government objectives, appeals to Besharov's conservative concepts.

5. "Respect for private choice, often in the form of markets." Individuals have the ability to make sound decisions about their lives, and private choices should be trusted as vehicles for social welfare services, Besharov believes.

6. "Humility bred from disappointing experiences—and the likelihood of unintended consequences." Besharov points out that many social welfare initiatives are failures or have consequences that negatively outweigh their benefits. (pp. 1–3)

Besharov (2008) also says that conservatives display "a preference for state action over federal action" (p. 3). Correcting mistakes at the state level, he suggests, is much less cumbersome than trying to do so at the federal level.

Other organizations give voice to the conservative perspective. In addition, several magazines are conservatively oriented. For example, *Forbes*, an influential business periodical, is edited by Steve Forbes, who was a candidate in 1996 for the Republican presidential nomination. He writes a column for each issue. The late Casper Weinberger, secretary of health, education, and welfare under President Richard Nixon, was the publisher of *Forbes*. Thomas Sowell has written columns for *Forbes*. *The National Review* is a magazine founded by William F. Buckley, Jr. Buckley, of course, was one of the earliest spokespersons for conservative viewpoints beginning in the 1950s and 1960s. Other magazines such as *The American Spectator* take decidedly conservative positions. *The Washington Times* newspaper is probably the leading consistently conservative newspaper in the nation, although many others take generally conservative editorial positions.

Conservative media are also critical of foundations that appear to pursue liberal objectives. For example, in 1996, *Forbes* published an article (McMenamin, 1996) that criticized the Annie E. Casey Foundation and the Robert Wood Johnson Foundation for their pursuit of liberal public policies. The two foundations are among those most involved in human services. The *Forbes* article charges that the two foundations combined spend $100 million annually to influence state and local social welfare policy.

Among the most influential of popular conservative voices are several radio and television talk show personalities. Among the best known are Rush Limbaugh (1992, 1993), who conducts a three-hour daily conversation with listeners and callers and who has also written books on his ideas. Some observers credit him with helping influence the 1994 Republican successes in congressional elections. G. Gordon Liddy (1991, 1997), one of the convicted perpetrators of the Watergate political crimes under President Richard M. Nixon (Johnson, 1998) hosted a daily radio talk show and is also a writer. Liddy was also a marine and, for a time, served with the Federal Bureau of Investigation. Oliver North, who was initially found guilty of crimes in the Iran-Contra scandals under President Ronald Reagan and whose conviction was reversed on appeal, has also been a media host. North, like Liddy, is a former marine and was involved in national defense programs under President Reagan. He has published a book (North & Roth, 1994) and videotapes. In addition, Tony Brown (1995), an African American television personality with a show called *Tony Brown's Journal* has also raised questions about affirmative action and especially about welfare programs. In addition, Fox television has become a major and popular source of news and commentary presented from a conservative position.

Conservative Thought and Social Policy

One manifestation of conservative thought in the area of social policy is the concept of mediating structures. The idea of mediating structures is propounded by a variety of conservative writers, particularly, sociologist Peter Berger (1986, 1990) and others who have suggested that local, community-based, community-run organizations have the best chance of overcoming some of the kinds of problems social welfare programs are designed to reduce. Such structures mediate between those in need and governments to solve problems with local solutions and without the massive structures associated with federal programs. Robert Woodson (1981), who was discussed earlier, is another advocate of the mediating structures solution to human welfare problems. Mediating structures are, very simply, non-governmental organizations that provide human services. The concern of some of their advocates is that governments, as they grow more rapidly into welfare states, require more and more resources to meet more and more perceived human needs. As government grows, albeit for humanitarian purposes, capitalism and free enterprise are undermined, they insist. Leaving the solutions to human problems in the hands of mediating structures provides mechanisms for dealing with human problems without leading to negative effects, such as the growth of government, mediating structures advocates would argue.

Economics and Public Social Policy

Much of the conflict over social welfare policy from an economic perspective has reflected differences between those who support theories of a market economy as opposed to those who value a planned, largely government-run economy, as contemplated by authors such as the late Michael Harrington (1962, 1976). Harrington believed that capitalism is inherently unjust and that social welfare made capitalism work by tempering its worst effects. The economic theories of John Maynard Keynes (1965, 1971), which proposes a system of balancing the economy through government policy, provides another example of this approach. Keynes's ideas were regularly used by American economic policy makers and were supported by presidents of both parties. However, traditional conservative thought, dating from the 1930s New Deal, doubted the validity of Keynesian economic theory, which suggests that, when an economy is in difficulty, government can help overcome the difficulties through public expenditures. But, in the modern era, conservative presidents such as Ronald Reagan and George W. Bush promoted economic growth through deficit finance measures, including tax reductions. Bill Clinton, a Democrat often described as liberal, presided over a balanced budget and the erasure of the federal deficit.

Whether or not a nation prospers has a great deal to do with a number of factors of geography, climate, and basic social systems even more than the nation's use of market or planning mechanisms, according to some writers (Landes, 1998). For example, communism never seemed to work well in Russia, despite decades of enforced central planning and control. In nearby Scandinavia, on the other hand, a kind of democratic socialism has been practiced for a long time, and the region has prospered while meeting the social welfare needs of its citizens.

Religion and Conservatism

Some religious groups also tend to associate with capitalism and, therefore, with conservatism. John D. Rockefeller, the founder of one of America's wealthiest families, acknowledged the close connection between his Protestant faith and practice (Baptist) and capitalism (Chernow, 1998). He said he was always trained to work and save. Some say that Rockefeller demonstrated the accuracy of Max Weber's thesis (1904/1980) that there is a close link between Protestantism and capitalism.

Opposition to social welfare programs may also be found in the writings and speeches of some religious conservatives, both Protestant and Roman Catholic. Religious fundamentalist leaders such as Reverend Jerry Falwell generally took a position against the social welfare programs of the federal and sometimes the state governments, which they consider as contributing to immorality and a lack of economic enterprise and self-sufficiency. Programs such as family assistance encourage people to have children, whether or not they are married, they say, which also conflicts with the basic values of most Protestant religious organizations. The former head of the Christian Coalition of America, Ralph Reed (1996a, 1996b) who was an unsuccessful candidate for elective office in Georgia in 2006, also takes negative positions on social welfare programs. For example, he has proposed chastity education programs in the schools to discourage teen pregnancy and supported abstinence as the birth control approach to be taught in schools, as opposed to family planning and birth control education. He also supported reducing welfare payments and making divorce more difficult. For some time, before he entered elective politics, Reed was a political consultant (Bandy, 1998).

Some Roman Catholic philosophers also tend toward opposing social welfare programs as having the effect of reducing or eliminating individual initiative and responsibility for behavior. Michael Novak (1993) believes that the Catholic ethic and capitalism are entwined. He quotes Pope John Paul II as suggesting that government involvement in dealing with community problems destroys the initiative of those communities to deal with their own problems. Novak also makes the case, as does Murray, that social welfare programs not only fail to resolve problems such as the underclass and urban crime but actually contribute to their growth. Although not all those who define themselves as conservatives would agree, religious conservatives generally oppose the recognition of same sex unions between gay and lesbian men or women. They also generally oppose the pro-choice position, which supports a woman's right to choose to have an abortion. Some conservatives also oppose mechanical and pharmaceutical means of birth control.

Business Interests and Conservative Thought

Business has traditionally supported conservative ideas about social welfare in some ways. However, business has also traditionally been the largest supporter, besides government, of social welfare programs, especially those offered by voluntary agencies. Many boards of social service agencies include business men and women, and many such individuals chair those boards. United Way organizations, nonprofit foundations, and corporations are all allies of human services. However, if there is conflict between business needs and social welfare needs, the assumption has been that the business and economic development needs should prevail. The fundamental idea is that a strong economy and business activity is the best antidote to social need and that poverty can be overcome by a strong economy. There is no substitute, economic development advocates suggest, for a strong economy. Government intervention may be harmful, as Adam Smith suggested, and certainly lacks the growth opportunities provided by free-enterprise economics.

Nonmarket or economically planned socialist governments have taken positions against the market-economy thinking of Smith and other free-enterprise economic theorists. But some (Elliott, 1998; Yergin & Stanislaw, 1998) say that business and the state no longer conflict and that almost all governments, such as India, the former Soviet bloc, and Western Europe, all now follow free-market ideas and programs. Margaret Thatcher, who was prime minister of Great Britain in the 1970s and 1980s, and Ronald Reagan are given the credit for the changes. As one writer put it, nations have learned "There never was nor ever will be a bureaucracy so omniscient that it can rival the market's subtlety" (Elliott, 1998, p. 37).

In any case, the United States is not alone in rejecting welfare growth and focusing on economic development, work programs for people who are disadvantaged, and pursuing personal responsibility for one's own well-being. Many other nations that might once have worked toward centrally planned economies are adopting, to some degree, strategies that have been effective in improving and building the economies of the United States and the United Kingdom.

Current Social Welfare Programs

One of Ronald Reagan's goals for social welfare policy was to disentangle the federal government from social programs. Although he and his supporters did not suggest total abandonment of social programs, they proposed and were successful in achieving a change in many programs from being federally run to being operated by the states with only minimal federal involvement and supervision. Blocks of funds, in smaller amounts than the programs that were "blocked" had commanded, were given to the states to use as they saw fit in solving or treating their own social problems. Block grants were developed in 1981 for many former categorical federal programs. And block grants are a critical part of the new financial assistance program for disadvantaged people.

The Personal Responsibility and Work Opportunity Reconciliation Act of 1996 (P.L. 104-193) made the most important changes in American social welfare since those programs began in 1935. Essentially, the act did away with the standardized, federal program of support called Aid to Families with Dependent Children, replaced it with block grants to the states, and gave the states greater latitude in designing and operating public assistance. The new legislation, which was implemented in 1997, allows for states to limit assistance to families to as few as two years. Under the federal legislation, states may not provide assistance using federal funds for more than five years of the client's whole lifetime. States have the option of providing assistance to up to 20% of their clients for more than five years if they deem it necessary to do so. And, of course, states, so long as they use no federal funds, can continue assistance to families with no limits.

There are also rigid requirements for work or training for those who are eligible for the TANF program, which replaced AFDC in the new legislation. In addition, there are many other features, such as requirements that teenage mothers live with their parents or other responsible adults if they are to receive benefits. Incentives are given to states that show a reduction in out-of-wedlock births without an increase in the abortion rate. Strict limits on assistance for immigrants and for single persons who are food stamp recipients were incorporated into the legislation but later softened. Thus far, the assistance rolls have been dramatically reduced in the United States. How much that is a function of the new law and how much it is a function of a very strong economy in the 1990s is uncertain. The George W. Bush administration (2001–2009) did not propose major changes in TANF.

Conclusion

Clearly, conservative positions have come to have a renewed and significant influence on American welfare policy. They are likely to continue to do so to an extent for the foreseeable future. This chapter has traced the origins of those positions, described some of the more important theories and theorists of recent decades that have informed those positions, and investigated the practical consequences of the influence of conservative social welfare policy. It should be clear, however, that conservative policy proponents are not necessarily against human services. Many social agency board members and officers may believe in traditionally conservative social policies while still serving as strong advocates for human services programs.

As mentioned earlier in this chapter, conservative policies have largely affected social welfare programs and economic policy. In addition, there are debates about national defense, which take on some of the coloration of conservative versus nonconservative philosophies. Support for the 21st-century war in Iraq seems to concentrate most heavily in the Republican Party, which is traditionally considered conservative, rather than in the Democratic Party, which is traditionally viewed as liberal or progressive. But defense and international relations are a different subject and beyond this discussion of conservatism and social welfare policy.

References

Armey, D. (1996). *The flat tax*. New York: Fawcett Columbine.

Axinn, J., & Levin, H. (1996). *Social welfare: A history of the American response to need* (4th ed.). New York: Longman.

Bandy, L. (1998, June 28). Fair set up own defeat. *The State*, p. D1.

Berger, P. L. (1986). *The capitalist revolution: Fifty propositions about prosperity, equality, and liberty*. New York: Basic Books.

Berger, P. L. (Ed.). (1990). *The capitalist spirit: Toward a religious ethic of wealth creation*. San Francisco: ICS Press.

Besharov, D. J. (2008, January 9). Social welfare conservatism. *On the Issues*, pp. 1–3. Retrieved February 14, 2008, from http://www.aei.org/publications/filter .all,pubID.27338/pub_detail.asp

Brown, T. (1995). *Black lies, white lies: The truth according to Tony Brown*. New York: William Morrow and Co.

Chernow, R. (1998). *Titan: The life of John D. Rockefeller, Sr*. New York: Random House.

Coll, B. D. (1977). Social welfare: History. In J. B. Turner et al. (Eds.), *Encyclopedia of social work* (16th ed., pp. 1503–1512). New York: NASW Press.

Coulter, A. (2006) *Godless: The Church of Liberalism*. New York: Random House.

Davis, A. F., & McCree, M. L. (1969). *Eighty years at Hull House*. Chicago: Quadrangle Books.

Day, P. (1997). *A new history of social welfare*. Boston: Allyn & Bacon.

D'Souza, D. (2007). *The enemy at home: The cultural left and its responsibility for 9/11*. New York: Doubleday.

Edelman, P. (1997, March). The worst thing Bill Clinton has done. *The Atlantic Monthly*, pp. 43–58.

Elliott, M. (1998, May 4). The romance of the marketplace. *Newsweek*, p. 37.

Friedman, M., & Friedman, R. (1980). *Free to choose: A personal statement*. New York: Avon Books.

Frohnen, B., Beer, J., & Nelson, J. O. (Eds.). (2006). *American conservatism: An encyclopedia*. Wilmington, DE: ISI Books.

Frum, D. (1996). *What's right*. New York: Basic Books.

Gilder, G. (1981). *Wealth and poverty*. New York: Basic Books.

Gilder, G. (1995, June). End welfare reform as we know it. *The American Spectator*, pp. 24–27.

Gillespie, E., & Schellhas, B. (1994). *Contract with America: The bold plan by Representative Newt Gingrich, Representative Dick Armey and the House Republicans to change the nation*. New York: Random House.

Gingrich, N. (1995). *To renew America*. New York: HarperCollins.

Gingrich Communications. (2008). *Official bio*. Retrieved February 11, 2008, from http://newt.org/AboutNewt/tabid/57/Default.aspx

Ginsberg, L. (1987). Economic, political, and social context. In A. Minahan et al. (Eds.), *Encyclopedia of social work* (18th ed., Vol 1, pp. xxxiii–xli). Silver Spring, MD: NASW Press.

Goldwater, B. (1990). *The conscience of a conservative*. Washington, DC: Regnery Gateway.

Harrington, M. (1962). *The other America*. New York: Macmillan.

Harrington, M. (1976). *The twilight of capitalism*. New York: Simon & Schuster.

Hernnstein, R. J., & Murray, C. (1994). *The bell curve: Intelligence and class structure in American life*. New York: Free Press.

Hoover, H. (1956). The welfare state: Road to collectivism. In A. Ebenstein (Ed.), *Great Political Thinkers: Plato to the present* (2nd ed., pp. 805–808). New York: Rinehart.

Johnson, P. (1998). *A history of the American people*. New York: HarperCollins.

Keynes, J. M. (1965). *The general theory of employment, interest, and money*. New York: Harcourt, Brace and World.

Keynes, J. M. (1971). *The collected writings of John Maynard Keynes* (Vols. 1–30). Cambridge, UK: Cambridge University Press.

Kristol, I. (1996). A conservative welfare state. In M. Gerson (Ed.), *The essential neoconservative reader* (pp. 283–287). New York: Addison-Wesley.

Landes, D. S. (1998). *The wealth and poverty of nations*. New York: W. W. Norton.

Liddy, G. G. (1991). *The monkey handlers*. New York: St. Martin's Press.

Liddy, G. G. (1997). *Will: The autobiography of G. Gordon Liddy*. New York: St. Martin's Press.

Limbaugh, R. H., III. (1992). *The way things ought to be*. New York: Pocket Books.

Limbaugh, R. H., III. (1993). *See, I told you so*. New York: Pocket Books.

Loury, G. C. (1987). Why should we care about inequality? In E. F. Paul et al. (Eds.), *Equal opportunity* (pp. 249–271). New York: Blackwell.

Luksik. P. (1996, Winter). *National parents commission: Up close* (Special ed.). Johnstown, PA: National Parents Commission.

McMenamin, B. (1996, December 16). Trojan horse money. *Forbes*, pp. 123–126.

Moynihan, D. P. (1969). *Maximum feasible misunderstanding*. New York: Free Press.

Murray, C. (1984). *Losing ground: American social policy, 1950–1980*. New York: Broadway Books.

Murray, C. (2006). *In our hands: A plan to replace the welfare state*. Washington, DC: The American Enterprise Institute.

North, O. L., & Roth, D. (1994). *One more mission: Oliver North returns to Vietnam*. New York: Harper Prism.

Novak, M. (1993). *The Catholic ethic and the spirit of capitalism*. New York: Free Press.

Rand, A. (1984). *Capitalism, the unknown ideal*. New York: New American Library.

Rand. A. (1989). *The virtue of selfishness: A new concept of egoism*. New York: New American Library.

Rathbone, C., & Stephenson, M. (1985). *Longman pocket companions guide to political quotations*. Essex, UK: Longman Group.

Reed, R. (1996a). *After the revolution: How the Christian coalition is impacting America*. Dallas, TX: Word Publishing.

Reed, R. (1996b). *Active faith: How Christians are changing the soul of American politics.* New York: Free Press.

Schlafly, P. (1977). *The power of the positive woman.* New Rochelle, NY: Arlington House.

Smith, A. (1991). *The wealth of nations.* New York: Alfred A. Knopf, Everyman's Library. (Reprint of the 5th edition published in 1789)

Social Security Administration. (n.d.). *George W. Bush statements on Social Security-2001.* Retrieved March 25, 2008, from http://www.ssa.gov/history/gwbushstmts .html

Sowell, T. (1983). *The economics and politics of race: An international perspective.* New York: William Morrow.

Sowell, T. (2005). *Black rednecks and white liberals.* San Francisco: Encounter Books.

Stearns, P. N. (2001). *The encyclopedia of world history* (6th ed.). New York: Houghton Mifflin.

Watson, P. (2005). *Ideas: A history of invention and ideas from fire to Freud.* New York: HarperCollins.

Weber, M. (1980). *The Protestant ethic and the spirit of capitalism.* Englewood Cliffs, NJ: Prentice Hall. (Original work published 1904)

Woodson, R. L. (1981). *A summons to life: Mediating structures and the prevention of youth crime.* Cambridge, MA: Ballinger.

Yergin, D., & Stanislaw, J. (1998). *The commanding heights: The battle between government and the marketplace that is remaking the modern world.* New York: Simon & Schuster.

14

Critical
Social Policy

Demetrius S. Iatridis

More and more in the new millennium, critical social policy is reflected in the discourse of social science—and in social policy and social work as well. More and more of the professional literature on social welfare theory and social work practice of interventions for planned change explores the impact of critical social policy in the context of social justice, equality, human rights, and empowerment in advanced global capitalism. More and more critical social policy is discussed in the context of global, national, and local issues. Recent global developments in advanced capitalism necessitated critical social policy approaches in a wider range of central areas including critical social work (Leonard, 2001), social work curricula (Allan, Pease, & Briskman, 2003), public policy (Woodside-Jiron, 2004), social welfare (Clarke & Islam, 2004; Leonard, 1997), poverty (MacGregor, 2005), theory and practice (Mooney, Scott, & Williams, 2006; Wahab, 2005), socioeconomic justice and equality (Dybicz, 2004), globalization (El-Ojeili & Hayden, 2007), clinical social work and therapy (Dow &.McDonald, 2003; Sands & Soloman, 2001), education (Healy & Leonard, 2000), diversity and inclusion (Brown, 2001; Hugman, 2001), housing and urban affairs (Martin, 2004), health and mental health (Mubarak, 2003), global development (Browne, 2002; Haacke, 2005), epistemology (Dow & McDonald, 2003; Fook, 1999; Gladstone, 2001), oppression and power (Baines, 2000; Mullaly, 2001; Profitt, 2000), and work-family issues (Martin, 2004).

Evolution of Critical Social Policy

The term *critical* is used in philosophy and social science literature to denote the analysis of capitalist change and the mutating forms of domination that accompany it. It is also associated with New Left, feminist, and antidiscriminatory policy analysis in the context of contradictions between the progressive rhetoric of egalitarianism and the reality of racial and class discrimination. Critical social policy traditions have drawn inspiration from many theorists, including Marx, Kant, Hegel, Weber, the Frankfurt school, Foucault, Habermas, Derrida, Freire, and Giroux (Kincheloe & McLaren, 1994).

Critical theory typically refers to theoretical traditions developed last century by the Frankfurt Institute of Social Research at the University of Frankurt in Germany (the Frankfurt school). Believing that injustice and subjugation shaped the world, its leaders—Theodor Adorno, Erich Fromm, Max Horkheimer, Leo Lowenthal, and Herbert Marcuse—focused on reinterpreting the forms of domination and oppression associated with Nazism, Fascism, and the changing nature of capitalism.

Critical social policy is fundamentally based on postmodern social science inquiries about social structures and the state in advanced capitalist societies. Their dominant statist, corporatist, and neoliberal institutions of capitalist societies serve primarily the profit interests of the oppressive classes (composed primarily of rich white males), which legislate for and control racial and ethnic groups, the poor, women, the powerless, and cultural minorities. In this view, state welfare represents typically ruling class, race, and gender interests (Forester, 1993; Foucault, 1972; Gough & Thomas, 1993; Leonard, 1997; Piven & Cloward, 1996). Critical perspectives, especially the liberating work of Marcuse, provided the philosophical voice of the New Left regarding political emancipation (Gibson, 1986; Marcuse, 1996; Wexler, 1991). Advocacy for liberation, emancipation, and the empowerment of underrepresented people in advanced capitalism is a central ideological theme and principle of the critical social policy approach (Popkewitz, 1990; Roberts, 1990).

In the United States, Britain, and Western Europe, critical social policy is associated with activism against socioeconomic oppression through restructuring the social economy and with social justice and reformist community approaches to social reconstruction. It is also concerned with human rights; social care; racial, age, ethnic, and gender equality; and social diversity and inclusion. Inherent contradictions and oppressive elements in statist, administrative welfare associated with Fabian and Titmussian policies are typical foci of critical analysis.

Critical social policy did not evolve suddenly and does not operate in a vacuum. Rather, it developed in three related contextual frames related to public policy controversies: first, critical theory as social inquiry; second, social policy as a discipline and practice in its own right; and, third, globalization and the transformation of the social economy after World War II. The combination of all three provided the context of public policy controversies and discourse. The controversies include the unprecedented expansion and transformation of capitalist modes following World War II, the globalization of the economy, the support for free market ideology, and the inextricable link between economic logic and social policy goals in advanced capitalist countries. The discourse has accelerated the role of critical social policy and enhanced its practice.

A Mode of Critical Theory

Critical social policy's unified dialectical critique of society and its discourse for human emancipation associated with postpositivism and postmodernism emerged as a result of multiple historical developments. They include the frustration of some of the movement's leaders with the American social science establishment and its a priori, traditional belief that empiricism and positivism can describe and accurately measure any dimension of human behavior (Kellner, 1990). Frustration was also fueled by the forms of domination emerging from post-Enlightenment culture nurtured by advanced capitalism (Billings, 1992).

Frustration with positivism opened the road to dialectical inquiries on the social construction of experience and to postpositivist and postmodern critical approaches. This disillusion with capitalist culture helped to identify critical theory with concerns about power relations, the state in a free market, and class structures. Together these concerns paved the way to the conviction that a reconstruction of social sciences, and the understanding of power relations in society, could eventually lead to a more egalitarian and democratic social order.

In this context, critical theory downgrades positivist, technicist, value-neutral, and rational views of reality as old views of knowledge, characterizing them as "dated," "raw empiricism," "mindless quantification," "antihumanism," "legitimation of the status quo," and "pretentiousness" (Turner, 1985). Notably, it rejects the positivist notions that science and scientific methods can acquire knowledge of human social reality by empirical knowledge alone (that is, only by sensory experience). It also rejects the idea that objective reality is separate from the observer and can be understood through objective observation independently of the observer (Ammassari, 1992; Greenwood, 1995; Tyson, 1992). It denies that social science, including policy science, can be scientific in the same way as physics or mathematics (Adler, 1964; Kolb, 1964). It does not accept that ethical concerns are meaningless in the context of scientific inquiry or that setting goals is non-rational and arbitrary because goals concern only ethics and philosophy (Turner, 1992) or that social science inquiry can only select means to an end, not goals.

Under strong criticism by several social science schools of thought (Kuhn, 1962), positivism has now dissolved into a plurality of approaches. At the same time, new postpositivist perspectives (Nagel, 1961) have emerged, including critical social science and, in turn, critical social policy. Postpositivism favors new perspectives based on the notion that all knowledge is constructed and consists of what individuals create and express.

This view is known as constructivism. Notably, postpositivists argue that, in the real world, the choice of goals is more important than the choice of rational technical means to achieve them. They claim that scientific methodology is not and cannot be value free and objective because opting for scientism, rationalism, and empiricism to the exclusion of other perspectives is itself a value orientation and an oxymoron (Eckstein, 1968; Lerner & Lasswell, 1951; Raymond, 1968). They believe that empiricism and rational technical models cannot resolve social issues of choice among conflicting but desirable social goals, offering no direction in interventions for social change. People, they contend, create knowledge from the interaction between their existing knowledge or beliefs and the new ideas or situations they encounter.

Critical theory relies heavily on several postpositive and postmodern schools of thought. For example, critical theorists are inspired by phenomenology in that they link knowledge to action and to the subjective meanings of the problem to the actors, suggesting that knowledge is constructed in a social context rather than having an independent existence. The notion that a given whole is problematic (not given) and that people create knowledge from the interaction between experience and their existing knowledge or beliefs and the assumption that there are a set of social structures that are unobservable but which generate observable social phenomena reflects structuralism (Habermas, 1970, 1971, 1973, 1974; White, 1988).

Social Policy Planning

Critical social policy as an advocacy mode of social policy planning is associated with developments regarding the nature and role of social planning in contemporary capitalist societies. In advanced capitalism, there are different contexts of social policy discourse. However, two contexts are crucial. These are economic rationality and advocacy for underrepresented groups. That is, social policy planning includes two fundamental strategic modes of intervention for social change or for maintaining the status quo. One is its economic-rational mode (technical rationality), and the other is its social justice–political mode. In its economic-rational mode, social policy planning seeks to identify issues of policy choice, to construct a search of options, to gather data relevant to the choice among options, to set up criteria for choice, and to recommend choices. Technical rationality is based mainly on asocial, ahistorical, and value-neutral technicist and empirical approaches. In its social justice–political mode, social policy planning seeks to identify issue frames in the policy discourse and to specify the forum in which the discourse occurs. In other words, it seeks to identify and analyze the political power game of interests and domination that is at stake in any given policy issue or controversy and to explore the social justice, ethical, and value structures that underlie the controversy.

Distributive socioeconomic justice and political power favoring empowerment of the disadvantaged, racial and gender equality, emancipation, self-determination, and advocacy for the powerless are at the epicenter of the critical social policy mode. Rather than focusing on economic technical rationality, critical social policy analyzes political power dominations in policy issues and explores their social justice structures. Hence, it rejects utilitarian models of social justice (maximization of aggregate utility based on satisfaction of individual demands), market justice models (proclaiming markets as just distributive systems), and libertarian models (opposing redistribution of goods and services). Instead, critical social policy incorporates Rawls's justice as fairness model: a social contract model requiring the fair redistributions of income, wealth, and power and favoring the poor and powerless (Iatridis, 1994).

Committed to the justice as fairness model and, therefore, to redistribution, critical social policy rejects society's gender oppression and inequality. Dubois and Duelli-Klein (1983) provide insights that transcend patriarchal and traditional societal gender roles. In this context, critical social policy practice is associated with social justice reform struggles, community radicalism, and antidiscriminatory movements for just and equal relations (Fenby, 1991; Forester, 1993; Leonard, 1997; Piven & Cloward, 1996; Rossiter, 1996; Tyson, 1992). The social justice–political mode is based mainly on advocacy, distributive social justice, racial and gender equality, and democratic self-determination for individuals, groups, and communities. Empowerment, emancipation, and liberation are central themes of these modes. Between the two poles (technical rationality and social justice) are several other modes of social policy planning, which constitute combinations of technological logic and social justice–political goals.

Critical social policy is best understood, and more accurately represented, in the context of the social justice and political mode of social policy planning. In this mode, it is concerned with both the social justice that underlies public policy controversies in capitalism and the historical social transformation of social economy. Planners enter into the policy arena as value-committed and value-critical actors, seeking strategically to advocate for social change of a kind that empowers ill-represented classes and social groups.

A Mode Emerging From Globalization and Post–World War II Developments

Critical social policy is not a newcomer in public policy discourse. The ancient origins of social policy planning reflect striking similarities with contemporary concerns regarding rationality, social justice, and equality. For example, ancient Mesopotamia established the legal Code of Hammurabi and female roles and equality in ancient Greece were debated in Plato's *Republic* and in Aristotle's *Politics* and *Ethics* (Lasswell, 1971).

However, contemporary perspectives on social policy planning's nature and approaches differ considerably from these older debates.

Four seminal socioeconomic developments in the post–World War II era have shaped recent modes of critical social policy and its discourse. The first is war technology, which includes operations research, as well as behavioral and management scientific investigations. These developments provided policy makers with ahistorical, asocial, and "value-free" technical frameworks and tools to guide their action in finding solutions to major problems (Lerner & Lasswell, 1951). In this sense, technological developments influenced the emergence of technical modes of social policy planning. They also contributed to the emergence of the technical aspects of social policy planning as a macro-level, positivist process of "objective" reality and rational choice in interventions for action by groups and communities (Dear, Briar, & Van Ry, 1986; Figueira-McDonough, 1993; Frey 1987; Haynes & Mickelson, 1986; Iatridis, 1995; Jansson, 1984, 1994; Nulman, 1983; Pierson, 1994; Tropman, 1987; Weimer & Vining, 1992; Wyers, 1991). The policy science movement is also seen as one outcome of this development. Perceived as a structured rationality and organized creativity in the interests of better policy making, the movement is concerned with the technical allocation of resources and with efficiency. However, Dror (1971) suggests that the movement is also concerned with relations between knowledge and power and the social significance of science.

The second development concerns the social consensus of dominant classes about worldwide reconstruction and ways to meet human needs within advanced capitalism, notably in the decades following World War II. The social consensus of major political groups in the postwar period supported the state as provider of social programs and services within the capitalist frames. The democracies of the West, chastened by the brutalities of pure capitalism, the two world wars, and the Great Depression, accepted the necessity of a mixed economy for socioeconomic reconstruction. They concluded that a market economy needed to be tamed and domesticated by an ever-expanding capitalist state welfare system and by checks to regulate the market's stability and its ethical and just operation. Inherent in this was the notion that states have responsibilities to improve social well-being and social structures while, at the same time, maintaining strong capitalist economies. In this context, Western societies, including the United States, Britain, and Scandinavian countries, expanded social reforms on the wave of worldwide reconstruction and a long economic boom. This development is associated with shifts of social policy planning approaches toward the social justice–political pole of the continuum.

The third development, occurring in the middle 1970s, concerns the disintegration of the postwar social consensus, the end of the expansion of labor demand, labor movements, the welfare state, and globalization. The economic stagnation and declining rates of economic growth of the 1970s, massive restructuring of capital and labor, new forces of production, mass communication, technology, globalization, and the resurgence of organized business as a political force undermined the social coalition of elite political forces.

The transformation of the global social economy and the consequent weakening of national policies are at the epicenter of the critical social policy mode. More specifically, globalization flattened the planet by collapsing time and distance (Friedman, 2005), while the global economy is self-regulating, operating almost independently of national political systems, which function mainly nationally. With only a few basic rules, liberal global capitalism is essentially unaccountable and free from social justice and traditional government policies, a situation that has generated new egalitarian challenges and critical social policy interventions at global, national, and local policy levels. For example, the implementation by 2015 of the United Nations Millennium Declaration requires critical social policy approaches that transcend the effectiveness of traditional, technical policy models. The eight Millennium Development Goals (eradicate extreme poverty and hunger; achieve universal primary education; promote gender equality and empower women; reduce child mortality; improve mental health; combat HIV/AIDS, malaria, and other diseases; ensure environmental sustainability; and develop a global partnership for development) are unique in complexity and scope and, thus, unlikely to be achieved with traditional positivist policy approaches.

National policies are also transformed by globalization. Some policies *shifted up* to international institutions (the European Union, the World Trade Organization, the World Bank, the International Monetary Fund and the North American Free Trade Agreement or NAFTA). Others *shifted down* to local institutions, generating what may be called "cosmopolitan localism": local self-governments with distinct global orientation to protect local development policies from global economic competition. This bifurcation reduced the effectiveness of national socioeconomic policies (Wilding, 1997), necessitating new critical social policy practice in several policy areas: global warming, pollution and waste disposal, global poverty, drug abuse, migration, sex slavery or tourism, and the imbalance between capital and labor. Unfettered global economic competition also generated the "public burden model of health and welfare" phenomenon that seeks to reduce welfare states at all levels and exerts strong downward pressure on social expenditure. Consequently, global and national social policies mainly enhance economic efficiency rather than temper unfettered capitalism.

Globalization is controversial. Supporters argue that, driven by three concerted technological revolutions (communications, transportation, and information technology), it stimulates worldwide socioeconomic development, ensures prosperity for all, brings real chances of prosperity to the impoverished in the world, and maximizes socioeconomic efficiency because of free movements of goods and services (Lewis, 2001; Seitz, 2002). Opponents argue that global competition harms the environment, concentrates wealth more than it creates broad opportunities, benefits mainly the industrialized countries, and causes growing social exclusion, discrimination, poverty, injustice, and inequality on the planet. Unregulated global capitalism fails to invest adequately in public goods and produces socially intolerable distributions of income, wealth, and power. Moreover, macroeconomic policies in one country compete with those of other countries, harming rather than benefiting development. In order to promptly "put the genie back into the bottle," opponents propose alternative globalization models at all levels, ones that will provide the same pro-corporate protection for workers, the environment, and the poor.

Fourth, the revived credulity in pure markets and a shift to Radical Right ideologies in the 1980s, brought about by radical socioeconomic developments, moved social policy planning away from the state to local governments and to residual, low-cost social programs. In this context, Keynesianism was attacked because it favored increased central government spending and social welfare programs in economic crises. At the same time, political forces of the Left and the Right intensified their assault against social policy planning's ideological orientations, notably state welfare provision of programs and services for well-being. The fragmenting of the social coalition and the shift to the ideological right moved the trend away from collective frames of social policy planning toward individualistic technological approaches of unfettered markets, which is the technicist mode of the social policy planning continuum.

Critical Social Policy Revisited

Critical social policy's canons for social change focus on community radicalism, democratic social liberation, empowerment, and emancipation. In the process, they challenge the capitalist institutional structures that dominate modern societies. In this context, critical social policy practice is associated with social reform struggles, community radicalism, and anti-discriminatory movements for just and equal social relations. Typically, such practice is characterized by radical analyses of community structures and institutions (Blaug, 1995; Code, 1991; Fenby, 1991; Forester, 1993; Ginsburg, 1979, 1992; Leonard, 1994, 1997; Piven & Cloward, 1996; Rossiter, 1996; Taylor, 1996; Tyson, 1992). Advocating distributive socioeconomic justice goals, equality, human emancipation, and community radical action, critical social policy is committed to social liberation goals rather than to empirical, value-neutral, apolitical, asocial technical interventions and research.

Power and Social Structure

Critical social policy assumes that contemporary advanced capitalist societies and their state institutions are oppressive in that they systematically represent the interests of certain societal groups at the expense of the interests of others. Explicit in analyses of socioeconomic issues are concerns with oppression, exploitation, and social injustice, including the foci of power, race, gender, income, wealth, poverty, and education. Critical perspectives contend that capitalist societies and their dominant institutions serve primarily the interests of an oppressive class of rich white males legislating for and controlling the poor, women, and the powerless as well as cultural and ethnic minorities. Using principles and ideas that serve their own interests, elite classes and governments pretend instead that their policies and programs protect the poor, women, the powerless, and the disadvantaged (Abramovitz, 1996; Ginsburg, 1992; Gough, 1979; Piven & Cloward, 1971, 1977).

Critical perspectives have also helped analyze state welfare and its crisis, critiquing the liberal, Fabian, social democratic, and democratic-centrist or communist approaches to social services that emerged in the post–World War II era. The critical social policy critique is directed at the policies of William Beveridge (1879–1963) and the Labour Party in Britain, as well as the New Deal and the Great Society programs in the United States. The welfare states of democratic centralism in the former Soviet Union are also challenged as top to bottom domination, devoid of citizens' participation in social policy making.

Critical perspectives are also used to respond to the Radical Right's attacks on state welfare (Ackerman, 1982; Ginsburg, 1992; Iatridis, 1983, 1988, 1994; Lekachman, 1982; Rousseas, 1982). Reaganomics and Thatcherism inspired policies in favor of the ruling, elite, corporate class and against the poor. Critical approaches, using class and power analyses and emphasizing empowerment, emancipation, caring, human needs, and Keynesian perspectives, critiqued the ideology and power interests of the Radical Right. Under the pretense of protecting the poor while, in fact, favoring the rich, Reaganomic policies and programs drastically reduced taxation on corporations, and high-income groups increased their profits and cut state social expenditures deeply. The shift to the ideological right revived residual, workfare, and lower-cost forms of social programs by delegating responsibility for state social care to local authority and control.

Critical social policy advocacy has also focused on society's gender oppression and inequality. Dubois and Duelli-Klein (1983) claim that critical approaches illuminate the ways in which dominant members of society have perpetuated hierarchical social structure assumptions in all aspects of institutional norms. Critical analysis has provided insights that transcend patriarchal and traditional societal gender roles. It refocused the way women and female welfare recipients perceive themselves and interpret their tasks (Bernstein, 1978; Code, 1991; Fenby, 1991). This encourages action based on what people actually do (transcending rationalism) and what their knowledge is (transcending positivism), and it considers a dialectic interplay between actors' values and rationalizations. From this perspective, the attention to values and the use of the self provides a different understanding of power relations in gender and feminist analyses and illuminates more accurately the women's situation and problems (Abramovitz, 1996; Davis, 1985; Ehrenreich & Piven, 1984; Pascal, 1991).

Critical social policy has been applied in several other domains, including housing and the bureaucratization of professional practice. In the field of housing and homelessness, its analysis indicates that mainstream social policy approaches are inadequate, simplistic, and atheoretical and that they cannot explain the relation between social structure or key institutions and the housing problem. Nor do they directly explain the lack of effective social policy and provision for low-cost housing and homeless people (Evans, 1991; Haar & Iatridis, 1974; Johnson, Murie, & Naumann, 1991; Neal, 1997). Instead, critical social policy uses alternative theoretical perspectives, which focus on subjectivity, power, powerlessness, and postmodernism (Neal, 1997; Sommervil, 1992).

Habermas's (1971) analysis of the crucial transformation of liberal capitalism to that of advanced monopolistic capitalism is associated with the changing role of the state in the economy. This change gave rise to the administrative state and to the decreased role of the public in decision making, notably in welfare discourse (Kellner, 1989; Koivisto & Valiverronen, 1996; Leonard, 1997). Habermas's theory of communicative action has been used to analyze the bureaucratization and quality of some forms of critical analysis. These analyses highlight dissatisfaction about solutions being offered by professionals and mainstream social policy and management experts. Critical social policy considers such solutions overly mechanical, instrumental conceptions of human reason and, therefore, as inappropriate for designing human care (Blaug, 1995). Habermas's work to improve communicative methods has implications for social work practice in the areas of supervision, agency policy, training, assessment and monitoring, staff support groups, action learning and empowerment groups, user involvement, and social work research (Forester, 1987; Lukacs, 1923/1971, 1993; Masson, 1990; Mullender & Ward, 1991).

Intervention for Social Change

Advocacy and empowerment interventions for social change call for the attainment of strong emancipatory, democratic, antidiscriminatory social liberation goals. Status quo frames and socioeconomic inequalities constitute social injustice and must be rejected. Accordingly, critical social policy encourages oppressed individuals, groups, and communities to examine societal structures as well as their own values and beliefs. The advocacy-empowerment approach exposes the ways in which social and cultural realities may hinder the human potential of all people (Lather, 1991).

Implicit in this perspective is the notion that individuals, groups, and communities do not need didactic experts to lead them because they are capable of becoming enlightened about hidden influences in their own situations of social economy. Emancipatory action and praxis leading to social change will occur once people, groups, and communities are enlightened, empowered, and organized. Responding to the experience and needs of communities and groups can inspire and guide the process of sociocultural transformation and liberation.

By explaining the links between society's institutions and the everyday behaviors of individuals, groups, and communities, the poor and powerless can see how ideology serves the interests and development of elites. Power, as a property of relationships, is transactional and dynamic. When power as force and dominance is the reality, the social systems that evolve become stratified. Power is viewed as a limited commodity that must be acquired (Marcuse, 1996). In most societies, hierarchical relationships are considered normal, and, typically, society's institutions (families, schools, community agencies, the media, government bodies, and churches) enforce the dominant values of the powerful.

Dynamic and Eclectic Inquiry

Critical social policy is dynamic, open-ended, qualitative, and constantly evolving to integrate empirical, interpretive, phenomenological, ethical, and other critical social science perspectives. Implicit in this assumption is the notion that critical inquiry—which includes observing, asking, acting, and reflecting—expands reflective practice (Comstock, 1982; Freire, 1986; Lather, 1991; Morgain, 1994; Schon, 1983; Tremmel, 1993). In this sense, it seeks to integrate styles of policy analysis and research in innovative ways. Rather than providing distinct explanations or hypotheses to test, it encourages emancipatory challenges in diverse domains, including social policy planning, public administration, housing, and urban planning (Adorno & Horkheimer, 1972; Bernstein, 1978; Fay, 1975, 1977; Forester, 1993; Fromm, 1941; Giddens, 1984).

Critical social policy as a process (Figure 14.1) differs distinctly from positivist processes in that it challenges socioeconomic injustice, inequality, and the status quo while it promotes income, wealth, and power redistributions favoring the powerless and disadvantaged:

The critical social policy cyclical process depicted above consists of three sequential phases: Inputs (A), Throughputs (B), and Outputs (C). Arrows 1 through 12 indicate the influence and direction of components and phases. Each phase leads to the next, framing its activities. Finally, feedback loops lead back to A. The cycle is then repeated until its goals are achieved. Thus, phase (A) sets specific societal values and ideologies (e.g., social justice, equality, empowerment, and self-determination) as inputs or intervention goals. These goals frame and guide the analysis of institutional power relations (phase B), including policy plans and their implementation. For example, the decrease of poverty (perceived as the power, income, class, and state dominance of societal elites) necessitates the design of institutional

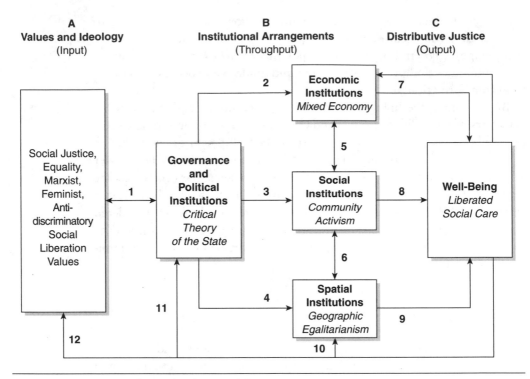

Figure 14.1   A Critical Social Policy Model

policy changes and implementation of plans to increase social inclusion and the incomes of the poor. Phase (C) is concerned with desired outputs and redistributive justice (power, income, and the well-being of groups and neighborhoods) to empower the poor. Through feedback loops (arrows 10 through 12) outcomes are evaluated by making comparisons to inputted goals (A). If poverty is not sufficiently reduced by given interventions, input and throughput adjustments are made, and the circular process (A to C) is repeated until desired goals are achieved.

Critical Social Policy in Welfare State Discourse

Critical social policy discourse is reflected in critical explanations of the nature, outcomes, and future of welfare states in advanced capitalist countries. These explanations have facilitated a major appraisal of government social welfare programs in these countries. The four socioeconomic developments in the post–World War II era, which were described earlier, explain fluctuations in the trend toward greater or lesser state interventions in the social welfare field. The social coalition of elitist forces in the early postwar decades about worldwide reconstruction, and ways to meet human needs, supported expansions of the welfare state in the 1950s and 1960s within advanced capitalist countries, including the United States, Britain, Sweden, and Denmark. Social welfare reform and the capitalist market seemed to coexist.

The disintegration of the social coalition in the 1970s and 1980s, the shift to the political right, and economic globalization supported radical right-wing constructions in welfare states and social expenditures. Understandably, this raised serious questions about the potential of market and welfare state coexistence, notably about the continuance of the welfare state as advocated by Fabian and Titmussian assumptions. Further analyses based on critical approaches and especially class, race, and gender power issues provide insightful and persuasive explanations of the nature and future of the welfare state in advanced capitalism. The central focus of such analyses relates to the key social divisions of class, race, and gender (Ginsburg, 1992; Iatridis, 1994; Leonard, 1997; Olofsson, 1988; Taylor, 1996; Williams, 1989).

Critical accounts of the welfare state in a post-Enlightenment culture have reached five major conclusions. First, it has been shown by critical scholars that welfare states operate in the context of a patriarchal and racially structured capitalism. Having institutionalized class, race, and gender divisions and inequalities, their structures are dominated by common elements shared by wealthy capitalist states, notably by patriarchally and racially structured capitalism. Second, the function of state welfare in advanced capitalism is the interpretation and application of the political consensus (ruling class) in order to contain or restructure class relations. A third conclusion is that the ruling class (the advantaged) favors residual, paternalistic, and sexist social welfare policies, while the working class (the disadvantaged) and social movements favor socially just, democratic approaches and adequate standards.

Fourth, welfare states are products of a combination of working-class struggle and capital's requirements for the reproduction of labor power. Capital is engaged in struggles for profits and fair competition, while the working class is involved in struggles for a decent standard of living and a more egalitarian sharing of society's output. Welfare states are structured by requirements necessary to the continued survival of modern capitalism. This contrasts sharply with functionalist analyses that see state welfare as fulfilling functions (functionalism) essential for the maintenance of political consensus, social integration, and economic equilibrium and growth. It also contrasts with the notion (Fabian and Titmussian in nature) that social welfare represents the rights of citizenship and promotes social solidarity.

Finally, social welfare expands or contacts as a response of governments to pressures from class conflicts, including organized labor, corporatist coalitions, and social movements. In brief, governments respond to pressures from the prerequisites of capitalist markets for profit and are thus pushed into (or away from) expansion of social welfare policies and programs. In this context, state welfare in the United States developed because of two peaks of popular pressure and social reform: the New Deal of the 1930s and the rapid expansion of social programs in the Great Society era of the 1960s.

Guidelines for Reconstructing Social Welfare

Critical social policy has typically focused most of its attention on providing a comprehensive critique of social welfare in welfare states under current conditions of advanced capitalism. As a brief analysis of critical social policy literature indicates, the future of state welfare and the articulation of specific proposals for its future have received less attention.

Notably, the conclusion that welfare states epitomize the requirements of capitalism for profit and survival at the expense of the poor and powerless does not suggest a bright future for reforms of current residual social welfare systems. Is it perhaps an oxymoron to perpetuate an inherently flawed system by cosmetic changes? The path "from critique to solution" is typically far more unpredictable, and most authors are understandably reluctant to predict future events. This includes providing solutions to complex and evolving issues that depend on rather uncertain socioeconomic parameters. Nevertheless, critical social policy writers have suggested some guidelines for restructuring social welfare.

The main thrust of these suggestions about the future of social welfare is organized around the issue of postmodernism, state power, and capitalist requirements (Ginsburg, 1992; Leonard, 1997). There are five overarching notions of this thrust. First, the old welfare state, once the epitome of moral progress in democratic societies, is no longer the ideal. Some of the basic ideological foundations of current welfare states have disintegrated as a result of challenges to modernism by profound social and cultural changes. These challenged principles include social democratic assumptions of a Fabian and Titmussian nature, which optimistically believe in an ever-expanding, universalistic welfare state based on altruism to improve standards of living of all citizens, notably the working class (Leonard, 1997).

Second, the goal of reconstruction reflects the tenets of critical social policy critiques of welfare states. These critiques aim to achieve an emancipatory social welfare that would be built from the ground floor upward rather than from a centralist plan dictated by those in positions of power. This goal contrasts sharply to typical cosmetic social reform efforts based on and implemented by administrative and professional expertise. Community participation is an absolute prerequisite for this new approach to social welfare.

Third, Marxist and feminist perspectives can provide adequate ethical guidelines for reconstructing an emancipatory postmodern welfare state. Postmodernism, in the context of Marxism and feminism, can provide the theoretical framework of action and political struggle in the field of social welfare (Leonard, 1997). Fourth, in the proposed emancipatory concept, social welfare is visualized as a process (rather than a plan), which is not exclusionary, respects diversity and diverse ways of meeting human needs, is not subordinated to old or new kinds of domination or expert power, and calls for the participation of people to determine their own welfare.

Finally, recognizing the central importance of political struggles and pressures, and considering the critique of state and political parties as instruments of domination, critical thinkers propose that the proposed emancipatory social welfare system requires the construction of a political party as a "confederation of diversities." This is viewed as an organized political alliance of a wide range of social movements, each pursuing its own vision—but representing a united front of solidarity committed to a struggle of mass politics to meet common human needs and interests (Leonard, 1997). In brief, social justice and liberal equality cannot be rejected. If either is, society is left with two bleak alternatives: rely on the logic and institutions of the economic market or on public provisions delivered by professionals and bureaucrats.

Conclusion

Critical analysis in social policy constitutes a philosophical and social science platform for egalitarian, insightful, and convincing explanations of the nature, the development, and consequences of social policies and programs in advanced capitalist societies. Despite current swings to the Radical Right and policies of drastic reductions in state social expenditures in most advanced capitalist countries (or maybe because of them), critical theory and social policy have maintained and increased their ability to challenge the status quo and have offered proposals for reforming the social economy. In the last seven decades, critical writers have made several innovative ontological and epistemological contributions to social science inquiry. Their commitment to social liberation movements and their compelling analyses of the changing nature of advanced capitalism have contributed to the understanding of the inherent socioeconomic domination reflected in current societal institutions. The social issues associated with current critical social policy analyses have long standing in social science literature, but critical theoretical frames for inquiry transcend the traditional approaches of the past.

Because these approaches clearly exceed the traditional limits of mainstream social policy planning, critical theory approaches have evoked loyalty from proponents and hostility from opponents. Whether for or against critical social policy, we must not ignore it. The fact that critical theory is still vibrant for almost seven decades after its development in Frankfurt, Germany, testifies to its utility.

However, certain methodological and conceptual questions in emerging critical approaches require further debate. Even those who support critical analysis argue for more methodological and theoretical clarity. Opponents argue that, in practice, critical social policy is less of a methodology than a commitment or vision. Its actual applications, in this view, are vague and unclear about the methodology and tools needed to guide specific operations. They also argue that its commitment to advocacy for the oppressed and powerless can be dysfunctional in a pluralistic society where many power conflicts prevail. By necessity, they argue, critical analysis ignores ideologies and interests of other social classes and population groups. Critical social policy literature reflects arguments both for and against welfare states. Is this an antithesis and oxymoron or rather a harmonious, symbiotic coexistence? While viewing the welfare state as fundamentally oppressive (notably for poor people, blacks, women, and ethnic minorities), supporters also argue that welfare states can generate positive gains in social justice and equality (notably as a result of pressure from low-income groups and the bottom of the social stratification pyramid) in the sense that racial and gender inequalities would be greater without the social policy interventions that characterize welfare states.

From a critical perspective, the welfare state embodies and reflects capitalist patriarchal and racist domination. Having institutionalized ruling class interests, welfare state policies and programs represent capitalist power structures. This raises the issue about the future of welfare states in capitalism. Can the welfare state be radically transformed within capitalist structures? Does egalitarian social welfare reform necessitate a different environment of social economy as a prerequisite for substantive change? Critical writers do not believe that the state or the economic market can be the principle around which to organize future social welfare. This leaves the community as the fundamental alternative for building radical social welfare reform. If so, what community-oriented approaches are both feasible and effective given the trend toward globalization? Community coalitions, partnerships, and federated action have yet to produce viable and new directions for reform. Are new political community or party organizations a realistic possibility in the immediate future? Only time will tell.

References

Abramovitz, M. (1996). *Under attack, fighting back: Women and welfare in the United States.* New York: Monthly Review Press.

Ackerman, F. (1982). *Reaganomics: Rhetoric vs. reality.* Boston: South End Press.

Adler, F. (1964). Positivism. In J. Gould & W. L. Kolb (Eds.), *Dictionary of the social sciences* (pp. 520–522). New York: Free Press.

Adorno, T., & Horkheimer, M. (1972). *The dialectic of the enlightenment.* London: New Left Books.

Allan, J., Pease, B., & Briskman, L. (2003) *Critical social work: An introduction to theories and practices.* Crows Nest, NSW, Australia: Allen & Unwin.

Ammassari, P. (1992). Epistemology. In E. F. Borgatta (Ed.), *Encyclopedia of sociology* (Vol. 1, pp. 550–554). New York: Macmillan.

Baines, D. (2000). Everyday practices of race, class, and gender: Struggles, skills, and radical social work. *Journal of Progressive Human Services, 11*(2), 5–27.

Bernstein, R. J. (1978). *The restructuring of social and political theory.* Philadelphia: University of Pennsylvania Press.

Billings, D. (1992). Critical theory. In E. F. Borgatta (Ed.), *Encyclopedia of sociology* (Vol. 1, pp. 384–390). New York: Macmillan.

Blaug, R. (1995). Distortion of the face to face: Communicative reasons and social work practice. *British Journal of Social Work, 25,* 423–439.

Brown, D. (2001). National belonging and cultural difference: South Africa and the global imaginary. *Journal of Southern African Studies, 27*(4), 757–769.

Browne, C. (2002, July 10). *Can democratization lead to another form of globalization? Habermas and Giddens on the discontinuities of late-modernity.* Paper presented at the International Sociological Association World Congress, Queensland University of Technology, Brisbane.

Clarke, M., & Islam, S. M. N. (2004). *Economic growth and social welfare: Operationalising normative social choice theory.* Amsterdam: Elsevier.

Code, L. (1991). *What can she know? Feminist theory and the construction of knowledge.* Ithaca, NY: Cornell University Press.

Comstock, D. E. (1982). A method for critical research. In E. Bredo & W. Feinberg (Eds.), *Knowledge and values in social and educational research* (pp. 370–390). Philadelphia: Temple University Press.

Davis, L. (1985). Female and male voices in social work. *Social Work, 30*(2), 106–113.

Dear, R. B., Briar, K. H., & Van Ry, A. (1986, March). *Policy practice: A "new" method coming of age.* Paper presented at the Annual Program Meeting, Council on Social Work Education, Miami, FL.

Dow, B., & McDonald, J. (2003). Social support or structural change? Social work theory and research on care-giving, *Australian Social Work, 56*(3), 197–208.

Dubois, B., & Duelli-Klein, R. (1983). Passionate scholarship: Notes on values, knowing, and method. In G. Bowles & R. Duelli-Klein (Eds.), *Theories in women's studies* (pp. 105–116). Boston: Routledge and Kegan.

Dror, Y. (1971). *Design for policy sciences.* New York: Elsevier.

Dybicz, P. (2004). Ethical consumption within critical social policy. *Journal of Progressive Human Services, 15*(2), 25–43.

Eckstein, H. (1968). Political science and public policy. In I. de Sola Pool (Ed.), *Contemporary political science: Toward empirical theory* (pp. 121–165). New York: McGraw-Hill.

Ehrenreich, B., & Pivin, F. F. (1984). *The feminization of poverty.* Washington, DC: Institute for Policy Studies.

El-Ojeili, C., & Hayden, P. (2007). *Critical theories of globalization.* London: Palgrave/Macmillan.

Evans, A. (1991). *Alternatives to bed and breakfast: Temporary housing solutions for homeless people.* London: National Housing and Town Planning Council.

Fay, B. (1975). *Social theory and political practice.* Birkenhead, UK: Allen & Unwin.

Fay, B. (1977). How people change themselves: The relationship between critical theory and its audience. In T. Ball (Ed.), *Political theory and praxis: New perspectives* (pp. 200–233). Minneapolis: University of Minnesota Press.

Fenby, B. L. (1991). Feminist theory, critical theory and management's romance with the technical. *Affilia 6*(1), 20–37.

Figueira-McDonough, J. (1993). Policy practice: The neglected side of social work intervention. *Social Work, 38,* 179–188.

Fook, J. (1999). *Transforming social work practice.* London: Routledge.

Forester, J. (Ed.). (1987). *Critical theory and public life.* Cambridge: MIT Press.

Forester, J. (Ed.). (1993). *Critical theory, public policy, and planning practice: Toward a critical pragmatism.* Albany: State University of New York Press.

Foucault, M. (1972). *The archeology of knowledge.* London: Tavistock.

Freire, P. (1986). *Pedagogy of the oppressed* (M. B. Ramos, Trans.). New York: Continuum.

Frey, G. A. (1987, March). *Toward a conceptual framework for policy-related social work practice.* Paper presented at the Community Organization and Social Administration Symposium, Council on Social Work Education, St. Louis, MO.

Friedman, T. L. (2005). *The world is flat*. New York: Farrar, Straus & Giroux.

Fromm, E. (1941). *Escape from freedom*. New York: Farrar & Rinehart.

Gibson, J. L. (1986). Pluralistic intolerance in America: A reconsideration. *American Politics Quarterly, 14*, 267–293.

Giddens, A. (1984). *The constitution of society: Outline of the theory of structuration*. Cambridge, UK: Polity Press.

Ginsburg, N. (1979). *Class, capital, and social policy*. London: Macmillan.

Ginsburg, N. (1992). *Divisions of welfare: A critical introduction to comparative social policy*. Newbury Park, CA: Sage.

Gladstone, D. (2001). Social policy at fifty: Postwar to postmodern. *Work, Employment and Society, 15*(3), 653–659.

Gough, I. (1979). *The political economy of the welfare state*. London: Macmillan.

Gough, I., & Thomas, T. (1993). *Cross-national variation in need satisfaction*. Manchester, UK: University of Manchester.

Greenwood, E. (1995). Social science and social work: A theory of their relationship. *Social Service Review, 29*, 20–33.

Haacke, J. (2005). The Frankfurt school and international relations: On the centrality of recognition. *Review of International Studies, 31*(1), 181–194.

Haar, C., & Iatridis, D. (1974). *Housing and the poor in suburbia: Public policy at the grass roots*. Boston: Bellinger.

Habermas, J. (1970). Towards a theory of communicative competence. *Inquiry, 13*, 360–375.

Habermas, J. (1971). *Knowledge and human interests*. (J. Shapiro, Trans.). Boston: Beacon Press.

Habermas, J. (1973). *Theory and practice* (J. Viestel, Trans.). Boston: Beacon Press.

Habermas, J. (1974). *Theory and practice*. London: Heinemann.

Haynes, K. S., & Mickelson, J. S. (1986). *Affecting change: Social workers in the political arena*. New York: Longman.

Healy, K., & Leonard, P. (2000). Responding to uncertainty: Critical social work education in the postmodern habitat. *Journal of Progressive Human Services, 11*(1), 23–48.

Hugman, R. (2001). Post-welfare social work? Reconsidering post-modernism, post-Fordism and social work education. *Social Work Education, 20*(3), 321–333.

Iatridis, D. (1974). *Housing the poor in suburbia: Public policy at the grass roots*. Boston: Bellinger.

Iatridis, D. (1983). Neoconservatism revisited. *Social Work, 28*, 101–103.

Iatridis, D. (1988). The new social deficit: Neoconservatism's policy of social underdevelopment. *Social Work Journal, 33*(1), 11–15.

Iatridis, D. (1994). *Social policy: Institutional context of social development and human services*. Monterey, CA: Brooks/Cole.

Iatridis, D. (1995). Policy practice. In R. L. Edwards & J. G. Hopps (Eds.), *Encyclopedia of social work* (19th ed., Vol. 3, pp. 1855–1866). Washington, DC: NASW Press.

Jansson, B. (1984). *Theory and practice of social welfare policy: Analysis, processes, and current issues*. Belmont, CA: Wadsworth.

Jansson, B. (1994). *Social policy: From theory to practice* (2nd ed.). Monterey, CA: Brooks/Cole.

Johnson, B., Murie, A., & Naumann, L. (1991). *A typology of homelessness: A report to Scottish Homes*. Edinburgh, UK: Scottish Homes.

Kellner, D. (1989). *Critical theory, Marxism and modernity.* Baltimore: Johns Hopkins Press.

Kellner, D. (1990). Critical theory and the crisis of social theory. *Sociological Perspectives, 33*, 11–33.

Kincheloe, J. L., & McLaren, P. L. (1994). Rethinking critical theory and qualitative research. In N. K. Denzin & Y. S. Lincoln (Eds.), *Handbook of qualitative research* (pp. 138–154). Thousand Oaks, CA: Sage.

Koivisto, J., & Valiverronen, E. (1996, Fall). The resurgence of critical theories of the public sphere. *Journal of Communication Inquiry, 20*(2), 18–35.

Kolb, W. L. (1964). Science. In J. Gould & W. L. Kolb (Eds.), *Dictionary of the social sciences* (pp. 620–622). New York: Free Press.

Kuhn, T. S. (1962). *The structure of scientific revolutions.* Chicago: University of Chicago Press.

Lasswell, H. D. (1971). *A preview of policy sciences.* New York: American Elsevier.

Lather, P. (1991). *Getting smart: Feminist research and pedagogy within the postmodern.* New York: Routledge.

Lekachman, R. (1982). *Greed is not enough: Reaganomics.* New York: Pantheon.

Leonard, P. (1994). Knowledge, power, and post-modernism: Implications for the practice of a critical social work education. *Canadian Social Work Review, 44*, 11–26.

Leonard, P. (1996). New approaches to welfare theory. *Canadian Social Work Review, 13*(2), 246–247.

Leonard, P. (1997). *Postmodern welfare.* Thousand Oaks, CA: Sage.

Leonard, P. (2001). The future of critical social work in uncertain conditions. *Critical Social Work, 2*(1). Retrieved February 8, 2008, from http://www.criticalsocialwork.com

Lerner, D. J., & Lasswell, H. D. (1951). *The policy sciences.* Stanford, CA: Stanford University Press.

Lewis, L. (2001, November 1–3). *Neoliberalism: Latin America's nightmare.* Paper presented at the Conference on Interrogating the Globalization Project, Iowa Memorial Union, University of Iowa, Iowa City, IA.

Lukacs, G. (1971). *History and class consciousness* (R. Livingstone, Trans.). Cambridge: MIT Press. (Original work published 1923)

Lucas, J. (1993). Searching for answers. *Open Mind, 63,* 17.

MacGregor, S. (2005). The welfare state and neo-liberalism. In A. Saad-Filho & D. Johnston (Eds.), *Neoliberalism: A critical reader* (pp. 142–148). London: Pluto Press.

Marcuse, H. (1996). *Eros and civilization.* Boston: Beacon Press.

Martin, J. A. (2004). Critical reflection and research on work-family issues in Saskatchewan and Canada: The case for caring with equality. *Dissertation Abstracts International, 64*(09), 3497A.

Masson, H. (1990). Training for competence in child protection work. *Social Work Education, 9*(1), 35–43.

Mooney, G., Scott, G., & Williams, C. (2006). Introduction: Rethinking social policy through devolution. *Critical Social Policy, 26*(3), 483–497.

Morgain, C. A. (1994). Enlightenment for emancipation: A critical theory of self-formation. *Family Relations, 43*, 325–335.

Mubarak, A. R. (2003). Malaysia's social policies on mental health: A critical theory. *Journal of Health & Social Policy, 17*(1), 55–72.

Mullaly, B. (2001). Confronting the politics of despair: Toward the reconstruction of progressive social work in a global economy and postmodern age. *Social Work Education, 20*(3), 303–320.

Mullender, A., & Ward, D. (1991*). Self-directed group work: Users take action for empowerment.* London: Whiting and Bird.

Nagel, E. (1961). *The structure of science.* London: Routledge and Kegan Paul.

Neal, J. (1997). Homelessness and theory reconstructed. *Housing Studies, 12*(1), 47–61.

Nulman, E. (1983). Family therapy and advocacy: Directions for the future. *Social Work, 28,* 19–22.

Olofsson, G. (1988). After the working-class movement: The new social movements. *Acta Sociologica, 31*(1), 15–34.

Pascal, G. (1991). *Social policy: A feminist analysis.* London: Routledge.

Pierson, P. (1994). *Dismantling the welfare state? Reagan, Thatcher, and the politics of retrenchment.* Cambridge, UK: Cambridge University Press.

Piven, F., & Cloward, R. (1971). *Regulating the poor.* New York: Vintage.

Piven, F., & Cloward, R. (1977). *Poor people's movements.* New York: Vintage.

Piven, F., & Cloward, R. (1996). Welfare reform and the new class war. In M. B. Lykes (Ed.), *Myths about the powerlessness: Contesting social inequalities* (pp. 72–86). Philadelphia: Temple University Press.

Popkewitz, T. S. (1990). Whose future? Whose past? Notes on critical theory and methodology. In E. Guba (Ed.), *The paradigm dialog* (pp. 46–66). Newbury Park, CA: Sage.

Profitt, N. J. (2000). Survivors of woman abuse: Compassionate fires inspire collective action for social change. *Journal of Progressive Human Services, 11*(2), 77–102.

Raymond, H. (1968, December 15). Sociologist sees intellectual peril. *New York Times,* p. 11.

Roberts, H. (1990). *Doing feminist research.* London: Routledge.

Rossiter, A. B. (1996). A perspective in critical social work. *Journal of Progressive Human Services, 7*(2), 23–41.

Rousseas, S. (1982). *The political economy of Reaganomics: A critique.* Armonk, NY: M. E. Sharpe.

Sands, R. G., & Soloman, P. (2001). Social work curriculum and psychiatric rehabilitation. *Psychiatric Rehabilitation Skills, 5*(3), 495–513.

Schon, D. A. (1983). *The reflective practitioner: How professionals think in action.* New York: Basic Books.

Seitz, J. (2002). *Global issues* (2nd ed.). Oxford, UK: Blackwell.

Sommervill, P. (1992). Homelessness and the meaning of home: Rooflessness or rootlessness? *International Journal of Urban and Regional Research, 16*(4), 529–539.

Taylor, D. (Ed.). (1996). *Critical social policy: A reader.* London: Sage.

Tremmel, R. (1993). Zen and the art of reflective practice in teacher education. *Harvard Educational Review, 63,* 434–458.

Tropman, J. E. (1987). Policy analysis: Methods and techniques In A. Minahan et al. (Eds.), *Encyclopedia of social work* (18th ed., Vol. 2, pp. 268–283). Silver Spring, MD: NASW Press.

Turner, J. H. (1985). In defense of positivism. *Sociological Theory, 3*(2), 24–30.

Turner, J. H. (1992). Positivism. In E. F. Borgatta & M. Borgatta (Eds.), *Encyclopedia of sociology* (Vol. 3, pp. 1509–1512). New York: Macmillan.

Tyson, K. B. (1992). A new approach to relevant scientific research for practitioners: The heuristic paradigm. *Social Work, 37*(6), 541–556.

Wahab, S. (2005). Motivational interviewing and social work practice. *Journal of Social Work, 5*(1), 45–60.

Weimer, D., & Vining, S. (1992, Spring). Welfare economics as the foundation for public policy analysis: Incomplete and flawed but nevertheless desirable. *Journal of Socioeconomics, 21*(1), 25–37.

Wexler, P. (1991). *Critical theory now.* Philadelphia: Falmer.

White, S. K. (1988). *The recent work of Jürgen Habermas.* Cambridge, UK: Cambridge University Press.

Wilding, P. (1997). The welfare state and the conservatives. *Political Studies, 46,* 716–726.

Williams, F. (1989). *Social policy: An introduction.* Cambridge, UK: Polity Press.

Woodside-Jiron, H. (2004). Language, power, and participation: Using critical discourse analysis to make sense of public policy. In R. Rogers (Ed.), *An introduction to critical discourse analysis in education* (pp. 173–205). Mahwah, NJ: Lawrence Erlbaum.

Wyers, N. L. (1991). Policy practice in social work: Models and issues. *Journal of Social Work Education, 27,* 241–250.

15 Welfare Pluralism and Social Policy

Neil Gilbert

Welfare pluralism, sometimes referred to as the "mixed economy of welfare" has played an increasingly prominent role in social policy discourse since the late 1970s. According to Johnson (1987), heightened interest in this idea began to build in Britain after publication of the 1978 Wolfenden report on *The Future of Voluntary Organisations,* which specifically referred to welfare pluralism in developing the notion that the voluntary sector was one of four sectors that could provide social welfare benefits. The Wolfenden report sought to expand the role of the voluntary sector, as part of pluralistic arrangements for the provision of social welfare, though not necessarily at the expense of state-sponsored provisions. As the idea of welfare pluralism gained currency, efforts were made to analyze the design of the mixed economy of social welfare and how it operates.

Structure and Function

At one level, the structure of welfare pluralism can be seen as composed of four sectors—government, voluntary, informal, and commercial—through which social provisions can be delivered to assist citizens in need. At another level, these four sectors can be seen as imbedded in the public and private domains of the social market of the welfare state, which is separate but overlaps with the economic market of capitalist society. From this perspective, welfare pluralism is analyzed not only as various modes for meeting needs through the four sectors, but also as a system for the finance and delivery of social provisions that functions outside the market economy. This view draws on Marshall's (1972) observation:

In contrast to the economic process, it is a fundamental principle of the Welfare State that the market value of an individual cannot be the measure of his right to welfare. The central function of welfare, in fact, is to supersede the market by taking goods and services out of it, or in some way to control and modify its operations so as to produce a result which it would not have produced itself. (p. 19)

Figure 15.1 illustrates the structure of welfare pluralism in the context of social and economic markets. The distinctions between social and economic markets rest on the principles and motives that guide the allocation of provisions. The social market of the welfare state allocates goods and services primarily in response to human need, dependency, altruistic sentiments, social obligations, charitable motives, and desires for communal security. In contrast, goods and services in a capitalist society are produced and distributed through the economic market, ideally on the basis of entrepreneurial initiative, productivity, consumer choice, ability to pay, and a desire for profit (Gilbert, 1983).

As shown in Figure 15.1, the social market contains both a public and a private domain. The public domain encompasses the government sector, which consists of federal, state, and local agencies and accounts for the largest portion of goods and services distributed in the welfare state. There are three methods of allocating social welfare transfers through the public domain: first, direct expenditures via government grants; second, indirect spending through special tax subsidies such as deductions and exemptions and credit subsidies; and, third, transfers achieved through the regulatory powers of government, for example, rent controls.

The private domain includes the informal sector made up of networks of family and friends that provide mutual aid and social support, the voluntary sector composed of nonprofit social welfare agencies, and the commercial sector of profit-oriented firms. The latter overlaps with the activities of the economic market, which, to some extent, blurs the boundary between the private domain of the social market and the economic market. The activities

Social Market of the Welfare State				Economic Market
Public Domain	*Private Domain*			
Direct provision of transfers by federal, state, and local government. Indirect transfers through tax expenditures. Regulatory transfers	Informal supports by family and friends	Services by voluntary (nonprofit)	Services by for-profit agencies	Goods and services produced by profit-making enterprise

Figure 15.1   Welfare Pluralism in the Social Market

of profit-oriented firms in the social market are usually devoted more to the delivery than the financing of social provisions. But there are cases in which profit-making firms subsidize social transfers, for example, when housing developers set aside a number of units for rent or sale below market value to low-income households. However, these cases are often in response to regulatory measures attached to government loans for housing development. Hence, they represent more a regulatory transfer promoted by the government sector than private acts of charity.

The example of how regulatory transfers are generated through the interaction of the government and commercial sectors reveals not only the permeable character of the different sectors but also some of the functional complexity of how pluralism operates in the social market. Not only are there different sectors, but each sector can exercise either partial or full responsibility for the financing and the delivery of various social provisions. A government agency, for example, can hire its own staff to provide day care services for low-income mothers or, through purchase-of-service arrangements, it may pay to have the service provided by a voluntary agency, a profit-making enterprise, or by members of the client's family. In this manner, the roles of government, voluntary, profit-oriented, and informal sectors are variously combined in the pluralistic or *mixed economy of welfare*. The extent to which these different sectors contribute to the mixed economy has changed over time. As the balance among these sectors shifts, new configurations emerge altering the distinctive nature of the social market and the character of the welfare state.

Trends: Decentralization and the Changing Balance of Public–Private Responsibility

An examination of the development of social welfare programs in the United States reveals three broad patterns of responsibility among the four sectors of welfare pluralism during the 20th century. From the turn of the century through 1935, welfare transfers were largely community based. Under these arrangements, local government, voluntary charitable institutions, families, and neighbors provided the major sources of aid for those unable to meet their needs through the market economy. Although the federal government had occasionally funded private welfare services as far back as 1819, when it provided support for the Hartford Asylum for the Deaf and Dumb, the federal role in social welfare did not take on the character of a large-scale systematic effort until the mid-1930s. Prior to the 1930s, allocations through the social market were a distinctly local affair, which relied heavily on voluntary charity organizations and informal sources to finance and deliver welfare transfers (Leiby, 1978).

Under the New Deal in the mid-1930s, the federal government assumed major responsibility for social welfare provisions financed and delivered mainly through public agencies. This was the start of the North American version of the welfare state. Direct federal and state government expenditures for social welfare climbed from 4% of the gross national product in 1929 to 9% in 1940 to 19.5% in 1976, after which social welfare spending declined slightly leveling off at about 18.5%. The structure of the welfare state that emerged between 1935 and the 1970s included a public domain, which financed and delivered welfare transfers through federal, state, and local units of government, and a private domain in which transfers flowed through voluntary nonprofit agencies and informal networks of families and friends. These government, voluntary, and informal sectors operated in separate spheres that only occasionally joined together, while profit-making enterprises were, for the most part, excluded from the main line of activity on the social market.

Compared to most European welfare states at that time, the role of the government sector was somewhat less vigorous, and voluntary nonprofit agencies performed more actively in the United States. Overall, through the early 1970s, the general pattern in the United States involved a system of welfare pluralism in which government directly financed and publicly delivered social welfare provisions that were supplemented by the private activities of voluntary nonprofit agencies and informal networks.

Since the early 1970s, the balance between activities in the public and private domains has undergone notable changes, with responsibilities for the delivery of social provisions increasingly transferred to agencies in the private domain. This trend toward privatization of social welfare was spurred by the 1974 Title XX amendments to the Social Security Act that permitted purchase-of-service arrangements under which government agencies could contract for welfare services to be produced and delivered by private organizations, whose donations qualified for part of the state's required local matching share of social services grants (Gilbert, 1983).

By 1980, as purchase of service arrangements multiplied, federal agencies provided over 50% of the financial support received by private nonprofit social service and community development organizations (Salamon & Abramson, 1982). The widely documented movement toward privatization not only enlarged the range of benefits provided under government contract with nonprofit welfare agencies, it also created an opportunity for the production and delivery of welfare services by profit-making organizations (Gilbert & Terrell, 1998; Johnson, 1995; Kamerman & Kahn, 1989). Indeed, by the mid-1990s, proprietary agencies were prominently represented among the service providers in the areas of nursing home care, homemaker aides, day care, child welfare, health care, and housing (Gilbert & Tang, 1995).

By 2001, not only were private agencies involved in the delivery of social welfare provisions, but private spending through voluntary measures such as employer provided health insurance as well as publicly mandated private spending accounted for almost one third of the social expenditures in the United States. As shown in Table 15.1, the United States had the second highest rate of private expenditures as a percent of total social expenditures

Table 15.1   OECD Countries Ranked by Use of Public and Private Channels of Expenditure, 2001

Country	Net Public Social Expenditure %	Net Private Social Expenditure %	Rank of Net Private Social Expenditure
Korea	61.00	39.00	1
United States	63.64	36.36	2
Netherlands	79.19	20.81	3
Australia	80.09	19.91	4
Canada	82.76	17.24	5
Japan	84.16	15.84	6
United Kingdom	84.55	15.45	7
Germany	90.22	9.78	8
Sweden	91.15	8.85	9
Belgium	91.81	8.19	10
France	92.96	7.04	11
Norway	93.78	6.22	12
Austria	94.50	5.50	13
Italy	94.52	5.48	14
Iceland	95.65	4.35	15
Finland	96.00	4.00	16
Ireland	96.00	4.00	16
New Zealand	96.86	3.14	17
Denmark	96.89	3.11	18
Slovak Republic	97.60	2.40	19
Spain	98.24	1.76	20
Mexico	98.39	1.61	21
Czech Republic	100.00	0.00	22

SOURCE: Organisation for Economic Co-operation and Development (2005), Table Annex 3: From gross public to total net social spending, 2001.

in the advanced countries of the Organisation for Economic Co-operation and Development (OECD).

This cross-sectional analysis of private expenditures shows how things currently stand but not where they are going. Is the relationship of public and private responsibility changing and, if so, in what direction? There are several reasons to think that mean scores on the indices of indirect methods and private social expenditure are going to rise. Data from the OECD indicate that between 1990 and 2003, on average, gross private social spending showed a slight increase as a percent of GDP in a sample of 28 countries. This may mark the beginning of a deeper long-term trend. Since 1992, 30 countries have incorporated private individual accounts into their mandatory pension systems, including Denmark, United Kingdom, Italy, Poland, Slovakia, and Hungary (Kritzer, 2005). As these private pension programs mature, it is likely that the proportions of private social expenditure will accelerate.

As illustrated in Figure 15.2, the shift toward privatization of the mixed economy of welfare has been accompanied by a related movement toward decentralization. In the public domain, this development is reflected in the devolution of authority from central government to local units. Devolution was initially promoted in the early 1970s under the Nixon administration's New Federalism, which sought, in Nixon's (1971) words, "to set states and localities free—free to set new priorities, free to meet unmet needs, free to make their own mistakes, yes, but also free to score splendid successes which otherwise would never be realized" (p. 170). The devolution of authority was achieved through a change in federal methods of financing social welfare that involved substituting block grants, which afford states wide discretion to set policies in response to local needs, for categorical grants, which set federal guidelines that limited local decision making.

The move toward decentralization was advanced under the Reagan administration in the 1980s and continued apace with the Clinton administration in the late 1990s, as seen in passage of the Personal Responsibility and Work Opportunity Reconciliation Act of 1996, under which categorical grants for the Aid to Families with Dependent Children program were replaced by block grant allocations for TANF—the Temporary Assistance for Needy Families program.

Another approach to decentralization involves the increasing use of tax expenditures, vouchers for housing, and credit subsidies (Gilbert & Gilbert, 1989). Although the distribution of these benefits is administered by the federal government, the locus of decision on how the cash benefits are actually consumed is highly decentralized, resting in the hands of individual recipients. From this perspective, social welfare policies that provide cash or voucher benefits represent a market model of decentralization, which as Alice Rivlin (1971) explains is "the most extreme form of decentralization" (p. 122). This form of decentralization (which focuses on the authority to decide what is consumed) is tightly linked to privatization of social welfare delivery, as the individual recipients of cash, tax expenditures, vouchers,

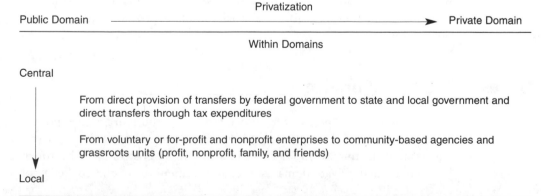

Figure 15.2 Trends in Welfare Pluralism: Privatization and Decentralization

and credit subsidies are free to purchase the goods and services they require in the private sector.

More generally, in recent years the movement toward decentralization and privatization under welfare pluralism has gained impetus from the collapse of command economies in Russia and Eastern Europe and the immense fiscal pressures coming to bear on the industrialized welfare states, which have diminished public faith in the capacity of central governments to ensure social well-being (and raised the stock of capitalism's public acceptance).

In the private domain, the move toward decentralization is driven, in part, by a growing interest in the revitalization of civil society (Berger & Neuhaus, 1996; Krauthammer, 1995; Osborne & Kaposvari, 1997). Community-based agencies and grassroots organizations are seen as mediating institutions that provide a cushion of civil society between the individual and the state. The value of such structural arrangements is not a new idea. Almost a century ago, the French sociologist Émile Durkheim (1893/1933) observed that

> where the State is the only environment in which people can live communal lives, they inevitably lose contact, become detached, and society disintegrates. A nation can be maintained only if between the State and the individual there are intercalated a whole series of secondary groups near enough to the individuals to attract them strongly in their sphere of action and drag them in this way into the general torrent of social life. (p. 28)

Today, both liberals and conservatives trumpet the virtues of civil society. "When civil society is strong," according to Senator Dan Coats (1996), "it infuses a community with its warmth, trains its people to be good citizens, and transmits values between generations. When it is weak no amount of police or politics can provide a substitute" (p. 25). In a similar vein, Putman (1993) observes that "focusing on the indirect effects of civic norms and networks is a much-needed corrective to an exclusive emphasis on the formal institutions of government as an explanation for our collective discontents" (p. 35). This interest in strengthening the mediating structures of local networks has stimulated efforts to contract with grassroots and community-based agencies for the delivery of social welfare provisions through the private domain.

Issues of Welfare Pluralism

As a theoretical perspective on the welfare state, the pluralistic approach conveys a model of descriptive neutrality. The discourse of *welfare mix* recognizes that the finance and delivery of social welfare is conducted through both public and private domains and draws attention to the challenge of finding the most efficient and effect combination of public and private efforts. There appears to be something here for everyone. Conservatives can advocate the merits of private efforts, and liberals can emphasize the virtues of public measures, while allowing that, in the end, there will always be some mix.

However, as Kvist and Torfing (1996) point out, implicit "in the academic and political endorsement of welfare mix/welfare pluralism is a belief that the state cannot adequately solve the social problems. Sometimes, the state is even seen as contributing to or augmenting social problems" (p. 13). Thus, they note that state failures are often discussed as reasons for the welfare mix. These concerns are more a criticism of the trends toward privatization and decentralization in welfare pluralism than a compelling case against the pluralistic model per se. It could equally be said that pluralists still recognize a basic role for the state (and that those favoring a statist model implicitly argue that only the state can adequately solve social problems).

The trends toward privatization and decentralization in welfare pluralism are supported by several popular assumptions that raise a number of issues. These assumptions are, first, that privatization offers the most efficient approach to the production and delivery of social services and, second, that local units of government are better able to serve the social welfare needs of citizens than central government because they are constituted closer to the people being served and bypass the impediments of massive federal bureaucracies. A third assumption is that grassroots and community-based organizations are still more effective than local public agencies because they are less bureaucratic, reside even closer to the people being served, and strengthen the mediating structures of civil society.

Regarding the first assumption, the case for the efficiency of privatization is based on both the presumed advantages of competition and the failings of public bureaucracies that operate outside the cost constraints and incentives to innovate spurred by competitive markets. Those who question this assumption note that the market metaphor does not apply to social welfare transactions, which involve services subsidized by public funds. When public funds are used to purchase services from private providers market discipline does not operate because these third-party purchases of service arrangements undermine the forces of competition responsive to consumer choice. The entire transaction is perceived by neither the individual consumer who receives private services that are publicly subsidized nor the purchasing body (public agency), which does not receive the service. Moreover, social service consumer populations are often vulnerable— children, the elderly, and the poor—and not well-informed consumers; in the absence of the market discipline imposed by well-informed consumers who pay for what they get, third-party purchase of services can have difficulties ensuring the quality of services being delivered. The question of ensuring quality leads into another potential problem of privatization, namely, that the transaction costs of contracting are quite high, requiring complicated measurement to determine the price of units of service being purchased and expensive procedures to then monitor the quality of what is delivered.

Still the issue remains, are private agencies more efficient and effective vehicles for the delivery of social welfare benefits than their public counterparts? And if private agencies are more efficient, is there a difference between those that are voluntary and those that operate for profit? On these formidable questions, the research findings are inconclusive, muddled by intervening factors such as agency size and geographic location, along with the difficulty of equating the substantive quality and effectiveness of social welfare services (Kantor & Summers, 1987). For example, research on day care finds that for-profit centers charge a lower hourly fee than nonprofit centers under religious and independent sponsorship. But the for-profit centers had a higher child-staff ratio, a lower percentage of teachers with college degrees, a higher rate of staff turnover, and offered fewer physical and cognitive examinations (Kisker, Hofferth, Phillips, & Farquhar, 1991).

Regarding the second assumption, it is often true that local governments are more knowledgeable than large, centralized units about problems in their areas and more responsive to the special needs of their constituencies. Also, small units can more easily experiment, and if they fail, all is not lost. However, there are also limits to what local units can accomplish and advantages that reside in working through larger units of national government. Localism can be parochial and oppressive. In small local units of government, it is easier to weld a cohesive majority that may disregard the interests of others. For example, through the late 1960s, the claims of states' rights were used to protect the power and privileges of whites in the South. Also, national units command greater resources than local governments, which amplify their technical and administrative capacity. And state and local units, by their very nature, can do little to affect problems of national scope.

The third assumption concerns the virtues of contracting with grassroots, community-based organizations to deliver publicly financed social welfare provisions. These organizations are thought to be effective in meeting local needs and accountable to people in their communities. Moreover, by shrinking the role of government in the delivery of social services and shifting of responsibility to community organizations, Krauthammer (1995) suggests that these "mediating institutions will once again have the space to flower, reclaiming their rightful place at the center of a revitalized civil society" (p. 17). But these claims often bear closer examination than is usually afforded by those who support the movements toward privatization and decentralization.

Whether community-based organizations are more effective in delivering social services than public bureaucracies is an empirical question. That they reside closer to the people being served, are less bureaucratic, and are more responsive to local influences may suggest that services will be more personal and, perhaps, intrusive, but these facts do not guarantee greater effectiveness in service delivery. McConnell (1966) offers a classic statement of some of the problematic aspects of localism:

> Impersonality is the guarantee of individual freedom characteristic of the large unit. Impersonality means an avoidance of arbitrary official action, the following of prescribed procedure, conformance to established rules, and escape from bias whether for or against any individual. Impersonality, and the privacy and freedom it confers, may be despised, and the human warmth and community concern for the personal affairs of individuals characteristic of the small community preferred. Nevertheless, the values involved are different, and are to a considerable degree antagonistic. (p. 107)

There is another consequence of shifting service delivery from the public domain to community-based organizations, which has not been fully articulated. Public bureaucracies represent the last stronghold of the union movement in the United States. From 1970 to 1991, union membership declined from 28% to 16% of the labor force. While union membership in the private sector was declining, the number of union members in government employment increased. In 1970, government workers accounted for 10% of union membership; by 1991, they accounted for 40% of unionized labor. One of the reasons, of course, is that organized labor in government is largely in the service sector; unlike industrial production, these service jobs could not be shipped overseas to be performed at lower costs. In terms of the provision of social welfare services, work once done by unionized government employees is now being contracted out to local community organizations, which are relatively small, voluntary, nonprofit units that have few ties to organized labor. The lower costs and greater flexibility of community organizations may be desirable. But in any analysis of the directions of welfare pluralism, the trade-offs should be made explicit, particularly the implications for the future of organized labor in the social services.

Finally, at a more general level, the changing balance between both public and private and central and local responsibility for the delivery of social provisions in the mixed economy of welfare raises a fundamental question as to whether the emerging character of welfare pluralism in the late 1990s represents a new paradigm for social protection (Gilbert, 1998).

References

Berger, P., & Neuhaus, J. (1996). *To empower people: From state to civil society* (2nd ed., M. Novak, Ed.). Washington, DC: AEI Press. (Original work published 1977)

Coats, D. (1996, January/February). Can Congress revive civil society? *Policy Review, 75*, 25.

Durkheim, É. (1933). *The division of labor in society* (G. Simpson, Trans.). New York: Free Press. (Original work published in 1893)

Gilbert, N. (1983). *Capitalism and the welfare state: Dilemmas of social benevolence.* New Haven, CT: Yale University Press.

Gilbert, N. (1998). Remodeling social welfare, *Society, 35*(5), 8–13.

Gilbert, N., & Gilbert, B. (1989). *The enabling state.* New York: Oxford University Press.

Gilbert, N., & Tang, K. L. (1995). The United States. In N. Johnson (Ed.), *Private markets in health and welfare: An international perspective* (pp. 203–224). Oxford, UK: Berg.

Gilbert, N., & Terrell, P. (1998). *Dimensions of social welfare policy* (4th ed.). Boston: Allyn & Bacon.

Johnson, N. (1987). *The welfare state in transition: The theory and practice of welfare pluralisms.* Amherst: University of Massachusetts Press.

Johnson, N. (Ed.). (1995). *Private markets in health and welfare.* Oxford, UK: Berg.

Kamerman, S., & Kahn, A. (Eds.). (1989). *Privatization and the welfare state.* Princeton, NJ: Princeton University Press.

Kantor, R., & Summers, D. (1987). Doing well while doing good: Dilemmas of performance measurement in non-profit organizations and the need for multiple-constituency approach. In W. Powell (Ed.), *The non-profit sector: A research handbook* (pp. 154–166). New Haven, CT: Yale University Press.

Kisker, E., Hofferth, S., Phillips, D., & Farquhar, E. (1991). *A profile of child care settings: Early education and care in 1990—Executive summary.* Washington, DC: U.S. Department of Education.

Krauthammer, C. (1995, Fall). A social conservative credo. *The Public Interest, 121,* 15–22.

Kritzer, B. (2005). Individual accounts in other countries. *Social Security Bulletin, 66*(1), 32–36.

Kvist, J., & Torfing, J. (1996). *Changing welfare state models* (Center for Welfare State Research Working Paper No. 5). Odense: University of Southern Denmark.

Leiby, J. (1978). *A history of social welfare and social work in the United States.* New York: Columbia University Press.

Marshall, T. H. (1972). Value problems of welfare capitalism. *Journal of Social Policy 1*(1), 19–20.

McConnell, G. (1966). *Private power and American democracy.* New York: Alfred Knopf.

Nixon, R. (1971, February 8). Message to Congress on general revenue sharing. *Weekly Compilation of Presidential Documents, 7,* 170.

Organisation for Economic Co-operation and Development. (2005). *Net social expenditure, 2005* (OECD Social, Employment, and Migration Working Papers No. 29). Paris: Author.

Osborne, S., & Kaposvari, A. (1997). Towards a civil society? Exploring its meaning in the context of post-communist Hungary. *Journal of European Social Policy, 7*(3), 209–222.

Putman, R. D. (1993). The prosperous community: Social capital and public life. *The American Prospect, 4*(13), 35–42.

Rivlin, A. (1971). *Systematic thinking for social action.* Washington, DC: Brookings Institution Press.

Salamon, L., & Abramson, A. (1982). The nonprofit sector. In J. Palmer & I. Sawhill (Eds.), *The Reagan experiment* (pp. 219–245). Washington, DC: Urban Institute.

16 Feminist Approaches to Social Policy

Cheryl Hyde

Feminist approaches to social policy are concerned with issues relevant to the social, economic, and political well-being of women and their families and to the structural apparatuses and collective processes that either empower or subordinate women. Such analyses are necessary correctives to gender blind and androcentric perspectives that dominate social policy discourse. Fortunately, there has been an explosion of multidisciplinary feminist scholarship on social policy. Central themes in these efforts are the reclamation of women's experiences and the illumination of gendered dynamics in social welfare.

Myriad policies touch the lives of women—child care, reproductive rights, workplace equity, income maintenance, divorce, educational access, and sexual violence, to name but a few (Blankenship, 1993; Gelb & Palley, 1996; Hill & Tigges, 1995; Hyde, in press/b; Miller, 1990; Orme, 2002; Petchesky, 1990; Peterson & Lieberman, 2001; Sapiro, 1990). This chapter is primarily concerned with feminist understandings of social policies and particularly of welfare policies in the United States. A focus on social welfare brings into sharpest relief the gendered biases within policy theories and practices. Women constitute most of the recipients and providers of what is generally termed *welfare*, and at the core of the controversial welfare debates is one on sexual politics and gender roles (Abramovitz, 2006; Fraser & Gordon, 1994; Gordon, 1990; Hill & Tigges, 1995; Kamerman, 1995; Koven & Michel, 1993; Miller, 1990; Mink, 1990, 1995, 1998; Orloff, 1993, 1996, 1998; Peterson & Lieberman, 2001; Sainsbury, 1996a, 1996b, 1996c; Sapiro, 1990; Sidel, 2000, 2006; Taylor, 2000; Williams & Cooper, 2004). While important feminist studies of social welfare policy in other countries have been undertaken, space limitations prevent more than cursory attention to these works (Christopher, England, Ross, Smeeding, & McLanahan, 2000; Cooke, 2006; Ehrenreich & Hochschild, 2004; Estes,

1998; Hill & Tigges, 1995; Kamerman, 1995; Koven & Michel, 1993; Orloff, 1996; Orme, 2002; Razavi & Hassim, 2006; Sainsbury, 1996a, 1996b; Zoelle, 2000).

The chapter begins with a summary of two predominant approaches to the understanding of social policy. This is followed by an overview of feminist responses to these arguments as well as theoretical innovations by feminist scholars. The chapter concludes with brief consideration of the next steps within this body of feminist knowledge and action.

Dominant Paradigms

Feminist approaches to social policy are, to a large extent, remedies to prevailing policy design and implementation. At present, social policy in the United States is strongly influenced by a conservative, increasingly fundamentalist and right wing agenda. At the core of this agenda are patriarchal views of gender roles and responsibilities. For the conservatives, social policy is an essential vehicle to the creation of a more traditional society (Abramovitz, 2006; Dinerman, 2004; Hyde, 1995; S. Marshall, 1995; Sidel, 1996, 2006).

A patriarchal family structure, with husband as breadwinner and wife as homemaker, is the bedrock of the conservative social agenda. Conservative groups oppose policies and programs that suggest the possibility of women's independence. For example, antiabortion rhetoric, in part, focuses on women going against "their true nature" as mothers. Opposition to domestic violence legislation was premised on the belief that shelters for battered women were unnecessary R&R (rest and relaxation) homes where they will be turned against family (Hyde, 1995; S. Marshall, 1995). Family friendly corporate policies, such as child care, are viewed as threats to family life because they allow women the option of employment.

Perhaps no policy issue captures conservative views on women and family better than welfare. Welfare discourse always has distinguished between "deserving" and "undeserving" women—the former who performed society's roles of wife and mother while the latter (typically, an unwed mother) did not (Abramovitz, 2006; Gordon, 1995; Kunzel, 1993; Sidel, 2006). Currently, conservative activists and policy makers (joined by some liberals and neoliberals) invoke an outright misogynistic portrayal of women who are welfare recipients.

For example, culture of poverty arguments condemned the "welfare culture" as pathological. By extension, women on welfare were deemed lazy, promiscuous, and deceitful. In his 1973 book *The Politics of Guaranteed Income*, the late Senator Daniel P. Moynihan foreshadowed current debates by arguing that welfare programs create an unnatural state of dependency that is antithetical to being a healthy, normal adult. This notion of "welfare dependency" is central to contemporary welfare policy discourse. Politicians and opinion makers rail against welfare recipients, likening their need for state assistance to a drug habit (Fraser & Gordon, 1994). Ruth Sidel (1996) notes that "the rhetoric has escalated to previously unimagined levels of hyperbole and vitriol" (p. 5) and serves only to scapegoat and stigmatize poor women (see also Abramovitz, 1996, 2006; Mink, 1998, Sidel, 2000).

This derogatory rhetoric, which now invokes the term "culture of illegitimacy" to describe welfare recipients and blame them for their circumstances, continues unabated. It is reflected in popular opinion and in the welfare policy changes of the Reagan, G. H. W. Bush, Clinton, and G. W. Bush administrations. Such an approach explicitly focuses on gender. Economic (and moral) salvation for women is through the patriarchal family structure that entails marriage and traditional gender roles, all of which is supported by conservative social policy (Abramovitz, 1996, 2006; Albelda & Tilly, 1996; Dinerman, 2004; Edin & Reed, 2005; Mink, 1995, 1998; Sainsbury, 1996c; Sidel, 1996, 2000).

There is another, seemingly more benign, approach to understanding social policy. Well represented in mainstream policy texts are the so-called *gender-blind* (or neutral) accounts. Discussions emphasize the issues, programs, and structures relevant to the design and implementation of social policy. Women, as a group, might be referred to as primary recipients of certain policy initiatives—but this is more a demographic than analytical point. Little attention is paid to the ways in which these policies differentially reward and punish men and women or to the distinctly gendered realities of the labor market and family (Abramovitz, 2006; Connell, 2005; Gordon, 1990; Nelson, 1990; Nichols, Elman & Feltey, 2006; Sapiro, 1990; Taylor, 2000). Gender, as it shapes and is shaped by social policy, is invisible as an analytical construct.

Even liberal and progressive accounts of social policy have often been blind to gendered realities (Abramovitz, 2006; Gordon, 1990, 1995; Hobson, 1993; Orloff, 1993; Sainsbury, 1996a, 1996c). Michael Harrington, in his classic *The Other America* (1962), did not discuss the distinct worlds of poor men and women. His concern was "the poor." Neo–Marxist analyses of the welfare state (O'Connor, 1973; Offe, 1984; Piven & Cloward, 1993) do little to illuminate the gendered dynamics of the state. Consideration of gender differences is largely absent in mainstream examinations of social rights, citizenship, and claims to state provisions (Esping-Anderson, 1990; Marshall, 1950). Yet, as discussed later, men and women do not share common experiences as the poor, the welfare recipient, or the citizen.

Neither conservative nor gender-blind approaches capture the historical or current economic, political, or cultural situations of women. Feminist theory and practice focus on remedying these distortions and omissions. Feminist scholarship on social policy directly challenges these approaches by capturing the realities of women's lives and revealing the gendered dynamics of policy practice.

Feminist Viewpoints

Despite a shared goal of correcting the misconceptions and inaccuracies of these prevailing views on social policy, feminist scholarship is multifaceted; there is no single feminist response to these accounts, no one feminist analysis of the state and its policies. There are many feminist perspectives—liberal, Marxist, psychoanalytic, radical, and cultural—each with its own assumptions and points of debate (Delmar, 1986; Miller, 1990; Pateman, 1986). Yet, fundamentally, feminist scholarship is a commitment to "address women's lives and experiences in their own terms, to create theory grounded in the actual experience and language of women" (DuBois, 1983, p. 108). Feminism is concerned with enlarging the choices that women have in their lives (Pateman, 1986).

Feminist understandings of social policy reflect these different perspectives and interpretations. Perspectives vary in emphasis regarding the regulatory role of the state, the state as a potential ally in the empowerment of women, the agency of women, the effectiveness of legislative versus protest strategies, and so forth. Yet, there is consensus that the state, through its policies and programs, reinforces traditional assumptions about gender roles and thus, supports a gender regime that privileges certain groups of men and, to varying degrees, subordinates virtually everyone else (Abramovitz, 1996, 2006; Connell, 2005; Cooke, 2006; Fraser, 1989; Fraser & Gordon, 1994; Gordon, 1990; Miller, 1990; Orloff, 1996; Sainsbury, 1996a, 1996b; Sapiro, 1990; Sidel, 1996, 2000).

Women's Realities

Perhaps the most direct response to gender-blind and (especially) conservative accounts is the documentation of the economic, social, and political conditions of women. In the last 40 years, feminists have engaged in extensive efforts to document and reveal the private troubles of women and reframe them as public issues. This documentation has occurred in spite of disinterest or opposition by the state and its functionary institutions, such as the police, the courts, and hospitals.

These efforts have spanned every imaginable issue or cause. New understandings of sexual violence shifted attention from blaming the victim to holding perpetrators responsible for their acts and institutions accountable for not re-traumatizing victims. Concern over the seriousness of women's illnesses has led to growing demand for better medical research on and care of, for example, breast cancer patients. Careful examination of the unique developmental needs of adolescent girls gives credence to calls for more antisexist educational measures. Extensive economic research continues to underscore the inequitable employment situations with which women contend, despite important policies such as the Equal Pay Act and Title VII.

There is, however, a constant tension between claiming small policy victories and remaining vigilant of the realities for women and their families (Albelda, 1997; Gelb & Palley, 1996; Gibelman, 2002; Hyde, in press/a; Josephson, 1997; Munch, 2006; Orme, 2002; Peterson & Lieberman, 2001; Silliman Fried, Ross, & Gutierrez, 2004).

Given current welfare debates, feminist scholars have been prodigious in research on the plight of poor women. Diana Pearce's germinal article, "The Feminization of Poverty" (1978), is a touchstone for much of this research. She argued, quite simply, that more women than men were impoverished and that this trend would increase at an alarming rate. It has continued—the majority of the poor remain women and their children. Moreover, recent years have witnessed a widening of the gender poverty gap. Based on 2003 census data, adult women were 39% more likely to be in poverty as compared to men; for adults over age 65, it is 71%; for single parents, it is 86%; and for wage earners, it is 41%. These effects are intensified for women of color, particularly black and Latino women; for rural women; for older women; and for women with no postsecondary education (Legal Momentum, 2004; see also Abramowitz, 2006; Henderson, Tickamyer, & Tadlock, 2005; Sidel, 2000; Snyder & McLaughlin, 2004). On the global stage, women in the United States fare worse than women in other Western democracies, as the United States has "the highest poverty rate and the highest ratio of women's to men's poverty among eight modern nations" (Christopher et al., 2000, p. 1).

Feminist scholars delve into the reasons for these disturbing poverty trends. Much of this work has focused on women's relationship to the workforce. Even with increased labor force participation, women's work is still marked by pay inequity, job segregation, and devalued occupations. Part-time and contingency work, framed as flexible job options, do not come with sufficient pay or benefits. Jobs for which poor women qualify do not provide adequate wages or benefits to lift them and their families out of poverty. The absence of comprehensive child care compounds women's employment difficulties. Essentially, the lack of work equity and employment-related social support programs heightens women's dependency on male wages (Albelda & Tilly, 1997; Blank, Danziger, & Schoeni, 2006; Blankenship, 1993; Crittenden, 2002; Edin & Lein, 1997; Ehrenreich & Hochschild, 2004; Gibleman, 2002; Goldberg, 1990; Goldberg & Kremen, 1990; Mink, 1998; Nichols et al., 2006; Sidel, 1996; Weigt, 2006; Williams & Cooper, 2004).

Others examine the relationship between labor expectations and family structure, specifically the ways in which domestic responsibilities undercut earning potential (Blankenship, 1993; Crittendon, 2002; Edin & Reed, 2005; Goldberg & Kremen, 1990; Kamerman, 1995; Nichols et al., 2006). Regardless of their particular economic situation, mothers are overwhelmingly responsible for child rearing; wives and daughters are the primary caregivers for elderly family members. Yet, women receive little economic compensation for this unpaid domestic and maternal labor, which further ties them to men's incomes (Connell, 2005; Fraser & Gordon, 1994; Hooyman & Gonyea, 1995; Pearce, 1990; Williams & Cooper, 2004).

Labor force participation and family roles not only influence peoples' economic health as young and middle-aged adults, but also account for it in old age. Women's labor force participation often is marked by periods of detachment (for child rearing or lack of jobs). This, coupled with lower wages, has a negatively cumulative effect on retirement income. Women, who were homemakers throughout their lives, depend on their spouses' earnings for income in old age. Because of these trends, older women are at twice the risk of being poor, compared to older men. Estes (1998) notes that these economic trends and social expectations, coupled with inadequate or shortsighted policies, constitute "a war on women." Older women will be more economically vulnerable if privatization plans for social security go forward (Estes, 2004).

Because women experience higher rates of poverty than men, feminist scholars also concentrate on documenting the conditions of women in poverty (Abramovitz, 1996, 2006; Albelda & Tilly, 1996, 1997; Amott, 1990; Gibelman, 2002; Goldberg, 1990; Goldberg & Kremen, 1990; Legal Momentum, 2004; Mink, 1998; Pearce, 1990; Sidel, 2000; Snyder & McLaughlin, 2004). These scholars seek to refute popular stereotypes of women on welfare and underscore the societal measures that stack the deck against them. For example, Edin and Lein (1997) detailed the work ethic, rational choices, and futile job searches of poor and near-poor women. Neither welfare nor work are sufficient to support a family, and consequently, women are often forced to engage in (technically) fraudulent behavior to secure needed resources, a situation that has intensified since the passage of the 1996 welfare "reform" legislation (Dinerman, 2004; Edin & Reed, 2005; Sidel, 2000; Taylor, 2000; Weigt, 2006). Other feminist scholars have focused on the challenges of single motherhood (Christopher et al., 2000; Mink, 1998; Sidel, 2006; Snyder & McLaughlin, 2004), homeless women (Arrighi, 1997; Kisor & Kendal-Wilson, 2002; Mulroy, 1995), paternity and child support (Connell, 2005; Josephson, 1997; Mink, 1998; Nichols et al., 2006; Teitler, Reichman, & Nepomnyaschy, 2004), and domestic violence in their unpacking of the reasons for women needing welfare assistance (Albelda, 1997; Davis & Kraham, 1995; Hagen, 2001; Pyles, 2006). Feminist scholarship paints a much different portrait of the economic and political status of women than do either the conservative or gender-blind theorists.

Women's Actions and Resistance

Women are not, however, passive recipients of economic, political, or social subordination. Feminist accounts of historical and contemporary policy development are replete with portrayals of women as policy advocates and activists. Feminist scholarship has examined and informed the different forms of women's collective action. While tensions exist between researchers and activists, progress in understanding women's resistance has been made.

Historically, women assumed important roles in developing policies that benefited other women and their children. Feminist historians situated these efforts in accounts of the larger feminist struggles of particular periods, rather than adopting the more masculinist style of focusing on "the influential person." For example, Kunzel's (1993) analysis of the emergence of social work as a profession is a tale of competing interest groups of women. Sarvasy (1992) details the debates between equality and difference feminists and how they informed welfare state development. Gordon's (1995) account of the events leading up to New Deal is an examination of varying feminist ideologies and political strategies of that time. White (1993), Giddings (1984), and Hine (1986) reveal the extensive nature of black female activism, especially in the post-slavery period. Both Boris (1993) and Gordon (1990, 1995) illuminate issue and strategy differences between white and black activists during the Progressive and New Deal eras. This research conveys the activism and leadership of women, particularly during the first decades of the 20th century (see also Crocker, 2006; Mink, 1995; Nelson, 1990; Sapiro, 1990; Sklar, 1993; Skocpol & Ritler, 1995).

The contemporary feminist movement has worked to expand women's economic, political, and social rights and halt the severe measures designed to undercut the progress of women. Legislative reforms have resulted in greater access to education, employment, credit, and pensions, though currently many of these advances are at risk (Gelb & Palley, 1996; Gibelman, 2002; Williams & Cooper, 2004). Demands have been made on the state to fiscally support feminist initiatives, such as antiviolence organizations (Hyde, 1992, 1995; Matthews, 1995; Reinelt, 1995). Feminist policy networks continue working for greater equity for women (see, for example, the National Organization for Women or the Feminist Majority Foundation, n. d.).

Feminist movement actions also extend to establishing alternatives to the welfare state (Hyde, 1992, in press/a; Peterson & Lieberman, 2001; Pyles, 2006; Sarvasy, 1992; Silliman, Fried, Ross, & Gutierrez, 2004). Feminist self-help efforts of the late 1960s and 1970s were, in effect, rejections of the state's treatment of women. Establishing a health center or battered women's shelter sent a message that women, not the state, would provide for the well-being of others. Since the late 1970s, a major source of contention within the movement has been the relationship between feminist service organizations and state funding. When resources are provided, the likelihood of co-optation makes these organizations vulnerable to state control, particularly in an era of conservative regulation (Hyde, 1992, 1995, in press/a; Matthews, 1995; Morgen, 2002; Munch, 2006; Reinelt, 1995).

With regard to welfare policies and programs, women have engaged in protest politics through the National Welfare Rights Organization and other welfare rights activities (Abramovitz, 1996; Dujon & Withorn, 1996; Piven & Cloward, 1979; West, 1981). These protest movements advocate for a living wage, expansion of welfare benefits, and the rights of women to receive adequate assistance in order to mother. Welfare rights activists are in a tenuous position. Feminist activists simultaneously critique the current system for its draconian measures while defending the rights of poor women to secure benefits from it (Abramovitz, 2006; Sidel, 2000).

Gendered Analyses of the State

By documenting the experiences, actions, and treatment of women, feminists have developed a comprehensive body of knowledge on the gendered dynamics of the state (Orloff, 1996). Gendered analyses deconstruct assumptions and actions, expose the differential treatment of men and women, and indicate how prevailing approaches serve the patriarchal structure of the state. Social policies aid in the reproduction of gender norms and roles and, thus, support male privilege within a gendered regime (Connell, 2005; Cooke, 2006; Gordon, 1990; Nelson, 1990; Petchesky, 1990; Sainsbury, 1996c; Taylor, 2000; Williams & Cooper, 2004).

The gender-blind social policy approach mentioned earlier reveals inherent biases. Feminist analysis contends that these accounts are not neutral but mask deeply embedded patriarchal assumptions. Within a gender-blind framework, terms such as *breadwinner*, *dependents*, and *the family* are discussed as if they were not associated with particular gender roles such as man/husband, wife and children, or nuclear unit headed by a male breadwinner. The structure of benefit provision through public insurance, private employers, and means-tested programs reflects these assumptions. This design clearly privileges workers with attachments to the primary labor market because they have greater access to social insurance and private employer plans. These workers are overwhelming men and usually white and skilled. This structure serves to reinforce a male breadwinner/female homemaker family model, and it sets a double standard for welfare provision (Abramovitz, 2006; Cooke, 2006; Fraser & Gordon, 1994; Gordon, 1990; Nelson, 1990; Orloff, 1993, 1996).

There are two related themes in gendered analyses of the state, specifically the welfare state. The first centers on its gendered origins particularly during the Progressive and New Deal eras. Feminist social histories, which were mentioned earlier, focus on the women's movements of these periods, with an emphasis on the maternalist reform measures designed to protect women as workers and, especially, as mothers, as well as to provide for the care of children (Crocker, 2006; Gordon, 1995; Koven & Michel, 1993; Nelson, 1990; Sklar, 1993). While espousing the sanctity of motherhood was useful in gaining some benefits for widows and deserted wives, this position essentially reified women's place in the domestic or private sphere.

A two-track gender system emerged in which women were viewed as charity recipients while men, as worker-citizens in the public sphere, were entitled to state compensation. This division remains largely in place today.

By the 1920s, the maternalist movements waned—falling victim to a male-dominated political arena, a resurgence of fundamentalist religious groups, the business boom, and a postwar backlash against social justice campaigns. These developments attenuated reformers' abilities to obtain full entitlements for women. By the time of the New Deal, it was virtually impossible to secure benefits for working mothers. Women were consigned to the home, while men were viewed as worker-citizens in the public arena. Nonetheless, early maternalist reforms provided the foundation for the welfare state (Crocker, 2006; Gordon, 1995; Koven & Michel, 1993; Nelson, 1990; Sklar, 1993; Skocpol & Ritler, 1995).

The other theme focuses on the ways in which the state regulates gender, which makes explicit the consequences of Progressive Era and New Deal developments. Through legislation, court decisions, and administrative mandates, the state shapes the options available for women and, indeed, for men. Consider reproductive rights and specifically abortion. In 1973, the court legalized abortion (*Roe v. Wade*), yet subsequent state measures and court decision have eroded women's choice. These decisions seek to regulate motherhood and sexuality (Petchesky, 1990). Efforts to restrict the availability of birth control reflect similar regulatory impulses (Dinerman, 2004; Mink, 1998; Silliman et al., 2004).

This regulatory function is quite pronounced in the provisions of welfare. Feminist analysis suggests ways in which political, cultural, and economic elites (and often the general public) blame society's ills on women on welfare—making poor women "the enemy" (Sidel, 1996, 2000). In stigmatizing welfare recipients, the policy process reinforces the retrenchment of state assistance and reliance on traditional family roles and structures (Abramovitz, 1996, 2006; Miller, 1990; Mink, 1990, 1998; Orme, 2002; Williams & Cooper, 2004).

However, the gendered messages of the current state are paradoxical and intersect with race and class. Poor women are now expected to work and to marry, that is, to be dependent on both a boss and a husband for economic security. A core component of welfare reform is workfare, which has altered the gendered division of labor for poor women (Blank, Danziger, & Schoeni, 2006; Orloff, 1998; Taylor, 2000; Weigt, 2006). As welfare rights advocates have discovered, arguing in favor of single poor women receiving "mothering" wages has met with a considerable backlash—in contrast to the reception given similar arguments in the Progressive Era. Public sentiment and political will has little sympathy for the "stay at home" mom if she can only do this with state assistance. That option is only open to a married woman with a husband who earns a sufficient income. In this way, the state regulates motherhood and, by extension, women (Abramovitz, 2006; Connell, 2005; Edin & Reed, 2005; Mink, 1995, 1998; Taylor, 2000).

The state, through welfare policies and procedures, also regulates the lives of women as workers. While some progress has been made in ending employment discrimination, women still lack wage equity (Albelda & Tilly, 1997; Blank et al., 2006; Blankenship, 1993; Gibelman, 2002; Goldberg, 1990; Miller, 1990). Under new workfare programs, women's labor is substantially devalued. Child care and health benefits remain unavailable to many women workers, furthering their dependence on a male wage (Edin & Reed, 2005; Teitler et al., 2004; Weigt, 2006).

Finally, the state regulates women's lives through its reliance on women as unpaid caregivers to meet societal health and social needs (Cooke, 2006; Crittenden, 2002; Hooyman & Gonyea, 1995; Sapiro, 1990). This unpaid caregiving labor occurs in family units that are expected to be self-sufficient. Thus, men's wages play an increasingly significant role in family security. This bolsters the male breadwinner/female homemaker family model. Economic and political forces collude to enforce a "family ethic" or "family wage ideology" in which men gain dominance because of their wage earning capacities (Abramovitz, 2006; Connell, 2005).

The labor market makes few allowances for these caregiving demands, and many employers benefit from the economic devaluation of women's labor at home and on the job. Women are economically trapped. Thus, the state and the labor market assume, depend upon, and reinforce a family structure that, in actuality, only reflects actual practice in 12% of American families. Gendered analyses of social policy clearly reveal how women's lives are regulated in ways that limit their options and simultaneously uphold patriarchal values.

Next Steps: Gender, Race, Class, and Globalization

Feminist understandings of social policy illuminate the experiences of women and the ways in which social policy theory and practice regulate gender. These are important and needed contributions to our understanding of U.S. state functioning, social rights, and citizenship. Yet, feminist scholarship still has many more steps to take before a fully gendered analysis is realized. In addition, feminist scholarship needs to more effectively link local, national, and global realities in social policy analyses.

Using feminist insights regarding the breadwinner model and its subordination of women, some researchers have begun to examine the lives of marginalized men who also do not benefit from the prevailing social policy system (Connell, 1995, 2005; Edin, 1998; Lerman & Ooms, 1993). Although, in popular accounts, these men are often referred to as "deadbeats," more comprehensive studies argue that anyone who fails to live up to the designated roles of the breadwinner model will not gain assistance. For men, this comes in the form of a lack of services and public degradation; the current welfare system is constructed to keep these men marginalized. This research suggests a more complex gendered analysis is needed.

Feminist research also needs to continue to grapple with the infusion of race, class, and other social categories such as citizenship and nationality into gendered accounts (for example, see Amott, 1990; Blankenship, 1993; Boris, 1993; Hill & Tigges, 1995; Hobson, 1993; Orloff, 1998; Quadagno, 1994, Silliman et al., 2004). Feminist scholarship risks reifying gender, without careful attention to other social milieu. Yet, to fully understand gender means attention to the ways in which all cultural attributes shape, and are shaped by, one another. Similarly, and arguments of American uniqueness aside, the conditions of women in the United States need to be placed within a broader global context so that more robust theoretical frameworks on the status and progress of women can be delineated (Ehrenreich & Hochschild, 2004; Razavi & Hassim, 2006; Zoelle, 2000).

These themes are likely to be central to future feminist analyses of social policy. The core of feminist scholarship, however, will remain focused on revealing the life choices of women and how these choices are enhanced or constrained by social policy. As the retrenchment and devolution of the public sector proceeds and conservatives continue to pursuer policy initiatives designed to limit gender options for women and men, the insights of feminist scholarship become all the more important.

References

Abramovitz, M. (1996). *Under attack, fighting back: Women and welfare in the United States.* New York: Monthly Review Press.

Abramovitz, M. (2006). Welfare reform in the United States: Gender, race, and class matter. *Critical Social Policy, 26*(2), 336–364.

Albelda, R. (1997). *In harm's way? Domestic violence, AFDC receipt, and welfare reform in Massachusetts.* Boston: Center for Social Policy Research (UMASS).

Albelda, R., & Tilly, C. (1996). It's a family affair: Women, poverty, and welfare. In D. Dujon & A. Withorn (Eds.), *For crying out loud: Women's poverty in the United States* (pp. 79–86). Boston: South End Press.

Albelda, R., & Tilly, C. (1997). *Glass ceilings and bottomless pits: Women's work, women's poverty.* Boston: South End Press.

Amott, T. (1990). Black women and AFDC: Making entitlement out of necessity. In L. Gordon (Ed.), *Women, the state, and welfare* (pp. 280–300). Madison: University of Wisconsin Press.

Arrighi, B. (1997). *America's shame: women and children in shelter and the degradation of family roles.* Westport, CT: Praeger.

Blank, R., Danziger, S., & Schoeni, R. (Eds.). (2006). *Working and poor: How economic and policy changes are affecting low-wage workers.* New York: Russell Sage Foundation.

Blankenship, K. (1993). Bringing gender and race in: U.S. employment discrimination policy. *Gender & Society, 7*(2), 204–226.

Boris, E. (1993). The power of motherhood: Black and white activist women redefine the political. In S. Koven & S. Michel (Eds.), *Mothers of a new world: Maternalist politics and the origins of welfare states* (pp. 213–246). New York: Routledge.

Christopher, K., England, P., Ross, K., Smeeding, T., & McLanahan, S. (2000). *Women's poverty relative to men's in affluent nations: Single motherhood and the state* (Joint Center for Poverty Research Working Paper No. 108). Chicago: Northwestern University.

Connell, R. W. (1995). *Masculinities.* Los Angeles: University of California Press.

Connell, R. W. (2005). A really good husband—work/life balance, gender equity and social change. *Australian Journal of Social Issues, 40*(3), 369–383.

Cooke, L. (2006). Policy, preferences, and patriarchy: The division of domestic labor in East Germany, West Germany, and the United States. *Social Politics, 13*(1), 117–143.

Crittenden, A. (2002). *The price of motherhood: Why the most important job in the world is still the least valued.* New York: Henry Holt.

Crocker, R. (2006). *Mrs. Russell Sage: Women's activism and philanthropy in gilded age and progressive era America.* Bloomington: Indiana University Press.

Davis, M., & Kraham, S. (1995, Summer). Protecting women's welfare in the face of violence. *Fordham Urban Law Journal, 22,* 1141–1157.

Delmar, R. (1986). What is feminism? In J. Mitchell & A. Oakley (Eds.), *What is feminism?* (pp. 8–33). Oxford, UK: Blackwell.

Dinerman, M. (2004). Grading George W. on women's issues. *Affilia, 19*(2), 129–133.

DuBois, B. (1983). Passionate scholarship: Notes on values, knowing, and method in feminist social science. In G. Bowles & R. Duelli-Klein (Eds.), *Theories of women's studies* (pp. 105–113). London: Routledge & Kegan Paul.

Dujon, D., & Withorn, A. (Eds.). (1996). *For crying out loud: Women's poverty in the United States.* Boston: South End Press.

Edin, K. (1998, August). *"Single" mothers and "absent" fathers: Real-life families, work, and social welfare categories.* Paper presented at the Annual Meeting of the American Sociological Association, San Francisco.

Edin, K., & Lein, L. (1997). *Making ends meet: How single mothers survive welfare and low-wage work.* New York: Russell Sage Foundation.

Edin, K., & Reed, J. (2005). Why don't they just get married? Barriers to marriage among the disadvantaged. *Future of Children, 15*(2), 117–137.

Ehrenreich, B., & Hochschild, A. (Eds.). (2004). *Global woman: Nannies, maids, and sex workers in the new economy.* New York: Owl Books.

Esping-Anderson, G. (1990). *The three worlds of welfare capitalism.* Princeton, NJ: Princeton University Press.

Estes, C. (1998, August 23). *Crisis, the welfare state, and aging: Capitalism and the post-industrial state.* Paper presented at the Annual Meeting of the American Sociological Association, San Francisco.

Estes, C. (2004). Social security privatization and older women: A feminist political economy perspective. *Journal of Aging Studies, 18,* 9–26.

Feminist Majority Online. (n.d.). [Homepage] Retrieved February 5, 2007, from http://www.feminist.org

Fraser, N. (1989). *Unruly practices: Power, discourse and gender in contemporary social theory.* Minneapolis: University of Minnesota Press.

Fraser, N., & Gordon, L. (1994). A genealogy of dependency: Tracing a keyword of the U.S. welfare state. *Signs: Journal of Women in Culture and Society, 19*(2), 309–336.

Gelb, J., & Palley, M. (1996). *Women and public policies: Reassessing gender politics.* Charlottesville: University Press of Virginia.

Gibelman, M. (2002). Progress or complacency? Pay equity for women circa 2001. *Affilia, 17*(3), 279–298.

Giddings, P. (1984). *When and where I enter: The impact of black women on race and sex in America.* Toronto: Bantam Books.

Goldberg, G. (1990). The United States: Feminization of poverty amidst plenty. In G. Goldberg & E. Kremen (Eds.), *The feminization of poverty: Only in America?* (pp. 17–58). New York: Greenwood Press.

Goldberg, G., & Kremen, E. (1990). The feminization of poverty: Discovered in America. In G. Goldberg & E. Kremen (Eds.), *The feminization of poverty: Only in America?* (pp. 1–16). New York: Greenwood Press.

Gordon, L. (1990). The new feminist scholarship on the welfare state. In L. Gordon (Ed.), *Women, the state, and welfare* (pp. 9–35). Madison: University of Wisconsin Press.

Gordon, L. (1995). *Pitied but not entitled: Single mothers and the history of welfare.* New York: Free Press.

Hagen, J. (2001). Women, welfare and violence: A look at the family violence option. In K. Peterson & A. Lieberman (Eds.), *Building on women's strengths: A social work agenda for the twenty-first century* (2nd ed., pp. 119–144). Binghamton, NY: Haworth Press.

Harrington, M. (1962). *The other America: Poverty in the United States.* New York: Penguin.

Henderson, D. A., Tickamyer, A. R., & Tadlock, B. L. 2005. The impact of welfare reform on the parenting role of women in rural communities. *Journal of Children and Poverty, 11*(2), 131–147.

Hill, D., & Tigges, L. (1995). Gendering welfare state theory: A cross-national study of women's public pension quality. *Gender & Society, 9*(1), 99–119.

Hine, D. (1986). Lifting the veil, shattering the silence: Black women's history in slavery and freedom. In D. C. Hine (Ed.), *The state of Afro-American history, past, present and future* (pp. 223–252). Baton Rouge: Louisiana State University Press.

Hobson, B. (1993) Feminist strategies and gendered discourses in welfare states: Married women's right to work in the United States and Sweden. In S. Koven & S. Michel (Eds.), *Mothers of a new world; Maternalist politics and the origins of the welfare state* (pp. 396–430). New York: Routledge.

Hooyman, N., & Gonyea, J. (1995). *Feminist perspectives on family care: Policies for gender justice.* Thousand Oaks, CA: Sage.

Hyde, C. (1992). The ideational system of social movement agencies: An examination of feminist health centers. In Y. Hasenfeld (Ed.), *Human services as complex organizations* (pp. 121–144). Newbury Park, CA: Sage.

Hyde, C. (1995). Feminist social movement organizations survive the new right. In M. Ferree & P. Martin (Eds.), *Feminist organizations: Harvest of the new women's movement* (pp. 306–322). Philadelphia: Temple University Press.

Hyde, C. (in press/a). Feminist health care in a hostile environment: A case study of the Womancare Health Center. *Journal of Health and Social Policy.*

Hyde, C. (in press/b). Feminist social work practice. In T. Mizrahi & L. Davis (Eds.), *Encyclopedia of social work* (20th ed.). New York: Oxford University Press.

Josephson, J. (1997). *Gender, families, and state: Child support policy in the United States.* Lanham, MD: Rowman & Littlefield.

Kamerman, S. (1995). Gender role and family structure changes in the advanced industrialized west: Implications for social policy. In K. McFate, R. Lawson,

& W. J. Wilson (Eds.), *Poverty, inequality and the future of social policy* (pp. 231–256). New York: Russell Sage Foundation.

Kisor, A., & Kendal-Wilson, L. (2002). Older homeless women: Reframing the stereotype of the bag lady. *Affilia, 17*(3), 354–370.

Koven, S., & Michel, S. (1993). Introduction: "Mother worlds." In S. Koven & S. Michel (Eds.), *Mothers of a new world: Maternalist politics and the origins of welfare states* (pp. 1–33). New York: Routledge.

Kunzel, R. (1993). *Fallen women, problem girls: Unmarried mothers and the profes-sionalization of social work, 1890–1945.* New Haven, CT: Yale University Press.

Legal Momentum. (2004). *Reading between the lines: Women's poverty in the United States.* Retrieved December 30, 2006, from http://www.legalmomentum.org

Lerman, R., & Ooms, T. (Eds.). (1993). *Young unwed fathers: Changing roles and emerging policies.* Philadelphia: Temple University Press.

Marshall, S. (1995). Confrontation and co-optation in antifeminist organizations. In M. Ferree & P. Martin (Eds.), *Feminist organizations: Harvest of the new women's movement* (pp. 323–337). Philadelphia: Temple University Press.

Marshall, T. H. (1950). *Citizenship and social class and other essays.* Cambridge, UK: Cambridge University Press.

Matthews, N. (1995). Feminist clashes with the state: Tactical choices by state-funded rape crisis centers. In M. Ferree & P. Martin (Eds.), *Feminist organiza-tions: Harvest of the new women's movement* (pp. 291–305). Philadelphia: Temple University Press.

Miller, D. C. (1990). *Women and social welfare: A feminist analysis.* New York: Praeger.

Mink, G. (1990). The lady and the tramp: Gender, race, and the origins of the American welfare state. In L. Gordon (Ed.), *Women, the state, and welfare* (pp. 92–122). Madison: University of Wisconsin Press.

Mink, G. (1995). *Wages of motherhood: Inequality in the welfare state.* Ithaca, NY: Cornell University Press.

Mink, G. (1998). *Welfare's end.* Ithaca, NY: Cornell University Press.

Morgen, S. (2002). *Into our own hands: The women's health movement in the United States.* New Brunswick, NJ: Rutgers University Press.

Moynihan, D. P. (1973). *The politics of a guaranteed income: The Nixon adminis-tration and the Family Assistance Plan.* New York: Random House.

Mulroy, E. (1995). *The newly uprooted: Single mothers in urban life.* Westport, CT: Auburn House.

Munch, S. (2006). The women's health movement making policy, 1970–1995. *Social Work in Health Care, 43,* 17–32.

National Organization for Women. (n.d.). [Homepage]. Retrieved February 5, 2007, from http://www.now.org

Nelson, B. (1990). The origins of the two-channel welfare state: Workmen's com-pensation and mothers' aid. In L. Gordon (Ed.), *Women, the state, and welfare* (pp. 123–151). Madison: University of Wisconsin Press.

Nichols, L., Elman, C., & Feltey, K. (2006). The economic resource receipt of new mothers. *Journal of Family Issues, 27*(9), 1305–1330.

O'Connor, J. (1973). *The fiscal crisis of the state.* New York: St. Martin's Press.

Offe, C. (1984). *The contradictions of the welfare state.* Cambridge: MIT Press.

Orloff, A. (1993, June). Gender and the social rights of citizenship: The comparative analysis of gender relations and welfare states. *American Sociological Review, 58,* 303–328.

Orloff, A. (1996). *Gender and the welfare state* (Institute for Research on Poverty Discussion Paper No. 1082-96). Madison: University of Wisconsin.

Orloff, A. (1998, August). *Ending the entitlement of poor mothers, expanding the claims of poor employed parents: Gender, race, class in contemporary U.S. social policy.* Paper presented at the Annual Meeting of the American Sociological Association, San Francisco.

Orme, J. (2002). Social work: Gender, care and justice. *British Journal of Social Work, 32,* 799–814.

Pateman, C. (1986). Introduction: The theoretical subversiveness of feminism. In C. Pateman & E. Gross (Eds.), *Feminist challenges: Social and political theory* (pp. 1–10). Boston: Northeastern University Press.

Pearce, D. (1978). The feminization of poverty: Women, work and welfare. *Urban & Social Change Review, 11,* 28–36.

Pearce, D. (1990). Welfare is not *for* women: Why the war on poverty cannot conquer the feminization of poverty. In L. Gordon (Ed.), *Women, the state, and welfare* (pp. 265–279). Madison: University of Wisconsin Press.

Petchesky, R. (1990). *Abortion and woman's choice: The state, sexuality and reproductive freedom* (2nd ed.). Boston: Northeastern University Press.

Peterson, K., & Lieberman, A. (Eds.). (2001). *Building on women's strengths: A social work agenda for the twenty-first century* (2nd ed.). Binghamton, NY: Haworth Press.

Piven, F., & Cloward, R. (1979). *Poor people's movements: Why they succeed, how they fail.* New York: Vintage Books.

Piven, F., & Cloward, R. (1993). *Regulating the poor: The functions of public welfare* (2nd ed.). New York: Vintage Books.

Pyles, L. (2006). Toward safety for low-income battered women: Promoting social justice strategies. *Families in Society, 87*(1), 63–70.

Quadagno, J. (1994). *The color of welfare.* New York: Oxford University Press.

Razavi, S., & Hassim, S. (Eds.). (2006). *Gender and social policy in a global context: Uncovering the gendered structure of 'the social.'* New York: Palgrave Macmillan.

Reinelt, C. (1995). Moving onto the terrain of the state: The battered women's movement and the politics of engagement. In M. Ferree & P. Martin (Eds.), *Feminist organizations: Harvest of the new women's movement* (pp. 84–104). Philadelphia: Temple University Press.

Sainsbury, D. (1996a). *Gender, equality and welfare states.* New York: Cambridge University Press.

Sainsbury, D. (Ed.). (1996b). *Gendering welfare states.* Thousand Oaks, CA: Sage.

Sainsbury, D. (1996c). Women's and men's social rights: Gendering dimensions of welfare states. In D. Sainsbury (Ed.), *Gendering welfare states* (pp. 150–169). Thousand Oaks, CA: Sage.

Sapiro, V. (1990). The gender basis of American social policy. In L. Gordon (Ed.), *Women, the state, and welfare* (pp. 36–54). Madison: University of Wisconsin Press.

Sarvasy, W. (1992). Beyond the difference versus equality policy debates: Postsuffrage feminism, citizenship and the quest for a feminist welfare state. *Signs: Journal of Women in Culture and Society, 17*(2), 329–360.

Sidel, R. (1996). *Keeping women and children last: America's war on the poor.* New York: Penguin Books.

Sidel, R. (2000). The enemy within: The demonization of poor women. *Journal of Sociology and Social Welfare, 27*(1), 73–84.

Sidel, R. (2006). *Unsung heroines: Single mothers and the American dream*. Berkeley: University of California Press.

Silliman, J., Fried, M., Ross, L., & Gutierrez, E. (Eds.). (2004). *Undivided rights: Women of color organize for reproductive justice*. Boston: South End Press.

Sklar, K. (1993). The historical foundations of women's power in the creation of the American welfare state, 1830–1930. In S. Koven & S. Michel (Eds.), *Mothers of a new world: Maternalist politics and the origins of welfare states* (pp. 43–83). New York: Routledge.

Skocpol, T., & Ritler, G. (1995). Gender and the origins of modern social policies in Britain and the United States. In T. Skocpol (Ed.), *Social policy in the United States: Future possibilities in historical perspective* (pp. 72–135). Princeton, NJ: Princeton University Press.

Snyder, A., & McLaughlin, D. (2004). Female-headed families and poverty in rural America. *Rural Sociology, 69*(1), 127–149.

Taylor, M. (2000). The potential impact of gender role socialization on welfare policy formation. *Journal of Sociology and Social Welfare, 27*(3), 135–152.

Teitler, J., Reichman, N., & Nepomnyaschy, L. (2004). Sources of support, child care and hardship among unwed mothers, 1999–2001. *Social Service Review, 78*(1), 125–148.

Weigt, J. (2006). Compromises to carework: The social organization of mothers' experiences in the low wage labor market after welfare reform. *Social Problems, 53*(3), 332–351.

West, G. (1981). *The national welfare rights movement: The social protest of poor women*. New York: Praeger.

White, D. (1993). The cost of club work, the price of black feminism. In N. Hewitt & S. Lebsock (Eds.), *Visible women: New essays on American activism* (pp. 247–269). Urbana: University of Illinois Press.

Williams, J., & Cooper, H. (2004). The public policy of motherhood. *Journal of Social Issues, 60*(4), 849–865.

Zoelle, D. (2000). *Globalizing concern for women's human rights: The failure of the American model*. New York: St. Martin's Press.

17

Race, Politics, and Social Policy

Lori Parham, Jill Quadagno, and Jordan Brown

Political theorists who attempt to trace the grand panorama of American politics have often failed to recognize the way racial issues have influenced America's social, economic, and political institutions (Morone, 1990). Yet American political development has been organized around the dynamics of race, and conflicts over race are embedded in the structure of all social policies (Katz, 2001). Although social policy does not reproduce racial inequality as directly as it did in the past, race remains an ambiguous moral force in contemporary American politics (Omi & Winant, 1994). It not only influences the strategies and tactics of elected officials and policy makers, it also shapes the way citizens define the functions and responsibilities of government. This chapter examines current policy trends in the context of the continuing political struggle to reshape social institutions that have been designed, intentionally or not, to reproduce racial inequality.

The Legacy of the New Deal

Racial inequality as a distinguishing feature of American exceptionalism became embedded in national social policy during the New Deal. The Social Security Act of 1935 created two social insurance programs, Old Age Insurance and Unemployment Insurance, and two means-tested programs for the poor, Old Age Assistance and Aid to Dependent Children (ADC). Southern Democrats would only support the Social Security Act if labor arrangements in the South were left undisturbed. As a result, workers in agricultural and domestic service, jobs held by three-fifths of all black workers, were excluded from the social insurance programs (Lieberman, 1998). Instead, they were relegated to the means-tested programs where local welfare authorities could determine benefit levels and set eligibility rules

(Quadagno, 1994). Because of local discretion, black woman and children were largely excluded from ADC, especially in the South (Amott, 1993).

Other New Deal programs also reproduced racial inequality in their rules and structure. The National Labor Relations Act (or Wagner Act) of 1935 granted workers the right to organize unions and bargain collectively (Domhoff, 1990). It also permitted labor organizations to exclude African Americans and to establish separate, racially segregated unions. From the 1930s to the 1960s, the skilled trade unions maintained policies of racial exclusion and segregation with the tacit approval of the federal government (King, 1995).

The New Deal also reinforced patterns of residential racial segregation through housing policy. The Federal Housing Authority (FHA) encouraged "redlining": a red line was drawn around areas of cities considered too risky for loans, and risk assessment was based on economic *or* racial reasons. Not surprisingly, most redlined areas were in predominantly black neighborhoods. Until 1949, the FHA also encouraged the use of restrictive covenants that banned African Americans from given neighborhoods, and it refused to insure mortgages in integrated neighborhoods. Public housing also extended racial segregation, as authorities located new projects in racially segregated neighborhoods and intentionally selected tenants by race (Quadagno, 1994).

Although the New Deal provided income security against job loss, injury, and old age to white working men and their families, it also reproduced the racial divisions that were embedded in the political and social institutions of the nation.

The Legacy of the Great Society

Following World War II, thousands of African Americans migrated from the rural South to urban areas, particularly in the Northeast and Midwest. In 1940, 77% of African Americans lived in the South; by 1970, only 53% still did. The presence of black migrants in northern cities moved the American dilemma from the periphery to the center of national politics and gave rise to the struggle for racial equality. As the civil rights movement swept across the nation, it demanded the dismantling of segregated institutions in the South but also equal opportunity in employment, education, housing, and health care.

The Civil Rights Act of 1964 represented a major victory with sweeping consequences. It outlawed segregation in public accommodations, banned racial discrimination in employment and in public education, and barred the use of federal funds in programs that operated in a discriminatory manner. What could not be alleviated through legal remedies were the social needs created through decades of discrimination and neglect. These needs were what President Lyndon Johnson sought to address when he embarked on his War on Poverty. The capstone legislation of the War on Poverty, the Economic Opportunity Act of 1964, provided federal funds for job training, community improvement, education, and health care. As antipoverty resources poured into local communities, they became absorbed into the struggle for racial equality, creating a white backlash against the welfare state.

Community Action

The key antipoverty program was community action, which was under the jurisdiction of the new Office of Economic Opportunity (OEO). The OEO, in turn, delegated responsibility to community action agencies, which established neighborhood health centers, emergency food and medical services, and job and literacy training. Many community action programs were developed by local civil rights organizations, which used the resources to pursue the struggle for political equality (Andrews, 2001). Throughout the South, community action programs undermined the patronage-based system of party politics, empowered racially integrated community organizations, and created new distributive networks. These programs also introduced a profusion of resources into urban ghettos, creating a network of affiliated agencies that provided the first source of jobs for African Americans that was independent from the local power structure.

As black men and women gained experience and visibility in community action programs, where they campaigned for the poverty boards, chaired meetings, lobbied, and litigated, they used these experiences to enter politics (Andrews, 1997). When Johnson declared the War on Poverty, there were no black mayors and only 70 elected black officials at any level of government. Five years later, there were 1,500 elected black officials; by 1981, there were 5,014 including 170 mayors. Many got their start in community action programs.

Although community action programs helped fuel the struggle for political equality, they also created controversy, because they challenged the local power structure and toppled white politicians. Following a 1967 New Jersey riot that was linked indirectly to the local community action agency, OEO shut down that program. Over the next few years, OEO's core programs went to other agencies, and in 1973, President Nixon unceremoniously abolished the agency, wiping the inner cities off the legislative agenda for the next 20 years.

Job Training and the Origins of Affirmative Action

Since the New Deal, the federal government had tacitly allowed the skilled trades unions to exclude African Americans. Title VII of the Civil Rights Act banned discrimination in employment on the basis of race, religion, national origin, or sex by private employers with 15 or more employees (Reskin, 1998). A clause specifically directed at trade unions prohibited discrimination in the admission of members, in admitting persons to apprenticeship programs, and in referring workers to jobs. The problem was that federal officials had no mechanism to force the unions to comply with the law.

Many of the federal job training programs created or expanded by the War on Poverty recruited trainees from urban ghettos and thus had a disproportionate number of black trainees. By 1968, African Americans constituted 47% of the Neighborhood Youth Corps, 81% of the Concentrated Employment Program, and 59% of the Job Corps. As poor, black men (and some women) moved out of federal job training programs and into the labor market, they were blocked from jobs in the skilled trades, where hiring was controlled by the unions, which gave preference to their members (Quadagno, 1994). These practices put the federal government on a collision course with the skilled trade unions most jealously guarded prerogative.

In 1968, the Department of Labor ruled that building contractors could not receive federal contracts unless they took "affirmative action." Taking affirmative action meant proving that minorities were represented in all trades on the job and in all phases of the work. Under the new regulations, the Equal Employment Opportunity Commission (EEOC) could require each union to report on whether it was complying with affirmative action and then decide if the union was discriminating. If it was, then the EEOC could turn the case over to the attorney general to bring a civil suit against the offenders. In practice, the right to sue had little significance, because few people with employment grievances could afford a lawsuit, and such grievances were difficult to prove (Quadagno, 1994).

As the skilled trade unions vehemently resisted federal intervention in hiring practices, job training programs became embroiled in the pursuit of civil rights. Over the long run, this conflict triggered a white backlash against the Democratic Party, undermining the party's support among a key constituency.

Housing Policy

From the New Deal to the 1960s, federal housing policy had encouraged private home ownership on a racially discriminatory basis. Title IV of the Civil Rights Act required that all newly constructed housing financed by the federal government engage in open housing practices (Massey & Denton, 1993). However, that ruling did not apply to the existing housing stock, which remained segregated, nor was it easily enforceable in housing under construction because of neighborhood segregation patterns. In 1968, following a week of rioting across the nation, Congress enacted a stricter and more encompassing fair housing bill, the Civil Rights Act of 1968. Title VIII banned discrimination in the sale, rental, or financing of most housing units and brought millions of single-family homes owned by private individuals under federal fair housing law. Title VIII also mandated that the Department of Housing and Urban Development (HUD) use its own programs to achieve open occupancy, reorient programs that had previously been used to improve housing for whites, and expand housing for the inner city poor.

Although federal housing officials tried to pressure suburban communities to integrate, the widespread opposition of white residents to this "open communities" policy quickened the pace of white flight to the suburbs and ultimately forced President Nixon to rescind enforcement orders. No progress was made in integrating subsidized housing in urban ghettos, which remained racially segregated. During the 1970s, the supply of federally subsidized housing declined, as funds for these programs were slashed (Katz, 2001). Since then, federal housing production has stagnated, and no president has advocated suburban housing integration (Orfield, 1988).

Health Care

Racial discrimination was as pervasive in the health care system as in other social institutions. Many hospitals maintained "white" and "colored" floors, labeled equipment by race, and reserved a certain number of beds for patients of each race. Throughout the South, black doctors were refused staff privileges, and black students were excluded from nurse training programs. The problem was not confined to the South. In northern cities, too, many hospitals segregated black patients from white patients and discriminated against black health care workers (Quadagno, 2000, 2005).

The Hill-Burton Act of 1946 was enacted to eliminate the shortage of beds in hospitals and other health care facilities. Provisions protecting the principle of "separate but equal" were written into the legislation by southern congressmen to ensure that federal officials could not regulate internal hospital policies. Federal statutes did require that institutions receiving Hill-Burton funds sign a nondiscrimination assurance agreeing that care would be available to all persons regardless of race, creed, or color. However, Section 622 allowed federal funds to be used to construct separate facilities for different population groups as long as the segregated facilities were of equal quality. It also allowed internal racial segregation as long as no patient was denied admission if beds allotted to the other population group were available. Further, doctors and other health care workers could be denied staff privileges and jobs based on race because these were issues of internal hospital policy outside the jurisdiction of the federal government. Fourteen southern states constructed entire hospital systems based on the principle of "separate but equal." Although the Hill-Burton Act did extend access to health care facilities to southern blacks, it was on a segregated basis (Thomas, 2006).

Title VI of the Civil Rights Act banned racial discrimination in any program or activity receiving federal funds. The problem was that the law only applied to hospitals currently receiving federal funds but not to those that had been constructed with Hill-Burton funds over the past 20 years. When Medicare was enacted in 1965, it included a provision that hospitals would not be eligible for Medicare if they discriminated in patient admissions and room assignments or in staff assignments. Within three weeks after Medicare was put into operation, only 0.5% of hospitals were not certified for Medicare eligibility. Most hospitals rapidly eliminated racial barriers because of the promise of desperately needed federal funds (Quadagno, 2005). Unlike racial integration in other social institutions, health care integration succeeded because of the leverage provided by federal resources.

Welfare for Poor Mothers

No program better exemplifies the racially divisive character of social welfare programs in the United States than Aid to Families with Dependent Children (AFDC), which evolved out of ADC. During the 1960s, African American women entered the program in record numbers in part due to rising need in inner cities but also because of assistance provided by legal advocates funded by Great Society programs (Amott, 1993). By 1974, 45% of all AFDC recipients were black, reversing the historical pattern of exclusion of African American women and children.

As state budgets rose in concert with the expanding welfare rolls, reducing spending became a major political issue. In 1972, the Nixon administration proposed the Family Assistance Plan (FAP), which would have replaced AFDC with a guaranteed annual income for all the working and nonworking poor (Quadagno, 1994). The Family Assistance Plan was passed in the House and initially had strong support in the Senate. Yet, the bill was never reported out of the Senate Finance Committee, and two years later, a substantially altered bill was defeated. Southern congressmen opposed the plan because they feared a guaranteed income would reduce the supply of low-wage labor in the South. Welfare beneficiaries in northern states also opposed the plan because their current benefits were higher than what the FAP would have provided. Ironically, after the bill's defeat, most states cut welfare benefits and removed many people from the rolls.

In retrospect, the War on Poverty was a key turning point in social provision in the United States. The community action programs that might have provided a precedent for extensive intervention in the inner cities and prevented the spiral of decline so painfully visible to observers on all sides of the political spectrum became embroiled instead in the task of extending political rights to African Americans. As a result, the nation turned its back on the cities. The job training programs that might have initiated a commitment to full employment and established a partnership between the federal government and the trade unions instead became the source of

internecine warfare within the trade union movement. The funds for housing that briefly poured into the inner cities might have improved the quality and expanded the quantity of the nation's housing supply. However, the
racial backlash that ensued when integration became linked to housing
undermined public support for a national housing agenda. A proposal to
provide a guaranteed minimum income to the poor instead resulted in cuts
in welfare for single mothers and children. The exception to this pattern
was health care; Medicare funds provided federal officials with the leverage
to force southern hospitals to integrate and vastly improved access to health
insurance for older people, regardless of race.

The Rise of the New Right

The implementation of social policies in the 1960s redefined liberalism with
racial equality as the central priority. This new racial liberalism took as its
central premise that equal opportunity for civil rights could only be achieved
through government intervention. The pursuit of equal opportunity, in turn,
provided a new rallying cry for antigovernment conservatives that inspired
the New Right movement of the 1970s. The New Right decried the targeted
policies of the 1960s and used negative racial symbols and code words to
mobilize conservative opinion and provide the justification for repealing
redistributive social programs. These tactics propelled the Republican Party
to victory in the 1980 election. Taking a conservative civil rights stance,
Republicans made gains at every level of electoral competition—from state
legislative seats to the White House. Racial conservatism had once again
become a political asset. Under the presidency of Ronald Reagan, the
policies and programs that were created in the 1960s, those whose primary
beneficiaries were African Americans, Latinos, and the working poor, experienced the deepest cutbacks (Williams, 1998). Targets of the New Right
agenda included affirmative action, AFDC, and housing programs.

The Dismantling of Affirmative Action

Affirmative action remains one of the most polarizing of civil rights
issues. A strong majority of African Americans favor preferences to correct
for past discrimination, while an overwhelming majority of whites oppose
such programs. In fact, polls show that white respondents believe they are
at greater risk of discrimination at work than African Americans are, by a
margin of two to one (Schuman, Steeh, Bobo, & Krysan, 1997).

Under the Reagan administration, opposition to race-based affirmative
action became a matter of policy and of partisan strategy. Republicans outlined two distinct and contradictory visions of America: a Republican
vision of individual ambition and equal opportunity and a Democratic
vision of welfare dependence and antidemocratic special preference (Edsall

& Edsall, 1992). The federal government actively participated by providing resources and leadership for movements that opposed affirmative action. For conservatives, racial inequity no longer existed—past injustices were not to be remedied by government action (Williams, 1998).

The assault on affirmative action also affected budgets. Between 1981 and 1983, the budgets of the Equal Employment Opportunity Commission and the Office of Federal Contract Compliance Programs were reduced by 10% and 24%, respectively. Both agencies had been important sources of pressure on the private sector in implementing affirmative action programs in employment (Edsall & Edsall, 1992).

By the early 1990s, opponents of affirmative action had obtained a number of high-level government offices. Supporters of affirmative action were forced, in order to prevent erosion of existing programs, to abandon advocacy of the preferences and set aside the orders that had become so unpopular. When Republicans won control of both houses of Congress in the midterm elections of 1994, the GOP put the Clinton administration on the defensive in regard to civil rights issues. Clinton responded with a White House review, which concluded that affirmative action should be mended but did not specify how the mending of affirmative action would be accomplished (Edley, 1996). When George W. Bush was elected president in 1980, he further reduced funding for the Equal Opportunity Commission, one of the major enforcement tools for affirmative action (Office of Management and Budget, 2007).

Affirmative action was also undermined by the courts. In 1995, in the case of *Adarand Constructors, Inc. v. Peña*, the U.S. Supreme Court limited the scope of affirmative action programs. Although the programs were not ruled unconstitutional, they had to be presented as remedies for demonstrated prior discrimination (Parikh, 1997). Two 1996 decisions altered the trajectory of affirmative action in higher education. In the first case, the Supreme Court refused to hear appeals from opponents of California's Proposition 209, ending affirmative action in college admissions. In the second, *Hopwood v. State of Texas* (1996), a federal appeals court affirmed Hopwood's suit and forbid race preferences in the University of Texas admissions process. Since then, colleges in other states have been forced to change their admissions policies to avoid similar lawsuits (Malveaux, 2004).

Does affirmative action have a future as a mechanism for improving the life chances of minorities, or will it suffer the same fate as other remedial efforts such as school busing? Many studies find that, although white Americans oppose affirmative action, they are not unilaterally opposed to all of its forms. For example, whites reject minority preferences in employment, but support "soft" forms of affirmative action, such as programs meant to reach out to disadvantaged groups or ones that provide training and education (Crosby, Iyer, & Sincharoen, 2006). According to Lowery, Unzueta, Knowles, and Goff (2006), whites support affirmative action policies targeted to minorities if they believe there will be no consequences for themselves or other whites. As debates about affirmative action continue, voters remain divided over its meaning, its effectiveness, and its constitutionality.

Racial Concentration in Housing

The passage of the Civil Rights Act in 1964 and the Fair Housing Act in 1968 were intended to remedy the inequalities resulting from segregation and discrimination. Yet, the fight for fair housing became more complex as whites fled the central cities. White flight dramatically changed the demographic composition of cities and led to high levels of urban black racial concentration. In 1960, the racial mix in urban areas was similar to that of the population as a whole (Wilson, 1996). By 1970, urban areas were characterized by a predominantly black central city surrounded by mostly white suburbs (Massey & Denton, 1993). Racial concentration has been accompanied by declining quality of life in decaying urban ghettos.

Racial discrimination by private lenders contributed to the deterioration of inner cities. Congress made an effort to confront the discriminatory practices of the lending industry in the 1970s. The Home Mortgage Disclosure Act of 1975 mandated that banks report which neighborhoods received home-improvement and mortgage loans, and the Community Reinvestment Act of 1977 required that banks prove they were providing credit to low-income areas that had a history of being unable to secure assets. Because these policies lacked direction for implementation and follow-up by the responsible agencies, discrimination continued (Massey & Denton, 1993).

In the 1980s, the Reagan administration and the National Association of Realtors (NHA) worked to weaken HUD's already limited authority to enforce fair housing policy. When Reagan took office, his cabinet appointees took an aggressive anti–civil rights position, reversing policies that HUD had adopted under the Fair Housing Act. Under Reagan, the number of cases prosecuted for defying the legislation dropped dramatically. Between 1968 and 1978, an average of 32 cases per year was prosecuted. During Reagan's first year in office, not one case was initiated (Massey & Denton, 1993).

Subsidized housing was also targeted during the Reagan era for being too costly and inefficient. The Section 8 Housing Assistance Program that was authorized in 1974 was the largest source of low-income housing in the United States. It provided housing assistance payments to low- and moderate-income families that were eligible (Coulibaly, Green, & James, 1998). The Reagan administration also cut funds for the construction of new subsidized housing units, except to construct housing for the elderly and handicapped. As a result of these cuts, federal spending on housing for the poor fell from $26.1 billion in 1981 to $2.8 billion in 1985 (Slessarev, 1988).

In 1988, the newly elected Democratic Congress passed an amendment that extended the time during which a housing discrimination complaint could be filed, increased the penalties for those who discriminated, gave HUD secretaries the authority to investigate discrimination without waiting for private complaints, and expanded the role of the Department of Justice in enforcing fair housing (Massey & Denton, 1993).

When Clinton took office in 1992, America's cities looked bleak. The cumulative effects of economic decline, poverty, crime, and fiscal distress could not be ignored. However, Democrats could not agree on urban policy proposals. Aware of the opposition that would come from linking the urban poor to the suburban middle class through metropolitan approaches, Democrats rejected traditional urban programs. Instead, they sought to promote community and economic development by creating empowerment zones and community credit financial institutions. These programs have been relatively unsuccessful, however, because they often got bogged down in local politics (Mollenkopf, 1998).

In 1996, President Clinton signed Republican-sponsored legislation that would deny any new Section 8 vouchers, which were originally created to reduce segregation. The theory was that supplementing housing costs would help low-income families to move out of areas where poverty was highly concentrated and allow welfare recipients to live in areas where more jobs were available. Instead, the vouchers only provided enough for families to move to other highly racially and poverty-segregated areas (McClure, 2004). Even though Section 8 vouchers had not lived up to expectations, they did serve the purpose of supporting nonprofit community development corporations, which typically account for most housing construction in poor neighborhoods. The resources of these corporations are derived from many sources, public and private, national and local, and they require some tenants to have Section 8 vouchers to guarantee long-term rent (Mollenkopf, 1998). Thus, any reduction in vouchers threatens the stability of these corporations. In the 1990s, many public housing units were also sold or demolished (Gotham, 1998).

The fight against housing segregation made no progress under the George W. Bush administration, which has deemphasized integration and the expansion of low-income housing properties. As a result, African Americans still live in more segregated communities than any other racial group. Persistence in racial neighborhood segregation has increased the concentration of poverty in African American neighborhood (Basolo & Nguyen, 2005). Poverty segregation, in turn, increases racism because it puts poor blacks in closer proximity to low socioeconomic status whites, the group most likely to feel threatened by their presence. The larger political effect is to diminish support for policies aimed at poor communities (Branton & Jones, 2005).

In the 1990s, housing segregation also increased among highly educated blacks (Iceland & Wilkes, 2006). The reasons are complex and include discriminatory practices by lenders, personal preferences among whites, and self-segregation (Dawkins, 2004). As a result, African Americans are the group least likely to own their own homes (Friedman & Rosenbaum, 2004). When they do become homeowners, they live in poorer quality homes but pay higher monthly payments because whites less frequently have to pay points on loans and have better credit ratings. Because their homes have high values, whites more readily qualify for a home-equity loan, which can see a family through a spell of unemployment, leverage an investment, or be used to buy rental property or to pay for a child's education. Depressed home values due to neighborhood segregation also mean that African Americans' homes grow more slowly in value. The consequences are likely to reverberate across the generations, perpetuating disadvantage by leaving African American baby boomers with less wealth to pass on to their children (Shapiro, 2004).

Health Care

Since the 1960s, overt racial barriers like separate white and colored entrances, wards, waiting rooms, and cafeterias have been removed, but that does not mean that racial inequality in health care has disappeared. As job-based benefits have become a surrogate for national policy, racial inequality in access to health insurance benefits has become a secondary effect of employment inequities. In 2002 and 2003, nearly 60% of Hispanic non-elderly adults were uninsured for some time as well as 43% of African American compared to just 23% of whites (Stoll & Jones, 2004). Both African Americans and Hispanics are less likely than whites to be employed in the kind of company that offers health benefits, but African Americans have a significant advantage over Hispanics because they are more likely to work for a state or the federal government (Carrasquillo, Himmelstein, Woolhandler, & Bor, 1999). In old age, Medicare is the great leveler, providing health coverage for 99% of people 65 and older (Schulz & Binstock, 2006).

Although the formal barriers to racial equality have been removed, racial discrepancies in access to care remain. From conception to death, African Americans receive less health care, and health outcomes remain profoundly unequal (Lado, 1994). To a large degree, racial differences in health care access are the result of the failure of the state to eliminate racial barriers in other institutional spheres. Continuing patterns of residential segregation sustain hospital segregation (Smith, 1999). Health care segregation is also the result of practices that are not directly discriminatory but that have the same effect as direct racial discrimination. Some health care facilities have moved from African American communities to the predominantly white suburbs. Other hospitals have closed or moved emergency rooms and obstetrical care units, the point of entry for the poor. Some have adopted highly restrictive admission policies or engaged in patient dumping (Lado, 1994). In many cases, the motivation is to change the patient mix to increase reimbursement from insurers. These tactics, which are designed to limit access for the poor, have a disproportionate impact on African Americans, who are perceived by private facilities as potential revenue losses.

Welfare Reform

In the 1980s, the racial nature of the welfare state was reflected in increasing public opposition toward social programs targeted to the poor and in rhetoric that equated the use of AFDC and food stamps with laziness and moral incompetence (Baca Zinn, 1989). Between 1978 and 1983, AFDC spending fell more than 10%, eligibility requirements were tightened, and nominal benefits failed to keep pace with the inflation rate (Burtless, 1994). Attacks on the program increased throughout the decade as New Right critics argued that redistributive programs caused more harm than good by creating a disincentive to work and that most social programs only worsened the conditions of people whose lives they were intended to improve (Joffee, 1998).

The Family Support Act of 1988 contained reforms designed to increase the potential earnings of welfare recipients. This act mandated that states provide more employment and training alternatives to AFDC recipients through a Job Opportunities and Basic Skills (JOBS) program (Handler & Hasenfeld, 1991). The Family Support Act had little effect on AFDC beneficiaries' work effort for several reasons. One problem was that most AFDC beneficiaries received no economic benefit from working unless they also received health care and subsidized child care (McFate, 1995). Another problem was that the act had been implemented during an economic downturn when unemployment was increasing and job growth was stagnant (Heclo, 1994). As a result, welfare reform remained a controversial political issue.

Several factors were moving the nation toward a major welfare reform initiative in the 1990s. In the 1992 presidential debates, Bill Clinton had promised to end welfare in its current form. The debate was made more contentious by the success of conservatives in portraying welfare recipients as black, promiscuous, and lazy, even though the percentage of AFDC beneficiaries who were African American had declined from 45% in 1973 to 36% by 1994 (Federico & Luks, 2005; Mink, 1998; Neubeck & Cazenave, 2001). It also became more difficult to defend a program that paid mothers not to work when the majority of women were in the labor force.

The Personal Responsibility and Work Opportunity Reconciliation Act (PRWORA), which was enacted in 1996, ended AFDC's status as a federal entitlement. PRWORA replaced AFDC with Temporary Assistance for Needy Families, a time-limited welfare program that includes mandatory work requirements, a performance bonus to reward states for moving welfare recipients into jobs, and comprehensive child support enforcement. PRWORA also severed the programmatic ties of categorical eligibility, which linked cash assistance receipt with eligibility for Medicaid and food stamp benefits. The decoupling of TANF from Medicaid reduced health coverage among poor, single mothers. One-third of women who left welfare for work subsequently became uninsured (Garrett & Holahan, 2000).

Because African Americans represent a disproportionate share of TANF recipients, program reforms have affected them more than other groups (National Congress of State Legislators, 1998). Further, although TANF increased incomes for white and Hispanic American recipients, household income among African American recipients steadily decreased through the end of the 1990s (Bitler, Gelbach, & Hoynes, 2003). Evidence also suggests that welfare reform was implemented more harshly for African Americans. According to Keiser, Mueser, and Choi (2004), under TANF, the percentage of African Americans who had welfare benefits discontinued rose from 1% in 1996 to 10% by 2000. In the majority of these cases, TANF recipients were penalized because they failed to find employment under the time limits. Child care and transportation continue to pose impediments for many poor mothers.

Conclusion

From the 1930s to the present, the United States has instituted three welfare regimes, each with different consequences for racial equality. The first national welfare programs of the New Deal protected the working class against the exigencies of old age and unemployment but also reinforced existing patterns of inequality in employment, housing, health care, income security, and political opportunity. The War on Poverty provided the means to undo the New Deal legacy and extend equal opportunity, but it inadvertently became embroiled in the civil rights struggle. This "equal opportunity" welfare state resulted in a white backlash against government intervention for social equality. The result was racial isolation and decades of stagnation of the welfare state. In the third phase, the task has been to maintain past gains without directly challenging white privilege. The point is not that there has been no improvement in racial attitudes and behaviors over the past century but rather that racial inequality remains a significant force that affects the social, economic, and political institutions in the United States.

References

Amott, T. (1993). *Caught in the crisis*. New York: Monthly Review Press.

Andrews, K. (1997). The impacts of social movements on the political process: The civil rights movement and black electoral politics in Mississippi. *American Sociological Review, 62*, 800–819.

Andrews, K. (2001). Social movements and policy implementation: The Mississippi civil rights movement and the War on Poverty, 1965–1971. *American Sociological Review, 66,* 71–95.

Baca Zinn, M. (1989). Family, race and poverty in the eighties. *Signs: Journal of Women in Culture and Society, 14*(4), 856–875.

Basolo, V., & Nguyen, M. T. (2005). Does mobility matter? The neighborhood conditions of housing voucher holders by race and ethnicity. *Housing Policy Debate, 16*(3/4), 297–324.

Bitler, M. P., Gelbach, J. B., & Hoynes, H. W. (2003). Some evidence on race, welfare reform, and household income. *American Economic Review, 93,* 293–298.

Branton, R. P., & Jones, B. S. (2005). Reexamining racial attitudes: The conditional relationship between diversity and socioeconomic environment. *American Journal of Political Science, 49,* 359–372.

Burtless, G. (1994). Public spending on the poor: Historical trends and economic limits. In S. Danziger, G. D. Sandefur, & D. Weinberg (Eds.), *Confronting poverty: Prescriptions for change* (pp. 51–84). New York: Russell Sage Foundation.

Carrasquillo, O., Himmelstein, D., Woolhandler, S., & Bor, D. H. (1999). A reappraisal of private employers' role in providing health insurance. *New England Journal of Medicine, 340*(2), 109–114.

Coulibaly, C., Green, R. D., & James, D. M. (1998). *Segregation in federally subsidized low-income housing in the United States.* London: Praeger.

Crosby, F. J., Iyer, A., & Sincharoen, S. 2006. Understanding affirmative action. *Annual Review of Psychology, 57,* 585–611.

Dawkins, C. J. (2004). Recent evidence on the continuing causes of black-white residential segregation. *Journal of Urban Affairs, 26*(3), 379–400.

Domhoff, G. W. (1990). *The power elite and the state: How policy is made in America* New York: Aldine de Gruyter.

Edley, C., Jr. (1996). *Not all black and white: Affirmative action and American values.* New York: Hill and Wang.

Edsall, T. B., & Edsall, M. D. (1992). *Chain reaction: The impact of race, rights, and taxes on American politics.* New York: W. W. Norton.

Federico, C. M., & Luks, S. (2005). The political psychology of race. *Political Psychology, 26,* 661–666.

Friedman, S., & Rosenbaum, E. (2004). Nativity status and racial/ethnic differences in access to quality housing: Does homeownership bring greater parity? *Housing Policy Debate, 15*(4), 865–901.

Garrett, B., & Holahan, J. (2000). *Welfare leavers, Medicaid coverage and private health insurance* (New Federalism: National Survey of America's Families No. B-13). Washington, DC: Urban Institute.

Gotham, K. F. (1998). Blind faith in the free market: Urban poverty, residential segregation, and federal housing retrenchment, 1970–1995. *Sociological Inquiry, 68*(1), 1–31.

Handler, J., & Hasenfeld, Y. (1991). *The moral construction of poverty: Welfare reform in America.* London: Sage.

Heclo, H. (1994). Poverty politics. In S. Danziger, G. D. Sandefur, & D. Weinberg (Eds.), *Confronting poverty: Prescriptions for change.* New York: Russell Sage Foundation.

Iceland, J., & Wilkes, R. (2006). Does socioeconomic status matter? Race, class, and residential segregation. *Social Problems, 53,* 248–273.

Joffe, C. (1998). Welfare reform and reproductive politics on a collision course: Contradictions in the conservative agenda. In C. Y. H. Lo & M. Schwartz (Eds.), *Social policy and the conservative agenda* (pp. 290–301). New York: Blackwell.

Katz, M. (2001). *The price of citizenship: Redefining the American welfare state.* New York: Henry Holt.

Keiser, L. R., Mueser, P. R., & Choi, S. W. (2004). Race, bureaucratic discretion, and the implementation of welfare reform. *American Journal of Political Science, 48,* 314–327.

King, D. (1995). *Actively seeking work?* Chicago: University of Chicago Press.

Lado, M. E. (1994). Breaking the barriers of access to health care: A discussion of the role of civil rights litigation and the relationship between burdens of proof and the experience of denial. *Brooklyn Law Review, 60,* 239–273.

Lieberman, R. (1998). *Shifting the color line: Race and the American welfare state.* Cambridge, MA: Harvard University Press.

Lowery, B. S., Unzueta, M. M., Knowles, E. D., & Goff, P. A. (2006). Concern for the in-group and opposition to affirmative action. *Journal of Personality and Social Psychology, 90,* 961–974.

Malveaux J. (2004). Know your enemy: The assault on diversity. *Black Issues in Higher Education, 21,* 32–33.

Massey, D. S., & Denton, N. A. (1993). *American apartheid: Segregation and the making of the underclass.* Cambridge, MA: Harvard University Press.

McClure, K. (2004). Section 8 and movement to job opportunity: Experience after welfare reform in Kansas City. *Housing Policy Debate, 15*(1), 99–131.

McFate, K. (1995). Trampolines, safety nets, or free fall? Labor market policies and social assistance in the 1980s. In K. McFate, R. Lawson, & W. J. Wilson (Eds.), *Poverty, inequality, and the future of social policy* (pp. 631–634). New York: Russell Sage Foundation.

Mink, G. (1998). *Welfare's end.* Ithaca, NY: Cornell University Press.

Mollenkopf, J. (1998). Urban policy at the crossroads. In M. Weir (Ed.), *The social divide* (pp. 464–505). New York: Russell Sage Foundation.

Morone, J. (1990). *The democratic wish.* New York: Basic Books.

National Conference on State Legislatures. (1998). *Tracking recipients after they leave welfare: Summaries of state follow-up studies.* Retrieved March 24, 1998, from http://www.ncsl.org/statefed/welfare/followup.htm

Neubeck, K., & Cazenave, N. (2001). *Welfare racism.* New York: Routledge.

Office of Management and Budget. (2007). Department of Housing and Urban Development (HUD). In *Budget of the United States Government: Fiscal year 2007.* Retrieved February 14, 2008, from http://www.whitehouse.gov/omb/budget/fy2007/hud.html

Omi, M., & Winant, H. (1994). *Racial formation in the United States.* New York: Routledge.

Orfield, G. (1988). Race and the liberal agenda: The Loss of the integrationist dream, 1965–1974. In M. Weir, A. Orloff, & T. Skocpol (Eds.), *The politics of social policy in the United States* (pp. 357–380). Princeton, NJ: Princeton University Press.

Parikh, S. (1997). *The politics of preference.* Ann Arbor: University of Michigan Press.

Quadagno, J. (1994). *The color of welfare.* New York: Oxford University Press.

Quadagno, J. (2000). Promoting civil rights through the welfare state: How Medicare integrated southern hospitals. *Social Problems, 47,* 68–89.

Quadagno, J. (2005). *One nation, uninsured: Why the US has no national health insurance.* New York: Oxford University Press.

Reskin, B. (1998). *The realities of affirmative action in employment.* Washington, DC: American Sociological Association.

Schulz, J. H., & Binstock, R. (2006). *Aging nation: The economics and politics of growing older in America.* Westport, CT: Praeger.

Schuman, H., Steeh, C., Bobo, L., & Krysan, M. (1997). *Racial attitudes in America.* Cambridge, MA: Harvard University Press.

Shapiro, T. (2004). *The hidden cost of being African American: How wealth perpetuates inequality.* New York: Oxford University Press.

Slessarev, H. (1988). Racial tensions and institutional support: Social programs during a period of retrenchment. In M. Weir, A. Orloff, & T. Skocpol (Eds.), *The politics of social policy in the United States* (pp. 342–351). Princeton, NJ: Princeton University Press.

Smith, D. B. (1999). *Health care divided: Race and healing a nation.* Ann Arbor: University of Michigan Press.

Stoll, K., & Jones, K. (2004). *One in three: Non-elderly Americans without health insurance, 2002–2003.* Washington, DC: Families USA Foundation.

Thomas, K. K. (2006, November). The Hill-Burton Act and civil rights: Expanding hospital care for black southerners. *Journal of Southern History, 72,* 823–879.

Williams, L. F. (1998). Race and the politics of social policy. In M. Weir (Ed.), *The social divide* (pp. 417–463). New York: Russell Sage Foundation.

Wilson, W. J. (1996). *When work disappears.* New York: Alfred A. Knopf.

The Social Development Perspective in Social Policy

18

James Midgley and Michael Sherraden

The social development perspective has attracted increasing attention in social policy circles in recent years. It originated in the developing countries of the Global South in the 1950s and has been actively promoted by international agencies such as the United Nations, UNICEF, and the International Labour Office. Interest in social development heightened because of the World Summit for Social Development, which was held in Copenhagen in 1995. The identification of poverty eradication targets at the conference resulted in the subsequent adoption of the United Nations Millennium Development Goals, which currently guide global social development efforts.

Social development seeks to integrate social welfare and economic development. It harmonizes economic and social policy making and creates institutional mechanisms for linking economic development and social welfare policies and programs. In addition to urging that economic and social policy be integrated, social development proponents insist that economic development promote the well-being of the population as a whole. They also require that social welfare programs be investment oriented and contribute positively to economic development.

Although better known today, much of the social development literature remains unfamiliar to Western scholars. Nevertheless, some have become knowledgeable about social development and have recognized its potential to inform social policy in their own countries, including the United States. Some believe that social development offers a viable challenge to the claim that government social expenditures harms economic growth. By advocating the integration of economic and social policy, the effective use of economic policy to achieve social goals, and the promotion of social investment strategies that encourage participation in the productive economy, social development's proponents argue convincingly that social welfare is not antithetical to economic progress but that the two are, in fact, interdependent. They also believe that social development's concern with economic and social progress may provide a useful basis for social policy in postindustrial economies faced with the challenges of globalization and rapid economic change.

Social development ideas have also been applied in social programs in Western countries. These programs include welfare to work, supported employment for people with disabilities, microenterprise projects, asset development, and community economic development programs. All are intended to enhance economic participation and capabilities and promote well-being. As the social development approach is being more clearly articulated, it may have wider appeal and challenge those who advocate social expenditure reductions, social service privatization, and the abolition of government involvement in social welfare.

This chapter describes the social development perspective in social policy, paying particular attention to the various programmatic strategies that characterize this approach. Key premises are also discussed. The chapter concludes with a brief discussion of some of the issues and controversies attending the social development perspective.

The Social Development Perspective

The social development perspective emerged in the developing countries around the time of World War II when the era of European imperialism and colonialism was coming to an end. The nationalist independence movements, which had grown in size and strength, were in the process of securing national sovereignty, and the territories that had been under the rule of the European powers were about to become independent nation states. In addition to their political goals, the leaders of the nationalist independence movements were committed to economic development, which they hoped would transform their predominantly agrarian societies into modern industrial countries and raise the standards of living of their people. Many independence leaders had studied in Europe and were familiar with the significant expansion of social welfare programs in these countries in the early 20th century. However, they recognized that the developing countries lacked the resources to establish comprehensive social security, social service, and welfare programs. In this context, the idea of specifically linking social policy to economic development gained support, and many also approved the adoption of social development.

Drawing on formative community-based economic projects in India, West Africa, and other parts of the developing world, welfare administrators in the Global South began to create local developmental activities, which had the objective of contributing to economic growth and, at the same time, meeting social needs and raising incomes and standards of living. Initially, the British government took the lead in promoting these projects, and the independence leaders of the emerging nations inherited this leadership role. The earlier programs were known as *community development*, but, later, the term *social development* emerged to connote a more holistic approach in which both community-based and national, governmental interventions were adopted to foster economic and social objectives (Midgley, 1995).

In the 1950s and 1960s, the United Nations became actively involved in social development and used its influence and resources to encourage new developing country members to adopt the social development perspective. The United Nations sent expert missions to advise governments of developing countries on social development, and it also published numerous reports and other documents on the subject. In addition, a series of international conferences to debate social development issues were convened (United Nations, 1969, 1971). In the 1970s, other international agencies, including UNICEF, the International Labour Organization, and the World Bank, also became actively involved. Information about social development innovations in the developing world was widely disseminated. Community-based health care, sanitation, and educational, nutritional, and other social programs were established in many parts of the Global South. Preventive maternal and child health programs and microenterprise and local economic projects expanded rapidly. Sustainable and environmentally sensitive projects such as communal forest management and cooperative agriculture became more commonplace. All were characterized by the integration of economic and social projects designed to tackle the poverty problem, address social needs, and raise standards of living.

Although the social development perspective was adopted in the Global South, the advocacy of neoliberal, free-market economic policies by the International Monetary Fund, the World Bank, and several Western governments in the 1980s undermined the social welfare gains that had been recorded in many parts of the world. As government spending for social development projects was slashed, and as user charges and fees for education and health care were imposed under structural adjustment programs, poverty and deprivation increased. In response, the United Nations convened the 1995 World Summit for Social Development. The summit, which took place in Copenhagen, was attended by 117 heads of state who affirmed, in the Copenhagen Declaration, their commitment to a number of key social development policies, such as eradicating poverty, achieving universal primary education, ending illiteracy, promoting gender equality, reducing the incidence of unemployment, and increasing access to primary health care (United Nations, 1996). In a special session of the United Nations General Assembly in the year 2000, delegates reaffirmed these commitments by formally adopting the Millennium Development Goals, which currently inform social development efforts around the world (United Nations, 2005).

It was noted earlier that the principles and strategies of social development are now more widely known in Western countries. This has come about because of the increasing global exchange of information and the diffusion of knowledge about policy innovations in different parts of the world. Social development has also been actively promoted by academics in both developing and Western countries and by professional staff at the international development agencies who believe that the social development perspective, with appropriate adaptation, can be applied universally. Research has also expanded rapidly, and information about social development projects and programs is now widely shared.

Social development proponents working in the field of social policy suggest that the neglect of economic factors in mainstream social policy discourse has been detrimental and that much can be learned by studying social development innovations in the Global South (Midgley & Livermore, 2004). They believe that the conventional income maintenance and "social service" approach that has dominated social policy for most of this century has failed to appreciate the extent to which economic considerations affect social policy debates and decisions. By neglecting economic issues, social policy advocates in the West in the 1980s were put on the defensive by market liberal and conservative critics of government social welfare programs who claimed that generous social spending, comprehensive social service programs, and extensive welfare regulations had harmed economic growth (Ginsberg, 1998). By shifting resources out of the productive economy to unproductive social expenditures, governments have stifled economic growth, created unemployment, and lowered standards of living. These arguments have resonated with the electorate, and in recent years, support for the conservative position has increased. In the current climate of budgetary retrenchment, privatization, and neglect, advocates of government social welfare have struggled to articulate a politically successful rationale for social welfare. Social development principles may help to meet the challenge.

Social Development Principles

As outlined earlier, the social development perspective offers an alternative view of social policy, one that is concerned with enhancing peoples' capacities to participate in the productive economy. Social development proponents believe that economic participation is the primary means by which most people meet their social needs. Unlike the traditional income maintenance and social service approaches, the social development perspective seeks to shift the emphasis from consumption-based and maintenance-oriented services to social programs that contribute directly to economic development (Sherraden, 1991). Instead of detracting from economic growth, these programs enhance economic participation and contribute to growth.

However, it must be stressed that social development advocates do not merely urge social welfare clients to become economically productive; they argue that adequate investments should be made to ensure that people have the skills, knowledge, resources, opportunities, incentives, and subsidies to participate effectively in the productive economy. Of course, this principle applies not only to the consumers of welfare services but also to the population as a whole. Social development advocates require that government regulations, subsidies, and supports be provided to all to ensure that economic participation results in adequate living wages, access to universal health care, full educational opportunities, affordable housing, and the other dimensions of a decent and satisfying living standard.

Three normative principles are usually emphasized in the social development literature. These relate firstly to the harmonization of economic and social policy; second, to the requirements that that economic development be inclusive and people centered and that it promote the well-being of the population as a whole; and, third, that social welfare programs are investment oriented and contribute positively to economic development. These principles reflect intense intellectual debates over the years about the best ways of enhancing social well-being in the development context (Midgley, 2003).

The emphasis on purposefully integrating economic and social policy is a key normative social development prescription. This requires the creation of formal arrangements that effectively link economic and social policies and programs. In many countries, governmental organizations concerned with social welfare have few ties to agencies engaged in economic development. The social development perspective seeks to end the bifurcation of economic and social policy and to ensure that social policy is not subsidiary to the economy. Instead, it advocates an integrative approach that regards economic and social policies as two essential elements of a sustainable and transformative development process.

The prescription that economic development should bring tangible benefits to ordinary people is another key feature of the social development perspective. Many countries are characterized by what may be described as a "distorted" process of economic development (Midgley, 1995) in which the benefits of growth accrues to economic and political elites, urban dwellers, and those in formal wage employment. A substantial proportion of the population is not brought into the economic development process and remains neglected and excluded. Many social development writers (Myrdal, 1970; Seers, 1969; Sen, 1999) have argued that economic growth is meaningless unless it improves standards of living among the population as a whole. This requires the adoption of a people-centered, inclusive economic development process in which governments actively promote economic participation and adopt measures that will increase employment, incomes, and educational skills and enhance standards of living.

Social development writers reject the argument that the free market will, of itself, create wealth and prosperity for all. They contend that governments have a key role to play in ensuring that people have the skills and knowledge to participate effectively in the economy. Governments should also ensure that employment and self-employment opportunities are maximized and that the benefits of economic growth are equitably distributed. They also believe that governments should protect the vulnerable from economic exploitation and encourage the payment of wages that support a decent standard of living. Although few social development advocates believe that the state should exert full control or assume ownership of the economy, they urge the creation of a climate in which the government, together with community groups and civil society organizations, promotes development strategies that are income maximizing, asset building, inclusive, and equitable.

A third normative principle is that social policies and programs should contribute positively to economic development. In this regard, social development proponents challenge the conventional income maintenance and social services approach in mainstream social policy thinking. As noted earlier, they argue that a shift in emphasis from consumption-based and maintenance-oriented social policies toward investment policies is needed. They urge the adoption of a number of strategies that encourage social investments to promote economic participation. Social investment strategies should benefit the population as a whole as well as the traditional recipients of welfare services. Although they obviously recognize that some groups will require maintenance services and interventions that address debilitating psychological and familial problems, they believe that the welfare system should not be based entirely on the provision of services, remedial interventions, and income transfers. They also believe that conventional services can be reconfigured so that they are investment oriented. For this reason, the social development approach is also known as the *social investment* or, more technically, as the *productivist* approach to social policy (Midgley, 1995, 1999). Work by Gilbert (1983), Esping-Anderson (1990), Giddens (1998), Sen (1985, 1999), Sherraden (1991), and others on the integration of social policy and market economies and the role of investments in social welfare helped lay the groundwork for thinking about the use of productivist approaches. As is shown in the next section of this chapter, a number of productivist intervention strategies have been identified and adopted in social development practice.

In addition to these normative principles, social development thinking draws on various value concepts and normative ideals. These are infused in social development theory and inform its programmatic activities. They include the concepts of social change and social progress as well as the idea of agency or interventionism, which underlie the view that social development policies and programs can bring about significant improvements in social conditions. Utopianism and a belief in inclusivity and universalism also inform social development ideas. With regard to interventionism, it will be shown that social development has historically advocated community-based interventions coupled with those of government. However, social development thinking has oscillated between statist and community-based populist preferences with some social development advocates preferring an extensive and proactive role for the government while others advocate a grassroots community development approach in which local people take responsibility for social development projects. In more recent times, an enterprise approach that stresses the role of market integration and entrepreneurship in social development has gained popularity (Rainford, 2001). In addition, feminist and critical thinking have also influenced social development theory and practice (Midgley, 2001). However, many social development writers adopt a pluralist approach, recognizing that social development goals can be achieved through the agency of the state, community, and market and that an appropriate balance between these agents should be found.

By giving expression to these value ideals and normative principles, social development is essentially optimistic, believing that steady improvements in human welfare are possible through judicious government intervention in combination with individual enterprise and community effort. Social development also stresses the importance of improving peoples' material welfare, which requires that social policy be primarily concerned with fostering improvements in incomes, assets, health, housing, and the other resources that comprise an acceptable standard of living and an ability to plan and invest for the future.

Social Investments and Social Policy

The principles and prescriptions informing the social development approach find expression in a number of policies, programs, and projects that are productivist, investment oriented, and committed to enhancing economic participation among the population as a whole and among individuals, groups, and communities that have traditionally been served by government social programs. Social development seeks to enhance capacities to participate and function effectively in the productive economy. It is in this regard that this social development perspective is particularly relevant to social policy.

In the following paragraphs are some of the social investment strategies that have been adopted in social development practice around the world. Although a good deal of information has been collected to show that these investment strategies are effective in promoting economic participation and enhancing people's capabilities, more research is needed to refine these approaches and ensure that their implementation will, in fact, promote economic participation and social well-being. Although the following strategies are enumerated separately, they can, of course, be combined. They can also be combined with traditional social services approaches so that clients can simultaneously be provided with the supports, services, and subsidies that facilitate participation in the productive economy.

Human Development and Human Capital Investments

Human development refers to increasing the capacities and functioning of individuals, which will, in turn, likely have multiple positive outcomes (Sen, 1985). Attention to human development as a central theme can be credited in part to Mahbub ul Haq (1995), who pioneered the human development reports of the United Nations. According to the *1990 Human Development Report*, "Human development is a process of enlarging people's choices. The most critical of these wide-ranging choices are to live a long and healthy life, to be educated, and to have access to resources needed for a decent standard of living . . ." (p. 1). The report goes on to say that development should create a conducive environment for people, individually and collectively, to develop their full potential and to have a reasonable chance of leading productive and creative lives in accord with their needs and interests (United Nations Development Programme, 1990).

Key human development factors are represented by the basic needs of nutrition, primary health care, literacy, and basic housing (Streeten, 1981). There is considerable empirical evidence that investments in nutrition, primary health care, education, and basic housing yield positive social returns in increased participation, increased connectedness, and increased social stability. These investments also generate positive economic returns in increased productivity, higher economic growth, and reduced income and asset inequality (Beverly & Sherraden, 1997). Early childhood interventions such as day care centers have been shown to have a particularly strong incentive effect on human capital development (Kirp, 2007).

Human capital refers to the store of knowledge and skills that individuals possess, although this term can also include other individual characteristics such as health, creativity, energy, and so on. Human capital is most often measured by level of education and skill training. There is a solid body of evidence that human capital investments yield high returns in economic performance (Becker, 1993). Indeed, estimates of human capital as a proportion of the total wealth of modern economies range to 75% and higher. In other words, most of the value in modern economies resides inside of people rather than in land, buildings, machines, and other forms of tangible assets. Moreover, the importance of human capital increases with technological development. In addition, there is evidence that human capital investments enhance human development in improved nutrition and health. Given its overwhelming role in the development of individuals, families, communities, and societies, investment in human capital should be in the forefront of social policy and should be a focus of social work and other applied social professions. This idea was suggested several decades ago by Schultz (1959).

Investments That Promote Employment and Self-Employment

Employment policy has been a central feature of the welfare states of Western Europe during the last half of the 20th century. In these nations, labor markets have been regulated to protect the incomes and job security of workers. The United States, in contrast, has not embraced strong labor market policies. Employment-related policies make up no more than 2% of total federal spending, and the regulation of incomes or the provision of job security is limited. An important exception is the federal minimum wage law. With the globalization of the world economy and the economic integration of the European Community at the end of the 20th century, national policies designed to protect workers and their rights have been challenged. The likely trend in most nations will be toward labor markets with weaker labor protection regulation. This will very likely promote low-wage employment, but at high costs to workers, who will bear the brunt of global wage competition and economic dislocation. Moreover, there are disturbing trends in the United States, showing increasing wage inequality over the past two decades, which may be due, in part, to higher skill demands in the information-age economy and to the lack of educational preparation on the part of many workers (Levy, 1999).

In this environment, there has been increasing emphasis on self-employment, sometimes in very small businesses called microenterprises, as an economic strategy for disadvantaged workers and communities. Community economic development specialists in the United States and other economically advanced nations have looked to international examples, most notably the Grameen Bank of Bangladesh, as models for adaptation (Jurik, 2005; Yunus, 1999). Some aspects of these models have been oversold, and it is often implied that microenterprise offers a new and dynamic approach to poverty alleviation. However, although microenterprise has a role to play in stimulating local economic activities, it is hardly a panacea. Many people in this "movement" refer to their work as *microcredit*, implying that only loans are needed for self-employment, which is unfortunately misleading. Also, peer lending has, by and large, not been successful in the United States. Nonetheless, for the small proportion of social welfare clients and poor people who are interested in pursuing this option, microenterprise can play an important role. Although income effects are typically modest, entrepreneurs report very positive impacts regarding satisfaction with the business, sense of control over their lives, learning, ability to take care of their families, and other social development factors (Sherraden, Sanders, & Sherraden, 2004). In recent years, the discussion of microenterprise has broadened to consider *microfinance*, which encompasses deposit, insurance, and other financial services (World Bank, 2006).

Social Capital Investments

Programs that promote social capital formation are suited to the needs of deprived low-income communities that are often the location of crime, poverty, deprivation, and neglect. Investments in social capital are intended to strengthen social networks, foster civic engagement, and promote community solidarity not only because these are desirable goals in their own right but because they have positive implications for economic development. Research indicates that enhanced community integration can promote local economic development. In an important book, Robert Putnam and his co-workers (1993) found that regions in Italy with well-developed civic traditions have higher rates of economic development than those regions where social integration is low. Their research suggests that social programs that promote civic engagement contribute positively to economic development.

Social programs directed at poor communities have tended to focus on the provision and coordination of social services or on mobilizing local residents for political purposes. Community organization, as this approach is known, has been infused with the notion of empowerment. Empowerment facilitates local political activism designed to secure resources to improve local conditions. Although community organization has not totally ignored the need for local economic development, the field has been dominated by the empowerment and social service approaches.

In more recent years, more attention has focused on the need for community economic development (Sherraden & Ninacs, 1998). Local enterprises, credit opportunities, employment generation, and asset building have been emphasized to a greater extent than before. It is in this context that community organizers are being urged to focus on projects that have direct relevance to economic development. This involves both the creation of social capital and the direction of social capital toward productive activities (Midgley & Livermore, 1998). Community workers should collaborate closely with planners and local economic development specialists to create new enterprises (particularly among women and low-income clients), encourage communities to support local enterprises, assist in the creation of local community development agencies, help to create networks for employment referral, and attract external investment for local economic development.

Investments in Individual and Community Assets

In the policies of modern states, welfare or well-being has been defined primarily in terms of income. Income is assumed to represent consumption (although the empirical relationship is not always strong), and consumption equals welfare, by definition, in welfare economics. On this narrow intellectual base, the welfare state was constructed in the 20th century, and for many decades, the assumption that consumption equals well-being went largely unchallenged. However, in the 1990s, questions have arisen about whether this income-and-consumption concept, taken by itself, is a sufficient policy definition for well-being. Sherraden (1991) has pointed out that income approaches are designed for maintenance rather than development. He has suggested that impoverished individuals and communities should build financial and tangible assets if they are to make investments in education, home ownership, businesses, and other strategies that will enable them to develop economically. As an instrument for asset-based policy, Sherraden has proposed individual development accounts (IDAs), which are matched savings accounts for the poor. The rationale behind IDAs is that saving is due, in large part, to structures and incentives rather than to personal preferences (Schreiner & Sherraden, 2007; Sherraden, Schreiner, & Beverly, 2003) and that assets have multiple positive effects in addition to deferred consumption. These effects may include stronger orientation toward the future, greater effort to enhance the value of assets, stronger social connectedness and community involvement, and improved well-being of offspring (Sherraden, 1991). Overall, research indicates that assets do have many such positive effects (Page-Adams & Sherraden, 1997; Scanlon & Page-Adams, 1998).

IDAs have a growing presence in public policy and community development. IDAs were included as a state option in the 1996 welfare reform law in the United States, and 40 or more states have included IDAs in their state plans. In addition, almost all states have now raised asset limits in welfare policies, allowing the welfare poor to accumulate somewhat more assets without losing eligibility for the program. In 1998, the Assets for Independence Act was passed, creating $125 million in federal funding for IDAs over five years.

In addition to federal resources, funding for IDA projects is coming from foundations, corporations, and state and local governments. In 2007, the United Way of America allocated $1.5 billion for family financial stability, including IDAs. This eclectic mix of private and public partnerships may signal a new form of social development policy in which the government and the private sector combine efforts in creative, almost entrepreneurial, fashion to respond to particular issues.

Investments That Remove Barriers to Economic Participation

If the participation of social welfare clients in the productive economy is to be enhanced, steps must be taken to remove the barriers that impede economic participation. Those who currently receive social benefits face serious barriers to economic participation, which limits their effective economic functioning. However, the removal of these barriers presents a formidable challenge. It is a matter not only of providing clients with the knowledge and skills they need to be employable or of helping them find employment but also of overcoming obstacles that impede economic participation. It is now widely recognized that those on income support face serious difficulties in securing transportation to work, access to affordable day care, and other resources that are available to many middle-class people. The barriers facing those with physical and mental disabilities who seek to become economically active are even more formidable, and as is widely recognized, many will require supports if they are to participate effectively in the productive economy. Barriers to asset accumulation, which have long characterized means-tested social welfare programs, are also a major impediment to the development of households and communities. Such asset limits should be liberalized and, where possible, eliminated altogether.

It is equally important that wider, socially institutionalized obstacles to economic participation be addressed. These include the problems of prejudice and discrimination based on race and ethnicity, gender, nationality, disability, age, and other factors that impede people's careers and life chances. Unless these challenges are met, the effectiveness of skills development, job placement, and employment programs and asset building will continue to be impeded.

Compared with many other countries, the United States has taken steps to address these concerns. Well-defined antidiscriminatory and affirmative action programs have been adopted and, in certain fields, such as employment for people with disabilities and racial discrimination in mortgage lending, much progress has been made. The Americans with Disabilities Act is widely regarded as a major step toward removing the barriers that limit economic participation among people with disabilities. The Community Reinvestment Act has broadened opportunities for home ownership and also supported local community economic development projects (Immergluck, 2004). Nevertheless, much more needs to be done to ensure that those who seek to be economically active attain this goal. The rise of anti-affirmative action sentiment and the popular notion that welfare clients are given unfair advantage through education, job training, and other investments that are not available to all are disturbing. If these attitudes become entrenched, many of those who strive to function in the productive economy will face increasing hardship. In addition, the importance of providing high-quality education so that citizens can participate fully in the productive economy remains critical. Unfortunately, as Sacks (2007) has shown, access to education, and particularly to higher education, has become increasingly unequal in recent times.

Investments in Cost-Effective Programs

The social development approach also requires that social programs be carefully evaluated to determine their cost effectiveness. The social services have often been accused of being wasteful, inefficient, and excessively bureaucratic. Critics have claimed that these programs are seldom subjected to careful, independent scrutiny. Indeed, it is often argued that they are perpetuated for political and other extraneous reasons. They may favor a particular constituency of clients who have a vested interest in their perpetuation. Politicians and bureaucrats may, for similar reasons, connive to maintain these programs irrespective of their effectiveness. The result is that resources are transferred out of the productive economy to maintain wasteful social services that harm economic development.

Although these claims are often exaggerated, efficiency is not always given as much precedence as it should get, and programs are not always rigorously evaluated to determine whether they do, in fact, meet their stated goals. Although sophisticated techniques of program evaluation are now available, they are not always properly implemented to determine the effectiveness of programs, and, sometimes, their findings are disregarded. This is often the case when political considerations play a major role in the development of particular programs.

Efficiency is a major consideration in social development. Because social development is primarily concerned with investments, it is obviously desirable that the effectiveness of these investments be assessed. Greater use should be made of technologies that calculate social investment returns. The future success of the social development model will, to a large extent, depend on whether it can be demonstrated that social investments do, in fact, bring positive returns of this kind.

Controversies in Social Development

Although there is growing interest in the social development perspective, many aspects of the social development approach remain controversial and different views about its usefulness have been expressed. Indeed, advocates of the social development approach have been criticized on several grounds, and the criticisms leveled against them should be carefully considered and addressed.

For example, they have been challenged on the political implications of their ideas. Some critics have claimed that social development is little more than an expedient effort to secure electoral support for social programs without addressing the fundamental challenges of poverty and inequality in society. While these critics come from the political left, others from the right claim that social development is a backdoor attempt to perpetuate government involvement in social welfare at a time when voters have rejected the failed welfare statism of the past. Yet, others are concerned that those who advocate social service retrenchments will exploit the social development approach, so it will result in little more than exhortations to the needy to find work and become self-sufficient. These critics are concerned that the emphasis on economic participation will overlook the real hardships that many welfare recipients face in securing employment and result in further deprivation and neglect.

Another controversy deals with some of the philosophical ideas attending the social development approach. For example, the emphasis placed on progress and, particularly, on material progress by social development writers has been challenged by those who claim that a continued emphasis on economic development will result in greater environmental damage, more mindless consumerism, and a weakening of traditional cultural values. Economic development should not, they believe, be confused with progress. Indeed, they argue that economic development has often caused more harm than good. Other writers are skeptical of the very notion of social progress embodied in social development. They accuse social development writers of being naively utopian. Social progress, they claim, is an illusion at a time when violence, ethnic conflict, inequality, and racism characterize the human condition. Until these fundamental issues are addressed, talk of social progress through social development is unrealistic. A similar argument is made by postmodernist writers who contend that proposals for social transformation are no longer possible in an increasingly fragmented world characterized by individualism, localism, and ethnocentrism. The prescriptions for large-scale planning contained in social development thinking are simply unworkable in the postmodern era.

Although other criticisms of social development have been made, those discussed previously are perhaps the most challenging to social development as a viable, innovative perspective in social policy. These criticisms are being taken into account as advocates of the social development approach seek to refine its principles and practice strategies and offer a viable alternative to conventional approaches to social welfare policy and, particularly, to the supporters of those approaches who believe that markets and individual effort alone are sufficient to ensure the welfare of all.

References

Becker, G. (1993). *Human capital: A theoretical and empirical analysis, with special reference to education* (3rd ed.). Chicago: University of Chicago Press.

Beverly, S., & Sherraden, M. (1997). Human investment as a social development strategy. *Social Development Issues, 19*(1), 1–18.

Esping-Anderson, G. (1990). *The three worlds of welfare capitalism.* Princeton, NJ: Princeton University Press.

Giddens, A. (1998). *The third way: The renewal of social democracy.* Cambridge, UK: Polity Press.

Gilbert, N. (1983). *Capitalism and the welfare state.* New Haven, CT: Yale University Press.

Ginsberg, L. (1998). *Conservative social welfare policy: A description and analysis.* Chicago: Nelson Hall.

Haq, M. U. (1995). *Reflections on human development.* New York: Oxford University Press.

Immergluck, D. (2004). *Credit to the community: Community reinvestment and fair lending policy in the United States.* Armonk, NY: M. E. Sharpe.

Jurik, N. C. (2005). *Bootstrap dreams: US microenterprise development in an era of welfare reform.* Ithaca, NY: Cornell University Press.

Kirp, D. (2007). *The sandbox investment: The preschool movement and kids-first movement.* Cambridge, MA: Harvard University Press.

Levy, F. (1999). *The new dollars and dreams: American incomes and economic change.* New York: Russell Sage Foundation.

Midgley, J. (1995). *Social development: The developmental perspective in social welfare.* Thousand Oaks, CA: Sage.

Midgley, J. (1999). Growth, redistribution and welfare: Towards social investment. *Social Service Review, 77*(1), 3-21.

Midgley, J. (2001). The critical perspective in social development. *Social Development Issues, 23*(1), 42–50.

Midgley, J. (2003). Social development: The intellectual heritage. *Journal of International Development, 15*(7), 831–844.

Midgley, J., & Livermore, M. (1998). Social capital and local economic development: Implications for community social work practice. *Journal of Community Practice, 5*(1/2), 29–40.

Midgley, J., & Livermore, M. (2004). Social development: Lessons from the global south. In M. C. Hokenstad & J. Midgley (Eds.), *Lessons from abroad: Adapting international social welfare innovations* (pp. 117–136). Washington, DC: NASW Press.

Myrdal, G. (1970). *The challenge of world poverty.* Harmondsworth, UK: Penguin.

Page-Adams, D., & Sherraden, M. (1997). Asset building as a community revitalization strategy. *Social Work, 42*, 423–434.

Putnam, R. D. (with Leonardi, R., & Nanetti, R. Y.). (1993). *Making democracy work: Civic traditions in modern Italy.* Princeton, NJ: Princeton University Press.

Rainford, W. (2001). Promoting welfare by enhancing opportunity: Individual enterprise approach to social development. *Social Development Issues, 23*(1), 51–57.

Sacks, P. (2007). *Tearing down the gates: Confronting the class divide in American education.* Berkeley: University of California Press.

Scanlon, E., & Page-Adams, D. (1998). Effects of asset holding. In R. Boshara (Ed.), *Building assets.* Washington, DC: Corporation for Enterprise Development.

Schreiner, M., & Sherraden, M. (2007). *Can the poor save?* New Brunswick, NJ: Transaction.

Schultz, T. W. (1959). Investment in man: An economist's view. *Social Service Review, 33*, 109–117.

Seers, D. (1969). The meaning of development. *International Development Review, 3*(1), 2–6.

Sen, A. (1985). *Commodities and capabilities.* New York: Elsevier.

Sen, A. (1999). *Development as freedom.* New York: Knopf.

Sherraden, M. (1991). *Assets and the poor: A new American welfare policy.* Armonk, NY: M. E. Sharpe.

Sherraden, M. (Ed.). (2005). *Inclusion in the American dream: Assets, poverty, and public policy.* New York: Oxford University Press.

Sherraden, M. S., & Ninacs, W. (Eds.). (1998). *Community economic development and social work.* New York: Haworth.

Sherraden, M., Schreiner, M., & Beverly, S. (2003). Income, institutions, and saving performance in Individual Development Accounts. *Economic Development Quarterly, 17*(1), 95–112.

Sherraden, M. S., Sanders C. K., & Sherraden, M. (2004). *Kitchen capitalism: Microenterprise in low-income households.* Albany: State University of New York Press.

Streeten, P. (with Burki, S. J., Haq, M. U., Hicks, N., & Stewart, F.). (1981). *First things first: Meeting basic human needs in developing countries.* New York: Oxford University Press.

United Nations. (1969). *Proceedings of the International Conference of Ministers Responsible for Social Welfare.* New York: Author.

United Nations. (1971). Social policy and planning in national development. *International Social Development Review, 3,* 4–15.

United Nations. (1996). *Report of the World Summit for Social Development: Copenhagen, 6–12 March 1995.* New York: Author.

United Nations. (2005). *Investing in development: A practical plan to achieve the millennium development goals.* New York: Author.

United Nations Development Programme. (1990). *Human development report 1990.* New York: Oxford University Press.

World Bank. (2006). *Microfinance consensus guidelines.* Washington, DC: Consultative Group to Assist the Poor.

Yunus, M. (1999). *Banker to the poor: Micro-lending and the battle against world poverty.* New York: Public Affairs Press.

19

Social Policy and the Physical Environment

Marie D. Hoff and John G. McNutt

This chapter describes how environmental problems affect social welfare and establishes the environmental components of a range of social policy issues. The discussion concludes with proposals for approaches to move beyond industrial social welfare to a social policy model grounded in the principles and practices of sustainable social development.

In this discussion, we argue that traditional models of social welfare, based on models of the economy that do not take into account the key role of the resource base, have outlived their usefulness for guiding social policy making. Despite their significant theoretical and ideological differences, all of these models fail to account for the physical environment as the necessary foundation of social well-being (McNutt, 1994). As environmental resources are increasingly depleted and degraded, we need a new paradigm to guide progress toward building caring, functional human societies. Sustainable social development, as the new model for social policy, is characterized by a simultaneous, integrated strategy to pursue environmental protection, economic development, and sociocultural well-being as one set of goals (Daly & Cobb, 1994; Hoff & McNutt, 1994; Olson, 1995; Speth, 2004).

Loss and Degradation of Environmental Resources

The most fundamental social problem in any society is lack of ready access to the basic necessities of life: clean air and water, a safe, adequate food supply, secure housing, and energy supplies for cooking and heating—all of which come directly from a sustaining natural environment. Yet, in every country in the world, the sources of life's basic necessities are threatened, depleted, or polluted at alarming and possibly irreversible rates.

A toxic mix of various chemicals causes constantly rising levels of air pollution. Most dangerous is the rising rate of carbon emissions—7.09 billion tons in 2006 (Black, 2006). In 1995, the Intergovernmental Panel on Climate Change (IPCC)—2,500 scientists sponsored by the United Nations—voiced overwhelming agreement that global warming and climate change due to carbon emissions pose substantial risks to the natural world and human society (IPCC, 1995). Their most recent recommendations in 2007 went considerably further than in the past (IPCC, 2007, p. 113; Vig & Kraft, 1997, pp. 369–370). The most serious consequence of climate change is the threat to food production, although recent disasters in the Far East and the U.S. Gulf Coast raise other issues as well.

The National Environmental Protection Agency estimated that it would cost $13 billion *per year* over 20 years to clean up and rebuild the nation's infrastructure for delivering safe, adequate water supplies (*Meeting Clean Water and Drinking Water Infrastructure Needs*, 1997). Clean, safe drinking water is a threatened commodity. As many as 1,000 deaths and 400,000 illnesses per year may be due to unsafe drinking water (Kraft & Vig, 1997, p. 21). Groundwater, the source of drinking water for about 50% of the nation, is being used up at rates far exceeding the rate of replenishment. Depletion of groundwater and underground aquifers is occurring most rapidly in some of the nation's major food producing areas, such as California and the High Plains (Postel, 1996; Reisner, 1993). Loss of clean water supply is due to inadequate treatment of industrial, agricultural, and municipal wastewater, while reduction in supply is attributable to wasteful irrigation methods and increasing industrial and urban residential demand. Worldwide, poor sanitation and waste treatment procedures leave perhaps 2 billion people without clean water. Pollution and depletion of water supplies also destroys world fisheries, which are a major source of protein for a billion people in Asia (Weber, 1993, p. 9). In the United States, two major threatened fisheries include Atlantic cod and Pacific salmon (McGinn, 1998, p. 60).

The United Nations estimates that between 1945 and 1990, soil degradation, due to unsustainable agricultural practices, affected 26% of agricultural land in North America and 74% in Central America (Gardner, 1996, p. 27). Highways, dams, industrial expansion, and residential sprawl also remove rich agricultural land from production. The Santa Clara Valley of California—once a rich fruit-growing region—is now renamed Silicon Valley—a center for the electronics industry. Grains are the staple of the human diet. Soil loss, along with growing population and slowing growth in crop yields, is contributing to a sharply declining world grain supply (Brown, 2005). Crop loss in one large producer country, such as China, can drive up the worldwide cost of food significantly (Brown, 1995; Gardner, 1996, p. 10).

Renewable resources, such as food and timber, come from interactive dynamic ecological systems. To understand the full magnitude of the impact of environmental losses, we must appreciate how loss or disequilibrium in one element of the ecosystem affects all others. Most pervasive are the threats from global warming and climate change (see Gore, 2006): loss of coastal lands from rising oceans, habitat loss and extinction or migration of species, disasters, and, perhaps, major collapses in agricultural productivity (Speth, 2004). The Kyoto Protocol, intended to deal with the problems of greenhouse gasses and their subsequent effects on climate change, has yet to be ratified by the United States.

Depletion of renewable and nonrenewable resources, including species extinction, is one major pole of environmental loss. The other is the massive poisoning and destruction of the global environment from the thousands of chemicals in use today in every facet of modern life: household and building construction, agriculture, industry (including electronics), transportation, health care, military, recreation, media, and entertainment. Of the thousands of chemical compounds on the market, only a few have been identified and tested for safety by the National Environmental Protection Agency (Rogge, 1994). The inadequate progress is especially worrisome in light of new evidence that some of these chemicals may disrupt human immune and reproductive systems and cause neurotoxic disorders (Kraft & Vig, 1997, p. 22).

Relationships Between Social Policy and Environmental Problems

Environmental conditions and social problems and needs have an oscillating, spiraling interaction: deficiencies in, losses from, and toxification of the physical environment lead to complex social problems; and social and economic policies and practices lead to increasingly serious threats to the basic sustainability of the physical environment. Figure 19.1 illustrates the critical role of the resource base in decisions for social welfare. Not only does the resource base provide the critical foundation for the economic system, but it also has an independent effect on well-being. The industrial and agricultural sectors of the economy (and even the information sector) are clearly dependent on extractive processes (e.g., mining, logging, and farming) for both raw materials and productive energy. The despoliation and depletion of natural resources are critical problems for most of the economic system. Additionally, the degradation of the natural environment leads to physical and psychological illnesses, community destruction, and the devastation of aesthetic values, all of which directly affect individual and community welfare (Hoff & McNutt, 1994; Rogge, 2000; Rogge & Combs-Orme, 2003; Wachtel, 1989). Social welfare policy is concerned with well-being (Iatridis, 1994), and environmental conditions have a direct effect on human well-being, in addition to their role in the economy. Many contemporary models of social welfare include the environment as part of the economy (Iatridis,

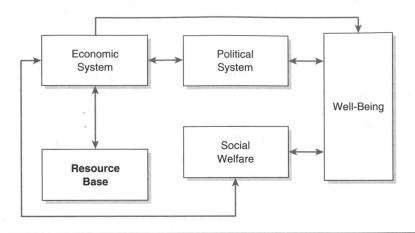

Figure 19.1   Relationship Between Social Welfare and the Resource Base

1994; Titmuss, 1974; Wilensky & Lebeaux, 1965). On balance, this view
ignores the direct impact of the environment on well-being and fails to
acknowledge that prevailing economic theories give little specific attention
to the role of the environment in the functioning of the economy (Daly,
1996; Daly & Cobb, 1994; Hawken, 1993; Lutz & Lux, 1988).

Policy makers and policy scholars must begin to explicitly integrate social,
economic, and environmental strategies and goals. This integration involves
the restoration and preservation of the natural environment and the development of industrial, agricultural, and consumer practices that do not damage or deplete the environment beyond sustainable levels. It also requires
measurable improvements in indicators of human welfare and development,
such as health, morbidity and mortality statistics, literacy and educational
levels, reduced crime and violence rates, improved housing quality and availability, full employment and reduction in poverty rates, and increased civic
participation and leisure (measures of social capital).[1] The effects of environmental problems on social well-being and social policy measures to
address these concerns are addressed in the following paragraphs.

Health Policy

Threats from various toxic chemicals constitute the most observable
health effects of environmental practices (Brulle & Pellow, 2006; Bullard,
2005; Rogge, 1994). Air pollution is considered to be the major environmental contributor to the 40% rise in asthma between 1981 and 1991 in
the United States (Centers for Disease Control and Prevention, 1995,
p. 952). Poor children in urban areas are at special risk from respiratory
problems related to air quality. Widespread radioactive fallout (which causes
thyroid disease) from nuclear bomb tests in the 1950s is now acknowledged
to be more pervasive than the government had previously acknowledged

(Ortmeyer & Makhijani, 1997). Navajo and white workers continue to suffer numerous forms of cancer from mining radioactive minerals (Dawson, 1994; Dawson, Madsen, & Spykerman, 1997; Madsen & Dawson, 2004).

Precise cause-effect relationships between exposure to specific toxic materials and cancer or other health problems are often difficult to establish. Various scientific investigations continue to explore the etiology of various diseases and the effects of chemicals on fetal and child development. What is certain is that most forms of cancer are rising (Misch, 1994). Therefore, national health policy—still largely devoted to funding secondary and tertiary medical care—needs to be reoriented toward a public health and education approach to disease prevention, including reduction of the heavy reliance on chemicals in both industry and households.

Poverty and Inequality

Progressive social policy values equity and fairness in the distribution of social costs and benefits across classes and groups (Titmuss, 1974). Significant environmental injustices exist within and between nations. Children face special risks of damage from environmental threats; and depletion of resources or extinction of species can be viewed as a form of theft—an ethical violation of the rights of future generations (Garbarino, 1992). Governmental research (U.S. General Accounting Office, 1983) and other studies (Brulle & Pellow, 2006; Bryant & Mohai, 1992; Bullard, 2005; Commission for Racial Justice, 1987; Rogge, 1994) have established that ethnic minority and low-income communities, urban and rural, are the recipients of highly disproportionate burdens of environmental threats of all kinds: dangerous industries and waste disposal sites; polluted soil, water, and air; and poor housing, which burdens residents with an increased risk of lead paint poisoning and with inefficient, costly energy systems. Globally, environmental injustices are manifested in several ways: for example, the shipment of waste products from wealthier nations to financially strapped poor nations around the globe and the disproportionate consumption of the world's natural resources by the wealthy nations of the world. The United States has 5% of the world's population yet uses 30% of the world's fossil fuel supplies. Thus, the United States also contributes disproportionately to climate change. Global warming will undoubtedly affect everyone, but disadvantaged groups, such as the poor, racial or class minorities, and island nations, will suffer the most (Hoff, 2004).

Violence

Environmentally and socially ravaged urban areas are afflicted with extraordinary levels of violence and other symptoms of social dysfunction, such as high rates of suicide, mental hospitalization, and juvenile crime

(Wilson, 1996). Much broad-based research demonstrates the nature of linkages among environmental exploitation, low levels of social spending, the impoverishment of peoples, and high levels of social violence within and between nations (Alvares, 1994; Athanasiou, 1996; George, 1988, 1992; Korten, 1995; Shiva, 1991; Thomas, 1995; Wolpin, 1986).

In the United States, economic and social struggles intensify over natural resources, such as fish, minerals, timber, water use, wildlife management, grazing rights, and a host of other local issues (Hoff, 1998; Reisner, 1993; Wilkinson, 1992; Zakin, 1993).[2] Numerous communities experience conflict over issues such as finding disposal sites for waste, where to locate sites for military bombing ranges, and the cleanup of past environmental damage from industry and the military (Bullard, 2005). The American tendency toward litigation has prolonged these disputes and has made them extremely costly. Some communities have turned toward voluntary community-level decision making to resolve environmental disputes (Johnson, 1998), but legislation and, in some cases, local government participation, could assist to legitimatize and fund these non-litigious conflict resolution methods.

It is also difficult to ignore the connections. While genocide, civil unrest, and ethnic cleansing are tied to other social forces, conflict over scarce environmental resources, such as water, is also a significant stressor.

Agriculture and Food Policy

Federal policies pertaining to food supply (hunger issues), food safety (food-borne disease concerns), and agricultural policy (economic concerns of producers) are regulated by an uncoordinated maze of government agencies. National policy makers should begin to develop explicit objectives that integrate and redirect strategies to achieve progress in all three of these areas. Currently, the majority of federal and state research funds and agricultural subsidies go toward large, primarily corporate, producers, for agricultural methods that are highly dependent on irrigation and heavy infusions of chemical fertilizers and pesticides. Family farming is in sharp decline over the past two decades, and food safety concerns are increasing among consumers. New, integrated approaches would begin with support for organic agriculture and restoration of diversified, family farming in the United States. Such a redirection of national agricultural policy would promote a number of goals: soil renewal through increased recycling of organic materials; decreased reliance on imported food and petroleum; decreased health risks to farm workers and consumers from toxic substances; increased employment, as such methods are more labor intensive; and rural community revitalization through population maintenance. Redirection of national agricultural policy away from dependence on imported food and petroleum products would constitute a new political conception of national security.

Urban gardening is a burgeoning community movement in many cities across the country. It is often a favored strategy for youth development and rehabilitation. It provides nutritional benefits from fresh, local produce;

reduces food costs and pollution by lessening dependence on produce trucked at great expense; encourages entrepreneurship, healthy exercise, and neighborhood socialization; contributes to ecological education; and aids the revitalization of often seriously damaged urban soils. Finally, urban gardening fosters aesthetic values, which support emotional well-being. Some local governments provide support in the form of land, site preparation and maintenance, materials, and gardening instruction. Local and state legislation could provide increased funds for this promising social and environmental trend (Lawrence & Milstein, 1997; Nelson, 1996).

Housing and Community Development Policy

National housing and community development policy ignores environmental considerations. Because housing is primarily viewed as a profit-generating commodity, most planning decisions are made without a commitment to preserve the environment or minimize the use of resources, especially nonrenewable resources such as minerals or fossil fuels. Housing development patterns in the United States are profligate in their use of environmental resources: the trend is toward larger houses, which use more land space and require more materials and energy to build and maintain. Urban and rural sprawl is a major contributor to loss of agricultural land in the United States. Public policy places few restrictions on these private preferences. Additionally, housing for the poor has been a declining national priority for the past two decades (Moroney & Krysik, 1998).

Redirection of national housing and community development policy toward environmental sustainability would potentially support the goals of decency and affordability for the poor and near-poor. And, like urban gardening, a shift in housing policy would have the potential to contribute to community revitalization. Municipalities and other levels of government need to strengthen housing policy instruments including zoning, planning, and taxation incentives to encourage more density; experimentation with renewable, low-cost building materials;[3] greater energy efficiency; utilization of renewable energy sources; and recycling of household waste. Density reduces transportation costs and increases social contact, while energy and materials efficiencies decrease costs and pollution. Community design can facilitate environmental goals and the building of social capital, which, in turn, fosters strong communities and economies (Midgley & Livermore, 1998; Putnam, 1993, 2000).

Energy and Transportation Policy

Since the oil embargo of 1973, policy makers and social welfare professionals are more aware of the high costs of heating and transportation, especially for the poor. Nevertheless, U.S. energy policy has continued to increase our dependence on imported oil and has neglected conservation and renewable energy development (Romm, 1991). As global warming and climate change are increasingly acknowledged as serious environmental threats, there is more general awareness of the negative impact of world-wide dependence on fossil fuels, which are the major source of air pollution. Nuclear power, once promised as a low-cost alternative energy source is coming to be recognized as a costly and dangerous alternative. However, some recent proposals have been made to construct new nuclear power plants. National investment in wind and solar energy is very limited in the United States, although increasing in some parts of the country. Development of public transit lags far behind the marked American preference for private automobiles, which consume enormous quantities of fuel, materials, and land space. Public policy redirection toward the development of renewable, nonpolluting energy, as well as energy efficiency, conservation, and public transit would promote environmental protection goals while supporting the social policy goals of providing low-cost transportation and home heating and electricity for working-class and poor population groups.

Waste Disposal

Many communities around the United States struggle with the safe disposal of waste generated by industrial, agricultural, and consumer activities. The issue has numerous facets. Older cities are faced with brownfields—urban areas severely poisoned by industrial waste. Rural areas face severe threats of air and groundwater pollution from animal "production" factories, which house intense concentrations of animals, such as hogs and dairy cows, in confined animal feeding operations (CAFOs). CAFOs also threaten the safety of the food supply for consumers because huge infusions of antibiotics are needed to prevent disease in such closely confined animals. Numerous rural communities, including Native American communities on reservations, are fighting the siting of solid waste (municipal garbage) disposal facilities in their communities (Bullard, 2005). The nuclear weapons and energy industries have created waste disposal and toxic threats that may persist for literally tens of thousands of years. American consumer habits—the "throw-away" mentality—contribute, as does the excessive packaging of consumer products.

Waste disposal policy has numerous social policy dimensions: social justice issues in the location of facilities; health and safety threats; and waste disposal battles that divide community members, creating intense conflict and consuming personal energy. Democratic decision making, open government, and fairness in burden and risk bearing are some of the social values at stake in the current management of waste disposal (Kauffman, 1994). Public policy redirection of waste disposal should be guided by three goals: reduction of the quantity and toxicity of waste generated by both consumers and producers of agricultural and industrial products; increased research and experimentation in the reuse (recycling) of materials that are wasted in production processes; and fairness in the location of necessary waste facilities (Bullard, 2005). Waste disposal policy provides a sharp illustration of how social policy requires both value changes and serious research foundations for success. Public policy measures can help redirect wasteful consumer values and habits into more productive behaviors. However, research is essential to provide the technological means to reduce waste in the production process, as well as to better understand behavioral responses to policy directives (i.e., to discover which measures actually result in consumers' reducing use of, recycling, and reusing material resources).

Population Policy

The world's population is currently over 6.5 billion people (U.S. Census Bureau, 2008) and is estimated to grow to 7.7 billion or more in the next 50 years. The current U.S. population of over 300 million (U.S. Census Bureau, 2008) is projected to grow to 333 million by the year 2025 (Tobin, 1997, p. 323). Population issues are one of the most complex and controversial components of both environmental and social policy. Poor nations resent the accusation that their population growth is the cause of global environmental depletion, pointing out that the affluent, industrialized nations of the North consume the largest share of natural resources of the Earth (Tobin, 1997). However, substantial international consensus has gradually developed that population stabilization is necessary to save the physical integrity of the planet and improve the quality of life for all humanity (Independent Commission on Population and Quality of Life, 1996). At the 1994 United Nations conference on population, held in Cairo, Egypt, representatives of nations gathered there reached substantial agreement that increased education and social and economic development opportunities for girls and women is the essential policy approach to population control (Independent Commission on Population and Quality of Life, 1996; United Nations, 1995).

In the United States, population policy is intertwined with political and religious division over abortion and birth control. It also overlaps with immigration policy, a perennial concern that is currently intensifying. Religious and cultural values must be acknowledged and respected in family planning policy and services. However, the principle agreed to at the Cairo conference also applies domestically: social policy must address more specifically the developmental needs of girls and women, particularly teenagers from disadvantaged socioeconomic backgrounds, as essential factors in population stabilization in the United States (Furstenberg & Brooks-Gunn, 1989; Wilson, 1996).

Social Policy Measures
for Sustainable Societies

In the United States, public social policy arose to respond to the most egregious effects of modern industrial capitalism, namely, unemployment and income loss for those unable to work for reasons of disability or old age. Social policy measures that promote individual and social development are largely separated from public policy measures to maintain the economic apparatus. Consequently, the social costs of industrial capitalism are not adequately accounted for, such as sickness and diseases resulting from workplace pollution and toxins or the promotion of excessive consumerism and of new perceptions of needs to maintain the complex system of production and continuous growth.

Nor have environmental costs been factored into some pricing equations. Environmental resources have been, until very recently, largely treated as externalities and often ignored in economic decision making (Repetto, 1992).

Although it would be impossible to internalize every degree of the social and environmental cost of economic production, public policy should begin to move toward that broad goal. Moreover, the environmental and social benefits of new economic methods and patterns of production should be assessed. A number of countries in Europe, as well as Canada and Japan, are developing national accounting systems to measure net progress toward environmental, economic, and social goals (Stead & Stead, 1992). Known as Quality of Life Indicators or the Index of Sustainable Economic Welfare (Daly & Cobb, 1994), such systems identify and subtract environmental losses as costs. Social problems such as crime or health problems due to environmental or employment practices are also counted as costs against net progress.

These types of indicators provide a foundation of information to support the integration of social and environmental policy with economic policy measures: social and environmental costs would be minimized by efficient firms, and they, in turn, would competitively drive out firms that deplete or pollute the environment or that cause severe social disruptions and human stress. In summary, social policy should move from a model in which it serves as a handmaid to deal with the unfortunate aftereffects of industrial capitalism to a positive model for environmentally sustainable social policy. Redirected national priorities to support this agenda include the following:

Significantly expanded government funding for research to develop sustainable techniques of production of food, energy, low-impact housing, and transportation. Previously, the term frequently used in relation to these techniques was *appropriate*; we needed appropriate technology. A better term that defines the goal is *sustainable*. Sustainable technology and techniques are methods of material production that neither destroy the renewable capacities of the environmental base nor destroy or diminish the human person and the community (Daly, 1996; Hawken, 1993; Stead & Stead, 1992).

Integrated urban and rural development policy. This goal involves planning for techniques to encourage greater urban density while also promoting the economic and social viability of rural areas. Little concerted policy or funding muscle is directed toward promotion of this goal of regional planning (Roberts, 1994). The environmental goals of regional planning are to preserve open space, resource quality (soil, water, and air), and the habitat of native biological species, while the social goals are to preserve viable rural and small communities and enhance human community, through community-based economic development, social networking, and improved supports for quality of life amenities. Regional planning also includes international diplomatic challenges, as the United States must cooperate with Canada to restore and jointly manage the Great Lakes region, with Mexico to develop mutually beneficial immigration policies, and with both countries to ensure social and environmental protections in industry, especially along the border.

Redirection of tax policy to penalize or encourage appropriately the use, pollution, depletion, or restoration of environmental resources. The fundamental objectives are to stop subsidies, penalize resource waste or depletion, and shift tax policy toward incentives and rewards for environmental protection, on the part of both consumers and producers (Roodman, 1997; Roseland, 1998). Examples include pollution and packaging taxes or tax incentives for use of recycled or more energy-efficient materials. Such changes are usually cost-efficient for both producers and consumers. Many European countries have made significantly greater progress on these objectives than has the United States, and they could be looked to for policy models.

Strengthening of regulatory agencies. It is critical to augment enforcement of environmental safety standards. This is difficult in a political climate resistant to active government, regulatory reform, and the improved monitoring of business and industry, yet it is a crucial social need (Freeman, 1997; Gore, 2006).

Strengthened public participation mechanisms for social, economic, and environmental decision making to support and enhance citizenship behavior. Public participation enhances the quality of public decision making. Modern technology such as television and Internet can be used creatively to structure and increase public participation (Schuler, 1996). Public policy can also support and encourage community-based, voluntaristic decision-making structures to solve environmental problems and conflicts. Community-based approaches, oftentimes perceived as less threatening, may also increase participation. A new term, *civic environmentalism* (John, 1994) describes these types of voluntary efforts, and case studies have been developed to evaluate their effectiveness for strengthening or decreasing democratic representation (Hoff, 1998; John, 1994; Johnson, 1998).

Public policy to enhance community building as an antidote to consumerism. Through increased public funding for the arts, amateur athletics, and voluntarism, public policy can enhance individual and social capital (skills and abilities). Such endeavors provide humanistic alternatives to environmentally destructive consumerism as a way of life.[4] A growing body of social research suggests that strong communities with engaged, active citizens also are more likely to achieve economic development (Midgley & Livermore, 1998; Putnam, 1993, 2000). The social policy of the United States cannot be developed in isolation in an increasingly interdependent world, and "emerging environmental threats on the national and international agenda are even more formidable than the first generation of problems addressed by government in the 1970s . . ." (Kraft & Vig, 1997, p. 26). The United States takes an aggressive, but not necessarily progressive, role in influencing several key international policy issues in which social and environmental considerations are inextricably interrelated. As discussed earlier, increased support is needed for (a) education and economic supports for girls and women and family planning technology, (b) the development of universal social security systems in every country to diminish reliance on large numbers of children for old-age insurance, and (c) increased health services in poor communities to improve child survival rates.

Debt reduction. It is essential, in order to improve social and environmental conditions in poor nations, for countries to be able to manage their debt without crippling austerity programs. International lending institutions frequently require countries to reduce social and health spending and sell off natural resources to service their external debts.[5] These harmful policies will require continued political pressure to reverse. The Jubilee 2000 international campaign resulted in debt forgiveness or reduction for a number of the world's poorest countries. This campaign demonstrated that citizen movements can influence even international policy. American social policy should also support the movement toward the democratization of global economic structures and the implementation of international standards for environmental protection and for the universal enforcement of human rights standards. Social welfare and the guarantee of a sustainable physical environment in any one country have become interdependent issues requiring acute redirection in local, national, and international policy making.

The environment represents a serious challenge to conventional thinking about social policy. Although its impact on the forces that determine human well-being is undeniable, theorists still resist taking it into account in their models about policy impact and policy analysis. This is both shortsighted and conceptually limiting. If we are to advance in our understanding of social policy, we must fill this important gap.

Notes

1. See Putnam's 1993 study of civic traditions in Italy, which developed historical, empirical evidence that regions and cities with strong civic participation have long been more economically prosperous also. Such studies of social capital, or the density of social relationships, are burgeoning in the United States (Midgley & Livermore, 1998). See also Livermore and Midgley's (1998) case study of how an intervention in one impoverished neighborhood in Baton Rouge, Louisiana, focused on strengthening human and social capital.

2. See the newspaper *High Country News* for regular coverage of the interaction between environmental issues and economic survival concerns of communities in the American West.

3. In several parts of the country, such as in the city of Tucson, Arizona, small-scale experiments in the utilization of alternative building materials, such as straw bales and cob, are taking place.

4. See Paul L. Wachtel's (1989) *The Poverty of Affluence* for a book-length treatment of the negative psychological impacts of affluence and consumption-oriented lives.

5. George (1992) analyzes how third world debt also harms citizens of wealthier nations. Issues include environmental effects, drugs, taxpayer subsidies for lending banks, lost jobs and markets, immigration, and conflict and war. See also Bruce Rich's (1994) *Mortgaging the Earth* for a comprehensive study of relationships among international lending, environmental depletion, and failed social development. See also *Confessions of an Economic Hit Man* by Perkins (2004) for a vivid personal reflection on the experiences of a formerly highly placed international consultant with these lending institutions. He examines how these policies actually affect the recipient countries.

References

Alvares, C. (1994). *Science, development, and violence.* Delhi: Oxford University Press.

Athanasiou, T. (1996). *Divided planet: The ecology of rich and poor.* Boston: Little, Brown.

Black, R. (2006, November 27). Carbon emissions show sharp rise. *BBC News.* Retrieved February 19, 2007, from http://news.bbc.co.uk/2/hi/science/nature/6189600.stm

Brown, L. R. (1995). *Who will feed China? Wake-up call for a small planet.* New York: W. W. Norton.

Brown, L. R. (2005). *Outgrowing the earth: The food security challenge in an age of falling water tables and rising temperatures.* New York: W. W. Norton

Brulle, R. J., & Pellow, D. N. (2006). Environmental justice: Human health and environmental inequalities. *Annual Review of Public Health, 27*(3), 1–22.

Bryant, B., & Mohai, P. (1992). *Race and the incidence of environmental hazards.* Boulder: Westview Press.

Bullard, R. (Ed.). (2005). *The quest for environmental justice: Human rights and the politics of pollution*. San Francisco: Sierra Club Books.

Centers for Disease Control and Prevention. (1995). Current trends in asthma—United States, 1982–1992. *Morbidity and Mortality Weekly Report, 43*(51), 952–955. Retrieved February 14, 2008, from http://www.cdc.gov/mmwr/preview/mmwrhtml/00035450.htm

Commission for Racial Justice, United Church of Christ. (1987). *Toxic wastes and race in the United States*. New York: Author.

Daly, H. E. (1996). *Beyond growth: The economics of sustainable development*. Boston: Beacon Press.

Daly, H. E., & Cobb, J. B., Jr. (1994). *For the common good: Redirecting the economy toward community, the environment, and a sustainable future* (2nd ed.). Boston: Beacon Press.

Dawson, S. E. (1994). Navajo uranium workers and the environment: Technological disaster survival strategies. In M. D. Hoff & J. G. McNutt (Eds.), *The global environmental crisis: Implications for social welfare and social work* (pp. 150–169). Aldershot, UK: Avebury Books.

Dawson, S. E., Madsen, G., & Spykerman, B. R. (1997). Public health issues concerning American Indian and non-Indian uranium millworkers. *Journal of Health and Social Policy, 8*(3), 41–56.

Freeman, A. M., III. (1997). Economics, incentives, and environmental regulation. In N. J. Vig & M. E. Kraft (Eds.), *Environmental policy in the 1990s* (pp. 187–207). Washington, DC: Congressional Quarterly Press.

Furstenberg, F. F., Jr., & Brooks-Gunn, J. (1989). Causes and consequences of teenage pregnancy and childbearing. In M. N. Ozawa (Ed.), *Women's life cycle and economic insecurity* (pp. 69–100). New York: Praeger.

Garbarino, J. (1992). *Toward a sustainable society: An economic, social and environmental agenda for our children's future*. Chicago: Noble Press.

Gardner, G. (1996, July). *Shrinking fields: Cropland loss in a world of eight billion* (Worldwatch Paper No. 131). Washington, DC: Worldwatch Institute.

George, S. (1988). *A fate worse than debt*. New York: Grove Press.

George, S. (1992). *The Debt boomerang*. London: Pluto Press.

Gore, A. (2006). *An inconvenient truth*. Emmaus, PA: Rodale Press.

Hawken, P. (1993). *The ecology of commerce: A declaration of sustainability*. New York: HarperBusiness.

Hoff, M. D. (1998). The Willapa Alliance: The role of a voluntary organization in fostering regional action for sustainability. In M. D. Hoff (Ed.), *Sustainable community development: Studies in economic, environmental, and cultural revitalization* (pp. 177–192). Boca Raton, FL: Lewis.

Hoff, M. D. (2004). Effects of global warming on human cultural diversity. In A. Yotava (Theme Ed.), *Encyclopedia of life support systems (EOLSS): Climate change, human systems, and policy* (Developed under the auspices of the UNESCO). Oxford, UK: Eolss. Retrieved February 14, 2008, from http://www.eolss.net

Hoff, M. D., & McNutt, J. G. (Eds.). (1994). *The global environmental crisis: Implications for social welfare and social work*. Aldershot, UK: Avebury Books.

Iatridis, D. (1994). *Social welfare policy*. Belmont, CA: Wadsworth.

Independent Commission on Population and Quality of Life. (1996). *Caring for the future*. Oxford, UK: Oxford University Press.

Intergovernmental Panel on Climate Change. (1995). *Climate Change 1995*. Geneva, Switzerland: IPCC Secretariat. Retrieved February 14, 2008, from http://www .ipcc.ch/

Intergovernmental Panel on Climate Change. (2007). *Climate Change 2007*. Geneva, Switzerland: IPCC Secretariat. Retrieved February 14, 2008, from http://www .ipcc.ch/

John, D. (1994). *Civic environmentalism: Alternatives to regulation in states and communities*. Washington, DC: Congressional Quarterly Press.

Johnson, K. (1998). The Henry's Fork Watershed Council: Community-based participation in regional environmental management. In M. D. Hoff (Ed.), *Sustainable community development: Studies in economic, environmental, and cultural revitalization* (pp. 165–176). Boca Raton, FL: Lewis.

Kauffman, S. E. (1994). Citizen participation in environmental decisions: Policy, reality, and considerations for community organizing. In M. D. Hoff & J. G. McNutt (Eds.), *The global environmental crisis: Implications for social welfare and social work* (pp. 219–239). Aldershot, UK: Avebury Books.

Korten, D. C. (1995). *When corporations rule the world*. West Hartford, CT: Kumarian Press.

Kraft, M. E., & Vig, N. J. (1997). Environmental policy from the 1970s to the 1990s. In N. J. Vig & M. E. Kraft (Eds.), *Environmental policy in the 1990s* (3rd ed., pp. 1–30). Washington, DC: Congressional Quarterly Press.

Lawrence, K., & Milstein, S. (1997). City farms: The Big Apple's city-wide network of urban food producers. *GEO Grassroots Economic Organizing, 28*(1), 3–4.

Livermore, M., & Midgley, J. (1998). The contribution of universities to building sustainable communities: The community university partnership. In M. D. Hoff (Ed.), *Sustainable community development: Studies in economic, environmental, and cultural revitalization* (pp.123–138). Boca Raton, FL: Lewis Publishers.

Lutz, M. E., & Lux, K. (1988). *Humanistic economics: The new challenge*. New York: Bootstrap Press.

Madsen, G. E., & Dawson, S. E. (2004). Unfinished business: Radiation Exposure Compensation Act (RECA) for post-1971 U.S. uranium underground miners. *Journal of Health & Social Policy, 19*(4), 45–59.

McGinn, A. P. (1998). Promoting sustainable fisheries. In L. R. Brown et al. (Eds.), *State of the World Report 1998* (pp. 59–78). New York: W. W. Norton.

McNutt, J. G. (1994). Social welfare policy and the environmental crisis: It's time to rethink our traditional models. In M. D. Hoff & J. G. McNutt (Eds.), *The global environmental crisis: Implications for social welfare and social work* (pp. 36–52). Aldershot, UK: Avebury Books.

Meeting clean water and drinking water infrastructure needs: Hearing before the Subcommittee on Water Resources and the Environment of the House Committee on Transportation and Infrastructure, 105th Cong., 1st session (1997, April 23) (testimony of R. Persiasepe, Assistant Administrator, Office of Water, U.S. Environmental Protection Agency). Washington, DC: Government Printing Office.

Midgley, J., & Livermore, M. (1998). Social capital and local economic development: Implications for community social work practice. *Journal of Community Practice, 5*(1/2), 29–40.

Misch, A. (1994). Assessing environmental health risk. In L. Brown et al. (Eds.), *State of the World Report 1994* (pp. 117–136). New York: W. W. Norton.

Moroney, R. M., & Krysik, J. (1998). *Social policy and social work: Critical essays on the welfare state* (2nd ed.). New York: Aldine de Gruyter.

Nelson, T. (1996). Urban agriculture. *World Watch, 9*(6), 10–17.

Olson, R. L. (1995). Sustainability as a social vision. *Journal of Social Issues, 51*(4), 15–35.

Ortmeyer, P., & Makhijani, A. (1997). Worse than we knew. *The Bulletin of the Atomic Scientists, 53*(6), 46–50.

Perkins, J. (2004). *Confessions of an economic hit man*. San Francisco: Berrett-Koehler.

Postel, S. (1996). Forging a sustainable water strategy. In L. R. Brown et al. (Eds.), *State of the world report 1996* (pp. 40–59). New York: W. W. Norton.

Putnam, R. D. (with Leonardi, R., & Nanetti, R. Y.). (1993). *Making democracy work: Civic traditions in modern Italy*. Princeton, NJ: Princeton University Press.

Putnam, R. D. (2000). *Bowling alone: The collapse and revival of American community*. New York: Simon & Schuster.

Reisner, M. (1993). *Cadillac desert: The American west and its disappearing water*. New York: Penguin.

Repetto, R. (1992). Accounting for environmental assets. *Scientific American, 266*(6), 94–100.

Rich, B. (1994). *Mortgaging the earth: The World Bank, environmental impoverishment, and the crisis of development*. Boston: Beacon Press.

Roberts, P. (1994). Sustainable regional planning. *Regional Studies, 28*(8), 781–787.

Rogge, M. E. (1994). Environmental injustice: Social welfare and toxic waste. In M. D. Hoff & J. G. McNutt (Eds.), *The global environmental crisis: Implications for social welfare and social work* (pp. 53–74). Aldershot, UK: Avebury Books.

Rogge, M. E. (2000). Children, poverty, and environmental degradation: Protecting current and future generations. *Social Development Issues, 22*(2/3), 46–53.

Rogge, M. E., & Combs-Orme, T. (2003). Protecting our future: Children, environmental policy, and social work. *Social Work, 48*(4), 439–450.

Romm, J. (1991). Needed—A no-regrets energy policy. *Bulletin of the Atomic Scientists 47*(6), 31–36.

Roodman, D. M. (1997). *Getting the signals right: Tax reform to protect the environment and the economy* (Worldwatch Paper No. 134). Washington, DC: Worldwatch Institute.

Roseland, M. (1998). *Toward sustainable communities* (Rev. ed.). Gabriola Island, BC: New Society Publishers.

Schuler, D. (1996). *New community networks: Wired for change*. Reading, MA: Addison-Wesley.

Shiva, V. (1991). *The violence of the green revolution*. London: Zed Books.

Speth, J. G. (2004). *Red sky at morning: America and the global environmental crisis*. New Haven, CT: Yale University Press.

Stead, W. E., & Stead, J. G. (1992). *Management for a small planet: Strategic decision making and the environment*. Newbury Park, CA: Sage.

Thomas, W. (1995). *Scorched earth: The military's assault on the environment*. Philadelphia: New Society Publishers.

Titmuss, R. (1974). *Social policy: An introduction*. London: Allen & Unwin.

Tobin, R. J. (1997). Environment, population, and the developing world. In N. J. Vig & M. E. Kraft (Eds.), *Environmental policy in the 1990s* (3rd ed., pp. 321–344). Washington, DC: Congressional Quarterly Press.

United Nations. (1995). *Population consensus at Cairo, Mexico City, and Bucharest: An analytical comparison* (United Nations Publication Sales No. E.96.XIII.2). New York: Author.

U.S. Census Bureau. (2008). *U.S. and world population clocks.* Washington, DC: Author. Retrieved February 18, 2008, from http://www.census.gov/main/www/popclock.html

U.S. General Accounting Office. (1983, June). *Siting of hazardous waste landfills and their correlation with the racial and socio-economic status of surrounding communities.* (Report No. GAO/RCED-83-168). Washington, DC: Government Printing Office.

Vig, N. J., & Kraft, M. E. (1997). The new environmental agenda. In N. J. Vig & M. E. Kraft (Eds.), *Environmental policy in the 1990s* (3rd ed., pp. 365–389). Washington, DC: Congressional Quarterly Press.

Wachtel, P.L. (1989). *The poverty of affluence: A psychological portrait of the American way of life.* Philadelphia: New Society Publishers.

Weber, P. (1993, November). *Abandoned seas: Reversing the decline of the oceans* (Worldwatch Paper No. 116). Washington, DC: Worldwatch Institute.

Wilensky, H. L., & Lebeaux, C. N. (1965). *Industrial society and social welfare.* New York: Free Press.

Wilkinson, C. F. (1992). *Crossing the next meridian: Land, water, and the future of the west.* Washington, DC: Island Press.

Wilson, W. J. (1996). *When work disappears.* New York: Alfred A. Knopf.

Wolpin, M. D. (1986). *Militarization, internal repression, and social welfare in the Third World.* London: Croom Helm.

Zakin, S. (1993). *Coyotes and town dogs: Earth First and the environmental movement.* New York: Viking/Penguin.

PART IV

Social Policy and the Social Services

Part IV is the largest of the handbook, containing 12 chapters that range over a number of social service and social policy fields. The social services are the primary mechanism by which the government implements social policies and seeks to enhanced peoples' welfare, so, obviously, these fields require extensive discussion. Some social services, such as child welfare, programs for the elderly, Social Security, and services to people with disabilities, are widely recognized to be at the core of social policy and are included in most accounts of American social welfare. However, activities not conventionally grouped with the mainstream social services are also discussed here. These include employment policies and services, correctional programs, and urban development policies. Although neglected by mainstream social work and social policy scholarship, these programs play an important role in social welfare in the United States today. Part IV also includes an overview of health, education, and housing programs, which are very large fields of social policy endeavor. Although they are often treated as separate specialized fields, to ensure that the book is as comprehensive as possible, these social services are included although, of course, they cannot be covered in great detail.

Generally, each chapter in this part of the book follows a standard format in which the historical evolution of each social service field is described briefly; the current legislative and administrative arrangements pertaining to service provision are outlined; and the social, political, and economic factors influencing policies and service delivery are considered. Each chapter also discusses various issues arising out of the descriptive account of each social service field. As will be seen, social service policy formulation and delivery raise complex and often contentious disagreements about which approaches are the most effective way of meeting human needs and promoting peoples' well-being today.

20 Child and Family Welfare Policies and Services

Katharine Briar-Lawson, Toni Naccarato, and Jeanette Drews

Vulnerable children have been among the most marginalized and under-served populations throughout the history of the United States. Their families and the systems that serve them often fail them. Policy makers have not deemed vulnerable children or their families as primary human resource investments. Moreover, the country does not have a comprehensive child and family policy or an integrative framework for investing in families and children.

Services to vulnerable children and their families have long been specialized and categorical. They are characterized by fragmentation and misalignment. Moreover, different eligibility criteria, funding streams, and enabling legislation dictate the type and duration of services. Which service sector children and families enter, such as welfare, child welfare, health, mental health, juvenile justice, schools, disabilities, or child care, will shape the nature of services. The needs of vulnerable children and families usually cross several service sectors, and children and families are often served at the same time by multiple service providers. Since there is no integrated policy for such children and families, service barriers, gaps, and conflicting approaches often impede desired outcomes. Child and family policy in the United States has been characterized as residual, crisis driven, and often child saving rather than family strengthening (Lindsey, 1994). Such policies have created high-cost human and fiscal outcomes that could have been avoided with lower-cost investments in vulnerable children and families (Holzer, 2007).

This chapter explores some of the policy and programmatic challenges facing 21st-century child and family welfare while addressing the historical antecedents. Special attention is placed on child protection and child welfare systems and their relation to poor children and families. This is because child welfare services often constitute the system of last resort, especially

315

when other service sectors, such as mental health, disabilities, welfare, and schools, are unable to serve children and their families effectively. In addition, innovations in one sector may have implications for more effective services in another, especially in child welfare. A cross-sector, comparative scan also suggests the need for more collaborative practices. Finally, such a scan leads to some design features for more innovative practices and for an integrative child and family policy for the 21st century.

Dominant Policies, Assumptions, and Approaches

Families perform 90% of all the caregiving, counseling, education, child protection, health care, and policing in the nation and around the world, yet many remain unaided when it comes to their dependent members (Briar-Lawson, Lawson, Hennon, & Jones, 2001). Since the late 1700s in the United States, parents have been charged with the protection and education of their children. During the 1800s, parents who were poor faced the removal of their child simply because of poverty. In 1874, the Society for the Prevention of Cruelty to Children was formed to protect children from maltreatment. Mothers' Pensions for poor families, child labor protections, infant and maternal feeding and health programs, and juvenile courts, along with public schooling, all emerged as Progressive Era innovations to address vulnerable children and families.

Although the 1935 Social Security Act required the protection of children as a focus of public social services, it was not until the discovery of the battered child syndrome in 1962 that child maltreatment emerged as a prominent policy and practice concern across the nation (Helfer, Kempe, & Krugman, 1997). Since then, states have developed a patchwork of programs that can be located somewhere along a continuum of prevention, early intervention, and crisis services (McCrosky, 2004). These include prevention programs such as family supports through prenatal and postnatal care, child care, and early childhood development programs and an array of child abuse prevention initiatives. Early intervention programs include nurse home visiting, Head Start, enhanced early childhood education programs, school-based services, and hotlines. Crisis services include child protection, family preservation promoting placement prevention and intensive family services, kin and non-kin foster care, as well as group and residential care services, adoption, guardianship, and independent living programs. Other crisis services include the detention, incarceration, or hospitalization of youth.

There are several dominant paradigms that undergird practice and policies involving vulnerable children and families. The first, drawn from prevention science, is risk assessment and resilience promotion (Jensen & Fraser, 2006). The evidence base is growing for services that address risk and foster protective factors. Jenson and Fraser (2006) effectively argue that more social policy for children and families should address risk and resilience. Growing knowledge about the developmental challenges, pathways, and trajectories of diverse, vulnerable children and their families should compel more comprehensive policies and programs (Wulczyn, Barth, Yuan, Harden, & Landsverk, 2006). Another approach involves strength-based strategies and services. This focuses on assets and often promotes social capital development and solution-focused practices (Matton, Schellenbach, Leadbeater, & Solarz, 2004; Saleeby, 1992). Such practices are dominant in family support oriented programs. Finally, family systems approaches assume that individuals must be served in the context of their families, with a change in one individual affecting others and the family as a whole. Accordingly, even though the child may have presenting problems, the whole family system requires interventions and services as well. Family therapy is one of several interventions that derive from this framework.

Notwithstanding the promise of these dominant approaches, the persistence of the patchwork of policies and programs across disparate service sectors is aggravated by the dearth of studies on their effectiveness. Many policies and programs draw from a hybrid of theories and strategies and undergo constant revision in trial-and-error improvements that may or may not be linked to evidence. Some are child centered, others family centered. Many are not tailored to the unique needs of children and their families, their cultures, and economic challenges.

Despite the relative lack of effectiveness studies, policy leaders at national, state, and local levels are increasingly expected to enact, foster, and fund more evidence-based practices and programs. Federal monitoring in child welfare now requires evidence of desired outcomes as measured, for example, by the Child and Family Services Reviews. Similarly, outcomes charting and the reporting of student performance are required for public schools in compliance with the No Child Left Behind Act of 2001. Such seemingly desirable practices may unintentionally add to the pressures on systems, families, and children themselves. Moreover, demonstrable improvements are not necessarily guaranteed as root causes such as poverty, inequality, marginalization, and exclusionary practices may go unaddressed or may worsen. Nonetheless, improvements can be seen on selected measures in some states' child welfare system performance over the past several years and in selected underperforming schools (U.S. Department of Education, 2008; U.S. Department of Health & Human Services, 2003).

Child Abuse and Neglect: Prevention and Service Response

There are many pieces of legislation governing child protection and child welfare systems in the United States. One major policy was the 1974 Child Abuse Prevention and Treatment Act (CAPTA). This act established the

National Center on Child Abuse and Neglect and mandated coordinated practices in prevention, identification, and treatment of abused and neglected children. States received funds to develop reporting systems for investigations and to support the Guardian Ad Litem (GAL) and Court Appointed Special Advocate (CASA) programs that provide court-based advocates for children. Since the passage of the Child Abuse Prevention and Treatment Act, there have been a number of amendments to strengthen prevention, detection, and reporting.

The Keeping Children and Families Safe Act of 2003 reauthorized the 1974 statute along with other provisions. For example, hospital staff must contact Child Protective Services (CPS) when a newborn is affected by substance abuse. In addition, children three years and under who are reported as experiencing child abuse or neglect must be screened for developmental delays and related disabilities. Children with these disabilities have higher rates of abuse (including sexual abuse) and neglect than those without have (Kendall-Tacket, Lyon, Taliaferro, & Little, 2005).

Offense Versus Service-Based Interventions

For the past several decades, safety and risk assessments have dominated much of the practice in child protection services. A safety assessment is conducted to determine if the child is in imminent danger. A risk assessment addresses the persistence and prevalence of the factors that affect safety. Safety and risk factors include domestic violence, mental illness, substance abuse, homelessness, environmental conditions, history of abuse, age of the child, skills of the caretaker, special needs of the child, and medical challenges. Many safety and risk assessment tools have been developed to counter the incident, offense-based focus of investigations. Only a few focus on family resilience, strengths, and cultural and community assets.

Debates are intensifying over the underlying practice and policy paradigms for child protection. One school of thought focuses on children's legal rights, with abusive parental behaviors seen as crimes requiring police-like rather than social work investigations (Pelton, 1989). Another school of thought seeks to replace the investigatory and abuse substantiation focus with services.

Such service approaches are consistent with research studies that show that, when biological parents receive the supports evidence-based approaches such as parenting classes, improved child welfare outcomes may eventuate (Barth, Berry, Yoshikami, Goodfield, & Carson 2005; Corcoran, 2000). In the last decade, such service-oriented approaches have resulted in child welfare systems called *multi* or *dual track* or *alternative response*. Such systems replace investigations with more supportive services for low- and moderate-risk families. Parents are not investigated for abuse. They are asked what supports and services they need to deal with their stresses. States testing such models show improved outcomes (Merkel-Holguin, Kaplan, & Kwak, 2006).

Family-Centered Practice

Over the years, states and counties have experimented with a variety of family-centered practices to address placement prevention and reunification. These include family preservation, family group conferences, family-to-family programs, and family team facilitation. Family preservation initiatives have varied in intensity, duration, worker-family ratios, and the skill of workers. So far, mixed results have emerged (Maluccio, Pine, & Tracy, 2002). Legislation that has helped to reinforce family preservation services includes the Indian Child Welfare Act of 1978, the Adoption Assistance and Child Welfare Act of 1980, and the Family Preservation and Support Services provisions of the Omnibus Reconciliation Act of 1993. Among other mandates, the Indian Child Welfare Act requires that "active efforts" be pursued to ensure that Indian children remain with their families and that tribal courts oversee decision making regarding Indian child welfare.

The Adoption Assistance and Child Welfare Act of 1980 required that "reasonable efforts" be pursued to ensure that children remain with their families. This act mandated preplacement efforts to divert children from going into out-of-home care and required that reunification be expedited and that permanent alternative supports through adoption, kinship care, guardianship, and independent living be provided if reunification is not possible. This act helped to spawn a number of family preservation demonstration projects including Homebuilders (Kinney, Madsen, Fleming, & Haapala, 1977).

The family preservation and support services provisions of the Omnibus Reconciliation Act promoted cohesive strategies to build community-based family supports and preservation strategies. As a result, some communities have experimented with neighborhood teams of child protection and child welfare workers who collaborate with other service providers in decision making and family-centered interventions (Van Wagoner, Boyer, Wiesen, Hinton, & Lawson, 2001). Other innovations being adopted include the Annie E. Casey Foundation's Family to Family Program model, which uses foster parents in the neighborhood where children reside to enable placement in proximity to the parent (Chahine, Van Straaten, & Williams-Isom, 2005). Children thus have fewer disruptions in school, child care, and with peers. Despite these developments, cautions have been recommended about neighborhood-based child welfare services (Berrick, 2006).

Family group conferencing is a strategy brought to the United States from the indigenous Maori communities in New Zealand. Families, however defined, are able to mobilize their own members to solve problems and design case plans. The practice addresses both problem solving and restorative justice, as perpetrators meet their victims and make amends (Burford & Hudson, 2000; Marsh & Crow, 1998; Van Wormer, 2003). Family team facilitation mobilizes service providers in joint meetings who are expected to foster collaborative case plans with the family. A professional facilitator, along with an advocate for the family, helps coordinate the conferences so that more tailored and coherent case plans can be devised.

About 10% of the children who are investigated for maltreatment are removed from their homes and placed in foster or group care (Wulczyn et al., 2006). Of these, higher rates of infants (60%) than of older children go on to be adopted (Wulczyn et al., 2006). Among those aged 1 to 14, 60% will be reunified (Wulczyn et al., 2006). Around 10% of children in foster care who return home re-enter foster care within 12 months (U.S. Department of Health & Human Services, 2003). High caseloads among child welfare workers, inadequate visitation, combined with parental difficulty in follow-through with court ordered case plans have created long stays in foster care, especially for children who are poor and of color. Moreover, disruptions in foster placements have increased over the years, signaling rising behavioral health challenges among abused and neglected children. In addition, rising numbers may be on medications for attention deficit and related disorders.

Support Services for Older Foster Youth

In the past few decades, new initiatives have been undertaken to better support foster care youth discharged to independent living. These responses attempt to address their barriers involving successful transitions to adulthood and independence. The federally funded Independent Living Program was enacted through the Consolidated Omnibus Budget and Reconciliation Act of 1985 and Title IV-E of the Social Security Act. A subsequent Foster Care Independence Act of 1999 (the Chafee Act) increased independent living financial entitlements and housing resources for youth ages 14 to 21 who have left foster care. Additional funds were to be used for education, vocational training, preparation for postsecondary education, training in daily living skills, substance abuse prevention, pregnancy prevention, preventive health, and training for foster and adoptive parents, group home staff, and others. The Promoting Safe and Stable Families Amendments of 2001 provided educational and training vouchers for youth who age out of foster care, as well as a mentoring program for children with incarcerated parents in federal, state, or local correctional facilities.

Service Time Limits and the Foster Care Crisis

In the 1990s, the U.S. General Accounting Office (1995) declared that the foster care system was in crisis because of the sharp increases of children in care. In addition, states experienced various forms of class action suits involving their child welfare systems. Rising numbers of children "adrift" and even "aging out" in foster care led to the enactment of the 1997 Adoption and Safe Families Act (ASFA). The act stressed that the child's well-being would be the prominent consideration in determining what was reasonable and consistent with a plan for a timely, permanent placement for a child. Time limits were set for children in care requiring that permanency decisions be made within 12 months of entering the foster care system. Accelerated permanency placement requires that states initiate court proceedings to free a child for adoption once that child has been waiting in foster care for at least 15 of the most recent 22 months unless there is an exception. Children's rights now were to take precedence over those of parents. The "reasonable efforts" requirement was to be waived if a parent had caused serious neglect or injury to a child, or already had rights terminated involving another child.

The Adoption and Safe Families Act gave the courts added responsibilities and tighter time frames for handling abuse and neglect cases, but it failed to provide the necessary resources. Thus, the Strengthening Abuse and Neglect Courts Act of 2000 was adopted to improve the efficiency and effectiveness of courts. It provides grants to courts to develop computerized case tracking systems, to reduce caseloads, and to expand the provision of court-based advocates in underserved areas.

Permanency, Kinship Care, and Adoption

Kinship foster care enables children to be placed with relatives who may become legal guardians. In some states, up to half of the children in out-of-home care may be in kinship arrangements (Hegar, 1998). Despite the promise of kinship care, reimbursement rates fall behind those granted to non-kin. Recent legislation introduced in Congress may help to rectify this. Kinship care has helped to offset the transracial adoption process by enabling extended family members to be resources for their children, especially in communities of color.

Adoption has long been part of the child welfare system. During the 1980s and early 1990s, attention was diverted away from adoptive services and toward a focus on child protection, family preservation, kinship, and foster and group care services. Despite this, adoption dissolution rates have been a concern of the child welfare system (Barth et al., 1988). Such disruptions, although often preventable, have not been the focus of much child welfare innovation. Thus, new adoption preservation practices and more post-adoption supports are expected to emerge in the near future.

In the 1990s, a controversy arose because, while African American children were in need of permanent homes, white parents were being denied the right to adopt them. This denial was based solely on race. Consequently, Congress passed the Multiethnic Placement Act of 1994, which asserted that race could not be a determining factor in adoption. It prevented discrimination in the placement of children based on race, color, or national origin. Moreover, this legislation was enacted to prevent children from remaining in care while same-race adoptive or foster homes were found.

In 1996, Interethnic Adoption Provisions were enacted that further favored factors other than race to determine the best adoptive or foster placement for a child. Although the evidence to support or refute the value of racial matching is inconclusive, many in the field continue to see children requiring cultural continuities as developmental requisites. Thus, in transracial placements, other kinds of cultural exposure and immersion are fostered whenever possible.

Since the inception of the Adoption and Safe Families Act, adoptions from foster care have nearly doubled from 31,000 in 1997 to approximately 51,000 in 2002 (Child Welfare League of America, 2004). Under the Adoption Promotion Act (2003), states receive financial incentives to increase adoptions, especially for children and adolescents with special needs. International adoptions also were supported through the passage of the Child Citizenship Act of 2000, which permits foreign-born, adopted children of American citizens to obtain American citizenship automatically.

Child Health, Disability, and Related Programs

Children's health needs have increased with the rise in traumatic brain injuries, attention deficit, autism, and related disorders. Consequently, the Children's Health Act of 2000 was passed. This act expanded, intensified, and coordinated research, prevention, and treatment activities for diseases and conditions having a disproportionate or significant impact on children. These include autism, diabetes, asthma, hearing loss, epilepsy, traumatic brain injuries, infant mortality, lead poisoning, and oral health. This act also addresses the problem of youth substance abuse and the violence associated with it and seeks to improve the health and safety of children receiving child care. The act also authorized the Healthy Start demonstration program, which is designed to reduce the rate of infant mortality and to improve birth outcomes in targeted communities by expanding access to health care services for pregnant women and infants.

Much of the family support movement draws its strength from the disability service sector. Without family supports, children with disabilities might be placed out of their homes or in institutions. Moreover, paralleling the principles of "reasonable efforts" in placement prevention in child welfare are other policy principles that derive from the disability field, such as a child's right to the "least restrictive" environment, to the "least intrusive" interventions, and to have supports that ensure "normalization" and "mainstreaming."

Policies governing children with disabilities mandate specialized care ranging from institutions to skilled nursing facilities, intermediate care facilities, community-based group homes, and family-based individualized support services. Similarly, children with mental health challenges may receive individualized, home, and community-based service options. Some of the most innovative practices have emerged with tailored, "wraparound services," which allow emotionally disturbed children to remain in their own homes and classrooms.

Some of these practice principles are reflected in laws such as the Education for all Handicapped Children Act of 1975 and its reauthorization in 1990 as the Individuals with Disabilities Act (IDEA). These landmark acts require that states provide education and special supports and services to meet the needs of all children—and to provide these supports and services in the least restrictive environments. Thus, children who might have been sent to institutions (including residential treatment facilities) for care and schooling are instead attending local public schools. Accommodations are required by law, ensuring that children are maintained in classrooms rather than sent to day treatment or to schools in residential care or shipped out of state for specialized treatment and confinement. Because of the expectations for the least restrictive setting for children's education and services, most of the mental health services provided to children are offered through schools.

Children's Mental Health

Children with mental health challenges have not been well served over the decades. Relative inattention to children's mental health, noted by the Joint Commission on Mental Health of Children (1969), Knitzer (1982), and others, has led to some modest reforms. Currently, one in five children may have a diagnosable disorder (Duchnowski, Kutash, & Friedman, 2002; English, 2002). Of these, only one in five will receive services (Gonzalez, 2005). There is wide variation in the definition of emotional and behavioral disturbances, as well as in detection, assessment, and service access.

Policy reforms in children's mental health have promoted "systems of care" that attempt to foster comprehensive and individualized assessment, effective treatment plans, service integration and coordination, and family-centered and evidence-based practices. Congressional support for "systems of care" resulted in the creation of the Comprehensive Community Mental Health Services for Children and their Families program in 1992. Studies of pilots have shown mixed results (Bickman et al., 1995; Bickman, Noser, & Summerfelt, 1999).

Children in impoverished environments lacking services and supports may have higher rates of serious emotional disorders. School-based services that address trauma and detect these disorders and an array of disabilities increasingly demonstrate that accommodation is possible so that children do not need to be placed out of the school (Austin, Briar-Lawson, King-Ingham, Spicer, & Davis, 2006). Despite some promising movements to build school-based services through the community schools, full-service schools, and related initiatives, accountability reforms for educational performance have upstaged if not impeded school-based service movements.

Educational Policy

The most recent federal legislation, which fosters standards-based educational reform, is the No Child Left Behind Act of 2001. This statute attempts to improve the performance of U.S. primary and secondary schools by boosting accountability standards for states, school districts, and schools and by affording parents increased flexibility when deciding on schools for their children. The No Child Left Behind Act is based on the belief that setting high expectations will result in success for all students.

The effectiveness and desirability of the statute's measures are controversial. Up for possible reauthorization, this legislation has caused considerable debate as Congress considers major changes, including revisions that would provide states much greater freedom from the No Child Left Behind Act's regulations and sanctions. Testing and educational performance have preempted, for many schools, a focus on the needs of children and on their learning barriers, which may stem from poverty and correlates such as community or family violence, substance abuse, unemployment, exclusion, and marginalization. Instead, school drop-out rates may run as high as 50% in urban schools. The Children's Defense Fund (2006) characterizes the trajectory for some poor children as pipelines to prison.

Juvenile Justice

Juvenile crime has been a long-term concern due to its social and human costs. The Juvenile and Delinquency Prevention Act of 1974 was established to reduce the number of status offenders in secure detention facilities and the number of juveniles in adult jails and, among other provisions, to address the disproportionate detainment of minority youth. Juvenile delinquency policy has experienced a shift in the past decade from retribution and rehabilitation approaches to the promotion of restorative justice. Given high rates of recidivism in juvenile justice institutions, such innovation is warranted. The retribution model views the juvenile offense as a crime against the state warranting punishment of the offender. The rehabilitation model focuses on the treatment of the offender with the assumption that interventions such as probation, multisystemic therapy, and cognitive skills training will alter behavior and reduce the frequency of juvenile offenses (Bradshaw & Roseborough, 2005). However, neither of these models shows significant evidence for reducing recidivism (Bradshaw & Roseborough, 2005; Lipsey, 1995). While the retribution and rehabilitative models focus on the offender, the needs of the victim are often neglected. Restorative justice models focus on the process of restoration and healing for the victim, offender, and community (Bradshaw & Roseborough, 2005; Fields, 2003). This may occur by holding the offender accountable, offering emotional assistance, and giving restitution to the victim (Bradshaw & Roseborough, 2005). Currently, three restorative justice program modalities are being tested, which include victim-offender mediation, family group conferencing, and peacemaking circles. The empirical work evaluating restorative justice approaches has been encouraging; however serious measurement problems exist (Lawson & Katz, 2004).

Co-Occurring Risk Factors

As attention increasingly focuses not just on children but on their parents for assessment and treatment purposes, mounting research shows the prevalence of co-occurring challenges. Nearly half the children being served by the juvenile justice and foster care system have mental health problems as severe as those children being served by the mental health systems. In fact, 80% of children in foster care (Clausen, Landsverk, Ganger, Chadwick, & Litrownik, 1998; Leslie et al., 2000) and 60% to 70% in juvenile justice have mental disorders (Teplin, Abram, McClelland, Dulcan, & Mericel, 2002). However, specialized treatment is not systematically pursued for these special needs foster care or juvenile justice youth. Moreover, there are no uniform national practices or policies ensuring that the mental health, developmental disabilities, health, and income support needs of children and families are systematically addressed regardless of which system they enter. In fact, a differential response, based on class, income, and ethnicity may be evident in many states and communities (Lindsey, 1994).

Similar co-occurring challenges are seen in parents. For example, it is estimated that between 50% and 70% of all child welfare families have substance abuse as a presenting problem (Ryan, Marsh, Testa, & Louderman, 2006). In many cases, referral resources for families are inadequate; child welfare families do not have "first call" on these resources. For example, few states have enacted policies enabling drug-using pregnant mothers to have priority access to substance abuse treatment beds. In substance abuse treatment, the focus may be on the parent with little attention to his or her role as a caregiver.

Evidence that anywhere from 30% to 50% of child welfare families may have domestic violence co-occurring with child maltreatment warrants far greater interdependence among the service systems addressing domestic violence and child abuse victims (Kohl, Barth, Hazen, & Landsverk, 2005). Instead, the philosophical clashes between child welfare and domestic violence service providers make such close articulation of services and supports often problematic. Philosophical differences stem from the belief that abused women need to leave the perpetrator at any cost; child welfare workers may be addressing the family as a unit and the services needed to keep it intact.

Disparities and Differential Policies and Services

Children who are poor and of color are disproportionately found in the child welfare and juvenile justice systems, while underserved in mental health. Disproportionalities have been a major concern in the child welfare system (Hill, 2007). A disproportionate number of African American children are referred and placed out of their homes even in areas where poverty is limited (Wulczyn et al., 2006). They are also left with fewer supports and options and encounter longer waiting times for adoption than Hispanic and white children. Rates of placement during adolescence do not show the same differentials as in the younger years, but Wulczyn et al. (2006) suggest that this may be because, during adolescence, a disproportionate number of African American youth are in the juvenile justice system rather than the child welfare system.

Youth of color have higher rates of entry into the juvenile justice system than their white counterparts. At each decision point in the juvenile justice system, they are more likely to be picked up by police and detained, to have less access to probation, and to be charged as an adult and sent to an adult prison (Poe-Yamagata & Jones, 2000). This is the case even when they are charged with lesser crimes than their white counterparts.

In mental health, some disproportionalities may be attributed to socioeconomic status (Gonzalez, 2005). However, with Hispanic youth, even when controlling for socioeconomic status, higher risks for mental health challenges are detected (Barbarin, McCandies, Coleman, & Atkinson, 2004). Rates of access to mental health treatment for children of color reflect severe disparities. Low-income children of color may be more likely to develop mental health problems and are less likely to receive requisite services (Gonzales, 2005).

In some states, children from nonpoor, nonminority families may be served in the mental health or developmental disabilities service systems. Families with children with mental or physical disabilities are less likely to be blamed or punished or to receive investigatory, policelike services than those in the child welfare system. Mental health and disabilities service systems have often sought to provide special supports, such as "wraparound" services, to help families accommodate the challenging behaviors of their children. In contrast, substitute care often has dominated child welfare systems. In some communities, a child with abuse, developmental, and mental health challenges might enter a variety of systems. If the child is first seen for mental health or developmental disabilities, the focus may be on services and specialized care. If a child enters detention and the juvenile justice system, the focus may be on restitution, restorative justice, and possible separation from the family. If the child enters the child welfare system due to abuse, the goal may be safety and permanence, requiring placement and expedited decision making regarding a permanent home.

Despite the fact that victims of abuse and neglect may also have co-occurring symptoms of mental illness and even disabilities, current policy does not ensure that all children, regardless of which system they enter, receive similar rights to and standards of care. Moreover, a child in out-of-home care in one state might receive in-home services if living in another state. Services for parents may vary or be nonexistent. In the child welfare system, many of the of court-ordered services for parents may not be available, especially given the time limits of 12 to 18 months for improvement in functioning.

Collaborative Practices

The rise of collaborative practices and attempts at service integration are, in part, a response to what are often called *cross systems* children and families. Because of the maze of often contradictory approaches and services for children and families, some states and counties have fostered experiments. These require that service providers collaborate on service plans and even pool funds to ensure that children receive appropriate and coordinated services from all relevant providers. None have achieved, on a large scale, integrated practices that address risk factors across the domains of child abuse and neglect, mental health, substance abuse, juvenile justice, disabilities, and special education.

Violence to Children by Systems Designed to Serve Them

Violence to children may occur not just in the home but also in systems designed to serve them. At the community systems level, for example, children who have been abused and neglected may face problematic out-of-home placements. Paradoxically, they may become harmed in some of these placements and deprived of requisite mental health and related services. Thus, the trauma of abuse and neglect may be compounded by the trauma of a succession of failed or injurious placements. Many well-intended foster and adoptive parents across the nation are insufficiently prepared for the challenges of caring for children whose abuse and neglect require intensely therapeutic and skilled care, multiple services, and many supports.

The chain of harmful experiences for children may have ripple effects and compounding consequences for their lifetimes. Research increasingly documents the high rate of comorbidities in adults stemming from adverse childhood experiences (Felliti et al., 1998). If untreated for truancy and substance abuse, for example, a third of juvenile offenders will become serious, chronic, violent offenders (Loeber & Farrington, 2001). Despite the fact that many vulnerable children experience trauma from abuse and neglect and related problems, few schools, hospitals, residential treatment and group care programs, or detention and juvenile justice facilities are trauma sanctuaries or draw on trauma informed strategies.

Poverty, Temporary Assistance to
Needy Families, and Child Welfare

Several authors, such as Gil (1970) and Lindsey (1994), argue that poverty is violence against children. Such claims are reinforced by research on brain and behavioral development. Poverty poses grave danger to children's healthy development (Tanner & Finn-Stevenson, 2002). The United States now has the highest income inequality in its history. In addition, the poverty rate remains persistently high. As the predictable stresses of poverty, unemployment, underemployment, substance abuse, mental illness, and intergenerational violence take their toll on parents, they, in turn, may neglect, harm, and hurt their children (Briar, 1988). Rather than promoting investments, such as family allowances, the United States is the only Western, industrialized nation that does not provide health insurance or family allowances for children or families. Welfare assistance was born out of the Mothers' Pension movement to ensure that no full-time caregiver be required to be a full-time employee and thus forced to place a child in an institution. While unevenly enacted across the states, and fraught with access barriers due to race, Mothers' Pensions were the forerunners of the federally provided Aid to Dependent Children (AFDC) program associated with the 1935 Social Security Act. Like Mothers' Pensions, AFDC was once a very critical child welfare service and a protective factor for reunification. Its successor, the Temporary Assistance to Needy Families (TANF) program has become a risk factor for child welfare (Paxon & Waldfogel, 2001).

Since wages have never been based on family income needs, many parents work full time and are still poor. Work-contingent income supplements through Earned Income Tax Credits are the primary vehicles, rather than wages alone, enabling some low-income working parents to rise above the poverty threshold. Research on children in poverty reveals that poor children suffer a higher incidence of adverse health, developmental disabilities, and other conditions than nonpoor children (Chase-Lansdale & Brooks-Gunn, 1995; Duncan & Brooks-Gunn, 2000). In addition, differential rates of child mortality are found between poor and nonpoor families (Duncan & Brooks-Gunn, 2000). Babies born into poverty are 1.4 times as likely as nonpoor counterparts to experience learning disabilities and developmental delays (Duncan & Brooks-Gunn, 2000). Negative outcomes for children's cognitive development have been attributed to maternal employment in the first three years of life (Brooks-Gunn, Han, & Waldfogel, 2002). Poor children also suffer from emotional and behavioral problems more frequently than do nonpoor children (Brooks-Gunn & Duncan, 1997; Duncan & Brooks-Gunn, 2000). Another problem is that childhood poverty creates the conditions for intergenerational transmission of risk factors. For example, children in poverty face higher risks for teen pregnancy (Duncan & Brooks-Gunn, 2000). Moreover, despite declining teen pregnancy rates in the United States, two-thirds of these pregnancies are attributed to rape (Kandakai & Smith, 2007).

Time limits in TANF and in child welfare, due to the Adoption and Safe Families Act, create double jeopardy families and children. First, the family may face loss of the TANF grant, impeding its capacity to parent and care for the child. Then, the family may face time limits in services to parents whose children are placed out of the home. For those who acquire and sustain employment with decent wages, the results may be beneficial (Golden, 1992). However, declining TANF benefits affect the demand for child welfare services (Paxon & Waldfogel, 2001). Like the clash of TANF with child welfare, similar misalignments are seen with child care subsidies. Federal funding for child care has not kept pace with need given that many TANF parents are now at work. Thus, states are forced to ration child care subsidies (Adams, Holcomb, Snyder, Koralek, & Capizzano, 2006).

Current Legislation and Administrative Features

One of the institutional symbols of the century-long struggle for child protection and well-being is the U.S. Children's Bureau. Established in 1912 to investigate child labor and to advocate for income supports for poor children, the U.S. Children's Bureau has been a source of advocacy and policy making for child welfare and for social work with families. Federal funds are funneled through state and county funding streams. These channels include Title XX of the Social Security Act, which provides block grants to the states for social services. Titles IV-E and IV-B of the Social Security Act primarily support substitute or out-of-home child welfare services. In addition, TANF has catalyzed the potential devolution of federal policy frameworks and entitlements for impoverished children and families. This has raised concerns that similar devolutions would occur with child welfare programs involving the block granting of IV-B and IV-E funds.

While there is a patchwork of public and private services for abused and neglected children across the nation, every state operates child protection, foster and group care, and adoptive services. Increasingly, the functions of child protection and foster care as well as adoption are being contracted out to voluntary social service agencies. Managed care has prompted states and localities to design alternative service delivery systems, to privatize much of the child welfare system, and to manage the cost through de facto service rationing.

Pressures to provide more effective services along with lawsuits have helped to reinforce efforts to reprofessionalize child welfare workforce with trained social workers. Reprofessionalization agendas have fostered two decades of partnerships between schools of social work and public child welfare. These partnerships have involved training for frontline staff, research, practicum programs, faculty and staff exchanges, curricular developments, and demonstration projects. In fact, at this time, most states have reprofessionalization partnerships between universities and child welfare agencies. Facilitators include IV-E funding, 426 funds from the Social Security Act, and commitments by child welfare administrators and schools of social work to reprofessionalize the workforce.

Collaborative efforts by advocates and organizations help to shape national directions for child welfare. Among the key collaborators are the National Association of Public Child Welfare Administrators, the American Public Human Services Association, the National Association of Social Workers, the Council on Social Work Education, the Child Welfare League of America, the American Humane Association, and the Children's Defense Fund. These organizations work together to lobby for child welfare funding, new legislation, child welfare staffing, and systems supports.

Several foundations have been at the center of child welfare and related system reform. The Annie E. Casey Foundation has invested in a collaborative community response to child welfare families and promotes grassroots neighborhood service and partnership approaches. More recently, the Pew Charitable Trust has invested in reform work. Ongoing investments have continued over the past two decades by the Edna McConnell Clark Foundation, focusing on family preservation, child protection reforms, and now youth development.

As policy companions to U.S. initiatives, reforms are underway in countries such as Sweden. The Swedish government, having made corporal punishment illegal, now works to aid families with the tools of child rearing so that the risk of abuse and neglect is reduced. Simultaneously, families in Sweden receive preventive and early intervention rather than just remedial services. For example, families are able to request respite care for exhaustion. This is provided by a "contact family" that can offer an array of respite and socially supportive services to both children and families. Devised to prevent the need for entry into the child welfare system, the Contact Family Program has demonstrated a sound and effective way to reach vulnerable families (Andersson, 1993).

Future Priorities

Twenty-first century child and family welfare policy paradigms need to be governed by new principles, programs, and approaches. Family capacity building and preventive approaches are urgently needed. Culturally and economically relevant supports rather than punishment and castigation should form the cornerstone of an effective child and family welfare approach. Extensive collaboration with all stakeholders is needed to formulate and advocate for an approach of this kind. More prevention and early intervention innovations such as Parents Anonymous are also needed.

There is an urgent need for the greater use of evidence-based solutions. These should be accompanied by continuous quality improvement frameworks augmented by the use of families, frontline practitioners, and others as key experts. They are well qualified to address the barriers that impede the well-being of children and families. Research into child welfare issues has made great progress in recent times, and ways need to be found of transferring tested knowledge to practitioners and to policy makers as well.

With regard to staffing, occupational ladders for economically disenfranchised parents and paraprofessionals are needed. Intensive services should be co-delivered by former clients trained as paraprofessionals, for example, as parent, reunification, foster care, and adoption support case aides. Much has been done to ensure that professionally qualified social workers are knowledgeable about the latest research and practice approaches in child welfare. The Title IV-E training program has been adopted in many schools of social work around the country and has been an extremely valuable resource. Nevertheless, more needs to be done to train paraprofessionals and parents in effective child welfare interventions.

Greater support for parents who are experiencing family and child welfare challenges is also needed. Neighborhood colleges that support parents in stress reduction should be encouraged. Long-term care supports for chronically fragile or vulnerable families, such as the supports that exist for those with disabilities and in special education, should be introduced. It is necessary to create a single point of entry into an integrated prevention and early intervention system for vulnerable families—a system that addresses the co-occurring challenges facing children and their parents. Vulnerable children's developmental needs and timely access to services should be critical priorities.

Finally, the government of the United States needs to ratify the United Nations Convention on the Rights of the Child. This important international human rights instrument has been ratified by all the Western industrial countries and by the majority of developing countries. The United States currently stands alone in the Western world in having failed to ratify this treaty. Child welfare activists, social workers, policy makers, and all concerned citizens should advocate vigorously for the ratification of this convention. In addition, there should be an end to corporal punishment in schools, and greater emphasis should be placed on promoting children's participation in the policies and services on which they depend.

References

Adams, G., Holcomb, P., Snyder, K., Koralek, R., & Capizzano, J. (2006). *Child care subsidies for TANF families: The nexus of systems and policies.* Washington, DC: Urban Institute.

Andersson, G. (1993). Support and relief: The Swedish contact person and contact family program. *Scandinavian Journal of Social Welfare, 2,* 54–62.

Austin, S., Briar-Lawson, K., King-Ingham, A., Spicer, J., & Davis, D. (2006). Role changes, learning enhancements and professional development through a university-school partnership. *Professional Development: The International Journal of Continuing Social Work Education, 8*(3), 84–97.

Barbarin, O., McCandies, T., Coleman, C., & Atkinson, T. (2004). Ethnicity and culture. In. P. Allen-Meares & M. W. Fraser (Eds.), *Intervention with children and adolescents: An interdisciplinary perspective* (pp. 27–53). Needham Heights, MA: Allyn & Bacon.

Barth, R. P., Berry, M., Yoshikami, R., Goodfield, R. K., & Carson, M. L. (1988). Predicting adoption disruption. *Social Work, 33*(3), 227–233.

Barth, R. P., Landsverk, J., Chamberlain, P., Reid, J., Rolls, J. A., Hurlburt, M. S., et al. (2005). Parent-training programs in child welfare services: Planning for a more evidence-based approach to serving biological parents. *Research on Social Work Practice, 15*(5), 353–371.

Berrick, J. D. (2006). Neighborhood-based foster fare: A critical examination of location-based placement criteria. *Social Service Review, 80*(4), 569–583.

Bickman, L., Guthrie, P. R., Foster, E. M., Lamber, E. W., Summerfelt, W. T., Breda, C. S., et al. (1995) *Evaluating managed mental health services: The Fort Bragg experiment*. New York: Plenum.

Bickman, L., Noser, K., & Summerfelt, W. T. (1999). Comparative outcomes of emotionally disturbed children and adolescents in a system of services and usual care. *Psychiatric Services, 48*, 1543–1548.

Bradshaw, W., & Roseborough, D. (2005). Restorative justice dialogue: The impact of mediation and conferencing on juvenile recidivism. *Federal Probation, 69*(2), 15–21.

Briar, K. (1988). *Social work with the unemployed*. Silver Spring, MD: NASW Press.

Briar-Lawson, K., Lawson, H., Hennon, C., & Jones, A. (2001). *Family centered policy and practice: International implications*. New York: Columbia University Press.

Brooks-Gunn, J., & Duncan, G. J. (1997). The effects of poverty on children. *The future of children: Children and poverty, 7*(2), 55–71.

Brooks-Gunn, J., Han, W. J., & Waldfogel, J. (2002). Maternal employment and child cognitive outcomes in the first three years of life: The NICHD study of early child care. *Child Development, 73*(4), 1052–1072.

Burford, G., & Hudson, J. (2000). *Family group conferencing: New directions in community centered child and family practice*. New York: Walter de Gruyter.

Chahine, Z., Van Straaten, J., & Williams-Isom, A. (2005). The New York City neighborhood-based services strategy. *Child Welfare, 84*(2), 141–152.

Chase-Lansdale, P. L., & Brooks-Gunn, J. (1995). *Escape from poverty: What makes a difference for children?* New York: Cambridge University Press.

Children's Defense Fund. (2006). *Juvenile justice and the cradle to prison pipeline*. Retrieved June 25, 2007, from http://www.childrensdefense.org/site/Page Navigator/c2pp_juvenile_justice

Child Welfare League of America. (2004, August). *The multiethnic placement act* [Issue Brief]. Washington, DC: Author.

Clausen, J. M., Landsverk, J., Ganger, W., Chadwick, D., & Litrownik, A. (1998). Mental health problems of children in foster care. *Journal of Child and Family Studies, 7*(3), 283–296.

Corcoran, J. (2000). *Evidence-based social work practice with families: A lifespan approach*. New York: Springer.

Duchnowski, A. J., Kutash, K., & Friedman R. M. (2002). Community-based interventions in a system of care and outcomes framework. In B. J. Burns & K. Hoagwood (Eds.), *Community treatment for youth* (pp. 16–37). New York: Oxford University Press.

Duncan, G. J., & Brooks-Gunn, J. (2000). Family poverty, welfare reform & child development. *Child Development, 71*(1), 188–196.

English, M. J. (2002). Policy implications relevant to implementing evidence–based treatment. In B. J. Burns & K. Hoagwood (Eds.), *Community treatment for youth* (pp. 301–326). New York: Oxford University Press.

Felliti, V. J., Anda, R. F., Nordenberg, D., Williamson, D. F., Spitz, A. M., Edwards, V., et al. (1998). Relationship of childhood abuse and household dysfunction to many of the leading causes of death in adults: The adverse childhood experiences (ACE) study. *American Journal of Preventive Medicine, 14*, 245–258.

Fields, B. (2003). Restitution and restorative justice. *Youth Studies Australia, 22*(4), 44–51.

Gil, D. (1970). *Violence against children*. Cambridge, MA: Harvard University Press.

Golden, O. (1992). *Poor children and welfare reform*. Westport, CT: Auburn House.

Gonzalez, M. J. (2005, August). Access to mental health services: The struggle of poverty affected urban children of color. *Child and Adolescent Social Work Journal, 22*(3–4), 245–256.

Hegar, R. L. (1998). The cultural roots of kinship care. In R. L. Hegar & M. Scannapieco (Eds.), *Kinship foster care: Policy practice and research* (pp. 17–27). New York: Oxford University Press.

Helfer, R. E., Kempe, R. S., & Krugman, R. D. (1997). *The battered child* (5th ed.). Chicago: University of Chicago Press.

Hill, R. B. (2007). *Disproportionality of minorities in child welfare: Synthesis of research findings*. Washington, DC: Westat, Race Matters Consortium. Retrieved March 7, 2007, from http://www.casey.org/resources/publications/disproportionalityResearch.htm

Holzer, H. (2007). *The economic costs of child poverty: Testimony before the U.S. House Committee on Ways and Means*. Retrieved March 3, 2007, from http://www.urban.org/url.cfm?ID=901032

Jensen, J. M., & Fraser, M. W. (2006). *Social policy for children and families*. Thousand Oaks, CA: Sage.

Joint Commission on Mental Health of Children. (1969). *Crisis in child mental health: Challenge for the 1970s*. New York: Harper & Row.

Kandakai, T. L., & Smith, L. C. R. (2007). Denormalizing a historical problem: Teen pregnancy, policy, and public health action. *American Journal of Health Behavior, 31*(2), 170–180.

Kendall-Tackett, K., Lyon, T., Talleferro, G., & Little, L. (2005). Why child maltreatment researchers should include children's disability status in their maltreatment studies. *Child Abuse & Neglect, 29*(2), 147–151.

Kinney, J. M., Madsen, B., Fleming, T., & Haapala, D. (1977). Homebuilders: Keeping families together. *Journal of Clinical and Counseling Psychology, 43*, 667–673.

Knitzer, J. (1982). *Unclaimed children: The failure of public responsibility to children and adolescents in need of mental health services*. Washington, DC: The Children's Defense Fund.

Kohl, P. L., Barth, R. P., Hazen, A. L., & Landsverk, J. L. (2005). Child welfare as a gateway to domestic violence services. *Children and Youth Services Review, 27,* 1203–1221.

Lawson, C. L., & Katz, J. (2004). Restorative justice: An alternative approach to juvenile crime. *The Journal of Socio-Economics, 33,* 175–188.

Leslie, L. K., Landsverk, J., Ezzet-Lofstrom, R., Tschann J. M., Sylmen, D. J., & Garland, A. F. (2000). Children in foster care: Factors influencing outpatient mental health service use. *Child Abuse & Neglect, 24*(4), 465–476.

Lindsey, D. (1994). *The welfare of children.* New York: Oxford University Press.

Lipsey, M. (1995). What do we learn from 400 research studies on the effectiveness of treatment with juvenile delinquents? In J. McGuire (Ed.), *What works: Reducing reoffending-guidelines from research and practice* (pp. 63–78). New York: John Wiley & Sons.

Loeber, R., & Farrington, D. P. (2001). *Serious and violent juvenile offenders: Risk factors and successful interventions.* Thousand Oaks, CA: Sage.

Maluccio, A. N., Pine, B. A., & Tracy, E. M. (2002). *Social work practice with families and children.* New York: Columbia University Press.

Marsh, P., & Crow, G. (1998). *Family group conferences in child welfare.* London: Blackwell Science.

Matton, K. I., Schellenbach, C. J., Leadbeater, B. J., & Solarz, A. L. (2004). *Investing in children youth, families and communities: Strengths based research and policy.* Washington, DC: American Psychological Association.

McCrosky, J. (2004). Social work with children and families. In A. L. Sallee (Ed.), *Social work and social welfare* (pp. 67–84). Peosta, IA: Eddie Bowers.

Merkel-Holguin, L., Kaplan, C., & Kwak, A. (2006). *National study on differential response in child welfare.* Washington, DC: American Humane Society and Child Welfare League of America.

Paxon, C., & Waldfogel, J. (2001). *Welfare reform, family resources, and child maltreatment* (Center for Health and Wellbeing Working Paper No. 264). Princeton, NJ: Princeton University, Woodrow Wilson School of Public and International Affairs, Center for Health and Wellbeing. Retrieved February 11, 2008, from http://ideas.repec.org/p/pri/cheawb/264.html

Pelton, L. H. (1989). *For reasons of poverty: A critical analysis of the public child welfare system in the United States.* New York: Praeger.

Poe-Yamagata, E., & Jones, M. A. (2000). *And justice for some: Differential treatment of minority youth in the justice system.* Washington, DC: Youth Law Center.

Ryan, J. P., Marsh, J. C., Testa, M. F., & Louderman, R. (2006). Integrating substance abuse treatment and child welfare services: Findings from the Illinois alcohol and drug abuse waiver demonstration. *Social Work Research, 30*(2), 95–107.

Saleeby, D. (Ed.). (1992). *The strengths perspective in social work perspective.* New York: Longman.

Tanner, E. M., & Finn-Stevenson, M. (2002). Nutrition and brain development: Social policy implications. *American Journal of Orthopsychiatry, 72*(2), 182–193.

Teplin, L. A., Abram, K., McClelland, G., Dulcan M., & Mericel, A. (2002). Psychiatric disorders in youth in juvenile detention. *Archives of General Psychiatry, 59*(12), 1133–1143.

U.S. Department of Education. (2008). *State and local implementation of the No Child Left Behind Act, Volume IV—Title I School choice and supplemental educational services: Interim report.* Retrieved April 1, 2008, from http://www.ed.gov/about/offices/list/opepd/ppss/reports.html

U.S. Department of Health & Human Services. (2003). *Child welfare outcomes 2003: Annual report to Congress—Chapter II. Achieving safety.* Retrieved April 1, 2008, from http://www.acf.hhs.gov/programs/cb/pubs/cwo03/chapters/chaptertwo2003.htm

U.S. General Accounting Office. (1995). *Child welfare: Complex needs strain capacity to provide services.* Retrieved July 1, 2007, from http://www.gao.gov/archive/1995/he95208.pdf

Van Wagoner, P., Boyer, R., Wiesen, M., Hinton, D., & Lawson, H. (2001). Introducing child welfare neighborhood teams that promote collaboration and community-based systems of care. In A. Sallee, H. Lawson, & K. Briar-Lawson (Eds.), *Innovative practices with vulnerable children and families* (pp. 323–360). Dubuque, IA: Eddie Bowers.

Van Wormer, K. (2003). Restorative justice's model for social work practice with families. *Families in Society, 84*(3), 441–448.

Wulczyn, F., Barth, R. P., Yuan, Y. Y., Harden, B. J., & Landsverk, J. (2006). *Beyond common sense.* New Brunswick, NJ: Aldine Transaction.

21 Income Maintenance and Support

The Changing Face of Welfare

Jill Duerr Berrick

At the turn of the 20th century, the economic circumstances of most single mothers in the United States were, at best, insecure. Heading into the second decade of the 21st century, the economic protections afforded single mothers have not improved substantially. Although a variety of local, state, and federal policies exist to assist unmarried women and their families, many of these mothers still struggle to offer their children sufficient protection from the vicissitudes of poverty.

The federal government's role in providing income assistance to low-income families underwent a profound transformation in 1996. In that year, the Personal Responsibility and Work Opportunity Reconciliation Act (P.L. 104-193 or PRWORA) was signed into law, heralding an "end to welfare as we know it." Variously called the *devolution revolution* (Kingsley, 1996; Weaver, 1996) or the *new federalism* (Corbett, 1996), the policy gave a large degree of flexibility and considerable authority to state and local governments for the design of poor people's income support. The program established under this policy, Temporary Assistance for Needy Families (TANF), provides time-limited cash assistance to poor families and requires, in turn, reciprocal obligations of mothers. Although TANF is available to single-parent and two-parent families, the great majority of recipients are women. In this chapter, women and mothers are referred to as recipient heads of household.

TANF reflects social values that center on the desirability of work, marriage, and positive parenting, values that have held currency throughout the social history of the United States (as described in greater detail earlier in this book). Today's income maintenance program for poor families is therefore both a departure from and a return to previous policies attempted in this country.

TANF is implemented with remarkable variability across the 50 states, giving rise to significant inequities among individuals based solely on geography, and in no state do TANF payments lift a family out of poverty. Services are available to link parents to the labor market, but, given the country's unstable low-wage economy, TANF offers little real protection from a capricious labor market. Recent evidence from various studies suggests that parents in low-income families are working more today than they did a decade ago but that, overall, their economic conditions have not improved appreciably.

The Historical Evolution of Welfare

Less than a century ago, single mothers had few socially appropriate avenues for supporting their children economically. Work was considered anathema to good parenting and was discouraged among "good" girls (Gordon, 1994). Instead, children were often forced into the labor market by circumstance, providing important financial support to the family during hard times (Gensler, 1996). With the introduction of child labor laws, children's employment prospects were severely curtailed, leaving single mothers as principal household earners. As many women and children faced destitution, legislators in a few states responded to the appeal for help and developed cash assistance programs to support women whose husbands had died or deserted or divorced them. These mothers' pensions quickly gained popularity across much of the country. The purpose of financial support was to supplant the loss of income from the primary breadwinner—the father—in order to encourage mothers to remain at home to parent their children (Abramovitz, 1988; Gordon, 1994). Aid was conditional; it was provided to those mothers who could show their worthiness to a social worker or community helper. Single women who gave birth to children, women of color, and women who had relationships with men outside of marriage were often considered undeserving of aid. Their children were sometimes removed from their homes or institutionalized, or the family was left to fend for itself in abject poverty (Abramovitz, 1988).

Mothers' pensions programs expanded dramatically across the country, particularly from 1910 to 1920. But in the 1930s, states were overwhelmed by rapidly rising caseloads in these programs as the country fell into a deep economic depression. Faced with rising costs and reduced capacity to fund mothers' pensions through government aid, state and local officials turned to the federal government for fiscal relief. The Social Security Act of 1935 launched several federally supported programs in aid of the poor, with Aid to Dependent Children (ADC) specifically targeted at single parents, generally poor women with children. With the introduction of ADC, which was renamed Aid to Families with Dependent Children (AFDC) in 1950, income support for poor families became a shared obligation among the federal, state, and local governments.

The AFDC program changed little from the 1930s through the 1950s. However, over time, the characteristics of AFDC families changed considerably. Whereas the majority of caregivers on aid in the early years of the program were widowed, deserted, or divorced, by the 1970s the AFDC caseload included large and rapidly growing numbers of never-married women (Rein, 1982; U.S. General Accounting Office, 1994). Welfare participants, in the early years, also were dominated by Caucasians—primarily due to state and local policies that precluded the participation of women of color (Abramovitz, 1988; Bell, 1965; Quadagno, 1994). In later decades, however, the AFDC caseload included large numbers of women of color, with disproportionate utilization of aid by African American families (Quadagno, 1994). These changes were accompanied by shifts in the labor force participation of women not receiving AFDC. Rather than shunning work, women were joining the labor market in droves. By 1983, more than 70% of women worked or were regularly looking for work (Ellwood, 1988).

Mirroring this shift in the labor market, federal policies from the 1960s onward placed a new emphasis on employment within the AFDC program. With each iteration of reform, new policies were overlaid onto AFDC, with an increasing emphasis on work participation among welfare recipients. The Work Incentive (WIN) demonstration of 1969, WIN II (1972), and the Job Opportunity and Basic Skills (JOBS) program of 1988 all reflected an increased orientation toward employment (Bane & Ellwood, 1994; Coll, 1995; Ellwood, 1988; Pappas, 1996). Yet funding constraints limited the number of AFDC parents allowed to participate in these new programs, and overall, each of the programs proved only modestly effective in supporting women's transitions from welfare to work (Gueron & Pauly, 1991).

By the early 1990s, changes in the characteristics and circumstances of women on aid, and shifting perspectives in public opinion (Blendon, 1995; Farkas, 1995; Farkas & Johnson, 1995; Weaver, Shapiro, & Jacobs, 1996), compelled state and federal lawmakers to reconsider the basis of the AFDC program, and they shifted its emphasis from a largely cash aid program to a work-based, short-term assistance program. On August 22, 1996, President Clinton signed P.L. 104-193, ushering in a new era of welfare.

Current Legislative and Administrative Arrangements

With the passage of the Personal Responsibility and Work Opportunity Reconciliation Act, the 60-year-old AFDC program was abolished and replaced with a program whose name conveys the meaning behind assistance.

Temporary Assistance for Needy Families, or TANF, includes several requirements that shape the symbols and provisions of public assistance for poor families. Receiving assistance is not an entitlement; instead, eligibility is conditional and time limited; exits off of aid are expected to be rapid, and employment is the preferred passage to economic self-sufficiency. In 2005, Congress reauthorized TANF under the Deficit Reduction Act, placing a greater requirement on the states to increase recipients' work participation and greater pressure on low-income parents to join the low-wage labor market.

Block Grants

Prior to the implementation of TANF, all poor, single-parent families that met income and asset tests were eligible to receive cash assistance. The entitlement to AFDC guaranteed that the poorest families could receive assistance until their personal income rose above a predetermined threshold or until their youngest child turned 18. Funding for aid was provided through a combined federal and state contribution. When AFDC caseloads grew, state officials applied to the federal government for increased funding. Significant expenditure increases were largely controlled through incremental benefit reductions or, in times of low unemployment, reduced caseloads.

Under TANF, the entitlement to aid was abolished. Instead, states receive an annual block grant of funding from the federal government. This funding replaces three previous federal programs including AFDC, JOBS, and Emergency Assistance (EA). State governments are required to maintain their financial commitment to recipient families through "maintenance of effort" requirements, thus ensuring that states will not withdraw their support from the TANF program. Combined federal and state resources have been sufficient to serve families applying for aid. However, the block grant structure of this program does not guarantee sufficient funding should caseloads rise above the block grant allocation. If this were to happen, state and local authorities would be fully responsible for the additional financial burden of assisting families. Given this financial disincentive, states may reduce costs either through benefit reductions, time limits, or targeting strategies (Berrick, 2001).

Time Limits

TANF is only available to families for a limited period of time. Federal funding for TANF payments may be used for only 60 cumulative months, regardless of the age of the child or the poverty status of the family. However, states are given latitude to reduce time limits further, and many states have more restrictive policies (Gallagher, Gallagher, Perese, Schreiber, & Watson, 1998; U.S. Department of Health and Human Services, 1997).

Work Requirements

Work requirements are also imposed on recipients in exchange for cash assistance. Work includes either unsubsidized or subsidized employment. Some other activities are considered allowable under limited conditions. Single parents are required to work 20 to 30 hours per week, depending on the age of their child, and two-parent families must work 35 to 55 hours (combined) per week (Center on Budget and Policy Priorities, 2007).

Economic Sanctions and Penalties

Participation in TANF is conditional on the applicant's characteristics and behaviors. For example, TANF is limited to applicants with very low income and assets. It is also only available to U.S. citizens and to permanent residents, refugees, or asylum seekers residing in the United States for more than five years. Unmarried minor parents may receive aid, but only if they live with an adult or in an adult-supervised setting. Sanctions to the TANF grant may apply under a variety of circumstances: to mothers who fail to submit to paternity establishment procedures, to women who give birth to an additional child while on aid (called the *family cap*), and to families when children are not immunized or do not regularly attend school. Unless the penalty is overturned by state law, adult recipients are barred from aid for life if they are convicted of a drug felony.

Safety Net Provisions

Although TANF can include income restrictions, some program elements also offer employment-related opportunities to low-income families. TANF gives state governments considerable discretion to develop work and training programs that match the needs of their welfare population. Block grant funds may be used to offer job clubs and other work preparation activities. These program components, when offered, may prepare welfare recipients for the demands of the labor market, offering them improved skills and employment support.

Funding for child care is also available to support parents' transitions to the labor market. Given that approximately half of all children on welfare are under age six (U.S. House and Ways Committee, 1996), the child care needs of these families can be substantial, and parents who are pressed to join the labor market quickly must find affordable and accessible care. Child care subsidies are available for a wide variety of child care types, depending on the state, and for many parental needs (Holcomb et al., 2006).

Health insurance is also critical to employment retention. Families that previously transitioned from AFDC to work often faced significant obstacles to economic self-sufficiency because health insurance was not available (Edin & Lein, 1997). The Balanced Budget Act of 1997 created the State

Children's Health Insurance Program (S–CHIP) to provide health insurance for low-income children whose families earn less than 200% of the poverty level. Today, most families that transition off of public aid should be eligible for continued health insurance.

And finally, under AFDC regulations, earned income was taxed at very high rates, reducing the economic allure of work. TANF instead offers states significant latitude to set these income disregards at various levels in order to induce greater work participation among welfare recipients.

Through economic benefits and sanctions, TANF regulations encourage women to work outside of the home, and they support appropriate parenting practices. More subtle is the symbolic message that low-income women should raise children within the context of heterosexual marriage. Indeed, the legislation itself targets marriage as the foundation of a "successful society" and an "essential institution . . . which promotes the interests of children" (PRWORA, 1996, § 101). Under the TANF reauthorization legislation of 2005, several hundred million dollars were devoted to marriage promotion activities, including media campaigns, public assemblies, brochures, and counseling sessions, all to encourage and support marriages for low-income parents (Berrick, 2005). The emphasis on marriage and positive parenting diverges little from the foundations of the AFDC program; the emphasis—indeed, the requirement—that women work, sets TANF apart from its predecessor policy.

Social, Political, and Economic Factors Influencing TANF Policy

Shortly after the TANF policy was introduced, many heralded the approach as an unabashed success. In 1997, President Clinton observed, "I think it's fair to say the debate is over. We know now that welfare reform works" (Broder, 1997). Indeed, reductions in the welfare caseload both before and shortly after passage of the law were dramatic. At its peak in 1994, welfare supported over 5 million families (U.S. Department of Health and Human Services, 1998). Almost a decade later, that number stood at about 2 million families (Blank & Haskins, 2002; Weil & Finegold, 2002)—a remarkable 50% drop in the welfare caseload, nationwide. Since the turn of the century, caseload decline has stalled—an important impetus for passing the TANF reauthorization legislation that pushes the work participation agenda more forcefully still.

Whether caseload declines were a product of welfare reform or a strong economy is a subject of significant debate, as these changes mirrored other trends, including the child poverty and unemployment rates. Nationwide, the child poverty rate shifted substantially. Falling from a high of 22.5% in 1993 (Bennett & Lu, 2000) to 16% in 2000, the child poverty rate then rose rapidly again from 2000 to 2004 (Institute for Research on Poverty, 2007).

Some evidence suggests that the steep decline in child poverty was largely due to improvements in labor market conditions—particularly for less-educated workers (Nichols, 2006). In 1996, the official unemployment rate stood at 5.4% and by the end of that decade had reached a strikingly low 3.9% (Solow, 2002). After the year 2000, economic conditions worsened, and many low-wage and less-educated adults lost employment and other means of support. Therefore, in spite of TANF advocates' applause for the policy's dramatic effects on welfare caseloads, a good deal of evidence indicates that an important proportion of caseload decline was probably due to the economy rather than TANF policy (Corcoran, Danziger, Kalil, & Seefeldt, 2000).

But measuring success solely or even primarily by caseload decline is of limited value. Evidence from a number of studies indicates that the vast majority of women leaving welfare are moving into jobs (Loprest, 2002). Large numbers of women have left welfare to find work, but work has not necessarily resulted in greater financial security for families. Generally, a range of studies suggest that women—even those working full-time, year-round—see their income rise but do not attain self-sufficiency (Cancian & Meyer, 2000; Hennessey, 2005). Indeed, most remain at or near the poverty level (Parrott & Sherman, 2006). In fact, in one study, although welfare leavers under TANF had similar if not somewhat better work-related outcomes compared to welfare leavers under AFDC, TANF welfare leavers were more likely to experience material hardships such as an inability to pay rent or missed meals (Loprest, 2001). Low educational attainment, few job skills, little work history, and other social and personal barriers collude to push women onto welfare in the first place. These challenges also limit women's employment options and their capacity to keep jobs long term.

In addition to women's limited income from work, most disconcerting are the numbers of families that do not work at all and those who receive no cash assistance. Recent estimates indicate that approximately 1 million women fall into this category, largely due to time limits and women's inability to locate work that matches their very low skill level (Parrott & Sherman, 2006). Women up against a time limit are very likely to possess one or more substantial barriers to employment, including a physical illness or disability, a mental health problem, or domestic violence (London & Mauldon, n.d.).

The families that reach the 60-month time limit are of special concern, as they no longer have access to the financial safety net once available under AFDC. In a handful of states, children can continue to receive benefits through a child-only grant. In these instances, the parent's portion of the aid payment is terminated, but the child's grant remains intact, resulting in a monthly reduction in family aid of about 20% to 30% (for more detail, see Berrick, 2005). The economic conditions of families exceeding TANF's time limits are precarious indeed. Although critics of TANF have argued that extreme financial deprivation may increase rates of child maltreatment and foster care entry (Courtney, 1999; Waldfogel, 1998), evidence on the effects of the TANF law on child maltreatment and child well-being are mixed. Overall, there have been no large effects on Child Protective Services involvement for families previously involved with the TANF system. Slack and her colleagues (2007) have found, however, that grant reductions and sanctions are to some extent related to greater child welfare involvement.

The effects of the TANF policy on global child well-being are also mixed. A summary of the findings from various studies shows that the essential point is that children whose parents' income rises as a result of the TANF policy largely have improved child well-being. This is because income is closely correlated with a number of positive benefits for children (Duncan & Brooks-Gunn, 1997; Haveman & Wolfe. 1995); improved economic conditions may mean better neighborhoods, better schools, improved health and nutrition, and improved parenting.

Children whose parents' income declines or remains the same largely experience negative effects (for a review, see Morris, Scott, & London, 2005). Decades of research on children show the profound effects of poverty on development and well-being. When family income falls, the effects for children are detrimental. Family poverty is associated with increased rates of maltreatment (Garbarino, Kostelny, & Grady, 1993; U.S. Department of Health and Human Services, 1996), more health conditions (Brooks-Gunn, Duncan, & Maritato, 1997; Halpern, 1993), poorer educational attainment (Benedersky & Lewis, 1994; Pagani, Boulerice, & Tremblay, 1997; Smith, Brooks-Gunn, & Klebanov, 1997), and other adverse outcomes. In short, the longer children are exposed to poverty, the younger their age at the time of exposure, and the deeper the poverty, the more significant are these negative effects (Duncan & Brooks-Gunn, 1997). Since welfare neither lifts children out of poverty nor contributes to families' economic security, it does little to support positive gains in children's development and well-being.

Conclusion

When PRWORA passed, many welcomed the flexibility offered by the block grant and the up-front infusion of funding to craft a new welfare program customized to the political and social constituencies of the states (Haskins, 2006). Since that time, TANF has evolved into at least 50 different programs, all operating within the constraints of the federal law but with many variations in approach, emphasis, and structure (Rowe & Giannarelli, 2006). Now that caseloads have stabilized and funding is contingent upon exceptionally high work participation rates, the shine has dulled considerably. "Welfare reform" has not met the promise of its most ardent supporters, nor has it ushered in large-scale deprivation across the country. Many families have indeed left the welfare program, but few have attained economic well-being. The daily challenges of family life have grown more severe (Scott, Edin, London, & Mazelis, 2001), and many children have been shut out of the American dream (DeParle, 2005). A decade into this new policy, it is easy to become complacent and accept the

TANF cash assistance program for poor families as a fait accompli. But the role of social workers in the postwelfare reform environment is as important as ever. Social work practitioners, policy makers, and researchers must continue to follow the effects of PRWORA on low-income children and families and to press for policy changes that move families out of poverty and into opportunity.

References

Abramovitz, M. (1988). *Regulating the lives of women: Social welfare policy from colonial times to the present.* Boston: South End Press.

Bane. M. J., & Ellwood, D. (1994). *Welfare realities: From rhetoric to reform.* Cambridge, MA: Harvard University Press.

Bell, W. (1965). *Aid to dependent children.* New York: Columbia University Press.

Benedersky, M., & Lewis, M. (1994). Environmental risk, biological risk, and developmental outcome. *Developmental Psychology, 30*(4), 484–494.

Bennett, N. G., & Lu, H.-H. (2000). *Child poverty in the states.* New York: National Center for Children in Poverty.

Berrick, J. D. (2001). Personal responsibility, private behavior, and public benefits: Targeting social welfare in the United States. In N. Gilbert (Ed.), *Targeting social benefits* (pp. 129–156). New York: Transaction Books.

Berrick, J. D. (2005). Marriage, motherhood, and welfare reform. *Social policy and society, 4*(2), 133–146.

Blank, R., & Haskins, R. (Eds.). (2002). *The new world of welfare.* Washington, DC: Brookings Institution Press.

Blendon, R. J. (1995). *Survey on welfare reform: Basic values and beliefs; support for policy approaches; knowledge about key programs.* Menlo Park, CA: The Henry J. Kaiser Family Foundation.

Broder, J. M. (1997, August 17). Big social changes revive the false God of numbers. *New York Times,* Section 4, p. 14.

Brooks-Gunn, J., Duncan, G., & Maritato, N. (1997). Poor families, poor outcomes: The well-being of children and youth. In G. Duncan & J. Brooks-Gunn, (Eds.), *Consequences of growing up poor* (pp. 1–17). New York: Russell Sage Foundation.

Cancian, M., & Meyer, D. (2000, June). Work after welfare: Women's work effort, occupation, and economic well-being. *Social Work Research, 24*(2), 69–86.

Center on Budget and Policy Priorities. (2007, February). *Implementing the TANF changes in the Deficit Reduction Act: "Win-win" solutions for families and states.* Washington, DC: Author.

Coll, B. D. (1995). *Safety net: Welfare and Social Security, 1929–1979.* New Brunswick, NJ: Rutgers University Press.

Corbett, T. (1996). The new federalism: Monitoring consequences. *Focus, 18*(1), 3–25.

Corcoran, M., Danziger, S., Kalil, A., & Seefeldt, K. (2000). How welfare reform is affecting women's work. *Annual Review of Sociology, 26,* 241–269.

Courtney, M.E. (1999). The economics. *Child Abuse & Neglect, 23*(11), 1019–1040.

DeParle, J. (2005). *American dream.* New York: Penguin.

Duncan, G., & Brooks-Gunn, J. (Eds.). (1997). *The Consequences of growing up poor.* New York: Russell Sage Foundation.

Edin, K., & Lein, L. (1997). *Making ends meet: How single mothers survive welfare and low-wage work.* New York: Russell Sage Foundation.

Ellwood, D. T. (1988). *Poor support*. New York: Free Press.

Farkas, S. (1995). *Public attitudes toward welfare and welfare reform*. New York: Public Agenda.

Farkas, S., & Johnson, J. (1995). *The values we live by: What Americans want from welfare reform*. New York: Public Agenda.

Gallagher, L. J., Gallagher, M., Perese, K., Schreiber, S., & Watson, K. (1998). *One year after federal welfare reform: A description of state Temporary Assistance for Needy Families (TANF) decisions*. Washington, DC: Urban Institute.

Garbarino, J., Kostelny, K., & Grady, J. (1993). Children in dangerous environments: Child maltreatment in a context of community violence. In D. Cicchetti & S. L. Toth (Eds.), *Child abuse, child development, and social policy*, pp. 167–190). New Jersey: Ablex.

Gensler, H. (Ed.). (1996). *The American welfare system: Origins, structure, and effects*. Westport, CT: Praeger.

Gordon, L. (1994). *Pitied but not entitled: Single mothers and the history of welfare*. New York: Free Press.

Gueron, J. M., & Pauly, E. (1991). *From welfare to work*. New York: Russell Sage Foundation.

Halpern, R. (1993). Poverty and infant development. In C. H. Zeanah (Ed.), *Handbook of infant mental health* (pp. 73–86). New York: Guilford.

Haskins, R. (2006). *Work over welfare: The inside story of the 1996 welfare reform law*. Washington, DC: Brookings Institution Press.

Haveman, R., & Wolfe, B. (1995). *Succeeding generations*. New York: Russell Sage Foundation.

Hennesey, J. (2005). Welfare, work, and famly well-being: A comparative analysis of welfare and employment status for single female-headed families post-TANF. *Sociological Perspectives, 48*(1), 77–104.

Holcomb, P., Adams, G., Snyder, K., Koralek, R., Martinson, K., Bernstein, S., et al. (2006). *Child care subsidies and TANF*. Washington, DC: Urban Institute.

Institute for Research on Poverty. (2007). *Who is poor?* Retrieved January 28, 2008, from http://www.irp.wisc.edu/faqs/faq3.htm

Kingsley, G. T. (1996, Autumn). Perspectives on devolution. *Journal of the American Planning Association, 62*(4), 419–426.

London, R., & Mauldon, J. (n.d.). *Time running out: A portrait of California families reaching the CalWORKs 60-month time limit in 2004*. Oakland: University of California, Office of Research.

Loprest, P. (2001, April). How families that left welfare are doing: A comparison of early and recent welfare leavers. *New Federalism: National Survey of America's Families* (Series B, No. B-36). Washington, DC: Urban Institute.

Loprest, P. (2002). Making the transition from welfare to work: Success by continuing concerns. In A. Weil & K. Finegold (Eds.), *Welfare reform: The next act* (pp. 17–31). Washington, DC: Urban Institute.

Morris, P. A., Scott, E. K., & London, A. S. (2005). Effects on children as parents transition from welfare to employment. In J. D. Berrick & B. Fuller (Eds.), *Good parents or good workers? How Policy shapes families' daily lives* (pp. 87–116). New York: Palgrave Macmillan.

Nichols, A. (2006, May). *Understanding changes in child poverty over the past decade*. Washington, DC: Urban Institute.

Pagani, L., Boulerice, B., & Tremblay, R. (1997). The influence of poverty on children's classroom placement and behavior problems. In G. J. Duncan &

J. Brooks-Gunn (Eds.), *Consequences of growing up poor* (pp. 311–339). New York: Russell Sage Foundation.

Pappas, A. (1996). Welfare reform: Child welfare or the rhetoric of responsibility? *Duke Law Journal, 45,* 1301–1328.

Parrott, S., & Sherman, A. (2006). *TANF at 10: Program results are more mixed than often understood.* Washington, DC: Center on Budget and Policy Priorities.

Quadagno, J. (1994). *The color of welfare: How racism undermined the war on poverty.* New York: Oxford University Press.

Rein, M. (1982). *Dilemmas of welfare policy: Why work strategies haven't worked.* New York: Praeger.

Rowe, G., & Giannarelli, L. (2006). *Getting on, staying on, and getting off welfare.* Washington, DC: Urban Institute.

Scott, E. K., Edin, K., London, A. S., & Mazelis, J. M. (2001). My children come first: Welfare-reliant women's post-TANF views of work-family trade-offs and marriage. In G. J. Duncan & P. L. Chase-Lansdale (Eds.), *For better and for worse* (pp. 132–153). New York: Russell Sage Foundation.

Slack, K. S., Lee, B. J., & Berger, L. M. (2007). Do welfare sanctions increase child protection system involvement? A cautious answer. *Social Service Review, 81*(2), 207–228.

Smith, J., Brooks-Gunn, J., & Klebanov, P. (1997). Consequences of living in poverty for young children's cognitive and verbal ability and early school achievement. In G. Duncan & J. Brooks-Gunn (Eds.), *Consequences of growing up poor* (pp. 132–189). New York: Russell Sage Foundation.

Solow, R. M. (2002). Why were the nineties so good? Could it happen again? *Focus, 22*(2), 1–7.

U.S. Department of Health and Human Services. (1996). *Results of the third national incidence study on child maltreatment in the United States.* Washington, DC: National Center on Child Abuse and Neglect.

U.S. Department of Health and Human Services. (1998). *Change in welfare caseloads.* Retrieved January 28, 1999, from http://www.acf.dhhs.gov/news/case load.html

U.S. Department of Health and Human Services, Office of the Assistant Secretary for Planning and Evaluation. (1997). *Setting the baseline: A report on state welfare waivers.* Washington, DC: Author.

U.S. General Accounting Office. (1994). *Families on welfare: Sharp rise in never-married women reflects societal trend.* Washington, DC: Author.

U.S. House Ways and Means Committee. (1996). *1996 Green Book: Background material and data on programs within the jurisdiction of the Committee on Ways and Means.* Washington, DC: Author.

Waldfogel, J. (1998). *The future of child protection: How to break the cycle of abuse and neglect.* Cambridge, MA: Harvard University Press.

Weaver, R. K. (1996, Summer). Deficits and devolution in the 104th Congress. *Plubius—The Journal of Federalism, 26*(3), 45–85.

Weaver, R. K., Shapiro, R. Y., & Jacobs, L. R. (1996). *Public opinion on welfare reform: A mandate for what? Looking before we leap: Social science and welfare reform.* Washington, DC: Brookings Institution Press.

Weil, A., & Finegold, K. (2002). *Welfare reform: The next act.* Washington, DC: Urban Institute.

22

Social Security

Martha Ozawa

The public's attitude toward Social Security has been positive, as public opinion surveys have indicated time and time again (Cook, Barabas, & Page, 2002; Cook & Jacobs, 2002). However, the public has become concerned about the financial solvency of Social Security. Will Social Security exist when young generations retire? (Baggette, Shapiro, & Jacobs, 1995; Friedland, 1994). Since the George W. Bush administration attempted to reform Social Security in its first term, the public has come to realize that there is a problem in Social Security financing, not just in abstract terms but in concrete terms. Thus, the current policy debate is no longer *when* or *if* but *how* to reform it.

This chapter discusses how the Social Security system works; the emerging problems, including demographic shifts and financial problems; benefit-cost analyses for different groups of beneficiaries; the reform agenda; and the link between social policy for the elderly and social policy for children.

The Social Security system in the United States includes social insurance programs to provide economic security for elderly persons, disabled workers, and workers' dependents and survivors. Specifically, the system includes, first, Old Age and Survivors Insurance (OASI), established under the Social Security Act of 1935 and its 1939 amendments to provide cash benefits for retired workers, dependents, and survivors, and, second, Disability Insurance (DI), enacted through the 1956 amendments to the Social Security Act and designed to provide cash benefits for disabled workers and their eligible family members.

However, when appropriate, the financial condition of Medicare will also be discussed in this chapter. Medicare is an insurance-funded health care program for retirees, which was introduced by the Johnson administration in 1965. Although Medicare is funded through the insurance mechanism, it is not usually included in discussions on Social Security.

During the 2005 calendar year, Old Age, Survivors, and Disability Insurance (OASDI) benefits amounting to $521 billion were paid to retired and disabled workers and their families and to the survivors of deceased workers. A total of 48.4 million persons received OASDI benefits at the end of December 2005. In 2005, an estimated 159 million people had earnings covered by OASDI (OASDI Board of Trustees, 2006a, 2006b).

Basic Principles

Social Security provides benefits as an earned right without a means test or an income test. Contributions are compulsory, unless workers are specifically exempt, such as those in states that have not opted to participate in Social Security. The provision of Social Security benefits is predicated on two principles: first, individual equity, which relates benefits directly to beneficiaries' prior earnings, and second, social adequacy, which provides for larger benefits to low-wage workers in relation to their contributions and extra benefits to auxiliary beneficiaries (for example, children, dependent parents, and spouses with no earnings of their own) without added contributions.

Social Security funding is based on the principles of compulsory contributions from employees and employers and from self-employed workers and pay-as-you-go financing. However, the 1983 amendments to the Social Security Act included a provision to build up the trust fund's assets in anticipation of the large number of baby boomers who will reach retirement age starting in 2010.

Provisions

Old Age and Survivors Insurance

To be eligible for OASI benefits, workers must be either fully insured or currently insured. To be fully insured, one must have earned the minimum amount of 40 quarters of coverage. In 2006, workers received one quarter of coverage for each $970 of covered annual earnings ($1,000 in 2007), with no more than four quarters credited to an individual in one year. The amount of earnings needed to gain a quarter of coverage increases at the rate of the increase in average wages.

The age at which full benefits are paid has been increased from 65 years, which was the original normal retirement age (NRA). For those who were born in 1937 or earlier, it remains 65 years. For those who were born between 1943 and 1954, the NRA will be 66. And for those who were born in 1960 or later, the NRA will be 67. It is possible to receive reduced benefits prior to these retirement ages. By 2027, the full, actuarial reduction in benefits at age 62 will increase to 30%.

To be currently insured, one must have acquired 6 quarters of coverage in the 13-quarter period ending in the calendar quarter of death, disability, or reaching age 62. This status entitles the worker's surviving spouse and children to survivors' insurance benefits, plus a lump-sum payment of $255 for burial expenses.

To be eligible for disability insurance benefits, one must be both fully insured and disability insured. Attaining the status of being disability insured requires that workers earn a certain number of quarters of coverage, depending on their age. However, having only fully insured status is required for workers whose disability is caused by blindness.

All Social Security benefits are based on the primary insurance amount (PIA), which is derived in two steps. First, the worker's average indexed monthly earnings (AIME) is obtained, which is calculated by indexing the taxable earnings for each year from 1951 to the average wage level in the second year before age 62, disability, or death. Indexed earnings (and unindexed earnings in years after age 60) are then added and the sum is divided by the number of months elapsed after 1950 (or age 21, if later) through age 61 (or the year before the year of disability or death). Five years of the lowest earnings are dropped from the calculation of AIME (fewer drop-out years apply to disabled workers). The benefit computation period is 35 years (fewer years apply to disabled workers).

The PIA is then calculated on the basis of AIME. For those who retired at age 62 in 2006, the PIA is calculated as follows:

$$\text{PIA} = 90\% \text{ of the first } \$656 \text{ of AIME} + \\ 32\% \text{ of the next } \$3{,}299 \text{ of AIME} + \\ 15\% \text{ of AIME in excess of } \$3{,}955$$

The bend points ($656 and $3,955) increase each year at the rate of the increase in the average wage. Benefits for workers who retire earlier than the normal retirement age are subjected to actuarial reductions in the PIA—a 25% reduction for those retiring at age 62 in 2006 and pro rata reductions for those retiring at ages 63 through the NRA, which was 66 in the same year.

Eligible members of a retired worker are each entitled to benefits equivalent to 50% of the PIA. But spouses who claim auxiliary benefits before age 65 face an actuarial reduction unless an eligible child is present. In addition, when spouses receive pensions that are based on their own federal, state, or local government work that is not covered by Social Security, their Social Security benefits are reduced by an amount equal to two-thirds of their public pensions. Total family benefits may not exceed the maximum family benefit. Widows or widowers of insured workers are entitled to 100% of the PIA of the deceased spouses if they claim benefits at the normal retirement age or later. Widows and widowers can claim benefits as early as age 60 (or age 50 if disabled), although the benefits are subjected to actuarial reduction.

Children younger than age 18 (or younger than 19 if still in high school) and the surviving spouse who is caring for them are entitled to survivor benefits. Each eligible survivor is entitled to benefits equal to 75% of the PIA, but the maximum family benefit rule applies. When the youngest child reaches age 18, benefits for the surviving spouse cease, but if any child has a disability that originated in childhood (before age 22), benefits for the child and caretaker parent continue without an age limit.

Disability Insurance

To receive disability benefits, a worker must be unable to engage in any substantial gainful activity (SGA) because of a severe physical or mental impairment that is expected to last for at least 12 months or to result in death. Education, work experience, and age are taken into account in determining disability. Disability insurance beneficiaries must accept rehabilitation services offered by state rehabilitation agencies if the Social Security Administration determines that these services are likely to be successful.

Eligible disabled workers are entitled to monthly benefits equal to the PIA. Eligible children and the spouse caring for a child under age 18 or children who became disabled before age 22 are each entitled to 50% of the PIA. The total family benefits may not exceed the disability maximum family benefit.

Unless they recover medically from their disability, disabled people generally are allowed to continue to receive benefits for up to nine months while they test their ability to work. Benefits are not terminated until the second month following the earliest month after the trial work period in which the individual engages in substantial gainful activity or is determined by the Social Security Administration to be able to engage in substantial gainful activities.

Other Rules for OASDI Beneficiaries

Earnings test. No retirement earnings test applies to people who are at the normal retirement age or older. For those who attain normal retirement age after 2007, the annual exempt amount in 2007 is $12,960. For those who reach normal retirement age in 2007, the annual exempt amount is $34,440. This higher exempt amount applies only to earnings that were made in months prior to the month of attaining normal retirement age.

Taxes on benefits. As was mentioned earlier, the 1983 amendments required beneficiaries to pay taxes on Social Security benefits. Currently, individuals filing a federal tax return with a combined income (ordinal income plus Social Security benefits) of between $25,000 and $34,000 have to pay taxes on 50% of the Social Security benefits. If the combined income is more than $34,000, up to 85% of the Social Security benefit is subjected to income tax. If the beneficiary files a joint return, the beneficiary pays taxes on 50% of the benefits if the couple has a combined income that is between $32,000 and $44,000. If the couple's combined income is more than $44,000, up to 85% of the Social Security benefit is subject to income tax. About one-third of Social Security beneficiaries are subjected to payment of taxes on the benefits.

Financing

OASDI is financed by payroll taxes on employers, employees, and the self-employed. The payroll tax is authorized by the Federal Insurance Contribution Act up to the maximum taxable earnings ($97,500 in 2007). The tax (or contribution) rate of 6.2% for OASI and Disability Insurance combined is levied on employees and employers, totaling 12.4% of the payroll. The self-employed pay at the 12.4% rate. The current allocation of funds is 5.30% for OASI and 0.90% for disability insurance. The allocation is changed from time to time.

Emerging Problems

Demographic Shifts

At the core of the financial problems associated with the Social Security program is the rapid change in the country's demographics. Gramlich (1996a, 1996b) explained how the old dependency ratio and the relationship between the number of beneficiaries and the number of workers determine the rate of taxes needed to support the beneficiary population at a desired level of income. The following equations determine the rate of taxes:

$$T = (B/W) \times (S/N),$$

where T is the OASDI tax, B is the average social security benefits, W is the average taxable wages, S is the number of social security beneficiaries, and N is the number of workers.

Observe that B/W (the ratio of average benefits to average taxable wages) is the same as the replacement rate, in aggregate terms. Observe also that S/N (the ratio of beneficiaries to workers in covered employment) is the dependency ratio. Thus, the tax rate is the product of the replacement rate and the dependency ratio. By deduction, controlling for the replacement rate, the tax rate increases with the increase in the dependency ratio.

According to data compiled by the OASDI Board of Trustees (2006a), the number of OASI beneficiaries, who are mostly elderly persons, per 100 covered workers—the dependency ratio—will increase from 20.0 in 2010 to 42.1 in 2080 (see Table 22.1). On the basis of this equation, the increase in the dependency ratio, while maintaining the level of benefits relative to wages intact (for example at 60%), will result in an increase in the tax rate of from 12.5% in 2010 to 25.3% in 2080. The financial problem stemming from the growing dependency ratio will not disappear even after the baby-boom generation passes away because the proportion of children will continue to decline (Bosworth, 1997).

Another way to characterize the impact of the demographic shift is to estimate the proportion of the total population that will be future beneficiaries of OASDI. As Table 22.2 indicates, the proportion will increase from 17.6% in 2010 to 26.0% in 2080. In absolute terms, the number of beneficiaries will increase from 53.6 million to 111.5 million.

Table 22.1   The Aged Dependency Ratio, 2010–2080

Year	Aged Dependency Ratio
2010	.209
2020	.270
2030	.349
2040	.372
2050	.380
2060	.396
2070	.411
2080	.421

SOURCE: OASDI Board of Trustees (2006a), Table V.A2, p. 78.

Table 22.2   Projected Numbers and Proportions of OASDI Beneficiaries, 2010–2080 (in thousands)

Year	Number of Beneficiaries Under OASI	Number of Beneficiaries Under DI	Total Number of Beneficiaries Under OASDI	Total Beneficiaries as a Percentage of the Population
2010	43,781	9,693	53,564	17.0
2020	58,025	11,178	69,203	20.4
2030	71,872	12,422	84,294	23.4
2040	78,401	13,083	91,484	24.3
2050	81,735	13,989	95,724	24.6
2060	86,072	14,532	100,604	25.0
2070	91,197	15,044	106,241	23.5
2080	95,819	15,673	111,492	26.0

SOURCE: OASDI Board of Trustees (2006a), Tables V.A2, V.C4, V.C6; pp. 78, 112, 119.

NOTES: Old-Age Insurance (OAI) beneficiaries include retired workers, spouses, and children. Survivors Insurance (SI) beneficiaries include widows and widowers, mothers and fathers, children, and parents. Disability Insurance (DI) beneficiaries include disabled workers, spouses, and children.

Two reasons for the enormous increase in the number of social security beneficiaries are, first, increasing life expectancy and, second, the increase in the proportion of covered workers who retire earlier than the normal retirement age. Life expectancy at birth is projected to increase from 81.0 years in 2010 to 85.9 years in 2080 for men and from 84.9 years in 2010 to 88.9 years in 2080 for women. Life expectancy at 65 is projected to increase from 17.4 years to 21.2 years for men and from 19.9 years to 23.6 years for women, over the same period (OASDI Board of Trustees 2006a, Table V.A4, p. 82). The proportion of those who retired earlier than the normal retirement age increased from 58% in 1980 to 74% in 2003 for men and from 70% in 1980 to 77% in 2003 for women (Ozawa, 2006).

Financial Problems

The OADSI Board of Trustees (2006a), which has oversight of the Social Security system, determined that the long-term financial solvency of OASDI is worsening. The board compared the annual income rates and cost rates for OASI and disability insurance and evaluated the actuarial condition of the OASI fund, the disability insurance fund, and a combination of the two, all in terms of the percentage of the taxable payroll. The data presented in the following tables are based on the assumptions established by the Office of the Actuary in the Social Security Administration.

Table 22.3 shows the actuarial status of the OASI Trust Fund, the Disability Insurance Trust Fund, and the combination of the two during the following incremental periods: 25 years from 2006 to 2030, 50 years from 2006 to 2055, and 75 years from 2006 to 2080.

Table 22.3 indicates that, except in the first 25-year period, the OASI Fund will have an actuarial imbalance: 0.99% of the taxable payroll during the coming 50 years and 1.68% of the taxable payroll during the coming 75 years. Thus, looking at a 75-year time frame, income has to increase by 1.68% of the taxable payroll, starting now. Otherwise, the OASI Trust Fund will be out of balance. In the same vein, income to pay for disability insurance benefits must increase by 0.33% of the taxable payroll to meet the actuarial balance in the Disability Insurance Trust Fund for the coming 75 years. OASI and disability insurance together will require an additional or 2.02% of the taxable payroll, starting now, to strike an actuarial balance in the coming 75-year period. If action is delayed, the rate of the payroll tax will have to increase even more substantially.

Table 22.4 shows the well-known demarcation points for OASI and disability insurance. Demarcation points for Medicare Health Insurance (Part A of Medicare) are also shown. Table 22.4 indicates that, beginning in 2018, the outgo for OASI will be higher than the income that excludes interest. In 2028, the OASI outgo will exceed the income, including interest. At this point, OASI will have to begin to use the trust fund assets. In 2042, the trust fund assets will be exhausted.

Table 22.3   Summarized Income Rates and Cost Rates for Valuation Periods, by Trust Fund, Under Intermediate Assumptions, Calendar Years 2006–2080 (As a Percentage of the Taxable Payroll)

Valuation Period	OASI			DI			Combined		
	Income Rate	Cost Rate	Actuarial Balance	Income Rate	Cost Rate	Actuarial Balance	Income Rate	Cost Rate	Actuarial Balance
25 years: 2005–2030	12.60	11.76	0.81	2.02	2.17	–.15	14.62	13.96	0.66
50 years: 2005–2055	12.10	13.08	–.99	1.95	2.23	–.27	14.062	15.31	–1.26
75 years: 2005–2080	11.95	13.63	–1.68	1.93	2.27	–.33	13.88	15.90	–2.02

SOURCE: OASDI Board of Trustees (2006a), Table IV.B4, p. 56.

Table 22.4   Key Dates for the Trust Funds

	OASI	DI	OASDI	HI
First year outgo exceeds income excluding interest	2018	2005	2017	2006
First year outgo exceeds income including interest	2028	2013	2027	2010
The year trust assets are exhausted	2042	2025	2040	2018

SOURCE: OASDI Board of Trustees (2006b).

NOTE: OASI = Old Age and Survivors Insurance, DI = Disability Insurance, OASDI = Old Age, Survivors, and Disability Insurance, HI = Health Insurance.

The financial condition of Disability Insurance Trust Fund will be even worse. In 2005, income that did not include interest was already smaller than the outgo. In 2013, disability insurance outgoes will exceed income including interest. Finally, in 2025, the Disability Insurance Trust Fund will be exhausted. In 2040, the combined OASDI and Disability Insurance Trust Funds will be exhausted. Note further, that the year of exhaustion of Medicare health insurance will be much earlier—2018.

In 2040, the year when the combined OASDI and Disability Insurance Trust Funds are exhausted, income from contributions will be sufficient to pay only 72% of benefits. Because the rate of growth in benefit obligations will continue to increase faster than the rate of growth in tax income, the percentage of the benefits that can be paid with current income will continue to decline, dropping to about two-thirds at the end of the 75-year period, and it is expected to continue to drop even after that.

The projections that are presented in Tables 22.3 and 22.4 indicate the funds needed to maintain the long-range actuarial balance for all the Social Security system, that is, to maintain or prevent the trust funds from being exhausted. However, given the fact that the government has not actually accumulated the surplus of the OASDI trust funds in the form of *real* assets, but only as special bonds, the more realistic way to assess the financial problem is to estimate whether the government can produce the financial resources to fill the gap between income and expenditures.

When we consider the financial situation of Social Security in this way, it is more instructive to assess the fiscal viability of Social Security by estimating the cost of financing OASI, disability insurance, *and* Medicare health insurance (Part A of Medicare) as a percentage of the gross domestic product (GDP). Table 22.5 shows the cost of these programs in particular years as well as for different periods of time.

As shown in Table 22.5, the cost of funding these programs, especially Medicare, will increase enormously. In 2010, the cost of funding OASDI will be equivalent to 4.32% of the GDP, and it will increase to 6.32% of the GDP in 2080—this is a 45% increase. The cost of funding Medicare will be even greater. In 2010, the program will cost the nation 1.58% of GDP, but this cost will surge to 4.90% of the GDP in 2080—a 120%

Table 22.5 OASDI and HI Income, Cost, and Balance in Selected Years and in Summarized Rates, 2010–2080 (As a Percentage of GDP)

				Percentage of GDP								
	OASDI			**HI**			**Combined**					
Year	Income	Cost	Balance	Income	Cost	Balance	Income	Cost	Balance			
2010	4.88	4.32	.56	1.48	1.58	-.10	6.36	5.90	.46			
2020	4.89	5.27	-.38	1.53	2.01	-.49	6.42	7.28	-.86			
2030	4.87	6.18	-1.31	1.54	2.77	-1.23	6.41	8.95	-2.54			
2040	4.80	6.36	-1.56	1.53	3.50	-1.97	6.33	9.86	-3.53			
2050	4.72	6.26	-1.54	1.50	3.96	-2.45	6.23	10.22	-3.99			
2060	4.65	6.26	-1.61	1.48	4.31	-2.82	6.13	10.57	-4.43			
2070	4.47	6.32	-1.74	1.46	4.65	-3.18	6.04	10.95	-4.92			
2080	4.50	6.32	-1.83	1.44	4.90	-3.45	5.94	11.22	-5.28			
Summarized Rates												
25 years: 2006–2030	5.52	5.27	.25	1.61	2.07	-.46	7.13	7.34	-.21			
50 years: 2005–2055	5.21	5.68	-.47	1.57	2.72	-1.15	6.78	8.40	-1.62			
75 years: 2005–2080	5.07	5.81	-.74	1.55	3.14	-1.60	6.62	8.95	-2.33			

SOURCE: OASDI Board of Trustees (2006a), Table IV.F4, p. 171.

NOTE: OASDI = Old Age, Survivors, and Disability Insurance, HI = Health Insurance.

increase. The cost of OASDI and Medicare health insurance combined will be equivalent to 5.90% of GDP in 2010 and 11.22% of GDP in 2080.

How significant is the 11.22% of the GDP? It is estimated that the cost of OASI, disability insurance, and Medicare health insurance, plus the payment of the interest on the national debt, will increase to 22.5% of the GDP in 2080, which will exceed the entire federal outlays at its historic high of 20.9% of the GDP in 1944 and 2000 (Steuerle, 2003). Moreover, the cost of financing Medicare Part D (insurance on drugs for the elderly) is yet to be factored in. Thus, in 2080, there will be nothing left in the federal budget to pay for any other federal programs, let alone other social welfare programs.

Benefit-Cost Analysis of OASDI and Medicare

How do individual beneficiaries fare under the current OASI and disability insurance programs and Medicare? How much do individual beneficiaries contribute to the system, and how much do they receive in their lifetime from benefits? Adam Carasso and C. Eugene Steuerle of the Urban Institute analyzed data that are used by the actuary of the Social Security Administration when producing the 2006 Annual Report of the Boards of Trustees of the Federal Old Age and Survivors Insurance and Federal Disability Insurance Trust Funds. Permission was granted to the author of this chapter to use their analysis.

Table 22.6 shows the results of the benefit-cost analysis for a single male, a single female, a two-earner couple, and a one-earner couple, thus effectively showing the gender differences and the difference when only one spouse works or two spouses work. In all cases, the beneficiaries were all average earners. The general findings follow.

Under the Social Security Program

- All things being equal, female beneficiaries received more from Social Security because they live longer; on the tax side, they paid equal amounts of taxes. The Social Security lifetime benefits for those who become 65 in 2030 will be $33,035 higher for female beneficiaries than for male beneficiaries.
- One-earner couples can anticipate receiving lifetime benefits of $489,000, compared with $601,000 for two-earner couples. Notice, however, that two-earner couples paid twice the taxes paid by one-earner couples. Thus, on balance, two-earner couples benefit less from social security because, although taxes are twice as much, benefits are less than twice the amount that a one-earner couple receives.
- Later cohorts benefit more from social security than do earlier cohort.

Table 22.6   Benefits and Taxes Under Social Security and Medicare Programs in 2006 Dollars

Year Cohort Turns 65	Social Security Annual Benefits	Social Security Lifetime Benefits	Medicare Lifetime Benefits	Total Lifetime Benefits	Social Security Lifetime Taxes	Medicare Lifetime Taxes	Total Lifetime Taxes	Lifetime Transfers
Single Male								
1960	$8,200	$100,000	$13,000	$113,000	$16,000	$0	$16,000	$97,000
1980	13,400	179,000	54,000	233,000	85,000	7,000	92,000	141,000
2005	15,800	214,000	152,000	366,000	233,000	41,000	274,000	92,000
2030	20,900	283,000	301,000	584,000	371,000	79,000	450,000	134,000
Single Female								
1960	$8,200	$130,000	$20,000	$150,000	$16,000	$0	$16,000	$134,000
1980	13,400	220,000	70,000	290,000	85,000	7,000	92,000	198,000
2005	15,800	241,000	175,000	416,000	233,000	41,000	274,000	142,000
2030	20,900	318,000	340,000	658,000	371,000	79,000	450,000	208,000
Average-Wage, Two-Earner Couple ($38,700) each								
1960	$16,600	$226,000	$34,000	$260,000	$32,000	$0	$32,000	$228,000
1980	26,800	399,000	124,000	523,000	170,000	15,000	185,000	338,000
2005	31,600	455,000	328,000	783,000	465,000	83,000	548,000	235,000
2030	41,800	601,000	641,000	1,242,000	742,000	158,000	900,000	342,000
Average One-Earner Couple Earnings ($38,700)								
1960	$13,000	$186,000	$34,000	$220,000	$16,000	$0	$16,000	$204,000
1980	20,000	326,000	124,000	450,000	85,000	7,000	92,000	358,000
2005	23,700	369,000	328,000	697,000	233,000	41,000	274,000	423,000
2030	31,400	489,000	641,000	1,130,000	371,000	79,000	450,000	680,000

NOTES: These are expected rather than realized benefits. Lifetime amounts are discounted to present value at age 65 using a 2% real interest rate and adjusted for mortality after age 65. Projections are based on intermediate assumptions of the 2006 OASDI and the Hospital Insurance and Supplemental Medical Insurance trustees reports. Calculations were done by Adam Carasso and C. Eugene Steuerle of the Urban Institute, 2006.

Under Medicare

- For those in the youngest cohort, caution is needed when interpreting the findings in Table 22.1. For them, Medicare has not "matured."
- As anticipated, female beneficiaries benefit more from Medicare than do male beneficiaries.
- It is anticipated that Medicare benefits will grow faster for later cohorts than under Social Security. One major reason for the faster growth in Medicare benefits is that they reflect not only growth in wages but also the escalating cost of medical goods and services, the greater intensity of the use of these items, and the higher quality of such items.
- On the tax side, one-earner couples are the clear "winners." Medicare provides the same value of goods and services to the spouse who did not earn income as to the spouse who did. Under Social Security, one-earner couples cannot expect to receive twice the benefits based on the one-earner's earnings record.
- At the aggregate level, Medicare has the greater impact on the cost of financing Social Security and health care.

Net Transfers From Social Security and Medicare Combined

The last column of Table 22.6 indicates which groups of beneficiaries have the larger amounts of *net transfers,* meaning lifetime benefits minus lifetime taxes. It shows the following:

- Later cohorts receive larger net transfers than do year cohorts.
- Female beneficiaries receive larger net transfers than do male beneficiaries. The net transfer for female beneficiaries who will become 65 in 2030 is estimated to be $208,000, compared with $134,000 for male beneficiaries.
- The average net transfers for one-earner couples who will become 65 in 2030 are estimated to be $680,000, compared with $342,000 for two-earner couples.

Special attention is needed in projecting the net transfers in the Social Security program. Although the level of Social Security will increase for future cohorts of beneficiaries, the rate of increase in Social Security taxes has been faster. Thus, the ratio of benefits to taxes will decline for future cohorts. Also, it should be noted that, for high-wage earners, the ratio of benefits to taxes will be lower than for low-wage beneficiaries.

The better benefit-tax ratio for one-earner couples than for two-earner couples or for single female beneficiaries may, indeed, reflect the rationale that the Committee on Economic Security, under the Roosevelt administration, took in developing the Social Security program in the United States: protection of women and the need to support married couples because of the assumption that women would not work outside the home (Altmeyer, 1966). The assumptions that were made in 1935, when the original Social Security Act was put into effect, may not hold in American society today or in the future.

Reform Agenda

It is clear that the cost of financing retirement and health care has increased enormously, creating a collision course between the public's wish to continue supporting the elderly population and its resistance to expanding the scope of the welfare state in the United States, notwithstanding the fact that the scope of the welfare state is one of the smallest among the industrialized societies, according to data from the Organisation for Economic Co-operation and Development (2001). The conflict between these two aims is the focal point of the American dilemma.

Over the past decades, several presidential commissions have been appointed to find viable solutions to Social Security reform. President Ronald Reagan established a bipartisan committee to reform Social Security. After intense policy deliberation, the 1983 amendments to the Social Security Act were put into effect. As a result of these amendments, a portion of the Social Security benefits became taxable; the normal retirement age was changed, so it would reach 67 in 2027; and benefits for those who postpone retirement to later years were increased. Most important, the social security contribution rate was increased considerably, so sizable assets would be accumulated in the trust fund to pay for the increasing cost of OASI when the baby-boom generation retires (Ozawa, 1984).

The 1994–1996 Advisory Council on Social Security (1997), established under President Bill Clinton, recommended three different plans: the Maintain Benefit (MB) plan, the Individual Account (IA) plan, and the Personal Security Accounts (PSA) plan. Of the three recommendations, the PSA plan was the most far reaching. It would require five percentage points of the Social Security payroll taxes to be *carved out* to enable workers to develop their own personal accounts to be used for their future financial security (PSAs), and it would change the traditional Social Security benefits, which are based on average indexed monthly earnings (AIME), to flat amount benefits. In essence, then, the PSA plan envisions a double-decker scheme for the future Social Security system: the first tier comprising flat-rate benefits and a second tier comprising a defined-contribution plan in the form of a savings account. The PSA plan was the forerunner of the concept of privatizing social security, now being debated among policy makers.

The Individual Account plan also included the concept of an individualized savings account, but the difference between the PSA plan and the IA plan is in the latter's use of *additional* contributions of 1.6% of taxable earnings to establish individualized retirement accounts (IRAs). This recommendation is based on an *add-on* approach. The carve-out versus the add-on approach is one of the focal points of current policy debate.

The adoption of the carve-out approach or the add-on approach would have different policy ramifications. The add-on approach would maintain the current provisions intact, thus leaving the current financial problems unresolved. Moreover, this approach would need to bring additional financial resources into the system. The carve-out approach would create different kinds of problems. Enormous transitional costs would be needed to implement this approach, and these would be financed by future generations of taxpayers. In addition, if the carve-out approach is adopted, the intra-cohort redistribution of financial resources built into the system will become smaller. That is, under the current system, sizable Social Security benefits are internally redistributed to certain groups who are considered financially needy, such as spouses, widows or widowers, and low-wage beneficiaries. Under a shrunken traditional Social Security system, the degree of internal redistribution would be limited when Social Security taxes are carved out to finance personal retirement accounts. Thus, there is no free lunch in implementing either the carve-out approach or the add-on approach.

The President's Commission to Strengthen Social Security (2001), established by President George W. Bush, recommended three plans. However, the introduction of some form of savings account was recommended under each plan. One plan (known as Plan 3) proposed an entirely new way of reducing Social Security benefits, thus lowering the cost of OASDI. This plan recommended the adoption of price indexing of earnings in prior years in calculating the AIME, which is the basis for calculating the primary insurance amount (PIA). Under the current system, wages earned in early years (since 1951 or at age 21, whichever is later) are adjusted to account for the rate of increase in average wages. For example, the index factor for earnings in 1951 is 11.9 to make them equivalent to the earnings made in 2002. To adjust the 1951 earnings for inflation to the 2002 price level, an index factor of only 9.9 needs to be used. Thus, the use of the price index, instead of the wage index, would result in lower average indexed monthly earnings (AIMEs), which would lead to lower Social Security benefits. The commission claimed that the adoption of wage indexing alone would not only help eliminate unfunded liability but also ensure permanent financial solvency of the system. Also note that the retention of wage indexing would maintain the built-in force that would guarantee higher benefits for later cohorts of beneficiaries. On the other hand, future cohorts may be required to pay more taxes than earlier cohorts; thus the question of who will benefit more from the system than others is an empirical question (see Table 22.6).

Regarding privatization, in general, the concept of introducing savings accounts has taken hold among policy makers and the public. Burtless (1998) warned, however, that there would be sizable between-cohort variations in the rates of return on the contributions that are made to these accounts. His study involving 88 hypothetical workers whose earnings increased by 1% a year and who contributed 2% of their wages to savings accounts throughout their working lives. He showed that the percentage of wages that could be replaced by annuities that were purchased by the accumulated assets in the IRAs differed enormously, depending on when the workers entered the workforce. He demonstrated that workers who entered the workforce in 1926 and retired in 1965 had the highest rate of return (40%), whereas those who entered the workforce in 1881 and retired in 1920 had the lowest rate of return (7%). On the other hand, Feldstein (1997) argued that, because the rates of return on contributions would be so high compared with the rates of return on the contributions to the traditional Social Security program, it is probable that every participant in a savings account would be better off. Furthermore, in support of the privatization of Social Security, Feldstein and Samwick (1996) argued that, because the rate of return on equities considerably exceeds that on the U.S. Treasury's special issues, the benefits that are financed by the existing 12.4% payroll tax can be financed by mandatory contributions of only 2.1% of the taxable payroll under a privatized system. Even after taking the cost of transition into account, Feldstein's model would generate better rates of return (Feldstein, 1997).

Linkage Between the Young and the Old

As policy makers and the public struggle to find ways to maintain the financial solvency of Social Security in the United States, it is important to address the economic conditions of the young. It will take economically vital future generations to address and solve the impending financial problems facing Social Security.

In this section, it is argued that the federal government is placing a low priority on dealing with the economic problems of children. Relative to other countries, the United States redistributes a disproportionately small amount of money to children in comparison to the amounts redistributed to the elderly and adult populations. In addition, the poverty rate of children is higher when compared with those of the elderly and adult populations.

Intervention on behalf of children is a lower priority of the federal government of the United States. Carasso, Steuerle, and Reynolds (2007) reported that federal spending for children increased from 1.9% to 2.6% of the GDP from 1960 to 2006, whereas spending for the elderly increased from 2.0% to 7.6% of the GDP. Clearly, the rate of growth in spending for children has been much slower during the past four decades.

The low priority placed on spending for children is reflected in the ratio of per capita public income transfers for children to those for elderly people and for adults. An analysis by Ozawa and Lee (n.d.), using data from the Luxembourg Income Study (LIS), showed that the United States is an extreme case: The ratio of transfers for children to that of the elderly is 1:8.12, meaning that for each dollar the United States transfers per child, it transfers $8.12 per elderly person. Only Italy and Spain have a more skewed distribution in favor of their elderly population. Countries that have distributional patterns in the mid-range (4.00 or higher) are France, Germany, Netherlands, and Spain. At the other extreme—those with a ratio lower than 4.00—are Sweden, Denmark, and Norway. These eleven countries were chosen for comparative purposes according to the scheme established by Esping-Andersen (1999).

The difference between public income transfers to children and to adults is significantly smaller than the difference between transfers to children and to the elderly. However, the pattern of differences is similar to the one explained previously. The degree of difference is the third highest in the United States (after Italy and Spain), again indicating the lower priority that the United States places on providing income transfers to children than that found in other industrialized societies, except Italy and Spain. Note that, in the United Kingdom and the Netherlands, per capita public income transfers are higher for children than for the adult population (see Table 22.7).

With regard to the poverty rate, children are losing ground in comparison to the elderly. The income status of the elderly has been improving during the past four decades, so much so that the poverty rates of the elderly and children crossed between 1973 and 1974. As of 2005, the poverty rate of children was 1.74 times that of the elderly. Note that, since 1993, the poverty rate of the elderly has been lower than that of adults except in 2000 (see Figure 22.1; U.S. Census Bureau, 2005). The poverty rate of children has been higher than that of the elderly or of adults during the past four decades.

A snapshot of income status by age groups is poignant. Governmental data indicate that as many as 39% of children, but only 17% of the elderly,

Table 22.7 The Ratio of Income Transfers per Elderly Person and per Adult to Income Transfers per Child

Country	Ratio(65+/0–17)	Ratio(18–64/0–17)
United States	8.12	1.37
Canada	4.82	1.06
United Kingdom	2.40	0.77
France	4.37	1.07
Belgium	3.80	1.04
Germany	4.62	1.09
Netherlands	4.77	1.13
Sweden	2.99	0.97
Denmark	3.03	1.08
Norway	3.79	1.00
Italy	13.28	3.68
Spain	6.76	2.02

SOURCE: Ozawa & Lee (n.d.).

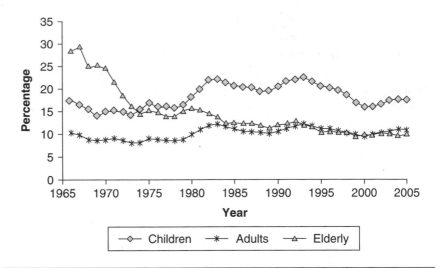

Figure 22.1   The Trend in Poverty Rates of Children, Adults, and Elderly,
1996–2005

SOURCE: U.S. Census Bureau (2005).

are in the bottom quintile of income distribution. Moreover, 48% and 52% of black children and Hispanic children, respectively, are in the bottom quintile (Ozawa, 1998; U.S. Census Bureau, 1994).

These data indicate that the child population is falling behind the adult and elderly populations in terms of poverty and income distribution. This situation is unacceptable in an adequate, effective, and fair Social Security system. It is important to ensure that policy makers and the public understand that there is a direct link between social policy for the elderly and social policy for children.

Although a relatively small number of policy analysts have related the problems of poverty and economic deprivation among children to the problems of Social Security financing, research on the relative deprivation of children in the United States is increasing (Brady, 2004; Gabel & Kamerman, 2006; Garfinkel, Rainwater, & Smeeding, 2006; Gornick, 2006; Lynch, 2001). Input from academic researchers will certainly provide important information to the debate on Social Security reform in the future.

References

Advisory Council on Social Security. (1997). *Report of the 1994–1996 Advisory Council on Social Security: Vol. 1. Findings and recommendations*. Washington, DC: Author.

Altmeyer, A. J. (1966). *The formative years of social security*. Madison: University of Wisconsin Press.

Baggette, J., Shapiro, R. Y., & Jacobs, L. R. (1995). The polls-poll trends: Social security—An update. *Public Opinion Quarterly, 59,* 424–425.

Bosworth, B. (1997). What economic role for the trust funds? In E. R. Kingson & J. H. Shulz (Eds.), *Social security in the 21st century* (pp. 156–177). New York: Oxford University Press.

Brady, D. (2004). Reconsidering the divergence between elderly, child and overall poverty. *Research on Aging, 26,* 487–510.

Burtless, G. (1998, June 18). The role of individual personal saving accounts in social security [Testimony before the Subcommittee on Social Security of the House Committee on Ways and Means. Washington, DC: Government Printing Office.

Carasso, A., Steuerle, C. E., & Reynolds, G. (2007, March 15). *Kids' share 2007.* Washington, DC: Urban Institute. Retrieved February 1, 2008, from http://www.urban.org/url.cfm?ID=411432

Cook, F. L., Barabas, J., & Page, B. J. (2002). Invoking public opinion: Policy elites and social security. *Public Opinion Quarterly 66,* 235–265.

Cook, F. L., & Jacobs, L. R. (2002). Assessing assumptions about Americans' attitudes about social security: Popular claims meet hard data. In P. Edelman & L. D. Salisbury (Eds.), *The future of social insurance* (pp. 82–110). Washington, DC: Brookings Institution Press.

Esping-Andersen, G. (1999). *Social foundation of postindustrial economies.* Oxford, UK: Oxford University Press.

Feldstein, M. (1997, July–August). The case for privatization. *Foreign Affairs, 76,* 24–38.

Feldstein, M., & Samwick, A. (1996). *The transition path in privatizing social security* (Working Paper No. 5761). Cambridge, MA: National Bureau of Economic Research.

Friedland, R. B. (1994). *When support and confidence are at odds: The public's understanding of the Social Security program.* Washington, DC: National Academy of Social Insurance.

Gabel, S. G., & Kamerman, S. B. (2006). Investing in children: Public commitment in twenty-one industrialized countries. *Social Service Review, 80*(2), 239–263.

Garfinkel, I., Rainwater, L., & Smeeding, T. M. (2006). *Welfare state expenditures and the redistribution of well-being: Children, elders, and others in comparative perspective* (Working Paper No. 387). Syracuse, NY: Syracuse University, Maxwell School of Citizenship and Public Affairs.

Gornick, J. (2006). Social expenditures on children and the elderly in OECD countries, 1980–1995. In A. H. Gauthier, C. Y. C. Chu, & S. Tuljapurkar (Eds.), *Allocating public and private resources across generation* (pp. 201–226). New York: Springer.

Gramlich, E. M. (1996a). Different approaches for dealing with social security. *American Economic Review, 86,* 358–362.

Gramlich, E. M. (1996b). Different approaches for dealing with social security. *Journal of Economic Perspectives, 10,* 55–66.

Lynch, J. (2001). The age-orientation of social policy regimes in OECD countries. *Journal of Social Policy, 30,* 411–436.

OASDI (Old Age, Survivors, and Disability Insurance) Board of Trustees. (2006a). *2006 annual report of the Board of Trustees of the federal Old Age and Survivors Insurance and Disability Insurance trust funds.* Washington, DC: Government Printing Office.

OASDI Board of Trustees. (2006b). *Status of the Social Security and Medicare programs: A summary of the 2006 annual reports.* Washington, DC: Government Printing Office.

Organisation for Economic Co-operation and Development. (2001). *OECD social expenditure database 1998–1998* [CD-ROM]. Paris: Author.

Ozawa, M. N. (1984). The 1983 amendments to the Social Security Act: The issue of intergenerational equity. *Social Work, 29,* 131–137.

Ozawa, M. N. (1998). Children's economic place in America. *Journal of Poverty: Innovations on Social, Political & Economic Inequalities, 2*(3), 1–12.

Ozawa, M. N. (2006). Social security. In J. Birren (Ed.), *Encyclopedia of gerontology* (2nd ed., pp. 541–551). London: Elsevier.

Ozawa, M. N., & Lee, Y. S. (n.d.). *The public income transfers for children vs. for the elderly and adults: Inter-country comparison.* Unpublished manuscript, Washington University, St. Louis, MO.

President's Commission to Strengthen Social Security. (2001). *Strengthening social security and creating personal wealth for all Americans.* Washington, DC: Author

Steuerle, C. E. (2003, December). *The incredible shrinking budget for working families and children* (National Budget Issue No. 1). Washington, DC: Urban Institute. Retrieved February 1, 2008, from http://www.urban.org/publications/310914.html

U.S. Census Bureau. (1994). *Survey of income and program participation, 1991.* Washington, DC: Author.

U.S. Census Bureau. (2005). *Historical income tables: Poverty statistics.* Washington, DC: Author.

23

Social Policy and the Elderly

Fernando M. Torres-Gil and Valentine Villa

T he contemporary nature of social policy and the elderly in the United States involves a unique amalgam of history, politics, public benefits, and demographic trends. These factors, in turn, have come to shape public discourse and actions for older persons, caregivers, and all who are approaching old age. Because of population aging, the emergence of elders as a political force, and the pending age wave, issues of social policy for the elderly will continue to be of major domestic concern for much of this century, even more so than in the past.

Social Security, Medicare, and the aging of the baby-boomer cohort highlight the contemporary importance of controversies about how individuals, government, the private sector, and society at large respond to aging and how existing social policies for the elderly will need to be altered and adapted. This chapter examines the factors affecting policies and programs for the elderly and the major issues facing these policies and programs. It describes the historical development of these policies and programs, the politics of aging, and the current set of public entitlements and services for the elderly.

Historical Overview: The Politics of Aging

The United States is unique among nations in the area of social policies predicated on age and in the influence of senior citizens in politics and public policy. In part, this is due to the tripartite American political system (executive, judicial, legislative), which makes for a permeable structure whereby interest groups and organized lobbies can "work the system" toward their own ends. The American sense of a civic culture and, as Alexis de Tocqueville (1835/1945) astutely observed, the tendencies of Americans to be involved in political and social affairs have created a climate whereby organized constituencies can have a powerful influence on laws and political decisions. More than most groups, the elderly exemplify interest group politics and have benefited from a host of entitlements, services, and legislative protections that have given them a prominent place in society. In contrast, nations with parliamentary and authoritarian forms of government do not have a "politics of aging" although many do have generous social welfare programs for the elderly. Although some nations, such as Canada, Denmark, Israel, Australia, and France are beginning to see pensioners mobilize, only the United States has an inextricable link among politics, old age, and social policy developments (Carmel, Morse, & Torres-Gil, 2007).

Population aging is hardening this link. According to the U.S. Bureau of the Census, "Today's older Americans are very different from their predecessors, living longer, having lower rates of disability, achieving higher levels of education and less often living in poverty" (National Institute on Aging [NIA], 2006).

The population aged 65 and over in the United States is expected to double in size within the next 25 years. By 2030, one in every five Americans (72 million people) will be 65 years or older. And as the United States becomes more diverse, a greater proportion of those 65 and older will be from minority populations. By 2030, the 65-plus group will include 11% Hispanic, 10% African American, and 5% Asian (NIA, 2006). Older persons may well continue to be a political force, assuming they continue their high rates of registration and voting (Binstock & Day, 1996).

Historical Developments

The politics of aging represents the coming of age of older persons as a political force and the rise of social policies predicated on age as a primary criterion. This was not always so. Life expectancy at birth was about 35 years when the nation was founded and increased to about 42 years by the mid-1800s (U.S. Bureau of the Census, 1996). Thus, it comes as no surprise that there were few very old people in those societies. Throughout much of human civilization, older persons (who could be in their 40s, depending on life expectancy) were few and privileged. In agrarian societies, those few who survived into old age acquired a measure of status and authority (Williamson, Evans, & Powell, 1982). In large and complex societies such as ancient China, gerontocracies developed where those in power were invariably the very old. Elders with authority were usually men with wealth, and rarely did women (with Sparta being one of the few exceptions) and the poor acquire influence in their old age. The advent of industrialization and modern societies in the 19th and 20th centuries, which was accompanied by movement toward cities and away from rural areas, broke down the inherent advantages of old age. Social mobility, the ascendancy of private property, industrial specialization, and urbanization served to break down customs that respected and valued elders. In these times, individualism and physical abilities became highly prized, and older persons and the disabled were often at the mercy of families, neighbors, and communal organizations.

Throughout history, regardless of whether societies were agrarian or urban and regardless of the extent of gerontocracies, old age was not a basis for collective organizing and political action. The advent of a politics of aging, whereby older persons advocated on behalf of older persons for the purpose of creating old-age laws, is a phenomenon unique to the United States in the last century. While the United States moved from its agrarian roots on the eastern seaboard toward cities and the West, older persons, especially the poor, frail, and those unable to compete, relied for support on the willingness and vagaries of their children, neighbors, and local charities. Poverty among elderly persons without those safety nets was widespread, and, by the 1930s, old age was synonymous with being poor. There were a few exceptions. Civil War veterans and widows did receive pensions, and some industries such as railroads provided retirement benefits (Blanck & Song, 2003). But generally, retirees and the elderly were dependent on others.

The Great Depression created a paradigm shift from historical ambivalence toward elders to the rise of social policies for older persons. The elderly were most vulnerable to the vagaries of economic dislocation and forced migration and found themselves cast adrift. Older persons and middle class families lost their homes, life savings, and a sense of stability. The radicalization of older folks and the subsequent advent of social policies for the elderly took place in the depths of the Great Depression. As early as the 1920s, a group called the Fraternal Order of the Eagles campaigned on behalf of old age pensions. By the 1930s, others followed that example, especially in areas with a high proportion of retirees (Day, 1990). California was a prominent stage upon which both individuals and organizations used the economic problems of older Americans for political organizing. Upton Sinclair's campaign for governor in 1933 with his "end poverty in California" agenda rallied retirees with a promise to provide a $50-per-month pension. The Townsend movement in the early 1930s, based in Long Beach, California, gained national notoriety. Dr. Francis Townsend proposed to give persons 60 and older $200 a month, on condition that it is spent within 30 days (Schulz & Binstock, 2006). Those and other efforts highlighted the isolation and social vulnerability of older folks and gave impetus to President Franklin Roosevelt's proposal for a national social insurance plan. The passage of the Social Security Act of 1935 represented the culmination of historical and demographic forces that gave shape to a social policy predicated, in part, on attaining old age. Paradoxically, the signing of the Social Security Act did not include representatives of the pension movements, whose advocates considered Social Security too tame. In fact, the passage of the Social Security Act had multiple goals: to provide a national safety net, to mitigate radical tendencies, to open up the labor force to younger workers, and to give elderly persons some measure of security. For whatever reasons, the stage was set for the philosophical and political acceptance of age as a basis for eligibility in social policies. Older persons were now considered the "deserving poor," and political organizing around pensions and national attention to the plight of the elderly gave impetus to a politics of aging that would shape social policy for the next 60 years.

Policies and Programs for the Elderly

Since the 1930s, a plethora of policies have been created to serve older persons and their families. They range from entitlement programs to social services to volunteer and advocacy programs, and they involve a separate service delivery system for the elderly. Few other constituency groups (with the possible exception of veterans) enjoy such a dedicated set of programs and benefits, and none has policies predicated on age.

Entitlements

Entitlement programs constitute the bedrock of social policies for the elderly. Social Security, Medicare, and Medicaid guarantee access to benefits, depending on eligibility and contributions, and provide a social safety net for most older Americans and their families. Yet entitlement programs are at the heart of heated political debates about the future of social policies for the elderly.

The Social Security Act of 1935 established the basic federal old-age benefits program and a federal-state system of unemployment insurance (Schulz, 1988). Since its inception, Social Security has come to exemplify a "social contract," whereby older persons expect the federal government (and the public) to provide a measure of retirement security in their old age, regardless of economic circumstances. The Social Security Act has evolved and expanded dramatically in subsequent years. In 1939, survivors' and dependents' benefits were added (Old Age and Survivors Insurance—OASI). In 1956, Social Security was expanded to include disability insurance to protect severely disabled workers (Old Age, Survivors, and Disability Insurance—OASDI). In 1965, Medicare was added, establishing a comprehensive health program for the elderly (Old Age, Survivors, Disability, and Health Insurance—OASDHI). Indexing of earnings used to compute benefits was legislated in 1972 (Schulz, 1988).

In 2007, the tax rate was 6.2% for workers and 6.2% for employers on salaries up to $97,500, with a Medicare tax of 1.45% paid by workers and employers on all salaried income (Social Security and Medicare Board of

Trustees, 2007). By 2006, more than 48 million American's were receiving approximately $539 billion in Social Security benefits. This included 30 million retired workers, 6.5 million disabled workers, and 6.7 million survivors (AARP, 2006).

Medicare and Medicaid, both passed in 1965, constitute a national health care system for older persons and the poor. Medicare is the federal program providing health care insurance for seniors and people with disabilities. Often called Part A (hospital insurance), it provides benefits financed by compulsory payroll taxes (1.45% on all income). Medicare covers all persons age 65 and older who are eligible for Social Security or Railroad Retirement benefits or who are spouses or former spouses of eligible persons. It also covers those under 65 who have been receiving Social Security disability benefits for at least two years or who have end-stage renal (kidney) disease. Supplementary medical insurance, often called Part B, is a voluntary program for non-hospital health care financed by participant premiums ($93.50 per month in 2007) and a matching contribution by the federal government out of general revenue.

A major addition to the Medicare program was the passage of the Medicare Prescription Drug, Improvement, and Modernization Act of 2003. This new drug benefit, Part D of Medicare, offers, for the first time, payments for out-of-pocket prescription drugs and enables Medicare beneficiaries to confront the escalating cost of these drugs (Kaiser Family Foundation, 2004). Yet, it is a complex benefit, with gaps in coverage, and utilizes private insurance plans. Its ultimate success in promoting affordable prescription drug coverage remains uncertain.

Medicaid, enacted in 1965 as Title XIX of the Social Security Act, is a means-tested entitlement program for persons in need. Medicaid is not limited to older persons; rather, it is a state and federally funded program that provides health insurance to persons with low incomes who meet certain eligibility requirements based on income and assets. It pays for health care services deemed "medically necessary," including physician visits, hospital and nursing home care, adult day health services, home health care, and hospice care. While initially intended for the very poor, regardless of age, Medicaid has become a de facto nursing home and long-term care program for older persons who have spent down their assets to qualify. Given the high costs of nursing homes (averaging $40,000 to $80,000 a year), 70% to 80% of the elderly cannot afford to stay in a nursing home (Schulz, 1988). Medicaid will pay for such care when private assets are exhausted. This "spend down" provision has enabled—or forced—middle-income elderly to become impoverished in order to qualify for Medicaid-financed nursing home care (Moody, 2006).

By 2004, Medicare was providing health insurance for 42 million people who were elderly or disabled, and Medicaid provided coverage for 52 million low-income people. Medicare and Medicaid accounted for approximately

$600 billion in that year, making those programs, along with Social Security, an extraordinarily visible segment of national social policy (Smith, Cowan, Heffler, Catlin, & National Health Accounts Team 2006). These entitlement programs affect the lives of most Americans, directly or indirectly, and are thus highly political and personal issues for the elderly, their caregivers, and their families. Medicare and Medicaid also represent an "industrial health complex" that lubricates a huge conglomerate of hospitals, nursing homes, medical suppliers, pharmaceutical companies, and health care professionals. Proposals to restructure these programs, then, become a matter of great national importance and political sensitivity.

Public Benefits and Social Services

While highly visible, Social Security, Medicare, and Medicaid are not the sole components of social policy for the elderly. A host of public benefits and social services provide crucial support to older persons, their families, and caregivers. In particular, two programs have an important impact on the economic and social welfare of the aged. Social Security's Disability Insurance (DI) program and the Supplemental Security Income (SSI) program provide benefits to people who have severe long-term disabilities. The Disability Insurance program became part of the Social Security Act in 1956. Disability protections under the program are provided to disabled insured workers and their dependents, disabled widows and widowers of insured workers, and adult (age 18 or older) sons and daughters, who become disabled before age 22, of insured disabled, retired, or deceased workers (Schulz, 1988). The Supplemental Security Income program (SSI), authorized in 1972 under Title XVI of the Social Security Act, provides cash benefits to aged, blind, or disabled individuals whose income and resources are below certain levels. It is administered by the federal government and financed from general revenues. In 2005, Disability Insurance and Supplemental Security Income together paid about $126 billion annually to 12.8 million disabled beneficiaries (U.S. Government Accountability Office [GAO], 2006).

The Older Americans Act (OAA) of 1965, as amended, constitutes a small but elaborate set of social and supportive services for the elderly. Unlike entitlement programs, the act is administered through a national network of state and local area agencies on aging. The act, funded for approximately $1.8 billion dollars in 2006, authorizes grants to state and community programs for the provision of ombudsman services, legal assistance, housing and transportation services, and employment training, as well as grants to Native American tribes (O'Shaughnessy & Napili, 2006). A popular component of the Older Americans Act is support for congregate and home-delivered meals (Meals on Wheels). The National Family Caregiver Support Program, enacted in 2000, was added to address growing needs in caregiving. Separate housing and transportation subsidies, albeit small in scale, are provided through the Department of Housing and Urban Development and the Department of Transportation. Taken together, these services enable older persons to stay in their homes and communities. The senior citizen centers developed through the Older Americans Act provide a social network and focal point for senior citizens to socialize, eat, and receive a variety of assistance. The prevalence of local and state offices on aging gives older persons an important infrastructure for advocacy, community organizing, and political visibility.

One more important source of social services for older persons is Title XX of the Social Security Act (Social Services Block Grants). In 1974, Title XX was included in the Social Services Amendments to the Social Security Act and authorized funds according to the size of states' populations (Gelfand, 1988). States, in turn, were required to design their own packages of service and define their eligible populations. Among services for the aging provided by Title XX are adult day care, foster care, homemaker services, and in-home supportive services.

Taken together, these benefits and social services constitute a set of social policies that provides a substantial system of services and programs giving older and disabled persons and their families a wide measure of support. State and local governments depend heavily on these federal disbursements to cope with the costs of social services to older persons. Although not all of these policies are strictly age based, older persons benefit immeasurably from their status as a deserving group and their ability to confront elected officials when these programs are threatened with cutbacks.

Volunteer, Advocacy, and Projections

Alongside these social supports lies another set of programs and activities that exemplify the success older persons have enjoyed in seeking public sympathy and crafting social policies. A host of volunteer programs provides older persons with a variety of opportunities to contribute their time and energies to civic activities. The Retired Senior Volunteer Program (RSVP), the Foster Grandparent program, the Senior Companion program, and the Service Corps of Retired Executives (SCORE) enlist and draw upon the talents, experiences, and good will of older persons who wish to help others. Advocacy by the elderly is encouraged and incorporated in many policies, programs, and agencies, including the Older Americas Act, the various state offices on aging, and the efforts of national organizations such as AARP, formerly called the American Association of Retired Persons. Educational programs in gerontology and geriatrics abound at colleges, universities, and medical schools. Travel and education grows in popularity, and Elderhostel remains the preeminent organization for travel and learning among older adults.

In addition, older persons enjoy a variety of legal and civil rights, safeguards, and legal protections. Ageism and fears that people will be discriminated against as they age have led to the passage of laws such as the Age Discrimination Employment Act of 1967 (ADEA). The act provides protections for persons 40 to 70 years of age who are seeking employment. It covers persons in the private and nonfederal sectors; mandatory retirement has been abolished for most federal employees. In 1986, amendments to the Age Discrimination Employment Act outlawed mandatory retirement at the age of 70. Further safeguards are provided through the Americans with Disabilities Act (ADA) of 1990 and the Olmstead case of 1999, a Supreme Court ruling that, under ADA, care should be provided in the least restrictive setting such as in the home or community rather than in a nursing home.

The New Aging: Changes and Pressures on Social Policies

Given this historical and descriptive overview, what do we make of this constellation of policies and programs for the elderly? What does it tell us about the nature of social policy and politics toward the elderly? What are the factors and forces likely to bring change?

Over the last 60 years, older persons have seen the development of an enviable set of benefits, programs, laws, and services. In many ways, social policy for the elderly has been extraordinarily successful. During the Great Depression, poverty rates among the elderly climbed as high as 70%. By 2002, the percentage of older people living in poverty declined to 10% compared to 35% in 1959 (AARP, 2006). Older persons have sophisticated lobbies in Washington, D.C., in state capitals, and in their local communities, and this political influence has given them the ability to promote an expansion of benefits and to protect their programs. However, these programs and services, by their very nature, are also a complex, fragmented, and increasingly controversial component of social policy. Older people and their families, and especially those who are poor, illiterate, and non-English speaking, find it difficult to access the multitude of agencies, eligibility criteria, and forms required to receive services. The proliferation of services and programs has created a vast and unwieldy system. Yet, even with this vast array of programs and services and the expenditures devoted to older persons directly or indirectly, there are still wide gaps. The elderly, for example, find themselves spending the same proportion of their incomes on health care as was the case before Medicare and Medicaid were enacted (Villers Foundation, 1987). Medicaid, SSI, and Title XX do not provide help to middle-income families struggling with the high costs of social, health, and long-term care. Most individuals and families find that home- and community-based services are more necessary and preferable than hospital and nursing home care; yet, unless they qualify for Medicaid or have long-term care insurance coverage, they must take care of themselves or do without. In addition, the move toward the devolution of federal responsibility to state and local governments has led to the consolidation of social services to include programs for older persons, the disabled, and those needing long-term care and thus has eroded the identity of old-age programs. The success of social policies predicated on age and geared toward the elderly, then, has sown the seeds of profound changes.

What does all of this say about the nature of policy and politics toward the elderly? Will public attitudes and social policy continue to support existing programs and benefits for older Americans? What are the forces that may change both the public perception of elderly people and the nature of social policies for older persons?

Several trends have created a major crossroads in the politics and policies of aging. These include the demographic imperative, the graying of the federal budget, the aging of the baby boomers, and generational tensions. Together, these trends are leading toward another paradigm shift in social policy and aging and are moving us into a new historical period in the politics of aging (Torres-Gil, 1992). Earlier periods can be characterized as the *young aging* and the *modern aging* periods. The young aging period (pre-1930) reflected much of human history: older persons, with some exceptions, did not expect or receive age-based support. With the 1930s came the modern aging period, a dramatic growth and acceptance of aged-based social policies. However, we are now witnessing a move toward a *new aging* period. Earlier successes in responding to the needs of older persons stemmed from their economic vulnerability, which elicited public sympathy. During this period, the 1930s to the 1990s, there was little opposition to or concern about expanding programs to the elderly. Their high propensity to vote and sophisticated lobbying made them a powerful force, and, through organizations such as AARP, their lobbying power is recognized alongside other well-known interest groups such as the American Medical Association and the National Rifle Association. By the 1990s, however, public opinion began to show discernible change toward older persons, their entitlements, and their use of political clout. This new trend suggests that a paradigm shift in social policy will be heavily influenced by three forces: longevity, diversity, and generational claims.

Longevity involves life expectancy and a redefinition of old age. Life expectancy at birth was 47 in 1900, but by 2006, it reached 77 years and continues to climb (Moody, 2006). Gender and racial differences remain; women live longer than men and some racial groups have lower life expectancy. Yet we can expect longer life expectancy not only at birth but after reaching the age of 65. The number of centenarians has more than doubled since 1980 (U.S. Bureau of the Census, 1996). This increased longevity is altering social views about old age. Sixty-five years of age is no longer considered "old," and we are seeing healthy and active aging among those 70 to 80 years of age. In the new aging period, we will see a trend to move back the years at which one is considered middle aged and old. At the same time, longevity is forcing a rethinking of eligibility. If we are living longer and healthier lives, does it still make sense to use the age of 65 as an eligibility factor for Medicare, ages 65 to 67 for full benefits under Social Security, age 60 to qualify for services under the Older Americans Act, and age 50 to join AARP?

Diversity relates to the tremendous heterogeneity in the American population. Those differences involve race, ethnicity, and language, as well as economic disparities and lifestyle choices. The growth of minority populations such as Hispanic, Asian/Pacific Islander, African American, and Native American is well documented. This growth will mean a much different America in the next century. For example the percentage of non-Hispanic whites as a proportion of the entire population has dropped from 70% in 2000 to 67% in 2005 (U.S. Bureau of the Census, 2007). The diversification of the United States will also see social and family changes. Women continue to outlive men, and the trends toward fewer children and continued geographic and social mobility will reinforce alternative lifestyles and households. More people will live alone and apart from family members, and three- and four-generation households will also be common. Single-parent families and grandparents caring for grandchildren will abound. The continued prevalence of economic disparities will haunt social policy. More people will do well, but more families will be poor as well. The baby-boom cohort, for example, while a relatively privileged generation socially and economically, has at least one-quarter of its members (out of 75 million) considered "at risk" today because they have failed to accumulate sufficient savings (Congressional Budget Office, 2004). Thus, in the next century, baby-boomer retirees will be both well-off and poor. Economic diversity will further complicate how social policy responds to the needs of an aging population.

It is around generational claims that more immediate controversies and policy debates are taking place. The United States is facing an unprecedented situation in which there are distinct cohorts of age groups within its population. These generations of individuals, born around the same period and sharing historical events and life-long experiences, also tend to have differing views about the role of government and politics in their lives: The New Deal generation is today's elderly and the greatest proponent for Social Security and Medicare. The baby-boomer generation has greater antipathy toward big government, big business, and big labor and has greatly influenced popular culture. Generation X (those born between 1965 and 1976) and Generation Y (born between 1978 and 1989) are today's youth and tomorrow's workers and elders. Thus, generational claims will greatly influence social policy and aging because each cohort may view old age differently and have different views about today's public programs for the elderly. As important, the members of each generation must support their elders' retirement through productivity and taxes and prepare for their own aging.

By the 1990s, generational debates became quite visible because of fears of "generational warfare," charges of generational inequity, and new interest groups, such as the Concord Coalition, Americans for Generational Equality, and the Third Millennium, arguing that the elderly were receiving too much and at the expense of younger generations. Propelling these fears was the growing recognition that longevity and the aging of the baby boomers would put unsustainable pressures on public entitlements. The "graying of the federal budget" had become such that, by 1994, one-third of the federal budget was expended on benefits to older Americans, even though older persons constituted only about 13% of the population. Thus, curtailing the costs of Social Security, Medicare, and Medicaid increasingly consumed the energies of elected officials at the federal and state levels. Generational claims began to exemplify a changing public and political attitude toward the programs of the modern aging period and set the stage for what may be major reforms in Social Security and Medicare.

Contemporary Debates and the Future of Social Policy

Longevity, diversity, and generational claims are interacting with a host of demographic, social, and political forces to reshape our views of old age, of how older persons are viewed as a political force, and of how to promote social policy for the elderly. These changes are reflected in the policy debates around Social Security and Medicare and give important clues about the future direction of social policy. Alarmist reports about Social Security's insolvency raised fears that the social insurance foundation of this entitlement program would be eroded. While Social Security continues to enjoy widespread support among all ages and cohorts, there are still growing concerns that it will be unable to pay benefits to future generations of retirees. At the end of 2005, Old Age and Survivors Insurance had assets of $1.6 trillion (U.S. Social Security Administration, 2007), yet those surpluses will be insufficient for the baby boomers approaching retirement. Although estimates vary, some experts believe that, by 2018, payments to beneficiaries may no longer equal incoming revenues, and the federal government will have to begin repaying interest and principal on treasury bonds. They also believe that, by 2042, the trust funds will be depleted, and new sources of revenue will be needed, although payroll taxes will still provide 75% of needed revenues at that time. Medicare is also facing severe fiscal problems and is already drawing on its trust fund. The continuing rise in health care and nursing home costs and the lack of long-term care will be a severe drain on the public and private sectors when baby boomers become old.

The pressures on Social Security and Medicare have led to a host of dramatic proposals to restructure entitlement programs and revise the "social contract." For the first time in its venerable history, bipartisan support is growing for some form of privatization of Social Security, which may include investing trust funds in the private market and allowing individuals to use part of their payroll taxes for individual security accounts. Although President Bush's efforts to privatize Social Security were defeated by 2006, the trend toward privatizing entitlement programs continues, as seen in the use of income testing for Medicare Part D and the use of private insurance companies. Proposals to raise the eligibility age, impose means testing, increase premiums, and move beneficiaries into managed care continue to gain adherents. State and local governments continue to consolidate and merge old-age services into agencies serving multiple populations.

How these proposals and trends will eventually unfold is uncertain. What is clear is that public attitudes toward the elderly have changed dramatically. Although the public continues to support Social Security, Medicare, and most programs for the elderly (especially the poor elderly), younger cohorts increasingly voice skepticism about receiving benefits, and thus they are more open to ideas of privatization and reforms. Public and private encouragement to save and prepare for one's own retirement is exemplified in the dramatic growth of defined contribution plans, such as 401K plans, and the demise of defined benefit, guaranteed pensions. The vaunted political power of the elderly no longer carries the same collective influence or puts the same pressure on politicians. The heyday of senior power may have been the passage and dismissal of the Medicare Catastrophic Coverage Act of 1988 when, within one year, the Congress passed and repealed legislation to protect seniors from the high cost of health care at the price of higher premiums for upper-income persons. Since then, diversity and a public backlash to the apparent material and economic gains of the elderly have diminished public sympathy for social policies based solely on old age.

What future changes might occur in social policy for the elderly? How might the politics and policies of aging respond to aging in the next century? Any expansion of social policy for the elderly, especially in health and long-term care, may well see the use of need, based on low income, disability (limitations in the activities of daily living or ADL), and old-old age (75 years and older), as the essential criterion. Programs for the elderly may move toward a merging of social services for persons with similar vulnerabilities including the blind, disabled people, and the homeless. Future cohorts of individuals may, in fact, not want to take advantage of old-age programs such as senior citizen centers. Healthy and affluent persons in their 70s and 80s will be more interested in recreation and travel within intergenerational groupings.

This somewhat optimistic scenario, however, cannot detract from a possible return to a politics of aging. If younger cohorts are unable to save and invest well for their retirement, if we face economic recession, if the stock market should perform badly, and if entitlement programs and social, health, and long-term care services are not available for individuals and families in their old age, we may see a return to renewed political demands by future elderly and their families for expanded benefits and programs.

The future of social policy for the elderly remains unclear, but the history and current programs make for a storied and successful model of interest group lobbying and public response to what have been very real needs of older persons. The pressures facing social policies today will force fundamental changes, but the aging of the population and the doubling of older persons will ensure that social policy for the elderly and the politics of aging will remain important elements in social welfare policy.

References

AARP. (2006) *The aging of America. Wow! Quick facts.* Washington, DC: Author.

Binstock, R., & Day, C. (1996). Aging and politics. In R. Binstock & L. George (Eds.), *Handbook of aging and the social sciences* (4th ed., pp. 362–387). New York: Academic Press.

Blanck, P., & Song, C. (2003, February). Never forget what they did here: Civil War pensions for Gettysburg Union Army veterans and disability in nineteenth century America. *William and Mary Law Review, 44*(3), 1109–1171.

Carmel, S., Morse, C., & Torres-Gil, F. (Eds.). (2007). *Lessons on aging from three nations.* Amitville, NY: Baywood.

Congressional Budget Office. (2004, March 18). *The retirement prospects of the baby boomers* (Economic and Budget Issue Brief). Washington, DC: Author.

Day, C. (1990). *What older Americans think: Interest groups and aging policy.* Princeton, NJ: Princeton University Press.

Gelfand, D. (1988). *The aging network: Program and services* (3rd ed.). New York: Springer.

Kaiser Family Foundation. (2004, March). *Medicare: The Medicare prescription drug law: Fact sheet.* Menlo Park, CA: Author.

Moody, H. R. (2006). *Aging: Concepts and controversies* (5th ed.). Thousand Oaks, CA: Pine Forge Press.

National Institute on Aging. (2006, March 9). *Dramatic changes in U.S. aging highlighted in new census, NIH Report.* Retrieved January 28, 2008, from http://www.nia.nih.gov/NewsAndEvents/PressReleases/PR2006030965PlusReport.htm

O'Shaughnessy, C., & Napili, A. (2006). *The Older American Act: Programs, funding, and 2006 reauthorization* (CRS Report for Congress No. RL31336). Washington, DC: Congressional Research Service.

Schulz, J. (1988). *The economics of aging* (4th ed.). Dover, MA: Auburn House.

Schulz, J., & Binstock, R. (2006). *Aging nation: The economics and politics of growing older in America.* Westport, CT: Praeger.

Smith, C., Cowan, C., Heffler, S., Catlin, A., & the National Health Accounts Team. (2006). National health spending in 2004: Recent slowdown led by prescription drug spending. *Health Affairs, 25,* 186–196.

Tocqueville, A. de. (1945). *Democracy in America.* New York: Vintage. (Original work published 1835)

Torres-Gil, F. (1992). Toward a new politics of aging in America. *In-Depth: A Journal for Values and Public Policy, 2*(3), 37–38.

U.S. Bureau of the Census. (1996). *65+ in the United States* (Current Population Reports, Special Studies No. P23-190). Washington, DC: Government Printing Office.

U.S. Bureau of the Census. (2007). Race and Hispanic origin in 2005 [Updated Feb. 2007]. In *Population profile of the United States: Dynamic version* (Internet release). Washington, DC: Government Printing Office. Retrieved February 20, 2008, from http://www.census.gov/population/www/pop-profile/profiledynamic .html

U.S. General Accounting Office (1995, August). *Supplemental Security Income: Disability program vulnerable to applicant fraud when middlemen are used.* Washington, DC: Author.

U.S. General Accounting Office. (1996, October). *Social Security Disability: Alternatives would boost cost-effectiveness of continuing disability reviews.* Washington, DC: Author.

U.S. Government Accountability Office. (2006, October). *Social Security disability programs: Clearer guidance could help SSA apply the Medical Improvement Standard more consistently.* Washington, DC: Author.

U.S. Social Security Administration, Social Security and Medicare Board of Trustees. (2007). *Status of the Social Security and Medicare programs: A summary of the 2007 annual reports.* Baltimore: Author.

Villers Foundation. (1987). *On the other side of easy street: Myths and facts about the economics of old age.* Washington, DC: Author.

Williamson, J., Evans, L., & Powell, L. (1982). *The politics of aging: Power and policy.* Springfield, IL: Charles C Thomas.

24 Social Policy and Health Care

Jennie Jacobs Kronenfeld

Detailed federal involvement in health is a fairly new occurrence in United States history. Although a few laws were passed prior to the 20th century, the bulk of the federal legislation that has health impact has been passed since 1900, and most of it has actually been passed in the past 50 or so years. This chapter focuses on health care in the United States and first reviews the history of federal government involvement in health care and health concerns and surveys some of the major pieces of legislation that link to health, describing both their historical development and, in the second section, their current features. The third section of the chapter discusses the importance in the health care arena of such values as freedom of choice, protection of the private sector, and aversion to socialized models of health care and rationing of care. The fourth section presents some current statistics on health insurance trends and health care costs. The final section discusses current controversies in the health care system about how to restructure health care delivery.

Review of Historical Evolution of Policies

This section reviews the historical evolution of health care policies in the Unites States. It outlines developments before and during World War II, changes in the role of the federal government during the Kennedy and Johnson administrations, and subsequent changes through the 1980s.

Health Care Policy Through the End of World War II

Neither public health nor health care were an important part of the role of the federal government in the period from the founding of the Republic to the time of the Civil War. Most books mark the beginning of federal involvement in health care by the passage of a law in 1798, the Act for the Relief of Sick and Disabled Seamen, which provided for health services for this group by imposing a 200 cent per month tax on seamen's wages to pay for their medical care (Kronenfeld & Whicker, 1984; Lee & Benjamin, 1993). Shortly thereafter, arrangements were made to care for sick and disabled seamen in most major coastal seaports through the building of what later became known as the Merchant Marine hospitals and still later as the Public Health Service hospitals.

Even during and after the Civil War, the role of the federal government in health was only gradually expanded as major changes in the overall involvement of the central government in many activities took place. At other governmental levels, most states began to establish state departments of public health, and by 1909, such agencies were established in all the states. Corresponding to this, local health departments also grew in size and responsibility in most areas. In 1902, a separate health act was passed, clarifying federal health functions and recognizing the expansion of the activities of the Marine Hospital Service by renaming it the Public Health and Marine Service of the United States. This act legitimated the dominant role of the federal government in public health by specifying a system of communications among state and territorial health officers.

One major piece of federal legislation was passed in 1906, the Federal Food and Drugs Act. Although the initial legislation was focused more on regulating the adulteration and misbranding of food and drugs, with an aim of protecting the pocketbook of consumers as much as their health, this act became the basis for most of the present day regulation of testing, marketing, and promotion of both prescription and over-the-counter medications.

Another major piece of legislation was the Maternity and Infancy Act, also known as the Sheppard-Towner Act. This act was passed in 1921 and provided grants to states to help them develop health services for mothers and their children. This legislation has served as a prototype of federal grants-in-aid programs in health. The act proved to be quite controversial, generating criticism and opposition from conservative groups and from medical groups such as the American Medical Association who openly called the Sheppard-Towner Act "an imported socialistic scheme" (Rosenberg, 1992, p. 77). Adding to the controversy of the act was a requirement that services provided under its aegis be available for all residents of a state, regardless of race. This particular piece of legislation was allowed to lapse in 1929, although many of the functions of the Maternity and Infancy Act were resumed under the passage of the Social Security Act in 1935 (Skocpol, 1992; Wallace, Gold, & Oglesby, 1982).

From the 1930s on, the role of the federal government expanded both generally and in health. First with the Depression, then with World War II, and then gradually over the next three decades, major programs were developed to help support the building of hospitals, the training of health personnel, research into important diseases and health care concerns, and, eventually, the provision of insurance and funds for health care. One of the most important pieces of legislation in this period was the Social Security Act of 1935, arguably the most significant piece of domestic legislation related to health passed up to that time. It did not include health care services for the elderly, although early drafts of the legislation had included such provisions. They were removed due to the threatened opposition of the American Medical Association. The act did solidify the principle of federal aid to the states for public health and welfare assistance, as had been started in health by the Shepard-Towner Act, and Titles V and VI included federal grants to the state for maternal and child health, for services for children with disabilities (Title V), and for public health (Title VI). The program for children with disabilities represented a new thrust in federal legislation. Included were demonstration monies that became the foundation of experience for innovative project grants amendments in later legislation.

Consumer protection in the drug arena was further expanded by the passage of the Food, Drug, and Cosmetic Act in 1938. This act required manufacturers to demonstrate the safety of drugs before marketing them. Other programs of the 1930s and early 1940s included a temporary program instituted during World War II to pay for the maternity care of wives of army and navy enlisted men. Some experts have concluded that this program was responsible for an improvement in infant and maternal health during World War II. Although discontinued after the war ended, its success became one factor considered in later debates about national health insurance.

One substantial accomplishment in this era was the beginning of a major role for the federal government in health research. The U.S. Public Health Service Hygienic Laboratory, established in 1901, was converted into the National Institute of Health (NIH) in 1930 with the passage of the Ransdell Act. This act, along with the ongoing activities of the lab, marked a departure from the originally constricted federal role of providing services to merchant seamen or to those directly affected by epidemics. With this act, the federal government edged into general health activities and began a very small role in manpower training (Kronenfeld & Whicker, 1984; Strickland, 1978).

A second act also expanded the federal role in health research. The first categorical institute within the overall NIH framework was created as part of the focus on cancer, which began with the passage of the National Cancer Institute Act in 1937 (Raffel, 1980; Strickland, 1978). The National Cancer Institute (NCI) was authorized to award grants to nongovernmental scientists and institutions, provide fellowships for the training of scientists and clinicians, and fund direct federal government cancer research. Representing a break with tradition, this federal funding of nongovernmental institutions and scientists became a pattern for all federal support of biomedical research.

Federal involvement in the direct provision of health care services for veterans emerged separately. The Veterans Act of 1924 codified and extended the role of the federal government in the provision of health care services to veterans. That act extended medical care to veterans not only for treatment of disabilities associated with military service but also for other conditions requiring hospitalization. Preference was given to veterans who could not afford private care. In 1930, the Veterans Administration was created as an independent U.S. government agency to handle disabled soldiers and other matters related to veterans, such as pensions.

A major piece of legislation, the Public Health Service Act, was passed in 1944 and became the foundation for most public health legislation after World War II, including the large expansion of hospital building funded under the Hill-Burton amendment. The Hill-Burton Act provided grants to assist states to inventory existing hospitals and health centers, to survey the need for the construction of additional health facilities, and, after state surveys were completed, to build new hospitals.

Title IV of the Public Health Service legislation relocated the National Cancer Institute (NCI) to within the Public Health Service, where it became part of the newly created subdivision labeled the National Institutes of Health. The Heart Institute was added as another specific institute in 1946, and, now, there are institutes to deal with most major categories of diseases, as well as ones linked to specific segments of life (the National Institute of Aging and the National Institute of Child Health and Human Development) and for general medical issues also.

Expansion of the Federal Role in Direct Provision of Services During Kennedy–Johnson Years

Many major federal health policy developments occurred during the Kennedy and Johnson years. The most important was the passage of the Medicare and Medicaid programs as amendments to the Social Security Act. The first amendment increasing the federal role in directly paying for health services was the Kerr-Mills Act in 1960, which established a new program of medical assistance for the aged. Federal aid was given to states to pay for medical care for medically indigent people 65 years of age and older. State participation was optional. The program became the forerunner of Medicaid and was implemented in 25 states before the passage of Medicare and Medicaid.

The Social Security Act Amendments of 1965 established the Medicare program, the program of national health insurance for the elderly, through a new title, XVIII. It also established a special program of grants to the states for medical assistance to the poor through Title XIX (Medicaid).

For the Medicare program, part A of the title provided basic protection against the cost of hospital and certain posthospital services. Inpatient hospital services of up to 90 days during any episode of illness and psychiatric and inpatient services for up to 190 days in a lifetime were included. Extended care services, such as nursing home care, were covered for up to 100 days during any episode of illness. Some home health services and hospital outpatient diagnostic services were covered initially (and these areas were expanded over time with new amendments). Part B provided supplemental medical insurance benefits and was a voluntary insurance program, financed by premium payments from enrollees and matching payments from general social security revenues. Initially, enrollment was very high (over 90%), and now it is generally above 98%. Physician and related services, such as x-rays, laboratory tests, supplies, and equipment, were covered, as were additional home health services. Claims and payments were not handled directly by the Social Security Administration but were paid through fiscal intermediaries such as Blue Cross and Blue Shield in many parts of the country. Institutional providers had to meet conditions of participation, such as utilization reviews, that were aimed at ensuring a minimum quality of service. This program is an important departure from many earlier federal health programs in that it provides direct services to citizens through a fiscal intermediary but not through states and localities, as had been the case with many other federal health-related programs. It was consistent with the model of Social Security, however, in which direct payments were sent to individuals from the federal government.

The Medicaid program is more complex in its administrative structure, although it follows the more standard pattern in health care of joint federal-state programs with a matching component in terms of funding. Medicaid was started as a program of medical assistance to public welfare recipients, and participation by any particular state was voluntary. Thus, from the beginning, there was variability in coverage and amount of service funded across the states, as well as in participation.

Under Medicaid, all states were initially required to provide at least five basic services: inpatient hospital care, outpatient hospital services, other laboratory and x-ray services, skilled nursing home services, and physician services. A large number of optional services, such as optometric services, could be made available, along with basic mental health coverage, ambulance transportation, and dental care.

Health Care Policy Changes From 1968 to 1980

Amendments to the Medicare and Medicaid legislation began only a few years after the initial passage of these laws, with many amendments having either the goal of extending the program or the number of services provided or modifying the institutional eligibility requirements and reimbursement schedules. The 1967 amendments featured expanded coverage for durable medical equipment and podiatry, for example. In 1972, new services such as chiropractic and speech pathology were added to Medicare, and family planning services were added to Medicaid. Eligibility was increased by adding persons to Medicare who were eligible for cash benefits under the disability provisions of the Social Security Act for at least 24 months. Additionally, Medicare services were extended to people who required hemodialysis or renal transplants for chronic renal disease, a program later known as the ESRD (end stage renal disease) program.

The 1972 amendments were also the first to address the growing costs of the Medicare program by establishment of Professional Standards Review Organizations (PSROs) to address problems of cost, quality case control, and medical necessity of services.

In 1976 and 1977, a separate agency, the Health Care Financing Administration (HCFA), was established to assume the primary responsibility for implementation of the Medicare and Medicaid programs. Policy changes in the late 1970s focused on antifraud and anti-abuse efforts in 1977 and cost control measures in 1978. Details are available from other sources (Kronenfeld, 1997; Longest, 1994). The 1980 Omnibus Budget Reconciliation Act or OBRA '80 included extensive modifications in Medicare and Medicaid, with 57 separate sections, many focused on controlling costs.

Two important programs dealt with education for health professionals and mental health concerns. The Health Professions Educational Assistance Act of 1963 authorized direct federal aid mostly in the form of construction aid to medical, dental, pharmacy, and other health professional schools, as well as scholarship and student loan aid to the students in the schools. In the mental health area, the 1963 Mental Retardation Facilities and Community Mental Health Centers Construction Act provided assistance through grants for construction of research centers and grants for facilities for persons with developmental disabilities. In addition, assistance was provided for construction of community health centers.

The basic Public Health Service legislation (although passed in 1944) has been amended many times, with new responsibilities added and old ones deleted. Constant shifting and changing of the organizational structure and location of the service has continued from 1967 to the present day, reflecting the crisis-oriented development of health policy. A typical response to a problem, either new or newly articulated, is to create a new bureau, restructure a bureau, or move a bureau around. Restructuring is further driven by the turnover of presidential administrations and political appointees within the bureaucracy. New administrations enter with fresh ideas about how to reorganize the bureaucracy in a hopefully more rational manner. As an example, the 12 years between 1967 and 1979 saw eight major reorganizations of the Public Health Service and related federal health activity. Tracing all of these detailed shifts can become tedious and is well covered in books that focus on this topic (Kronenfeld, 1997; Kronenfeld & Whicker, 1984; Longest, 1994; Raffel, 1980).

The division of the Public Health Service the least affected by organizational relocation and structural turmoil has been the National Institutes of

Health. Most of the changes there have been the addition of new functions and new institutes in additional research areas. Although the creation of each new institute has involved the movement of some grants and research away from older institutes, reorganizational shifts have been minimal compared to those in some of the other divisions. Not totally coincidental, research promulgated and funded by this division has been regarded as one of the more successful areas of national health policy.

One interesting fact about many of the new programs enacted during this time is that few, even including ones such as Medicaid, were directly administered by the federal government. Medicare was one of the very few exceptions. Many of the other programs involved grants to states or to private health-related agencies. Grant-in-aid programs grew during the Johnson administration (excluding Medicare and Social Security) from 7 billion dollars at the beginning of the presidency of John F. Kennedy in 1961 to 24 billion in 1970 (Lee & Benjamin, 1993). These programs became the prototypes for federal government involvement in health care. Federal funds for biomedical research, health personnel development funds, hospital construction funds, health care financing, and a large range of categorical programs all grew in this time, one of an expanding role for the federal government in health care.

_____ Current Programs and Administrative Features

This section reviews how current health care policies developed during the Reagan, Bush, Clinton, and George W. Bush administrations.

Reagan Administration Efforts

The series of amendments in Medicare and Medicaid noted above set the stage for the Reagan administration's efforts in health. Reagan pushed for a significant reduction in federal domestic social expenditures, including health care. Revenue sharing funds were eliminated, and block grants were created for what had been many separate category-specific programs (Lee & Benjamin, 1993). The Omnibus Budget and Reconciliation Act of 1981 included extensive budget reductions and program revisions for the Public Health Service. One major change was a move away from specific categorical grants dealing with special programs and diseases to the consolidation of these programs under block grants. Budget cuts were included in the block grant process. Total funding for the programs in each block grant was reduced by 21%. Given inflation, the real size of the cut was probably closer to 30%.

Concern over rapidly rising costs led to hospital care reimbursement by diagnosis-related groups (DRGs), a Medicare hospital payment reform that increased the amount of federal regulation of hospitals as a way to control costs, despite the plan being a regulatory solution at odds with much of the philosophical orientation of the Reagan presidency. The new system based payments to hospitals on predetermined rates per discharge for diagnosis-related groups as contrasted to the earlier cost-based system of reimbursement.

A recent summary of this system argues that inpatient hospital care use declined initially and then stabilized in 1987 while outpatient hospital care continued to increase, as did costs for physician care (Edwards & Fisher, 1989). Many analysts contend that piecemeal reforms of the health care system generally lead to disappointing results after a few years.

The other major area of reform within the Medicare program has been control of physician costs through a new physician payment program. Although begun in 1989, the legislation was implemented in the 1990s. The Health Care Finance Administration was directed to begin implementing a resource-based relative value scale (RBRVS) using a system initially developed by Hsiao (Hsiao, Yntema, Braun, & Becker, 1988). Previously, physicians had been paid based on what their charges were for various services. By 1996, payments for family physicians were increased by almost 30%, whereas payments for procedure-oriented specialties dropped a similar amount (McIlrath, 1991). Changes were gradual from 1992 to 1996. The implementation of this new payment program led some physicians to argue that the health care system was becoming increasingly bureaucratic and was limiting the options for practice in the name of cost control.

More in line with the overall philosophy of his adminstration, health planning was eliminated under Reagan. The Omnibus Budget and Reconciliation Act of 1981 also included an elimination of all federal funds for Health Maintenance Organizations (HMOs). All new HMO funds were eliminated in 1982. This may also appear a contradictory move, given the emphasis in the Reagan administration on a pro-competition model of health care. The stance of the Reagan administration, however, was that federal funds were unnecessary to stimulate competition and that private market forces would be sufficient to facilitate HMO growth. Renamed and broadened to manage care, this type of organization has continued to grow, and growth accelerated in the second half of the Clinton years.

Implications of Changes During the Reagan–Bush Administrations

The period from 1969 until the present has been an era of controversy regarding the appropriate role of the federal government in health care. This was especially true during the G. H. W. Bush term and the first term of Clinton due to the pressure of the growing federal debt and the need to constrain growth in all government programs, including health care. The conflict included more than Medicare and Medicaid because the federal role in funding training and development of health professionals had grown from a minuscule one to a substantially greater effort by the late 1970s. Expansion of the federal role ended, however, and substantial retrenchment began with the Reagan administration.

The amendments to the Public Health Service Act again illustrate the turmoil and rapid changes that have occurred at times in both health legislation and health agency structure. Instability has undercut the development of a coherent and chronologically consistent federal policy. Often, shifts in administration, as with the shift to the Reagan administration, have changed the role of the federal government vis-à-vis states, local governments, and private health-related organizations. During the 1980s, the federal government moved, in a relatively short span, from being supportive of HMOs through financial and organizational assistance to a more neutral role in terms of actual support, even though the approach was still viewed positively by many in important health policy positions within the administration. While the federal categorical grant programs had encouraged local health departments to develop a multitude of specialized and separately organized programs, often independent of the state health department, the block grant procedure forced local health departments to work through their state units and encouraged consolidation rather than separation of program functions. These federally required rapid shifts in program focus and in state-local relationships have been deleterious to ongoing continuity in agencies and to smooth administrative functioning. Chaotic federal changes have led to a public perception that state and local health officials are ineffective managers. In reality, the atmosphere of chaotic changes and crisis development of policy is federal in origin.

Clinton and George W. Bush Achievements and Failures

Clinton won election to the presidency initially in November 1992, and he started a discussion of health care reform with a goal of improving access to health care for all while containing costs. To accomplish this, a special task force was created. Although the creation of such a task force could have been productive, most experts now agree that the task force became problematic, with the attempt at openness and discussion backfiring (Blendon, Brodie, & Benson, 1995; Kronenfeld, 1997; Starr, 1994). The public became confused, the initial momentum needed to push reform was lost, and negative ads by some interest groups further lowered the chances of the reform plan passing (Johnson & Broder, 1996).

Although major health care reform did not pass, some new health-related legislation was passed in the 1990s under President Clinton, and a smaller amount became law more recently under President George W. Bush. Overall, in the G. W. Bush administration, there was very little attention paid to health care, partially because of the focus on terrorism and security after the September 11, 2001 attacks on the World Trade Center in

New York City and the Pentagon in Washington, D.C. The major piece of legislation under Clinton was the State Children's Health Insurance Program (SCHIP), and under Bush, it was the Medicare Prescription Drug, Improvement, and Modernization Act. These two are discussed in more detail following the general discussion of Clinton and G. W. Bush administration successes and failures. Some new legislation saw the creation of a commission to deal with border health issues. A Freedom of Access to Clinic Entrances law was passed for abortion clinics. Definitions of dietary supplements were clarified by new legislation, and small changes in Medicare and Medicaid (often clarifying benefits and improving fraud control efforts) were passed under Clinton. Federal health, primary care, and prevention programs were consolidated by a new Health Centers Consolidation Act in 1996. The Ryan White CARE Act that deals with AIDS was expanded. Minor improvements in mental health care access were passed, requiring that annual lifetime caps on mental health benefits be the same as those for physical illness. Another law prohibited employers who offer health insurance from excluding an employee because that specific person has very high health care expenses, and it removed the problem of people receiving limited coverage because of preexisting conditions when they switch jobs and therefore health insurance. The HIPAA or Health Insurance Portability and Accountability Act of 1996 was another important new piece of legislation that had the goal of improving efficiency in health care delivery by standardizing electronic data interchange and providing protection of patient confidentiality. This legislation has led to some sweeping changes in health care administrative information systems and the release of information to the general public and clergy about people in hospitals, although experts differ on whether these administrative changes have impacted patient care overall.

One of the trends in health care over the past decade has been the growth of managed care in all parts of the country and the questioning of such care (Kleinke, 1998; Rauber, 1998; Robinson, 2001). Terms are not always clear in the HMO-managed care areas, but managed care is a broader term that covers point of enrollment plans and preferred provider plans. This includes the switch of many state Medicaid programs to a managed care approach and the encouragement of managed care within the Medicare program. Consumer satisfaction has been declining, however. Consumers have expressed concern about care that is denied, inability to see specialists, and limitations on certain drugs. Kleinke (1998) argues that the profitability that gave rise to the growth of large, national, for-profit managed care companies, which were expanded in the 1980s as a way to deal with rising health care costs and then continued after the failure of Clinton health care reform, has only been temporary. One piece of legislation related to managed care passed under Clinton to deal with some of the concerns of the public about the growth of managed care after the failure of major health care reform. It was a bill that required health insurance companies to allow overnight hospital stays for maternity visits.

Profits have begun to decline and managed care now appears to have fewer solutions regarding successful cost control than was once believed (Rauber, 1998). There has been discussion of a managed care backlash and the end of managed care (Gold, 1999; Mechanic, 2001; Robinson, 2001). Robinson has argued that managed care can be characterized as "an economic success but a political failure" (Robinson, 2001, p. 2622). By this, he means that the image of comprehensive benefits has conflicted with the reality of restricted access and has ended up making patients and providers unhappy. Despite these concerns, managed care remains an important way in which care is delivered and is estimated to provide health services to 85% of insured employees (Kuttner, 1999) and to over half of all Medicaid recipients (Rosenbaum, 2003).

State Child Health Insurance Program (SCHIP)

The largest expansion of health coverage since the passage of Medicare and Medicaid in 1965 is the State Child Health Insurance Program, created by the Balanced Budget Act of 1997 under President Clinton. Over five years, beginning in fiscal year 1998, 24 billion dollars became available to cover health care for children. Some sources estimated that free or low cost health insurance became available to almost half of the nation's children (Kilborn, 1997). More recently, estimates are that more than half of the nation's children are now eligible for SCHIP. As with Medicaid, this is a joint federal-state program, and states had several options as to how to implement the plan. States could use funds to expand Medicaid eligibility, set up a "stand-alone" program, or combine the two approaches. Some states have mostly added more children to Medicaid, especially those whose families earn too much to qualify for cash welfare benefits. Other states have added many children of the working poor, a number of states have added children whose families earn up to 300% of the federal poverty level, and one state (New Jersey) covers children whose families earn up to 350% of the federal poverty level. States can also set up special programs or require children to enter managed care plans. States have great flexibility in the ages of children covered, the income limitations applied, and the application process (Kronenfeld, 2006). Over 2 million children were enrolled in SCHIP programs by May 2000 (Friedrich, 2000). Although most experts agree that, as with Medicaid, not all eligible children are enrolled, the program has increased health insurance coverage rates among children and therefore improved access to care (Aston, 1998; Kronenfeld, 2006; Reschovsky & Cunningham, 1998). An examination of coverage rates for children using 2005 Current Population Survey data reported that 74% of all uninsured children are eligible for coverage through Medicaid or SCHIP, although not all of these are enrolled (Dubay, Holahan, & Cook, 2007). The percentage of children without health care coverage has decreased since the implementation of the SCHIP program.

One essential activity for the second Bush administration was the need in 2007 to pass legislation to reauthorize the program, and there was controversy over this because the Bush administration proposed only covering children up to 200% of the federal poverty level (Pear, 2007). Although the SCHIP program needed reauthorization in 2007, the attempt to pass the reauthorizations with some expansions in coverage failed, due to presidential vetoes of the legislation at the end of 2007. The program continues to be funded, however, through continuing resolutions, without the expansions proposed by the Democrats in Congress. A more detailed consideration of major modifications in this program will be left for the next Congress, after the 2008 presidential elections.

Medicare Prescription Drug, Improvement, and Modernization Act

This legislation, which passed in 2003, has been described as the largest addition to the Medicare program since its initial establishment, although, as with SCHIP, this legislation represents an incremental type of reform that helps certain groups of people; it is not a major overhaul of the health care system such as was proposed in the first Clinton term. Experts believe that this legislation passed near the end of Bush's first term due to the desire of the Bush administration to have some type of health care policy success. This plan is quite complicated, however, with a variety of different plans available depending upon the state in which a Medicare recipient resides and with complex variation in costs of the plan depending upon the income of the elderly as well as what medications they are currently using. Given this variety, in the initial sign-up period, many elderly were confused about options and upset about the complexity of choosing a plan. Several major criticisms of this legislation exist. One is that it did not allow Medicare to use its purchasing power to negotiate discounted drug prices for the elderly but instead used private insurance plans that vary by state as the mechanism of implementation of the program. This has been viewed as an inappropriate payoff to powerful pharmaceutical interests (Mechanic, 2006). Another critique is a gap in benefit coverage often called the *doughnut hole* that leaves people who have high but not the highest drug costs without coverage for part of the year. The motivation for this aspect of the policy was to keep costs down. A recent analysis argues that the vast majority of Medicare beneficiaries in 2007 and in 2006 will have a coverage gap (Cubanski & Neuman, 2007). Other aspects of the legislation increased costs, however, by providing subsidies to private health plans to encourage them to offer prescription drug coverage and also to employers to encourage them to retain coverage already being provided to their retirees (Mechanic, 2006).

Political, Social, and Economic Factors That Influence Health Care

Many different types of factors influence the organization of health care. Health care policy is part of broad social policy, and the overall beliefs of the country are reflected in its health care system. In the past, certain values have been central to the health care system. These have included a right to choice of provider, a basic principle in the early Medicare legislation; protection of the private sector; and an aversion to "socialized" models of care, which are seen to exist in other countries such as Great Britain, and to the concept of rationing of care. Another important value has been an emphasis on technology.

The growth of managed care has already changed the concept of the right to choose a provider, as has the importance of employment-based insurance and the push by employers to limit their costs for health insurance. Many employers now offer only one plan, and many of these plans limit choice of provider. These trends have not led to the elimination of the private sector involvement in health care, and, in fact, the past decade has seen a growth of for-profit companies in the HMO field and in the hospital field. The protection of the private sector of health care providers has continued in this way except for physicians. Some experts think that a majority of physicians by 2020 will work for groups rather than being self-employed, as most physicians were in 1950. This is one area in which the health care system is currently evolving.

Given the basic ideological orientation of the United States toward capitalism and the greater emphasis on the independent role of local and state governmental units, an emphasis on avoiding a centralized or government-controlled medical care system is not surprising. Unlike the citizens of other countries with capitalist economies, all with some form of comprehensive, universal health insurance, Americans have not viewed this form of health coverage as a value or desire for most of the last half century. Similarly, rationing as a way to allocate limited resources is not a popular idea here. Instead of explicit rationing, the allocation of health care resources relies on implicit rationing based on the possession of health insurance, a good job (with health insurance), and income that enables the purchase of noninsurance-supported care.

Last, the culture has long been enamored of new technology in many areas. This is also true in health care. The United States has the most technologically sophisticated health care, and this is more widely available (to people who can afford it) than carefully controlled. Whether the health care system of the future will continue to reflect high technology is not clear. One way to control costs is to limit access to the most expensive technology, and this is an unsolved health care system dilemma.

Health Insurance and Health Care Costs

Because the costs of health care are increasing, a subject too large to be covered in any detail in this chapter, the costs of health insurance are increasing and more Americans are either losing coverage at their workplace or paying much higher costs for health care insurance. In 2000, about 40 million Americans did not have health insurance, a figure that increased to 45 million by 2004, and 46.6 million people in 2005 or about 18% of the population under 65 (almost all people 65 and over have coverage through the Medicare program). As a percentage of the overall population, the percentage without health insurance increased slightly from 2004 to 2005, from 15.6 percent to 15.9 percent (Denavas-Walt, Proctor, & Lee, 2006; U.S. Census Bureau, 2006). The percentage of people with employment-based health insurance continues to decline a bit each year, and was 59.5 percent in 2005. Ethnicity plays an important role in variation in health insurance coverage, with one-third of Hispanics and one-quarter of Native Americans uncovered. About 21% of African Americans are uncovered versus only 11% of white Americans (Denavas-Walt, Proctor, & Lee, 2006; Holohan & Cook, 2006). Rates of coverage also vary by state, partially because Medicaid (the program that covers some of the poor) is more generous in some states than in others. People in the South and Southwest are twice as likely to be uninsured as those in better-covered regions, such as the Upper Midwest.

Results from the *Employer Health Benefits 2004: Annual Survey* and the 2006 data help to demonstrate some of the current concerns in health care insurance coverage and rising costs both to employees and employers (Clemans-Cope, Garrett, & Hoffman, 2006; Gabel et al., 2004). Employee-sponsored health insurance premiums have been continuing to increase, although the rate of increase has moderated over the last three years. In 2004, premiums increased an average of 11.2%. The rate of increase was 9.2% in 2005 and 7.7% from 2005 to 2006. Thus, there is some improvement in the rate of increase for each of these three years, but there remains a sign of continuing problems with rising health insurance rates. While the rate of increase is down from the double-digit rates of increase from 2000 to 2004, this has been a period of low overall inflation in the U.S. economy (Gabel et al., 2004). Premiums have continued to increase much faster than overall inflation (3.5 %) and wage gains (3.8 %) (Clemans-Cope, Garrett, & Hoffman, 2006). Another way to view this trend is that, from 2001 to 2004, health insurance premiums have increased 59%, employee contributions have increased 57% for single coverage and 49% for family coverage, and the percentage of workers covered by their own employer's health insurance plan has decreased from 69% in 2000 to 61% in 2006.

The costs of obtaining health care are on the rise for the typical American, and the costs of health insurance coverage represent a very real expense, in addition to payments required for visits to doctors, hospitals, or for prescription and nonprescription drugs. The average monthly cost of single coverage in the recent employer health benefits survey was over $50 a month or over $600 a year. For family coverage, the cost is much higher, averaging over $250 a month or almost $3,000 a year. This is a rough average for the amount that employees actually pay. The amount employees actually pay varies widely, based on the benefits that particular employers provide. Although it is difficult to generalize about all employers, typically, more of the cost of the individual's coverage is provided than is that of the family's. Often, larger firms cover more of the cost. The dollar amount mentioned above is what the employee pays not the overall costs of the health insurance coverage. That figure is much higher, about $4,242 for single coverage in all plans and $11,480 for family coverage in all plans. These are the estimated overall costs of these types of health insurance coverage, a substantial figure (Gabel et al., 2004).

Current Controversies: Access, Costs, _____ Medicare and Medicaid, and the Structure of Care

What is likely to happen to the U.S. health care system in the future? What will be the federal role? Most of the major problems of the health care system that were discussed in 1992, at the beginning of the debate about major health care reform, still remain almost 15 years later. Some incremental reforms have been passed, of which the child health provisions and the Medicare prescription drug benefit may have the largest impact on access to care, but major overall reform or restructuring of the health care system has not occurred. Some reports indicate that lack of health insurance is growing among adults, although down some among children. The failure to pass major reform legislation has not caused major problems to disappear. Access to health care is still a substantial issue, fears of increased costs abound, and problems in the funding of Medicare and Medicaid are real.

Given the presence of divided government for the second half of Bush's second term (one party in the White House, another controlling both branches of Congress), most experts have not believed that major federally led changes in health care would occur. In fact, the 2006 off-year election was more of a referendum on the Iraq War than an election with discussion of domestic policy concerns, including health. A Kaiser Family Foundation poll in October 2006, before the election that resulted in the Democrats retaking control of Congress, found that, although 46% of voters said they were very worried about having to pay more for their health care, a figure putting worries about the cost of health care at the top of voters' personal worries, Iraq dominated the overall concerns of voters. When people were asked to report the most important election issue, 30% chose the war in Iraq, with health care and the economy both a distant second at 15% each (Kaiser Family Foundation, 2006).

Not all changes in the health care system come from federal legislation. Some experts believe that, in the past decade, we have observed major restructuring led not by federal legislation but by reaction to the need to cut costs and control growth. Relationships in the health care market are in the midst of major changes. Competitive market forces have been dominating the system. Two important aspects of this restructuring are continued changes in our views about HMOs and managed care and the emergence of new organizational structures among physicians, hospitals, and insurers that is resulting in a redefinition of the role of the hospital ("Complexity Defines Relationships," 1996).

Several different health policy experts have argued that the current situation provides special contradictions. Employers of all sizes have reduced the choice of health care plans available to their workers. Traditional fee-for-service medicine is on the decline, but now, this decline is due to pushes from the marketplace rather than pushes from government. One health policy expert argues that "what we're getting is managed care but without the consumer protection and patients' rights that people have a right to expect" (Starr as quoted in Toner, 1996). As Drew Altman, president of the Kaiser Foundation, states, "There are a lot of people out there who feel, or should feel, that they fought off the government monster only to find themselves faced with changes in the marketplace that they care about a lot more" (as quoted in Toner, 1996).

This chapter has mentioned some current trends in managed care and competition. None of these trends or solutions will resolve one of the major concerns that began the health care reform debate in 1992, problems in access to care. That these trends will even hold down rising costs in health care now appears unlikely. In Medicare, the aging of the population and the growth in the number of the elderly insured by Medicare will represent a major pressure point on the health care delivery system, even with some short-term reforms in Medicare financing. Some of those reforms (limitations on payments to hospitals and HMOs) may cause financial and thus perhaps quality problems. Current estimates are that, over the next decade, health care spending will double from today's level and consume almost 20 cents of every dollar spent (Poisal et al., 2007).

Public opinion data demonstrate that most Americans see health care and insurance costs as the top health care concern (Kaiser Family Foundation, 2006). Other surveys show that a majority of Americans believe that the health care needs of children and the elderly are not being met despite SCHIP and the recently enacted drug benefit for Medicare (Berk, Schur, Chang, Knight, & Kleinman, 2004). About 59% of adults did not believe the health care needs of children were being addressed, and 67% did not believe that the health care needs of the elderly were being met. In a democracy, at some point, public opinion and public attitudes should result in public policy changes, but the movement from public concern about an issue to new legislation is not simple, sure, or fast. Although rising costs of health care and rising rates for health insurance are likely, at some point in the future, to lead to greater demand for major change in health care, such comprehensive reform is uncommon and difficult to achieve. During the second term of President George W. Bush, major health care reform seems most unlikely. The rising federal deficit, the commitment to the tax cut and its impact on overall federal revenues, the high spending on the war in Iraq and on approaches to deal with terrorism, as well as a general philosophical commitment to less rather than more government makes major overall health care reform led at the federal level unlikely for the rest of the Bush term.

In a recent book, Quadagno (2005) argues that the fight to enact some type of national health insurance in the United State has generally been a one-sided contest that reformers have perennially lost. She argues that the best chance for reform in the future is a three-tiered coalition: national leadership at the top would be responsible for mapping out a grand plan; at the middle level, coalitions such as senior citizens groups, state labor coalitions, and others would disseminate the ideas for reform; and, at the local level, grassroots efforts would relate to and inform the political groups at the top or the mid-level organizations that influence state and local level politics. She sees a greater chance of such a coalition occurring as people's fears of being uninsured and concerns about members of their extended family being uninsured rise, giving people a motivation to want reform.

Experts differ on how likely they think it is that the United States will enact major health care reform or on whether changes will need to come with small steps, such as the recent measures that added coverage for some children and improved drug coverage for the elderly. There is another option: individual states can enact health reform laws. This legislation can serve two functions: it can benefit a state's residents while serving as a blueprint for future national reforms. Massachusetts has just passed legislation supposed to guarantee coverage for virtually all residents of Massachusetts by July 2007, including about 550,000 people in the state currently not insured. The legislation will provide subsidies and sliding-scale premiums to encourage the poor and those with low incomes to sign up for a plan. Current state funds that are being used to pay for free care for the uncovered will help subsidize insurance. If this program is successful, it might become a model for future national-level reform. California Governor Arnold Schwarzenegger has recently suggested exploring a similar program in that state. Calls to extend care to all children in the state have occurred in New York, Illinois, and Pennsylvania. Any major national reform will probably not happen during the rest of the George W. Bush administration, despite some proposals by President Bush that would focus on a market-based health insurance reform approach and some Democratic proposals that would focus on making a Medicare-type benefit available to all. It is more likely that health care reform may become a major part of the political debate in the choosing of the next president in 2008, and depending on the outcome of that election, there may be more pushes for major reform. Whether major reform and overhaul of the health care system will occur after that depends a great deal on overall political trends in the United States.

References

Aston, G. (1998, June 5). Getting insurance for kids. *American Medical News*, pp. 5–6.

Berk, M. L., Schur, C. L., Chang, D. I., Knight, E. K., & Kleinman, L. C. (2004, September 14). Americans' views about the adequacy of health care for the children and elderly. *Health Affairs* [Web Exclusive No. W4-446]. Retrieved February 1, 2008, from http://content.healthaffairs.org/cgi/content/full/hlthaff.w4.446/DC1

Blendon, R. J., Brodie, M., & Benson, J. (1995). What happened to Americans' support for the Clinton health plan? *Health Affairs, 14*, 7–23.

Clemens-Cope, L., Garrett, B., & Hoffman, C. (2006). *Changes in employees' health insurance coverage, 2001–2005* (Kaiser Commission on Medicaid and the Uninsured Issue Paper No. 7570). Retrieved February 1, 2008, from http://www.kff.org/uninsured/7570.cfm

Complexity defines relationships in increasingly competitive marketplaces. (1996, November). *Health Care Financing and Organization News and Progress*, pp. 1–4. (Available from the Alpha Center, Washington, DC)

Cubanski, J., & Neuman, P. (2007). Status report on Medicare enrollment in 2006: Analysis of plan-specific market share and coverage. *Health Affairs, 26*(1), w1–w12.

Denavas-Walt, C., Proctor, B. D., & Lee, C. H. (2006). *Income, poverty and health insurance coverage in the United States, 2005* (U.S. Census Bureau Current Population Reports No. P60–231). Washington, DC: Government Printing Office.

Dubay, L., Holahan, J., & Cook, A. (2007). The uninsured and the affordability of health insurance coverage. *Health Affairs, 26*(1), w22–w30.

Edwards, W. O., & Fisher, C. R. (1989). Medicare physician and hospital utilization and expenditure trends. *Health Care Financing Review, 11*, 111–116.

Friedrich, M. J. (2000). Medically underserved children need more than insurance card. *Journal of the American Medical Association, 283*, 3056–3057.

Gabel, J., Claxton, G., Gil, I., Pickreign, J., Whitmore, H., Holve, E., et al. (2004). Health benefits in 2004: Four years of double-digit premium increases take their toll on coverage. *Health Affairs, 23*(5), 200–209.

Gold, M. (1999). The changing U.S. health care system: Challenges for responsible public policy. *The Milbank Quarterly, 77*, 3–37.

Holohan, J., & Cook, A. (2006). *Why did the number of uninsured continue to increase in 2005?* (Kaiser Commission on Medicaid and the Uninsured Issue Paper No. 7571). Menlo Park, CA: Kaiser Family Foundation. Retrieved February 1, 2008, from http://www.kff.org/uninsured/7571.cfm

Hsiao, W. C., Yntema, D. B., Braun, P., & Becker, E. (1988). Resource-based relative values: An overview. *Journal of the American Medical Association, 260*, 2347–2353.

Johnson, H., & Broder, D. S. (1996). *The system: The American way of politics at the breaking point*. Boston: Little, Brown.

Kaiser Family Foundation. (2006). *Health poll report survey: Voters on health care and the 2006 elections*. Menlo Park, CA: Kaiser Family Foundation. Retrieved February 1, 2008, from http://www.kff.org/kaiserpolls/pomr102306pkg.cfm

Kilborn, P. T. (1997, September 21). States to provide health insurance to more children. *The New York Times*, pp. 1, 22.

Kleinke, J. D. (1998). *Bleeding edge: The business of health care in the new century.* Gaithersburg, MD: Aspen Press.

Kronenfeld, J. J. (1997). *The changing federal role in U.S. health care policy.* Westport, CT: Praeger.

Kronenfeld, J. J. (2006). *Expansion of publicly funded health insurance in the United States.* Lanham, MD: Lexington Books.

Kronenfeld, J. J., & Whicker, M. L. (1984). *U.S. national health policy: An analysis of the federal role.* New York: Praeger.

Kuttner, R. (1999). The American health care system: Employee-sponsored health coverage. *New England Journal of Medicine, 340,* 248–252.

Lee, P. R., & Benjamin, A. E. (1993). Health policy and the politics of health care. In S. J. Williams & P. R. Torrens (Eds.), *Introduction to health services* (4th ed., pp. 399–420). Albany, NY: Delmar.

Longest, B. B., Jr. (1994). *Health policymaking in the United States.* Ann Arbor, MI: AUPHA Press.

McIlrath, S. (1996, December). HCFA issues final RBRVS rules. *American Medical News,* pp. 1, 26–47.

Mechanic, D. (2001). The managed care backlash: Perceptions and rhetoric in health care policy and the potential for health care reform. *Milbank Quarterly, 79,* 35–54.

Mechanic, D. (2006). *The truth about health care: Why reform is not working in America.* New Brunswick, NJ: Rutgers University Press.

Pear, R. (2007, February 27). Child health care splits White House and states. *New York Times,* p. A1. Retrieved February 1, 2008, from http://www.nytimes.com/2007/02/27/washington/27govs.html

Poisal, J. A., Truffer, C., Smith, S., Sisko, A., Cowan, C., Kecha, S., et al. (2007, March/April). Health care spending projections through 2016: Modest changes obscure Part D's impact." *Health Affairs, 26*(2), w242–w253.

Quadagno, J. (2005). *One nation uninsured: Why the U.S. has no national health insurance.* New York: Oxford University Press.

Raffel, M. W. (1980). *The U.S. health system: Origins and functions.* New York: John Wiley and Sons.

Rauber, C. (1998, October 19). Evolution or extinction: Experts say HMOs must reinvent themselves if they are to survive. *Modern Healthcare, 28*(42), 36–40.

Reschovsky, J. D., & Cunningham, P. J. (1998, August). *CHIPing away at the problem of uninsured children* (Issue Brief No. 14). Washington, DC: Center for Studying Health System Change.

Robinson, J. C. (2001). The end of managed care. *Journal of the American Medical Association, 285,* 2622–2628.

Rosenbaum, S. (2003). Racial and ethnic disparities in health care: Issues in the design, structure, and administration of federal health care financing programs. In B. D. Smedley, A. Y. Stith, & A. R. Nelson (Eds.), *Unequal treatment: Confronting racial and ethnic disparities in health care* (pp. 664–698). Washington, DC: National Academy Press.

Rosenberg, R. (1992). *Divided lives: American women in the 20th century.* New York: Hill and Wang.

Skocpol, T. (1992). *Protecting soldiers and mothers: The political origins of social policy in the United States.* Cambridge, MA: Harvard University Press.

Starr, P. (1994). *The logic of health care reform.* New York: Penguin.

Strickland, S. (1978). *Research and the health of Americans: Improving the public policy process.* Lexington, MA: Lexington Books.

Toner, R. (1996, November 24). Harry and Louise were right, sort of [Editorial]. *New York Times,* Section 4, pp. 1, 3.

U.S. Census Bureau. (2006). *Health insurance coverage, 2005.* Retrieved February 1, 2008, from http://www.census.gov/hhes/www/hlthins/hlthin05.html

Wallace, H., Gold, E. M., & Oglesby, A. C. (1982). *Maternal and child health practices: Problems, resources, and methods of delivery* (2nd ed.). New York: John Wiley and Sons.

25

Housing Policy

Kevin Fox Gotham and James D. Wright

The history of federal housing policy in the United States is much more than a history of government programs pertaining to physical shelter, real estate, and home building. As the famous poet Robert Frost once remarked, "Home is the place where, when you have to go there, they have to let you in" (quoted in Jackson, 1985, p. 73). As Frost recognized, housing is not just a dwelling and a place to live; it is a symbol of personal worth, social status, and security. The selection of a home represents the selection of a neighborhood that, in turn, can influence the nature of one's friends and styles of social interaction with them. In addition to lifestyle and social status, housing and neighborhood heavily impact upon the types and kinds of jobs and cultural amenities one has access to (Bratt, 2002). Moreover, housing and neighborhood not only determine the quality of schools children attend but also the quality of other public services, including fire and police protection, parks and recreation, and transportation. As many scholars have recognized, housing policy affects a broad range of public and private activities including housing availability, affordability, and quality; real estate and banking activities; taxation policy; and local building codes and zoning, subdivision regulations, and insurance laws (Belsky & Prakken, 2004; Bratt, Stone, & Hartman, 2006; De Souza Briggs, 2005; Schwartz, 2006; Shlay, 1995). Indeed, in the case of housing policy, it is important to understand just how the programmatic orientation of federal housing policy plays a crucial role in the structuring of market relations as well as in reinforcing the trajectories of social inequality, including uneven metropolitan development, homelessness, and poverty.

The institutional structure of housing and housing policy is an underresearched component of social stratification and inequality. This is a significant omission given that housing is the average household's single largest expenditure and asset. As a key source of investment for many American families, housing represents the most visible insignia of social rank and prestige that people present to the larger world. Moreover, housing is the physical entity that defines "families," which are, in turn, the most basic unit of society. In addition, housing reflects and reinforces the polarization of race and social class in the larger society, a process that few scholars acknowledge in empirical studies on the causes and consequences of social stratification. As the gap between the haves and the have-nots continues to widen in the United States, racial minorities and the poor will likely face a higher incidence of poor physical conditions, overcrowding, and severe housing cost burdens. Recent years have witnessed a sharp increase in the number of working poor families needing housing assistance, persistent rental housing affordability gaps, and increases in housing foreclosures (Colton, 2003; Immergluck & Smith, 2006; Lee, Price-Spratlen, & Kanan, 2003; National Low-Income Housing Coalition, 2006b). Overall, a long history of research has shown that housing patterns tend to reinforce the segregation of classes and races that simultaneously perpetuates educational segregation and impedes access to employment opportunities and upward mobility for disadvantaged groups (Goldring, Cohen-Vogel, Smrekar, & Taylor, 2006; Gotham, 2002; Johnson, 2006; Orfield & McArdle, 2006). In this way, housing expresses and perpetuates the stratification of classes and races that exists within the society as a whole.

This chapter is organized into four sections. We begin by examining the historical development of federal housing policy from the 1930s through the 1970s. We focus on the origin of New Deal housing programs, including the creation of the Federal Housing Administration (FHA) through the National Housing Act of 1934 and the beginnings of public housing via the United States Housing Act of 1937. Our historical narrative then traces the development of federal housing policies and programs through the immediate post–World War II era. We focus on the 1949 Housing Act that promised a "decent home and suitable living environment" for all citizens and embraced other policy initiatives pertaining to public housing and suburban home building. Next, we explore the creation of the cabinet-level Department of Housing and Urban Development (HUD) in 1965, the Housing and Urban Development Act of 1968 that established the Section 235 and Section 236 programs, and President Nixon's 1973 moratorium on public housing construction and housing subsidies.

In the second section of the chapter, we examine legislative and administrative arrangements pertaining to housing policy from the 1970s to the present. Three major goals define federal housing policy since the 1970s: first, to deconcentrate poverty by requiring demolition of public housing units; second, to encourage low-income homeownership through novel and creative mortgage finance mechanisms; and, third, to develop, through public–private partnerships, new mixed-income neighborhoods that integrate public housing with surrounding neighborhoods. Overall, these policy efforts dovetail with trends toward the devolution of authority, responsibility, and funds from the federal government to state governments and, then, to local municipalities for low-income housing assistance. We examine the content, evolution, and significance of the Section 8 program, the 1987 McKinney-Vento Homeless Assistance Act, the 1990 Cranston-Gonzalez National Affordable Housing Act, the 1992 Housing and Community Development Act, the 1992 Housing Opportunities for People Everywhere (HOPE) VI program, and the 1998 Quality Housing and Work Responsibility Act (QHWRA), among other housing-related programs.

The third section of the chapter explores the major population and demographic trends affecting the formulation and implementation of federal housing policy. First, we examine the impact of increasing poverty and homelessness, abandonment, and escalating housing costs on housing policy. Second, we investigate the impact of racial discrimination and residential segregation on federal housing policy. Third, we examine the consequences of the federal government's heavy reliance on the private sector to address housing problems.

The last section and conclusion explore some of the major issues arising from our descriptive account. We examine recent programmatic developments on the federal level, the implications of current policy trends, and future directions in housing policy. Our discussion addresses three major questions. First, can increasing housing mobility through housing voucher programs be an effective antipoverty strategy? Second, can housing programs to encourage low-income homeownership promote asset accumulation among the poor and stimulate urban revitalization? Third, what are the opportunities and limitations of recent policy reforms surrounding public housing (e.g., tenant self-sufficiency and the recent emphasis on mixed-use and mixed-income developments)? In conclusion, we address the limitations of market-centered strategies and discuss policy recommendations for meeting the housing needs of U.S. citizens.

Historical Review of Federal Housing Policy, 1930s–1970s

The housing acts of 1934 and 1937 marked the beginnings of federal involvement in housing and finance markets, in subsidizing suburban development, and in housing policy formulation. The National Housing Act of 1934 created the Federal Housing Administration (FHA) and provided mortgage insurance guarantees to encourage banks to make loans for single-family homes to middle-income people. Designed and run by representatives of the real estate and banking industries, the FHA was created to salvage the home-building and finance industries that had collapsed in the early years of the Great Depression. The FHA, and later the Veterans Administration (created in 1944), lowered home down payments to 10%, established minimum standards for home construction, and eliminated lending institutions' risk in providing mortgage financing by lowering interest rates (Federal Housing Administration, 1959; Gotham, 2002; Radford, 1996, pp. 179–180).

During the 1930s, the FHA, along with the Federal Home Loan Bank Board and the Home Owners' Loan Corporation (HOLC) introduced the long-term, self-amortizing mortgage with uniform payments spread over the life of the housing debt and extended national appraisal norms and training to realtors, builders, developers, and banks throughout the United States (Crossney & Bartelt, 2005; Hays, 1985; Jackson, 1980). The effect of this new mortgage system was to fully amortize all home loans and reduce the average monthly payment, thereby substantially increasing the number of families that could buy a home. As a result of the FHA's home-building and home-ownership subsidies, housing starts rose from 93,000 in 1933 to 332,000 by 1937, to 619,000 per year by 1941. After World War II, the numbers increased substantially, and, by 1972, the FHA had helped 11 million families become home owners (Jackson, 1985, p. 205). Indeed, from the 1930s to 1959, the FHA proudly proclaimed that it had financed three out of every five homes purchased in the United States (Federal Housing Administration, 1959, p. 21). Thus, the long-term effect of the establishment of the FHA and the modern mortgage system was to transform a nation of renters (52% of the population) before the 1930s into a nation of home owners (65%) by the mid-1980s (Bartelt, 1993, p. 138).

The 1937 United States Housing Act established the public housing program to provide rental units to low-income households through local public housing authorities (Vale, 2002). The act decentralized the administration of public housing and empowered local communities to create local housing authorities with the legal power of eminent domain to acquire privately owned land for slum clearance and rehousing (Hoffman, 1996). Interestingly, public housing was originally conceived as temporary way stations for working class families on the road to upward mobility and home ownership (Bauman, 1987). Following World War II, however, population and demographic changes affecting the United States and opposition from real estate interests gradually transformed public housing into modern-day asylums for the poorest of the urban poor (Gelfand, 1975). Real estate and building interest groups, such as the National Association of Home Builders (NAHB) and the National Association of Real Estate Boards (NAREB), successfully lobbied Congress to impose budget cuts on public housing from the 1930s onward, and production was curtailed throughout the ensuing decades (Gotham, 2002). Moreover, local officials and real estate interests in many cities prevailed in getting public housing located away from affluent white neighborhoods and built near poor and deteriorating areas of the inner city (Hirsch, 1983; Kirp, Dwyer, & Rosenthal, 1995; Silver & Melkonian, 1995).

The decentralized nature of public housing coupled with the tendency to segregate public housing tenants by race also served to reinforce racial residential segregation and concentrate poor minorities, especially African Americans, in central cities throughout the United States. Up to 1964, almost all housing authorities segregated their public housing residents by race. Although Title VI of the Civil Rights Act of 1964 banned discrimination in housing receiving federal assistance, programmatic changes in tenant selection during the 1960s reinforced racial segregation. Many cities adopted a "freedom of choice" tenant selection policy that allowed prospective tenants to choose among housing projects when an opening became available. However, in direct violation of federal law, many housing authorities maintained a separate waiting list for each project and refused to take affirmative steps to undo segregation in their projects. The segregative impact of public housing was reinforced by the passage of the Brooke amendments in 1969, 1970, and 1971, which capped public housing rentals at 25% of income and opened admission to welfare recipients. While the purpose of these amendments was to open public housing to more poor families, the legislation also reduced the amount of funds available for maintenance and upkeep. Caught between increasing costs and declining rents, the public housing stock deteriorated rapidly, projecting an image of social disaster and impoverishment.

By the 1970s, public housing was being criticized by scholars for creating "vertical ghettos," concentrating poverty, and reinforcing the chasm between the predominantly white suburbs and the increasing black inner city—an image that Reynolds Farley and associates referred to as "Chocolate City, Vanilla Suburbs" (Farley, Schuman, Bianchi, Colasanto, & Hatchett, 1978). Whereas from 1944 to 1951 nonwhite families represented between 26% and 39% of all public housing tenants, by 1978, over 60% of the residents of public housing were African Americans (Bratt, 1986, p. 339). Recent research suggests that, despite a modest decline in racial segregation in public housing since the 1970s, the majority of African American public housing residents live in poor, racially isolated neighborhoods while white tenants typically live in less isolated neighborhoods. Racial isolation in public housing combined with white avoidance of mixed and predominantly nonwhite areas help maintain high levels of white and black segregation (Dawkins, 2004; Fischer, 2003; Rosenbaum & Argeros, 2005; Squires, Friedman, & Saidat, 2002). These and other findings corroborate research showing that racial segregation in housing is fundamental to the structuring of market relations and to patterns of capitalist investment and disinvestment that have created the class and racial geography of American metropolitan areas (Denton, 2006; Massey & Denton, 1993; Squires, 1994; Wright, Rubin, & Devine, 1998).

In addition to the segregative effect of public housing, the FHA's housing subsidies that were established during the 1930s had a major impact on post–World War II migrations of middle-income whites to suburban areas and on the concentration of low-income, mostly African American families in deteriorating inner cities. Racial minorities, especially African Americans, were officially excluded from FHA subsidies and segregated by the agency's refusal to underwrite mortgages in predominantly minority areas (Myrdal, 1944). From the 1930s through the 1950s, the FHA's underwriting manuals considered African Americans to be "adverse influences" on property values and warned against the "infiltration of inharmonious racial or nationality groups" in racially homogeneous all-white neighborhoods (Federal Housing Administration, 1936; 1952, p. 233). The FHA alerted land developers and realtors that "[i]f a neighborhood is to retain stability it is necessary that properties shall continue to be occupied by the same social and racial classes. A change in social or racial occupancy generally leads to instability and a reduction in values" (Federal Housing Administration, 1936, p. 233).

Local and national real estate boards followed the lead of the FHA in adopting a code of ethics stating that "a Realtor should never be instrumental in introducing into a neighborhood . . . members of any race or nationality . . . whose presence will clearly be detrimental to property values in that neighborhood" (Helper, 1969, p. 201). Agency officials, realtors, land developers, banks, and appraisers all embraced the belief that the highest appraisal value goes to homes in all-white neighborhoods, with lesser values to homes in racially mixed neighborhoods, and lesser values still in all-black neighborhoods. Although the FHA's underwriting manuals were revised in the 1950s and 1960s to delete explicit reference to racial groups, the agency continued to trumpet the merits and necessity of maintaining and creating racially homogeneous neighborhoods (Abrams, 1965; Federal Housing Administration, 1952, 1959; Massey & Denton, 1993). As a result, the housing policies and practices of the FHA influenced lending and home mortgage financing decades after World War II, thus subsidizing suburban housing construction, contributing to and exacerbating neighborhood deterioration in inner cities, and institutionalizing a racially segregated housing market on a national scale (Gotham, 2002; Oliver & Shapiro, 1995).

The Housing Act of 1949 promised a "decent home and suitable living environment for every American family." The Act authorized construction of 810,000 public housing units over the next six years and provided the legal regulations (eminent domain) and funding for large-scale slum clearance through the new urban renewal program (Hoffman, 1996, pp. 430–431). Urban renewal used the model of federal funding and local decision making provided in the 1937 National Housing Act and empowered localities to create urban renewal authorities to designate and clear "blighted" areas (Gelfand, 1975, chapter 6; Wilson, 1966). The Housing Act of 1959 broadened the urban renewal program, increased funding for FHA home financing activities, and established the first specific housing for elderly citizens through the public housing program. Due to opposition from the real estate industry and conservative members of Congress, public housing never came close to the construction levels provided in 1949 (810,000 units). By 1960, only 250,000 units had been made available, and by 1979, only about 1 million total units had been built across the nation (Mitchell, 1985, pp. 9–11). The urban renewal program destroyed thousands more units than it replaced and became the target of intense civil rights protest from leaders who labeled it "black removal" due to the large number of African American residents and neighborhoods cleared under the guise of "urban renewal" (Gans, 1962; Jacobs, 1961).

Three major programmatic developments in the 1960s transformed the role of federal involvement in housing and the implementation of housing policy. First, the cabinet-level Department of Housing and Urban Development (HUD) was established in 1965 to coordinate and streamline the federal government's housing-related activities and programs. HUD was designed to replace the old Housing and Home Finance Agency (HHFA) that had been the umbrella of all federal housing agencies and programs since World War II. Second, the passage of Title VIII of the Civil Rights Act of 1968 established the national goal of fair housing and provided the first administrative mechanisms to combat housing discrimination through litigation.

Third, the 1949 goal of a "decent home" for every American family was reaffirmed in the Housing and Urban Development Act of 1968 (Keith, 1973, pp. 165–167). Praised as a solution to the urban riots and housing shortages plaguing the nation, the 1968 legislation signaled the beginnings of a long-term shift in federal housing policy away from dispensing aid to local housing authorities for building public housing to providing direct supply-side subsidies to the private sector to stimulate home ownership for the poor. The 1968 act directed the FHA to relax standards so that the poor could obtain mortgages for home ownership (e.g., the Section 235 program) or rent subsidies (e.g., the Section 236 program) to move into affordable apartments rather than public housing. After decades of underwriting mortgages for middle-income, mostly white families in the suburbs, the FHA was now required to shoulder the risk of making loans to moneylenders in inner city areas. The home-ownership provision provided lending institutions with mortgage insurance and reduced the home owners' housing costs by making payments directly to the lenders on behalf of the owners. The newly created Government National Mortgage Association (Ginnie Mae) was the conduit for the housing subsidy while the Federal National Mortgage Association (Fannie Mae) was to provide a secondary market for federally insured mortgages. The 1968 housing programs were designed to attract private lenders and developers to participate in supplying low-cost housing for poor people. However, reports of scandals in the programs provided the impetus for the discontinuation of the housing subsidy programs and the decision by the Nixon administration to impose a moratorium on all federally subsidized and public housing construction in 1973 (Bonastia, 2006; Lamb, 2005).

_____ Federal Housing Policy Since the 1970s

Shrinking federal housing resources, declining supplies of public housing units as a result of demolition, lax enforcement of fair housing and antidiscrimination statutes, and increased reliance on market-centered strategies (e.g., tax subsidies) have been the core features of housing policy since the 1970s (Gotham, 1998; Hartman, 1986; Hays, 1994; Rubin, Wright, &

Devine, 1992). During this time, virtually all federal housing programs that provide housing to low-income residents, through new construction or rehabilitation, have witnessed severe funding cutbacks. Plans are currently underway, and have been since the 1980s, to demolish, convert, or privatize substantial portions of the existing federally subsidized housing stock (Crump, 2003). Since the 1990s, Congress has proposed to end subsidies for public housing construction, repeal the United States Housing Act of 1937 that created the public housing system, and promote low-income home ownership as a vehicle for eliminating poverty (Denton, 2001; Shlay, 2006).

Two major components of low-income housing policy since the 1970s have been the Section 8 program, established through the Housing and Community Development Act of 1974, and the Housing Opportunities for People Everywhere (HOPE) VI program launched in 1992. The Section 8 program works by allowing local housing authorities to issue housing vouchers to low-income renters to give to landlords who then receive rental subsidies from HUD to make up the difference between "fair market" rents and what poor households can afford to pay. Participating landlords charge the approved "prevailing market rate" for apartments, while low-income tenants pay 30% of their income for rent, and HUD pays the rest. Low-income renters use the housing voucher to search for affordable housing that meets HUD-approved minimum quality standards. The goal of the HOPE VI program is to replace severely distressed public housing projects with mixed-income housing and provide housing vouchers to enable some of the original residents to rent apartments in the private market (Popkin, Katz, Cunningham, Brown, Gustafson, & Turner, 2004). Other important federal housing programs include the Low Income Housing Tax Credit (LIHTC) established in 1986 to encourage the private sector to build low-income housing; the 1990 Cranston-Gonzalez National Affordable Housing Act and the 1992 Housing and Community Development Act, which provide block grants to states and local governments to subsidize low-income housing construction, rental, and homeowner assistance; and the Quality Housing and Work Responsibility Act (QHWRA) of 1998 to encourage public housing residents to work and become self-sufficient.

The only major legislative response to the scarcity of accessible and affordable low-income housing for homeless people has been the 1987 McKinney-Vento Homeless Assistance Act. Increasing homelessness during the 1980s prompted the passage of this legislation to provide shelter and housing provisions to homeless and near-homeless people (Wright, 1989). Amendments in 1988, 1990, 1992, and 1994 expanded the scope, reach, and funding of the original McKinney Act so that programs reached the mentally ill, homeless veterans and children, rural homeless persons, and other needy citizens. In 2001, Congress reauthorized the McKinney Education of Homeless Children and Youth Program as the McKinney-Vento Homeless Education Assistance Improvements Act in the No Child Left Behind Act (P.L. 107-110), signed by President George W. Bush on January 8, 2002. Currently, the McKinney-Vento Act consists of a series of programs including emergency shelter, transitional housing, job training, health care, education, and permanent housing. However, in recent years, funding and support for these programs, as for other low-income housing assistance programs, have decreased, and attempts have been made to repeal the authorization of the original act. A number of McKinney Act program evaluations conducted in 1995 and 1996 found that the homeless programs aided in providing permanent housing at reasonable costs for significant numbers of homeless persons (Fuchs & McAllister, 1996). Other program evaluations, however, have noted that resources allocated to McKinney programs are insufficient to meet demand. Moreover, the lack of stable funding severely limits the programs' effectiveness. In addition, other studies have argued that homelessness policy does little to address the determinants of homelessness, which include metropolitan variability in median rent levels and percentage of single person households (Lee & Price-Spratlen, 2004; Lee et al., 2003).

In sum, since the 1970s, federal housing policy has undergone a dramatic transformation. The Reagan, G. H. W. Bush, Clinton, and G. W. Bush administrations have all worked to transform public housing sites into mixed-income developments, reduced the number of units available to low-income families, and compelled needy people to rely on rental vouchers to find affordable housing in the private market. Today, low-income housing policies fail to meet the need for affordable housing in the United States. Moreover, the much trumpeted government efforts to reduce the spatial concentration of poverty through home-buyer finance programs have had modest and limited success (McClure, 2005). In recent years, the George W. Bush administration has proposed ending the HOPE VI program, replacing the Section 8 program with block grants to state governments instead of public housing authorities, and setting minimum rent levels for low-income families that live in public housing or receive housing assistance (Crump, 2003). These steps on the federal level have climaxed a two-decade long transformation of federal housing policy that has included privatizing federally supported mortgage markets, substituting housing vouchers for public housing construction, partially privatizing remaining public housing projects while unilaterally demolishing others, tightening eligibility requirements, and attempting to use housing policy to move low-income people into the workforce.

Population and Demographic Trends Affecting Federal Housing Policy

A major trend affecting federal housing policy is increasing poverty and homelessness in the face of escalating housing costs and declining supplies of low-income housing units in U.S. cities. As numerous studies have documented, inner-city housing costs have been increasing more rapidly than people's incomes, creating an affordability gap for low- and even moderate-income households (Joint Center for Housing Studies, 2006; National Low-Income Housing Coalition, 2006b; Stone, 2006). In addition, foreclosures of single-family mortgages have increased dramatically in many parts of the United States in recent years. Much of this has been tied to the rise of higher-risk sub-prime mortgage lending (Immergluck & Smith, 2006). As a result, the problems of market volatility and worsening housing marketing conditions threaten the financial fortunes of a large segment of the American population and create new risks for lenders, mortgage originators, policy makers, and government officials.

In addition to the problems of housing availability and affordability, racial residential segregation continues to be a tenacious and enduring feature of metropolitan housing markets and public housing, despite the passage of fair housing and a host of antidiscrimination statutes (Denton, 2006). Racial segregation and discrimination in housing today are somewhat different than they were decades ago. State and federal laws make official discrimination illegal, and a few African American families now live, or have tried to reside, in historically white neighborhoods in almost all U.S. cities (Keating, 1994; Maly, 2005). Informal patterns and institutionalized mechanisms of housing discrimination, however, remain a persistent and undeniable characteristic of American society. Institutional housing discrimination refers to actions prescribed by the norms of public agencies, private firms, and social networks of actors within the housing industry, actions that have a differentiated and negative impact on members of a subordinate racial group. *Linguistic profiling*—defined as the identification of a person's race from the sound of his or her voice and the use of that information to discriminate on the basis of race—has been documented in the property insurance industry and in many local housing markets around the nation (Massey & Lundy, 2001; Squires, 2003; Squires & Chadwick, 2006). In addition, much research has shown that housing prices and rents are generally higher for racial minorities, especially African Americans, than whites (even when income is controlled for) (Fischer, 2003). Moreover, a vast array of housing data indicates that conventional loans for home purchases and remodeling are available to whites, but racial minorities are forced to buy with cash, on contract, through predatory and sub-prime lenders, or through federal loan programs (Apgar & Calder, 2005; Bradford, 2002).

Trends in housing affordability, overcrowding, homelessness, and poverty and persistent racial residential segregation have been exacerbated by the federal government's increasingly heavy reliance on the private sector to address housing problems. Interestingly, most federally assisted housing in the United States, unlike that in other industrialized nations, is provided by the private sector. In many European nations, by contrast, a third or more of all units are owned and operated by government housing authorities. Since the New Deal, home builders, bankers, and other housing and real estate interests have been more or less unified in their opposition to federal intervention in the housing market, particularly when that intervention involves subsidies or programs for low-income citizens (Gotham, 2002). Throughout the postwar era, conservative politicians and real estate elites attacked public housing as a "socialist" program and opposed it on the grounds that it would put the government in competition with private housing construction and real estate. In the 1960s and 1970s, the National Association of Real Estate Brokers continued to resist new housing subsidy programs for the poor at the same time as they championed an expansion of FHA resources to benefit upper- and middle-income home owners and real estate and home-building interests. Since its inception in 1965, HUD programs have relied mainly upon the private housing market for the production, distribution, and rehabilitation of low-income and public housing (Bratt & Keating, 1993).

Implications and Future Developments in Federal Housing Policy

In recent years, two major programs—the HOPE VI program and the Section 8 program—have been promoted by public officials as promising antipoverty strategies to increase housing mobility for low-income, inner-city residents. Others have championed these programs as effective vehicles for deconcentrating racial minorities and creating racially mixed and economically mixed neighborhoods. According to promoters, Section 8 and HOPE VI can enable low-income residents and racial minorities to leave high-poverty areas and segregated neighborhoods and to move to middle- and high-income areas and racially integrated neighborhoods. The potential benefits of increasing housing mobility through Section 8 and HOPE VI supposedly include greater access to employment opportunities and quality schools, reduced crime, enhanced cultural amenities and entertainment venues, and enrichment of the lives of white, middle-class residents through increased interaction with more diverse groups of people. From 1992 through 2003, HUD awarded 446 HOPE VI grants in 166 cities. As of 2004, 63,100 severely distressed units had been demolished and another 20,300 units had been slated for redevelopment. Yet, after a decade of implementation, as of 2002, only 15 of 165 funded HOPE VI programs were fully complete (Popkin et al., 2004, p. 2).

Despite the fanfare, there is little evidence to indicate that increasing housing mobility through Section 8 vouchers and certificates or through the HOPE VI program is an effective antipoverty or housing desegregation strategy. Several program evaluations have provided a mixed picture of the advantages and limitations of these programs. On one hand, existing research suggests that the HOPE VI program has achieved its goals of demolishing severely distressed public housing units, erecting high-quality housing, and relocating residents to better housing in safer neighborhoods (Popkin et al., 2004). On the other hand, in a study of the spatial pattern of Section 8 recipients relocated from 73 HOPE VI sites in 48 cites, Kingsley, Johnson, and Pettit (2003) found that, although the majority of those who were relocated did move to neighborhoods with lower poverty rates than those they left behind, the impacts in reducing racial concentration were modest. Most relocated persons, according to Kingsley et al. (2003), tended to spread across many different neighborhoods although significant clustering was found in a few neighborhoods in most cities. In a comparative analysis of four HOPE VI sites in Cincinnati, Louisville, Baltimore, and Washington, D.C., Varady, Raffel, Sweeney, and Denson (2005) found that none of the four public housing developments explicitly sought to attract middle-income families with children as part of its marketing. This finding supports other studies that find that, although vouchers and certificates scatter subsidized tenants into suburbs better than conventional public housing, these suburbanized tenants nonetheless tend to concentrate in areas whose socioeconomic status and proportions of white residents are below average (Hartung & Henig, 1997; Pardee & Gotham, 2006). More problematic is the lack of clarity on the definition, benefits, and impact of the HOPE VI program and its relationship with the Section 8 program. According to Popkin et al. (2004),

> HOPE VI has not been "one program" with a clear set of consistent and unwavering goals. Rather, the program has evolved considerably during the past decade—in legislation, regulation, implementation, and practice. To an unusual extent, the program has been shaped more through implementation than by enactment. What was initially conceived as a redevelopment and community-building program evolved over time into a more ambitious effort to build economically integrated communities and give existing residents more choice in the private housing market. Because of the flexible nature of the program, local housing authorities have had tremendous latitude in how they chose to design and implement their local HOPE VI initiatives. It is impossible, therefore, to provide simple answers to general questions about programmatic effectiveness and "lessons learned." The response to such questions is usually another question: "Which HOPE VI program are you asking about?" (p. 2)

Both the Section 8 and HOPE VI programs are part of larger strategy of public housing reform that has evolved from providing shelter to providing opportunities for escaping high poverty areas (Basolo, 2007; McClure, 2005; Santiago & Galster, 2004). Yet, both programs have been the targets of intense criticism by housing and civil rights activists throughout the country due to the displacement caused by HOPE VI revitalization efforts and the persistent and multiyear waiting lists for embarrassingly few Section

8 vouchers. The average waiting time nationwide for Section 8 housing vouchers is over two years, and many housing agencies have much longer waits. Indeed, many have closed their waiting lists entirely. The Section 8 program gives a few qualifying low-income people inadequate housing resources to compete with other needy citizens for a dwindling supply of affordable housing. Not surprisingly, studies throughout the country indicate that many residents fail to use their vouchers because of an inability to locate quality housing and the dearth of landlords willing to participate in the voucher program (Shlay, 2006). In addition, although inadequate funding clearly impedes the effectiveness of the Section 8 voucher program, the program's greatest weakness is its focus on increasing the housing "choice" for low-income residents rather than addressing the problem of housing affordability that many low-income citizens face.

Recent trends in housing policy suggest decreasing funds and less emphasis on the Section 8 and HOPE VI programs and more government promotion of low-income home ownership to reduce urban poverty, revitalize cities, and promote self-sufficiency among the poor. Over the decades, Section 8 funds have been cut while other tax subsidy programs, such as the Low Income Housing Tax Credit (LIHTC) program, have failed to meet massive needs for rental housing assistance. At the same time, the federal government has encouraged low-income home ownership based on the expectation that it will remedy urban ills and other social problems. Various tools to promote low-income home ownership include low or no down payments, use of adjustable rate mortgages (ARMs), and reliance on sub-prime markets for mortgage financing (Duda & Belsky, 2001). Although much research has shown the social benefits of home ownership for the middle and upper classes, little evidence exists on whether low-income people experience positive social changes as a result of owning rather than renting their homes. Moreover, the recent surge of foreclosures suggests limited growth in low-income home ownership. Broadly, there are few studies to support the notion that promoting low-income home ownership can be a viable tool for asset accumulation or neighborhood redevelopment. Even more problematic, according to Shlay (2006), the alleged positive impacts of low-income home ownership may be based on measurement error and the conflation of home ownership with other unobserved features coincident with buying homes. Thus, ongoing budget cuts to low-income rental assistance programs combined with the elevation of low-income home ownership narrows the policy debate and limits the range of housing options available for the needy.

Conclusion

Today, housing policy in the United States is at a crossroads. On one hand, housing conditions, as a whole, are better than they were fifty years ago, and various federal housing programs and subsidies have enabled millions of families to become home owners (Belsky & Prakken, 2004; Colton, 2003; Di,

2007; Schwartz, 2006). Since the 1930s, federal intervention in housing markets has been an effective policy, stimulating private-sector housing construction and improving the quality of home building in this country. Indeed, despite trends toward fiscal retrenchment in federal housing provision, the federal commitment to housing remains enormous when tax expenditures and credit enhancements for home ownership and housing construction are considered. On the other hand, the goal of a decent home in a suitable living environment that Congress adopted more than fifty years ago remains elusive and unattainable for millions of low-income American families, both those who are homeless and those living in marginal, overcrowded, or otherwise substandard conditions. Very few households below the poverty line receive direct housing assistance, and escalating housing costs and affordability are still a problem for homeless persons and other low-income citizens.

Interestingly, the bulk of federal intervention in housing—tax laws that allow mortgage interest and property taxes to be deducted—continues to benefit upper- and middle-income home owners at the expense of the needy (Bratt, 2003; Dreier, 2006). According to the National Low-Income Housing Coalition (NLIHC, 2006a), in 2005, the federal government spent over $39 billion on housing assistance for low-income Americans. This is in stark contrast to $121 billion in tax expenditures in 2005 to subsidize home ownership through mortgage interest, capital gains, and property tax deductions, which disproportionately serve the home owners with the highest incomes. When both housing assistance and tax benefits are taken into account, the poorest one-fifth of American households—those earning less than $19,000 per year—received a paltry $34 billion in housing subsidies in 2006 in contrast to the richest fifth of American households (those earning over $92,000) who received approximately $94 billion in subsidies. Thus, the vast majority of federal tax expenditures and appropriations benefit those who least need housing assistance.

In contrast to federal tax expenditures for middle- and upper-income groups, many of the federal government's housing programs fail to meet the housing needs of low-income residents. Inadequate funding and a tendency to attack the symptoms of homelessness (e.g., substance abuse and mental illness) rather than its causes (lack of affordable housing) hamper the effectiveness of the McKinney-Vento Act programs. Moreover, while the 1990 Cranston-Gonzalez National Affordable Housing Act and the 1992 Housing and Community Development Act emphasize home ownership and tenant-based assistance, these programs have been underfunded and fail to satisfy the housing needs of low-income persons. In addition, a 1998 HUD report found that an estimated 12.5 million rental households that qualify for HUD housing aid are unable to get it because the department does not have the funding to help them (U.S. Department of Housing and Urban Development, 1998).

Overall, low-income housing assistance programs have fared poorly in the Bush administration's budget in recent years, according to a 2007 report from the Center on Budget and Policy Priorities (Rice & Sard, 2007). By 2006, inflation-adjusted funding for HUD programs had declined by $3.3

billion (or 8%) in comparison to 2004 funding. For 2007, the administration has proposed further cutbacks of $1.3 billion that will likely affect nearly every low-income housing assistance program. The funds to public housing have been cut the most: funding declining by 20%, 16%, and 11%, respectively, from 2004 to 2006. The result has been a noticeable reduction in housing assistance resources available to local communities, including the loss of more than 150,000 housing vouchers since 2004.

Many of the policy recommendations being put forth by scholars and researchers to remedy the nation's housing problems are based on market-centered strategies designed to increase housing options for the poor and stimulate greater private-sector participation in the production of housing. However, we believe that scholarly debates must move beyond discussions over the relative merits of market-centered housing policies and expose the conservative thrust of public policy that seeks to convince us of the beneficence of the private market. In particular, the recent focus on opening up supposedly free and benevolent housing "markets" through various federal tax credits, or Section 8 vouchers and certificates, ignores the fact that markets are not necessarily open to all those who wish to participate as buyers and sellers. What unites these otherwise different tax incentives and subsidies is that they are all based on the notion that market forces will cure housing ills if only the barriers to investment and growth are removed. However, despite more than two decades of ostensibly open housing markets, antidiscrimination ordinances, and the universal adoption of market-centered housing policies in metropolitan areas throughout the United States, "markets" routinely fail to provide adequate quality housing for all citizens. The history of housing policy indicates that market-based strategies have never been successful in revitalizing cities, ameliorating poverty and disinvestment, or providing housing for the needy. What market-centered policies have traditionally been quite successful at is distributing wealth and income upward, reinforcing the segregationist tendencies of the private market, and perpetuating geographic patterns of investment and disinvestment. Thus, we believe that the faith that scholars, policy researchers, and elected officials place in market-centered policies to remedy the problems of housing affordability, homelessness, and segregation is misplaced. As the history of federal housing policy shows, the problems, instead, are market induced (Gotham, 2002; Squires, 1994).

Given the massive cutbacks in HUD's budget over the last two decades and the general anti-poor sentiment in the nation, it is unlikely that there will be any increased housing expenditures or substantial new housing programs on the federal level in the near future. New and innovative housing policies and programs, although necessary and laudable, are unlikely to meet with much support and enthusiasm from government officials, given the current political climate. Thus, housing advocates should try to protect current government funding and shore up political support for existing housing programs while calling for additional policies to increase the supply of low-income housing. Another approach could be to coordinate existing housing programs with local social service agencies, schools, and other educational services. In addition, housing advocates could concentrate their efforts on state and local governments to tap new sources of government funding and support. However, although the above initiatives are important for attacking the housing problems of the poor, such efforts, by themselves, will not be sufficient to address the major population and demographic trends and programmatic changes that are contributing to increased the abandonment, escalating costs, and deterioration of the inner-city housing stock. Thus, we believe that the goal of providing decent and affordable housing to low-income people does not lie just in housing programs themselves but, rather, in an effort to coordinate housing programs with a comprehensive welfare policy. As we see it, the housing problems of low-income people can only be addressed through a comprehensive program that includes the creation of jobs that pay a living wage, adequate benefits for those who cannot work, access to affordable health care, and an increased supply of affordable housing.

References

Abrams, C. (1965). *The city is the frontier.* New York: Harper & Row.

Apgar, W. C., & Calder, A. (2005). The dual mortgage market: The persistence of discrimination in mortgage lending. In X. de Souza Briggs (Ed.), *Geography of opportunity: Race and housing choice in metropolitan America* (pp. 101–149). Washington, DC: Brookings Institution Press.

Bartelt, D. (1993). Housing the "underclass." In M. Katz (Ed.), *The underclass debate: Views from history* (pp. 118–157). Princeton, NJ: Princeton University Press.

Basolo, V. (2007). Explaining the support for homeownership policy in US cities: A political economy perspective. *Housing Studies, 22*(1), 99–119.

Bauman, J. F. (1987). *Public housing, race, and renewal: Urban planning in Philadelphia, 1920–1974.* Philadelphia: Temple University Press.

Belsky, E., & Prakken, J. (2004). *Housing wealth effects: Housing's impact on wealth accumulation, wealth distribution, and consumer spending* (Joint Center for Housing Studies Report No. W04–13). Cambridge, MA: Harvard University.

Bonastia, C. (2006). *Knocking on the door: The federal government's attempt to desegregate the suburbs.* Princeton, NJ: Princeton University Press.

Bradford, C. (2002). *Risk or race? Racial disparities and the subprime refinance market.* Washington, DC: Center for Community Change.

Bratt, R. G. (1986). Public housing: The controversy and contribution. In R. G. Bratt, C. Hartman, & A. Meyerson (Eds.), *Critical Perspectives on Housing* (pp. 362–377). Philadelphia: Temple University Press.

Bratt, R. G. (2002). Housing and family well-being. *Housing Studies, 17*(1), 13–26.

Bratt, R. G. (2003). Housing for very low-income households: The record of President Clinton, 1993–2000. *Housing Studies, 18*(4), 607–635.

Bratt, R. G., & Keating, W. D. (1993). Federal housing policy and HUD: Past problems and the future prospects of a beleaguered bureaucracy. *Urban Affairs Quarterly, 29*(1), 3–27.

Bratt, R. G., Stone, M. E., & Hartman. C. (Eds.). (2006). *A right to housing: Foundation for a new social agenda.* Philadelphia: Temple University Press.

Colton, K. W. (2003). *Housing in the twenty-first century: Achieving common ground.* Cambridge, MA: Harvard University Press.

Crossney, K. B., & Bartelt, D. (2005). The legacy of the Home Owners' Loan Corporation. *Housing Policy Debate, 18*(3/4), 547–574.

Crump, J. R. (2003). The end of public housing as we know it: Public housing policy, labor regulation, and the U.S. city. *International Journal of Urban and Regional Research, 27*(1), 179–187.

Dawkins, C. J. (2004). Recent evidence on the continuing causes of black-white residential segregation. *Journal of Urban Affairs, 26*(3), 379–400.

De Souza Briggs, X. (Ed.). (2005). *The geography of opportunity: Race and housing choice in metropolitan America.* Washington, DC: Brookings Institution Press.

Denton, N. (2001). Housing as a means of asset accumulation: A good strategy for the poor? In T. M. Shapiro & E. N. Wolff (Eds.), *Assets for the poor: The benefits of spreading asset ownership* (pp. 232–268). New York: Russell Sage Foundation.

Denton, N. (2006). Segregation and discrimination in housing. In R. G. Bratt, M. E. Stone, & C. Hartman (Eds.), *A right to housing: Foundation for a new social agenda* (pp. 61–81). Philadelphia: Temple University Press.

Di, Z. X. (2007). *Growing wealth, inequality, and housing in the United States* (Joint Center for Housing Studies Report No. W07-1). Cambridge, MA: Harvard University.

Dreier, P. (2006). Federal housing subsidies: Who benefits and why? In R. G. Bratt, M. E. Stone, & C. Hartman (Eds.), *A right to housing: Foundation for a new social agenda* (pp. 105–139). Philadelphia: Temple University Press.

Duda, M., & Belsky, E. S. (2001). *The anatomy of the low-income homeownership boom in the 1990s* (Joint Center for Housing Studies Low-Income Homeownership Working Paper Series No. LIHO01-1). Cambridge, MA: Harvard University.

Farley, R., Schuman, H., Bianchi, S., Colasanto, D., & Hatchett, S. (1978). Chocolate city, vanilla suburbs: Will the trend toward racially separate communities continue. *Social Science Research, 7,* 319–344.

Federal Housing Administration. (1936). *Underwriting manual.* Washington, DC: Government Printing Office.

Federal Housing Administration. (1952). *Underwriting manual.* Washington, DC: Government Printing Office.

Federal Housing Administration. (1959). *The FHA story in summary, 1934–1959.* Washington, DC: Government Printing Office.

Fischer, M. J. (2003). The relative importance of income and race in determining residential outcomes in U.S. urban areas, 1970–2000. *Urban Affairs Review, 38*(5), 669–696.

Fuchs, E., & McAllister, W. (1996). *The continuum of care: A report on the new federal policy to address homelessness.* Gaithersburg, MD: Community Connections.

Gans, H. (1962). *Urban villagers.* Glencoe, IL: Free Press.

Gelfand, M. I. (1975). *A nation of cities: The federal government and urban America, 1933–1965.* New York: Oxford University Press.

Goldring, E., Cohen-Vogel, L., Smrekar, C., & Taylor, C. (2006). Schooling closer to home: Desegregation policy and neighborhood contexts. *American Journal of Education, 112,* 335–362

Gotham, K. F. (1998). Blind faith in the free market: Urban poverty, residential seg-regation, and federal housing retrenchment, 1970–1995. *Sociological Inquiry, 68*(1), 1–31.

Gotham, K. F. (2002). *Race, real estate, and uneven development: The Kansas City experience, 1900–2000.* Albany: State University of New York Press.

Hartman, C. (1986). Housing policies under the Reagan administration. In R. G. Bratt, C. Hartman, & A. Meyerson (Eds.), *Critical perspectives on housing* (pp. 362–377). Philadelphia: Temple University Press.

Hartung, J., & Henig, J. (1997, January). Housing vouchers and certificates as a vehicle for deconcentrating the poor. *Urban Affairs Review, 32*(3), 403–419.

Hays, R. A. (1985). *Federal government and urban housing: Ideology and change in public policy.* Albany: State University of New York Press.

Hays, R. A. (1994). Housing privatization: Social goals and policy strategies. *Journal of Urban Affairs, 16*(4), 295–317.

Helper, R. (1969). *Racial policies and practices of real estate brokers.* Minneapolis: University of Minnesota Press.

Hirsch, A. R. (1983). *Making the second ghetto: Race and housing in Chicago, 1940–1960.* Cambridge, UK: Cambridge University Press.

Hoffman, A. von. (1996). High ambitions: The past and future of American low-income housing policy. *Housing Policy Debate, 7*(3), 423–446.

Immergluck, D., & Smith, G. (2006). The impact of single-family mortgage foreclo-sures on neighborhood crime. *Housing Studies, 21*(6), 851–866.

Jackson, K. T. (1980). Race, ethnicity, and real estate appraisal: The Home Owners' Loan Corporation and the Federal Housing Administration. *Journal of Urban History, 6*(4), 419–452.

Jackson, K. T. (1985). *Crabgrass frontier: The suburbanization of the United States.* New York: Oxford University Press.

Jacobs, J. (1961). *The death and life of great American cities.* New York: Vintage Books

Johnson, H. B. (2006). *The American dream and the power of wealth: Choosing schools and inheriting inequality in the land of opportunity.* New York: Routledge.

Joint Center for Housing Studies. (2006). *State of the nation's housing, 2006.* Cambridge, MA: Harvard University.

Keating, W. D. (1994). *Suburban racial dilemma: Housing and neighborhoods.* Philadelphia: Temple University Press.

Keith, N. S. (1973). *Politics and the housing crisis since 1930.* New York: Universe Books.

Kingsley, G. T., Johnson, J., & Pettit, K. L. S. (2003). Patterns of Section 8 relocation in the HOPE VI program. *Journal of Urban Affairs, 25*(4), 427–451.

Kirp, D. L., Dwyer, J. P., & Rosenthal, L. A. (1995). *Our town: Race, housing, and the soul of suburbia.* New Brunswick, NJ: Rutgers University Press.

Lamb, C. M. (2005). *Housing segregation in suburban America since 1960: Presidential and judicial politics.* Cambridge, MA: Cambridge University Press.

Lee, B. A., & Price-Spratlen, T. (2004). The geography of homelessness in American communities: Concentration or dispersion. *City and Community, 3*(1), 3–27.

Lee, B. A., Price-Spratlen, T., & Kanan, J. W. (2003). Determinants of homelessness in metropolitan areas. *Journal of Urban Affairs, 25*(3), 335–359.

Maly, M. T. (2005). *Beyond segregation: Multiracial and multiethnic neighborhoods in the United States.* Philadelphia: Temple University Press.

Massey, D. S., & Denton, N. A. (1993). *American apartheid: Segregation and the making of the underclass.* Cambridge, MA: Harvard University Press

Massey, G., & Lundy, G. (2001). Use of black English and racial discrimination in urban housing markets: New methods and findings. *Urban Affairs Review, 36*(4), 452–469.

McClure, K. (2005). Deconcentrating poverty through homebuyer finance programs. *Journal of Urban Affairs, 27*(3), 211–233.

Mitchell, J. P. (Ed.). (1985). *Federal housing programs: Past and present.* Rutgers: State University of New Jersey Press.

Myrdal, G. (1944). *An American dilemma: The Negro problem and modern democracy.* New York: HarperTorchbooks.

National Low-Income Housing Coalition (NLIHC). (2006a). *Housing crisis fact sheet: Misplaced federal budget priorities.* Washington, DC: Author. Retrieved April 24, 2007, from http://www.nlihc.org/detail/article.cfm?article_id=3730&id=21

National Low-Income Housing Coalition (NLIHC). (2006b). *Out of reach, 2006.* Washington, DC: Author. Retrieved April 23, 2007, from http://www.nlihc.org/oor/

Oliver, M. L., & Shapiro, T. M. (1995). *Black wealth, white wealth: A new perspective on racial inequality.* New York: Routledge.

Orfield, G., & McArdle, N. (2006). *The vicious cycle: Segregated housing, schools and intergenerational inequality* (Joint Center for Housing Studies Report No. W06-4). Cambridge, MA: Harvard University.

Pardee, J. W., & Gotham, K. F. (2006). HOPE VI, Section 8, and the contradictions of low-income housing policy. *Journal of Poverty, 5*(2), 24–56

Popkin, S. J., Katz, B., Cunningham, M. K., Brown, K. D., Gustafson, J., & Turner, M. A. (2004). *A decade of HOPE VI: Research findings and policy challenges.* Washington, DC: Urban Institute.

Radford, G. (1996). *Modern housing for America: Policy struggles in the New Deal era.* Chicago: Chicago University Press.

Rice, D., & Sard, B. (2007, February 1). *Cuts in federal housing assistance are undermining community plans to end homelessness.* Washington, DC: Center on Budget and Policy Priorities.

Rosenbaum, E., & Argeros, G. (2005). Holding the line: Housing turnover and the persistence of racial/ethnic segregation in New York. *Journal of Urban Affairs, 27*(3), 261–289.

Rubin, B. A., Wright, J. D., & Devine, J. A. (1992). Unhousing the urban poor: The Reagan legacy. *Journal of Sociology and Social Welfare, 19*(1), 111–148.

Santiago, A. M., & Galster, G. C. (2004). Moving from public housing to homeownership: Perceived barriers to program participation and success. *Journal of Urban Affairs, 26*(3), 297–324.

Schwartz, A. F. (2006). *Housing policy in the United States: An introduction.* London: Routledge.

Shlay, A. (1995). Housing in the broader context in the United States. *Housing Policy Debate, 6*(3), 695–720.

Shlay, A. (2006). Low-income homeownership: American dream or delusion? *Urban Studies, 43*(3), 511–531.

Silver, M. L., & Melkonian, M. (Eds.). (1995). *Contested terrain: Power, politics, and participation in suburbia.* Westport, CT: Greenwood Press.

Squires, G. D. (1994). *Capital and communities in black and white: The intersections of race, class, and uneven development.* Albany: State University of New York Press.

Squires, G. D. (2003). Racial profiling, insurance style: Insurance redlining and the uneven development of metropolitan areas. *Journal of Urban Affairs, 25*(4), 391–410.

Squires, G. D., & Chadwick, J. (2006). Linguistic profiling: A continuing tradition of discrimination in the home insurance industry. *Urban Affairs Review, 41*(3), 400–415.

Squires, G. D., Friedman, S., & Saidat, C. E. (2002). Experiencing segregation: A contemporary study of Washington, DC. *Urban Affairs Review, 38*(2), 155–183.

Stone, M. E. (2006). Housing affordability: One-third of a nation shelter-poor. In R. G. Bratt, M. E. Stone, & C. Hartman (Eds.), *A right to housing: Foundation for a new social agenda* (pp. 20–37). Philadelphia: Temple University Press.

U.S. Department of Housing and Urban Development. (1998). *Rental housing assistance—The crisis continues.* Washington, DC: Government Printing Office.

Vale, L. J. (2002). *Reclaiming public housing: A half century of struggle in three public neighborhoods.* Cambridge, MA: Harvard University Press.

Varady, D. P., Raffel, J., Sweeney, S., & Denson, L. (2005). Attracting middle-income families in the HOPE VI public housing revitalization program. *Journal of Urban Affairs, 27*(2), 149–170.

Wilson, J. Q. (Ed.). (1966). *Urban renewal: The record and the controversy.* Cambridge: MIT Press.

Wright, J. D. (1989). Address unknown: Homelessness in contemporary America. *Society, 26*, 45–53.

Wright, J. D., Rubin, B. A., & Devine, J. (1998). *Beside the golden door: Policy, politics, and the homeless.* Hawthorne, NY: Aldine de Gruyter.

26 Social Policies and Mental Health

James W. Callicutt

I n the United States, the provision of services to persons with mental illness and their families is inextricably tied to mental health policy. In this chapter, I identify and briefly discuss some of the major issues dealing with the organization and delivery of services in the mental health field vis-à-vis mental health policy. In addition, I review the historical evolution of services for persons with mental illness; describe the current mental health service system; identify, define, and discuss the major forces that interact in formulating and forging mental health policy; and, finally, examine the major issues and trends in this arena.

Mental Illness and Mental Health

It is impossible to discuss the term *mental illness* without at the same time considering the concept of *mental health*. Mental illness is a synonym for mental disorder, which is defined as

> Impaired psychosocial or cognitive functioning due to disturbances in any one or more of the following processes: biological, chemical, physiological, genetic, psychosocial or social. Mental disorders are extremely variable in duration, severity, and prognosis, depending on the type of affliction. The major forms of mental disorder include *mood disorders, psychosis, personality disorders, organic mental disorders,* and *anxiety disorder.* (Barker, 1995, p. 231)

Mental health, on the other hand, defies uniform definition. Vague and imprecise, it has multiple meanings that differ with the context. For example, in one instance, it may be used as a euphemism for mental illness; in another, it may be used to indicate emotional or psychological well-being; and, in yet a third, it may be used to mean both well-being and mental illness (Callicutt, 1987; Callicutt & Lecca, 1983). It is interesting to note how terminology and rhetoric change over time in the broad arena of social welfare, including in the field of mental illness. In part, terminology is changed with a conscious effort to destigmatize the population served. For example, insane asylums became mental hospitals, then psychiatric institutes, and, subsequently, behavioral health care facilities. Also, we talk about a mental health service system rather than a mental illness service system. Consequently, in this chapter, I at times use the terms *mental illness* and *mental health* interchangeably.

Historical Evolution of Services for Persons With Mental Illness

Cruel, harsh, and inhuman treatment, reflecting the views of society about the causes of mental illness, characterized the care of persons with mental illness for centuries. Called *mentally deranged,* these persons were thought to be possessed by demons or spirits, and they were subjected to devices of coercion and restraint including manacles, chains, and whips in order to instill fear and awe and to promote discipline and order, and thus restore reason (Callicutt, 1987).

Colonial America

Sparsely populated, with a largely rural, agrarian economy, colonial America provided care for persons with mental illness by the family or community primarily on an ad hoc, informal basis (Grob, 1994). The methods of caring for dependent persons, including the *distracted* and the poor, were basically modeled after England's Poor Laws. According to Deutsch (1949), provision for persons with mental illness in colonial America was characterized by punishment, indifference, and oppression. In contrast, Grob (1973) observed that "all that can be said is that each community, depending on its circumstances, improvised or attempted to do the best that it could under prevailing conditions" (p. 12).

Persons with mental illness were first received by the Pennsylvania Hospital, the first general hospital in America, completed in 1756. There, in the cellar, they were confined by chains to the cell walls (Deutsch, 1949). In Williamsburg, Virginia, the first state hospital for persons with mental illness was opened in 1773. Subsequently, state hospitals for persons with mental illness were established throughout the United States, and they continue to provide the bulk of inpatient services in the public sector.

Moral Treatment

Moral treatment, the kind and considerate treatment of patients with mental illness as human rather than as subhuman and incurable, is associated with the names of Vincenzo Chiarugi, an Italian; Phillipe Pinel, a Frenchman; and William Tuke, an Englishman. Benjamin Rush and Dorothea Dix, Americans, also merit inclusion in this discussion. While presiding over a large mental hospital, Chiarugi (1759–1820), a physician in Florence, put his ideas into effect, arguing that "medical personnel had a moral duty to treat persons with mental illness as individuals and to treat them tactfully and humanely" (Cockerham, 1989, p. 19).

Pinel (1745–1826), also a physician, asserted that patients with mental illness would respond favorably to kindness and sympathy administered in the context of firm guidance (Cockerham, 1989). After being appointed as a physician to the insane asylum of Bicetre in 1779, he went from cell to cell unchaining the 53 male patients, then referred to as lunatics. He ordered beatings and other forms of physical abuse stopped; "food was improved and the patients were treated with a new drug: kindness" (Cockerham, 1989, p. 21). Often the responses of the patients were dramatically salutary. Three years later, Pinel instituted the same reforms at the women's mental institution in Paris (Callicutt, 1987). Pinel articulated the philosophy and precepts of moral treatment.

At virtually the same time, William Tuke (1732–1822), a layman, obtained formal support from Quakers in York, England, to start an institution that would offer gentle and wholesome treatment to fellow believers (Duetsch, 1949). Then, in 1796, the Retreat was established in York (Glover, 1984). There, chains were prohibited; patients were treated as guests rather than inmates. Exercise and work and a family environment were emphasized. Firm guidance emanating from the physician, clinician, and/or superintendent of the mental hospital was a hallmark of the ideology of treatment.

Earlier, in America, Benjamin Rush (1745–1813), a physician considered to be "the father of American psychiatry" (Deutsch, 1949), played a prominent role in improving the care of persons with mental illness. In 1783, he adopted kinder and more humane treatment practices at the Pennsylvania Hospital than were usually accorded patients with mental illness. In this process, Rush gave attention to employing well-qualified attendants to serve as friends and companions to the patients. Rush's positive impact on the treatment of persons with mental illness is undeniable. Yet, he was a product of his time and practiced bloodletting and invented treatment devices including the *tranquilizer,* which "consisted of a chair to which the patient was strapped hand and foot, together with a device for holding the head in a fixed position" (Deutsch, 1949, p. 79). While his approaches were not completely consistent with the philosophy of moral treatment as espoused by Chiargui, Pinel, and Tuke, his contributions were remarkable.

Born in Hampden, Maine, Dorothea Lynde Dix (1802–1887), acclaimed as "one of the most famous women in American history," was a "teacher, writer, social reformer, religious poet, nurse [and] friend to the poor" (Stroup, 1986, p. 123). Frail and subject to periods of physical and mental collapse, her sensitivity and zeal were forged into a consuming force of advocacy for persons with mental illness when, after conducting Sunday school services for women offenders, she found prisoners with serious mental illness in unheated quarters in the East Cambridge, Massachusetts, jail. She gathered facts about the callous and inhumane confinement of persons with mental illness in institutions, including agencies, jails, and private homes. In presenting memorials (addresses citing the facts that she had collected) to many state legislatures, she succeeded in establishing asylums for the care of this population. Ironically, Dorothea Dix's efforts, which resulted, in part, in the expansion of large state hospitals together with the increasing popularity of the view that insanity was incurable, contributed to custodial functions becoming more dominant and moral treatment declining. Certainly, moral treatment was never applied universally in America where it was practiced primarily by private hospitals "or by only the most progressive public asylums" (Cockerham, 1989, p. 21). Unquestionably, Dorothea Dix's work had a profound impact on mental health policy in the United States, and its effects and implications continue today.

Early 20th Century

In the late 1800s, state hospitals continued to increase in number and size. Overcrowding "due to the large influx of poor immigrants and the emptying of jails and almshouses into the state facilities at the urging of Dorothea Dix" contributed to the failure of state hospitals (Krauss & Slavinsky, 1982, p. 70). Again, custodial care became the overriding role of state mental institutions.

One milestone in the history of the care of persons with mental illness was the publication of a remarkable autobiography. In 1908, Clifford Whittingham Beers, a New Haven, Connecticut, businessman, published *A Mind That Found Itself,* a book that dramatically chronicled the abusive and harsh treatment he received when hospitalized in 1900 for three years for manic-depressive mental illness (Beers, 1913). Also, in 1908, he played a major role in establishing the Connecticut Society for Mental Hygiene and was named its executive secretary (Deutsch, 1949). The next year, the National Committee for Mental Hygiene was founded primarily as the result of Beers's vision, energy, and talents. This citizen's movement identified mental illness as a problem requiring government intervention (Langsley, Berlin, & Yarvis, 1981). It evolved into the National Mental Health Association, a major advocacy organization in the mental health and mental illness arena. Now it is known as Mental Health America.

In the 1920s, demonstration child guidance clinics were established throughout the country, financed as a project of the Commonwealth Fund (Stroup, 1960). Predicated on the concept that meeting the mental health needs of children would prevent adult psychopathology, this movement employed an interdisciplinary team-staffing model consisting of a psychiatrist, psychologist, and psychiatric social worker (Callicutt, 1983).

World Wars I and II

As Deutsch (1949) notes, "It is one of the grotesque ironies of history that wars, with their frightful carnage in lives lost and wrecked, do tend to give impetus to various health movements" (p. 317). In this context, the high incidence of mental disorder in the military and the recognition of the need to deal with this issue in terms of the war effort led to the formation of a division of neurology and psychiatry as part of the Office of the Surgeon General. The responsibility for organizing this division was allocated to the National Committee for Mental Hygiene. Screening, diagnostic, and treatment services, and the development of facilities, were among the major functions of the division of neurology and psychiatry (Deutsch, 1949).

Psychiatric disorders caused over a million draft registrants to be rejected for military service by August 1, 1949, according to testimony by the director of the Selective Service System (Deutsch, 1949). Similarly, during the period of January 1, 1941, through December 31, 1945, approximately one million patients with neuropsychiatric disorders were admitted to U.S. Army hospitals (Menninger, 1947). These experiences set the stage and provided an impetus for federal government actions and policies related to mental illness and mental health, as presented in a subsequent section of this chapter.

Community Mental Health Movement

Penetration of the concepts of public health into the field of mental health was identified as "mental health's third revolution" by Hobbs (1964). Hobbs associated the names of Pinel, Tuke, Rush, and Dix with mental health's first revolution (see previous discussion of moral treatment) and the name of Sigmund Freud and the consequent preoccupation with intrapsychic life with mental health's second revolution (Hobbs, 1964).

The community mental health movement, embracing the concepts of public health including the early identification and treatment of mental disorders and attention to the realm of prevention, represented, in part, an outcome of the publication *Action for Mental Health*. This report of the Joint Commission on Mental Illness and Health (1961), a report sponsored by thirty-six organizations making up the commission, was a political and ideological document setting forth recommendations of experts after a five-year study process. In 1963, Congress passed the Mental Retardation Facilities and Community Mental Health Centers Construction Act. This legislation committed "the federal government to help support easily accessible and locally controlled mental health centers" and "reflected the objective of modern treatment to support mental patients in their own communities" (Cockerham, 1989, p. 280). Although the initial legislation excluded staffing grants, provision for staffing was included in subsequent amendments.

In order to receive federal funds, local centers had to provide five essential elements of service. Four of these elements were clinical or direct service in nature: inpatient, outpatient, twenty-four hour emergency, and partial hospitalization services. The remaining element—consultation and education—was nonclinical or indirect in nature. Through this service component, mental health centers provided services to the schools, social service agencies, professional groups such as the clergy, and the general public.

By 1982, there were 691 community mental health centers in the United States, up from about 300 in 1972. One of the expectations of the community mental health movement was to reduce admissions to state hospitals and serve patients more effectively and at less cost in the community. However, a well-recognized shortcoming was, for the most part, the failure of publicly funded centers to serve the chronic mental patient.

Deinstitutionalization

Deinstitutionalization is defined as "The process of releasing patients, inmates, or people who are dependent for their physical and mental care from *residential care facilities,* presumably with the understanding that they no longer need such care or can receive it through community based services" (Barker, 1995, p. 93). Community mental health centers were expected to be the linchpin in the deinstitutionalization of mental patients. Although state hospital admissions fell and outpatient and partial care admissions increased dramatically (as discussed in my subsequent discussion of the de facto mental health system), there is evidence that community mental health centers contributed little to the remarkable reduction of the number of patients populating state hospitals (Isaac & Armat, 1990)

Explosion of Private Psychiatric Hospital Services

Dramatic increases in the number of private psychiatric hospitals, from 150 to 475, accompanied by an increase in the number of psychiatric beds in these facilities occurred between 1970 and 1992 (Foley et al., 2006). Accounting for only 2.7% of inpatient beds in 1970, by 1992, psychiatric hospitals had 43,684 beds (down from a peak of 44,871 in 1990), which equaled 16.1% of the total of 270,867 beds in mental health organizations (Foley et al., 2006). Legislative and judicial decisions; funding policy changes, based, in part, on cost containment issues; and the scandalous abuses and unethical practices of some private psychiatric hospitals, which filled beds without regard to patients' needs for inpatient treatment, have resulted in the consolidation, downsizing, and closing of many of these hospitals (Callicutt, 1997; Sharkey, 1994). Thus, the trend involving the expansion of private psychiatric hospitals has now been reversed as further revealed by the fact that, in 2002, private psychiatric hospital beds had declined to 25, 095 or 11.9% of the total (211,199) of 24-hour hospital and residential treatments beds (Foley et al., 2006).

Managed Care

Currently, managed care is recognized as a potent, even dominant, force relative to the provision of services across the full spectrum of health and mental health services. As Ross and Croze (1997) observed, "Today, both the public and private sectors are attempting to manage care in an effort to deliver appropriate care that meets the patient's clinical needs under a fixed budget" (p. 359). Managed care is further discussed in Chapter 24 of this handbook.

It is clear that there are many issues, including accessibility to services and lack of service, as mental health care is extended further under the umbrella of managed care. There are hazards in terms of potential abuses, but there are challenges and opportunities to develop broader, better integrated, and more effective systems of mental health care (Mechanic, 1999).

The Current Mental Health System

A wide array of mental health programs and services proliferate across the United States today. They provide services to individuals and, to a lesser extent, families on a selective basis. The concept of *system* embraces the notion of interdependent or interrelated parts forming a unified or organized whole (Anderson & Carter, 1990). Rather than constituting a unified whole, the extant programs and services are often disjointed, fragmented, and lacking in cohesion. As they are driven by political, philosophical, professional, and ideological forces that may be neutral or even antagonistic instead of supportive of the development of an authentic, organized mental health system, it is reasonable to assume that what exists is basically a nonsystem (Callicutt, 1997). Nevertheless, there is wide recognition that the broad scope of mental health services provided under public, not-for-profit, and for-profit corporate and proprietary auspices in a multiplicity of settings, results in the existence of a de facto mental health service system (Bevilacqua, 1991; Regier, Goldberg, & Taube, 1978).

Components of the Mental Health System

The two major components of the mental health system are inpatient care and outpatient care. Partial care is also an important category. Currently, the practice is to classify patient care in two categories: 24-hour hospital and residential treatment care and less-than-24-hour care.

Inpatient. "Around-the-clock care is indicated when people are so seriously mentally disturbed that they pose a significant threat to themselves or others" (Callicutt, 1987, p. 126). The 32-year period from 1970 to 2002 showed a major change in the number of psychiatric beds in mental health organizations providing inpatient and/or residential treatment services. From an estimated 524,878 psychiatric beds in 1970, the number decreased by more than half to 211,199 in 2002 (Foley et al., 2006). This startling drop reflected decreases in the number of beds in state and county mental hospitals; accounting for about four-fifths of the beds in 1970, these beds represented only 27% of all psychiatric beds in 2002 (Foley et al., 2006).

Decreases in inpatient and residential treatment services beds are related to the deinstitutionalization movement, increases in outpatient services, increases in the number of community mental health centers, and the use of psychotropic medications. The influence of managed care and other cost containment policies and measures is also discerned in the reduction in 24-hour hospital and residential treatment beds.

Outpatient. I have asserted that outpatient services are the backbone of the mental health system (Callicutt, 1987). More extensive and effective use of outpatient care has both averted admissions to inpatient facilities as well as shortened inpatient stays (Callicutt, 1997).

Outpatient or less-than-24-hour care treatment options include short-term individual counseling or therapy, group and family therapy, extended supportive treatment, medication, and case management services. These and other services are available to a wide range of patients reflecting a broad spectrum of mental health problems (Callicutt, 1997).

Outpatient service settings include child and family guidance clinics, community mental health centers, outpatient departments of freestanding mental health agencies, and private practice offices of mental health professionals, including social workers, psychologists, and psychiatrists. Furthermore, primary care clinicians also treat a large number of patients with mental health problems.

As shown in Figure 26.1, a stunning shift has occurred in mental health organizations from 1955 to 2002. This shift relates to the number of patient care episodes—a duplicated count of the number of persons

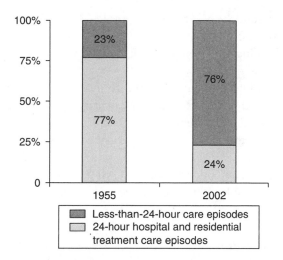

Figure 26.1   Patient Care Episodes in Mental Health Organizations in 1955 (1.7 Million Patient Care Episodes) and 2002 (9.5 Million Patient Care Episodes)

SOURCE: Reprinted from Foley et al. (2006, p. 209).

under care throughout the year. In 1955, inpatient episodes accounted for 77% of a total of 1.7 million episodes while outpatient episodes claimed the remaining 23%. Remarkably, in 2002, episodes in less-than-24-hour care facilities were 76% of a total of 9.5 million episodes while episodes in 24-hour hospital and residential treatment facilities were 24%. Impressively, the percentages are almost exactly reversed from 1955 to 2002 (Foley et al., 2006).

Major Mental Health Settings

This section describes the principal settings in the specialty mental health system. It includes those organizations designed to provide mental health services per se as distinct from the general health care system, which also includes mental health services.

Community Mental Health Centers. Passage of the Mental Retardation Facilities and Community Mental Health Centers Construction Act of 1963 (known as the CMHC Act) and its later amendments was a powerful stimulant to the growth in the number of community mental health centers (CMHCs)—from 205 in 1969 to 789 in 1980 (Lecca, 1983). However, the Omnibus Budget Reconciliation Act of 1981, passed during the Reagan administration, changed the course of federal financial support of community mental health centers from direct funding to the provision of block grants to the states, which would then allocate the funds. Although the federal initiative of providing staffing and construction grants was discontinued, the influence of the funding support that stimulated the development of community mental health centers from 1963 to 1981 continues. The organization, structure, and funding of CMHCs varies from state to state, as does the funding of mental health programs from state sources (Callicutt, 1987).

The de jure policy of deinstitutionalization (discussed in a previous section and discussed further in a subsequent section on policies) had a positive impact on the development of CMHCs, originally mandated to provide five essential elements of service: inpatient services, outpatient services, 24-hour emergency services, partial hospitalization, and consultation and education. Later, amendments to the CMHC Act of 1963 provided for staffing grants and added other service requirements. These requirements no longer apply as federal funds come to the states via block grants.

Department of Veterans Affairs. In 2002, the Department of Veterans Affairs (VA) provided psychiatric services to veterans at 140 VA medical centers. Of this number, 131 provided 24-hour hospital or residential treatment care, and 116 provided less-than-24-hour care (Foley et al., 2006). (See Price [1997] for a more detailed discussion of mental health services for veterans.)

State and County Mental Hospitals. From 1970 to 2002, the number of state and county mental hospitals declined from 310 to 273. Even more telling, for the same period, the number of beds in these facilities shrank from 413,066 to 93,058. In 1970, they accounted for almost 79% of inpatient beds available in all mental health organizations, whereas, in 2002, their ratio had decreased to 27.1%. Still, in 2002, these facilities had 52,612 inpatient residents, 29.1% of the inpatient and residential treatment residents in all mental health organizations (Foley et al., 2006). Again, although the number of hospitals, wards, and beds has witnessed a precipitous drop and the number of inpatient additions and inpatient residents likewise has declined, state and county mental hospitals continue to play a vital role in the care of the persons with serious mental illness and the poor. Lutterman (1994) indicated that state mental health agencies provide planning, policy making, and other functions in addition to direct client care services. In 2002, there were 222 state and county hospital, 88 fewer than in 1970, reflecting the trend from 24-hour care to ambulatory care (Foley et al., 2006).

Private Psychiatric Hospitals. The number of private psychiatric hospitals increased markedly between 1970 and 1992, from 150 to 475, and declined to 253 in 2002 (Foley et al., 2006) As mentioned previously, 2002 also saw a decline in the number of beds in private psychiatric hospitals to 25,095 (Foley et al., 2006).

Psychiatric Units in General Hospitals. Nonfederal general hospitals with psychiatric units increased from 797 in 1970 to 1,674 in 1990 and then dropped to 1,285 in 2002 (Foley et al., 2006). Similarly, the number of inpatient additions increased from 478,000 in 1969 to 1,094,715 in 2002. The most

additions—1,109,730—occurred in 1998. It now seems that the shift in the
locus of mental health care to nonfederal general hospitals is continuing, as
the growing use of these facilities accounts for nearly half of the 2002 additions to all mental health organizations providing 24-hour hospital and residential treatment (Foley et al., 2006).

Residential Treatment Centers. Residential treatment centers for emotionally
disturbed children, which numbered 261 in 1970, nearly doubled to 501 in
1990, declined to 497 in 1992, and then rose to 508 in 2002.

   In 2002, these facilities had 35,709 inpatients at the end of the year, up
from 13,489 in 1969 and accounting for 19.8% of all 24-hour hospital and
residential treatment residents (Foley et al., 2006).

Other Organizations. Freestanding psychiatric partial care organizations
and multiservice mental health organizations, which include community
mental health centers unless they are part of psychiatric or general hospitals,
are included in this category. In 2002, there were 1,893 such organizations,
with more than one-third (686) providing 24-hour hospital or residential
care services and 1,881 providing less-than-24-hour care (Foley et al., 2006).

Freestanding Psychiatric Outpatient Clinics. The number of freestanding
psychiatric outpatient clinics declined from 1,109 in 1970 to 743 in 1990 but
increased to 862 in 1992. Outpatient additions decreased from 538,426 in
1969 to 464,499 in 1992, but these facilities cared for 16% of the outpatient
care episodes in mental health organizations in 1992 (Redick, Witkin, Atay,
& Manderscheid, 1996). They are now included in the category of all other
mental health organizations, which also includes partial care organizations
and multiservice mental health organizations. In 2002, there were 1,893
organizations in this category with a total of 2,262,810 additions or 63.3%
of less-than-24-hour care additions to all organizations (Foley et al., 2006).

Private Practice, Nontraditional Settings, and Innovative Services. Mental
health professionals in private practice settings play an important role in the
mental health service system. Although systematic service statistics are not
available relative to this component of care, the role of primary care clinicians is clearly recognized, with Regier et al. (1978) observing that 54.1% of
people with mental disorders received services in the outpatient or primary
care medical sector. Primary care clinicians (e.g., general practitioners,
family practitioners, pediatricians, and internists) frequently are the sole
source of care for people with mental disorders (Manderscheid, Rae,
Narrow, Loch, & Regier, 1993).

   Self-help and mutual aid groups, as well as advocacy organizations and
consumer groups, continue to play an important role in the mental health
arena (Watkins & Callicutt, 1997). In addition, mental health services are
provided within occupational, educational, and other organizational settings, including in jails, prisons, and the workplace.

Homeless Shelters, Jails, and Prisons. Although they are not a part of the specialty mental health system as such, I have asserted that homeless shelters, jails, and prisons are uneasy components of the de facto mental health system (Callicutt, 2006). Moreover, Rochefort (1997) called attention to the "'localization' of mental health care, in the form of greater reliance on county, municipal, and other local resources, from general hospitals, to homeless shelters, to jails" as an important dimension of the deinstitutionalization shift (p. 149).

Torrey (1988, 1997) graphically depicted the harsh reality of homelessness all too often faced by persons with mental illness. Although the National Coalition for the Homeless (2006) notes two trends as "largely responsible for the rise in homelessness over the past 20–25 years: a growing shortage of affordable rental housing and a simultaneous increase in poverty" (p. 1), there is a disproportionate number of persons with serious mental illness, estimated at 23%, in the population of persons who are homeless (U.S. Conference of Mayors, 2003).

In the *Survey of Mental Health Organizations and General Hospital Mental Health Services*, Manderscheid and Berry (2006) reported a total of 4,301 mental health organizations in 2002, down from a peak of 5,722 in 1998. However, clearly absent in the statistics compiled via this survey are the homeless shelters, jails, and prisons: uneasy components of the de facto mental health system.

Staffing: The Mental Health Professions

Traditionally, the recognized core mental health professions are psychiatry, psychology, mental health nursing, and social work. (See Callicutt and Price [1997] for a fuller discussion of these four mental health core professions.) In addition, other important patient care professions involved in the provision of mental health services have been clearly acknowledged. For example, Dial et al. (1992) discuss marriage and family therapy, clinical mental health counseling, and psychosocial rehabilitation in the context of developing areas of practice. More recently, school psychology has been included in "An Update on Human Resources in Mental Health" published in *Mental Health, United States, 1996* (Peterson et al., 1996). The revival of the practice movement in sociology is also outlined (Peterson et al., 1996).

In 2000, there were 569,187 full-time equivalent staff members employed in all mental health organizations. Table 26.1 shows the number and percent distribution of these positions by staff discipline for selected years from 1972 to 2000. In 2000, among the traditional core professions, registered nurses accounted for 12.4%; social workers, 12.3%; psychologists, 3.3%, and psychiatrists, 3.6%. The peak year shown for full-time equivalent staff was 1998 with a total of 680,310 (Foley et al., 2006).

Table 26.1 Number and Percent Distribution of Full-Time Equivalent Staff[1] in All Mental Health Organizations by Staff Discipline: United States, Selected Years, 1972–2002[2]

Staff discipline	1972	1976	1978	1986[2,3]	1990	1992	1994	1998	2000
	Number of FTE staff								
All staff	375,984	373,969	430,051	494,515	563,619	585,972	577,669	680,310	569,187
Patient care staff	241,265	251,756	292,699	348,630	415,719	432,866	370,635	531,532	426,558
Professional patient care staff	100,886	117,190	153,598	232,481	273,374	305,988	225,250	304,449	243,993
Psychiatrists	12,938	12,888	14,492	17,874	18,818	22,803	20,242	28,374	20,233
Other physicians	3,991	3,055	3,034	3,868	3,865	4,949	2,692	3,561	2,962
Psychologists[4]	9,443	10,587	16,501	20,210	22,825	25,000	14,050	28,729	19,003
Social workers	17,887	18,927	28,125	40,951	53,375	57,136	41,326	72,367	70,208
Registered nurses	31,110	33,981	42,399	06,180	77,635	78,588	82,620	78,562	70,295
Other mental health professionals	17,514	27,977	39,363	56,245	84,071	102,162	57,982	78,854	53171
Physical health professionals and assistants	8,203	9,767	9,684	27,153	12,785	16,350	6,338	14,002	8,023
Other mental health workers[5]	140,379	134,566	139,101	114,149	142,345	126,878	145,385	227,083	182,566
Administrative, clerical, and maintenance staff	134,719	122,213	137,352	147,885	147,800	153,106	207,034	148,778	142,627
	Percent distribution of FTE staff								
All staff	100.0	100.0	100.0	100.0	100.0	100	1010	100.0	100.0
Patient care staff	64.2	67.3	68.1	70.1	73.8	73.9	64.2	78.1	74.9
Professional patient care staff	26.8	31.3	35.7	47.0	48.5	512	310	448	42.9
Psychiatrists	3.4	3.4	3.4	3.6	3.3	3.9	3.5	4.2	3.6
Other physicians	1.1	0.8	0.7	0.8	0.7	0.7	0.5	0.5	0.5
Psychologists[4]	2.5	2.8	3.8	4.1	4.0	4.3	2.4	4.2	3.3
Social workers	4.7	5.1	6.5	8.3	9.5	9.8	7.2	10.6	12.3
Registered nurses	8.3	9.1	9.9	13.4	13.8	114	14.3	11.5	12.4
Other mental health professionals	4.7	7.5	9.2	11.4	14.9	17.4	10.0	11.6	9.4
Physical health professionals and assistants	2.2	2.6	2.3	5.5	2.3	2.8	1.1	2.1	1.4
Other mental health workers[5]	37.3	36.0	32.3	23.1	25.3	21.7	25.2	33.4	32.1
Administrative, clerical, and maintenance staff	35.8	32.7	31.9	29.9	26.2	26.1	35.8	21.9	25.1

SOURCES: Reprinted from Foley et al. (2006, p. 211). Published and unpublished inventory data from the Survey and Analysis Branch, Division of State and Community Systems Development, Center for Mental Health Services.

1. The computation of full-time equivalent staff is based on a 40-hour work week.
2. For 1986, some organizations had been reclassified as a result of changes in reporting procedures and definitions.
3. Includes data for CMHCs in 1978. In 1986, 1990, 1992, and 1994, these staff were subsumed under other organization types. Data for CMHCs are not shown separately.
4. For 1972–1978, this category included all psychologists with a BA degree and above; for 1986–1994, it included only psychologists with an MA degree and above.
5. Workers in this category have less than a BA degree.

It is obvious that the specialty mental health industry utilizes a broad array of human resources in staffing organizations. Expanded use of personnel from the various professions is likely to produce both competition and conflict among the patient care professions as this process continues.

Mental Health Policy

As mentioned previously, mental health service provision is a reflection of mental health policy. For the most part, public mental health policy is a product of legislative, regulative, and judicial processes—that is, laws, regulations, and court decisions (Callicutt, 1997). In addition, customs and mores of the community shape public policy. Beyond these forces, there is also the impact of program spending patterns in both the public and voluntary sectors, which further contour mental health policy and services.

Making a useful distinction between de jure and de facto public policy, Keisler and Sibulkin (1987) observe, "*De jure* policy is intentional in nature and usually legislated into law. The *de facto* policy is the net outcome of overall practices whether the outcome is intended or not" (p. 17). In this context, the de jure mental health policy of the United States is deinstitutionalization and its presumedly concomitant community-based approach emphasizing outpatient services. However, de facto mental health policy, shaped by the underfunding of community-based programs and resources, has led, in part, to the flood of persons with mental illness who are homeless, an unintended negative consequence of deinstitutionalization (Callicutt, 1997). This tragic national phenomenon is attributed, in part, to the misguided efforts of civil libertarians to *free* persons with mental illness (Grob, 1994; Isaac & Armat, 1990; Kuhlman, 1994; Rochefort, 1997; Torrey, 1988). Isaac and Armat (1990) assert that psychiatry, as well as the law, abandoned persons with mental illness and contributed to the surge of persons with mental illness *in the streets*. As discussed earlier, the United States has a de facto mental health system; also, we have a de facto mental health policy.

Federal Government Leadership and Initiatives

Historically, the states have played a prominent role in providing care for persons with mental illness and consequently in the establishment of mental health policy (see Hudson & Cox, 1991). World War II created an increased awareness of both the high cost of mental illness and the potential effectiveness of psychiatric intervention. This set the stage for the passage of the National Mental Health Act of 1946, which provided for the funding of research, the training of professional personnel, and assistance to the states in establishing pilot and demonstration projects and studies. It focused on the cause, diagnosis, treatment, and prevention of mental disorders.

In 1949, the National Institute of Mental Health (NIMH) was formed after funds were appropriated to carry out the act's provisions. This agency has had a major impact on the development of the mental health system in the United States.

As a result of the Mental Health Study Act of 1955, the Joint Commission on Mental Illness and Health was formed to study the problems of mental and emotional illness. A series of important monographs was published by the commission. Its final report, *Action for Mental Health* (Joint Commission on Mental Illness and Health, 1961), listed the major barriers to the development of mental health programs and recommended the establishment of full-time mental health clinics and general hospital psychiatric units, the development of intensive psychiatric treatment centers, increased recruitment of professional personnel, and investment in long-term basic research.

Based on experience, including the successful treatment of military personnel on the front lines, new community mental health centers focused on treating the patient in the community not in an isolated institution away from family, job, and friends (Callicutt, 1987). The intent was to provide seed money for initiating programs, with the expectation that the state and local community would cover the operating costs as federal support was withdrawn.

In 1977, President Jimmy Carter signed Executive Order No. 11793 establishing the President's Commission on Mental Health "to review the mental health needs of the Nation and to make recommendations to the President as to how the Nation might best meet these needs" (President's Commission on Mental Health, 1978, p. 1). After holding public hearings across the country, the commission submitted its report in 1978.

The commission suggested that 15% of the population, rather than the previous estimate of 10%, needed mental health services. However, estimates of prevalence rates in 1990 suggested that 40.4 million persons experienced a nonaddictive mental disorder with an additional 10.9 million persons affected by an addictive disorder (Bourdon, Rae, Narrow, Manderscheid, & Regier, 1994). Other recommendations addressed the needs of underserved populations, including persons with chronic mental illness and racial and ethnic minorities. Subsequently, the Mental Health Systems Act of 1980 authorized the continuation of grants for community mental health centers and for special populations. Case management was stressed for persons with chronic mental illness discharged or diverted from inpatient facilities. Also, it required that performance contracts be executed.

The Omnibus Budget Reconciliation Act of 1981, passed under the Reagan administration provided that federal funds cut by 25% be allocated directly to the states, which would have the responsibility for distributing them. This legislation set a different tack relative to the course of mental health policy and the interface of the federal government and the states.

Individual states have considerable mental health policy leeway, in terms of the influence of the state mental health agency director, office of the governor, state legislators, as well as local elected officials, boards, and staff members in molding, interpreting, directing, and implementing decisions regarding program funding and service provisions (Fellin, 1996).

Other federal policy initiatives have been directed to specific populations, especially persons with chronic mental illness. Community support programs were developed, and service emphases included the "clubhouse" model for the rehabilitation of former patients from psychiatric hospitals. Fountain House in New York City was the first. Psychosocial rehabilitation programs, such as Assertive Community Treatment (ACT) developed in Madison, Wisconsin, were also replicated with variations throughout the country (Fellin, 1996).

Other federal legislation targeting persons with chronic mental illness and focusing on the states establishing an organized community-based system of care is seen in the State Comprehensive Mental Health Services Plan Act of 1986 (P.L. 99-660) (Fellin, 1996).

Patterns of funding for programs including Medicare and Medicaid have also impacted patient care, shifting many elderly patients from state hospitals to nursing homes or board and care homes in the community. In some respects, the operative term is transinstitutionalization rather than deinstitutionalization.

President George W. Bush's Executive Order 13263 of April 29, 2002, established the President's New Freedom Commission on Mental Health. The commission, consisting of 15 members appointed by the president and seven ex officio members, was chaired by Michael F. Hogan (PhD), director of the Ohio Department of Mental Health. It was directed "to study the problems and gaps in the mental health system and make concrete recommendations for immediate improvements that the Federal government, state governments, local agencies, as well as public and private health care providers can implement" (New Freedom Commission on Mental Health, 2003, p. 1).

In its *Interim Report to the President*, the New Freedom Commission on Mental Health (2002) declared ". . . the [mental health delivery] system is fragmented and in disarray . . . lead[ing] to unnecessary and costly disability, homelessness, school failure, and incarceration" (p. 2).

Its final report, *Achieving the Promise: Transforming Mental Health Care in America*, was submitted to President Bush on April 22, 2003. In it, the commission specified recovery as the goal of a transformed system and identified six intertwined goals for transforming mental health care in America:

Goal 1: Americans Understand that Mental Health is Essential to Overall Health.

Goal 2: Mental Health Care is Consumer and Family Driven.

Goal 3: Disparities in Mental Health Services are Eliminated.

Goal 4: Early Mental Health Screening, Assessment, and Referral to Services are Common Practice.

Goal 5: Excellent Mental Health Care is Delivered and Research is Accelerated.

Goal 6: Technology is Used to Access Mental Health Care and Information. (New Freedom Commission on Mental Health, 2003, p. 5)

Among the serious health challenges underscored in the commission's final report is the sobering fact that "mental illnesses rank first among illnesses that cause disability in the United States, Canada, and Western Europe" (New Freedom Commission on Mental Health, 2003, p. 3). It stated that "the World Health Organization (WHO) recently reported that suicide worldwide causes more deaths every year than homicide or war" (p. 3).

In addition, it reported that the economic cost of mental illness is remarkably high: an estimated $79 billion annually in indirect cost that includes the "loss of productivity as a result of illnesses, . . . almost $12 billion in mortality costs (lost productivity resulting from premature death) and almost $4 billion in productivity losses for incarcerated individuals and for the time of those who provide family care" (p. 3).

Achieving the Promise: Transforming Mental Health Care in America presents a chapter on each goal and discusses the recommendations formulated to reach the goal. Thus, the document may be considered as a proposed blueprint for transforming mental health care in America (New Freedom Commission on Mental Health, 2003).

Events in the United States prior to and since the publication of this report have resulted in the consumption of an enormous amount of fiscal and human resources. The war on terror, homeland security issues, and the war in Iraq have emerged as high priorities for the Bush administration. Nevertheless, there has been some movement in the mental health arena. For example, nine states have received Mental Health Transformation State Incentive Grants "to help change the mental health service delivery system in each state to reflect consumer and family needs and to focus on building resiliency and facilitating recovery" (Substance Abuse and Mental Health Services Administration, 2005, p. 2).

In 2005, seven states selected from among 33 applicants received awards totaling 92.5 million over five years. In 2006, two more states were awarded Mental Health Transformation State Incentive Grants totaling $21.9 million over five years (Substance Abuse and Mental Health Services Administration, 2006, p. 3). Thus, the combined total awarded to the nine states is $114.4 million.

Texas's Mental Health Transformation State Incentive Grant (Ganju, 2006), characterized as the Comprehensive Mental Health Plan for the State of Texas, was among the first seven awarded. The grant application addressed, in order, the goals specified by the New Freedom Commission on Mental Health. Several emphases stand out in the plan:

> The approach to transformation is to build on current strengths and initiatives; to focus on key, pivotal areas; to place initiatives in a learning framework; and to be opportunistic.
>
> An essential aspect is the development of a transformation partnership culture, which builds on new technologies, collaboration among agencies, and a strong and vibrant consumer and family member voice.
>
> A basic assumption of the plan is that transformation must occur at both state and local levels. Activities at that state level alone will not result in improved access or outcomes. The focus on local community behavioral health collaboratives is critical. (p. 5)

The explicit thrust is to promote partnerships at the state and local levels, to sanction and reward multiple collaborations, and to integrate funding across the [transformed] system.

How this overall incentive strategy will play out remains to be seen. Will it lead to by-products of more operational control by private managed care companies and possibly more regional centralization or to increased reliance on and exploitation of local unique opportunities, incentives, and collaborations? In any event, the experiences of the nine states awarded the transformation grants will provide some answers to these and other questions as the 50 states and other entities struggle to fix the nation's broken mental health system.

Role of the Courts

Judicial decisions have had a profound impact on mental health policy. Only a few instances will be mentioned to highlight the significance of the court's influence. For example, when the courts held that persons involuntarily committed should receive care according to the concept of the least restrictive alternative, this principle challenged mental health professionals to determine the need for institutional treatment as opposed to a form of community care; it also required that similar consideration be given the range of limitations and restrictions in structuring a person's care in the hospital (Crain, 1983; Shannon, 1997).

In another important decision, the courts have also held that patients may not be exploited for their work in mental institutions. If they work, it must be performed voluntarily, and they must be compensated (Crain, 1983).

In 1971, a federal court found in *Wyatt v. Stickney* that the Alabama state mental health facility was providing woefully inadequate care, and the court subsequently conducted an extensive bearing, ultimately resulting in the stipulation of an array of treatment conditions to provide an acceptable treatment program (Shannon, 1997). A broad array of treatment issues were addressed including the right to be free from excessive or unwarranted medication and a right to informed consent before the use of invasive procedures such as electroconvulsive treatment. It was this case in which the least restrictive alternative issue was spelled out (Shannon, 1997).

Many other court decisions speak to mental health issues, including the insanity defense, competence to stand trial, and the diversion of offenders with mental illness out of the jail setting to more appropriate treatment facilities pending further criminal proceedings. In addition, there are decisions affecting the potential liability of mental health professions; for example, there are the legal questions around the "duty to warn" when the professional has direct knowledge of the patient posing a risk to harm someone (Shannon, 1997). These examples illustrate the enormous impact of the courts in forming mental health policy.

Issues and Trends

In this section, I underscore some of the basic issues in the sphere of mental health policy. Likewise, selected trends will be highlighted. First and foremost, inpatient and residential treatment services are declining—in terms of the number of facilities, the number of beds, the number of treatment episodes, and length of stay. This trend started in 1955, and the locus of patient care has shifted from inpatient to outpatient as a consequence of the deinstitutionalization movement and the use of psychotropic medications. Sadly, we are continuing to witness the spectacle of "The Tragic Odyssey of the Homeless Mentally Ill" (Torrey, 1988). The forces involved in this problem are complex: political, economic, philosophical, ideological, and more. Although the need for housing for the homeless is obvious, the need for providing treatment resources for those suffering from mental and/or addictive disorders is also apparent. We are not yet close to addressing this problem adequately.

The environment of managed mental health care is a current reality, but its parameters are not fixed. Although this movement is, in fact, inexorable, its effects are uncertain. It is safe to predict that the competition for managed care contracts will be keen, as the stakes are high. Special provision should be made to ensure that persons with severe and persistent mental illness will receive the necessary treatment and community support services to permit them to have a reasonably safe and acceptable life in the community. While this is an appropriate goal, inpatient care should be accessible when needed. Not every acute mental disturbance is responsive to community-based interventions.

Persons with addictive disorders, by and large, require treatment services. Persons involved in crimes related to substance abuse are taxing the resources of state and federal prisons in the United States. In 1993, drug offenders made up 30% of newly sentenced inmates as opposed to 7% in

1988 (Turnbo & Murray, 1997). As noted by Turnbo and Murray (1997), "Because of the deinstitutionalization of the mentally ill, the criminal justice system now increasingly has become the destination of mentally ill and developmentally disabled individuals" (p. 298). This unsettling trend should compel policy makers to make mental health treatment services available to this group. However, it seems that elected officials are responding to their constituents' views that support the building and maintenance of prisons at the expense of providing an adequate range of treatment services. Advocacy organizations must be more aggressive in *educating* the public as well as pushing for policy reforms.

Advances in the neurosciences offer one foundation for optimism regarding the treatment of people with mental disorders. New, more effective medications offer increased hope for providing mental stability for persons with schizophrenia, depression, anxiety, or bipolar affective disorders. As Wilson (1997) asserts, "Neuroscience now provides an essential perspective regarding the causes and treatments of mental disorders." He goes on to conclude, "Effective humanistic treatments for mental illness will be heavily influenced by neuroscientific research" (p. 105). Here, the call is for policy makers and funding organizations to continue, and even increase, support for neuroscientific research. Furthermore, social research legitimately has a claim for funding (Millard, 1997) in terms of its potential impact in preventing and combating mental illness.

Perhaps one of the more compelling issues deals with the balance between the right to receive treatment juxtaposed against the right to refuse treatment. This complex equation, at one point, seemed to pit the fields of mental health law, fueled by the passion of the civil rights movement, against the ideology involving psychiatry's responsibility to provide appropriate treatment services to the mentally disordered. As lawyers fought to free persons from confinement occasioned by mental problems, psychiatrists, it is suggested, acquiesced to the onslaught of the mental health bar (Isaac & Armat, 1990). Shannon (1997) captures the essence of the issue, placing it within our cultural context:

> As greater knowledge is acquired about the diagnosis and treatment of serious mental illness, the courts and judicial system will eventually catch up. Unfortunately, however, there is often a time lag between medical learning and judicial acceptance of new developments. As old stigmas and inaccurate assessments of serious mental illnesses as somehow not being real diseases fade away, the courts and advocates will likely become more attuned to appropriate treatment needs. (p. 66)

Judicial decisions, then, will continue to be prominent in the mental health policy arena and, thus, will impact the system of mental health service delivery.

References

Anderson, R. E., & Carter, S. (1990). *Human behavior in the social environment: A social system approach* (4th ed.). New York: Aldine de Gruyter.

Barker, R. L. (1995). *The social work dictionary* (3rd ed.). Washington, DC: NASW Press.

Beers, C. W. (1913). *A mind that found itself* (3rd ed., Rev.). Norwood, MA: Plimpton Press.

Bevilacqua, J. J. (1991). Overview of state mental health policy. In C. G. Hudson & A. J. Cox (Eds.), *Dimensions of state mental health policy* (pp. 73–83). New York: Praeger.

Bourdon, K., Rae, D., Narrow, W., Manderscheid, R. W., & Regier, D. (1994). National prevalence and treatment of mental and addictive disorders. In R. W. Manderscheid & M. A. Sonnenschein (Eds.), *Mental health United States, 1994* (CDHHS Publication No. SMA 94–3000, pp. 22–51). Washington, DC: Government Printing Office.

Callicutt, J. W. (1983). Contemporary settings and the rise of the profession in mental health. In J. W. Callicutt & P. J. Lecca (Eds.), *Social work and mental health* (pp. 30–41). New York: Free Press.

Callicutt, J. W. (1987). Mental health services. In A. Minahan et al. (Ed.), *Encyclopedia of social work* (18th ed., Vol. 2, pp. 125–135). Silver Spring, MD: NASW Press.

Callicutt, J. W. (1997). Overview of the field of mental health. In T. R. Watkins & J. W. Callicutt (Eds.), *Mental health policy and practice today* (pp. 1–16). Thousand Oaks, CA: Sage.

Callicutt, J. W. (2006). Homeless shelters: An uneasy component of the de facto mental health system. In J. Rosenberg & S. Rosenberg (Eds.), *Community mental health: Challenges for the 21st century* (pp. 169–180). New York: Routledge.

Callicutt, J. W., & Lecca, P. J. (1983). The convergence of social work and mental health services. In J. W. Callicutt & P. J. Lecca (Eds.), *Social work and mental health* (pp. 3–10). New York: Free Press.

Callicutt, J. W., & Price, D. H. (1997). Personnel: The professionals and their preparation. In T. R. Watkins & J. W. Callicutt (Eds.), *Mental Health policy and practice today* (pp. 69–85). Thousand Oaks, CA: Sage.

Cockerham, W. C. (1989). *Sociology of mental disorders* (2nd ed.). Englewood Cliffs, NJ: Prentice Hall.

Crain, P. M. (1983). Civil law. In J. A. Talbott & S. R. Kaplan (Eds.), *Psychiatric administration: A comprehensive text for the clinician-executive* (pp. 369–383). New York: Grune & Stratton.

Deutsch, A. (1949). *The mentally ill in America* (2nd ed.). New York: Columbia University Press.

Dial, T. H., Pion, G. M., Cooney, B., Hohout, J., Kaplan, K. O., Ginsberg, L., et al. (1992). Training of mental health providers. In R. W. Manderscheid & M. A. Sonnenschein (Eds.), *Mental health, United States, 1992* (CDHHS Publication No. SMA-92-1942, pp. 142–162). Washington, DC: Government Printing Office.

Fellin, P. (1996). *Mental health and mental illness: Policies, programs, and services.* Itasca, IL: F. E. Peacock.

Foley, D. J., Manderscheid, R. W., Atay, J. E., Maedke, J., Sussman, J., & Cribbs, S. (2006). Highlights of organized mental health services in 2002 and major national and state trends. In R.W. Manderscheid & J. T. Berry (Eds.), *Mental health, United States, 2004* (DHHS Publication No. SMA-06-4195, pp. 200–236). Rockville, MD: Substance Abuse & Mental Health Services Administration.

Ganju, V. (2006). *Mental health transformation states incentive grant: Comprehensive mental health plan for the state of Texas* (Grant No. SM-05-009). Austin: Texas Department of State Health Services.

Glover, M. R. (1984). *The Retreat York: An early experiment in the treatment of mental illness.* York, UK: William Sessions Limited.

Grob, G. N. (1973). *Mental institutions in America.* New York: Free Press.

Grob, G. N. (1994). *The mad among us: A history of the care of America's mentally ill.* New York: Free Press.

Hobbs, N. (1964). Mental health's third revolution. *American Journal of Orthopsychiatry, 34,* 822–833.

Hudson, C. G., & Cox, A. J. (Eds.). (1991). *Dimensions of state mental health policy.* New York: Praeger.

Isaac, R. J., & Armat, V.C. (1990). *Madness in the streets: How psychiatry and the law abandoned the mentally ill.* New York: Free Press.

Joint Commission on Mental Illness and Health. (1961). *Action for mental health.* New York: Science Editions.

Kiesler, C. A., & Sibulkin, A. E. (1987). *Mental hospitalization: Myths and facts about a national crisis.* Newbury Park, CA: Sage.

Krauss, J. B., & Slavinsky, A. T. (1982). *The chronically ill psychiatric patient and the community.* Boston: Blackwell Scientific.

Kuhlman, T. L. (1994). *Psychology on the streets: Mental health practice with homeless persons.* New York: Brunner/Mazel.

Langsley, D. G., Berlin, F. N., & Yarvis, R. M. (1981*). Handbook of community mental health.* Garden City, NY: Medical Examination Publishing.

Lecca, P. J. (1983). Current trends in mental health services and legislation. In J. W. Callicutt & P. J. Lecca (Eds.), *Social work and mental health* (pp. 11–29). New York: Free Press.

Lutterman, T. C. (1994). The state mental health agency profile system. In R. W. Manderscheid & M. A. Sonnenschein (Eds.), *Mental health, United States, 1994* (CDHHS Publication No. SMA 94-3000, pp. 165–187). Washington, DC: Government Printing Office.

Manderscheid, R. W., & Berry, J. T. (Eds.). (2006). *Mental health, United States, 2004* (Center for Mental Health Services DHHS Publication No. SMA 06 4195). Rockville, MD: Substance Abuse & Mental Health Services Administration.

Manderscheid, R. W., Rae, D. S., Narrow, W. E., Loch, B. E., & Regier, D. A. (1993). Congruence of service utilization estimates from the epidemiologic catchment area project and other sources. *Archives of General Psychiatry, 50,* 108–114.

Mechanic, D. (1999). *Mental health and social policy: The emergence of managed care* (4th ed.). Boston: Allyn & Bacon.

Menninger, W. C. (1947, March). Psychiatric experience in the war, 1941–1946. *American Journal of Psychiatry, 103,* 577–586.

Millard, D. W. (1997). Research into social factors in mental health. In T. R. Watkins & J. W. Callicutt (Eds.), *Mental health policy and practice* (pp. 107–128). Thousand Oaks, CA: Sage.

National Coalition for the Homeless. (2006). *Why are people homeless?* (NCH Fact Sheet No. 1). Washington, DC: Author.

New Freedom Commission on Mental Health. (2002). *Interim report*. Retrieved October 26, 2006, from http://www.mentalhealthcommission.gov/reports/Interim_Report.htm

New Freedom Commission on Mental Health. (2003). *Achieving the promise: Transforming mental health care in America* (DHHS Publication No. SMA-03-3832). Rockville, MD: Author.

Peterson, B. D., West, J., Pincus, H. A., Kohout, J., Pion, G. M., Wicherski, M. M., et al. (1996). An update on human resources in mental health. In R. W. Manderscheid & M. A. Sonnenehein (Eds.), *Mental health, United States, 1996* (CDHHS Publication No. SMA 3098, pp. 168–204). Washington, DC: Government Printing Office.

President's Commission on Mental Health. (1978). *Report to the president* (Vol. 9). Washington, DC: Government Printing Office.

Price, D. H. (1997). Mental health services to America's veterans. In T. R. Watkins & J. W. Callicutt (Eds.), *Mental health policy and practice today* (pp. 209–234). Thousand Oaks, CA: Sage.

Redick, R. W., Witkin, M. J., Atay, J. E., & Manderscheid, R. W. (1996). Highlights of organized mental health services in 1992 and major national and state trends. In R. W. Manderscheid & M. A. Sonnenschein (Eds.), *Mental health, United States, 1996* (CDHHS Publication No. SMA 96–3098, pp. 90–137). Washington, DC: Government Printing Office.

Regier, D. A., Goldberg, J. D., & Taube, C. A. (1978). The de facto U.S. mental health services system: A public health perspective. *Archives of General Psychiatry, 35,* 685–693.

Rochefort, D. A. (1997). *From poorhouses to homelessness: Policy analysis and mental health care* (2nd ed.). Westport, CT: Auburn House

Ross, E. C., & Croze, C. (1997). Mental health policy and practice today. In T. R. Watkins & J. W. Callicutt (Eds.), *Mental health policy and practice today* (pp. 346–361). Thousand Oaks, CA: Sage.

Shannon, B. (1997). The impact of the courts on mental health policy and services. In T. R. Watkins & J. W. Callicutt (Eds.), *Mental health policy and practice today* (pp. 49–68). Thousand Oaks, CA: Sage.

Sharkey, J. (1994). *Bedlam.* New York: St. Martin's.

Stroup, H. S. (1960). *Social work: An introduction to the field.* New York: American Book Co.

Stroup, H. (1986). *Social welfare pioneers.* Chicago: Nelson-Hall.

Substance Abuse and Mental Health Services Administration. (2005, November/December). SAMHSA awards final 2005 grants. *SAMHSA News, 13*(6). Retrieved October 26, 2006, from http://www.samhsa.gov/SAMHSA_News/VolumeXIII_6/NovDec2005.pdf

Substance Abuse and Mental Health Services Administration. (2006, September/October). SAMHSA awards final 2005 grants. *SAMHSA News, 14*(5). Retrieved October 26, 2006, from http://www.samhsa.gov/SAMHSA_News/VolumeXIV_5/septoct2006.pdf

Torrey, E. F. (1988). *Nowhere to go.* New York: Harper & Row.

Torrey, E. F. (1997). *Out of the shadows: Confronting America's mental illness crisis.* New York: Harper & Row.

Turnbo, C., & Murray, D. W., Jr. (1997). The state of mental health services to criminal offenders. In T. R. Watkins & J. W. Callicutt (Eds.), *Mental health policy and practice today* (pp. 298–311). Thousand Oaks, CA: Sage.

U.S. Conference of Mayors. (2003). *Hunger and homeless survey 2003.* Washington, DC: Author.

Watkins, T. R., & Callicutt, J. W. (1997). Self-help advocacy group in mental health. In T. R. Watkins & J. W. Callicutt (Eds.), *Mental health policy and practice today* (pp. 146–162). Thousand Oaks, CA: Sage.

Wilson, W. H. (1997). Neuroscientific research in mental health. In T. R. Watkins & J. W. Callicutt (Eds.), *Mental health policy and practice today* (pp. 89–106). Thousand Oaks, CA: Sage.

Wyatt v. Stickney, 325 F. Supp. 781 (M.D. Ala. 1971), 334 F. Supp. 1341 (M.D. Ala. 1972), 344 F. Supp. 373 (M.D. Ala. 1972), 344 F. Supp. 387 (M.D. Ala. 1972), aff'd sub nom., Wyatt v. Aderholt, 503 F.2d 1305 (5th Cir. 1974).

27 Social Policies for People With Disabilities

Elizabeth Lightfoot

Many varied social policies, at both the federal and state levels of the United States, currently affect the lives of people with disabilities. The current core goals for U.S. disability policy, as outlined in the Americans with Disabilities Act of 1990, are *equality of opportunity, full participation, independent living,* and *economic self-sufficiency.* The policies include civil rights laws, entitlement programs, discretionary grant-in-aid programs, and regulatory statutes (Silverstein, 2000). The policies take the form of cash benefits, in-kind benefits, social services, and regulations. The disability policy framework is now so complicated that, in the federal code alone, there are 67 different sections that define disability, with a total of 35 separate definitions of disability (Cherry Engineering Support Services Inc., 2003). This chapter briefly outlines the paradigm shifts relating to disability policy that occurred in the 20th century, provides an overview of the major federal social policies affecting the lives of people with disabilities, and describes current and future trends related to disability policy.

Historical Background

Prior to the 20th century, people with disabilities in the United States were routinely excluded from virtually every aspect of society, including education, employment, religion, and community life. There were neither policies protecting them from discrimination nor ones providing them with services, subsistence, or supports. During the 20th century, a labyrinth of federal and state policies were developed that helped protect people with disabilities from discrimination, promote community inclusion, and provide financial support. Although these policies have helped to improve the lives of people with disabilities, those with disabilities still routinely face poverty, social exclusion, discrimination, and high unemployment rates.

Through the ages, many have viewed the concept of *disability* through a moral or religious lens (Clapton & Fitzgerald, 1997). Disability has been conceived of, in some religious or cultural traditions, as being a reflection of some sort of moral flaw that is associated with an individual or his or her family (Barnes, 1997). As such, many people with disabilities were either hidden by their families or banished. Other religious or cultural traditions have viewed disability as a blessing and have thus treated people with disabilities with reverence. In early U.S. history, there is evidence of both moral views of disability. Additionally, people with disabilities were often viewed in a charitable fashion. They were the "deserving" poor in the Elizabethan Poor Laws, deserving of public charity and public pity. Indeed, the primary public support that people with disabilities received during the early 20th century was through the giving of alms.

With the rise of the medical profession in the late 19th and early 20th century, the medical model began to dominate views of disability. Under the medical model, disability is viewed as a pathological individual attribute linked to incapacity and dependence. The focus of the medical model is to rehabilitate or cure the individual, in other words, to help an individual overcome his or her disability. The rise of the medical model fit with the increasingly industrialized society, which increasingly valued participation in paid employment (Clapton & Fitzgerald, 1997). People with disabilities, who could not be rehabilitated enough to participate in the paid labor market, were often institutionalized, either for further training or for receiving specialized care. These two trends led to the large focus on institutionalizing people with disabilities, a focus that continued through the mid-twentieth century. These trends also coincided with the rise of the eugenics movement in the Unites States, when many state laws were passed allowing forced sterilization of people with disabilities as a means of preventing more disabilities (Kevles, 1995). The subtext of the medical model is that a person with a physical, sensory, or mental impairment has a tragic flaw and needs help to overcome this flaw and that having such a flaw should be prevented at all costs. The focus is squarely on the individual, without focus on the connections between that individual and society (Brisenden, 1986).

While the medical model still holds ground in many sectors of the United States, a gradual shift in societal attitudes toward disability began during and after World War II, as many injured war veterans returned home, and this shift took hold in the United States in the 1970s. After World War II, there were a number of federal programs developed to help rehabilitate injured war veterans, which were expanded to provide for other people with disabilities. This culminated with the inclusion of disability benefits into the Social Security Act in 1956 and the creation of Medicaid in 1965.

In the 1950s and 1960s, people with disabilities and their family members also began advocating for the rights of people with disabilities, mirroring the social trends toward civil rights for people of color and women in that era. The concept of normalization for people with intellectual disabilities arose, and many people with all kinds of disabilities joined in expressing the desire for a "normal" life (Wolfensberger, 1972). New federal programs emerged, including programs providing vocational rehabilitation, housing, training, and research. However, prior to the 1970s, most of the disability policies in the United States did not include the concept of rights, and they have been characterized as reflecting "benevolent paternalism" toward people with disabilities (Hull, 1979, p. 21).

In the 1970s, a number of disability self-advocacy groups formed and advocated for an independent living approach to disability. According to the independent living model, the professionals and the government are viewed as some of the main barriers to people with disabilities living independently (DeJong, 1979). Adults with disabilities desired to gain independence from professionals who were placing them in institutions and otherwise excluding them from society, and they wanted consumer control of services as the antidote to the problems associated with impairments. Likewise, people with disabilities also became organized as an oppressed group and began advocating for policies that promoted community inclusion and protections from discrimination. In the period from the early 1970s to the early 1990s, we saw the rise of a new federal policy framework centered on equal opportunity laws for people with disabilities in the areas of education, employment, transportation, housing, and communication (Shapiro, 1993). In addition, the majority of the residential institutions were closed, and the segregated services that were developed earlier in the 20th century were mostly abandoned in favor of providing services and supports in community settings to people with disabilities.

In the 21st century, a very extensive federal policy network has evolved that aims to protect people with disabilities against discrimination; support their inclusion in education, work, and the community; and provide appropriate income and shelter. Despite these great advances, people with disabilities are still among the most impoverished and least included groups in the United States.

There are a myriad of disability policies at the federal, state, and local levels. The following section will outline some of the major policies, including antidiscrimination legislation, public assistance and social insurance programs, policies that promote community or residential living, education policies, and employment policies. There are many other smaller federal programs in each of these areas, as well as a multitude of state programs and regulations that affect the lives of people with disabilities.

Antidiscrimination Legislation

The United States was the first country in the world to adopt sweeping antidiscrimination legislation for people with disabilities: the Americans with Disabilities Act of 1990. The passing of the Americans with Disabilities Act was predated by some state-level antidiscrimination legislation, by some more limited federal-level antidiscrimination legislation, and by a series of federal court decisions that increasingly protected the rights of people with disabilities.

The earliest federal antidiscrimination laws for people with disabilities were targeted to provide them with access to specific activities or locations. The first federal law, initiated by a policy entrepreneur, was the Architectural Barriers Act of 1968 (Katzmann, 1986). This law mandated that all federally owned or leased buildings be accessible to people with physical disabilities. Other early federal antidiscrimination laws included the Voting Accessibility for the Elderly and Handicapped Act of 1984, mandating accessible polling places; the Air Carrier Access Act of 1986, prohibiting commercial airlines from discriminating based on disability; and the Fair Housing Act Amendments of 1988, which added people with disabilities to the groups protected from discrimination in housing. While these laws initially had minimal impacts and were often difficult to enforce, they did help lay the building blocks for future antidiscrimination legislation.

Rehabilitation Act of 1973

The most notable early antidiscrimination legislation, which was the major precursor to the Americans with Disabilities Act, was Section 504 of the Rehabilitation Act of 1973. Section 504 stated that "No otherwise qualified handicapped individual in the United States . . . shall, solely by reason of his handicap, be excluded from the participation in, be denied the benefits of, or be subjected to discrimination under any program or activity receiving federal financial assistance" (Rehabilitation Act of 1973, 29 U.S.C. §700 *et seq.*, section 504, 1976). The Rehabilitation Act required such programs and activities to provide reasonable accommodations to employees, to make their programs accessible to the public, and to make sure that new construction of facilities were accessible. This was the first time civil rights for people with disabilities were essentially encapsulated in federal legislation. Section 504 was so controversial at the time that the federal government refused initially to release the regulations implementing this legislation. It was not until protests three years later, including sit-ins at the Department of Health Education and Welfare by members of the burgeoning disability rights movement, that the regulations were released in 1977 (Scotch, 2001). The civil rights language in the Rehabilitation Act helped fuel the disability rights movement, and a number of states developed state-level antidiscrimination laws containing language similar to that of the Rehabilitation Act in the 1980s.

Americans with Disabilities Act of 1990

The Americans with Disabilities Act (ADA) is the primary antidiscrimination law for people with disabilities in the United States. The ADA was passed in 1990 with bipartisan support and support from a broad coalition of disability groups. The law was intended as a sweeping civil rights law that works to eliminate discrimination against people with disabilities in the areas of employment, public accommodations, state and local government, transportation, and communications (Americans with Disabilities Act, 1990). The following outlines the definition of disability in the ADA, and the four major components of the ADA.

Definition of Disability. Under the Americans with Disabilities Act, an individual with a disability is defined as (a) an individual who has a physical or mental impairment that causes a substantial limitation in one or more major life activities—such as walking, speaking, hearing, or learning; (b) an individual who has a record of an impairment—such as a person who has a history of an impairment and no longer has one or has been misclassified as having an impairment; or (c) an individual who has been regarded as having such an impairment—such as a person who has an impairment with no substantial limitation but is perceived as having a limitation. The Americans with Disabilities Act does not have a specific list of qualifying impairments, and judgments on disability are on an individual basis. This definition is broad enough to include people who have no limitations but still face discrimination, such as a person with a facial disfigurement. The Americans with Disabilities Act also specifically lists certain personal characteristics as not being a disability, including current abuse of drugs or alcohol; sexual behavior disorders such as pedophilia, exhibitionism, or voyeurism; or compulsive gambling, kleptomania, or pyromania. This ADA definition has become a common definition, and it is used by many other federal and state statutes.

Title I: Employment. The first title of the ADA bans employment discrimination against qualified persons with a disability by employers that have more than 15 workers. According to the ADA, a qualified person with a disability is a person with a disability that has the knowledge, skills, abilities, and qualifications necessary to perform the essential functions of a particular job. The ADA bans all types of employment discrimination against qualified people with disabilities, including hiring, compensation, training, promoting, and termination. Title I also requires employers to provide reasonable accommodations to assist a person with a known disability to carry out a job, such as modifications to a work environment, changes to a work schedule, restructuring of job responsibilities, or provision of a qualified interpreter.

Title II: Public Services. Title II of ADA bans discrimination against people with disabilities in the provision of public services by state and local governments, and it also prohibits discrimination in any form of public transportation. Under Title II, state and local governments must make reasonable modifications to their policies, practices, and procedures, as long as doing so does not fundamentally alter the nature of these services. State and local governments must also not discriminate in the area of employment. Further, all new construction must be accessible. Essentially, Title II mandates that governmental services be accessible to people with disabilities.

Title III: Public Accommodations. Title III bans discrimination by places of public accommodation. A public accommodation is a private business or organization that owns or operates a place of public accommodation, such as a retail store, restaurant, theater, hotel, medical provider, museum, recreation program, private school, therapist, park, or day care provider. Private clubs and private religious organizations are exempt from Title III. Title III requires public accommodations to make reasonable modifications in policies, practices, and procedures that deny equal access to persons with disabilities, as long as these modifications do not fundamentally alter the nature of the service; to provide goods or services in an integrated setting; to make all new construction accessible; to remove architectural, structural, and communication barriers in existing facilities where readily achievable; to furnish communication aids; and to eliminate discriminatory eligibility standards.

Title IV: Telecommunications. Title IV of the ADA requires all telecommunication companies to provide functionally equivalent services for persons who are Deaf or hard of hearing and for those with speech impediments. In essence, this required telecommunication carriers to install public Telecommunication Devices for the Deaf (TDD) and led to the creation of Telecommunication Relay Services (TRS) in all states, which enables people who are deaf to communicate via the telephone.

International Antidiscrimination Policy

Since the passage of the Americans with Disabilities Act, a number of other countries have passed similar antidiscrimination laws, notably Australia's Disability Discrimination Act of 1992 and the United Kingdom's Disability Discrimination Act of 1995. The European Union passed the Racial Equality Directive and the Employment Equality Directive in 2000, which mandated that the 25 member European Union states implement antidiscrimination policies related to racial or ethnic origin, religion or belief, sexual orientation, age, and disability. As a response to these directives, most of the member EU states now have federal antidiscrimination policies banning discrimination against people with disabilities (Bell, Chopin, & Palmer, 2006).

Income Maintenance and Support

The Social Security Act of 1935 is the main source of income transfer and social insurance policy for people with disabilities. The Social Security Act did not directly include provisions for people with disabilities, aside from the federal Aid to the Blind program, until the adoption of Social Security Disability Insurance in 1956 (Berkowitz, 2000). Now, the Social Security Act is the main policy source for social insurance, public assistance, and health insurance for people with disabilities.

Social Security Disability Insurance

Social Security Disability Insurance (SSDI) is a social insurance program that provides cash assistance to workers who have contributed to the Social Security Trust Fund and become unable to work due to a disability before retirement age. Social Security Disability Insurance was initially only for people who were over age 50, but now it is available to people of all ages if they have worked for a certain period of time. SSDI is also available to spouses and dependents of an insured worker who acquires a work disability. The definition of disability under SSDI differs substantially from that in the Americans with Disabilities Act. Under SSDI, an individual is classified as having a disability only if he or she has a total, permanent disability that makes a person unable to work at his or her previous job or at another job. As SSDI is a social insurance program, it is an entitlement program that is not means tested.

Supplemental Security Income

Supplemental Security Income (SSI) was established in 1974 as a means-tested public assistance program that is financed by the general funds of the treasury. SSI is not funded by Social Security contributions and is not based on an individual's previous work history. To be eligible for SSI, a person must be either over age 65, blind, or have a disability. The definition of disability varies for children and adults. For children under age 18, a person has a disability if she or he has a permanent physical or mental impairment that results in severe functional limitations. For individuals 18 years or older, a disability must also limit their ability to engage in substantial gainful activity. SSI is only available to people who have both a very limited income and very limited resources. In general, for an unmarried adult to receive SSI, he or she should make less than the total allowable per month and have less than $2,000 in resources, not including one car, a house, and several other exclusions. The exact amount of SSI a person will receive depends on that person's earned and unearned income, with SSI benefits lowered in correspondence to the amount of total income a person receives. Although there is a standard SSI monthly payment, $623 for single adults and $934 for a married couple in 2007, some states augment this amount (Social Security Administration, 2006). In many states, qualifying for SSI automatically qualifies an individual for Medicaid and food stamps.

Medicaid

Medicaid, the major health insurance program for people with disabilities, was established in 1965. Unlike SSDI and SSI, Medicaid is a state-administered program that is jointly funded through the federal and state governments. The federal government provides guidelines and some of the funding, with states setting their own income and eligibility requirements and providing additional funding. The federal government mandates certain health care services that the states must provide, with many states covering and paying for additional services. In general, the federal government requires states to provide medical care under Medicaid, including physician services, hospital care, home health care, diagnosis and treatment, and nursing home care. States can pay for additional services, such as personal assistance services and intermediate care facilities for the mentally retarded (ICF/MRs).

Like SSI, Medicaid is a means-tested program available to people who meet certain categorical requirements. In 32 states, people who are eligible for SSI are automatically eligible for Medicaid. In other states, people with disabilities who meet other categorical and means tests are eligible for Medicaid. Many states have special eligibility requirements for people who are determined to be medically needy, meaning they have too much income or resources to be eligible under the means tests but are in need of Medicaid. Children with disabilities are often covered under Medicaid through this medically needy category.

Medicare

Some people with disabilities are also eligible to receive health insurance coverage under Medicare. While both Medicaid and Medicare were adopted in 1965 to provide health insurance under the Social Security Act, they are very different programs. Medicare is a social insurance program that is funded and administered at the federal level. Medicare is not a means-tested program but instead is available to people who have worked for a certain period of time and either are over age 65 or have a permanent work disability. Generally, people who receive SSDI are eligible for Medicare after a two-year waiting period. Medicare pays for fewer services than Medicaid. A number of people with disabilities are eligible for both Medicare and Medicaid.

Community and Residential Living Policies _____

A major trend in social policy for people with disabilities is the emphasis currently placed on community care. Although seclusion, largely in residential facilities, was widely used in the past, people with disabilities are now living in the community and taking charge of the process of care by actively campaigning for the services they need. This development has been supported by policy decisions.

Medicaid Waiver

Although it was initially conceived as primarily a health program, Medicaid has evolved into the policy that provides the major source of public funding for residential living for people of all ages with disabilities. In 1981, the first Medicaid waiver program, the Home and Community-Based Services (HCBS) Waiver, was passed, which authorized states to use Medicaid funds to pay for home and community-based services for people or people with disabilities (Duckett & Guy, 2000). Under the Medicaid waiver program, the United States Department of Health and Human Services waives certain Medicaid requirements, allowing people who would require institutional care in a nursing home or an ICF/MR to instead receive supports in community-based settings. Waivers may be used to pay for such supports as home health care, personal care services, respite care, targeted case management, or home modifications, and must cost no more than the costs of providing institutional care. In order to receive waiver services, an individual must meet the same category and income tests required for Medicaid and choose to enroll in the waiver as an alternative to an institution. Currently, approximately 1.4 million people with disabilities use a Medicaid waiver to support their living in community settings (Harrington & Kitchener, 2003). Unfortunately, the demand for Medicaid waiver slots and other community living opportunities far exceeds the current supply, with more than 157,000 people on state Medicaid waiver waiting lists in 2002 (Harrington & Kitchener, 2003). Thus, paradoxically, while our federal Medicaid program is an open-entitlement program for qualified individuals to receive care in institutions, the Medicaid waiver program that supports people to live in community-based settings is generally not.

Olmstead Decision

While community residential services are in limited supply for people with disabilities, the U.S. Supreme Court ruled in an ADA case known as the *Olmstead* decision (*Olmstead et al. v. L.C. et al.*, 1999) that people with disabilities should not be institutionalized unnecessarily. The Supreme Court ruled that states could not place people unnecessarily in institutions simply because there were not community slots available. In response to *Olmstead,* the federal government released the New Freedom Initiative of 2001 (Executive Order 13127, June 2001), which ordered states to provide care to people with disabilities in the least restrictive environment and most integrated setting possible. It also required states to ensure that they had community-based alternatives to institutional placements.

Education Policy

Although there were a number of early federal and state education laws that provided funding for special education, the Education of All Handicapped Children Act of 1975 was the first law that guaranteed children and adults with disabilities between the ages of 3 and 21 were entitled to a free education. This law required that states provide a free, appropriate education to all children in the least restrictive environment. The concept of the least restrictive environment meant that children with disabilities were to be included in regular classrooms to the maximum amount appropriate. It also required states to provide special services or special education as required by children with disabilities. This law has been amended and expanded a number of times since 1975, and it was renamed in 1990 as the Individuals with Disabilities Education Act, commonly known as IDEA.

IDEA establishes policy that is federally mandated; jointly funded by federal, state, and local governments; and locally implemented. Through IDEA, the federal government provides states funding for local education authorities to provide free and appropriate education to children and youth with disabilities. To be eligible for services under IDEA, a child has to fit within one of 13 disability categories, including such categories as autism, deafness, mental retardation, orthopedic impairment, serious emotional disturbance, or specific learning impairment, and be in need of special education services. Children up to age 2 can receive early intervention services under Part C of IDEA, while children and youth ages 3 to 21 qualify for special education services under Part B of IDEA. Although most other disability policies require people with disabilities to self-identify as having a disability or to request disability benefits, under IDEA, the state local education authority is required to identify, locate, and evaluate children with disabilities to determine eligibility for services and to provide appropriate assessments or evaluations. This includes both early identification screening for infants and toddlers, as well as identification in schools for older children.

A key aspect of IDEA is that services to children and youth are individualized based on a student's need and that there is a plan outlining the specific services that will be provided. Under Part C, families are entitled to an Individualized Family Service Plan (IFSP), developed in conjunction with families and professionals, with established performance goals and a service plan to meet these goals. Similarly, Under Part B, children and youth have an Individualized Education Program (IEP), developed in conjunction with the family, teachers, and professionals, which determines annual goals and services needed to reach these goals.

IDEA also requires schools to provide transition services to youth once they reach age 16 and to include transition goals and activities in a youth's IEP. Transition services are services that help students with disabilities move as smoothly as possible from attending school to participating in post-school activities, such as employment, vocational education, postsecondary education, adult services, and community living.

IDEA has detailed procedural regulations, and parents and children have due process rights under IDEA. In conjunction with the No Child Left Behind legislation, IDEA was amended in 2004 to require that teachers providing special education services be "highly qualified," essentially entailing that they have received certification or a license in special education. The 2004 reauthorization of IDEA also included provisions related to behavior and discipline, such as allowing schools to consider a student's disability when determining disciplinary procedures and regulations for removing children with disabilities for disciplinary reasons.

A chronic concern raised about IDEA is the notion that IDEA is an underfunded mandate (Rothman, 2002). Currently, the federal government provides less than 20% of the funding required to pay for the mandates in IDEA, despite its previous commitment to pay for 40% of the mandates, leaving states to pay for the rest of the services.

Employment Policy

Unemployment has been a chronic problem for people with disabilities. Current estimates show that only approximately 25% to 30% of people with disabilities are employed (McNeil, 2001). The major policies intended to support people with disabilities in securing and maintaining employment are antidiscrimination laws, primarily Title I of the Americans with Disabilities Act, discussed above, and vocational rehabilitation programs.

Vocational rehabilitation is a joint federal-state service authorized primarily by the Rehabilitation Act of 1973. The Rehabilitation Services Administration (RSA) is a federal agency within the United States Department of Education, and it funds vocational rehabilitation offices to provide vocational rehabilitation services within each state. Vocational rehabilitation services include recruitment, eligibility determination, career counseling, job training, job placement, assistance with job searches, and case management. Unfortunately, many people with disabilities receiving public assistance programs, such as Supplemental Security Income (SSI) or Social Security Disability Insurance (SSDI), are not referred to vocational rehabilitation programs, nor do they receive any assistance in securing employment (Social Security Administration, 2006). Further, there are may disincentives for people with disabilities to obtain paid employment, most notably that, for many people with disabilities, obtaining paid employment would result in their lose of essential benefits, such as Medicaid or SSDI (Stapleton, Livermore, Scrivner, & Tucker, 1997).

Two recent laws passed that have attempted to support people with disabilities in finding paid employment and to reduce the employment disincentives are the Workforce Investment Act of 1998 and the Ticket to Work and Work Incentives Improvement Act of 1999. The Workforce Investment Act (WIA) of 1998 is designed to help states establish consolidated statewide or local workforce investment systems. A primary aspect of WIA is the development of one-stop systems for employment services, which are accessible to any person eligible for such services, including people receiving Temporary Assistance for Needy Families (TANF), SSI, or SSDI. Under WIA, all people who receive SSDI or SSI are automatically eligible for vocational rehabilitation services. WIA also requires that workforce centers are physically and programmatically accessible for people with disabilities and that states include people with disabilities in their state plans as a major customer group.

The Ticket to Work and Work Incentives Improvement Act of 1999 (TTWWIIA) was designed primarily to remove the work disincentives that people with disabilities face and to promote competition among employment services providers. Under the TTWWIIA, people with disabilities are given a work ticket, which essentially is a voucher that they can use to refer themselves for rehabilitation services. People with disabilities are able to use their ticket to purchase employment services from a variety of private and public providers, known as employment networks. The TTWWIIA also allows states the option of enabling people with disabilities to maintain health insurance coverage under Medicaid or Medicare while participating in paid employment. While the TTWWIIA was promising, very few people with disabilities actually are using their tickets, and only a limited number of providers have accepted any tickets (Thornton et al., 2006). There is still a great need for more effective policies supporting the participation in paid employment of people with disabilities.

Although the United States generally relies on vocational rehabilitation and antidiscrimination laws, there are other approaches used in different countries. In many nations, employment quotas are used for promoting employment of people with disabilities (Mont, 2004). For example, France has an employment quota in which all employers with 20 or more employees must have at least 6% of their employees be people with disabilities, either through competitive or supported employment. A problem with quota programs is that, in most countries that use quotas, the quotas are not readily fulfilled and there are not structures to help train and support workers with disabilities. Another approach used internationally is to provide wage subsidies to people with disabilities (Mont, 2004). For example, in Sweden, the government pays as much as 80% of an individual's wage depending on the severity of the disability, which provides an incentive for employers to hire people with disabilities. The United States has a similar policy in the form of a tax credit to employers, but this is at a much smaller scale and has not been used extensively.

Current and Future Issues

Social policy for people with disabilities is a rapidly evolving field, and policy changes are taking place all the time. Nevertheless, a number of significant ongoing issues can be identified that show the future direction of social policy for people with disabilities. These involve both domestic and international trends.

Consumer-Directed Care

A growing trend in the area of disability policy is for people with disabilities to direct their own services. The move toward consumer-directed services, also known as consumer-controlled services, emanates from the concern that agency-controlled services often do not meet the individual needs of people with disabilities and further increase the dependence on professionals and systems that people with disabilities experience. When agencies control services, people with disabilities have little choice over the personnel providing services, including services that are quite personal in nature. Consumer-directed services allow people with disabilities to hire, train, supervise, and fire their own staff with public money. Many states are now allowing consumer-controlled options under the Medicaid waiver program, and there are consumer-directed demonstration projects across the country that allow people of all ages who have disabilities to control the services they use (Benjamin, Matthias, & Franke, 2000; Mahoney, Simone, & Simon-Rusinowitz, 2000). Public social services policies for people with disabilities are likely to increasingly allow consumer-directed options, particularly as baby boomers age and desire more control over the supports they receive.

Aging and Disability

There is a large overlap between disability and aging policies, both in populations served and policy issues. According to the U.S. 2000 Census, about 48% of people with disabilities are over the age of 55 (McNeil, 2001). Likewise, about 54% of the total population of people over age 65 is categorized as having a disability. As the population demographics shift to an increasingly aging population, we can expect an even greater percentage of people with disabilities to be older. Further, many people with developmental disabilities, who in the early 20th century did not live into old age, now experience greatly lengthened life spans. There were approximately 641,000 people with developmental disabilities in the year 2000, and this number is expected to double by the year 2030 (Heller, Janicki, Hammel, & Factor, 2002). Thus, the total population of people with disabilities currently includes many older people with both life-long and age-related disabilities, and this number will only rise.

Many of the key issues for people with life-long and age-related disabilities are similar, including community-residential living; consumer-directed services; appropriate personal care services and care giving supports; and accessible housing, public services, public accommodation, and transportation

(Lightfoot, 2007). The growing convergence of disability policy issues and aging policy issues requires more collaboration between disability and aging services. Some of the more recent disability policies have recognized the common issues of these populations, such as the New Freedom Initiative's authorization of joint aging and disability resource centers, and financing of aging and disability services is often commingled (Ansello, 2001). We can expect to see more convergence of disability and aging policies as the population continues to age.

Universal Design

As the population of people ages and there are more people with disabilities, there will be an increasing need for policies that promote the universal design of both buildings and programs. Universal design is the concept that, whether one is designing buildings or programs, accessibility for people of all ages and abilities should be included as an integral part of that design (Center for Universal Design, 1997). For example, a universally designed building would include accessible features into the core design, such as an entryway that had no stairs, which would make the entrance accessible to all people in the same manner, rather than the creation of an alternative side entrance for the use specifically of people with disabilities. Although the Americans with Disabilities Act Accessible Design Guidelines support universal design, the principles of universal design go further than the current regulations (Osterberg & Kain, 2002). We can expect to see future policy development in the area of universal design in architecture and programs as the population ages.

Supported Parenting

Since the end of the forced sterilization laws in the 20th century, more people with disabilities are becoming parents. Current disability policy provides little support to people with disabilities in parenting activities, and programs that provide financial assistance or supports to individuals with disabilities for completing their individual activities of daily living, such as Medicaid, currently do not allow funds to be spent to support parenting or interdependent parenting. Many states also have policies that discriminate against parents with disabilities in child custody and child welfare proceedings (Lightfoot & LaLiberte, 2006a), and many child welfare agencies have a lack of knowledge regarding disability issues (Lightfoot & LaLiberte, 2006b). There is a growing interest in changing disability policies to support parents with disabilities (National Coalition for Supporting Parents with Cognitive Challenges, 2006), and we can expect policy changes in this domain in the near future.

Workforce Issues

As there are more people with disabilities of all ages who are living in community settings, there is a growing need for highly qualified and trained direct support staff to provide services, such as personal care assistance funded through Medicaid or employment supports funded through a vocational rehabilitation program. Unfortunately, the recruitment and retention of direct support staff has been a chronic problem associated with community supports (Hewitt & Lakin, 2001). Direct support workers are usually paid low salaries, have little training, have little opportunity for job advancement, and have job duties that are sometimes highly stressful. There is a growing concern that community-based services that rely on direct support professionals are not sustainable with these high turnover rates, both due to high turnover costs and the costs in the quality of services provided. As the society continues to age, we will likely see an even greater demand for direct care workers. While there are a number of small policies addressing this issue, the workforce crisis will likely require federal and state policy attention in the coming years.

International Disability Efforts

While the disability movement for independence and civil rights emerged most forcefully in the United States, there has been growing international attention to policies that protect people with disabilities from discrimination and promote economic and social well-being of people with disabilities by local and national advocacy groups, national governments, and international organizations. There are several worldwide disability advocacy networks, such as Disabled People's International, Inclusion International, and the World Federation of the Deaf, which advocate for international disability policy and share information on national policies.

The United Nations has been the international organization at the forefront of attempting to incorporate disability issues into national policies. As early as 1971, the United Nations' General Assembly adopted the *Declaration on the Rights of Mentally Retarded Persons*, and this was followed in 1975 by the *Declaration on the Rights of Disabled Persons*. Another publication, the *United Nations Decade of Disabled Persons, 1983–1992*, both publicized the issues faced by people with disabilities and promoted policies that supported equality and full participation of people with disabilities (World Health Organization, 1992). The United Nations has continued this work with specific regional campaigns, notably the *Asian and Pacific Decade of Persons with Disabilities* (1993–2002) and the *African Decade of Disabled Persons* (2000–2009). Further, the World Health Organization, in conjunction with people with disabilities and disability organizations worldwide, developed a new *International Classification of Functioning, Disability, and Health* (ICF) in 2002 (World Health Organization, 2002). The ICF recognizes both medical and social models of disability, and it is intended to be a common international means of classifying disability. Finally, there is a current effort by the United Nations to promote the rights of people with disabilities through the new *Convention on the Rights of People with Disabilities,* which was adopted by the United Nations in December 2006, with the highest number of opening-day signatories for a United Nations' convention (United Nations, 2007). Similar regional efforts have included the Organization of American States' *Convention on the Rights of Disabled Persons* and the European Union's *European Disability Strategy.* The efforts of the United Nations, regional international organizations, and national governments, combined with advocacy efforts of international, national, and local disability organizations, have led to more comprehensive disability policy that aims to promote the inclusion and well-being of people with disabilities internationally. Although these policies have not been entirely successful in reaching their goals, they have helped change the environment in which many people with disabilities live.

References

Americans with Disabilities Act of 1990, 42 U.S.C.A. § 1210 *et seq.* (West 1993).

Ansello, E. (2001, July). Building intersystem cooperation to benefit aging adults with lifelong disabilities and their families. In *Family caregiving with lifelong disabilities: Research, practice and policy.* Symposium conducted at the 17th World Congress of the International Association of Gerontology, Vancouver, Canada.

Barnes, C. (1997). A legacy of oppression: A history of disability in Western culture. In L. Barton & M. Oliver (Eds.), *Disability studies: Past, present and future* (pp. 3-24). Leeds, UK: The Disability Press.

Bell, M., Chopin, I., & Palmer, F. (2006). *Developing anti-discrimination law in Europe: The 25 member EU states compared.* Utrecht–Brussels: European Network of Independent Experts in the Non-Discrimination Field.

Benjamin, A. E., Matthias, R. E., & Franke, T. M. (2000). Comparing consumer-directed and agency models for providing supportive services at home. *Health Services Research, 35*(1), 351–66.

Berkowitz, E. (2000). Disability policy and history. Statement before the Subcommittee on Social Security of the House Committee of Ways and Means, July 13, Washington, DC.

Brisenden, S. (1986). Independent living and the medical model of disability. *Disability, Handicap & Society, 1*(2), 173–178.

Center for Universal Design. (1997). *The principles of universal design: Version 2.0.* Raleigh: North Carolina State University, Center for Universal Design.

Cherry Engineering Support Services Inc. (CESSI). (2003). *Federal statutory definitions of disability.* McLean, VA: The Interagency Committee on Disability Research. Retrieved May 4, 2007, from http://www.icdr.us/documents/definitions.htm

Clapton, J., & Fitzgerald, J. (1997). The history of disability: a history of 'otherness.' *New Renaissance, 7*(1). Retrieved May 15, 2007, from http://www.ru.org/artother.html

DeJong, G., (1979) Independent living: From social movement to analytic paradigm. *Archives of Physical Medicine and Rehabilitation, 60,* 435–446.

Duckett, M., & Guy, M. (2000). Home and community-based services waivers. *Health Care Financing Review, 63,* 123–125.

Harrington, C., & Kitchener, M., (2003). *Medicaid long-term care: Changes, innovations, and cost containment.* San Francisco: University of California, San Francisco. Retrieved February 17, 2006, from http://www.ncsl.org/programs/health/harrington/sld001.htm

Heller, T., Janicki, M., Hammel, J., & Factor, A. (2002). *Promoting healthy aging, family support and age-friendly communities for persons aging with developmental disabilities: Report of the 2001 Invitational Research Symposium on Aging with Developmental Disabilities.* Chicago: University of Illinois at Chicago, Department of Disability and Human Development, Rehabilitation Research and Training Center on Aging with Developmental Disabilities.

Hewitt, A., & Lakin, C. (2001). *Issues in the direct support workforce and their connections to the growth, sustainability, and quality of community supports.* Minneapolis: University of Minnesota, Research and Training Center on Community Living.

Hull, K. (1979). *The rights of physically handicapped people.* New York: Avon.

Katzmann, R. (1986). *Institutional disability: The saga of transportation policy for the disabled.* Washington, DC: Brookings Institution Press.

Kevles, D. (1985). *In the name of eugenics: Genetics and the uses of human heredity.* New York: Knopf.

Lightfoot, E. (2007). Disability. In J. Blackburn & C. Dulmus (Eds.), *Handbook of gerontology: Evidence based approaches to theory, practice, and policy* (pp. 201–229). New York: John Wiley & Sons.

Lightfoot, E., & LaLiberte, T. (2006a). The inclusion of disability as grounds for termination of parental rights in state codes. *Policy Research Brief, 17*(2). (Available from the Research and Training Center on Community Living, Institute on Community Integration, College of Education and Human Development, University of Minnesota)

Lightfoot, E., & LaLiberte, T. (2006b). Approaches to child protection case management for cases involving people with disabilities. *Child Abuse & Neglect, 30*(4), 381–391.

Mahoney, M., Simone, K., & Simon-Rusinowitz, L. (2000). Early lessons from the Cash and Counseling demonstration and evaluation. *Demonstration and Evaluation, 23*(3), 41–46.

McNeil, J. (2001). Americans with disabilities: 1997. In *Current Population Reports* (U.S. Census Bureau Publication No. P70–73). Washington, DC: U.S. Department of Commerce.

Mont, D. (2004). *Disability employment policy.* Washington: The World Bank, Human Development Network, Social Protection Unit.

National Coalition for Supporting Parents with Cognitive Challenges. (2006). *A chance to parent: National summit about supporting parents with cognitive challenges and their families.* Retrieved May 1, 2007, from http://www.mscd.edu/~family/

Osterberg, A., & Kain, D. (2002). *Access for everyone: A guide to accessibility with references to ADAAG.* Ames: Iowa State University.

Rehabilitation Act of 1973, 29 USC § 700 *et seq.* (1976).

Rothman, A. (2002). The politics of IDEA funding. *Education Week, 22*(6), 34–36.

Scotch, R. (2001). *From good will to civil rights: Transforming federal disability policy.* Philadelphia: Temple University Press.

Shapiro, J. (1993). *No pity: People with disabilities forging a new civil rights movement.* New York: Random House.

Silverstein, R. (2000). Emerging disability policy framework: A guidepost for analyzing public policy. *Iowa Law Review, 85,* 1691–1797.

Social Security Administration. (2006). *SSI federal payment amounts.* Washington, DC: Author. Retrieved May 15, 2007, from http://www.ssa.gov/OACT/COLA/SSI.html

Stapleton, D., Livermore, G., Scrivner, S., & Tucker, A. (1997). *Exploratory study of health care coverage and employment of people with disabilities: Literature review.* Washington, DC: U.S. Department of Health and Human Services.

Thornton, C., Fraker, T., Livermore, G., Stapleton, D., O'Day, B., Silva, T., et al. (2006) *Evaluation of the Ticket to Work Program: Implementation experience during the second two years of operations (2003–2004).* Washington, DC: Mathematic Policy Research, Inc. and the Cornell University Institute for Policy Research.

United Nations. (2007). *Information on the Convention on the Rights of Persons with Disabilities and Optional Protocol.* New York: Author. Retrieved May 15, 2007, from http://www.un.org/esa/socdev/enable/conventioninfo.htm

Wolfensberger, W. (1972). *The principle of normalization in human services.* Toronto: National Institute of Mental Retardation.

World Health Organization. (1992). *The work of WHO, 1990–1991; Biennial report of the Director-General.* Geneva, Switzerland: Author.

World Health Organization. (2002). *Toward a common language for functioning, disability and health: ICF.* Geneva, Switzerland: Author.

28 Social Policy and the Correctional System

Margaret Severson

No single chapter can fully capture the historical and present day complexities of the correctional system in the United States. This system is not a single definable entity; it is a complex array of infinite physical and philosophical influences, designs, services, products, and functions. Likewise, there is no simple list of social policies driving the vast assortment of correctional prototypes; the sheer number and magnitude of these policies impact separate and joint parts of a system that is undergoing profound transition in the early years of the 21st century. Although the violent prison disturbances of the last century in the United States have thankfully not become commonplace, the "uprisings" we see now are of the political and philosophical types, and their impact extends far beyond U.S. borders. Whether considering Abu Ghraib or Guantanamo Bay or New Castle, Indiana, all eyes are focused on how we say we will treat prisoners and how we actually treat prisoners. Since the founding of this nation, the politics of punishment have provided fascinating material for students and scholars of social policy.

The modern day correctional system, narrowly defined for the purposes of this chapter as including only jails and prisons, operates on two sometimes contradictory levels. Although federal, state, and local legislation and judicial rules and case law may regulate the lives of both the governed and the governors in these institutions, how these regulations are carried out are intrasystem functions that are obscure, generally attracting public scrutiny only over piecemeal issues and publicized revolts. Many historical examples of this exist: the disparity between the length of one's prison sentence and the actual time served given intrasystem allocations of good time credits, the admonition against incarceration of persons with mental illnesses and the "mercy bookings" that occur when access to the community mental health system is denied or curtailed, the officially declared functions of jails and prisons and the internal pressures and procedures that exist to force the institution to turn a profit. Contemporary examples of the duality exist as well. Our expressed national concern with human rights and the provocative pictures of the inhumanity of Abu Ghraib along with the stories of so-called protective incarceration or "preventive detention" at Guantanamo Bay have brought critical commentary from around the world and judicial intervention here at home.

As the terms are traditionally construed, prisons are federal- or state-sponsored—though not necessarily owned and/or operated—facilities constructed to house prisoners who have been convicted of a crime and sentenced to a period of punishment, of isolation from society. Jails are detention facilities intended primarily for the purpose of housing pretrial detainees who have been assessed as presenting a continuing risk of danger to society or of flight from the jurisdiction of the court and who have been unable to post the bail required to assure the court of their presence at trial. Although burgeoning prison populations have, to some extent, altered these traditional jail functions so that jails now provide the isolation, the mission of the pretrial detention facility is to act as the safekeeper of the accused so that justice can be served through the means of a speedy trial and the rendering of the procedural process due each defendant.

Increasingly, in the booming corrections industry, the line between the pretrial and post-conviction milieu is blurred, and the line is further blurred as to the nature of imprisonment. Although the government has always had the power to detain preventively, particularly in matters that affect the public health, the "war on terror" is the 21st century's example of the practice of detaining persons without charges and without appreciable rights, for an uncertain period of time. Where necessary in this chapter, distinctions between jails and prisons will be made. But the contemporary reality is, whether in the United States or in Iraq, in prison or jail, sentenced or detained for criminal charges or for protection, there is little distinction made between types of prisoners. Readers are encouraged to keep their eyes on the driving policy issues that affect both types of institutions and prisoners rather than focusing more narrowly on the system types.

Social Policy and the Development of Jails and Prisons

It has been suggested that, as a matter of public policy, prisoners are supposed to live in poverty (Sykes, 1958), and, in the early days of incarceration in this country, austerity was often used as an excuse for unconscionable environmental conditions. Through most of the 18th century, deterrence was the guiding principle when it came to the handling of criminals. Banishment, brutality, and the frequent use of barbaric forms of punishment and execution ultimately gave way in the late 1700s to a treatment philosophy espoused by the Quakers in Pennsylvania, who opposed the undisciplined management and violent conditions of the Philadelphia jail. In 1790, the Pennsylvania Prison Society opened the Walnut Street Jail, the first prison to operate with the philosophy that the proper objective of punishment was rehabilitation.

The first large prisons opened in the United States in the 1820s: the Auburn State Prison in New York and the Pennsylvania prisons located in Pittsburgh and Philadelphia. The organizational and treatment philosophies of these early prisons were centered on differing beliefs about the impact of social influences and the principles of resocialization as they affect the individual person. The Auburn prison, a congregate system, had prisoners sleeping alone but working alongside each other each day, albeit in total silence. In contrast, the Pennsylvania prisons operated so that prisoners were totally segregated from each other for the duration of their sentences (Rothman, 1998). The emphasis of each system on preventing communication between prisoners, believing that such contact would defeat the rehabilitation objective, meant that external control mechanisms, such as architectural design and types of work projects, became the "treatment" influences. This approach can be contrasted with the rehabilitative efforts made in the late 19th century and periodically throughout the 20th century, when treatment of the individual became a more popular form of trying to achieve rehabilitation. In any case, like many individual treatment experiments of the 20th century, these early programming endeavors in the prisons in New York and Pennsylvania have been declared failures in accomplishing their rehabilitative objectives. The failure of these prison models is, in part, attributed to the rise in mental health problems experienced in physically isolated prisoners, seen in suicides, self-mutilations, and other self-destructive and unusual behaviors, and to the "bizarre, obsessive prison practices" that grew out of desperate attempts to enforce silence in the institutions (Fogel, 1975, p. 56).

While model prisons were being discussed and developed in the 19th century, the proliferation of local jails was paid little notice. In fact, local jail conditions were often every bit as deplorable as those found in state prisons, but, because jails were deemed to be short-term holding facilities, policy making and advocacy efforts were instead directed toward the operations of the larger institutions (Welch, 1991). Even today's references to "jail reform" speak primarily to reformation of mid-20th century jail management strategies and are largely a result of judicial intervention as opposed to being the products of the righteous indignation of social reformers. One notable exception merits attention.

Since the late 1600s, a variety of state and local laws have authorized the incarceration of individuals with serious mental illnesses. In one example bearing startling resemblance to events happening in 2007, the governor of Virginia was forced to approve the confinement of persons with mental illnesses in the Williamsburg jail in 1773, because of the unavailability of appropriate psychiatric services elsewhere in the area (Deutsch, 1937). In the mid 1800s, these practices came to the attention of Dorothea Dix, a teacher turned progressive social reformer who took up and led the campaign to remove persons with mental illnesses from prisons, jails, and almshouses and place them instead into special hospitals (Deutsch, 1937). Dix's work is looked upon as being the type of advocacy that lies at the very roots of the social work profession, and in fact, by the end of the 19th century, she and her colleagues witnessed the creation of a number of psychiatric hospitals into which persons with mental illnesses could be diverted.

Still, in recent years, similar laws and practices, known generally as protective custody and vagrancy laws, serve to undo Dix's efforts (Torrey et al., 1992). If there is one connecting thread that ties together the penal philosophies and practices of colonial America and those of the 21st century, it is that of jails and prisons becoming repositories for those with serious mental illnesses or those who present threatening personal characteristics. Of course, what is threatening is a matter of perception and so, by virtue of stigma and ignorance, might include people who are homeless, annoying, or who are of certain ethnic and racial backgrounds.

Other social policies were also helping to shape the operations of the country's penal systems in the 19th century. The prison at Auburn charged its six to eight thousand annual spectators a fee to tour the penitentiary; these fees were applied toward the prison's budget (Fogel, 1975). Elsewhere, while enlightened reformers like Edward Livingston, Alexis de Tocqueville, and Jeremy Bentham were working to instill humanitarian interests in the prisons in the United States and other areas of the world, in some states, money making or money saving missions became the driving force behind correctional policy. In post–Civil War America, after what the late scholar Mark Carleton (1971) called "the most decisive event in the history of southern penology" (p. 13), the southern state legislatures were confronted with a growing prisoner population consisting of former slaves and an accompanying increase in expenses associated with providing these prisoners with the basic necessities of life. By the 1880s, all of the southern states, Nebraska, and the New Mexico Territory turned to convict leasing or a contract system of prison management in order to cut costs and, ideally, to make money (Carleton, 1971). Under these systems, private operators were allowed to either enter into a lease with the state for inmate labor or contract with the state to actually operate the prison itself. Vestiges of these private management schemes, which include private mental health interests, are seen in today's proliferation of private correctional operations, wherein 7.2% of all state and federal prisoners were held at midyear 2006 (Sabol, Minton, & Harrison, 2007). Further, the legacies of the convict leasing and prison contract systems include the underlying tensions that remain between present-day correctional policies and political agendas: are prisoners the subjects of a national policy that furthers public safety or the objects of an exercise for political gain?

In the 20th century, social policy practitioners, in part led by the former president of the American Association of Social Workers, Kenneth Pray, had the opportunity to contribute to the development of the modern correctional era. Instead, the development of contemporary penal policies and practices were forfeited to criminal justice and behavioral science experts. Rehabilitation through therapeutic treatment, particularly through the use of psychotherapy, has been emphasized (McNeece, 1995). Though a few social workers such as Pray, who also served as dean of the Pennsylvania School of Social Work, advocated for penal reforms and for social work professionals to provide services to prisoners (Pray, 1951), the social work practice and academic communities never wholly embraced this cause. Pray suggested that the "disciplined skill [of casework] in helping individuals make an adequate and satisfying social adjustment within relatively narrow limits is the distinctive potential contribution of professional social work to prison administration" (Pray, 1951). Instead, social work was work destined to be done elsewhere and certainly with more amenable patients. Social worker and proponent of the justice model for corrections David Fogel (1975) asserted that "the prison monolith was basically unshaken by the entry of professionals; rather, it absorbed social workers, psychologists, psychiatrists, teachers, chaplains, and others to help insulate itself from criticism . . ." (p. 61).

All in all, the social policies driving corrections up through the 20th century, including those emphasizing the popular rehabilitation ideals of corrections, seem largely to have been inspired by penologists and politicians. Even professionals eager to provide the treatment services thought to be the key to true prisoner rehabilitation approached this task with the unrealistic idea that, ultimately, jailers would be replaced by nurses and judges by psychiatrists—professionals who would treat and cure rather than punish the individual (Fogel, 1975).

Contextual Influences on Correctional Policies and Practice

The most recent correctional population data compiled by the United States Department of Justice reveals that, at midyear 2006, there were over 2.2 million persons incarcerated in adult prisons and jails in the United States (Sabol et al., 2007). Approximately two-thirds of these prisoners were incarcerated in federal and state prisons and the remaining one third were held in local jails. Sabol et al. (2007) indicate that 1 in every 133 U.S. residents was imprisoned in a state or federal prison or a local jail on June 30, 2006, and on that date, on average, jails were operating at 94% of their rated capacity.

As the number of persons locked up continues to increase at an alarming rate, the policies driving correctional services are seen in the outcomes of three primary and interrelated courses of action. The first, labeled here as *public commitments*, is shaped by a variety of social pressures. The business of corrections falls victim to the whims of politics and public opinion. The "lock 'em up" public sentiment is realized through the enactment of sentencing laws and in certain forms of involuntary detention and treatment. Pressure from crime victims (read voters) has made it easier for elected officials as well as elected judges to err on the conservative, more restrictive side of sentencing. And the federal courts in particular, tasked with determining the constitutionality of legislation and with safeguarding human rights, have shaped their own interventions, seen in the 30 years of judicial activism in prison and prisoner rights cases from the latter 1960s into the 1990s. Thus, the combination of more severe sentencing laws, more demonstrative public and victim advocacy, and more hands-on management of prison and jail systems by the federal courts has resulted in three decades of rapid change in the corrections industry.

The second course of action includes conservation of resources. Included here are the efforts to conserve tangible corrections resources, such as the number of trained personnel, the number of custodial beds, and the amount of physical space required by institutions. These efforts have been made through legislative activity at all levels of government.

Finally, the third course of action, containment, is related to the ever-increasing incarcerated population and to the social and fiscal costs associated with incarcerating so many people. These containment issues are crystallized in various pieces of legislation and service delivery system configurations. The most notable example is the Serious and Violent Offender Reentry Initiative that was initiated in 2001 under the Clinton administration and later revised and implemented under the Bush administration in 2003. (See, for example, the official site of the U.S. Department of Justice, www.ojp.usdoj.gov/reentry.)

Not surprisingly, given their inherently contradictory natures, the process and results of the activities springing from these three policy catalysts are mixed, and one might conclude that some have played out with a zero-sum result. A look at a few of many such legislative and administrative action strategies is illustrative.

Public Commitments

Political Forces. The smart politician always includes the anticrime agenda as part of her campaign platform. Regardless of the veracity of the claim, proclaiming oneself as a champion of public safety is an expedient way to gain favor among voters. The motivations of politicians who are in the position of being able to pursue get-tough-on-crime legislative strategies may be influenced more by emotional public opinion than by reasoned analysis of the facts and the potential consequences of the strategies advanced. California's Polly Klaas murder case, which was the catalyst behind the politically popular three-strikes laws, led to an increased prison population even though, in reality, these laws have been only infrequently used (Sorensen & Stemen, 2002). Megan's Law, Section 170101(d) of the Violent Crime Control and Law Enforcement Act of 1994 (42 U.S.C. §14071(d)), mandating sexual offender notification, has raised concerns about privacy, stigma, and treatment effectiveness (Lehman & Labecki, 1998). Kansas's sexual offender law, upheld by the U.S. Supreme Court in *Kansas v. Hendricks* (1997), changed the standards for involuntary detention and treatment of persons charged with certain predatory crimes. Truth-in-sentencing laws and passage of the Prisoner Litigation Reform Act of 1995, which curtailed the litigious activities of the jailhouse lawyer and limited the power of the federal courts to declare whole systems as being unconstitutional and to continue, ad infinitum, their supervision of such systems, are other examples. In short, although all of these laws, examples of the politicization of correctional policies, were enacted with the belief that public safety would be enhanced, new evidence suggests that this may not always be the case (Sorensen & Stemen, 2002).

When this chapter was first written, it would have been the rare politician who spoke against locking up every offender. But, in a 21st-century twist of fate, the focus has changed, and a small but significant sector of legislators are looking at the fiscal and social costs of incarceration and at the outcomes of restrictive sentencing practices. There is growing evidence that few of the harsh sentencing policies of the last two decades have had a significant impact on incarceration rates (Sorensen & Stemen, 2002). For example, new legislation is now focused on getting and keeping those with mental illnesses, many of whom could be better and more fiscally responsibly served by the public mental health system, out of jails and prisons. The Mentally Ill Offender Treatment and Crime Reduction Act of 2004 (PL 108–414) is still alive with significant legislative support for funding in 2007.

Victims' Rights. Victims, as a group and a status, have gone from being an afterthought to a force to be reckoned with, in the last two decades. The directives of the Victim and Witness Protection Act of 1982, the Victims of Crime Assistance Act (VOCA) of 1984, the Violent Crime Control and Law Enforcement Act of 1994, and many other legislative mandates have ensured that the needs of crime victims are addressed from a variety of fronts. Aside from being informed of the perpetrator's status in the significant stages of the criminal justice process, victims have also witnessed advancement of their rights to a more personal justice. In the United States, there is a national crime victims agenda, an Office for Victims of Crime (the government's advocacy resource for victims of crime), financial support for victim assistance and compensation programs, and initiatives to ensure the fair treatment of victims in the legal system as well as in other areas of public life (Adams, 1997). One excellent example of how victim concerns are at the fore in policy and practice decisions is in the area of sex offender management, where a "victim-centered approach" is integrated throughout (Center for Sex Offender Management [CSOM], 2007).

"Broken Windows." Some scholars are "convinced that there are too many prisoners and prisons in the United States today not because we overuse imprisonment but . . . because in the past we have not been willing enough to imprison serious offenders" (Block, 1997, p. 10). In their "broken windows" thesis, criminologists Wilson & Kelling (1982) argued that crime erodes neighborhoods and pulls apart communities that are already struggling to maintain some measure of stability. As Blagg & Smith (1989) explain, "instead of social workers and community activists 'mobilising' the poor and disadvantaged, the forces of law and order are invited to step in and fill the 'vacuum' left by the lack of appropriate social authority: the police become the guardians of a collapsing moral order" (p. 16). Thus, a policy of zero tolerance for even the slightest criminal activity is needed if troubled communities are to be morally reclaimed.

In 2007, the debate over the actual impact of zero-tolerance policing continues, with some arguing that alternative anticrime policies are equal to or more effective than those of the broken windows genre (Center on Juvenile and Criminal Justice, 2002) and others voicing public support for the broken windows approach ("Broken windows," 2007). However, that debate turns out, the crime-control policing strategies implemented in the 1980s and 1990s, some of which have had the impact of increasing prison and jail populations, have morphed into new ideas about reducing risk by understanding who should be institutionalized (controlling risk), what services they should receive while institutionalized that will reduce criminogenic risks (identifying needs), and who is likely to benefit from both (individual responsivity). In this regard, the work of Andrews and Bonta (2003) and others has moved prison administrators, worried about the seemingly endless volume of sentenced prisoners, to adopt assessment and treatment strategies that will effectively interdict in the onslaught. Andrews and Bonta (2003) believe that providing services that address dynamic and changeable personal factors and delivering the services in ways that individual offenders can receive them will reduce criminal thinking and behaviors.

While several other treatment and rehabilitative approaches are currently set forth in the literature, one other bears mention here. Lowenkamp and Latessa (2004) at the University of Cincinnati are working to identify the elements of interventions that work with particular kinds of offenders and, in so doing, are moving away from a blanket rehabilitation approach toward a more individualized program of assessment and intervention. Lowenkamp et al. argue that, contrary to popular thinking, doing something may not be better than doing nothing. Indeed, their research suggests that some persons under correctional supervision are left worse off when plied with interventions before the individual's measures of risk, needs, and responsivity are fully understood (see, for example, Lowenkamp & Latessa, 2004; Lowenkamp, Latessa, & Holsinger, 2006). Further, not all interventions are alike; unstandardized interventions with variations in dosage and duration—that is, the type, timing, and length of treatment—may make a person better or worse as a result (Wilson, 2007).

Judicial Activism. Many of the policy and practice changes witnessed in corrections over the last three decades have been accomplished as a direct result of judicial intervention. The federal courts did not involve themselves in prison operations until the late 1960s, when, in many cases, deplorable conditions of confinement and individual cases of maltreatment came to the attention of judges who were reading the Eighth Amendment's prohibition of cruel and unusual punishment with new energy (Ackerman, 1991). The bloody prison riots, the unsafe conditions, the growing number of prisoner suicides and mentally disturbed inmates seen over the next 15 years spurred the courts into a reformation mindset. In this process, the courts found that prisoners have fundamental constitutional rights to basic medical and mental health care while held in the custody of a corrections system. (See, for example, the prison cases of *Ruiz v. Estelle* [1980] and *Ramos v. Lamm* [1980] and the jail cases of *Campbell v. McGruder* [1978], *Bell v. Wolfish* [1979], and *Tittle v. Jefferson County Commission* [1992].)

Although the work of the courts today may be influenced by a different kind of activism than what was seen in the 1960s and 1970s, litigation seeking prison reforms is still being filed in this country, and the pursuit of those reforms has increasingly global implications. One need only read a small portion of the history of prisoner litigation advanced by the prisoners at Guantanamo Bay (e.g., *Rasul v. Bush* [2004], *Hamdan v. Rumsfeld* [2006], and *Hamdan v. Gates* and *Khadr v. Bush* [heard together in 2007]), to understand the global implications of the U.S. detention of foreign prisoners, many of whom were and are being held without charges.

Although court activism over time has forced correctional systems to change their operational and treatment policies, it has been unable to change the course and pace of population and institutional growth. Regardless of the amount of activism in the courts, the larger the correctional system becomes, the greater the burden will be to manage it effectively. Not only do the courts have less ability to do so now, in part due to the legislative constraints put on judges in the Prisoner Litigation Reform Act of 1995, but the judges may not have the internal support and that of political leaders to carry on in the change-agent fashion that made judicial intervention so interesting to watch in the 1970s and 1980s. That being said, the U.S. Supreme Court's surprise turnabout in its decision to hear the appeals of the Guantanamo Bay detainees (*Boumediene v. Bush* [2007]) may signal a new day in judicial intervention.

Conservation of Resources

Trained Correctional Personnel. The last three decades of the 20th century brought about a professionalization of the rank and file in corrections. The development of nationally recognized standards for the operation and management of correctional facilities, such as those promulgated by the American Correctional Association (1991), and the enactment of various state-based standards for certification of correctional officers have been catalysts for this professionalism. Professional and trade journals as well as conferences designed to assist officers and managers in doing their jobs more efficiently are commonly available. The federal government subsidizes training and technical assistance opportunities and a resource clearinghouse for state and local corrections professionals through its National Institute of Corrections, which has separate jail, prison, and community corrections divisions.

Unfortunately, recent publicized events threaten the perception of officer professionalism. The narrative depictions and provocative pictures of prisoner abuses that occurred at the Abu Ghraib prison (Hersh, 2004) had prison officials in the United States scrambling to distinguish their own operations from those in Iraq. New data on officer–prisoner sexual misconduct show the number of incidents rising in the two years of incident reporting required under the Prisoner Rape Elimination Act of 2003 (P.L. 108-79; Beck & Harrison, 2006). And recruitment challenges have led prison and local jail authorities to alter their job qualifications and advocacy organizations to generate new recommendations to (re)professionalize corrections' staff. Turnover rates among prison and jail officers are very high and are correlated with low salaries (Vera Institute of Justice, 2006). Recruitment demands mean that some systems now hire officers as young as age 18, creating an odd dynamic of vesting power and authority in people who arguably may be the least maturationally and experientially equipped to exercise it fairly.

Physical Space and the Availability of Beds. A "new generation" correctional philosophy emerged in the last 20 years under the theory that changes in the physical design of jails and prisons would force changes in management practices, which would, in turn, result in changes in inmates' behaviors (Zupan & Menke, 1991). These new generation facilities are streamlined in that supervision is easier to provide because the officer stands in closer proximity to the prisoners. Program space is built in, so program and living areas often merge within a certain physical boundary. When designed well and staffed to provide direct supervision of inmates, these newer institutions can provide better operational and personal security, good supervision, and more program opportunities while requiring fewer numbers of staff. Finally, though many new generation style facilities were designed to house inmates in single occupancy cells, conversion to two-person cells has been accomplished with minimal disruption to the operation and the safety goals of many of these institutions.

These advances in environmental design and equipment, however, have been threatened by the use of the correctional facility as a political tool. A few examples are illustrative. Some correctional agencies determined that a return to the fortress prisons of the past would serve them well, resulting in the "super max" prisons commonly found and touted in the state and federal systems. These locked-down institutions minimize staff–inmate and inmate–inmate verbal and physical contact and are reminiscent of the early prison era in this country. Litigation alleging that the environmental deprivation experienced in these prisons results in severe mental health problems has been argued and, in one well-known California class action suit, *Madrid v. Gomez* (1995), resulted in system changes.

Construction or utilization of "extra" local jail beds to house certain federal prisoners has put money into the general funds of some cities or has increased the profit margins of private corrections firms. Once a community becomes dependent on this additional income to support its basic services, it is difficult to alter the course. In 2005, local jails held about 5% of state and federal prisoners (Harrison & Beck, 2006).

Full discussion of the problems with using chemical and physical restraints in prisons and jails is beyond the scope of this chapter, but many facilities and officers have been met with litigation as a result of the improper use of these devices. In prisons, jails, and, until recently, psychiatric hospitals, the frustrations of dealing with persons with acute mental illnesses often led to the inappropriate application of restraints. New behavior management strategies that do not include restraints are being advanced by the federal government (U.S. Deptartment of Health and Human Services, 2005), but there is no evidence of their having been widely embraced in prisons and jails.

Containment of the Growth in Correctional Populations

Alternative Sentencing. In light of the steadily increasing correctional population, legislators and criminal justice experts have worked to reevaluate what types of crimes require incarceration of the perpetrator and whether, for other types of crimes, alternatives to incarceration are feasible. As a result, programs authorized by local legislation and judicial approval include house arrest, electronic monitoring, community service, victim–offender mediation, crisis intervention teams, diversion into mental health and substance abuse programs, halfway houses, day treatment centers, and the relatively new concept of "reentry programs." Good time credits, granted often solely on the authority of the incarcerating agency, also serve to get people out of institutions more quickly so that bed space is freed for the more serious offender. Many jurisdictions no longer support the incarceration of the misdemeanant, unless she or he has committed a politically volatile crime such as drunk driving or domestic assault or is someone with an apparent mental illness for whom necessary services cannot be as easily accessed. Eligibility for early release and diversion programs may be determined by a mental health or corrections' professional who has been vested with the authority to predict each particular prisoner's propensity to commit a new and perhaps more serious offense.

Sentencing is a public event, so a judge's decision to implement an alternative sentence can quickly raise the public's ire. The 2007 Paris Hilton sentencing fiasco comes to mind, and on close examination, it becomes apparent that what the media captured only scratched the surface of the vexing issues facing the entire criminal justice system. Should Paris Hilton have been sentenced and forced to serve jail time? Should anyone in the same circumstances be sentenced and forced to serve the same amount of jail time? Would justice have been meted out differently had a different person—of a different color, different gender, different attitude, different family—been in court? Who rules in the criminal justice system, and who should and when? These are clearly complex issues, and although the substance of the Paris Hilton case may have been lacking, the very personal, political, and judicial tensions that underlie correctional policy cannot be mistaken (see, for example, Winton & Blankstein, 2007).

Rehabilitation/Habilitation Strategies. Despite controversial assessments of the outcomes of various offender treatment programs (Lipton, Martinson, & Wilks, 1975; Martinson, 1974), work, educational, and therapeutic opportunities are offered to prisoners in the hope of reducing their risk of reoffending. In the 1990s, correctional managers were invested in being able to offer these types of services in their institutions as much or more for the purpose of keeping inmates busy as for habilitation. In the 2000s, these opportunities are offered to inmates while they are still incarcerated and as the inmate makes his or her transition into the community and a "free" life.

These "reentry programs" had their start under the Clinton administration and were brought to reality under the Bush administration's Serious and Violent Offender Reentry Initiative (SVORI). Seven federal agencies provided the initial funding for the evidence-based adult and juvenile offender programs that were ultimately initiated, though not always successfully, in every state. The development of cognitive thinking skills, job training and skill development, education, housing, health and mental health care, and substance abuse treatment have been emphasized. Despite a national evaluation and the requirement that states and local jurisdictions receiving SVORI funds evaluate the outcomes of their programs, the data have proved difficult to generate. Few outcome evaluations are available (see, for example, Severson, 2007; Wilson & Davis, 2006). While some state programs have ended, the concept of a coordinated reentry strategy holds promise in both reducing the rate of returns and new admissions to prison and helping released persons successfully reintegrate into their communities.

One important lesson of the SVORI era is that reentry efforts must be multifaceted. Although rehabilitation strategies in the 1970s were largely psychologically driven, in the 21st century, they are driven by a more holistic and public health approach and include an emphasis on employment, education, housing, health and mental health, and family, to name just a few components. And, clearly, just having a program is not enough; program fidelity, dosage, and duration are thought to be the keys to risk reduction and ultimate (ex) offender success in re-entering the free society (Wilson, 2007).

Further, even though prison-based mental health programs survived Martinson's and others' critical research findings, actually attracting and employing mental health professionals in corrections has proven difficult. In 1965, a national survey of correctional institutions revealed that there were a total of 167 "social workers or counselors" working in the institutions in this country or one for every 846 prisoners. Further, there was only one psychologist for every 4,282 inmates and one psychiatrist for every 2,436 inmates (President's Commission on Law Enforcement and the Administration of Justice, 1967, p. 178). A National Institute of Mental Health survey completed 25 years later revealed little change: There were only 297 social workers employed in prison mental health services throughout the United States in 1988 (U.S. Department of Health and Human Services, 1991). A survey published by the National Association of Social Workers (NASW) completed in 1991, showed that only 1.3% of NASW members identified the correctional setting as the site of their primary practice, a drop from 1.5% in 1988 (Gibelman & Schervish, 1993, p. 28). Further, this same survey found that those providing social work services in correctional settings were most likely to hold bachelor degrees in social work, leading the authors to comment that such data "reinforces the view that clients with the most complex and intractable socioeconomic and psychosocial problems are served by the least educated members" of the profession (Gibelman & Schervish, 1993, pp. 64–65). The popularity of 21st-century prisoner reentry programming offers the opportunity to practice social work at both micro and macro levels, in the prison and in the community, giving hope that social workers will reengage with this important population and societal institution.

Current Issues and Controversies

Corrections is an industry that serves clients on both the front and back steps of the criminal justice system. The industry itself is both shaping and being shaped by correctional policy, and it endures as an institution even though the ultimate social objective might be said to be to no longer need (so many) prison and jail beds. In addition to the ambiguities inherent in the correctional industry's mission, there are social policy ambiguities that perpetuate the proliferation and perhaps overutilization of correctional beds. The guiding policies of these two forces come together in the non-exhaustive list of critical issues discussed in the following pages.

Incarceration of Persons With Mental Illnesses

At the fore of any discussion of social policy and corrections stands the issue of the transinstitutionalization of persons with mental illnesses. Soon after the first wave of deinstitutionalization in the United States, when state hospitals radically downsized subsequent to the passage of the Mental Retardation Facilities and Community Mental Health Centers Construction Act of 1963, researchers began remarking about the possibility that a "criminalization" process involving persons with mental illness had resulted from this shift in government policy (Abramson, 1972; Teplin, 1983). The reduction in the nation's state hospital patients from 559,000 in 1955, when the total national population was 165 million, to a patient population of 72,000 out of the 250 million people nationally in 1994 (Lamb & Weinberger, 1998) meant that people with mental illnesses were going somewhere unseen or undetected, because they were not all being served in their communities. Briar (1983) identified the jail as being the "recycling station for some deinstitutionalized persons" (Briar, 1983, p. 388)

The bulk of the research into the incarceration of persons with severe and persistent mental illnesses has been completed within the last 20 years, and the evolving statistical picture is an interesting study. In 1987, Steadman, Fabisiak, Dvoskin, and Holohean found that 8% of inmates required immediate psychiatric treatment and another 16% of those evaluated required some type of periodic mental health service. Steadman (1990) suggested that 679,000 jail admissions in 1988 were of people with severe mental illnesses, and up to 672,000 releases from jails into the community that same year were persons "who were severely mentally ill upon admission" (p. 1). In 1999, reporting on 1995 survey data, Ditton found that nearly 16% of incarcerated males and 23% of incarcerated females had some form of mental illness. In 2006, James and Glaze reported that nearly 75% of women inmates in jails and prisons and between 55% and 63% of similarly situated males had a mental health problem and, in most cases, a substance dependence or abuse problem as well.

The "urgent problem" (Lamb & Weinberger, 1998, p. 483) of the increasing number of persons with severe and persistent mental illnesses housed in local jails may be attributable to the perception of jails as being safe havens when there are inadequate community-based mental health services. But recent research suggests that people are generally not incarcerated because of their mental illnesses; rather, they land in jail (and prison) because of the social and economic conditions (e.g., substance abuse, homelessness, poverty, unemployment) that precede the development of mental illness and that constitute the risk factors for criminal behavior (Draine, Salzer, Culhane, & Hadley, 2002; Junginger, Claypoole, Laygo, & Crisanti, 2006).

In an effort to cut costs and deliver constitutionally adequate health and mental health care, increasing numbers of jails and prisons are contracting with private providers to manage their institutional medical and mental health departments. As a result, public mental health agencies, such as community mental health centers and state psychiatric facilities, must find ways to work cooperatively and collaboratively with profit-driven corporations. In a time of fierce competition for diminishing fiscal resources, although it may be difficult to keep the professional focus on the care and treatment of those with mental illness no matter where they reside, public and private systems must especially find ways to do so.

Correctional Treatment. Nearly 20 years ago, Steadman and colleagues proposed five principles for planning effective mental health services in jails (Steadman, McCarty, & Morrissey, 1989). Included was the suggestion that the care and treatment of mentally disturbed inmates be seen as a community issue. Steadman et al. (1989) and others proposed that interventions be initiated before the person is brought to jail (diversion), that holistic treatment programming be offered to those incarcerated (Severson, 1992), and that discharge planning should begin in anticipation of an inmate's release, with community case management services to follow. Boundary spanning activities designed to bridge the communication and cooperation gap between institutional and community providers was recommended. Some progress has been made in these areas when viewed from the vantage point of policy and reentry practice initiatives (Pettus & Severson, 2006). For state and federal prisoners, the possibility and value of longer term, more intensive treatment services has been recognized and, in fact, has been supported both by legislation and case law.

Complicating the process of bringing these schemes to reality, however, are the legislative and judicial actions that make targeting dollars and therapeutic efforts to the seriously mentally ill population more difficult. For example, sexual offender treatment laws such as those in effect in Kansas (see *Kansas v. Hendricks,* 1997), require the state to dedicate expensive inpatient psychiatric beds and adequate numbers of mental health professionals to treat a condition for which a cure—or even symptom reduction—is elusive. A double bind is created by these types of laws: mental health professionals must effectively treat predatory sex offenders, at least to the extent of showing they are no longer dangerous, in order for hospital beds to be made available, only to have those beds filled again with offenders whose conditions may not respond to treatment. The burden falls on the mental health professional to treat the (perhaps untreatable) sex offender as well as the treatable person with a mental illness, but the clearer legislative mandate is geared toward the more difficult objective. It may be redundant, then, to suggest that social policies guiding corrections must also prioritize, by both need and potential, the objectives of intervention.

Women Prisoners. The number of women in prison and jail continues to climb at alarming rates. Annual rates of incarceration for women have been outpacing men's since 1996 (Gilliard & Beck, 1998). Between 2000 and

2006, the female prison population grew 3.3% on average, compared to a 2.0% growth in the male prison population. On June 30, 2006, women composed 7.2% of the prison population. Something similar is seen in the jails. Between 2000 and 2006, the number of adult females in local jails increased by 40%. Women now constitute 12.9% of the jail population (Sabol et al., 2007).

More so than men, women present unique mental health and social challenges within the corrections environment and are met with different standards of care and intervention. Teplin, Abram, and McClelland (1996) found that over 80% of the incarcerated women in their jail sample met the criteria for one or more lifetime psychiatric disorders; 17% of these women were diagnosed with a severe psychotic or affective disorder and less than one-fourth of females with severe mental disorders received services while incarcerated.

Correctional facilities, particularly jails, rarely have available to women programs that are comparable to those provided male inmates. Further, when such programs are available, they are often based on the models developed and used to treat males (Veysey, 1998).

Research has clearly illustrated the fact that women bring with them into the correctional facility gender dominant histories of being victims of sexual and physical abuse and domestic assault, as well as the problems associated with being single parents, being pregnant, or having to separate from their children physically if not emotionally while serving out their prison sentences (Severson, Postmus, & Berry, 2005).

Racial Disparities. The relationship between racial group membership and incarceration is made clear by the data. Persons belonging to a racial minority group are locked up in greater numbers and in greater percentages than ever before. While the incarceration of white individuals in prisons declined in the six-year period from 1990 through 1996, from 50.1% to 47.9%, the incarceration of persons of African American descent steadily rose during the same time period, from 48.6% to 49.4% (Gilliard & Beck, 1998). By the end of 1996, there were more black males in prisons across the country than white males (Gilliard & Beck, 1998). In the latest data available, Sabol et al. (2007) estimate that 4.8% of black men were in prison or jail on June 30, 2006, much higher incarceration rates than are found for Hispanic men (1.9%) and white men (0.7%). Black women have not escaped the phenomenon of disproportionate incarceration rates; these women were incarcerated at more than twice the rate of Hispanic women and nearly four times the rate of white women (Sabol et al., 2007).

Regarding the "racialisation of crime" in Britain and in the United States, Blagg and Smith (1989) suggest that the "dominant tradition in social work of perceiving black families as essentially pathological, inadequate and unstable" (p. 24) has worked its way into the suggestion that criminality springs from a culture of "frustrated aspirations amongst black youth" (p. 26). At least one of the dangers with this thinking about culture is that it can lead to entire communities being identified as "criminally inclined" (p. 26) and thus to differential treatment based on this assumption. This differential treatment does not just affect how law enforcement operations are carried out, it also impacts the social and economic perceptions of the neighborhood, potentially resulting in lost business opportunities, a decline in the types of social activities that support youth and families, and a weakening of other fundamental neighborhood supports.

Certainly, any interdiction of the racialization of the correctional system must begin before we get to the front steps of the system itself, namely, by increasing our understanding of and tolerance for expressions of racial and cultural diversity in the world community. This diversity must be considered when planning the physical, educational, commercial, and service components of communities, components that will support children and youth as they search for ways to express their differences.

Once we are on the steps of the system, however, at the point of contact between the citizen and law enforcement, and throughout the adversarial process, those with power must work to create social policies so that a color-blind, justice-seeking approach to correctional system management is the norm.

Alternative Sanctions and Diversion. In terms of serving the needs of persons with mental illnesses, diversion programs are generally designed to screen defined groups of detainees for mental disorders and negotiate with system players, including the courts, "to produce a mental health disposition as a condition of bond, in lieu of prosecution, or as a condition of a reduction in charges (whether or not a formal conviction occurs); and link the detainee directly to community-based service" (Steadman, Morris, & Dennis, 1995, p. 1630). The diversion of those with mental illnesses to more appropriate treatment milieus represents the humanitarian sentiments of some segments of society. By completing the collaborative loop that ties together the community and the correctional system, diversion programming is meant to ensure continuity of care and reduce the extent of disruption in the system and in the individual's and family's lives.

Although in the 1990s talk of diversion programming was often met with resistance from system officials as well as the public, in the 21st century it has gained some favor. Diversion strategies fit well with a public health risk reduction philosophy, which begs for a healthy body–healthy community mindset and for the thoughtful deployment of limited institutional and health resources (U.S. Department of Health and Human Services, 1999). As jails and prisons fill with persons at risk for physical, mental, and social problems, including women, persons with chronic health and mental health challenges, violent and habitual offenders, and others, questioning status quo solutions becomes all the more important. Is there a better *place* to treat this person? Is there a better *way* to treat this person? Is there a better *time* to treat this person? And is there a better *team* to treat this person?

Although attempts have been made to evaluate diversion programs, there still is relatively little evidence that supports the efficacy of any one model (Washington State Institute for Public Policy, 2006), and researchers have commented on the challenges of designing and executing this kind of evaluation (Draine & Solomon, 1999). The fact remains that, where diversion program outcomes have been identified to date, the data are still either missing or so incomplete as to make any statements about program success more speculative than evidence based. The evaluations that have been completed suggest that, though recidivism rates might not differ between diverted and non-diverted persons, there may well be other appropriate objectives reached by implementing a diversion program. Those objectives include reductions in criminal justice costs, increasing public safety by ensuring access to the treatment resources needed by an individual, and—in essence—doing the right thing: making sure those whose behavior is directed by their mental status receive the right intervention at the right time.

The Future of Correctional Social Policies and Practices

> The extent to which the existing social system works in the direction of the prisoner's deterioration rather than his rehabilitation; the extent to which the system can be changed; the extent to which we are willing to change it—these are the issues which confront us and not the recalcitrance of the individual inmate. (Sykes, 1958, p. 134)

Much remains to be done in the correctional realm. Although advances in inmate management, staff professionalism, and physical security of institutions have been realized, the humanistic aspects of corrections still require considerable work. The dangers that lurk ahead are the very same dangers that plagued the past: allowing punishment for profit to be a guiding concept in correctional management; assuming these institutions are endless resources that can continue to absorb and banish society's misfits, as well as society's ill-fits, with an "out of sight, out of mind" perspective; and using corrections as a political tool to be wielded as a reward or as a punishment depending on who is inquiring. Sykes was right—the social policy issues of the future and our focus must be on creating systemic change not on producing change in any given (recalcitrant) individual.

The presumptive sentencing practices of the last two decades of the 20th century, particularly those mandating certain sentences for drug, sex, and multiple felony convictions, promise to keep the population of jails and prisons increasing. Those increases will necessarily include more persons with mental illnesses and will mean significantly higher societal costs— fiscal and social—the costs of locking up a substantial number of young black males, increasing numbers of women, and hoards of juveniles.

History has repeated itself. Twenty-five years ago, Briar (1983) remarked that the jail is among society's most enduring institutions and suggested that "its uses and its future should be a major issue in social work communities across the United States" (p. 393). There is little doubt that the social policies driving and guiding corrections are major issues with which social workers must grapple. Though we are now well into the first decade of the 21st century, the question still remains: Will we choose to do so?

References

Abramson, M. F. (1972). The criminalization of mentally disordered behavior: Possible side-effect of a new mental health law. *Hospital and Community Psychiatry, 23*(4), 101–107.

Ackerman, H. A. (1991). The New Jersey jail crisis: The judicial experience. *Rutgers Law Review, 44,* 135–164.

Adams, A. (1997). *Victims of Crime Act of 1984 as amended: A report to the president and the congress.* Washington, DC: U.S. Department of Justice Office of Justice Programs, Office for Victims of Crime.

American Correctional Association. (1991). *Standards for adult detention facilities* (2nd ed.). Fairfax, VA: Commission on Accreditation for Law Enforcement Agencies.

Andrews, D. A., & Bonta, J. (2003). *The psychology of criminal conduct* (3rd ed.). Cincinnati, OH: Anderson.

Beck, A. J., & Harrison, P. M. (2006). *Special report. Sexual violence reported by correctional authorities, 2005.* Washington, DC: U.S. Department of Justice, Bureau of Justice Statistics.

Bell v. Wolfish, 441 U.S. 520 (1979).

Blagg, H., & Smith, D. (1989). *Crime, penal policy and social work.* Essex, UK: Longman.

Block, M. K. (1997, July). *Two views on imprisonment policies: Lethal violence and the overreach of American imprisonment: Supply side imprisonment policy presentations from the 1996 Annual Research and Evaluation Conference.* Washington, DC: U.S. Department of Justice, Office of Justice Programs, National Institute of Justice. Retrieved February 8, 2008, from http://www.ncjrs.gov/txtfiles/165702.txt

Boumediene v. Bush, No. 06–1195, 2007 U.S. LEXIS 8757 (2007).

Briar, K. H. (1983). Jails: Neglected asylums. *Social Casework: The Journal of Contemporary Social Work, 64*(7), 387–393.

Broken windows and crime [Editorial]. (2007, May 6). *Chicago Tribune.* Retrieved June 24, 2007, from http://www.chicagotribune.com/

Campbell v. McGruder, 580 F.2d. 521, 188 U.S. App. D.C. 258 (D.C. Cir. 1978).

Carleton, M. T. (1971). *Politics and punishment" The history of the Louisiana State penal system.* Baton Rouge: Louisiana State University Press.

Center on Juvenile and Criminal Justice. (2002). *Shattering "broken windows": An analysis of San Francisco's alternative crime policies.* Retrieved June 23, 2007, from http://www.cjcj.org/pubs/windows/windows.html

Center for Sex Offender Management. (2007). *Managing the challenges of sex offender reentry.* Washington, DC: U.S. Department of Justice, Office of Justice Programs.

Deutsch, A. (1937). *The mentally ill in America.* New York: Doubleday, Doran and Co.

Ditton, P. (1999). *Mental health and treatment for inmates and probationers.* Washington, DC: Bureau of Justice Statistics.

Draine, J., Salzer, M. S., Culhane, D. P., & Hadley, T. (2002). Role of social disadvantage in crime, joblessness, and homelessness among persons with serious mental illness. *Psychiatric Services, 53*(5), 565–572.

Draine, J., & Solomon, P. (1999). Describing and evaluating jail diversion services for persons with serious mental illness. *Psychiatric Services, 50*(1), 56–61.

Fogel, D. (1975). *". . . We are the living proof . . .": The justice model for corrections.* Cincinnati, OH: W. H. Anderson.

Gibelman, M., & Schervish, P. H. (1993). *Who we are: The social work labor force as reflected in the NASW membership.* Washington, DC: National Association of Social Workers.

Gilliard, D. K., & Beck, A. J. (1998). *Prisoners in 1997* (Bureau of Justice Statistics Bulletin No. NCJ–170014). Washington, DC: U.S. Department of Justice.

Hamdan v. Rumsfeld, 126 S. Ct. 2749 (2006).

Hamdan v. Gates/Khadr v. Bush, No. 06-1169 (2007).

Harrison, P. M., & Beck, A. J. (2006). *Prisoners in 2005* (Bureau of Justice Statistics Bulletin No. NCJ-215092). Washington, DC: U.S. Department of Justice.

Hersh, S. M. (2004, May 10). Torture at Abu Ghraib. *The New Yorker.* Retrieved June 22, 2007, from http://www.newyorker.com/

Junginger, J., Claypoole, K., Laygo, R., & Crisanti, A. (2006). Effects of serious mental illness and substance abuse on criminal offenses. *Psychiatric Services, 57*(6), 879–882.

Kansas v. Hendricks, 117 S. Ct. 2072, 138 L.Ed.2d 501 (1997).

Lamb, H. R., & Weinberger, L. E. (1998) Persons with severe mental illness in jails and prisons: A review. *Psychiatric Services, 49*(4), 483–492.

Lehman, J. D., & Labecki, L. S. (1998) Myth versus reality: The policies of crime and punishment and its impact on correctional administration in the 1990s. In T. Alleman & R. L. Gido (Eds.), *Turnstile justice: Issues in American corrections* (pp. 42–70). Saddle River, NJ: Prentice Hall.

Lipton, D., Martinson, R., & Wilks, J. (1975). *The effectiveness of correctional treatment: A survey of treatment evaluation studies.* New York: Praeger.

Lowenkamp, C. T., & Latessa, E. J. (2004). *Understanding the risk principle: How and why correctional interventions can harm low-risk offenders* (Topics in Community Corrections). Washington, DC: U.S. Department of Justice, National Institute of Corrections.

Lowenkamp, C. T., Latessa, E. J., & Holsinger, A. (2006). The risk principle in action: What we have learned from 13,676 offenders and 97 correctional programs. *Crime and Delinquency, 52*(1), 77–93.

Madrid v. Gomez, 889 F. Supp. 1146 (N.D. Cal. 1995).

Martinson, R. (1974). What works?—Questions and answers about prison reform. *The Public Interest, 35,* 22–54.

McNeece, C. A. (1995). Adult corrections. In R. L. Edwards & J. G. Hopps (Eds.), *Encyclopedia of social work* (19th ed., Vol. 1, pp. 60–68). Washington, DC: NASW Press.

Pettus, C., & Severson, M. (2006). Paving the way for effective reentry practice: The critical role and function of the boundary spanner. *The Prison Journal, 86*(2), 1–24.

Pray, K. L. M. (1951). Social work in the prison program. In P. W. Tappan (Ed.), *Contemporary corrections* (pp. 204–210). New York: McGraw-Hill.

President's Commission on Law Enforcement and the Administration of Justice. (1967). *The challenge of crime in a free society*. Washington, DC: Government Printing Office.

Ramos v. Lamm, 639 F.2d 559 (10th Cir. 1980), cert. denied, 450 U.S. 1041, 101 S. Ct. 1759, 68 L.Ed.2d 559 (1981).

Rasul v. Bush, 542 U.S. 466 (2004).

Rothman, D. J. (1998). The invention of the penitentiary. In T. Flanagan, J. W. Marquart, & K. G. Adams (Eds.), *Incarcerating criminals: Prisons and jails in social and organizational context* (pp. 15–23). New York: Oxford University Press.

Ruiz v. Estelle, 503 F.Supp. 1265 (S.D. Texas 1980), aff'd in part, 679 F.2d 1115 (5th Cir. 1982), cert. denied, 40 U.S. 1042 (1983).

Sabol, W. J., Minton, T. D., & Harrison, P. M. (2007). *Prison and jail inmates at midyear 2006* (Bureau of Justice Statistics Bulletin No. NCJ-217675). Washington, DC: U.S. Department of Justice.

Severson, M. (1992). Redefining the boundaries of mental health services: A holistic approach to improving inmate mental health. *Federal Probation, 56*(3), 57–63.

Severson, M. (2007). *Final report: Federal partners' Coming Home Initiative: The Shawnee County Reentry Project*. Retrieved February 7, 2008, from http://www.dc.state.ks.us/reentry/information-folder/research-references-related-to-reentry

Severson, M., Postmus, J., & Berry, M. (2005). Incarcerated women: Consequences and contributions of victimization, risk, and resiliency. *International Journal of Prisoner Health, 1*(2–4), 223–240.

Sorensen, J., & Stemen, D. (2002). The effect of state sentencing policies on incarceration rates. *Crime & Delinquency, 48*(3), 456–475.

Steadman, H. J. (1990). Introduction. In H. J. Steadman, *Jail diversion for the mentally ill: Breaking through the barriers—Effectively addressing the mental health needs of jail detainees* (pp. 1–9). Seattle, WA: National Coalition for the Mentally Ill in the Criminal Justice System.

Steadman, H. J., Fabisiak, S., Dvoskin, J., & Holohean, E. J. (1987). A survey of mental disability among state prison inmates. *Hospital and Community Psychiatry, 38,* 1086–1090.

Steadman, H. J., McCarty, D. W., & Morrissey, J. P. (1989). *The mentally ill in jail: Planning for essential services*. New York: Guilford.

Steadman, H. J., Morris, S. M., & Dennis, D. L. (1995). The diversion of mentally ill persons from jails to community-based services: A profile of programs. *American Journal of Public Health, 85*(12), 1630–1635.

Sykes, G. M. (1958). *The society of captives. A study of a maximum security prison*. Princeton, NJ: Princeton University Press.

Teplin, L. A. (1983). The criminalization of the mentally ill: Speculation in search of data. *Psychological Bulletin, 94*(1), 54–67.

Teplin, L. A., Abram, K. M., & McClelland, G. M. (1996). Prevalence of psychiatric disorders among incarcerated women. *Archives of General Psychiatry, 53,* 505–512.

Tittle v. Jefferson County Commission, 10 F.3d 1535 (11 Cir. 1994), en banc, vacating a contrary opinion appearing at 966 F.2d 606 (11th Cir. 1992).

Torrey, E. F., Stieber, J., Ezekiel J., Wolfe, S. M., Sharfstein, J., Noble, J. H., et al. (1992). *Criminalizing the seriously mentally ill: The abuse of jails as mental hospitals*. Arlington, VA: National Alliance for the Mentally Ill and Public Citizen's Health Research Group.

U.S. Congress. (1963). P.L. 88-164. *Mental Retardation Facilities and Community Mental Health Centers Construction Act of 1963.*

U.S. Congress. (1982). P.L. 97-291. *The Victim and Witness Protection Act of 1982.*

U.S. Congress. (1984). P.L. 98-473 *Victims of Crime Assistance Act of 1984* (VOCA).

U.S. Congress. (1994). P.L. 103-322. *The Violent Crime Control and Law Enforcement Act of 1994.*

U.S. Congress. (1996). P.L. 104-134. *Prisoner Litigation Reform Act of 1995.*

U.S. Department of Health and Human Services. (1991). *1988 inventory of mental health services in state adult correctional facilities.* Rockville, MD: U.S. Department of Health and Human Services, National Institute of Mental Health.

U.S. Department of Health and Human Services. (1999). *Mental health: A report of the surgeon general—Executive summary.* Rockville, MD: U.S. Department of Health and Human Services, Substance Abuse and Mental Health Services Administration, Center for Mental Health Services, National Institutes of Health, National Institute of Mental Health.

U.S. Department of Health and Human Services. (2005). *Roadmap to seclusion and restraint free mental health services.* Rockville, MD: U.S. Department of Health and Human Services, Center for Mental Health Services, Substance Abuse and Mental Health Services Administration.

Vera Institute of Justice. (2006). *Confronting confinement. A report of the Commission on Safety and Abuse in America's Prisons.* Retrieved June 24, 2007, from http://www.prisoncommission.org/

Veysey, B. M. (1998). The specific needs of women diagnosed with mental illnesses in U.S. jails. In B. L. Levin, A.K. Blanch, & A. Jennings (Eds.), *Women's mental health services: A public health perspective.* Thousand Oaks, CA: Sage.

Washington State Institute for Public Policy. (2006). *Evidence-based adult corrections programs: What works and what does not.* Retrieved May 23, 2006, from http://www.wsipp.wa.gov

Welch, M. (1991). The expansion of jail capacity: Makeshift jails and public policy. In J.A. Thompson & G.L. Mays (Eds.), *American jails: Public policy issues* (pp. 148–162). Chicago: Nelson-Hall.

Winton, R., & Blankstein, A. (2007, June 27). Paris is freed: Now it's Baca's turn. *Los Angeles Times.* Retrieved June 30, 2007, from http://www.latimes.com/

Wilson, J. A. (2007). Habilation or harm: Project Greenlight and the potential consequences of correctional programming. *NIJ Journal, 257,* 2–7. (Available from the U.S. Department of Justice, Office of Justice Programs, National Institute of Justice, Washington, DC)

Wilson, J. A., & Davis, R. C. (2006). Good intentions meet hard realities: An evaluation of the Project Greenlight Reentry Program. *Criminology & Public Policy, 5*(2), 303–338.

Wilson, J. Q., & Kelling, G. L. (1982, March). Broken windows: The police and neighbourhood safety. *The Atlantic Monthly,* pp. 29–38.

Zupan, L. L., & Menke, B. A. (1991). The new generation jail: An overview. In J. A. Thompson & G. L. Mays (Eds.), *American jails: Public policy issues* (pp. 180–194). Chicago: Nelson-Hall.

29

Employment Policy and Social Welfare

Michelle Livermore and Younghee Lim

For the majority of persons in the United States, work provides individuals with enough resources to ensure their own welfare. For others, however, jobs that provide an income adequate enough to support a family are illusive. This chapter addresses the mechanisms by which the U.S. government has acted to maximize work and the benefits of work to individuals. Current employment policies are reviewed in a historical context.

A range of policies exist to intervene in labor market processes to benefit individuals. In the most general terms, strategies promoting the welfare of workers either address factors affecting the supply and demand for workers or regulate the treatment, wages, or benefits of workers. Like all markets, labor markets are seen by neoclassical economists as regulated by two forces: supply and demand. The supply of labor involves the number and characteristics of workers. Related employment strategies focus on improving worker quality, linking workers to employers, and providing work supports. They include education and training programs and job search and placement assistance. The demand for labor involves the amount and type of labor needed by an employer for production. Labor demand strategies attempt to increase employers' ability and desire to hire workers. These include macroeconomic policies that aim to improve the market and subsequently create jobs, employer tax credits that reward employers for hiring certain categories of workers, and policies aimed at preventing discrimination. Regulatory policies focus on preventing worker exploitation and insuring workers against job loss. These include job loss protection, worker safety and benefits, and wage protection.

The history of employment policy in the United States involves a mix of these three types of policies. The first three sections of this chapter discuss each type of policy as implemented in the United States. The final section summarizes current issues and controversies related to these policies.

Labor Supply Policy

Augmenting the quantity or quality of the labor supply is the most common employment policy strategy implemented in the United States. Such policies include employment training, placement strategies, and providing workers with supports that enable them to enter and remain in the labor force.

Employment Training

Numerous employment and training programs exist in the United States with the goal of increasing the skills of current and potential workers. These include comprehensive high schools, vocational education classes and schools, apprenticeship programs, the military, community colleges, colleges, universities, and targeted employment training programs. The focus of this section is on targeted employment and training programs. Although all of the institutions mentioned above are relevant to the welfare of individuals in society, targeted employment and training programs have been most closely associated with social welfare policy because they specifically target individuals having difficulty in the labor market. Also, another chapter in this book discusses educational policy in the United States in more detail.

Federal intervention focusing on employment training emerged during the War on Poverty. Policies implemented during this era were based on assumptions that unemployment was an individual problem since jobs were plentiful. Therefore, targeting the poor was seen as the most effective strategy to combat unemployment, as policy makers strove to promote equality of opportunity. Human capital theory, on which this type of policy is based, posed that training would remedy individual deficiencies that prevented full labor market participation (Mucciaroni, 1990).

Employment and training programs begun during this period were small and fragmented. The 1962 Manpower Development and Training Act (MDTA) sought to prepare unemployed and displaced blue-collar workers for the new high-skilled jobs being created by the economy; MDTA made provision for vocational and on-the-job training, testing, counseling, job placement services, and living allowances (Janoski, 1990). The Economic Opportunity Act (EOA) of 1964 created its own manpower development system under the Office of Economic Opportunity (OEO), which used community action agencies to provide a centralized outreach point for employment training and placement, with specialized skills training provided by independent contractors (Janoski, 1990). Later that decade, the Work Incentive Program (WIN) was implemented to increase the work effort of recipients of Aid to Families with Dependent Children (AFDC). From 1967 until 1989, the program required public assistance recipients to register for work and training program unless they had young children. Although training and placement were the intentions of the program, only rarely did these activities follow registration (Bane & Ellwood, 1994).

Pressure to consolidate employment programs in the 1970s resulted in the Comprehensive Employment and Training Act (CETA). CETA decategorized federal and state "single issue" employment programs, placing all programs for special populations under the control of prime sponsors, which could be city or county governments. It required these entities to develop a comprehensive policy for manpower development in their local areas. This transfer of responsibility to the local level marked the decentralization of employment training. The amount of direct employment training also declined during this period. The Work Incentive Program, the Job Corps, and On-the-Job-Training (OJT), which involved a subsidy paid to employers for hiring and training workers, were the only programs remaining that provided job training (Janoski, 1990).

In 1982, the Job Training and Partnership Act (JTPA) replaced CETA, decreasing program expenditures and placing local business at the center of employment policy decision making through private industry councils (PICs) in various regions and municipalities (Guttman, 1983). The act eliminated on-the-job-training and limited the value of the wages that trainees could receive (Janoski, 1990). JTPA provided resources to poor, uneducated adults and youth through public and private training institutions. Program regulations were enforced by the Department of Labor and overseen by private industry councils, state job training coordinating councils, or, in some states, workforce development departments (Levitan, Magnum, & Magnum, 1998).

The JTPA legislation targeted a variety of different groups. It provided employment training for impoverished and undereducated adults and year round and summer employment and training programs for youth. Migrant and seasonal farm workers were provided with skill enhancement and job placement services, and funds were allocated for grants to Native American tribes to offer basic skills training, occupational skills training, work experience, and on-the-job training to their members. Also, the Job Corps program targeted impoverished youth with severe educational deficits and other employment barriers. This intensive, long-term job training and remedial education program included health care, counseling, and job placement assistance in a residential setting (General Accounting Office [GAO], 1995).

In 1996, the Temporary Assistance for Needy Families (TANF) program replaced the Aid to Families with Dependent Children (AFDC) program and its training program, Job Opportunities for Basic Skills (JOBS). The JOBS program required states to implement programs to increase the self-sufficiency of AFDC recipients; these included assessment, basic skills training, job skills training, job development, and job placement (Bane & Ellwood, 1994). Instead of the basic education strategy promoted in the JOBS program, TANF regulations required participants to work (U.S. House Committee on Ways and Means, 2004a). Currently, the amount of work required ranges from 20 to 30 hours per week for single parents and 35 to 55 hours per week for two-parent families (Center on Budget and Policy

Priorities, 2007). By requiring TANF recipients to work, TANF increases the supply of workers in the labor market. The plethora of categorical employment programs continued to be a primary issue of congressional concern in the 1990s (GAO, 1995). To address this, the Workforce Investment Act of 1998 (P.L. 105-220) uses block grants for employment, training, and literacy to coordinate activities of over 60 federal employment programs. It repealed the Job Training and Partnership Act and coordinated multiple federal programs through locally controlled workforce development systems (Social Legislation Information Service, 1998). By 2003, the number of federally funded employment programs declined to 44 (GAO, 2003).

One key component of the legislation is the one-stop service delivery system. This requires that each workforce investment area have at least one location where the public can gain access to different levels of services. Second, the work-first focus gives priority to "core services" that link individuals immediately to employment, such as job readiness, placement, and retention services. "Intensive services," such as assessment and counseling, and "training services," such as on-the-job and classroom training, are reserved for those who are unable to obtain employment. Priority for allocation of these services is given to public assistance recipients and other low-income individuals. A third component of the legislation is the Individual Training Account. Eligible participants are given these accounts to purchase training services from eligible providers. A fourth component is the development of state and local workforce investment boards, which are responsible for developing strategic plans for workforce investment and evaluating performance (Social Legislation Information Service, 1998; U.S. House Committee on Ways and Means, 2004b).

Job Placement

While employment training focuses on improving the labor supply, job placement focuses on labor supply management. Although both have often been offered by the same agencies and in the same programs, this has not always been the case. The history of job placement services actually began in the private sector. Labor shortages accompanying early American settlement during the early 19th century led to the emergence of private employment agencies that recruited workers from Europe and Africa (Janoski, 1990; Martinez, 1976). Public labor exchanges began at the state level in Ohio in the 1890s, and, soon after, employment offices were opened in 20 other states (Guzda, 1983; Janoski, 1990). Another 24 states began to regulate private labor exchanges but were discouraged by numerous Supreme Court actions. These judicial decisions reflected the typical laissez-faire view that government should limit its interference in the economy. In spite of this, job placement became a political issue prior to World War II, with demands for labor exchanges coming from both labor organizations and state unemployment offices (Janoski, 1990).

In response to this political pressure, President Woodrow Wilson created the United States Employment Service (USES) with an executive order in 1918. The USES took the place of the Division of Information, which had relocated immigrants throughout the country earlier in the century. It opened employment offices in 40 states and relied on state advisory boards for advice regarding the operation of these offices. High union–employer tensions present at this time weakened support for the USES, leading to its deterioration during the Hoover administration and to its subsequent sidelining when the National Reemployment Agency assumed its duties during the Roosevelt administration (Leschohier, 1919, cited in Janoski, 1990).

In 1933, the Wagner-Peyser Act reestablished the USES. Its duties were undertaken through a voluntary confederation of state employment offices, governed loosely by federal regulations. The USES recruited labor for the New Deal work relief programs in states without employment services. However, because the USES was also responsible for processing the large number of claims made for Unemployment Insurance during this time, its placement duties were much more limited than intended (Mucciaroni, 1990).

The importance of labor supply management again increased during World War II, as workers were in scarce supply. At this time, the federal government took over the USES, highlighting the importance of government employment programs to national interests (Janoski, 1990). Employment programs were viewed as important to society at large, because they helped maintain a productive economy in a world of increasing education levels and changing organizational structures and management (Mucciaroni, 1990).

The USES continued to operate during the 1950s. However, it listed only a small number of actual vacancies and focused only on the white lower-middle and working classes. Its decline during this time was due to a lack of organization; increasing competition from private employment agencies, union hiring halls, and civil service offices; and decreased funding due to the discontinuation of the local match requirement and the diversion of USES funds into the unemployment trust fund (Janoski, 1990). Although President Kennedy expanded the USES in 1961, it did not have a large impact later in the decade because alternative programs were created during the War on Poverty; civil rights activists viewed the USES as incapable of handling disadvantaged individuals (Janoski, 1990).

During the 1970s and early 1980s, placement services, in addition to training services, were under the control of the Comprehensive Employment and Training Act (CETA). During this period, the USES began computerizing job listings and making this information widely available. The 1976 CETA amendments provided incentives for prime sponsors to use the USES to place workers, but it was usually not the agency of choice, and this incentive was not continued in subsequent legislation (Janoski, 1990).

Under the Job Training and Partnership Act (JTPA), the Job Service was the entity that assisted individuals in finding jobs through a nationwide network of over 1,800 offices. In recent years, the service experienced budget cuts, decreased the amount of counseling services, and relied on a self-help approach to job placement. This included America's Job Bank, which listed available jobs nationwide, and America's Talent Bank, which provided resumes for employers. The Workforce Investment Act of 1998 incorporates the placement and information dissemination functions of the Job Service into a one-stop delivery system. Job search and placement assistance are core services prioritized in the act. Other core services include career counseling, skills assessment, and job retention services (GAO 2003; U.S. House Committee on Ways and Means, 2004b).

Work Supports

For low-wage workers, labor force attachment is often a challenge because work does not always meet the needs of their families (Edin & Lein, 1997). Numerous policies provide supports and incentives to assist and encourage labor market participation, including food stamps, Medicaid and the State Children's Health Insurance Program (SCHIP), child care subsidies, and the Earned Income Tax Credit (EITC) (Zedlewski & Zimmerman, 2007). We discuss EITC in this chapter, but health and income supports are covered by other chapters in this book.

Enacted in 1975 as a refundable tax credit for low-income workers, the EITC appeared to be a viable, work-oriented alternative to existing welfare programs (U.S. Senate, 1975, p. 33, as cited in Ventry, 2002). The federal EITC targets low-income individuals based on their family size and tax filing status, and it is considered a refundable tax credit because it subsidizes the low wages of workers without tax liability. The program began modestly with a credit equaling 10% of earned income up to $4,000 with a maximum credit of $400 (Ozawa & Hong, 2003), but it has been continuously modified with major expansions during the 1990s. Important EITC legislation includes the Tax Reform Act of 1986, which indexed the EITC for inflation; the Omnibus Budget Reconciliation Act (OBRA) of 1990, which increased the maximum amount of the credit and differentiated credit rates based on family size; the OBRA of 1993 that increased the subsidy rate for families with two children to 40%, which translated to an increase in the maximum credit from $1,511 to $3,556 (U.S. Office of Management and Budget, 2005); and the Economic Growth and Tax Relief Reconciliation Act of 2001, which reduced the marriage penalty for low-income married couples by increasing the point where EITC phase-out begins (Burman, Maag, & Rohaly, 2002). The fully phased-in EITC is the largest cash transfer program (U.S. Office of Management and Budget, 2005). In 2004, the adjusted gross income (AGI) limit for single filers with one child was $30,338, and, for single filers with two or more children, it was $34,458 (Hoynes, 2005). In addition to the federal EITC policy, as of July of 2007, 22 states had implemented their own state supplemental EITCs in addition to the federal EITC (Lim, in press).

A vast body of research consistently showed that the EITC provided unambiguous incentives for single mothers with children to participate in the labor force and increased their earnings (e.g., Blank, 2002; Eissa & Liebman, 1996; Eissa & Nichols, 2005; Ellwood, 2000; Grogger, 2003, 2004; Meyer & Rosenbaum, 2001). While providing a work incentive for those who were not in the labor market or who were working only a few hours (Eissa & Hoynes, 2005; Meyer, 2002), the EITC creates a disincentive to increase work for those already in the labor market due to high marginal tax rates in the phase-out region (Eissa & Hoynes, 2005; Hoffman, 2003). Research indicated, however, that this negative effect was small (Hotz & Scholz, 2003), and it may be due to lack of knowledge about the phase out of credit or to a lack of flexibility in adjusting hours.

A body of more recent research also found that the EITC played the most important role in decreasing welfare use among female-headed families (e.g., Grogger, 2003, 2004; Lim, 2007; Looney, 2005). Further, the EITC leads to significant reductions in poverty (Nagle & Johnson, 2006). The EITC, together with programs such as Supplemental Security Income and food stamps, help those who receive little or no help from the social insurance programs to meet basic needs. These means-tested programs are estimated to lift 11 million Americans out of poverty (Sherman, 2005). Although highlighting the difficulty in separating out the effects of welfare policy from general economic effects and the consequences of other policy changes, such as the expansion of the EITC, Blank (2002) attributed to the EITC some moderate increases in cash income and declines in poverty among less-skilled, single-mother families during the late 1990s. Gundersen and Ziliak (2004) also indicated that a large portion of improvement in after-tax poverty among the poorest families occurred through the EITC, especially among the female-headed families.

Labor Demand Strategies

Whereas labor supply strategies focus on workers, labor demand strategies focus on the availability of jobs. Government policies can attempt to stimulate labor demand through the private market, by creating jobs directly or by increasing demand for disadvantaged workers.

Private Market Approaches

Economic policy addressing labor demand through the private market is rooted in Keynesian economics, which has two branches. Secular stagnationists believe that, as the economy becomes unable to generate growth, policies that stimulate the economy are needed. Related interventions include increasing public investments and budgetary deficits. Federal policy during the Great Depression used spending on public works projects and direct job creation to curb the human effects of the economic downturn (Mucciaroni, 1990). Although the federal interventions of this period were viewed as temporary emergency measures, subsequent legislation made the role of the federal government in maintaining employment permanent. The Employment Act of 1946 requires the president to submit to Congress each year an economic report and policy proposals that address any problems related to employment, pricing, and production identified in this report. In the Full Employment and Balanced Growth Act of 1978, full employment is articulated as the goal of federal economic policy, and numeric targets for unemployment rates are specified (Santoni, 1986).

Commercial (or American) Keynesians have a more optimistic view of the market. Where secular stagnationists see stagnation, commercial Keynesians see a simple downturn in an economic cycle. Policy prescriptions for shortening the duration of these downturns include tax cuts, which quickly increase the amount of money available for consumer spending during recessionary periods (Mucciaroni, 1990). Even though the ideological foundations of commercial Keynesianism were lain during the late 1940s, the tax cut was completely absent as an economic recovery policy during the 1950s and emerged as an option in 1962 as recovery from the 1960–1961 recession slowed. When President Kennedy recognized the level of support for this idea in the business community, he and his Council of Economic Advisors embraced it. The tax cut remains a popular economic stimulation policy alternative offered by conservatives (Mucciaroni, 1990).

Other policies attempt to stimulate labor demand at the local level. Local economic development projects focus on areas that have unusually low levels of business activity and high levels of unemployment. Beginning in the 1930s, the federal government, in the New Deal, enacted legislation aimed at creating jobs in poor areas. These programs were expanded during the War on Poverty and again during the Carter administration. Community Development Block Grant funding emerged through the Department of Housing and Urban Development to support housing, public works, and economic development projects in these areas. Although the program continues today, funding was cut drastically during President Reagan's tenure (Levitan et al., 1998).

Focusing specifically on businesses, the enterprise zone programs created in most states during the Reagan administration provided a variety of incentives to businesses that opened in designated disadvantaged areas. The specifics related to incentives and target areas varied by state (Bird, 1989, as cited in Hirasuna & Michael, 2005). The Clinton administration changed the name of these incentives to the Empowerment Zone and Enterprise Community program and provided designated areas with federal funding to attract businesses that create jobs in impoverished areas. Currently, the Department of Housing and Urban Development's Community Renewal Initiative provides businesses with incentives such as tax credits for hiring, tax waivers to open in 20 designated Renewal Communities, and similar tax incentives, plus low-interest loans in 30 Empowerment Zones (U.S. Department of Housing and Urban Development, 2007). Critics of such initiatives claim that these programs do not actually create jobs. Rather, they move businesses from one location to another and actually hurt existing businesses in these and adjacent areas. Also, incentives offered are often not sufficient to overcome barriers to business relocation in these areas, such as an unskilled workforce, poor infrastructure, and a lack of amenities (Levitan et al., 1998).

In addition to these programs, the U.S. Department of Commerce's Economic Development Administration (2007) has a goal of increasing business investment and creating jobs in labor surplus areas that are experiencing many business failures and high levels of foreclosures. The Economic Development Administration (EDA) provides grants, loan guarantees, and technical assistance for public works as well as business development assistance. Also, the USDA Rural Development's Business and Cooperative Programs (BCP) and Business Programs (BP) fund grants, loans, loan guarantees, and technical assistance to develop business activities in low-income rural areas (U.S. Department of Agriculture, 2007).

Beyond influencing overall job creation at the national and local levels, government can attempt to increase jobs available to disadvantaged groups by making these individuals more desirable to employers. One mechanism for doing this is offering monetary incentives to employers. In the United States, the Targeted Job Tax Credit program was enacted in 1978 to entice employers to hire members of hard-to-employ target groups in exchange for federal tax credits. Findings of an evaluation done by the U.S. Department of Labor (1994), however, showed that the program failed to induce employers to hire target group members, projecting that employers would have hired 92% of the individuals in question without the tax incentive. In addition, the program was not cost effective, returning 37 cents to the dollar. Finally, it provided participants only with entry-level, low-paying, low-skilled, part-time jobs without benefits (U.S. Department of Labor, 1994). The program expired in 1994 and, at the recommendation of Secretary of Labor Robert Reich, was not reauthorized.

Public Job Creation

Government policy has also focused on direct public job creation to increase labor demand during times of large surpluses in labor. During the Depression, for instance, mass unemployment of one quarter of all workers created a crisis in the United States (Mucciaroni, 1990). It was then that job creation programs emerged for the first time since before the Civil War. President Hoover's 1932 Emergency Relief and Construction Act loaned money to states and cities to create jobs. Franklin D. Roosevelt's New Deal included numerous programs that created jobs. The Civilian Conservation Corps targeted single men between 18 and 25 years of age from needy families. The Public Works Administration dispensed loans and grants to federal, state, and local government units to undertake construction projects aimed at stimulating industrial growth. The Federal Emergency Relief Administration (FERA) provided direct unemployment relief and work programs (Janoski, 1990). The Civil Works Administration was created as a massive temporary public works project paying minimal benefits to over 16 million people (Jansson, 2000). The Works Progress Administration (WPA), although initiated to create self-liquidating capital-intensive projects, became the largest New Deal work program, focusing primarily on providing public employment through labor intensive projects. This New Deal approach to employment problems ended by World War II, when labor was again in demand (Janoski, 1990).

Except for a minor effort by President Truman to target defense contract procurement to high unemployment areas in his 1952 Defense Manpower Policy Executive Order, public job creation was absent in the United States from the beginning of World War II until its re-emergence in the 1970s. Then, high levels of unemployment led to a series of laws authorizing public job creation programs. Constructors of the Emergency Employment Act of 1971 saw the market failing to create enough jobs and viewed guaranteed public sector employment as a temporary solution to the temporary unemployment problem. The act created 140,000 jobs. In addition, Title II of the Comprehensive Employment and Training Act provided public employment to counter the predicted effects of the imminent oil embargo (Mucciaroni, 1990). The simultaneous existence of high rates of inflation and unemployment during the 1974–1975 recession, known as stagflation, was a new condition in the modern economy, which made increasing spending to stimulate the economy an unpopular position. This led policy makers to seek a new route to decrease unemployment. At the time, public sector employment was viewed positively, and, with the support of Congress, President Ford increased the number of public sector jobs to 170,000 (Janoski, 1990).

The 1974 Emergency Jobs and Unemployment Assistance Act, then, was considered a countercyclical measure that provided public service employment for all unemployed people during periods of economic downturns, but this endorsement of public service employment was short-lived. The 1976 Emergency Jobs Programs Extension Act limited program eligibility to the disadvantaged and enrollment to one year. In addition, the Full Employment and Balanced Growth Act (FEBGA) of 1978 set specific goals for reducing unemployment and inflation and noted that policies intending to reduce inflation should not increase unemployment. Again demonstrating the anti-interventionist ideology of the bill's supporters, FEBGA stressed that jobs should come only from the private sector, with public jobs being a last resort and paying low wages so as not to interfere with wages in the private sector (Mucciaroni, 1990).

The 1978 amendments to the Comprehensive Employment and Training Act tightened eligibility for public employment even further, focusing on the severely disadvantaged. The result of this intense focus was a decrease in the participation of local government in CETA programs. Consequently, community-based organizations with limited technical program knowledge or administrative capacity were left as the sole implementers of the programs (Janoski, 1990).

Just after the second oil shock hit the nation in 1979, Ronald Reagan entered the White House. His opposition to direct government intervention in the labor market led to severe cuts in the budgets of labor market programs during the early part of his administration. Job creation projects enacted by CETA, for instance, were slashed by over 75% (Janoski, 1990).

Since the Reagan administration, public employment programs have not regained wide political support. One remnant of government job creation programs, however, is the Senior Community Service Employment Program. This program provided 92,000 part-time jobs to individuals over 55 who had an income below 125% of the poverty line in the program year ending June 30, 2006 (U.S. Department of Labor, Employment & Training Administration, 2007a).

Equal Employment Opportunity

Another way to increase demand for certain categories of workers is to increase the cost of employer discrimination against these groups. Antidiscrimination legislation attempts to prevent wage or hiring discrimination on the basis of race, gender, ethnicity, religion, or disability status. Thus, it increases the demand for labor for groups that are often not preferred in the labor market.

Laws attempting to prevent discrimination in the workplace began with legislation at the state level. For example, in 1884, the state of Massachusetts passed a law protecting those seeking employment from discrimination on the basis of religion. By 1945, 22 states had laws against religious discrimination pertaining to civil service employees, and 11 states had provision against discrimination on the basis of race (Skrentny, 1996, p. 28).

At the federal level, equal employment opportunity policy is relatively new. The 1963 Equal Pay Act was the first major federal equal employment opportunity legislation enacted by Congress. It requires that employers pay equal pay to men and women undertaking equal work (Levitan et al., 1998). The next year, the Civil Rights Act of 1964 was passed. This Act, among other things, mandates nondiscrimination in employment on the basis of race, creed, or color (Rose, 1994). Unfortunately, the effectiveness of the legislation was limited by the lack of enforcement authority given to the Equal Employment Opportunity Commission (EEOC). Initially, the only way to implement the act was through lawsuits filed by the attorney general or private people. Thus, the success of the act depended on the willingness of the attorney general to file lawsuits and on the opinions of the courts. Substantive decisions did not emerge from the law until 1969, when the Supreme Court prohibited practices that were discriminatory in effect, not just intent. These included instituting employment tests for positions that did not previously require them. To broaden the scope of the act, President Johnson's 1965 Executive Order 11246 required businesses acquiring federal contracts over $10,000 to abide by the law and also to act affirmatively in ensuring the employment and fair treatment of individuals of all races (Harvey, 1973).

Other categories of workers have been added to those protected by the original legislation. Employment discrimination on the basis of age was made illegal by the 1967 Age Discrimination in Employment Act. The 1973 Vocational Rehabilitation Act added individuals with disabilities to the list by prohibiting discrimination against them in promotion and hiring decisions in businesses and programs receiving federal money. The 1990 Americans with Disabilities Act made employment discrimination on the basis of disability illegal in general and called for reasonable accommodations to be made to allow such individual to work (EEOC, 1998a; Levitan et al., 1998).

The Equal Employment Act of 1972 amended Title VII of the Civil Rights Act to include state, local, and federal governments and granted the Equal Employment Opportunity Commission the authority to file discrimination lawsuits, strengthening the power of the law considerably. Between 1972 and 1975, numerous court decisions against large companies, such as American Telephone and Telegraph (AT&T), Albermarle, and others, "captured the attention of business across the country" (Rose, 1994, p. 47), encouraging them to promote equal opportunity employment. Court decisions supported past wage remuneration for discrimination and prohibited the use of employment screening devices that led to discriminatory outcomes (Levitan et al., 1998).

While most of the laws implemented during the 1960s focused on making the hiring and promotion practices of employers fair, two Supreme Court decisions in 1979 targeted the outcome of these practices. *Griggs v.*

Duke Power Company found seemingly neutral employment practices to be illegal if their result negatively impacted targeted groups when the criteria involved were not job related. Thus, education requirements and tests not related to the job in question could not be used in hiring and promotion decisions if target groups were disadvantaged as a result. In *United Steelworkers v. Weber et al.*, the Supreme Court supported affirmative action plans as long as these plans were designed to overcome an existing imbalance, they were temporary, and did not infringe on the rights of majority workers (Levitan et al., 1998).

The tide turned against race-conscious hiring and promotion goals in the 1980s. This reversal was led by decisions of the U.S. Department of Justice, by the Reagan administration's requirement that intent to discriminate be demonstrated before laws were enforced, and by substantial cuts in the budget of the EEOC (Levitan et al., 1998). As a result, the EEOC failed to bring forward any suits regarding testing or adverse impact between 1983 and January of 1989 (Rose, 1994). Recent changes in equal employment opportunity laws have been mixed. In 1989, the Supreme Court overturned *Griggs*, weakening EEOC's power to enforce legislation. Congress responded with the 1991 Civil Rights Act, which increased penalties for violation of the equal employment opportunity legislation. Since the mid 1990s, increased criticism has emerged against affirmative action, in particular, with opponents arguing that women and minorities no longer need legal protection (Levitan et al., 1998). Related U.S. Supreme Court decisions regarding racial preference in educational institution admissions provide evidence of continued ambivalence about affirmative action. *Gratz v. Bollinger* (2003) ruled that awarding points for race is unconstitutional while *Grutter v. Bollinger* (2003) allows race to be considered as universities attempt to create diverse learning environments.

Regulatory Laws Protecting Workers

In addition to laws that attempt to prepare workers for jobs or make jobs available to workers, several types of laws have been enacted to protect workers from a variety of difficult circumstances. These include jobs loss, dangerous working conditions, and unfair wages and benefits mismanagement.

Job Loss Protections

Before the Depression, the United States had neither a system of unemployment insurance nor a system of labor exchange. The Unemployment Compensation Program was created by the Social Security Act of 1935

(P.L. 74-271). The goal of the program, which is still in effect, is "to provide temporary and partial wage replacement to involuntarily unemployed workers who were recently employed . . . and . . . to help stabilize the economy during recessions" (U.S. House Committee on Ways and Means, 2004b, p. 4-1). The basis of the system is outlined in the Federal Unemployment Tax Act of 1939 and in titles II, IX, and XII of the Social Security Act. Unemployment insurance is funded by taxes paid by employers on the first $7,000 paid to each worker. Although eligibility varies by state, the amount of recent employment, earnings of the workers, and ability and willingness to look for work are key factors in all states. Individuals are usually disqualified if they left their pervious job without good cause, were terminated for misconduct, or left due to a labor dispute. Benefits are a fraction of the individual's income and limited to a 26-week state benefit that can be extended to 36 weeks with the Extended Benefits Program. An additional 7 weeks is also available under a rarely used trigger option in times of high unemployment (U.S. House Committee on Ways and Means, 2004b; U.S. Department of Labor, Employment & Training Administration, 2007b).

In addition to unemployment insurance, other job loss protection programs target specific types of workers. To protect workers from layoffs due to foreign trade, several programs have been implemented since the 1970s. The Trade Adjustment Assistance (TAA) program, legislated under section 221-50 of the Trade Act of 1974, provides a trade adjustment allowance, employment service, training, job search assistance, and a relocation allowance to certified workers. This program is administered by the Employment and Training Administration of the Department of Labor in each state. Eligible individuals include those in firms or in portions of firms in which a significant proportion of the workers are in danger of layoff or have already been laid off due to a decline in the firm's sales and/or production resulting from increased imports of like or competitive items (U.S. House Committee on Ways and Means, 2004c).

The NAFTA Worker Security Act, or subchapter D of Title II of the Trade Act of 1974, established the North American Free Trade Agreement (NAFTA) Transitional Adjustment Assistance Program for workers adversely affected by NAFTA. Providing the same benefits as Trade Adjustment Assistance, this program targets individuals faced with lay offs due to a decline in the firm's sales or production in the face of Mexican or Canadian imports or a shift in the firm's production to a company subsidiary in Canada or Mexico (U.S. House Committee on Ways and Means, 2004c).

In addition, the 1988 Worker Adjustment and Retraining Notification Act requires businesses with over 100 employees to give two months notice to employees who will lose their jobs due to layoffs or plant closings (Employment and Training Administration, 2003). Also, the

Uniformed Services Employment and Reemployment Rights Act (USERRA) guarantees that persons who have served in active duty in the armed forces have a right to be rehired by their employer once they return from service (USERRA, 1994). The Workforce Investment Act continues these programs but encourages linkages between them and other programs at the local level.

Work Conditions

Beyond dislocation subsidies and retraining programs, government policy places limits on the environment in which individuals work in order to protect their health and physical well-being. The Occupational Safety and Health Administration (OSHA) or OSHA-approved state systems administer the Occupational Safety and Health Act, which regulates safety and health conditions in most industries in the private sector. The regulations require employers to maintain healthful and safe work environments and workers to adhere to workplace conduct guidelines (Hartnett, 1996; Mintz, 1984). The Occupational Safety and Health Act was passed into law in 1970 and amended in 1990. It supersedes original safety legislation enacted under the Walsh-Healy Act, the Services Contract Act, the Contract Work Hours and Safety Standards Act, the Arts and Humanities Act, and the Longshore and Harbor Workers Compensation Act (Hartnett, 1996; U.S. Department of Labor, Occupational Safety & Health Administration, 2007).

Benefit and Wage Protection

Other policies aim to ensure fair treatment of workers by employers regarding their benefits and wages. In order to protect retirement or pension benefits, the Employee Retirement and Income Security Act (ERISA) regulates pension administration, disclosure, and reporting for employers that chose to offer pensions to employees (U.S. Department of Labor, 2007).

In order to protect workers' jobs in times of family illness, the Wage and Hour Division of the Employment Standards Administration of the Department of Labor administers the Family and Medical Leave Act of 1993. This act requires employers with 50 or more employees to allow up to 12 weeks of unpaid leave to eligible employees for the serious illness of a family member or the birth or adoption of a child (EEOC, 1998b; U.S. Department of Labor, Employment Standards Administration Wage and Hour Division, 2007).

Since many Americans remain poor despite working full time, some policies have been enacted to increase the monetary returns for work. The Fair Labor Standards Act, enacted in 1938, requires that employers pay the minimum wage to covered employees and an overtime rate of 1.5 times the regular wage for hours worked over 40 in one week. It also restricts the number of hours worked and the type of jobs worked by children under 16 years of age. The federal minimum wage began at 25 cents per hour in 1938 (Nordlund, 1997) and has been increased numerous times since then. Evaluations of the impact of the 1996–1997 increases in the minimum wage found that the wages of 10 million workers were increased. About 46% of workers who benefited worked full time, gains were realized disproportionately by low-income working householders, and no significant job losses resulted (Bernstein & Schmitt, 1997). Unfortunately, for individuals attempting to raise a family, the minimum wage is often insufficient to bring their income above the poverty line (Levitan et al., 1998), and many workers are not covered by the law (Bernstein & Schmitt, 1997). The Fair Minimum Wage Act of 2007 raised the federal minimum wage to $5.85 in July 2007 and has scheduled two successive incremental increases ($6.55 in July 2008 and $7.25 in July 2009). The effects of the latest increase have not been evaluated.

Issues and Controversies

Amid the wide range of employment policies enacted in the United States, numerous issues and controversies remain. Some are timely and address the structure of current policy, whereas others address more basic, philosophical concerns. The most fundamental question is whether or not the government should mediate disparities in the labor market. Many economists would argue that any intervention by the government in these economic issues is harmful because it impedes the operation of the market. The market is seen as a natural system that will work out irregularities. Others, like the secular stagnationist Keynesians and commercial Keynesians, propose that government can effectively enact policy to stimulate labor demand (Mucciaroni, 1990).

Once the reality of government intervention in the labor market is accepted, the goal of employment policy determines appropriate policy action. Some argue that the proper goal is full employment, whereas others argue that the only appropriate goal is to protect workers from harm or severe market fluctuations or to raise individuals out of poverty. Clearly, throughout history, policy makers in the United States have responded to a multitude of goals, and these disparate goals are reflected in the complex conglomeration of employment policies that exist. According to Mucciaroni (1990), confused and conflicting objectives are one of the key reasons for the political "failure" of employment policies. Very little has changed since the early 1990s in this regard.

Providing employment for all who are willing and able to work is a goal of some employment policies. However, government must decide which strategy to use to increase employment. The structure of this chapter actually reflects this debate: Policy can either target labor supply or labor demand. The decision to focus on either of these depends on the perceived cause of unemployment. Labor supply policies are enacted when unemployment is seen as a product of an unskilled, unmotivated workforce with few social supports or of a breakdown in informal systems that connect individuals to jobs. Many of the 40 employment programs noted in the 2003 GAO report addressed the lack of skills of potential workers. The education and training components aim to invest in the human capital of workers. "Job readiness" programs assume that individuals are not working because they are unmotivated or lack the soft skills necessary to find a job. These programs aim to motivate individuals to enter the labor force. Job placement and job information services such as those offered by the Department of Labor's one-stop shops assume that individuals are not working because they lack information about available jobs. Such programs provide employment information to individuals and assist them in applying for jobs.

In contrast, labor demand policy views the undersupply of jobs as the primary cause of unemployment. To remedy this, job creation is the goal. However, the best way to create these needed jobs is another point of contention. Traditional Keynesians advocate increasing government expenditures to stimulate the economy, while commercial Keynesians favor tax relief to businesses. Some see employment generation as a private sector activity in which government has only a small facilitating role, whereas others see the role of government as including job creation. Although such activity was not popular in recent years, the federal government has directly provided jobs for workers during different periods of high labor supply including the New Deal era and during the high unemployment of the 1970s.

Those in favor of protecting workers from harm as a main goal of employment policy support regulatory policies such as those advanced by the Occupational Safety and Health Act. When protection from unanticipated job loss induced by market forces is the goal, policies such as the Unemployment Insurance Act and the Trade Adjustment Assistance program are supported. Those who think policy should protect workers' benefits from employer negligence support policies such as the Employee Retirement Income Security Act and the Family Medical Leave Act. If the goal of employment policy is to reduce poverty, policies such as the minimum wage and the Earned Income Tax Credit are supported.

Additional issues arise once the desired type of policy is chosen. One is the target population of the policy. Many policies are categorical, targeting the poor, minorities, and women. Proponents of this approach argue that spending scarce resources on the most needy is the best tactic. Opponents note that the political ramification of this is to alienate constituencies that would support universal programs.

Since the 1960s, one of the most consistent criticisms of employment policy is its chaotic administrative design. Programs teetered between being overly centralized and overly decentralized. During times of overly centralized policy, the federal government funneled grant money from numerous programs directly to local areas, bypassing state administrative structures and maintaining federal oversight over each contract. The subsequent overly decentralized period was characterized by regional Department of Labor offices overseeing local programs. The ineffectiveness of this strategy was primarily due to a lack of knowledge at the local level about how to run employment and training programs (Mucciaroni, 1990). The Workforce Investment Act attempts to achieve a balance by giving control to both local and state entities and by allocating funds for technical assistance and program evaluation.

Another commonly cited problem is program duplication. Past duplication of administrative structures and a few cases of blatant corruption have led to a public perception of employment training programs as being inefficient, ineffective, and suffering from gross mismanagement (Mucciaroni, 1990). Recent changes have consolidated federal programs and devolved authority to local entities through the one-stop delivery system (General Acounting Office, 2003).

References

Bane, M. J., & Ellwood, D. T. (1994). *Welfare realities: From rhetoric to reform.* Cambridge, MA: Harvard University Press.

Bernstein, J., & Schmitt, J. (1997). *Making work pay: The impact of the 1997–98 minimum wage increase.* Retrieved February 8, 2008, from http://www.epi.org/content.cfm/studies_stmwp

Blank, R. M. (2002). Evaluating welfare reform in the United States. *Journal of Economic Literature, 40*(4), 1105–1166.

Burman, L., Maag, E., & Rohaly, J. (2002). *EGTRRA: Which provisions spell the most relief?* Washington, DC: Urban-Brookings Tax Policy Center.

Center on Budget and Policy Priorities. (2007). *Implementing the TANF changes in the Deficit Reduction Act: "Win-win" solutions for families and states.* Washington, DC: Author. Retrieved September 15, 2007, from http://www.cbpp.org/2-9-07tanf.htm

Edin, K., & Lein, L. (1997). Work, welfare, and single mothers' economic survival strategies. *American Sociological Review, 62*(2), 253–266.

Eissa, N., & Hoynes, H. W. (2004). Taxes and the labor market participation of married couples: The Earned Income Tax Credit. *Journal of Public Economics, 88,* 1931–1958.

Eissa, N., & Hoynes, H. W. (2005). *Behavioral responses to taxes: Lesions from the EITC and labor supply* (Working Paper No. 11729). Cambridge, MA: National Bureau of Economic Research.

Eissa, N., & Liebman, J. B. (1996). Labor supply response to the Earned Income Tax Credit. *Quarterly Journal of Economics, 34*(2), 605–637.

Eissa, N., & Nichols, A. (2005). Tax-transfer policy and labor-market outcomes. *American Economic Review, Papers and Proceedings, 95*(2), 88–93.

Ellwood, D. T. (2000). The impact of the Earned Income Tax Credit and social policy reforms on work, marriage, and living arrangements. *National Tax Journal, 53*(4), 1063–1106.

Equal Employment Opportunity Commission. (1998a). *Disability discrimination: Employment discrimination prohibited by the Americans with Disability Act of 1990.* Washington, DC: Equal Employment Opportunity Commission, Technical Assistance Program.

Equal Employment Opportunity Commission. (1998b). *The Family Medical Leave Act, the Americans with Disabilities Act, and Title VII of the Civil Rights Act of 1964.* Washington, DC: Equal Employment Opportunity Commission, Office of Legal Counsel.

Fair Minimum Wage Act of 2007, Pub.L. 110-028, § 8101 121 Stat. 188 (2007). Retrieved November 11, 2007, from http://www.gpoaccess.gov/plaws/index.html

General Accounting Office. (1995). *Multiple employment and training programs: Major overhaul needed to reduce costs, streamline the bureaucracy, and improve results* (Testimony of Clarence Crawford before Senate Committee on Labor and Human Resources). Washington, DC: Author.

General Accounting Office. (2003). *Multiple employment and training programs: Funding and performance measures for major programs* (Report No. GAO-03-589). Washington, DC: Author. Retrieved October 3, 2007, from http://www.gao.gov/new.items/d03589.pdf

Gratz v. Bollinger, 539 U.S. 244 (2003).

Grogger, J. (2003). The effects of time limits, the EITC, and other policy changes on welfare use, work, and income among female-headed families. *The Review of Economics and Statistics, 85*(2), 394–408.

Grogger, J. (2004). Welfare transitions in the 1990s: The economy, welfare policy, and the EITC. *Journal of Policy Analysis and Management, 23*(4), 671–695.

Grutter v. Bollinger, 539 U.S. 306 (2003).

Gundersen, C., & Ziliak, J. P. (2004). Poverty and macroeconomic performance across space, race, and family structure. *Demography, 41*(1), 61–86.

Guttman, R. (1983). Job Training Partnership Act: New help for the unemployed, *Monthly Labor Review, 106*(3), 3–10.

Guzda, (1983). The US employment service at 50. *Monthly Labor Review, 106*(6), 12–19.

Hartnett, J. (1996). A political history of workplace safety. In J. Harnett, *OSHA in the real world* (pp. 5–41). Santa Monica, CA: Merritt.

Harvey, J. C. (1973). *Black civil rights during the Johnson Administration,* Jackson: University and College Press of Mississippi.

Hirasuna, D., & Michael, J. (2005). *Enterprise zones: A review of the economic theory and empirical evidence* (Minnesota House of Representatives Research

Department Policy Brief). Retrieved February 18, 2008, from http://www
.house.leg.state.mn.us/hrd/pubs/entzones.pdf

Hoffman, S. D. (2003). *The EITC marriage tax and EITC reform* (Working Paper
No. 2003-01). Newark: University of Delaware, Department of Economics.

Hotz, V., & Scholz, J. K. (2003). The Earned Income Tax Credit. In R. Moffitt (Ed.),
Means-tested transfer programs in the United States (pp. 141–197). Chicago:
University of Chicago Press.

Hoynes, H. W. (2005). *The Earned Income Tax Credit.* Paper presented to the
President's Advisory Panel on Federal Tax Reform, New Orleans, LA. Retrieved
August 2, 2007, from http://www.econ.ucdavis.edu/faculty/hoynes/working_
papers/Tax%20 Panel%20EITC%203-23-05.ppt

Janoski, T. (1990). *The political economy of unemployment: Active labor market
policy in West Germany and the United States.* Berkeley: University of
California Press.

Jansson, B. S. (2000). The early stages of the New Deal. In B. S. Jansson, *The reluctant welfare state: A history of American social welfare policies* (4th ed.,
pp. 166–192). Pacific Grove, CA: Brooks/Cole.

Levitan, S. A., Mangum, G. L., & Mangum, S. L. (1998). *Programs in aid of the poor*
(7th ed.). Baltimore: Johns Hopkins University Press.

Lim, Y. (2007). *Can "refundable" state Earned Income Tax Credits explain reductions in child poverty?* Manuscript submitted for publication.

Lim, Y. (in press). The mid-1990s Earned Income Tax Credit (EITC) expansion:
EITC and welfare caseloads. *Social Work Research.*

Looney, A. (2005). *The effects of welfare reform and related policies on single mothers' welfare use and employment in the 1990s* (Finance and Economics
Discussion Series No. 2005-45). Washington, DC: U.S. Board of Governors of
the Federal Reserve System.

Martinez, T. (1976). *The human market place.* New Brunswick, NJ: Transaction
Books.

Meyer, B. D. (2002). Labor supply at the extensive and intensive margins: The EITC,
welfare and hours worked. *American Economic Review, Papers and
Proceedings, 92*(2), 373–379.

Meyer, B. D., & Rosenbaum, D. T. (2001). Welfare, the Earned Income Tax Credit,
and the labor supply of single mothers. *Quarterly Journal of Economics, 116*(3),
1063–1114.

Mintz, B. W. (1984). *OSHA: History, law and policy.* Washington, DC: Bureau of
National Affairs.

Mucciaroni, G. (1990). *The political failure of employment policy, 1945–1982.*
Pittsburgh, PA: University of Pittsburgh Press.

Nagle, A., & Johnson, N. (2006). *A hand up: How state Earned Income Tax Credits
help working families escape poverty in 2006.* Washington, DC: Center for
Budget and Policy Priorities.

Nordlund, W. J. (1997). *The quest for a living wage: The history of the federal minimum wage program.* Westport, CT: Greenwood Press.

Ozawa, M. N., & Hong, B. (2003). The effects of EITC and children's
allowances on the economic well-being of children. *Social Work Research,
27*(3), 163–178.

Rose, D. (1994). Twenty-five years later: Where do we stand on equal employment opportunity law enforcement? In Paul Burstein (Ed.), *Equal employment*

opportunity: Labor market discrimination and public policy (pp. 39–58). New York: Aldine de Gruyter.

Santoni, G. J. (1986). *The Employment Act of 1946: Some history notes.* St. Louis, MO: Federal Reserve Bank of St. Louis. Retrieved November 10, 2007, from http://research.stlouisfed.org/publications/review/past/1986/

Sherman, A. (2005). *Public benefits: Easing poverty and ensuring medical coverage.* Washington, DC: Center for Budget and Policy Priorities.

Skrentny, J. D. (1996). *The ironies of affirmative action: Politics, culture, and justice in America.* Chicago: University of Chicago Press.

Social Legislation Information Service. (1998). *Washington Social Legislation Bulletin, 35*(40), 157–158.

Uniformed Services Employment and Reemployment Rights Act of 1994, 38 U.S.C. § 4301 (1994).

U.S. Department of Agriculture, Rural Development. (2007). *Business programs.* Retrieved October 1, 2007, from http://www.rurdev.usda.gov/rbs/busp/bpdir.htm

U.S. Department of Commerce Economic Development Administration. (2007). *About EDA.* Retrieved October 1, 2007, from http://www.eda.gov/AboutEDA/AbtEDA.xml

U.S. Department of Housing and Urban Development. (2007). *Welcome to the community renewal initiative.* Retrieved October 1, 2007, from http://www.hud.gov/offices/cpd/economicdevelopment/programs/rc/

U.S. Department of Labor. (1994). *Targeted jobs tax credit program: Employment inducement or employer windfall?* Washington, DC: Author.

U.S. Department of Labor. (2007). *Health plans & benefits: Employee Retirement Income Security Act—ERISA.* Retrieved November 10, 2007, from http://www.dol.gov/dol/topic/health-plans/erisa.htm

U.S. Department of Labor, Employment & Training Administration. (2007a). *About SCSEP.* Retrieved November 11, 2007, from http://www.doleta.gov/seniors/html_docs/AboutSCSEP.cfm

U.S. Department of Labor, Employment & Training Administration. (2007b). *Unemployment insurance extended benefits.* Retrieved November 1, 2007, from http://workforcesecurity.doleta.gov/unemploy/extenben.asp

U.S. Department of Labor, Employment Standards Administration Wage and Hour Division. (2007). *Compliance assistance—Family and Medical Leave Act (FMLA).* Retrieved November 10, 2007, from http://www.dol.gov/esa/whd/fmla/

U.S. Department of Labor, Occupational Safety & Health Administration. (2007). *OSH Act of 1970.* Retrieved October 10, 2007, from http://www.osha.gov/pls/oshaweb/owadisp.show_document?p_table=OSHACT&p_id=2743

U.S. House Committee on Ways and Means. (2004a). Temporary assistance for needy families (TANF). In *2004 Green Book* (Sec. 7, pp. 1–98). Retrieved November 10, 2007, from http://www.gpoaccess.gov/wmprints/green/index.html

U.S. House Committee on Ways and Means. (2004b). Unemployment compensation. In *2004 Green Book* (Sec. 4, pp. 1–36). Retrieved November 10, 2007, from http://www.gpoaccess.gov/wmprints/green/index.html

U.S. House Committee on Ways and Means. (2004c). Trade adjustment assistance. In *2004 Green Book* (Sec. 6, pp. 1–16). Retrieved November 10, 2007, from http://www.gpoaccess.gov/wmprints/green/index.html

U.S. Office of Management and Budget. (2005). *Analytical perspectives: Budget of the United States government, fiscal year 2006*. Washington, DC: Government Printing Office.

Ventry, D. J., Jr. (2002). The collision of tax and welfare politics: The political history of the Earned Income Tax Credit. In B. D. Meyer & D. Holtz-Eakin (Eds.), *Making work pay: The Earned Income Tax Credit & its impact on America's families* (pp. 15–66). New York: Russell Sage Foundation.

Zedlewski, S., & Zimmerman, S. (2007). *Trends in work supports for low-income families with children* (Perspectives on Low-Income Working Families Brief No. 4). Washington, DC: Urban Institute.

30

Education and Social Policy

Susan Stone

Very broadly, the term education refers to the system of inputs and institutional goals, structures, and processes designed to transmit socioculturally relevant knowledge to members of a given society. The transmission of this knowledge takes place in many ways. In addition to socialization through the family, children acquire knowledge from their community networks, from religious institutions, and in other ways. In earlier times, very few children benefited from formal education. Indeed, only a few were formally educated through the use of tutors or through religious schools. In modern times, education has been extended through the involvement of government, which is now the primary provider of formal education today.

It is in this context that educational policy and social policy are closely associated. Joel Samoff (1999) contends that "education is perhaps the most public of public policies" (p. 52). His assertion reflects three key characteristics of the public education system. The first is its institutional breadth. For example, over the last century, the United States rapidly achieved nearly universal primary and secondary school enrollment. Compulsory education increasingly became a state and federal versus a local responsibility, and as such, public education represents an integral feature of the modern welfare state. Second, few question the notion that education and educational attainment constitute social goods, at both individual and societal levels. Indeed, public education expenditures are conceived as both social and economic investments. Perhaps most fundamentally, even amid enduring questions about the extent of equity in the distribution of educational resources, opportunities, and outputs and outcomes, few question the primary role of public education as a core socializing institution. There is clearly an underlying American ethos that all children possess a fundamental right to basic education.

The public education system is, of course, complex. Multiple, and often conflicting, forces shape its aims, directions, and hoped-for outcomes.

Compulsory education necessitates complex institutional and organizational forms. As a consequence, there are a variety of options for assessing the processes and outputs of public education. Reflecting this complexity, this chapter summarizes multiple frameworks for analyzing the public education system by focusing exclusively on schools. Although governments are also extensively involved in the provision of postsecondary education, the chapter, primarily because of space limitations, does not discuss the role of colleges and universities in creating opportunities for social mobility.

The chapter begins with a brief historical overview of public schooling in the United States, including a selective review of major federal legislation relevant to public education. It then provides a summary of the various ways that the goals and aims of public education might be conceptualized. Policy studies traditionally analyze either the structural attributes and governance or the outputs and outcomes of the system. Thus, the chapter also reviews relevant scholarship in these areas. Subsequent sections discuss emergent educational equity issues and characterize the set of policy strategies forwarded to address these. The chapter concludes with a discussion of enduring issues in public education reform. Throughout this discussion, focus is placed on key domains of social policy questions and concerns.

A Brief History of Schooling in the United States

This section reviews key landmarks, including key federal laws, throughout the history and development of the American public education system (see Cohen, 1984; Graham, 2005; Ravitch, 2000; Tyack, 1974). This section is divided into four rough time periods that capture (1) the inception of compulsory primary schooling, (2) the inception of compulsory secondary education, (3) educational reforms related to the civil rights movement, and (4) the move toward standards-based reform.

Developments During the Colonial Period Through the 19th Century

Kernels of a public primary education system were evident in colonial America. However, schooling at this time largely reflected local efforts and interests. Thus, it was highly variable across regional areas, often organized by religious denomination, and, though public, was not always free. It wasn't until the mid-19th century that free public schools spread throughout the United States, a development largely attributed to the advocacy of Horace Mann. Mann championed the free common secular primary school through the publication of the *Common School Journal*. He asserted that school attendance could enhance democratic values and civic participation and ultimately prevent social ills such as crime and delinquency. Although there were critics of the common and secular orientation inherent in Mann's vision and propositions, states largely adopted compulsory primary education laws by the 1850s.

Early 20th Century: The Emergence of the High School

Demographic, economic, social, and political forces at the turn of the century also solidified state movement toward compulsory secondary education. Mass immigration, industrialization, urbanization, and a rapid expansion of the child population led educators and social reformers alike to advocate for secondary education, primarily as a social reform strategy. Indeed, there was a strong focus on socializing immigrant populations and selecting and sorting the college bound.

During this time, progressive educators, such as John Dewey, and social reformers alike agreed that schools should and could play a role in bettering the conditions of poor and immigrant children and families. "Scientist" perspectives, such as the ascendancy of formal IQ testing, which suggested techniques that could be used for educational assessment and intervention with what was perceived to be a heterogeneous student population, bolstered these views.

Ravitch (2000) contends that developments during this period set in motion an enduring educational debate about how best to serve a diverse student population. While some argued for a classic and foundational liberal arts education, progressive educators such as John Dewey forwarded the notion of a differentiated curriculum, in which content could be matched to student abilities and interests. Vocational education, academic and curricular tracking systems, and the multicultural education movement, for example, trace back to progressive educational principles.

The Civil Rights Movement and Great Society Programs

Immediately prior to and after the civil rights movement, concerns about inequitable distribution of social and, in particular, educational opportunities set in motion a series of foundational pieces of federal legislation. During this time, and largely as a result of the efforts and advocacy of affected groups, several federal milestones were put into place. The seminal *Brown v. Board of Education* Supreme Court decision (1954) challenged the "separate but equal" educational provisions for African Americans embedded in Jim Crow laws, ultimately ruling that "separate educational facilities are inherently unequal." In part, the decision also responded to the vast school resource and quality differences particularly evident in southern states.

Subsequent federal legislation included the Bilingual Education Act (1968) and the Education of All Handicapped Children Act (1975). The Bilingual Education Act, originally focused on Spanish speakers, emphasized

English language instruction and supports as well as attention to cultural differences. Special education legislation safeguarded the provision of free and appropriate education in the least restrictive educational environment for students with disabilities.

This period also witnessed the solidification of the Elementary and Secondary Schools Act (ESEA, 1965), which asserted a key federal role in the oversight and funding of public primary and secondary education. In particular, Title I of ESEA earmarked funds for schools and districts serving a critical density (approximately 40%) of poor and minority children. The act has subsequently been reauthorized every five years and is currently referred to as No Child Left Behind (2002).

The 1980s and Beyond

In 1983, the federally commissioned report *A Nation At Risk* drew attention from both the public and policy makers alike about the under-performance of American students relative to their international counterparts. It also raised concern about the persistent achievement gaps between middle-class, white students and poor and minority youth, despite federal educational legislation enacted during the civil rights era. In many ways, its publication represents the inception of standards-based reform, where all students are expected to achieve at internationally competitive standards. The standards-based reform movement recently culminated in the 2002 reauthorization of ESEA, titled No Child Left Behind (NCLB, 2002). Under NCLB, some would argue that there is an unprecedented federal role in compelling states to specify standards and implement school accountability systems. Specifically, states must set rigorous academic standards, periodically assess progress toward those standards so that all students are proficient in reading and mathematics by 2014. While calls for educational standards are not necessarily new, state-implemented systems to make indicators of student and school progress "transparent" to the public represent a novel school reform strategy. Students and families are offered alternative school choices if their school or district consistently underperforms.

Varying Conceptions of the Aims and Outcomes of Schooling

Although few would disagree that there should be public provision of compulsory education, there is not necessarily explicit or implicit agreement about what, exactly, the system should provide and, consequently, what expected outcomes—at both individual and systems levels—should be. Over time, several not necessarily exclusive outcomes include (1) initiation to societal mores and values, (2) survival skills such as the promotion of health and safety, (3) basic literacy and numeracy, (4) vocational training or preparation, (5) liberal or general knowledge generally associated with higher or postsecondary education, (6) civic understanding (e.g., rules and tools for participating as a citizen), and (7) knowledge relevant to the development human potential (e.g., skills for making informed decisions and for lifelong learning), including *humanitarian* skills that facilitate functioning, largely from a human rights perspective, in an increasingly technologically complex, global, and diverse world (Thomas, 1990). Among these varying potential educational goals and outcomes, student academic performance has been a central focus since the mid-1950s, with progress typically assessed through student performance on standardized achievement tests

Educational historian Patricia Albjerg Graham (2005) argues that, over the past century, the public education system has been charged with at least three inherently different missions, including (1) expanding enrollments and assimilating the first wave of immigrant families in the early part of the century, (2) effectively serving poor and minority children, and, most recently, (3) educating all children to achieve internationally competitive academic performance standards. As we discuss further in subsequent sections, the social, political, and economic forces that combine to shape the direction of system goals vary over time, and these forces may often be loosely related to the aims and expectations of the children and families served by the system or educators (Ravitch, 2000).

Even in the absence of consensus, such a diverse set of potential goals and outcomes clearly suggests that a diverse or flexible institutional and organizational structure or structures would likely be necessary to enact such goals and achieve such outcomes over time. However, the basic institutional, structural form of the common modern school generally has been quite persistent not only over time but also cross-nationally, leading many critics to question the relevance of the *modern* school (Torres, 2002).

Structurally, education systems display a remarkable degree of homogeneity. Virtually all countries require (or aspire to have) all children attend school for at least a fixed amount of time. In the United States, states typically set compulsory education laws for youth up to age 16, 17, or 18. As in the United States, international educational systems are vertically graded, consisting chiefly of a three-tiered system: primary, secondary, and postsecondary levels (although it is important to acknowledge that this system has generally expanded to include early childhood and adult educational tiers as well). There is regulation of the teaching corps in terms of credentialing and professional development and the implementation of a uniform curriculum. Within the United States, in particular, current public education remains age and peer segregated (Tyack, 1974). The curriculum is separated by subject matter and sequentially organized, with particular topics within subject areas typically introduced in a standard order. Moreover, students who perform or behave poorly relative to their peers are often segregated and served in alternative settings (Deschenes, Cuban, & Tyack, 2001).

Analyzing and Mapping Public Education

Given these basic institutional and structural attributes, analysis of the public education system generally focuses on either its governance structures or its structural and organizational attributes, or on both. Both public and scholarly discourse around governance and organization focus upon the overall *efficiency* and/or *quality* of the educational system.

School Governance

The core policy concern related to governance is what (and how) social agencies control the delivery, including funding, of educational services. Educational governance structures vary considerably cross-nationally, ostensibly reflecting unique sociocultural and political histories. These range from statist, bureaucratic structures to functionally or territorially decentralized systems to nongovernmental, including privatized, administrative structures. An enduring dilemma inherent in the governance and financing of mass education is that, as enrollments in educational systems increase, there is considerable pressure to constrain public educational expenditures (Arnove & Torres, 1999; Farrell, 1999)

It is important to note that assessment of governance structures must be approached from multiple units of analysis. The education system is shaped through multiple tiers of influence: federal, state, and local (including both district and schools). Scholarship indicates that these levels often undertake specific functions. Traditionally, the federal government plays a key role in planning and structural issues, such as goal and standard setting, and as a source of funding for schools. States and districts tend to focus on resource allocation. Local schools generally take on primary responsibility for the delivery of instruction.

Competing groups or coalitions within and across these levels press for different interests, often using control of education as a bargaining position. Moreover, conceptions of appropriate governance structures change as a function of overall sociocultural and economic changes. Decisions to create or alter school governance structures are not necessarily driven by educationally focused goals, and perhaps not surprisingly, relationships between governance structures and educational efficiency, equality, or equity typically are weak (McGinn, 1992).

The central dynamics of educational governance structures require social policy analysts to assess critically, on a conceptual level, the social forces and processes that produce *both* centralization and decentralization within the public education system. Two sets of factors shape governance structures (Bray, 1999). The first set of factors includes what are broadly termed *motives*. Motives include political trends and movements, administrative capacity and efficiency, the domain to be controlled (e.g., curriculum, teacher credentialing, school maintenance), and the degree to which system and particular system levels are pressured to adjust to meet local needs. The second set of factors is characterized as contextual. Contextual factors include underlying governmental structures, the extent of diversity within regions (e.g., socioeconomic, racial, ethnic, or linguistic diversity), overall system and population size (e.g., the considerable state and regional variation in age distributions), and the underlying communication infrastructures, which affect, broadly speaking, how efficiently information can be diffused. Thus, a key set of policy questions does not center explicitly on the underlying governance structure but on how particular school and systemic governance structures—considered in terms of both motivational and contextual forces—distribute power among various stakeholders to produce particular educational outcomes.

Mapping Key School System Variables

Given that educational governance in the United States is somewhat decentralized and generally enacted at the state and local district and school levels (e.g., the majority of educational funding is provided at the local and state levels), school systems are typically mapped or framed in terms of their inputs, organizational structures and processes, and outputs and outcomes (Monk, 1989).

Inputs. For a given school or district, inputs essentially refer to the set of variables that are often termed as *exogenous* or *fixed*. Essentially, these are conditions that a school or district is given and likely cannot alter. Perhaps most centrally, public schools vary as a function of the preexisting characteristics of the students or families they serve. These include the underlying ability and overall well-being of students and the sociodemographic background and characteristics of their families and immediate communities. For example, a key federal education report authored by educational sociologist James Coleman and titled *Equality of Educational Opportunity* (1966) offered evidence suggesting that child and family background characteristics largely explained the achievement distribution of children. A second set of inputs refers to available system resources. These include material resources (e.g., funds) as well as the characteristics, qualities, and capacities of the available teaching corps in a given school district or state.

Organizational Structures. Unlike inputs, school structural features are not necessarily fixed. That being said, evidence presented previously suggests that the basic structural and organizational form of both primary and secondary schools is largely invariant across localities and states. Such structural features generally capture how students within a given system level are organized for learning. As examples, the features that are commonly referenced include the grade span, enrollment, the physical size of the school, and class-room size. Other structural features include the extent of academic and curricular tracks and school start and end times (Eccles & Roeser, 1999).

Organizational Process. Schools, districts, and states vary tremendously in terms of their organizational process characteristics. Such characteristics include the style and quality of management, including the extent to which available resources are prioritized and utilized; the nature and extent of staff relationships and development; academically related goals, missions, and priorities; and the nature and extent of staff relationships with students, families, and local communities.

Outputs and Outcomes. Finally, an additional set of key variables includes what have been called *outputs* and *outcomes* (Farrell, 1999). Broadly, these refer to products of the education system. Outputs refer to proximal learning related outcomes whereas outcomes often are framed distally (income, occupational status in adulthood).

Assessing Progress Toward Educational System Outputs

In the early 1980s, educational systems worldwide were confronted with two dilemmas: (1) rising costs of education that accompanied increasingly universal provision of and expanded enrollments in primary and secondary education and (2) persistence of systemic educational inequity, although the nature of that inequality varied across nationalities (Arnove, Altbach, & Kelly, 1992; Arnove & Torres, 1999). Concerns about the equity of the American public education system—particularly for poor and minority children—have been voiced since the inception of the common school at the turn of the century (Tyack, 1992). These range from initial concern about the accommodation of the first waves of immigrants, differential access to educational resources evidenced in the *Brown v. the Board of Education* decision and in subsequent Federal legislation, and, most recently, persistent achievement gaps between poor and minority versus nonpoor and nonminority youth. This section presents a basic framework for assessing educational inequality and a summary of various accounts of the causes of such inequalities. Finally, I discuss key education reforms, within the context of the map presented in the previous section, that have been forwarded to address such inequalities.

Conceptualizing Educational Inequality

Farrell (1999) argues that educational inequalities, however defined, may have their source at one or more public education system levels. In the

United States, questions of inequality largely center on poor and minority (particularly African American and Latino) students. *Equality of access* refers to the extent to which children of various social subgroups participate equally across levels of the school system. For example, although there is near equality of access to the public primary and secondary system among key subgroups, much concern has been placed on access of poor and minority to students to postsecondary education. *Equality of survival* refers to relative rates of persistence within a particular systemic level. Thus, the disproportionately high dropout rate among Latino students (Fry, 2003) represents such a survival issue. *Equalities of output and outcome* refer to disproportionate levels of learning and labor force attachment, respectively.

Alternative Accounts of the Achievement Gap

The question of why poor and minority (especially African American and Latino children) persistently underperform relative to their peers has received a great deal of scrutiny by both American educators and policy makers. This section briefly outlines major explanations of why this may be the case.

Structural Explanations. Structural explanations contend that larger sociostructural forces explain the achievement gap. Perhaps the leanest explanation is that the achievement gap reflects inequitable societal distribution of goods and resources, particularly vast income inequalities and, importantly, the racialized nature of these inequalities in the United States (Anyon, 1995; Berliner, 2006). Some structuralists suggest that public schooling alone can neither remedy nor equalize these differences and that these inequalities constrain children's life chances before they enter school. Others suggest that these inequalities, more fundamentally, reflect a class-based economic system (Bowles, 1976). From this perspective, schools inevitably reproduce these larger structural forces.

System Inflexibility. Another explanation is that the persistent structure of the public school system contributes to inequities. The modern school system was created under a unique set of historical conditions that match neither the current diversity and needs of the student population nor current social and economic conditions (Deschenes et al., 2001; Tyack, 1974).

Inequality in School Resources. A third explanation is that schools and districts do not enjoy an equitable distribution of resources. That is, poor and minority children, on average, attend schools of poorer quality across a wide array of indicators (Darling-Hammond, 2006). The schools they attend have fewer resources, are more likely to employ poorer quality teachers, and have larger class sizes and enrollments. Schools with such attributes also are unlikely to enact effective organizational processes (Anyon, 1995; Sebring,

Allensworth, Bryk, Easton, & Luppescu, 2006). Moreover, such schools and districts tend to enroll disproportionate rates of socially vulnerable students. Unequal resources likely have not only direct but also interactive influences on the achievement of poor and minority children. In other words, resource inequalities may further accentuate academic risk among poor and minority children as they progress through school (Lee & Burkam, 2002).

Sociocultural Mismatches. A final explanation attends to various levels of sociocultural mismatch. A first area of mismatch occurs between students and their families and teachers. Such mismatch is enacted through day-to-day interactions within classrooms (Delpit, 1995; Heath, 1983). Teachers, who predominantly represent majority and middle-class values, do not necessarily value or capitalize on the different sociocultural experiences of students. These differences may contribute to student disengagement over time. Weinstein (2002) similarly argues that student race and class often condition teacher expectations and behaviors linked to student performance and achievement.

John Ogbu (1987) attends to sociostructural levels of analysis in framing sociocultural mismatch. Members of involuntary minority groups (those in a particular host society as a result of being enslaved or because of colonization) have experienced long-standing social and school discrimination and become, over time, highly distrustful of the educational system. Such experiences—which are often supported through explicit and implicit messages conveyed by families and communities—lead minority students to question whether educational participation will actually benefit them and, ultimately, to disengage from school.

In summary, this brief review of varying accounts of the achievement gap is compelling in that each of the explanations suggests a very different set of educational and social policies—from school input level reforms to educational institutional change to sociostructural change. Overall, scholarship has been mixed in terms of gauging the extent of singular support for any one of these explanations. Thus, addressing the achievement gap will likely require a multipronged effort, incorporating several of these explanations simultaneously.

Education Reform Strategies

Over the past three decades, the achievement gap has sparked heightened scrutiny of the performance of public schools, which is often assessed in terms of student performance on standardized tests of achievement. Reflecting the map articulated in the previous section, reforms have focused on school resources, organizational structure and processes, addressing or ameliorating student characteristics that place them at academic risk, and market-oriented strategies.

As noted previously, many critics question the capacity of the modern school system, which emerged in a postwar, postcolonial, industrially based context. Its original purpose was to train workers to compete in a nationally localized, skills-based economy. As such, it is argued that the infrastructure has become obsolete, with especially little relevance within the context of a global economy (Torres, 2002). It is therefore important to note that educational reform strategies largely attempt to adjust, but do not fundamentally alter, the basic public school infrastructure to produce desired outcomes and outputs.

School Resource Inputs

There is great debate in the academic literature about whether and how school resources matter to student and school performance. Educational economist Eric Hanushek's empirical work finds that school expenditures (and investments in public education expenditures) alone may not matter much to overall student achievement (Hanushek, 1998). Similarly mixed findings have emerged regarding building teacher capacity—that is, on the recruitment, training and retention of high quality teachers through postsecondary education, professional development, professionalization, and credentialing. For example, a recent large-scale study of elementary classrooms revealed that classroom quality did not vary significantly as a function of indicators of teacher experience (NICHD, 2005).

There are at least two potential interpretations of such findings. A first interpretation is that much of the variation in student achievement outcomes is explained by exogenous factors, by things related to the students, for example, rather than to teacher training. Echoing findings from the Coleman report (1966), Rutter and Maughan (2002) recently reviewed contemporaneous research assessing the influence of school effects on both pupil academic achievement and adjustment to school. They estimate that a substantial amount of the variability in child ability, achievement, and behavioral adjustment is explained by child and family sociodemographic characteristics, such as socioeconomic status. Thus, schools have a limited potential range of influence on student outcomes. However, an equally compelling interpretation is that schools vary tremendously in how they utilize resources and to what ends. This interpretation is perhaps best reflected in reforms centered on school organization and process.

School Organization and Process

Reforms focused on school organization and process generally assume that change in particular elements of the educational infrastructure will produce better quality educational outputs, without additional financial resources. This infrastructure includes school and classroom organization (including school size), within-tier streaming or tracking, curriculum and teaching materials, and the qualities and characteristics of the teaching corps. The small school movement and class-size reduction strategies are examples of such reforms. Class-size reductions appear to matter most for young children's achievement, but the effects of class size diminish as students move up grade levels. Biddle and Berliner (2002) argue, however, that a smaller class size increases the probability that effective school process can be enacted.

A robust set of scholarship highlights several school-level attributes that have been linked to both student and school achievement. This body of research, often referred to as the *essential* or *effective* schools literature suggests that, given a set of inputs and structural features, schools that (1) have strong principal leadership, (2) enact "ambitious instruction," (3) are characterized by a student-centered learning climate that combines high staff expectations for students with adequate supports for learning, (4) create strong parent and community partnerships, and (5) cultivate the professional development of teachers are more likely to be high achieving (Rutter & Maughan, 2002; Sebring et al., 2006). In short, this strategy suggests the modification of within-school organizational attributes. This strategy is evidenced in the proliferation and cross-national sharing of materials documenting empirically based "best practices"—in terms of strategies to improve the delivery of instruction and cultivate effective school leaders.

Student Inputs

Another adjustment focuses on student inputs—preexisting student attributes such as the background characteristics that shape student ability or opportunity to learn. Examples of this include specialized services for students with specialized learning needs, involving parents in their children's education, and the provision of comprehensive health and social services to children and families through schools.

Specifically, scholars from a range of disciplinary backgrounds assert that the psychosocial needs of students represent a salient concern of educational practice and policy. Over the past few decades, a diverse set of models to address these needs has emerged, for example, curriculums focused on social-emotional learning, school-based health and mental health centers, family resource centers, Comer schools, community schools, school-based prevention of risk behaviors, and systems-of-care models (Stone, 2008). These developments share several core assumptions: (1) that there is consensus about what nonacademic needs are as well as their related outcomes, (2) that addressing pupils' psychosocial needs can influence academic progress at either the student or school level, and (3) that the school, albeit in varying forms and levels, represents the logical point of intervention. In recent years, this set of strategies has garnered increasing attention from policy makers. Historically, however, such approaches appear to have made little progress, and programs addressing these needs have been particularly difficult to sustain in schools. These segregated settings may offer suboptimal learning opportunities and set conditions for iatrogenic peer-mediated effects. Finally, the education system often functions as a conduit for various interests, many of which are loosely coupled with the actual capacity of the system as a whole, underscoring the importance of careful deliberation when implicating schools as programmatic levers.

Output/Market

A final type of adjustment centers on outputs. Reform centered on knowledge outputs, for example, focuses on curriculum innovations and pedagogical strategies that develop the skills needed for computer literacy and understanding of information technology. The proliferation of standards across Western nationalities reflects attention on quality of student outputs (versus the quality of system attributes). Standards-based approaches include such requirements as mandatory grade promotion criteria and secondary leaving exams. Finally, in recent decades, there is an overall trend toward increased state responsibility for the expansion of postsecondary education, and greater enrollments have resulted.

An extension of output-driven reform intends to subject educational outputs to market-related controls. Two recent and controversial examples include (1) efforts to privatize what have traditionally been public education functions and (2) initiatives to expand opportunities for greater school choice, utilizing such strategies as vouchers (see Chubb & Moe, 1990; Fuller, 2000). Such strategies conceptualize educational systems as accountable to consumers (e.g., children and families) oftentimes as a function of student achievement.

Interpretative Summary

Looking across these various reform strategies, we see clearly that particular strategies tend to focus on one particular element of a given public education system. There is growing consensus among contemporary education scholars that such piecemeal policy approaches are problematic. Three central concerns have emerged. A first concern is that achievement outcomes are simply too narrow a criterion upon which to judge student, school, and system progress (Grubb, 2008). Rather, a broadened set of criteria for evaluating student and school progress is necessary.

Even when it centers on student performance outputs, recent evidence suggests that differing sets of resources, school structures, and organizational processes may have very different relationships to school performance outcomes (Rumberger & Palardy, 2005). Specifically, school characteristics related to achievement productivity over time are quite different from school characteristics related to graduation rates. This evidence implies that there are complex and heterogeneous relationships between school characteristics and qualities and various school outputs.

A third concern is that the relationship between school inputs, school organizational and process features, and particular outputs is much more dynamic than currently conceptualized. This perspective suggests that there are substantial "individual" differences between schools, districts, and states and that the nature and extent of these differences evolve over time. Thus, the process of matching reforms to particular schools and school conditions is essential, but often overlooked (Tyack & Cuban, 1995).

Conclusion: Policy Issues

This chapter provided an overview of the history and basic institutional features of the American public education system. It centered on the performance of poor and minority children as a key area of concern and described basic reform strategies designed to address this concern. In conclusion, several enduring social policy issues are discussed in light of material presented.

Educational Aims, Goals, Outputs, and Outcomes

Several sections within this chapter noted that a complex set of social forces shape the aims and desired outputs of the public education system. These issues speak broadly to the intersection between social policy and education. Education systems are in constant flux, especially in terms of their roles in and relationships to other societal structures. It is critical to underscore that school and educational systems are institutions that transmit dominant societal values. Clearly, social policies related to these systems reflect these overall values. A significant role of social policy is to struggle with how schools and educational systems represent a key tableau of inter- and intranation ideological, sociocultural and sociopolitical conflict and how these relate to systemic governance, structures, and outputs.

Jencks (1988) argues that there are pervasive but incorrect assumptions that there is societal consensus about the aims and purposes of education. The same applies for the conceptualization of desired outputs and outcomes. As noted above, education is conceived of as a social and economic investment. Recent scholarship takes a critical look at the dominance of such models in educational policy making and stresses careful rethinking of links (and of the desirability of such links) between the education system and the labor market. Perhaps most critically, there do not appear to be shared understandings of what constitutes equality and equity in educational context. Thus, there is an emergent need to reflect critically on and engage in deep dialogue about the concept of education itself (Ball, 1998).

Educational Inequality

A central policy concern relates to the nature and determinants of educational inequalities. These inequalities potentially include those of access (differential entry into various system levels), survival (differential completion rates), and output (differential distribution of learning or educational achievement). Educational systems initially grapple with access issues, then subsequently with survival and output issues. One policy lesson is that investments in education—especially primary and secondary education—generally have diminishing returns (Farrell, 1999). It is also clear that there are resource-related trade-offs between universalizing access and ensuring equality in output. Of note, issues related to inequality will generally persist given political and economic change, migration, and racism.

A related consideration is that global social, economic, and market dynamics shift the role of education—especially in western and northern developed nations such as the United States. This new role—to support competition in a "world market"—places an increased focus on standards (i.e., on the quality of outputs) at the expense of access and survival issues. Social critics worry that this shifting educational role will lead to increased distributional inequalities over time—especially among the most socially vulnerable students served by the most socially vulnerable educational subsystems.

System and Reform Strategy Limitations

A final policy concern attends to the limits of education systems, in terms of both fiscal and administrative capacity, to produce necessary or desired educational outputs. On one hand, questions have been raised as to the capacity of the education system to address social ills in the absence of other social policies, particularly those focused on inequities in overall income distribution. This also involves acknowledgement of the inherent complexity and imperfection related to educational policy making itself. As Ball (1998) notes, "Most policies are ramshackle, compromise, hit and miss affairs, that are reworked, tinkered with, nuanced, and inflected through complex processes of influence, text production, dissemination and, ultimately, re-creation in contexts of practice" (p. 126).

References

Anyon, J. (1995). Race, social class and educational reform within an inner city school. *Teachers College Record, 97,* 69–94.

Arnove, R., Altbach, P., & Kelly, G. (1992). *Emergent issues in education: Comparative perspectives.* Albany: State University of New York Press.

Arnove, R., & Torres, C. (Eds.). (1999). *Comparative education: Dialectic of the global and the local.* Boston: Rowman & Littlefield.

Ball, S. (1998). Big policies/small world: An introduction to international perspectives in education policy. *Comparative Education Review, 34,* 119–130.

Berliner, D. C. (2006). Our impoverished view of educational reform. *Teachers College Record, 108,* 949–95.

Biddle, B. J., & Berliner, D. (2002). Small class size and its effects. *Educational Leadership, 59,* 12–23.

Bowles, S. (1976). *Schooling in capitalist America: Educational reform and the contradictions of economic life.* New York: Basic Books.

Bray, M. (1999). The control of education: Issues and tensions in centralization and decentralization. In R. F. Arnove & C. A. Torres (Eds.), *Reframing comparative education: The dialectic of the global and the local* (pp. 207–232). Lanham, MD: Rowman & Littlefield.

Brown v. Board of Education, 347 U.S. 483 (1954).

Chubb, J., & Moe, T. (1990). *Politics, markets, and America's schools.* New York: Brookings Institution Press.

Cohen, R. (1984). American public schooling. In Institute for Research in History (Ed.), *History of Education* (pp. 1–14). New York: Haworth Press.

Coleman, J. S. (1966). *Equality of educational opportunity.* Washington, DC: U.S. Department of Health, Education, and Welfare, Office of Education.

Darling-Hammond, L. (2006). Securing the right to learn: Policy and practice for powerful teaching and learning. *Educational Researcher, 35*(7), 13–24.

Delpit, L. (1995). *Other people's children.* New York: New Press.

Deschenes, S., Cuban, L., & Tyack, D. (2001). Mismatch: Historical perspectives on schools and students who don't fit them. *Teachers College Record, 103,* 525–547.

Eccles, J., & Roeser, R. (1999). School and community influences on human development. In M. Bornstein & M. Lamb (Eds.), *Developmental psychology: An advanced textbook* (pp. 503–554). Mahwah, NJ: Lawrence Erlbaum.

Farrell, J. (1999). Changing conceptions of equality of education: Forty years of comparative experience. In R. Arnove & C. Torres (Eds.), *Comparative education: Dialectic of the global and the local* (pp. 149–177). Boston: Rowman & Littlefield.

Fry, R. (2003). *Hispanic youth dropping out of U.S. schools: Measuring the challenge.* Washington, DC: Pew Hispanic Center.

Fuller, B. (2000). *Inside charter schools: The paradox of radical decentralization.* Cambridge, MA: Harvard University Press.

Graham, P. A. (2005). *Schooling America.* New York: Oxford University Press.

Grubb, W. N. (2008). Families and schools raising children: The inequitable effects of family background on schooling outcomes. In J. Berrick & N. Gilbert (Eds.), *Raising children: Emerging needs, modern risks and social responses* (pp. 221–249). New York: Oxford University Press.

Hanushek, E. A. (1998). Conclusion and controversies about the effectiveness of school resources. *Economic Policy Review, 4,* F11–F28.

Heath, S. B. (1983). *Ways with words.* New York: Cambridge University Press.

Jencks, C. (1988). Whom must we treat equally for educational opportunity to be equal. *Ethics, 98*(83), 518–533.

Lee, V. E., & Burkam, D. T. (2002). *Inequality at the starting gate: Social background differences in achievement as children begin school.* Washington, DC: Economic Policy Institute.

McGinn, N. (1992). Reforming educational governance: Centralization/decentralization. In R. Arnove, P. Altbach, & G. Kelly (Eds.), *Emergent issues in education: Comparative perspectives.* Albany: State University of New York Press.

Monk, D. (1989). The education production function: Its evolving role in policy analysis *Educational Evaluation and Policy Analysis, 11,* 31–45.

National Institute of Child Health and Human Development Early Child Care Research Network (NICHD). (2005). A day in third grade: A large-scale study of classroom quality and teacher and student behavior. *Elementary School Journal, 105,* 305–323.

Ogbu, J. U. (1987). Variability in minority school performance: A problem in search of an explanation. *Anthropology and Education Quarterly, 18,* 312–334.

Ravitch, D. (2000). *Left back: A century of failed education reform.* New York: Touchstone.

Rumberger, R. W., & Palardy, G. J. (2005). Test scores, dropout rates, and transfer rates as alternative indicators of high school performance. *American Educational Research Journal, 41,* 3–42.

Rutter, M., & Maughan, B. (2002). School effectiveness findings, 1979–2002. *Journal of School Psychology, 40*(6), 451–475.

Samoff, J. (1999) Institutionalizing international influence. In R. Arnove & C. Torres (Eds.), *Comparative education: Dialectic of the global and the local* (pp. 51–90). Boston: Rowman & Littlefield.

Sebring, P. B., Allensworth, E., Bryk, A. S., Easton, J. Q., & Luppescu, S. (2006). *The essential supports for school improvement.* Chicago: Consortium on Chicago School Research.

Stone, S. (2008). Non-academic needs of children: How can schools intervene. In J. Berrick & N. Gilbert (Eds.), *Raising children: Emerging needs, modern risks and social responses* (pp. 201–220). New York: Oxford University Press.

Thomas, R. (Ed.). (1990). *International comparative education: Practices, issues, prospects.* Oxford, UK: Pergamon Press.

Torres, A. (2002). Globalization, education, and citizenship: Solidarity versus markets? *American Education Research Journal, 39,* 363–378.

Tyack, D. B. (1974). *The one best system: A history of American urban education.* Cambridge, MA: Harvard University Press.

Tyack, D. B. (1992). Health and social services in public schools: Historical perspectives. *The Future of Children, 2,* 19–31.

Tyack, D. B., & Cuban, L. (1995). *Tinkering towards utopia: A century of public school reform.* Cambridge, MA: Harvard University Press.

Weinstein, R. S. (2002). *Reaching higher: The power of expectations in schooling* Cambridge, MA: Harvard University Press.

31 Urban Development Policy

Robert Waste

This chapter describes the historical evolution and contemporary ramifications of place-based social policy, policies designed to address the concerns of the vast majority of Americans. More than 80% of America's residents are crowded into the urbanized 2% of our collective landscape—urban areas that historically we have referred to as *cities*.

More recently, urban policy scholars have begun to concentrate not only on cities but also on the larger region in which cities are embedded. Terms to describe this larger urban policy arena vary. Urban regions are referred to as "metropolitan statistical areas" by the U.S. Census Bureau or, in the more scholarly terms used by urban policy scholars, as "multinucleated metropolitan regions" (Gottdiener, 1985), "technoburbs" (Fishman, 1987, p. 184), "edge cities" (Garreau, 1991), "postsuburban regions" (Kling, Olin, & Poster, 1991), "polycentric metropolitan forms" (Blakeley & Ames, 1992, p. 436), "citistate" regions (Hill, Wolman, & Ford, 1995; Peirce, 1993; Peirce, 1995; Savitch, Collins, Sanders, & Markham, 1993; Voith, 1992), interdependent "regional economic commons" (Barnes & Ledebur, 1997), and, finally, as "metropolitical regions" (Orfield, 1998) or even as "edgeless cities" (Lang, 2003).

As the foregoing list of academic terms for describing the urban arena for social policy illustrates, the study of cities—and the development of American social policy to address the challenges facing urban residents—has undergone a gradual evolution from policies (and academic concepts) that once focused primarily upon center cities and center-city residents to a more recent focus on the shared policies and concerns, the "interwoven destinies" (Cisneros, 1993, p. 24), of both the central city and suburban residents of America's sprawling metropolitan regions.

Both America's center cities and the suburban fringe are facing tremendous challenges. As one study has indicated, 44 of the largest metropolitan areas in the United States, containing over 40% of the nation's residents, have, since the early 1980s, been seemingly locked into a "permanent urban crisis"; a crisis of hunger, crime, poverty, and infrastructure decay (Waste, 1998, pp. 1–19). Thirty million Americans suffer from hunger on a daily basis. Every 15 minutes, a child in an American city is killed by gunfire. Twenty percent of the bridges, highways, and basic infrastructure of American cities is obsolete. America has responded to these more recent placed-based urban problems, and to urban problems in general, with a series of policies and programs dating back to the Great Depression and the post–World War II era.

A recent authoritative Brookings Institution study draws a sharp contrast between America's center cities and their sprawling suburban "edge cities" (Berube, Katz, & Lang, 2006). Center-city poverty is higher than poverty in the suburbs—11% to 13% for center cities but only 6% to 8% for the suburban or regional fringe. American social policy has long attempted to address urban poverty, beginning with early programs such as the Social Security Act in 1935 and the federal "alphabet soup" employment programs (e.g., the WPA—Works Progress Administration and the CCC—Civilian Conservation Corps) associated with the Great Depression of the 1930s.

The Historical Evolution of Urban Development Services and Policies

Although America's city residents benefited from universal social welfare entitlement policies such as the Social Security Act (1935) and the "alphabet soup" employment programs that accompanied the Great Depression and the New Deal era, American social policy to aid urban development was quite limited. A small set of national grants-in-aid programs to local governments during the early 1930s, funded at an annual level of $30 million, grew by the 1960s to annual federal–local transfer levels averaging $7 billion—approximately 8% of all federal spending—in the 1960s and to a historic high of $91 billion or 16% of all national government spending by 1980 (Ross & Levine, 1996; Ross & Stedman, 1991, p. 338). Federal expenditures on behalf of urban areas declined dramatically in the Reagan and G. H. W. Bush years, declining to $88 billion or 11% of all federal spending nationally. Federal urban spending increased slightly in the Clinton years, averaging $200 billion annually, a figure equal to 14% of all federal spending annually. Federal urban spending dropped in key areas under the George W. Bush administration, with cuts in numerous federal urban aid programs including social services, community development, food stamps, energy assistance, and public housing—the latter most notably in the HOPE VI program (Housing Opportunities for People Everywhere VI). HOPE VI was adopted by Congress in 1992 to tear down low-income housing projects and replace them with needs-based low-rise apartments and townhouses. The George W. Bush administration first proposed eliminating the $570 million per year HOPE VI program but settled for reducing the annual HOPE VI appropriation to $150 million per year in 2004 (Popkin et al., 2004).

1940s and 1950s Era Urban Aid Programs Lead to Suburban Growth

The initial grants-in-aid programs grew modestly at first. Congress enacted the National Housing Act in 1934. This legislation created a Federal Housing Administration (FHA) to create government-insured home mortgages to prop up the failing home building industry and the Federal Saving and Loan Insurance Corporation (FSLIC) to insure the savings of individual savers who had lost their confidence after the bank failures and savings crises of the Great Depression. These early federal urban aid service strategies signaled a trend that was to remain constant in federal policies toward cities for several decades; assistance was directed toward industries such as home builders, banking and the saving and loan industry and, only indirectly, to places such as center cities. In fact, these early policies and later urban development policies proved to aid suburban growth as much or more than urban or center growth and development.

The social policies aimed at urban aid in the 1940s and 1950s exacerbated this urban fringe or suburban bias in urban aid programs. The federal Housing Act of 1949 created the Urban Renewal Agency and signaled the beginning of a decade of urban renewal in center cities. This renewal effort was called "Negro removal" or the "federal bulldozer" by its detractors (Anderson, 1964; Lemann, 1994). From 1950 to 1960, urban renewal funds were spent to raze over 120,000 substandard center-city housing units, which, in turn, were replaced with fewer than 30,000 housing units. Many of the newer units were consolidated in low-income public housing complexes, units which eventually became a source of controversy. Since the late 1990s, the federal government has been renovating, selling to tenets, or demolishing these units.

The eradication of low quality but affordable center-city housing stock via the Urban Renewal Agency program indirectly promoted suburban growth at the expense of the center city, as did two other post–World War II programs, the GI Bill of Rights and the Veterans Administration (VA) Home Loan Program. These latter two programs provided low cost loans requiring no down payments for World War II veterans on new homes, most of which were to be found in the suburban housing market of post–World War II America. The outer fringe areas of cities and the newly created suburban housing markets—the postwar "Levittown" phenomenon suburbs—were made all the more accessible due to an unparalleled era of freeway construction promoted by the federal government by the passage of the Highway Act of 1956.

Urban development services created in the 1940s and 1950s, ironically, created a boom market for suburban housing, a decline in affordable center-city housing stock, and a federally subsidized freeway system and home loan purchase program that left center-city residents increasingly isolated from their more affluent suburban or metropolitan neighbors. During the War on Poverty, the 1960s would see an effort by the federal government to frame urban development programs that would assist the increasingly isolated inner city poor.

Urban Services and the 1960s War on Poverty

The 1960s saw the enactment of several key universal social welfare measures that indirectly assisted the urban poor, including the Food Stamp program (1964), the Civil Rights Act (1964), the Voting Rights Act (1965), and Medicare (1965). The impact that enactment of these programs had on poorer Americans in general, as well as on Americans in urban areas, can hardly be exaggerated. Although the specific causal relationships between these programs and the dramatic reduction in American poverty levels during the 1960s is still the cause of lively debate in some quarters (Lockhart, 1986; Murray, 1984; Schwarz & Volgy, 1992), the dramatic results of these federal programs seem factually indisputable. Urban and rural poverty levels were cut in half in the Lyndon Johnson years, from a high of 22% in 1960 to a low of 12% by the time that LBJ left office in January of 1969. As I have observed elsewhere (Waste, 1998, p. 54), this is noteworthy given that no president since Johnson has reduced the federal poverty level by more than 1.5%. Poverty nationally declined 0.7% under Richard Nixon, increased 0.2% under Gerald Ford, increased 2.4% under Jimmy Carter, decreased 1.2% under Ronald Reagan, increased 2.3% under George Bush, and decreased less than 2% during the Clinton years.

The Rise of the Community Action Program (CAP) and Model Cities

Each of these 1960s era civil rights or antipoverty programs had positive if indirect impacts on cities, as did the key War on Poverty legislation—the Economic Opportunity Act of 1964, which created the food stamp and the low-income school lunch programs, Head Start, Upward Bound, Volunteers in Service to America (VISTA), and the Legal Services program. To this antipoverty package, the Johnson administration added a Community Action Program (CAP). Unlike the earlier universal civil rights or antipoverty approaches of the LBJ years, the Community Action Program was place-based, funding services and programs in poor neighborhoods directly by creating local community action agencies designed to operate without the assistance or interference of elected or appointed state or local officials. Unpopular with mayors, governors, and local officials, the Community Action Program gave way in 1966 to a second targeted urban aid approach, the Model Cities program. Originally created to target only a few cities with extremely poor neighborhoods, the 1966 Model Cities legislation eventually covered 60 cities, was funded with $1 billion in grants, and required clear coordination with local, state, and even regional elected and appointed officials. Originally designed to aid targeted high poverty neighborhoods, in a small number of cities, Model Cities grew to include far more "targets" than originally designated, and Model Cities funds were used by many cities for city-wide services including schools, sewers, sanitation, and police (Herson & Bolland, 1990).

General Revenue Sharing (GRS), Special Revenue Sharing (SRS), and Cities

With the election of a new and more conservative president in 1968 and because of the general unpopularity of targeted programs with many urban local and elected officials (Caputo, 1976), Congress adopted general revenue sharing (GRS) in the State and Local Government Assistance Act of 1972, allocating over $30 billion over a five-year period to state and local governments based not on need, per se, but on the population of the political unit in question. Supported later by both Presidents Gerald Ford and Jimmy Carter, GRS was eventually eliminated in 1986 under President Ronald Reagan.

Soon after the creation of GRS, Congress enacted a follow-up "special revenue sharing" urban service package. These two block grant programs, the 1974 Housing and Community Development Block Grant (CDBG) program and the 1977 Urban Development Action Grant (UDAG) program, were slightly more targeted than the earlier population-based GRS program. The 1974 CDBG program "blocked" seven earlier grant-in-aid programs for cities for such spending projects as sewers and urban renewal and allowed cities to receive funding automatically for any city over 50,000 in population that applied for CDBG funding. Extremely controversial with academic urban policy scholars (DeLeon & LeGates, 1976; Lovell & Korey, 1975; Marshall & Waste, 1977; Nathan & Domel, 1978; Nenno, 1974) because of the loose federal oversight of local spending and the automatic nature of the grants to all applying jurisdictions, CDBG continues to be funded and popular in both city and national political circles.

Urban Policy and Services in the Jimmy Carter, Ronald Reagan, and George Bush, Sr. Years: 1976 to 1992

The Carter administration attempted to move away from the loose oversight of the GRS and CDBG urban aid approach with the Urban Development Action Grant program enacted in 1977. Under this program, federal funding to cities would be provided only if cities could show that the money would be spent in designated distressed areas and demonstrate the presence of a local partnership to leverage the funds provided by the federal government. The "high strings" highly targeted Urban Development Action Grant approach was terminated by the Reagan administration, which dramatically reduced funding and services aimed at American cities. The Reagan administration reduced annual federal spending to urban areas by 57%, reduced the budget of the U.S. Department of Housing and Urban Development from 7% of the federal budget to 1% by 1989, reduced the authorization for assisted housing funding from annual levels of $27 billion in 1980 to $7.5 billion annually in the later Reagan years, and reduced the number of public units of housing from 129,000 to 19,000 between 1980 and 1989—reductions so sharp that one prominent critic charged the Reagan and Bush administration with "abandoning cities" (Ross & Levine, 1996, pp. 426–429).

The George H. W. Bush administration (1989–1992) saw few federal urban service initiatives, despite a dramatic urban riot in South Central Los Angeles in 1992. Tax incentive areas created in distressed urban areas, known as "urban enterprise zones," were discussed by Jack Kemp, the Bush administration secretary of HUD, but were not actually implemented during this time. Rather, they were implemented as "empowerment zones" by the subsequent Bill Clinton administration. The Bush administration is notable in the urban policy arena primarily for the passage of the "Ice Tea Act"—the Intermodal Surface Transportation Efficiency Act (ISTEA) in 1991. ISTEA mandates that urban regions, in order to receive millions of dollars in federal highway and transportation funds, create a Metropolitan Planning Organization (MPO) to insure regional coordination on transportation issues for cities. Renewed and expanded in 1998—and again in 2005—ISTEA has encouraged region-wide cooperation in America's metropolitan areas on transportation issues.

The Clinton Urban Aid/ Service Policy Package: 1992–2000

The Clinton administration urban service policy package was notable for four accomplishments: (1) the creation of empowerment zones (EZs) in six cities (Atlanta, Baltimore, Chicago, Detroit, New York City, and Philadelphia), two "supplemental zones" (Cleveland and Los Angeles), three "rural zones," and sixty-five "enterprise communities"; (2) the passage of the 1994 Crime Bill, which attempted to place 100,000 police on city streets; (3) an October 1998 budget compromise with Congress in which the Clinton administration extracted a $1.1 billion funding authorization for 100,000 teachers aimed at reducing class sizes in K–3 public schools from a national average of 22 students to an average of 18 students per classroom; and (4) The renewal of "Ice Tea" as "TEA-21," which directed more than $217 billion into state highway projects, including $198 billion for highway projects, $20 billion to rehabilitate and replace old bridges, $8 billion for congestion mitigation and air quality improvements, and $42 billion for transit development including pedestrian and bicycle trails.

Perhaps the most significant urban policy initiative of the Clinton administration was what one set of urban policy experts have labeled "a stealth urban policy of pursuing urban goals through 'nonurban' means, through programs that were not perceived to be focused on cities" (Ross & Levine, 2006, p. 455). The leading example of stealth urban policy in the Clinton administration was the Earned Income Tax Credit (EITC) program, a program that distributed millions annually in income assistance to the nation's working poor. Like negative income tax, which was proposed but not adopted in the Nixon Administration, the Clinton-era EITC provided a refundable tax credit of $3,370 to families with a single parent and two or more children (Ross & Levine, 2006, p. 456).

The George W. Bush Urban Aid/ Service Policy Package: 2000–2008

The George W. Bush administration urban service policy package has been notable for four accomplishments: (1) the 2006 renewal of the landmark transportation "Ice Tea Act" (SAFETEA-LU), which provided more than $200 billion for transportation projects, primarily for freeway construction but also $35 billion for railroad rehabilitation, $7 billion for smaller roads, and $4.5 billion for bicycle-related projects; (2) an emphasis by the Bush administration to shift federal funding to include funding for efforts by faith-based churches and organizations; (3) an emphasis on home ownership, as witnessed in the 2005 budget proposal to include $200 million for the American Dream Down Payment Initiative (enacted in 2003), in the beefed-up funding for the Self Help Home Ownership Opportunity program, and in the over $15 million allocated for new-buyer housing counseling; and, finally, (4) the No Child Left Behind (NCLB) Act. The Bush administration will probably be best remembered for the NCLB program, which required extensive school testing, accountability (including publication of school test scores), and counseling and assistance for students and school sites with low scores. NCLB has a mixed track record with some notable successes but more frequent charges of "teaching to the test," relaxed standards, and a lack of funding for remediation and intervention efforts for failed students and failing campuses.

The Evolution of Federal Urban Social Policies and Services: A Summary

From World War II to the present, federal assistance to urban areas has evolved from early grants-in-aid to broad needs-based entitlement programs for disadvantaged city residents in such programs as Head Start and food stamps. Early needs-based programs to aid needy cities and urban regions such as Model Cities and Urban Development Action Grants were eventually replaced by population (versus needs-based) formula grant programs such as general revenue sharing (GRS) and Community Development Block Grants (CDBG). After the demise of revenue sharing, the population-based formulaic CDBG program and the more decentralized "Ice Tea" (ISTEA) MPO program remain the key urban federal programs of the late 2000s. Against the backdrop of CDBG and ISTEA, the limited use of empowerment zones in the Clinton administration represented a small step back into targeted needs-based urban aid strategies in the late 1990s.

Thus, from World War II to the present, federal urban aid strategies have swung from small specific grants to broad universal entitlements, back to more targeted grants briefly in the Clinton years, and back again in both the Clinton and George W. Bush administrations to a steady increase in population-based entitlements and a reliance on broad or universal benefits (e.g., CDBG, ISTEA).

Service Delivery: Current Legislation and Administration Arrangements

The primary urban service program at the federal level is the continuing CDBG or Community Development Block Grant program, administered centrally by the U.S. Department of Housing and Urban Development (HUD). The key decentralized program, as noted earlier, is "Ice Tea" (ISTEA)—the Intermodal Surface Transportation Efficiency Act of 1991, which was renamed TEA-21 (the Transportation Equity Act for the 21st Century) and reauthorized by Congress in 1998 and reauthorized and renamed again by Congress in 2005 as SAFETEA-LU (the Safe Accountable, Flexible, Efficient Transportation Efficiency Act—A Legacy for Users).

ISTEA—now SAFETEA funded by a federal gasoline tax and administered nationally by the Department of Transportation—is administered within each urban region by the regional Metropolitan Planning Organization authorized under the ISTEA Act. Although states are either donor or donee states—meaning that they either get less or more back from the gas tax funds that they send to Washington, D.C.—every state receives ISTEA funding, with the average state receiving back only 92 cents for every dollar sent to the nation's capital (Boulard, 2003).

HUD also administers the limited Community Renewal Initiative for Renewal Communities and Empowerment Zones described above, a "Section 8" low-income housing assistance and voucher program, and the "Continuum of Care" homeless assistance programs developed by HUD to respond to spending and programs authorized by Congress in the McKinney-Vento Homeless Assistance Act of 1987 and its subsequent congressional reauthorizations of the 1987 act.

To remain eligible for CDBG funding, cities and counties are required to file annual Comprehensive Housing and Affordability Survey reports to HUD. Cities compete for McKinney Act funding by submitting Continuum of Care applications to HUD, and they have also competed in the past for designation as an empowerment zone or enterprise community. Cities and counties also apply to the Department of Justice for funding for additional police officers under the mechanism established by the 1994 Crime Bill. Funding for and administration of the Clinton 100,000 teachers initiative, presumably administered nationally by the U.S. Department of Education, is, as of this writing, not yet clear.

Because the United States federal government administration was divided up into ten regional offices under the New Federalism approach pioneered by President Richard Nixon in 1969, cities and counties have typically developed close working relations with one or more HUD and Department of Justice offices and with officials centered in one of the 10 regional offices nearest the given city or county in question.

Larger cities also regularly maintain liaison and information-seeking activities with the Washington-based national headquarters of HUD and the Department of Justice. The latter task has not been made easier for cities in either the Clinton or George W. Bush administrations due to a downsizing of the Washington HUD office staff, budget, and mission. Threatened with the elimination of HUD after the congressional elections of 1994, then-Secretary Henry Cisneros began a program of "reinventing HUD" that continues to the present. The Clinton administration's reinvention efforts included a streamlined or "reinvented" HUD administrative structure with a decidedly reorganized look. Over 60 categorical grants were combined into three broad, flexible performance-based grant programs. Local managers were given more authority to dismantle, sell, or rehabilitate federally funded housing projects. Many of these sites were turned over to residents in experimental resident/manager programs, while other residents were given vouchers in Move to Opportunity demonstration projects. More recently, HUD reinvention efforts of the George W. Bush administration have included a push to emphasize home ownership rather than apartment rental efforts in Section 8 and other housing programs.

Social, Political, and Economic Factors Influencing Policies: Crime, Hunger, Poverty, and Infrastructure Needs Remain Challenges

The social conditions of cities and the challenges faced by American cities have changed very little over the past two decades. As we noted at the outset of this chapter, cities are experiencing significant challenges on several fronts: violent crime, hunger, poverty, and infrastructure decay. These challenges have remained so fixed in American urban life over the past decade that one observer has labeled it a "permanent crisis" for American cities (Waste, 1998, pp. 1–9).

That observation, now over a decade old, remains accurate today. If the scope of the permanent crisis in American cities has remained relatively stable over the past several decades, the shape of that crisis has changed, if only slightly. Although still above post–World War II to early 1960s levels, violent crime has decreased slightly while urban poverty, which earlier characterized impoverished urban core areas, is to be found, increasingly, in suburban areas and inner ring suburban neighborhoods. Beginning in 1990, 42% of all metropolitan poor persons lived not in the center city but in suburban or inner ring neighborhoods. By the end of the current decade, suburban poverty continues to be a problem with America's suburbs exhibiting 6% to 8% poverty rates while center cities suffer even higher rates, with 11% to 13% in poverty households (Berube et al., 2006).

Urban crime—which dropped dramatically in the late 1990s to an average of 6.9 homicides per 1,000 people, the lowest rate in three decades (Butterfield, 1999)—is once again on the rise. The late '90s decline was due to (1) innovations in community-policing in large cities with populations exceeding 1 million, (2) a drop in gun-related violence among juveniles in that period, (3) changing demographics in youth and adults earlier involved in gun-related crime and crack cocaine trafficking, and, in part, (4) the limited success of "three strikes" incarceration laws enacted by state legislatures. After a decade of dropping crime rates from 1995 to 2005, urban crime began to rise again in 2005. In that year, the FBI reported a 1.8% increase, followed, in turn, by a 4.2% increase in 2006, according to the Police Executive Research Forum (Johnson, 2006). There are several factors contributing to the recent rise in urban crime rates, including the national focus on terrorism following the 9/11 attacks in New York City, the state of the national economy, overcrowding in many state prison systems, and the decline of the Clinton-era assistance for additional local police officers.

Cities Lack National Political Clout

Politically, cities and urban problems and policy proposals have lacked clout for several decades in American national politics and policy making. Urban issues lacked clout because suburban voters were widely perceived as more important to presidential and congressional elections than center-city voters (Barnes, 1990; Phillips, 1994). As one Stanford scholar has noted, "This is the age of the 'great dispersal' . . . voters, living in suburbia and exurbia, do not give a hoot about urban politics or are positively hostile to it. Congress, as noted, has little attachment to urban causes and is not likely to vote for programs sold as city-based" (Hendrickson, 2004, p. 8).

Urban areas also lack political clout because of the structural rural bias of the U.S. Senate, which, as Robert Dahl (1980) and others (Waste, 1998, p. 23) have pointed out, has an absolute voting majority drawn from the

26 smallest states, a figure equivalent to only 17% of the 1990 U.S. population. In this sense, the Senate serves as an antiurban anchor functionally preventing the emergence of urban issues and policies in American national politics.

Controversy Over Best Service Delivery Strategy for Urban Programs

Finally, even when social welfare or urban policy proposals are advanced in the presidential or congressional national policy arena, serious differences separate both politicians and social welfare scholars over the best approach to deliver such services and benefits. Advocates such as Harvard's W. J. Wilson (1988, 1989, 1990, 1992, 1996a, 1996b) and Skocpol (1985, 1990a, 1990b, 1994, 1996) have argued that social welfare reforms require broad universalistic benefits and political alliances such as those on which Social Security (1935) and Medicare (1965) were premised. However, the precise reform mechanism is disputed, with Wilson favoring "universalism within targeting" and Skocpol's favoring a far more expensive "targeting within universalism" approach, which suggests policy similar to that of the 1930s and 1960s—wide-scale, national assistance to impoverished groups in urban areas and elsewhere.

Other scholars such as Massey and Denton (1987, 1988, 1989, 1994) and Massey and Eggers (1990, 1994) have argued that social conditions vary significantly from ethnic group to ethnic group and between and within regions. Commentators supporting this position argue that the political and economic climate of the late 1990s and early 21st century requires either a more place-based or targeted approach.

This controversy in the scholarly and policy-making community was mirrored in the urban policies and programs enacted in Congress during the Clinton administration, which enacted both place-based targeted programs, such those addressed to empowerment zones, and more universalistic—if still somewhat limited in scope and scale—programs such as the 100,000 police or 100,000 teacher initiatives. Importantly, the Clinton administration failed to secure passage of the largest universal social welfare program proposed, the national health insurance proposal, a program directly relevant to urban policy since, as one observer noted, the "vast majority of the 37 millions without health-care insurance are urban residents" (Peirce et al., 1993, p.7).

Issues Arising From the Descriptive Account: "Think Nationally, Act Locally"

There has been an ironic result of the policy-making gridlock caused by the impact of the structural suburban, antiurban bias in American national politics and the disagreement among politicians and the scholarly community over targeted or place-based versus universal or entitlement approaches to social policy in general and urban policy specifically—the emergence of a number of local initiatives to aid local metropolitan regions. Urban areas have constructed several local or regional alternatives to nationally advanced or nationally funded urban social welfare policies. Several cities, with local and philanthropic foundation funding, have utilized Community Development Corporations (CDCs) to allow neighborhood residents to fund and direct limited neighborhood redevelopment projects. Urban areas have used CDCs in a limited fashion since the 1960s but, more recently, several cities—including, notably, New York City, Newark, and Baltimore—have used CDCs to aid low-income neighborhood revitalization efforts and to provide increased access to and increased housing units for low-income residents. Urban scholar Georg Gar notes "chain reactions" of investment lead to increased property values and neighborhood improvement by developing projects, engaging businesses and civic organizations, and helping public agencies to improve urban neighborhood conditions.

Second, several urban areas are exploring "livable cities" or "sustainable cities" considerations. These include cleaning up urban brownfields, regional cooperation in job creation, and addressing the "spatial mismatch" between where many impoverished urban area residents reside and where employment opportunities exist within their given urban areas. Although the "sustainable cities" dialogue has just begun, these local and regional efforts to coordinate and provide leadership in addressing problems within given American urban regions is likely to constitute a key focus of emerging urban policy in the early 21st century. If, as some pundits observed in the 1970s, 1980s, and 1990s, cities were "thinking globally and acting locally," in this century, urban areas may well turn to a focus in which they are "thinking nationally" but, given the constraints of American national politics and policy making, "acting locally." Two urban policy scholars have labeled the most successful of these "acting locally" "bootstrap" urban areas as *Comeback Cities* and cited remarkable numbers of individual Comeback City locales and accomplishments ranging from New York City to the West Coast (Grogan & Proscio, 2001).

In the coming years, the U.S. Conference of Mayors will continue to lobby, as in the past, for large-scale "Marshall Plan" urban aid programs for America's cities—"thinking nationally" and "acting nationally"—but such cities and their mayors will have to settle for a composite mix of local and regional "Comeback" efforts and limited federal efforts such as CDBG and ISTEA to alleviate the problems of cities in the foreseeable future.

Current Controversies

The current controversies in urban social policy are three in number. First, are the two leading national urban social programs—CDBG and "Ice Tea" (SAFETEA-LU)—sufficient in scope and funding to address the infrastructure, transportation, poverty, and public safety needs of America's center cities and suburban "edgeless" regions? Second, why, after a decade of dropping crime rates from 1995 to 2005, has America's urban area witnessed a surge in crime, and what ought to be the national government's response to this alarming rise in crime? Is a Clinton-era police officer augmentation bill needed, or, given the current cost and challenges of terrorism following 9/11, can the national government afford to focus on aiding cities in their urban crime fight? Finally, in a political context—as described earlier—that often marginalizes urban social policy and the urban area's political clout, how might Congress and the president be expected to address urban social policy issues in the coming decade? In presidential elections, suburban voters often trump urban voters; in senatorial elections, rural voters have more impact than do urban voters. Given these structural disincentives, how much federal aid to America's cities is likely to be forthcoming in the years ahead?

Conclusion: Urban Policy—History, Current Policies, and Future Prospects

As this chapter has illustrated, in the post–World War II period, America has embraced an evolving and deepening policy responsibility for the growth, decline, and social conditions of America's urban areas. The present decade and the decades of the 1970s to the late 2000s represent a retreat from the national activism in urban problem solving and urban policies and programs advanced in the 1960s. The period from 1990 to the present has been characterized by a long-term "permanent crisis" in America's cities, featuring high levels of poverty, hunger, crime, infrastructure decay, and eroding public schools and low-income neighborhoods. Recent efforts by Congress, the administration of President George W. Bush, and a "reinvented" U.S. Department of Housing and Urban Development (HUD) to address urban social conditions have resulted in two urban programs or approaches: (1) federal urban monetary assistance via programs such as CDBG and ISTEA/TEA-21 and SAFETEA-LU and the Metropolitan Planning Organizations funded under this legislation and (2) local place-based initiatives including "Comeback City" efforts such as the Community Development Corporation (CDC) programs and local and regional efforts at promoting "livable" and "sustainable" cities. Whether these limited federal urban policy efforts and programs, coupled with the local and regional efforts at producing sustainable "Comeback" urban regions, will suffice to address the seemingly intractable presence of a "permanent crisis" in America's urban areas is the central question facing urban policy analysts for the both the short- and long-term future.

References

Anderson, M. (1964). *The federal bulldozer: A critical analysis of urban renewal, 1949–1962.* Cambridge: MIT Press.

Barnes, W. (1990). Urban policies and urban impacts after Reagan. *Urban Affairs Quarterly, 25,* 562–573. (Reprinted in Caves, R. W. [Ed.]. [1995]. *Exploring urban America* [pp. 110–118]. Thousand Oaks, CA: Sage)

Barnes, W., & Ledebur, L. (1997). *The new regional economics.* Thousand Oaks, CA: Sage.

Berube, A., Katz, B., & Lang, R. (2006). *Redefining urban and suburban America: Evidence from* Census 2000). Washington, DC: Brookings Institution Press.

Blakely, E. J., & Ames, D. L. (1992). Changing places: American planning policy for the 1990's. *Journal of Urban Affairs, 14*(3/4), 423–446.

Boulard, G. (2003, March). States will miss TEA-21. *State Legislatures Magazine,* pp. 20–23.

Butterfield, F. (1999, October 18). F.B.I. study finds gun use in violent crimes declining. *New York Times,* p. A19.

Caputo, D. (1976). *Urban America: The policy alternatives.* San Francisco: W. H. Freeman.

Cisneros, H. (Ed.). (1993). *Interwoven destinies: Cities and the nation.* New York: W. W. Norton.

Dahl, R. A. (1980). *Democracy in the United States: Promise and performance* (3rd ed.). Chicago: Rand McNally.

DeLeon, R., & LeGates, R. (1976). *Redistribution effects of special revenue sharing for community development* (Working Paper No. 17). Berkeley: University of California, Institute of Governmental Studies.

Fishman, R. (1987). *Bourgeois utopias.* New York: Basic Books.

Garreau, J. (1991). *Edge cities: Life on the frontier.* New York: Doubleday.

Gottdeiner, M. (1985). *The social production of urban space.* Austin: University of Texas Press.

Grogan, P., & Proscio, T. (2001). *Comeback cities: A blueprint for urban neighborhood revival.* Boulder, CO: Westview Press.

Hendrickson, K. (2004, August–September). Bush and the cities. *Policy Review, 126,* 65–78.

Herson, L. J. R., & Bolland, J. M. (1990). *The urban web: Politics, policy and theory.* Chicago: Nelson-Hall.

Hill, E. W. N., Wolman, H. L., & Ford, C. C., III. (1995). Can suburbs succeed without their central cities? Examining the suburban dependence hypothesis. *Urban Affairs Review, 31*(2), 147–174.

Johnson, K. (2006, October 10). Dozens of cities see jump in murders, robberies. *USA Today.* Retrieved February 10, 2008, from http://www.usatoday.com/news/nation/2006-10-12-violent-crime_x.htm

Kling, R., Olin, S., & Poster, M. (Eds.). (1991). *Postsuburban California: The transformation of Orange County since World War II.* Berkeley: University of California Press.

Lang, R. (2003). *Edgeless cities: Exploring the elusive metropolis.* Washington, DC: Brookings Institution Press.

Lemann, N. (1994, January 9). The myth of community development. *New York Times Magazine*, pp. 27–31, 50, 54, 60.

Lockhart, C. (1986). *Gaining ground.* Berkeley: University of California Press.

Lovell, C., & Korey, J. (1975). The effects of general revenue sharing on ninety-seven cities in Southern California. In National Science Foundation, Research Applied to National Needs, *General revenue sharing utilization project: Vol. 2. Summaries of impact and process research* (pp.81–86). Washington, DC: Government Printing Office.

Marshall, D. R., & Waste, R. J. (1977). *Large cities responses to the Community Development Act.* Davis: University of California, Davis, Institute of Governmental Affairs.

Massey, D. S., & Denton, N. A. (1987). Trends in the residential segregation of blacks, Hispanics, and Asians. *American Sociological Review, 52,* 802–825.

Massey, D. S., & Denton, N. A. (1988). Suburbanization and segregation in U.S. metropolitan areas. *American Journal of Sociology, 94,* 592–626.

Massey, D. S., & Denton, N. A. (1989). Hypersegregation in U.S. metropolitan areas. *Demography, 26,* 373–391.

Massey, D. S., & Denton, N. A. (1994). *American apartheid: Segregation and the making of the underclass.* Cambridge, MA: Harvard University Press.

Massey, D. S., & Eggers, M. L. (1990). The ecology of inequality: Minorities and the concentration of poverty, 1970–1980. *American Journal of Sociology, 95,* 1153–88.

Massey, D. S., & Eggers, M. L. (1994). The spatial concentration of affluence and poverty during the 1970s. *Urban Affairs Quarterly, 29,* 299–315.

Meckler, L. (1996, November 6). Crime bill doesn't always put more cops on the street. *Sacramento Bee,* p. A6.

Murray, C. (1984). *Losing ground: American social policy, 1950–1980.* New York: Basic Books.

Nathan, R. P., & Domel, P. R. (1978). Federal-local relations under block grants. *Political Science Quarterly, 93,* 421–442.

Nenno, M. (1974). Housing and Community Development Act of 1974: An interpretation. *Journal of Housing, 31,* 345–362.

Orfield, M. (1998). *Metropolitics: A regional agenda for community and stability.* Washington, DC: Brookings Institution Press.

Peirce, N. (1995, November 21). In Indianapolis, a mayor and unions work together to streamline government. *Sacramento Bee,* p. B7.

Peirce, N. (with Johnson, C. W., & Hall, J. S.). (1993). *Citistates: does the American city have a future? How urban America can prosper in a competitive world.* Washington, DC: Seven Locks Press.

Phillips, K. (1994). *Boiling point.* New York. HarperPerennial.

Popkin, S., Katz, B., Cunningham, M., Brown, K., Gustafson, J., & Turner, M. (2004). *A decade of HOPE VI: Research findings.* Washington, DC: Brookings Institution Press.

Ross, B. H., & Levine, M. A. (1996). *Urban politics: Power in metropolitan America* (5th ed.). Itasca, NY: F. E. Peacock.

Ross, B. H., & Levine, M. A. (2006). *Urban politics: Power in metropolitan America* (7th ed.). Belmont, CA: Thomson Wadsworth.

Ross, B. H., & Stedman, M. S. (1991). *Urban politics: Power in metropolitan America* (4th ed.). Itasca, NY: F. E. Peacock.

Savitch, H. V., Collins, D., Sanders, D., & Markham, J. P. (1993). Ties that bind: Central cities, suburbs, and the new metropolitan region. *Economic Development Quarterly, 7*(4), 341–357.

Schwarz, J. E., & Volgy, T. J. (1992). *The forgotten Americans.* New York: W. W. Norton.

Skocpol, T. (1985, August 17). *Brother can you spare a job? Work and welfare in the United States.* Paper presented at the annual meeting of the American Sociological Association, Washington, DC.

Skocpol, T. (1990a, August 30–September 2). *Targeting within universalism: Politically viable policies to combat poverty in the U.S.* Paper presented at the Annual Meeting of the American Political Science Association, San Francisco.

Skocpol, T. (1990b). Sustainable social policy: Fighting poverty without poverty programs. *The American Prospect, 1*(2), 58–70.

Skocpol, T. (1994). *Protecting soldiers and mothers: The political origins of social policy in the United States.* Cambridge, MA: Harvard University Press.

Skocpol, T. (1996). Delivering for young families: The resonance of the GI Bill. *The American Prospect, 7*(28), 66–72.

Voith, R. (1992, September). City and suburban growth: Substitutes or complements? *Business Review,* pp. 21–31.

Waste, R. J. (1998). *Independent cities: Rethinking U.S. urban policy.* New York: Oxford University Press.

Wilson, W. J. (1988). American social policy and the ghetto underclass. *Dissent, 35,* 57–64.

Wilson, W. J. (Ed.). (1989). The ghetto underclass: Social science perspectives. *Annals of the American Academy of Political and Social Science, 501,* 26–47.

Wilson, W. J. (1990). Race-neutral policies and the Democratic Coalition. *The American Prospect, 1*(1), 74–81.

Wilson, W. J. (1992, March 17). The right message. *New York Times,* p. A15.

Wilson, W. J. (1996a, August 18). When work disappears. *New York Times Sunday Magazine,* pp. 26–33, 48–53.

Wilson, W. J. (1996b). *When work disappears: The world of the new urban poor.* New York: Knopf.

PART V

Conclusion

International and Future Perspectives on Social Policy

This final part of the handbook deals with two issues, namely the broader international context in which American social policy operates and the future of social policy in the United States.

Although discussions about social policy in the United States are seldom related to international trends, the first chapter in Part V shows that domestic social policy has long been affected by international developments. The evolution of social policy in the United States has often been influenced by international circumstances. Social policy in the United States has often been influenced by the flow of information about policies elsewhere. For example, some important social policy innovations, such as Social Security, reflected earlier developments in Europe. Similarly, the government of the United States is a signatory to many international conventions and treaties and because of these concords, it agrees to comply with minimum standards of social service delivery and entitlement. However, it must also be recognized that the government has declined to ratify several of these conventions. The chapter urges social policy makers and scholars to be more cognizant of innovations in other parts of the world and, where appropriate, to learn from them.

Chapter 33, the final chapter of the handbook, tentatively speculates on the future of social policy. It draws on the book's earlier chapters to examine the factors that will influence social policy in the future and considers the role that normative theory will play in shaping social policy. It examines the views of social policy scholars and contrasts optimistic and pessimistic scenarios. It concludes that social policy in the future will continue to reflect a pluralistic mix in which multiple agents will contribute to social well-being but that the role of the federal government will not be as significant as it was in the past. It also predicts that higher income groups will increasingly make use of commercial provisions and that social service programs catering to the poor and vulnerable will become increasingly meager and fragmented. However, it stresses that new ideas that may reinvigorate social welfare may emerge and significantly alter the prevailing situation.

32 International Aspects of Social Policy

Sheila B. Kamerman and Alfred J. Kahn

This chapter will focus on the ways in which international developments and institutions impinge on social policy developments within the United States. In an era of economic and social globalization, can social policy be purely national? The chapter argues that this was not the case in earlier eras, is not the case in the present, and is likely to be even less so in the future. Social policy can no longer be thought of in solely national terms in an economically and politically globalized economy.

Why the need to make the case? In the post–World War I euphoria about American economic and political leadership, and in reaction to the cynicism of Versailles as contrasted with the idealism of Wilson, strong isolationist themes appeared in the United States and were overcome only by the imperatives of World War II. The nation's economic and military achievements during the war, and subsequently, supported doctrines about a unique American character. That, and an underlying belief in the *specialness* of the history of this "first new nation" and in an American *exceptionalism*, tended to define the country as set apart and, to some, as morally superior (Lipset, 1963). We might export goods, technology, knowledge, and our experience with government, as we might import goods, styles, cultural materials and even workers, scholars, and performers. But large numbers of Americans doubted and still doubt that we have policy lessons to learn.

Let us look at the record.

The Earlier Record

Pre–Revolutionary War America was settled overwhelmingly by the English, and unsurprisingly, England's Poor Law set the main public pattern in the 17th and 18th centuries in the colonies and, later, in the states. Subsequently, during the 19th century, the country continued to be influenced by English and occasionally German and other continental developments through visitors and reports, as it experienced the transition to a wage economy as required by the Industrial Revolution and shared with Victorian England the problem of *taming* the exploding cities and their poverty populations (Boyer, 1978). Americans were much influenced by England as they developed public workhouses and private (church and nonsectarian) associations to help the poor, such as the Association for the Improvement of the Conditions of the Poor; provident societies; YMCAs and YWCAs; boys' and girls' clubs; and child protection agencies, as well as charity organization societies, settlement houses, and kindergartens. Le Play's studies of expenditures and budgets in Belgium in the mid-19th century, Booth's studies of the life and labor of the people of London between 1886 and 1907, and the later work of Rountree in York inspired and guided late 19th-century social problem and poverty studies, including the 1905 poverty report of Hunter in Chicago and the famous Pittsburgh Survey (Polansky, 1975). When American states began social insurance and labor legislation in the Progressive Era, they had reports of European developments in hand (Skocpol, 1992).

After World War I, when the United States became a more powerful nation, some social policy borrowing began to occur from America to Europe, west to east, in particular with regard to social work education and casework practice. Nonetheless, east-to-west borrowing continued to be dominant. Thus, for example, the Social Security Act of 1935 was clearly influenced by what had been developed in Europe, again with special attention to Germany and England and with American adaptations required by our federal system and the political strategies of President Franklin D. Roosevelt.

Post–World War II to the 1980s: The Shared Experiences of Modern Industrialized Societies

Following World War II, social policy learning and borrowing became increasingly active in both directions across the Atlantic. Although the experience of World War II was felt far more directly in Europe than in the United States and led to major new social policy initiatives in many countries, which set a standard that America has yet to achieve, subsequent experiences were far more likely to be shared.

Common demographic, economic, and technological trends have confronted all the advanced industrialized societies with similar challenges. For example, more than half of all births in the Scandinavian countries are now out of wedlock, as are more than one-third in Finland, France, and Britain. American rates are similar. Marriage rates in Europe are about half those in the United States, but so are divorce rates, although they are rising. Traditional families continue to decline in significance in Europe as in

America. Two-earner husband and wife families, reconstituted families, and families headed by cohabiting but not legally married couples now dominate the family environments in which children are reared. Yes, there are differences in female labor force participation rates, swings in fertility, differences in teen pregnancy rates, and different definitions of what some things (e.g., long-term stable cohabitation without marriage) signify. But important, even then, are the similar directions and challenges and the possibility of learning from differences. And some important differences (teen childbearing) occasion special interest and exploration. The advanced industrialized countries are a single demographic universe, and, thus, most must face similar issues.

The two most visible current illustrations are, first, the aging of the population while birthrates fall and, second, the rising rates of labor force participation among women with very young children. The industrial world is facing the shared issue of pension costs and pension financing while, at the other end of the age spectrum, because most mothers of infants, toddlers, and preschoolers are now in the paid labor force, there is the issue of what kind of early childhood care and education to provide, under what auspices to provide such care, how to finance this, how to staff such a program, and what curricular and program concepts to use.

On another front, all relatively rich and stable countries among the pluralistic democracies are the obvious destinations of asylum seekers, refugees, and immigrants from the poor, conflict-torn, authoritarian, underdeveloped, or transitional lands everywhere. Policies and programs in response are a high priority everywhere, even though the scale of the challenge, whether measured in sheer numbers or as a percentage of native population, varies considerably.

To move to another part of the policy spectrum, we refer to postsecondary education. Technological advances, the explosion of knowledge, and economic factors face countries with the issue of the normative levels of the education of youth. Whether out of concern for the quality of human capital with which it responds to economic challenges, out of a perspective on justice and equal opportunity, or with a view to preserve the country's cultural and civil traditions, each nation of the advanced industrialized world has been "churning" in this area: access, financial support to students and to higher education institutions, opportunities for advanced study and research, transitions into employment, and the nature of the core curriculum or whether there should be one.

There is no need to labor the point. Whatever the needs and differences of the developing and transitional worlds, there is considerable sharing of experiences in the advanced industrialized world and therefore considerable sharing of problems, issues, and tasks. And given the shared levels of education, research, and sophistication (despite historical, religious, and cultural differences) and the value systems of pluralistic democracies, it is hardly surprising that countries know about, consider, and sometimes adopt or adapt one another's solutions and innovations. In this context, the United States, for all of its economic and political power and the many areas of technology, science, and popular culture in which it is seen in a leadership role, is also a learner, a cooperator, a borrower, and a participant. For example, as we began to design child support legislation in the 1970s and to discuss family policy, we learned much from Europe, and at one point relatively recently, there was intensive examination of German apprenticeship programs in this country. Our thesis is that this is a growing, increasing, and inevitable process. Some of the mechanisms, vehicles, and pathways of the process merit attention.

The Mechanisms of Internationalization

Demonstration of Effects

We visit one another's countries as tourists, as professionals, as business people, as scholars, as exchange students, as members of delegations of one sort or another, or to retrace ancestral roots. Americans, who did most of the international visiting until relatively recently, discovered that their friends and colleagues were entitled to paid and job-protected leaves following childbirth, one-month and longer paid vacations from work, healthy and happy children in universal preschool programs, and health care that is readily available to all. None of this information exchange is formal or systematic, but it introduces a different world of other experiences and options, and it raises new issues for policy discussion.

The media, too, have facilitated more shared experiences. Television, in particular, has brought war, famine, floods, and earthquakes into the living rooms of Americans, Europeans, Asians, and others—and stimulated widespread concern about natural and man-made disasters. Societal responses, we hope, will also be far more immediate and personal than ever before.

Competitiveness

As professionals, scholars, or citizen consumers of the media, we are exposed to international rankings with regard to infant mortality, low birth weight, child inoculation rates, child poverty, literacy, reading-math-science scores, and rates of high school completion revealed in annual reports such as UNICEF's *The Progress of Nations* or *The State of the World's Children* and its Innocenti Research Center report cards, the United Nation's *Human Development Report,* and the World Bank's *World Development Report.* Some of these numbers instigate professional exploration, political action, and interest-group advocacy. We are distressed at our ranking 28th out of the 30 countries in the Organisation for Economic Co-operation and

Development (OECD) in infant mortality rates when all of our European counterparts and a mix of transitional economies and newly industrializing Asian countries rank ahead of us with significantly lower rates (UNICEF, 2006).

Mandates

The International Labour Organization, headquartered in Geneva, Switzerland, has a long history of setting norms, targets, and labor and industry standards, which have affected the United States along with the rest of the world. Conventions, agreements, and covenants adopted by the United Nations have had even more significant impacts. *The Economist* magazine noted in connection with the 50th anniversary of the Universal Declaration of Human Rights that the "world's central legal institution, the United Nations, was the brainchild of Franklin Roosevelt who began planning for it soon after the United States entered the war. His wife, Eleanor, was one of the prime movers behind the adoption of the Universal Declaration of Human Rights" ("World Law," 1998, p. 16).

But the United States public, in some instances, and its Congress, in others, do not readily accept and adopt international mandates, even when our citizens contribute substantially to their formulation. Traditionally, there has been suspicion of foreign involvement, and it can reach paranoid intensity under some circumstances. Moreover, unlike the many unitary parliamentary systems that find ratification of covenants relatively easier for parliamentary majorities, the United States federalism and our separation of powers offer a major obstacle course for all major covenants. For example, can the Senate provide all the assurances called for in the 1989 Convention on the Rights of the Child, given the preeminence of state law in most areas of family law, child welfare, and education?

Yet, the failure to ratify, often after signing, is not the whole story. What is also relevant is that these various internationally adopted instruments create international norms. Even where we are well in advance of world practice, as we are in many of these fields, such as the status of women, the covenants nonetheless are useful in some instances. Where we do not conform, reformers and advocates have a point of departure. The subject gets into public discussion. Sometimes it goes further. Commenting on the Universal Declaration of Human Rights, Wronka (1995) observes that "this document, which was originally meant to be hortatory, is increasingly referred to, at least in the United States, as 'customary international law'" (p. 1407). He buttresses his argument with a series of U.S. court decisions, including a finding against a military commander for torturing and murdering a Paraguan high school student. In short, without "authoritative legal status in the United States" the declaration "is beginning to substantively affect U.S. legal jurisprudence" (p. 1407).

The United States participates as well in many other United Nations' activities and projects, often initiatives of the General Assembly or the Economic and Social Council. The special "years" and "decades" dedicated to spotlighting the elderly, the handicapped, or children highlight policy and program issues often in the context of elaborate factual reporting and trend analysis as well as international comparisons. While the developing world is often in focus, the rich countries are not ignored—whether at the World Summit on Social Development (Denmark), the Beijing conference on women, or in other initiatives—or in the annual United Nations' reports on human development. Mandates and commitments aside, all of this keeps some United States issues visible and offers challenges—and rallying points—for leaders and advocates.

Collaboration

The United States plays a leading role in the Organisation for Economic Co-operation and Development (OECD), which has expanded to include 30 advanced, industrialized, pluralistic democracies. Although formally focused on economic policy, over the years, this organization has carried out projects, convened expert groups, and conducted ministerial level inter-governmental meetings with regard to female labor force participation, child care, aging, lone-mother families, income transfers, work training, youth policy, education at all levels, tax policy, urban policy, and various interrelationships among these. The rationales have stressed the relation-ships of various of these arenas, and others, to a conception of an active "labor market" policy or to equal opportunity, or technological progress, or human capital investment—and even to pension finance.

In fact, in the past several years, concerned about pension financing under almost universally experienced population aging, OECD has pro-moted, among other things, facilitating female labor force participation through adequate child-care policy, thus improving the ratio of currently employed workers to retirees.

OECD's regular data series (including expenditure and tax data and var-ious social indicators), its annual national accounts reports, the analyses of the tax situations of "average" worker families in different countries—as well as the conferences and project reports—play an important role in dis-seminating valuable information to public officials in all countries. Although the organization is not as visible to the media as is the UN, and although public officials and civil servants in all countries—especially in the executive branch—who are exposed to it rather than the public at large, it is extraor-dinarily successful in creating an ongoing international conversation about critical issues in economic and social policy. For example, see the following OECD publications *Family, Market, and Community: Equity and Efficiency in Social Policy* or *Starting Strong: Early Childhood Education and Care,*

2001–2006 or *Babies and Bosses, 2002–2007*, a five-volume description, assessment, and analysis of family-friendly child and family policies focused on the reconciliation of work and family life in more than a dozen member countries.

One could wish for more congressional exposure as well. None of this is to ignore the neoliberal slant of OECD, the considerable American and British influence, especially during the restructuring of the 1980s and 1990s, but in the spirit of balanced debate and eclectic policy making, and in appreciation of international exchange, one must value this organization, which exposes the United States to world developments, thinking, and viewpoints about country opportunities. Indeed, in some sense, each of the sources of information and exchange is controversial for some Americans, but the sum total of interactions means that we are hardly alone in thinking about our social policies.

Cross-National Research and Societal Learning

We here offer a personal illustration of learning from other countries. Although, in our own professional careers we have been involved with all of the above from time to time and in varied capacities, our own efforts at systematic contributions to the domestic social policy debate from the broader international experience have taken the form of a cross-national research program that parallels and feeds into our United States policy research and activity. We realized long ago that one can no more develop a full perspective on policy systems and policy substance by studying policy in one country than a clinician can conceive and elaborate a personality theory if limited to one case. The political science answer is the comparative study. The world is an arena of natural experiments.

For over 30 years, we have conducted studies of social policy issues, many in child and family policy, encompassing income transfers (cash and tax benefits), employment-related policies (maternity and parental leaves), and personal social services—all with a view toward enriching the policy debate in the United States. Because of the objective of immediate relevance, most of this work has been in the advanced industrialized world, much of it in Europe, but recently it has covered some developing countries as well. We have been concerned more with understanding the consequences of policies for families, children, and, sometimes, the community and the work environment than with accounting for country choices, but that, too, has sometimes been the question. We understand that policies must fit into the cultural, societal, and political context and therefore are often not directly transferable, but we see the value of enriching and elaborating the option menus in fields in which the United States *needs to act* (Kamerman & Kahn, 1995).

At one time, we were pioneers and among the few with such preoccupations. More recently, as Europe has organized itself more formally and, then, as what are called the *countries in transition* entered the picture, such work became more popular and has been systematized and expanded, as we note below.

First, to clarify, we offer some personal illustrations. Our studies in the industrial world, from the 1970s to those currently under way, have been concerned with various topics. We have asked what types of policies and programs have been developed in western and northern Europe on behalf of typical families, not for the poor alone (Kahn & Kamerman, 1975). We have also examined the issue of whether governments deliberately or implicitly undertake to develop family policy and, if so, in what domains and how (Kamerman & Kahn, 1978). Another issue has been how personal social services are organized and delivered in industrial societies. This study included a look at socialist Europe, which had labeled social work a capitalist instrument (Kahn & Kamerman, 1980). We have also examined international experiences with child care services and family benefits as alternatives or possibly complementary strategies for coping with family needs when both parents (or a single parent) work (Kamerman & Kahn, 1981). Our research has also focused on how public (social) assistance fits into a full income maintenance and tax package in helping families at different earnings levels (or without earnings) and how generous income transfers are elsewhere as compared with those in the United States (Kahn & Kamerman, 1983). We have questioned how countries cope with the child support question when parents separate and divorce and whether advance maintenance (government support guarantees or child support assurance) is a successful program when the noncustodial parent does not contribute (Kahn & Kamerman, 1988). Another issue is what the experience with more extended parental leaves is and how such leaves affect child care policies, maternal labor force participation, and child-conditioned income transfer packages (Kamerman & Kahn, 1991). We asked what the policy options are for responding to the needs and problems of lone mothers and their children, as seen in the European experience (Kamerman & Kahn, 1988). Finally, we have speculated on what the United States can learn about "starting right" in the rearing of its youngest children from countries with exemplar programs and policies relating to income, time, and services (Kamerman & Kahn, 1995).

Of course, the study and report writing are only a beginning. Contributions to domestic programs and policy require dissemination, education, and advocacy. Impact, if any, can be limited and slow.

Major Current Vehicles

Interchange, cross-national contacts, and collaboration are at all-time highs, and data about other parts of the world, particularly the industrial world, are more available in more systematic form than ever. This is inevitable given the technology of the information age and the great values recently placed on national and international transparency with regard to the economy, the polity, health, and human rights.

In our brief sketch, we note, first, that, where once there was little European interest in cross-national policy research and data collection, the European Community, now the European Union (EU), began, as it grew, to attend to child-care services and family policy. Although not formally in the EU's "competence," such social policy issues as parental leave and child care are relevant to its concerns with regard to the labor force and the status of women. A European Child Care Observatory with country reporters and, later, a European Observatory on Poverty and a European Family Observatory, similarly structured, have provided annual updates on developments in member countries as well as special reports on topics of general interest. (The European Child Care Observatory has been discontinued and the European Poverty Observatory has been replaced by a European Observatory on Social Exclusion.) A growing system of statistics and social indicators out of Eurostat enriches the picture of demography, programs, expenditures and various aspects of policy. What is more, the growth of the European Union and the fall of the east–west wall stimulated a rich array of cross-national research by European scholars, where once interest was limited. We might mention studies of poverty and social exclusion, child support, social assistance, lone mothers, and the workforce.

In brief, there is now a significant body of information and evaluated experience for cross-national learning and stimulation. On a smaller scale, but with much interest in family policy, there is also relevant output from the Council of Europe.

By now, the two-way flow is extensive. There are visiting scholars at universities and think tanks, often at work on cross-national issues and always available to clarify developments in their own countries. The major learned societies and professional groups are an active arena of shared and joint learning. We might cite the long-term deliberations and projects related to poverty of the International Sociological Association; the family policy, divorce, child support, and other deliberations of the International Society of Family Law; and the range of topical themes at the International Council on Social Welfare.

Associated with international and learned societies and associations, but also independent of them, is an extraordinary roster of international journals covering the fields under discussion. Indeed, the proliferation poses both a cost problem for libraries and a time challenge for interested policy scholars and officials.

A major international collaboration with very strong American presence, the Luxembourg Income Study, has not only built up an extensive micro database over the past two decades, which includes data from 25 modern industrialized states, but also perfected the adaptations to ensure comparability and supplied the associated institutional and program information that permits the most extensive comparative studies of poverty, family income packages by family type, and specific income-related policy questions. Researchers all over the world are supplied with disks of constantly updated data and codes. Summer conferences and workshops provide the occasion for exchange and for training young scholars. A parallel program, the Luxembourg Employment Study, is now being implemented as well. All these research initiatives now have rich Web sites as well that provide current information about important policy-relevant developments.

Knowing about other countries is not any longer a monopoly of scholars, specialists, public officials, or travelers. The media have discovered aspects of social policy on which they can report to interested audiences, whether in the daily press, general magazines, or on television and radio. The casual reader or audience member learns about welfare, social security, health systems, child care, or parental leaves, sometimes in sophisticated coverage and, at other times, in oversimplified and brief presentations.

Globalization and the Impact on Social Policy

Globalization is the current buzzword used to describe the growing internationalization of the production of goods, services, and the flow of capital. Economists, political scientists, sociologists, area specialists, and policy analysts are discussing the world economy and the implications of global economic developments for the future of social policy (Clayton & Pontusson, 1997; Cohen, 1998; Daly, 1998; Garrett, 1997; Pierson, 1994, 1995; Taylor-Gooby, 2004). There is a debate regarding whether globalization applies only to the changes occurring to the world economy as national economies are internationalized or whether it applies as well to current changes in political, social, and cultural institutions. Despite widespread agreement that worldwide competition means that economies with high wage costs will lose jobs to those with cheaper labor, there continues to be debate as well about whether such job loss is limited to unskilled work; whether, ultimately, it is good or bad for national economies; whether it will affect the composition of the wage package or just the overall size; and whether a "race to the bottom" among welfare states will follow, reducing wages and cutting social expenditures. Most important, there is a debate regarding the overall process of globalization, whether it is the cause of welfare state retrenchment and whether it will lead to high rates of dependency either on unemployment benefits or social assistance or both, thereby raising social expenditures, reducing social security contributions, and leading to cuts in benefits and services. The ultimate concern for many is how will these developments affect social policy?

There are many who believe that globalization is ultimately a positive process, even though they see the difficulties it creates. Difficulties may include, for example, jobs migrating from high-wage and high-benefit countries to

low-wage and low-benefit labor markets, country budgets and economic policies being undercut by currency speculation and developments in world equity
and bond markets, and precious aspects of national identity being eroded.
Others are much concerned about the impacts on population. As the president
of the Washington-based Economic Policy Institute observed,

> The mobility of private capital has now outstripped the capacity of
> governments and international agencies to keep markets from self-
> destructing or to shield their people from the brutal consequences. One
> result . . . is a rising hostility to globalization. A precondition to any
> solution is the building of institutions and policies that serve the inter-
> ests of the world's workers. (Faux, 1998, p. 1)

Even *The Economist* magazine, a proponent of the free market, commented, in noting the unexpected problems generated in the East Asian
economies and by the recklessness of hedge funds, that "the idea of globalization as irreversible inevitably will face stiff challenges" ("Human Rights,"
1998, p. 16).

Whichever the correct assessment of globalization, there is no denying
that, for the advanced industrialized societies, there are now shared policy
agendas with answers to be discovered by joint learning, learning from one
another, exchange and consensus, and through experience. We can debate
about contours and likely governance, but—to shift the metaphor—we are
in the same boat. A potentially helpful process is under way, but it will be
a hesitant one because countries are not sure whether to trust it and how
far. But they need to understand it together.

Societal learning is no longer a question of east–west learning or of trans-
Atlantic two-way learning. Instead, it is an issue of shared experiences and
problems and the need to work together to participate in the development of
policy and program responses. Social policy can no longer be purely national;
it requires international or regional or multinational initiatives. It involves
countries working together to respond to the same or similar challenges.

To illustrate: A June 1998 Stockholm meeting on pension policy jointly
sponsored by the Swedish government and the International Social Security
Association, one in a series, capped a consultative process and drew on a
specially commissioned study (Thompson, 1998). The sessions probed a
series of social security, public pension, and private pension models for the
future, as these were evolving in Europe, North America, Central and South
America, and East Asia in the light of economic and demographic developments. In a context of sophisticated understanding of the consequences of
free international markets, it was possible to examine the known advantages and caveats for systems based on advance funding, individual
accounts, and public management, with special attention to what can be
said about pension impacts on the economy. The meeting's purpose was put
by the organizers on these terms: "to assist policy makers and social security

organizations throughout the world to understand the issues, to widen the debate on the future of social security, and to chose alternatives best suited to their circumstances" (International Social Security Association, 1998).

For a second illustration, from 2001 to 2006, the OECD carried out a 20-country review of early childhood education and care (ECEC) policies and programs, exploring why countries are increasingly interested in the subject and what can be learned from the experiences of different industrialized countries (OECD, 2001–2006). The study was carried out by teams of international and national experts and scholars and covered the economic and demographic contextual factors driving these policies as well as the major policy developments and lessons learned from the other countries. The review culminated in an international conference and a two-volume report. The major conclusion was the importance of universal ECEC programs for children's education and well-being and the importance of integrating child care and early childhood education into one early childhood system.

A third illustration is the multiyear and multicountry OECD (2002–2007) study of "family friendly" child and family policies, a study that targets the reconciliation of work and family life. Family friendly policies are those policies that facilitate the reconciliation of work and family life by ensuring the adequacy of family resources, enhancing child development, facilitating parental choice about work and care, and promoting gender equality in employment opportunities (OECD, 2002–2007). The specific policies include parental leaves; affordable, decent quality ECEC; child-conditioned income transfers; and flexible work schedules.

There is also reverse learning occurring, from South and Central American countries to North America. An interesting example is the child-conditioned cash income transfer program. These conditional cash transfers (CCTs) developed first in Mexico and are now established in about half the Latin American countries (Kamerman & Gatenio-Gabel, 2007). CCTs are cash benefits provided monthly to families with young children, contingent on the children being enrolled in and attending school and the parents obtaining regular free health checkups for the children and other family members. The objective is to reduce income poverty and to increase human capital by expanding children's access to education and health care. In April 2007, New York City's Mayor Michael Bloomberg announced the launch of a CCT pilot program called Opportunity NYC, the first such program launched in the United States and modeled after the Mexican program.

There are parallel undertakings under way in many fields related to child and family policy, such as early child care and education or youth training and education; and there is shared work on needed technologies and data systems, such as childhood social indicators and poverty measures. In addition, there are studies of the impacts of these policies on children's well-being (Kamerman, Neuman, Waldfogel, & Brooks-Gunn, 2003).

Therefore, in conclusion, the answer to our original question is that, early on, the United States learned and borrowed from others. Later on, it continued to learn and borrow, but it also provided opportunities for others to learn and promoted initiatives that others borrowed from too. Now, we all learn and borrow, sometimes from one another but more often as part of the same global pool of knowledge, experience, and ongoing exploration. Social policy is a shared arena.

References

Boyer, P. (1978). *Urban masses and moral order in America, 1820-1920.* Cambridge, MA: Harvard University Press.

Clayton, R., & Pontusson, J. (1997). *Welfare retrenchment and public sector restructuring in advanced capitalist societies.* Ithaca, NY: Cornell University, Department of Government.

Cohen, D. (1998). *The wealth of the world and the poverty of nations.* Cambridge: MIT Press.

Daly, M. (1998, July). *Globalization and Bismarkian welfare states,* Paper presented at the Conference on Globalization and Social Policy, Lincoln, England.

Faux, J. (1998). Fools rush in: Unfettered global finance threatens prosperity at home and abroad. *Economic Policy Institute Journal,* p. 1.

Garrrett, G. (1997). *Partisan politics in a global economy.* New York: Cambridge University Press.

Human rights law survey [Special section]. (1998, December 5). *The Economist,* pp. 3–16.

International Social Security Association. (1998). *The Future of Social Security: The Stockholm Conference, June 29- July 1, 1998* [Meeting Announcement]. Somerset, NJ: Transaction.

Kahn, A. J., & Kamerman, S. B. (1975). *Not for the poor alone: Social services in Europe.* Philadelphia: Temple University Press.

Kahn, A. J., & Kamerman, S. B. (1980). *Social services in international perspective.* Rutgers, NJ: Transaction Books. (Reprinted from 1977 report published by U.S. Government Printing Office)

Kahn, A. J., & Kamerman, S. B. (1983). *Income transfers for families with children: An eight-country study.* Philadelphia: Temple University Press.

Kahn, A. J., & Kamerman, S. B. (Eds.). (1988). *Child support: From debt collection to social policy.* Beverly Hills, CA: Sage.

Kamerman, S. B., & Gatenio-Gabel, S. (2007). Social protection for children and their families: A global overview. In A. Minujin & E. Delamonica (Eds.), *Social protection initiatives for women, children, and their families.* New York: New School University.

Kamerman, S. B., & Kahn, A. J. (Eds.). (1978). *Family policy: Government and families in fourteen countries.* New York: Columbia University Press.

Kamerman, S. B., & Kahn, A. J. (1981). *Child care, family benefits and working parents: A study in comparative family policy analysis.* New York: Columbia University Press.

Kamerman, S. B., & Kahn, A. J. (1988). *Mothers alone: Strategies for a time of change.* Dover, MA: Auburn House.

Kamerman, S. B., & Kahn, A. J. (Eds.). (1991). *Child care, parental leave, and the under 3s: Policy innovation in Europe.* Westport, CT: Greenwood.

Kamerman, S. B., & Kahn, A. J. (1995). *Starting right: How America neglects its youngest children and what we can do about it.* New York: Oxford University Press.

Kamerman, S. B., Neuman, M., Waldfogel, J., & Brooks-Gunn, J. (2003). *Social policies, family types, and child outcomes in selected OECD countries* (OECD Social, Employment and Migration Working Paper No. 6). Paris: Organisation for Economic Co-operation and Development.

Lipset, S. M. (1963). *The first new nation.* New York: Basic Books.

OECD (Organisation for Economic Co-operation and Development). (1997). *Family, market, and community: Equity and efficiency in social policy.* Paris: Author.

OECD (Organisation for Economic Co-operation and Development). (2001–2006). *Starting strong: Early childhood education and care* (Vols. 1–2). Paris: Author.

OECD (Organisation for Economic Co-operation and Development). (2002–2007). *Babies and bosses: Reconciling work and family life* (Vols. 1–5). Paris: Author.

Pierson, P. (1994). *Dismantling the welfare state.* New York: Cambridge University Press.

Pierson, P. (1995). *The new politics of the welfare state* (Working Paper No. 3/95). Bremen, Germany: Center for Social Policy Research, University of Bremen.

Polansky, N. (Ed.). (1975). *Social work research.* Chicago: University of Chicago Press.

Skocpol, T. (1992). *Protecting soldiers and mothers: The political origins of social policy in the United States.* Cambridge, MA: Harvard University Press.

Taylor-Gooby, P. (2004). *New risks, new welfare: The transformation of the European welfare state.* Oxford, UK: Oxford University Press.

Thompson, L. (1998). *Older and wiser: The economics of public pensions.* Washington, DC: Urban Institute.

UNICEF. (2006). *State of the world's children, 2007.* New York: Author.

World law and world power. (1998, December 5). *The Economist,* p. 16.

Wronka, J. (1995). Human rights. In R. L. Edwards & J. G. Hopps (Eds.), *Encyclopedia of social work* (19th ed., Vol. 2, pp. 1405–1418). Washington, DC: NASW Press.

33

The Future
of Social Policy

James Midgley and Michelle Livermore

I n seeking to provide a comprehensive overview of American social policy, the authors of this book have addressed many diverse aspects of the social welfare field. They have dealt with the nature of social policy and the policy-making process, the history of social policy, the political economy of social policy, and social policy and the social services. By covering a wide field, the book's authors have sought to provide a state of the art account of American social policy at the beginning of the 21st century.

As social policy faces the challenges of a new century, it is appropriate that some tentative, speculative comments on its future direction be made. However, social policy is subject to many complex influences and events, so it is extremely difficult to predict future trends. As is well known, social scientists' attempts to discern the future have not been very successful. Nevertheless, some of the factors that will affect social policy development in the years to come can be identified. These include demographic, economic, cultural, and political factors, among others. By examining these factors, it may be possible to glimpse the future of social policy.

The task is complicated by the fact that the policy-making process is subject not only to the forces of economics, demography, cultural change, and electoral politics but also to beliefs and ideologies that offer very different prescriptions for the future direction of social welfare. These factors exert an indirect but powerful influence on social policy makers. Although social policy is often regarded as a technical process in which rational policy makers identify problems and dispassionately formulate cost-effective solutions, they are influenced by ideologies as well as wider economic, demographic, political, and other forces.

An understanding of these forces is relevant to any attempt to speculate on the future of social policy in the United States. As this brief chapter endeavors to show, many complex factors will shape and determine social policy's future trajectory. It will also show that social policy commentators have reached different conclusions about these factors and their effects on the future of social policy. Generally, their opinions tend to be either pessimistic or optimistic. Since the 1980s, liberal scholars have tended to take a pessimistic view about the future of social policy while those on the political right have been more optimistic, claiming that the changes introduced over the last two decades have reduced the role of government and encouraged greater personal responsibility in social welfare. On the other hand, there is some agreement about the role of economic, demographic, cultural, and political factors in shaping future trends. These trends, the role of ideologies and normative theories, and the views of social policy commentators about their importance are essential in attempting to discern the future of social policy.

Forces of Change and Social Policy

Economic factors are obviously very influential in determining current and future social policy events. Significant and often dramatic economic changes have certainly shaped the evolution of social policy in the past. This has been particularly evident in times of economic difficulty. As was shown in Chapter 9 of this book, the Great Depression created pressing social needs that exerted pressures on government to respond. Similarly, the economic difficulties of the 1970s, which were associated with high inflation and unemployment, contributed to the redirection of social policy thinking in the 1980s. By blaming economic difficulties on social expenditures, conservative thinkers legitimated the retrenchment of social programs and, many commentators believe, redirected the social policy trajectory from one of incremental expansion to one of containment if not retrenchment.

The economic boom of the late 1990s created a very different climate for social policy. With prosperity and a balanced budget, the alarmist claims of conservatives about the economic and fiscal problems created by social service expenditures lost credibility. The Clinton administration had managed to balance the budget, and, despite significant shifts in welfare thinking and pressures to partially privatize Social Security, various social programs expanded, including the Earned Income Tax Credit (EITC), child care, and the state-managed health insurance program for children of low-income families. Despite the termination of the Aid to Families with Dependent Children program and the sharp decline in AFDC expenditures, the expansion of the EITC in the 1990s resulted is a sizable increase in public wage subsidies. In 1990, the program cost approximately $7.5 billion. By the end of the decade, its cost had risen to approximately $30 billion (Hoffman & Seidman, 2003).

Faced with a sharp economic downturn in the wake of the tragedy of September 11, 2001, the Bush administration did not seriously retrench social service budgets even though the federal government again accumulated a sizable budgetary deficit that was hugely exacerbated by the invasion of Iraq in 2003. Despite criticisms from traditional conservatives who decried the administration's profligate spending, the social services were not subjected to the same threats of budgetary retrenchment as during the Reagan years. However, this did not mean that the Bush administration approved of state welfare. On the contrary, a major initiative to promote faith-based social services was launched by the White House shortly after George W. Bush's election in 2000 (Bartokowski & Regis, 2003; DiIulio, 2007; Kuo, 2006), and efforts to partially privatize Social Security redoubled during his years in office. In addition, the president's decision, in October 2007, to veto two bills designed to extend the Children's Health Insurance Program attracted widespread condemnation. In these and other cases, opposition to state welfare was not driven primarily by budgetary but by ideological considerations.

Nevertheless, the Bush administration has bequeathed a major budgetary deficit that will in all likelihood require fiscal austerity to remedy in the future. It is also likely that the challenge of balancing the federal budget will again invoke calls for the retrenchment of the social services. The severity of future fiscal retrenchment will, of course, depend on the health of the economy. If the economy continues to enjoy steady rates of growth since recovering from the post–September 11 recession, the challenge of balancing the budget may not be all that great. On the other hand, if economic conditions worsen, the prospect of balancing the budget in the near future may be slim. In addition, the vast recurrent costs of the occupation of Iraq will present a major challenge.

At the time of writing, economic growth had for many years been steady, and confidence in the economy, as revealed in stock market activity, had been strong. However, in early 2008, stock values fell sharply as it became increasingly apparent that many Americans who had purchased homes with subprime credit faced serious financial problems. The number of home foreclosures increased rapidly, and, although the unemployment rate remained relatively low at about 5%, anxieties about the health of the economy grew. In addition, these events mirrored wider economic concerns about the comparatively low value of the dollar, the trade deficit, and the continued inflow into the United States of low-cost consumer goods, particularly from Asian producers. These factors continue to pose a major challenge to the manufacturing sector, which has found it increasingly difficult to compete in a global economy. In addition, many manufacturers have employed strategies of relocation and outsourcing, which have placed downward pressure on domestic wages.

The intensification of economic globalization is likely to exert a significant influence on the future of American social policy. With its relatively open economy and a commitment to international trade among many political and business leaders, the United States is particularly exposed to these forces. This is not to deny that the federal government continues to protect certain sectors of the economy, particularly agriculture, from international competition, but it is likely that the manufacturing sector, which had previously created steady and remunerative employment opportunities, will continue to shrink and that the proportion of workers employed in comparatively well-paid blue-collar jobs will further decline.

Whether the traditional services sector and the expanding financial services sector can provide the same opportunities for millions of Americans to enjoy a good standard of living is questionable. The services sector is characterized by low-wage employment while the economically buoyant financial services sector has created well-paid employment opportunities for more highly educated workers. Indeed, the expansion of high-end employment opportunities and the stagnation of wages for unskilled workers have been identified as major reasons for the extraordinarily high rates of inequality that characterize income distribution in the United States.

The economic changes that have taken place with deindustrialization have significantly altered employment and income patterns in the United States. Obviously, as low-wage employment persists, poverty will remain an ever-present reality. Similarly, the proportion of the population in steady, lifetime employment is likely to decline. Indeed, increasing numbers of workers now cycle between jobs, and a growing number are also self-employed. These structural changes will continue to have significant implications for social policy in the future. Also relevant is the impact of information technology. Economic activities have been transformed through the information revolution and the advent of computers and other technologies, which have had a major impact on productivity and economic growth. It is clear that productive employment and self-employment will increasingly require skills and expertise suited to the utilization of these technologies and an understanding of the importance of information in society today.

Although economic globalization is often portrayed in the social science literature as a naturally occurring set of processes that are unresponsive to government regulation, governments are able to influence international economic activities through trade agreements, tariffs, control over currencies, and, indeed, through exerting political influence on multilateral international bodies such as the International Monetary Fund (IMF) and the World Bank. The extent to which the processes of globalization can be directed to promote social well-being at the domestic level thus reflects the influence that the government is able to exert and the extent to which it desires to shape global economic forces for the benefit of its citizens.

With regard to the former, the belief that the United States is the world's only superpower and that it exerts unrivaled economic, political, and military influence—which was so fervently advocated by neoconservative intellectuals in the 1990s (Midgley, 2007)—is now greeted with skepticism in view of the disastrous consequences of the invasion of Iraq and the emerging economic and political power of nations such as China, India, and Brazil, among others. On the other hand, the government of the United States is still able to exercise considerable international influence. In addition, opportunities for increased multilateral action through international cooperation are also available. It is possible that the pressing problems of poverty and deprivation that characterize the lives of millions of people around the world may be addressed if wise and committed leaders choose to foster a truly global perspective on social policy (Deacon, 2007). A perspective of this kind will have positive benefits not only for the world's citizens but for the citizens of the United States as well.

Demographic factors will continue to play an important role in shaping social policy in the future. Of these, the aging of the population is perhaps the most significant. It is generally recognized that, as the population continues to age, pressure for enhanced services will increase. In addition, population aging is widely believed to be creating pressures on the Social Security retirement program, which will soon result in a major fiscal crisis. Claiming that the Social Security system is unsustainable, critics have called for the current government-run program to be replaced with commercially managed individual retirement accounts. As a first step, advocates of privatization have urged that a portion of the payroll contribution be diverted to these accounts. On the other hand, it has also been claimed that the program is indeed sustainable provided that incremental adjustments to contribution rates and benefit levels are made. Another factor, which is relevant to an analysis of the effects of population aging on social policy, is the likelihood of people over the age of 65 years continuing to work. If real labor shortages occur, incentives to encourage some form of employment among elderly people may well be widely used.

Immigration will also affect social policy in the future. A proportion of immigrants are highly skilled workers whose expertise is sought after by employers, but many are unskilled, undocumented workers engaged in low-wage employment. Despite stringent immigration controls, the numbers of undocumented immigrants has risen steadily. Although immigrants do not place major demands on the social services, it is likely that social policy making will need to respond to their needs and to the increased cultural diversity of American society. The influence of increased diversity and the need to offer responsive services are already being felt in many fields, especially in education and health care.

The population of the United States will continue to diversify as many new immigrant groups with different cultures become established not only in the major metropolitan areas but in many other parts of the country as well. The traditional approach to cultural diversity, which identified two or three major ethnic groups, has now been compounded by the addition of many more distinctive cultural groupings with links to many different parts of the world. An awareness of the multicultural realities of contemporary American society is now more frequently reflected in social policy discourse.

Social policy debates have increasingly focused on multicultural issues, and, in addition to being more aware of racial and ethnic diversity, the field is increasingly cognizant of issues of gender and sexual orientation.

These developments have been characterized by some social policy scholars as reflecting the realities of a new postmodern era in which the values and ideals of Enlightenment modernism—as exemplified by a belief in rationalism and progress, the acceptance of encompassing ideologies, and strong, centralized government—are giving way to decentralization, fragmentation, and localism. They contend that issues of ethnicity, gender, religious belief, and traditionalism are becoming more important than the grand ideologies of modernist thought and that mass consumerism has become a dominant cultural and economic preoccupation. Today, they believe that people are increasingly cynical about the possibility of progress and that fewer participate in the political process.

This interpretation of current social and cultural realities has enjoyed some popularity, and more social policy scholars today are persuaded that the emergence of a postmodern culture will significantly influence the future of social policy. In addition to according a far more important role to gender, ethnicity, culture, sexual orientation, and other expressions of identity, social policy making is likely to become more decentralized and receptive to localism. The grand normative theories of social welfare that previously found expression in all encompassing federal legislative and administrative actions are likely to be undermined by local and state initiatives. Indeed, with the enactment of the 1996 welfare reform legislation, decentralization is now well established, and its effects will be felt even more strongly as federal funding for state and local social services continues to decline.

Current postmodern social and culture realities are also characterized by a tendency toward depoliticization and a lack of interest in major ideological controversies. There is evidence that people today are more influenced by consumerism and popular culture than by ideological and political issues. They are also increasingly focused on local rather than national and international events. Additionally, electoral turnout has declined, and political campaigns are increasingly targeted at the relatively small proportion of the people who actually vote. Generally, those who vote are disproportionately white, middle class, suburban and conservative. The changing nature of electoral politics now influences political decision making to a significant extent. These realities were evident in the congressional election of 1994 when the Republican Party secured a substantial majority in Congress and again in the 2004 presidential election when a relatively small proportion of the electorate decided in favor of George W. Bush. Electoral realities of this kind are obviously important in determining the future of social policy. However, the role of political factors can be overstated, and as experience has shown, electoral politics can be mercurial. In addition, the political process is governed not only by the voting strength of parties but also by popular opinion, the influence of the media, and, of course, by wider economic and social forces.

Changing electoral realities, the media, and public opinion also play key roles in shaping social policy. Media messages that oversimplify complex social issues but appeal to middle-class people can have a powerful effect on policy makers. For example, media images about welfare and crime have been used effectively in national elections and have created pressure on policy makers to adopt increasing punitive positions. Today, few politicians will openly oppose the death penalty, mandatory imprisonment for minor drug offenses, or other stringent penal measures that have a major impact on social policy. The future direction of social policy will be significantly influenced by these electoral realities and by the way social welfare services are presented in the media and perceived by those who exert electoral influence of the political process. Just as progressive social policy making previously depended on the labor movement for support, current social policy increasingly depends on and is determined by middle-class preferences.

The Role of Ideologies and Normative Social Policy Theories

In addition to the demographic, economic, cultural, electoral, and other forces that will shape the future of social policy, ideological beliefs and normative social welfare theories are also important influences. As was shown in Part II of this book on the history of social policy, ideological beliefs have exerted a powerful influence on the way social policies have evolved over the years. The social policies that were adopted at the time of the New Deal drew on collectivist ideology to offer a coherent, normative theory that legitimated extensive government intervention in social welfare. Ideological beliefs played an equally important role in shaping the social policy changes introduced during the Reagan era. Not imbued with the collectivism of the New Deal, these policies gave expression to the values and ideals of individualism. Clearly, attempts to discern the future trajectory of social policy must pay attention to the way ideologies and normative theories appeal to policy makers, interest groups, and the public at large.

For many years, social policy debates were characterized by juxtaposing institutionalism versus residualism as opposing normative social welfare choices. The New Deal legitimated institutionalist thinking, but, as many social policy scholars have shown, institutionalism never directed social policy in the United States to the extent that it did in Europe. Although many hoped that institutional ideas would be adopted and that social policy in the United States would evolve incrementally and conform to the European model, the Reagan era effectively challenged this vision and instead advocated a radical return to the residualism of the 19th century.

However, if it had been fully implemented, the shift toward residualism would have resulted in a massive curtailment of government involvement in social welfare and reduced the role of the state to one of providing limited assistance to the most desperately needy. But this goal was never realized. Although the social services were retrenched, a more fragmented, pluralist system of provision emerged, rather than a truly residualist "Poor Law state." As shown in Chapter 15 on welfare pluralism, privatization did not significantly reduce government involvement but instead resulted in widespread contracting with private providers. Contrary to the residualist tenet of reducing social expenditures to a bare minimum, the state has continued to meet the costs of social provision. The new pluralism not only sustained the nonprofit sector but also created a new commercial welfare industry that has reaped significant profits in fields as diverse as elder care, corrections, and child welfare.

Social policy during the Clinton era gave expression to welfare pluralism. Although New Democrat policy strategists at the Progressive Policy Institute and elsewhere sought to formulate a coherent approach to social policy that could inform the Clinton administration's agenda, David Stoesz (1996) has shown that they did not succeed in forging a new social policy paradigm. Instead, social policy under the Clinton administration may be viewed primarily as an eclectic reaction to the more coherent agenda of the Right and an attempt to respond to its electoral challenge. Despite the influence of communitarian and "Third Way" ideas on the Clinton administration, its approach was essentially eclectic and pluralistic. Indeed, both communitarianism and Third Way thinking are expressions of ideological centrism and compatible with the welfare pluralism of the Clinton presidency.

Although welfare pluralism was institutionalized under the Clinton administration, alternative normative perspectives were vigorously advocated by scholars on the political right. The Republican majority in Congress under House Speaker Newt Gingrich attacked the alleged welfare statism of the Clinton administration and promised to introduce social policies that would replace the welfare state with the "opportunity society" (Gingrich, 1995). It was in this context that the new paternalism of Lawrence Mead (1986, 1997) and his colleagues informed the Republican alternative to the Clinton administration's welfare reform efforts. The eclecticism and pluralism that characterize the original Clinton legislation was replaced with the dogmatic advocacy of a work first model, and it was with reluctance, and the resignation of key social policy advisors, that the President signed the Temporary Assistance for Needy Families (TANF) program into law in 1996. The Clinton administration also faced intense pressures from commercial and political interests to partially privatize Social Security. Although the president fended off the Social Security privatization campaign, it seemed that the initiative lay with the advocates of privatization and that the Clinton administration's position was essentially defensive.

The Bush administration moved quickly to implement a more coherent social policy approach which, as was shown earlier, was marked by the introduction of the faith-based initiative. This development represented a significant shift in normative social policy thinking. Based on the writings of Marvin Olasky (1992, 1996), the Bush administration argued that the churches and religious charities are more able to respond to social needs and social problems than the government, which, because of its bureaucratic nature, unresponsiveness, and wastage, was unable to implement the "compassionate conservative" agenda. Despite the appeal of this argument, the creation of a new office of faith-based services in the White House was controversial, and disputes soon arose about the allocation of resources to faith-based social agencies (DiIulio, 2007). It was alleged that evangelical Protestant religious groups were disproportionately favored and that the welfare activities of the black churches as well as non-Christian religious groups were neglected. Nevertheless, the faith-based initiative revealed an ability on the part of the political right to offer coherent normative alternatives to both the institutionalist welfare statism of the New Deal and the welfare pluralism of the Clinton era.

Similarly, the campaign to partially privatize Social Security was vigorously pursued by the Bush administration and only failed because of the stock market collapse after September 11, the high costs of the Iraq invasion, and the reluctance of Republican representatives to support the president's initiative for electoral reasons. However, the administration's single-minded ideological commitment to privatization and its effective communication of messages about the alleged unsustainability of Social Security have created a climate that will nurture future privatization endeavors.

The formulation of innovative and clearly articulated normative perspectives on social policy by the political right poses a challenge to the prevailing welfare pluralist system. It may be argued that the adoption of behavioral regulationist policies in the TANF program is indicative of a shift toward an increasingly punitive and controlling social policy regime. On the other hand, it may be claimed that the vigorous advocacy of the partial privatization of the Social Security system is indicative of a shift away from welfare pluralism toward welfare consumerism. It may also be argued that the new emphasis on faith-based social welfare is indicative of a shift toward traditionalism in social policy. But while these normative perspectives and their popularity during the Bush administration's time in office exerted considerable influence, social policy in the United States remains essentially pluralist. However, the future trajectory of social policy will depend on the extent to which the prevailing pluralist regime can be shaped and influenced by market, regulationist, or traditionalist ideologies or on whether it will sustain a viable equilibrium between institutionalism and residualism. In addition, it is difficult to predict whether alternative normative perspectives will emerge to offer a radically different direction for social policy and move the pluralist welfare system in new directions.

The Future: Optimists and Pessimists

It has already been argued that attempts to discern future trends in social policy will need to take account of a large number of factors that interact in complex ways to shape the future. As was explained earlier, these include the impersonal forces of economics, demographics, cultural change, and electoral politics, as well as normative welfare prescriptions based on ideological preferences. New normative perspectives have become quite influential, and their proponents are seeking to shape the prevailing pluralist welfare system.

Different social policy commentators have assigned greater importance to some of these factors than others. Some are persuaded that economic and fiscal realities will play a paramount role while others conclude that the future of social policy will be determined by electoral politics. Some believe that ideological factors are of vital importance while others contend that the future of social policy will be shaped largely by cultural change. Of course, some social policy scholars base their predictions on more than one of these factors, and other factors not discussed in this chapter may also emerge as likely determinants of social policy's future trajectory.

In addition to attempts to dispassionately identify the factors that are likely to influence the future of social policy, predictions have also been influenced by the personal dispositions of commentators, who may view future trends in either positive or negative terms. Social policy scholarship has, in the past, been liberally infused with preferences of this kind, and both pessimistic and optimistic dispositions have characterized past analyses. As was noted at the beginning of this chapter, these dispositions reflect ideological preferences. For example, the changes introduced during the Reagan administration in the 1980s were viewed by many liberal scholars in gloomy terms even though the effects of these changes did not result in massive retrenchments or in the dismantling of the New Deal legacy, as many believed they would. On the other hand, social policy scholars on the political right are persuaded that these changes have brought positive consequences by restoring self-reliance and personal responsibility and reducing the heavy fiscal burden imposed by excessive social expenditures. Obviously, accounts of the future of social policy will be influenced by these personal and ideological dispositions.

Despite these differences, and a tendency toward either pessimistic or optimistic predictions, there is some consensus about the impact of the different factors discussed earlier. For example, many social policy scholars agree about the role of economic change on the future of social policy. Although the economic situation at the time of writing in 2008 is ambiguous, attention has already been drawn to the challenges posed by the housing slump, the credit crisis and declining value of the dollar, and the possibility of a major economic downturn.

Although it is difficult to predict medium-term economic trends, there is more agreement about the effects of long-term economic changes on social policy. Most commentators agree that the contribution of manufacturing to the economy will continue to decline and that this will have an effect on employment patterns, which, as noted earlier, are already flexible, volatile, and cyclical. There is agreement also among scholars that social policy will continue to face the challenges posed by a postindustrial society and that policies previously based on steady, long-term employment will need to change to take account of labor flexibility, self-employment, and similar trends. However, the implications of these changes for incomes and poverty are disputed. While some pessimistically believe that the persistence of low-income employment and poverty presents a major challenge, others optimistically contend that low-paid workers, and immigrants in particular, are living the American dream and that they and their children will invariably seize the opportunities that will propel them into the middle class. These optimists argue that, if educational opportunities are freely available, the problems of low-wage employment and poverty will take care of themselves—provided the economy continues to grow and the culture of opportunity that characterizes American society is maintained. Others believe that more targeted interventions are needed to raise the standards of living of low-income families. They contend that the expansion of the Earned Income Tax Credit, a further increase in the minimum wage, and the restoration of wage bargaining through a reinvigorated union movement will serve this purpose.

There is agreement also among social policy scholars about the importance of demographic trends, and particularly population aging, on social policy. Most believe that the aging of the population will create greater demands for services in the future. However, with economic uncertainty, the fiscal resources to meet these needs are likely to be increasingly strained. As public revenues come under greater pressure, middle-class people will have to rely increasingly on their own resources. In keeping with the prevailing pluralistic climate, many commentators conclude that elderly people with higher incomes will make increasing use of private and commercial services while services for those with low incomes will be provided from governmental and voluntary resources. In this situation, it is likely that services to poor elderly people and, indeed, to poor people in general will continue to be badly funded, haphazardly implemented, and increasingly fragmented.

Discussions about the effects of population aging on the future of social policy invariably involve Social Security and intense debates about the system's long-term sustainability. Although many social policy scholars have shown that Social Security contributions will continue to exceed expenditures for at least three more decades, predictions from those on the political right contend that the system is on the verge of collapse. As noted earlier, this view has informed the Bush administration, which successfully communicated negative images about the future of Social Security. These images have been uncritically conveyed by the media with the result that many people today believe that the system is already bankrupt. In this climate, it is likely that some form of partial privatization will emerge in the future. Even though the Bush administration did not achieve this goal, pressures on future Republican political leaders to pursue the privatization agenda will undoubtedly continue. Of course, the Democrat alternative of creating an add-on system of mandatory accounts, which leaves the current Social Security program intact, may prevail.

There is consensus also about the continuing importance of immigration trends for social policy. Many commentators believe that efforts to restrict undocumented immigration will have limited success and that policies and procedures for legitimizing the importation of unskilled workers will be introduced. In addition, legal immigration will also continue to foster the further diversification of American society. For this reason, many believe that the social services will become increasingly responsive to the cultural needs of immigrant groups although, of course, the extent to which they are able to effectively meet the growing needs of low-income families is debatable. It is possible that the growing political activism of immigrant groups may create new political pressures for expanded social programs or, at least, for higher subsidies to nonprofit and community-based organizations that serve these communities.

With regard to electoral politics, many commentators are persuaded that the current disinclination among a sizable proportion of the electorate to engage in political activity will not be reversed even though there is scope for the greater political participation of immigrant groups in the future. It is likely that electoral politics will result in marginal shifts in the electoral strength of the two major parties although, as noted earlier, the political process can be mercurial. Nevertheless, national electoral campaigns will probably continue to focus on relatively small groups of swing voters. Policies articulated during major elections will generally focus on these groups, which, as mentioned earlier, tend to be predominantly white, suburban, and conservative.

Although, as was discussed earlier, social policy scholars on the political right have formulated innovative normative social policy proposals, it is likely that the prevailing pluralistic welfare approach will continue to characterize social policy making in the foreseeable future. This is not to deny the significance of attempts by those on the political right to shape the prevailing pluralist welfare regime so that it becomes increasingly dominated by a market-based welfare consumerism, or by traditionalism or regulationism, or even by a combination of these approaches. But despite these efforts, many social policy scholars believe that welfare pluralism will continue to characterize American social policy. It is also likely that the pluralistic position will be nurtured and sustained by wider social demographic and economic forces that will require multiple interventions appropriate to the demands of different situations. In addition, the expansion of faith-based welfare and the subsidization of the nonprofit sector are likely to continue and to give expression to social policy's pluralist impetus.

In this context, it is also likely that future social service provision will be characterized by greater decentralization and localism. As noted earlier, the trend from federalism to devolution is already revealed in the way responsibility for the TANF program has been transferred to the states. Some scholars take a pessimistic view of this trend, believing that increased devolution and localization will result in further fragmentation and unevenness in social service provision. Social policy scholars of a more optimistic disposition challenge this view, arguing that increased devolution will foster greater democratic participation and involvement in social policy making and implementation.

However, in view of the huge deficit accrued by the federal government since the Bush administration came to office, it is likely that federal funding for the social services will decline and that the states will be asked to assume greater responsibility for social welfare. This development, pessimists believe, will foster the further retrenchment and privatization of social programs and the disengagement of the middle class from the public social services. Although the social services may become more responsive to the cultural needs of ethnic minorities, their identification with low-income minority groups will result in less support from members of the white, suburban middle class, whose willingness to pay the taxes needed to fund these services will be increasingly strained. On the other hand, optimists claim that this trend will foster greater personal and community responsibility for social welfare. They view the shift toward devolution and pluralism as a welcome attempt to balance the excessive statism of the past with the increased participation of commercial and nonprofit providers. Middle-class people, they believe, will have new opportunities to meet their needs through the market in ways that are compatible with current social and economic realities. For example, the possible introduction of individual savings accounts as a part of Social Security reform will promote greater choice and responsibility and free up public resources to meet the needs of those who are not able to care for themselves.

These factors are likely to result in a perpetuation of welfare pluralism, and the trend toward localism and residualism will, in all likelihood, continue. It is highly unlikely, as some social policy advocates hope, that there will be a return to the golden age of welfare statism as exemplified by the New Deal and the social policy innovations of the Johnson administration. It is also unlikely that any of the normative prescriptions advocated by the political right will dominate social policy. Pluralism, decentralization, and inadequate funding will probably characterize the social services for the foreseeable future. However, it may also be the case that unforeseen factors and new normative theories will emerge to shape the future direction of social policy. It is also possible that social welfare may again emerge as a central and positive preoccupation of American political and social life and be characterized by a greater sense of collective responsibility and solidarity. But, if this is to be the case, it will require new, visionary ideas that are responsive to current realities as well as the leadership and resolve to ensure their implementation.

References

Bartokowski, J. P., & Regis, H. (2003). *Charitable choice: Religion, race, and poverty in the post-welfare era.* New York: New York University Press.

Deacon, B. (2007). *Global social policy and governance.* Thousand Oaks, CA: Sage.

DiIulio, J. (2007). *Godly republic: A centrist blueprint for America's faith-based future.* Berkeley: University of California Press.

Gingrich, N. (1995). *To renew America.* New York: Harper.

Hoffman, S. D., & Seidman, L. S. (2003). *Helping working families: The earned income tax credit.* Kalamazoo, MI: W. E. Upjohn Institute for Employment Research.

Kuo, D. (2006). *Tempting faith: An inside story of political seduction.* New York: Free Press.

Mead, L. (1986). *Beyond entitlement: The social obligations of citizenship.* New York: Basic Books.

Mead, L. (Ed.). (1997). *The new paternalism: Supervisory approaches to poverty.* Washington, DC: Brookings Institution Press.

Midgley, J. (2007). Global inequality, power, and the unipolar world: Implications for social work. *International Social Work, 50*(5), 613–626.

Olasky, M. (1992). *The tragedy of American compassion.* Washington, DC: Regnery Gateway.

Olasky, M. (1996). *Renewing American compassion.* Washington, DC: Regnery.

Stoesz, D. (1996). *Small change: Domestic policy under the Clinton presidency.* White Plains, NY: Longman.

Index

NOTE: Page references indicate figures and tables where appropriate.

About the Editors

James Midgley is Harry and Riva Specht Professor of Public Social Services and former dean of the School of Social Welfare, University of California, Berkeley. He previously taught at the University of Cape Town, the London School of Economics, and Louisiana State University. He has published widely on social development and international social welfare. His most recent books include *Social Policy for Development* (with Anthony Hall), *Lessons from Abroad: Adapting International Social Welfare Innovations* (with M. C. Hokenstad), and *International Perspectives on Welfare to Work Policy* (editor with Richard Hoefer).

Michelle Livermore is Assistant Professor of Social Work at Louisiana State University. She has published numerous articles and book chapters on poverty, social development, and community social capital. Her most recent research focuses on the government and social support factors affecting the employment of single mothers and TANF work program outcomes in Louisiana. She was coeditor of the first edition of the *Handbook of Social Policy* (2000) and has published in numerous journals including *Social Development Issues, Journal of Community Practice*, and *Journal of Sociology and Social Welfare*.

About the Contributors

Jill Duerr Berrick is Professor of Social Welfare and a codirector of the Center for Child and Youth Policy at the University of California at Berkeley. She conducts research on low-income children and families, child welfare consumers, and foster parents, and she has written several articles that highlight findings from her studies. She has authored or coauthored nine books on child abuse, foster care, and family poverty. Her latest book, *Take Me Home*, is forthcoming from Oxford University Press.

Katharine Briar-Lawson is a professor and the dean of the School of Social Work at the University of Albany. She has undertaken extensive research into child welfare policy and practice and has been a coprincipal investigator on numerous child welfare grants and a consultant on child welfare issues. She has recently coedited *Evaluation Research in Child Welfare* and *Charting the Impacts of University-Child Welfare Collaboration,* as well as a special issue of the journal *Child Welfare* on the subject of community building. She is President of the National Association of Deans and Directors of Schools of Social Work (NADD).

Jordan Brown is an advanced graduate student in the Department of Sociology at Florida State University. He is in the beginning stages of his dissertation, and his recent research interests focus on historical/comparative sociology and emotions and emotional culture in social movement activities. His previous research includes collaborative projects focusing on the use of media framing and the Internet in social movements.

James W. Callicutt is Professor Emeritus at the School of Social Work of the University of Texas at Arlington, where he previously served as the associate dean, the interim dean, and a professor. He has held social work positions in mental health settings in Tennessee and Massachusetts and has served as a consultant for community mental health centers in eastern Maine and Texas. He coedited *Mental Health Policy and Practice Today* (with Ted Watkins) and *Social Work and Mental Health* (with Pedro Lecca).

Pranab Chatterjee is Grace Longwell Coyle Professor of Social Work at the Mandel School of Applied Social Sciences, Case Western Reserve University. He has published numerous books and journal articles including *Approaches to the Welfare State, Repackaging the Welfare State,* and *Contemporary Human Behavior Theory.* His recent research includes the experience of adolescence and aging in different cultures, the relationship between justice and culture, and the consequences of increased expenditures by the state in modern societies.

Phyllis J. Day is a retired professor of social policy. She is the author of *A New History of Social Welfare* and coeditor of *Social Working: Exercises in Generalist Practice* (with Sandra Shelley).

Diana M. DiNitto is Professor of Alcohol Studies and Education and Distinguished Teaching Professor at the School of Social Work, University of Texas at Austin. She has published *Social Work: Issues and Opportunities in a Changing Profession, Chemical Dependency: A Systems Approach,* and *Social Welfare: Politics and Public Policy.*

Jeanette Drews is a consultant for community agencies serving person with developmental disabilities. She formerly was the acting dean and associate professor at the College of Social Work, University of Utah. Her work focused on inclusion and choice in service provision for people with disabilities. She was key author of a 1990 report to Congress that evaluated the state of state services. She also developed a service delivery model for the state of Utah's Services for People with Disabilities agency that included choice making for people with mental retardation.

Neil Gilbert is Chernin Professor of Social Welfare at the University of California at Berkeley and Director of the Center for the Comparative Study of Family Welfare and Poverty. He has published widely on social welfare policy, social security, and international social welfare. His recent books include *Welfare Justice: Restoring Social Equity, Combating Child Abuse,* and *The Transformation of the Welfare State.*

Leon Ginsberg is Professor of Social Work and Program Director at Appalachian State University in Boone, North Carolina. He was formerly the dean of social work at West Virginia University and the University of South Carolina. He has written extensively on rural social work and social welfare policy. His latest book, coauthored with Julie Miller-Cribbs, is *Understanding Social Welfare Problems, Policies, and Programs.*

Kevin Fox Gotham is Associate Professor of Sociology at Tulane University. His research focuses on the political economy of real estate, tourism, and urban redevelopment. He is author of *Authentic New Orleans: Race, Culture, and Tourism in the Big Easy.*

John M. Herrick is Professor Emeritus of Social Work at Michigan State University. He has undertaken research into health care policy and multicultural mental health practice in Michigan, the history of U.S. social policy, the history of the use of volunteers in social services during the Great Depression, and rural social work. His latest book is *The Encyclopedia of Social Welfare History in North America* (with Paul Stuart). He is active in several community social service agencies.

Richard Hoefer is Professor of Social Work at the University of Texas at Arlington. He writes on advocacy, interest groups, and Swedish social policy, as well as on nonprofit administration topics such as program evaluation. His articles have appeared in journals such as *Social Work, Administration in Social Work,* and *Social Service Review.* He is the editor of *The Journal of Policy Practice.* His most recent edited books include *Advocacy for Social Justice, Cutting Edge Social Policy Research*, and *International Perspectives on Welfare to Work* (with James Midgley).

Marie D. Hoff was formerly Professor of Social Policy and Macro-Practice at the School of Social Work, Boise State University. She has published widely on social welfare and environmental issues. Her major books include *The Global Environmental Crisis: Implications for Social Welfare and Social Work* (with John McNutt) and *Sustainable Community Development: Studies in Economic, Environmental, and Cultural Revitalization.*

Cheryl Hyde is Associate Dean for Professional Development and Director, Field Education at the School of Social Administration, Temple University, where she also serves as an associate professor. She has published widely in the areas of feminist theory and practice, community organizing and capacity building, civic society, organizational development, and multicultural education. She is the past chair of the Association of Community Organization and Social Administration.

Demetrius S. Iatridis is Professor of Social Policy Planning at the Boston College Graduate School of Social Work. His research focuses on social policy for the development of health and welfare organizations. He has published *Social Policy: Institutional Context of Social Development and Human Services* and *Social Policy and Privatization in Central and Eastern Europe* (with June G. Hopps).

Bruce Jansson is Margaret W. Driscoll/Louise M. Clevenger Professor of Social Policy and Administration at the School of Social Work of the University of Southern California. He has written extensively on social policy. His most recent books are *Becoming an Effective Policy Advocate: From Policy Practice to Social Justice; The Reluctant Welfare State: Using Policy Advocacy to Make it More Humane, Past, Present, and Future;* and *The Sixteen-Trillion-Dollar Mistake: How the United States Bungled Its National Priorities from the New Deal to the Present.*

Alfred J. Kahn is Professor Emeritus of Social Work at Columbia University. He also serves as codirector of the Cross National Studies Research

Program at the school. He is the author, coauthor, or editor of more than 30 books and 250 journal articles and book chapters. He has consulted widely in the United States and abroad for state and local governments, international organizations, private agencies, the State Department, and United Nations agencies.

Sheila B. Kamerman is Compton Foundation Centennial Professor for the Prevention of Children and Youth Problems at the School of Social Work at Columbia University. She is the author, coauthor, editor, or coeditor of more than 30 books and about 300 journal articles and book chapters. Her most recent books are *Early Childhood Education and Care: International Perspectives* (with Alfred J. Kahn) and *Beyond Child Poverty: The Social Exclusion of Children*.

Jennie Jacobs Kronenfeld is a professor in the Sociology Program of the School of Social and Family Dynamics at Arizona State University. She conducts research in the areas of health policy, health across the life course, and health behavior. Her recent books include *Schools and the Health of Children, Health Care Policy: Issues and Trends, Healthcare Reform in America*, and *Expansion of Publicly Funded Health Insurance in the United States: The Children's Health Insurance Program and Its Implications*. She is the editor of the Elsevier series *Research in the Sociology of Health Care* and coeditor of the journal *Health*.

Leslie Leighninger is a professor in the School of Social Work at Arizona State University. She has written many articles and books on social work and social welfare history, including *Social Work: Search for Identity* and *Creating a New Profession: The Beginnings of Social Work Education in the United States*. She is currently working on a book on the impact of the social work profession on state and national policies in health, mental health, aging, housing, and community development.

Robert Leighninger is the editor of the *Journal of Sociology and Social Welfare*. He is based at the School of Social Work at Arizona State University. He has undertaken extensive research into the New Deal and its public works programs. His latest book is *Long-Range Public Investment: The Forgotten Legacy of the New Deal*.

Elizabeth Lightfoot is an associate professor and director of the doctoral program at the University of Minnesota's School of Social Work. Her research has focused broadly on disability policy and services, with current research interests in the intersections of disability policy with child welfare, aging, and HIV prevention policies.

Younghee Lim is Assistant Professor of Social Work at Louisiana State University. Her research on social welfare policy includes antipoverty policies and programs, family structure, and welfare reform, in particular, the provision of work support policies as a means to support low- to moderate-income families. Her recent policy and program evaluations include studies of the Earned Income Tax Credit, of Voluntary Income Tax Assistance sites, and of welfare-to-work policies and programs in Louisiana.

John G. McNutt is Professor at the School of Urban Affairs and Public Policy and at the Center for Community Research and Service, University of Delaware. He is a specialist in the application of high technology to political and social engagement. His work focuses on the role of technology in lobbying, political campaigning and deliberation, organizing, and other forms of political participation. He has coedited or coauthored four books and many journal articles, book chapters, and web review articles. He regularly presents at national and international conferences.

Toni Naccarato is Assistant Professor of Social Welfare at the State University of New York at Albany. Her research focuses on the emancipation, welfare, and human capital accumulation of adolescents; social and economic policies and reforms; and research methods for increasing social and political changes in the social work arena. She is currently collaborating with the New York State Office of Children and Family Services to better integrate research and data management emphasizing child welfare practitioners.

Martha Ozawa is the Betty Bofinger Brown Distinguished Professor of Social Work at the George Warren Brown School of Social Work, Washington University. She writes widely on policy analysis and social issues related to older adults, women, and children. Her current research focuses on volatility in American families, inequality and child well-being, child allowances, and service use by elderly persons. She is the founder and director of the School's Martha N. Ozawa Center for Social Policy Studies. She is coeditor in chief of the *Asian Social Work and Policy Review*.

Lori Parham is Director of AARP Florida. She was formerly the advocacy manager for state affairs and the lead lobbyist for AARP on state issues affecting people 50 and older. She has also worked as a legislative analyst for the Florida Senate, Committee on Health, Aging, and Long-Term Care and at the Florida Agency for Health Care Administration in the Medicaid Research Bureau.

Jill Quadagno is Professor of Sociology at Florida State University, where she holds the Mildred and Claude Pepper Eminent Scholar Chair in Social Gerontology. She has served as a senior policy advisor on the President's Bi-Partisan Commission on Entitlement and Tax Reform. She conducts research on aging and health policy. Her most recent book is *One Nation, Uninsured: Why the U.S. Has No National Health Insurance*.

Michael Reisch is the Daniel Thursz Distinguished Professor of Social Justice at the University of Maryland where he also directs the Multicultural Social Welfare History Project. He is the author or editor of over 20 books and monographs and has published nearly 100 articles and chapters on the history and philosophy of social welfare, community organization theory and practice, the nonprofit sector, and contemporary social policy issues. His work has been translated into French, Spanish, Italian, Chinese, Korean, Japanese, and Bulgarian, and he has lectured and consulted widely in Europe, Asia, Australia, and Latin America.

Margaret Severson is Associate Professor of Social Work at the University of Kansas. She has served as a principal investigator on two research endeavors funded by the National Institute of Justice, one on jail-based suicide risk assessment strategies and another, more recently, on exploring the life trajectories of incarcerated and "free" women who have histories of violent victimization. She has published extensively in the area of correctional social work policy and practice. She serves as an expert witness in institutional litigation and as a consultant for federal and state authorities, helping jails and prisons develop and enhance their mental health and suicide prevention programs.

Michael Sherraden is Benjamin Youngdahl Professor of Social Development at the George Warren Brown School of Social Work, Washington University and Director of the Center for Social Development. He has published widely on youth service, social development, and assets. His work on asset policy is internationally recognized. His book on this subject, *Assets and the Poor*, proposes universal and progressive saving, beginning at birth, in individual development accounts (IDAs). Research and policy in asset building are discussed in *Inclusion in the American Dream: Assets, Poverty, and Public Policy* and *Can the Poor Save? Savings and Asset Accumulation in IDAs* (with Mark Schreiner).

David Stoesz is Professor of Social Policy at Virginia Commonwealth University. He has published widely on social policy issues, and his textbook *American Social Welfare Policy* (with Howard Karger) is widely used. His most recent book, *Quixote's Ghost, the Right, the Liberati, and the Future of Social Policy,* won the 2005 Pro-Humanitate Literary Award. Currently, he is finishing a book on social work education.

Susan Stone is an assistant professor in the School of Social Welfare at the University of California at Berkeley. Her substantive interest is in areas of overlap between the fields of social welfare and education, with a specific focus on the school progress of socially and academically vulnerable students. She has published on the educational needs of foster children, elements of effective schools, and area-level effects on student and school achievement outcomes.

Fernando M. Torres-Gil is Acting Dean of the UCLA School of Public Affairs (SPA). He holds appointments as Professor of Social Welfare and Public Policy in the SPA and is the director of the Center for Policy Research on Aging. He has undertaken research in the fields of health and long-term care, the politics of aging, social policy, ethnicity, and disability. He is the author or editor of six books and more than 80 articles and book chapters, including *The New Aging: Politics and Change in America* and *Lessons on Aging From Three Nations* (volumes 1 and 2).

Diwakar Vadapalli is doctoral student and adjunct faculty member at the Mandel School of Applied Social Sciences. He has a variety of research and practice experiences, including being a team member for a statewide pilot project that recruited foster families, conducting social surveys in the slums of India, and working as an Indian Child Welfare Act worker for the Native Village of Sleetmute, a federally recognized Alaskan Native tribe.

Valentine Villa is Professor of Social Work at California State University, Los Angeles, an adjunct associate professor with the UCLA School of Public Health, Department of Community Health Sciences, and a senior researcher with the UCLA Center for Health Policy Research. She undertakes research about aging and social policy and particularly about issues of minority aging. Her work assesses the effects of public policies on the health and economic status of the elderly population. She has authored and coauthored numerous journal articles, book chapters, and policy briefs.

Jane Waldfogel is Professor of Social Work and Public Affairs at the Columbia University School of Social Work and a research associate at the Centre for Analysis of Social Exclusion at the London School of Economics. She has written extensively on the impact of public policies on child and family well-being. Her most recent book is *What Children Need*.

Robert Waste is a professor and former chair of the Department of Public Policy and Administration at California State University, Sacramento. He has held fellowships at both Harvard and Yale University, and is the author of several articles and books on public policy and local government—including *The Ecology of City Policymaking* and *Independent Cities: Rethinking U.S. Urban Policy*. He has served as the chair of both the City of Sacramento Planning Commission and the City of Sacramento Campaign Reform Commission and has sat on the editorial board of the *Journal of Urban Affairs*.

James D. Wright is Provost's Distinguished Research Professor in the Department of Sociology at the University of Central Florida. He also serves as the director of the University's Institute for Social and Behavioral Sciences and is editor-in-chief of the journal *Social Science Research*. He has published eighteen books and more than 300 journal articles, book chapters, essays, reviews, and polemics on topics ranging from American politics to poverty to homelessness to guns to NASCAR. He also serves on the boards of the Coalition for the Homeless of Central Florida and of the Orlando Area Trust for the Homeless.